Advanced Programming with Mic

Visual Basic®.NET

A CASE-BASED APPROACH

Bob Spear

THOMSON

COURSE TECHNOLOGY ™

Australia • Canada • Mexico • Singapore • Spain • United Kingdom • United States

THOMSON

COURSE TECHNOLOGY

Advanced Programming with Microsoft Visual Basic .NET: A Case-Based Approach

by Bob Spear

Managing Editor:
Jennifer Muroff

Acquisitions Editor
Roberts Apse

Product Manager
Alyssa Pratt

Development Editor:
Laurie Brown

Production Editor:
Brooke Booth

Editorial Assistant:
Amanda Piantedosi

Product Marketing Manager:
Brian Berkeley

Senior Manufacturing Coordinator:
Laura Burns

Cover Designer:
Nancy Goulet

Disclaimer
Course Technology reserves the right to revise this publication and make changes from time to time in its content without notice.

ISBN 0-619-15916-2

Preface

Advanced Programming with Microsoft Visual Basic .NET: A Case-Based Approach is designed for the following students and readers:

- The primary audience consists of students who have completed an introductory course in Visual Basic .NET.
- For anyone who has learned an earlier version of Visual Basic, this book includes a chapter introducing the Visual Studio .NET IDE and its customization for developing projects in Visual Basic .NET.
- This book may be appropriate for professional programmers who already know how to program but need to update their skills in the VB.NET arena.
- Finally, this book is suitable for self-study, and for a distance-learning (Web-based) course.

Organization and Coverage

Advanced Programming with Microsoft Visual Basic .NET: A Case-Based Approach contains 11 tutorials that present hands-on instruction, and two appendices. In the tutorials, students with basic programming experience learn how to plan and create well-structured programs. By the end of the book, students will have learned how to write programs using Windows Forms, Web Forms, Console applications, class libraries, and external data sources (traditional sequential and random-access data files as well as relational databases using ADO.NET and ADO).

In the running case, the student is a member of a small group of civic-minded programmers who are helping the city of Friendsville prepare to host an international summer games event. The specific applications all revolve around the Friendsville International Games, from dining services to villager accommodations, scheduling and scoring of competitive events, and selling tickets. The case holds the reader's interest throughout.

In terms of the order of the material:

Tutorials 0, 1, 2, and 3 provide a review of the fundamentals of programming in Visual Basic .NET. This should be a review for students who recently completed an introductory Visual Basic .NET course, and it provides a solid but rapid introduction to Visual Basic .NET for programmers previously trained in Visual Basic 6.0. These tutorials cover the Integrated Development Environment (IDE), the three basic interfaces (Console, Windows Forms, and Web Forms), event-based programming, control structures (sequence, selection, and iteration), traditional file structures (sequential and random access), printing, and fundamental notions of objects.

Tutorials 4, 5, and 6 focus on more advanced techniques in Windows Forms applications, including multiple document interface applications, Windows Explorer-style and Microsoft Outlook-style applications, class libraries and reusable code, user-designed controls, and advanced notions of object-oriented programming.

Tutorial 7 focuses on Web-based applications. Students experience the notion of client-server programming, since Visual Basic .NET Web Forms applications run on both a client machine and a server (perhaps virtual) machine.

Tutorial 8 deals with data structures: pseudo-ISAM files, table and file-sorting algorithms, sequential and binary search techniques, and linked lists.

By the end of Tutorial 8, students have all of the tools they need to deal with and comprehend the last three tutorials in the book, which focus on databases. Tutorial 9 introduces ADO.NET, Microsoft's newest and most comprehensive data access technology; the example databases in this chapter use Microsoft Access, while the discussion covers the relational database model and the various ADO.NET objects that permit data retrieval and manipulation. Tutorial 10 expands the discussion of databases to Web-based applications, and focuses especially on the security considerations of these applications. The example databases in Tutorial 10 are SQL Server databases, created with the Microsoft Desktop Engine and the facilities of Server Explorer in Visual Studio .NET. Tutorial 11 again uses databases, but the focus here is on error handling, data validation, and the design of help files for an application, including the HTML Help Workshop.

Approach

Advanced Programming with Microsoft Visual Basic .NET: A Case-Based Approach is distinguished from other textbooks because of its unique approach, which motivates students by creating a realistic programming scenario—The Friendsville International Games, which offers them the opportunity to build programs not unlike those that programmers develop in a real-world environment. "Real World" (RW) applications evolve. All the requirements are not known at the outset. Some requirements are discovered in the process of development, and other requirements change. Reflecting that RW experience, students begin the development of a fairly simple and straightforward application, then discover hidden complexities or encounter new user requirements, and learn to adjust the project scope or alter the application design. Because this book teaches programming concepts using a task-driven, rather than a command-driven, approach, students learn how to create programs and solve problems they are likely to encounter in the workplace. This is much more effective than memorizing a list of commands out of context.

Features

Advanced Programming with Microsoft Visual Basic .NET: A Case-Based Approach is an exceptional textbook because it also includes the following features:

- **"Read This Before You Begin" Section** This section is consistent with Course Technology's unequaled commitment to helping instructors introduce technology into the classroom. Technical considerations and assumptions about hardware, software, and default settings are listed in one place to help instructors save time and eliminate unnecessary aggravation.
- **Application Preview** The first section of each tutorial previews the completed application that the student will develop in that tutorial. This provides a direction and focus to the whole tutorial, and motivates the student to develop the previewed application. Each tutorial is built around a specific application development project given to the Friendsville Games Development Team.
- **Lessons** Following the application preview, each tutorial is divided into three lessons—one Concept Lesson and two Application Lessons. The Concept Lesson introduces various programming concepts, including programming syntax and code examples. The Application Lessons work the case, giving students an opportunity to apply the concepts in a realistic scenario. Here the student creates the program that solves the case problem or goal. Concepts are combined in later Application Lessons so that the student has the opportunity to use multiple

programming features to efficiently solve programming tasks. Each lesson begins with a set of Learning Objectives. The material within the lesson is organized around these learning objectives.

- **Step-by-Step Methodology** The unique Course Technology methodology keeps students on track. They click or press keys always within the context of solving a specific problem or demonstrating the Application Lesson case. The text constantly guides students, letting them know where they are in the process of solving the problem. The numerous illustrations include labels that direct students' attention to what they should look at on the screen.
- **NOTE** Notes provide additional information about a procedure—for example, an alternative method of performing the procedure.
- **Tip** Tip notes provide caveats—things the programmer must be aware of when using a programming element.
- **Summary** Following each lesson is a summary, which recaps the programming concepts and commands covered in the lesson.
- **Questions and Exercises** Each lesson concludes with meaningful, conceptual Questions that test students' understanding of what they learned in the lesson. The Questions are followed by Exercises, which provide students with additional practice of the skills and concepts they learned in the lesson. Many of the exercises provide practice in applying cumulative programming knowledge or allow the student to explore alternative solutions to programming tasks.
- **Key Terms** Concluding each tutorial is a comprehensive listing of all the new terms, classes, controls, and concepts introduced in the tutorial. This list is a useful resource for students and teachers, helping them quickly locate topics in each tutorial.

Instructor's Resources

The following supplemental materials are available when this book is used in a classroom setting. All of the resources available with this book are provided to the instructor on a single CD-ROM.

Electronic Instructor's Manual The Instructor's Manual that accompanies this textbook includes:

- Additional instructional material to assist in class preparation, including suggestions for lecture topics.
- Solutions to all end-of-lesson Questions and Exercises.

ExamView® This textbook is accompanied by ExamView, a powerful testing software package that allows instructors to create and administer printed, computer (LAN-based), and Internet exams. ExamView includes hundreds of questions that correspond to the topics covered in this text, enabling students to generate detailed study guides that include page references for further review. The computer-based and Internet testing components allow students to take exams at their computers, and also save the instructor time by grading each exam automatically.

PowerPoint Presentations This book comes with Microsoft PowerPoint slides for each tutorial. These are included as a teaching aid for classroom presentation, to be made available to students on the network for tutorial review, or to be printed for classroom distribution. Instructors can add their own slides for additional topics they introduce to the class.

Data Files Data files, containing all of the data necessary for steps within the tutorials and the end-of-lesson Exercises, are provided through the Course Technology Web site at **www.course.com**, and are also available on the Teaching Tools CD-ROM.

Solution Files Solutions to end-of-lesson Questions and Exercises are provided on the Teaching Tools CD-ROM and may also be found on the Course Technology Web site at **www.course.com**. The solutions are password protected.

Distance Learning Course Technology is proud to present online courses in WebCT and Blackboard, to provide the most complete and dynamic learning experience possible. When you add online content to one of your courses, you're adding a lot: self tests, links, glossaries, and, most of all, a gateway to the twenty-first century's most important information resource. We hope you will make the most of your course, both online and offline. For more information on how to bring distance learning to your course, contact your local Course Technology sales representative.

Acknowledgments

I would like to thank all of the people on the Course Technology team, especially Laurie Brown, my Development Editor, Alyssa Pratt, the Product Manager, and Vitaly Davidovich, who created many of the solutions to end-of-lesson Exercises. Thanks to the reviewers: Tina Ostrander, Highline Community College; David Fullerton, Yeshiva University; David Grebner, Lansing Community College; Joseph Otto, California State University Los Angeles; Chris LaBounty, Brown College; and Chris Panell, Heald College.

I would also like to thank my most patient wife, Mary Helen, whose husband has been ensconced at the computer for the last 18 months.

Brief Contents

Contents

tutorial 2

CODING OF WINDOWS FORMS APPLICATIONS, AND THE TRANSITION TO OBJECTS 75

t u t o r i a l 3

VISUAL BASIC .NET FUNDAMENTALS 141

case ▶ Software Security at the Friendsville International Games 141

t u t o r i a l 4

PROGRAMMING WITH OBJECTS: CLASS LIBRARIES AND REUSABLE CODE *221*

tutorial 5

ADVANCED WINDOWS FORMS CONTROLS AND CODING *271*

t u t o r i a l 6

MORE ADVANCED WINDOWS FORMS CONTROLS AND CODING *343*

t u t o r i a l 7

WEB FORMS: WEB PAGES WITH SERVER CONTROLSS 409

t u t o r i a l   10

WEB FORMS WITH DATABASE INTERACTIVITY *619*

case ▶

t u t o r i a l   11

ERROR TRAPS AND HELP FILES 697

Read This Before You Begin

To the User

Data Files

To complete the steps and exercises, you will need data files that have been created for this book. Your instructor will provide the data files to you. You also can obtain the files electronically from the Course Technology Web site by connecting to **www.course.com**, and then searching for this book title or ISBN. The file VB.NET.Student.zip contains all of the zipped files together.

Each tutorial in this book has its own set of data files, contained in a single folder whose name identifies the tutorial to which it belongs. You can use a computer in your school lab or your own computer to complete the tutorials and Exercises in this book. If you are installing the student data files on your own computer, then create a folder called VB.NET\Student, and extract all files to that folder. Then open the data files for each tutorial as you come to it. In this way, the data files for Tutorial 3 will appear in the Tut03 folder, the files for Tutorial 4 will appear in Tut04, and so on. Throughout this book, you will be instructed to open files from or save files to these folders.

If you are using a computer in the student lab, you will need to copy the data files into a folder where you have read/write access.

As you peruse the data files, you will encounter a number of executable (exe) files, which, as the name suggests, are indeed executable. In some cases, you have been given an executable in order to see what the completed application should look like. Then, as you progress through the tutorial, you will build that application yourself.

You will often need to examine the contents of a folder, and you will need to know the filename extensions of the files you are looking at. Therefore, you want Windows Explorer to display (rather than hide) all filename extensions. To select this option, open Windows Explorer; from the Start menu, select Tools | Folder Options, or View | Folder Options, or View | Options (depending on which operating system you have); click the View tab; uncheck the checkbox that reads "Hide extensions for known file types;" and click OK.

Using Your Own Computer

You may wish to install Visual Studio .NET on your own computer. Before this decision is taken—and before you go out and purchase the software—you will want to be cognizant of the minimum system requirements for Visual Studio .NET.

The minimum PC must have a 450 MHz Pentium II processor, Microsoft Windows NT 4.0 or later operating system, 3.5 GB hard disk space (including 500 MB on the system drive), CD-ROM, and Super VGA or higher resolution monitor with 256 colors. The amount of RAM required for Visual Studio .NET depends on your operating system:

- Windows NT 4.0 Workstation: 64 MB RAM
- Windows NT 4.0 Server: 160 MB RAM
- Windows 2000 Professional: 96 MB RAM
- Windows 2000 Server: 192 MB RAM
- Windows XP: 160 MB RAM

Visual Studio .NET Console and Windows Forms applications will execute under the Windows 98 and Windows 2000 ME operating systems, but they cannot be developed using that system. These operating systems cannot run Web Forms applications. Windows 95 is not supported at all.

Web Forms Applications

Web Forms applications run on a server, which is a separate computer from the local machine you are using for Windows Forms applications. The server can be on a network, or it may be a "virtual" machine (named *localhost*) that is physically the same computer you are using to run Visual Studio .NET. In either case, files cannot be copied directly to the server from the local machine. Instead, you must install each Web Forms application by running a Setup.exe program for that application.

Web Forms applications can only be installed on a computer that is running Internet Information Server (IIS). You must have permission to run the installer on the computer, and you must have IIS permissions as well.

NOTE: Visual Studio .NET Console and Windows Forms applications can be developed on computers using the Windows XP Home Edition. The Home Edition, however, does not support Internet Information Server (IIS), and so you cannot develop or execute Visual Studio .NET Web Forms applications using Windows XP Home Edition. For Web Forms applications development and execution under Windows XP, you must have Windows XP Professional Edition.

Database Management Systems

Tutorials 9, 10, and 11 deal with relational database applications, primarily using Microsoft Access. Visual Studio .NET ships with the Microsoft Desktop Engine (MSDE), a limited version of Microsoft SQL Server. Tutorial 10 uses the MSDE to create and populate SQL Server databases. Of course, if the full SQL Server database is installed, then students may use the full (far more functional) SQL Server package instead of MSDE.

In addition, because the main application in Tutorial 10 (FigTickets) uses an SQL Server database, you must have installed Microsoft Data Access Components version 2.6 or higher before attempting to install it on any computer. If MDAC 2.6+ is not present on your system, the install of FigTickets will fail. If Visual Studio .NET is installed on your computer, then you already have MDAC 2.6+.

Figures

Many of the figures in this book reflect how your screen will look if you are using a Microsoft Windows XP system. Your screen will look similar to these figures if you are using a Microsoft Windows 2000 or Windows NT 4.0 system.

Visit Our World Wide Web Site

Additional materials designed especially for you might be available for your course on the World Wide Web. Go to **http://www.course.com**. Periodically search this site for more details.

Visual Studio .NET Editions

Visual Studio .NET is available in four editions: the Standard Edition, the Professional Edition, the Enterprise Edition, and the Enterprise Architect Edition.

All editions include Microsoft's Visual Studio .NET languages: Visual Basic .NET, Visual C++ .NET, Visual C# (read "C Sharp") .NET, and Visual J# .NET. Compatible languages and services from other vendors, designed for the .NET platform, are also becoming available.

Visual Studio .NET Professional Edition includes all of the components and functionality needed for this course, and indeed all of the programs in this text were written using Visual Studio .NET Professional Edition. The Professional Edition includes these essential features:

- Windows Forms — for the development of Windows-based applications
- Web Forms — for the development of Internet-based applications
- Console applications — for the development of applications without a graphical user interface
- Shared Integrated Development Environment (IDE) — the same development environment is used for all languages and for Console, Windows Forms, and Web Forms applications

- .NET Framework and Common Language Runtime — over 6000 classes (objects, properties, methods, inheritance, and overrides) underlie true object-oriented programming
- HTML and XML Designers — develop HTML and ASP .NET Web Forms graphically, without learning HTML code or scripts
- Visual Basic .NET Upgrade Wizard — provides assistance in rewriting Visual Basic 6.0 applications in Visual Basic .NET
- Microsoft SQL Server Desktop Engine — creates and/or connects to an SQL Server database
- Crystal Reports report program generator from Crystal Decisions, Inc.

As this book was being completed, Visual Basic .NET 2003 became available. The impact on application development is that you cannot switch back and forth between the original (2002) Visual Basic .NET and the 2003 release. That is, if you develop an application in the original package, and then convert it to the 2003 version, you will no longer be able to work on it in the original version. That said, both versions of the files are included with this text to circumvent any programming limitations.

To the Instructor

To complete the tutorials in this book, your students must use a set of data files. These files are included in the Teaching Tools CD-ROM. They may also be obtained electronically through the Course Technology Web site at **http://www.course.com**. Follow the instructions in the Help file to copy the data files to your server or standalone computer. You can view the Help file using a text editor such as WordPad or Notepad. Once the files are copied, you should instruct your users how to copy the files to their own computers or workstations, and how to unzip them.

The Tutorials and Exercises in this book were tested using the final version of Visual Studio .NET on a Microsoft Windows XP system.

Course Technology Data Files

You are granted a license to copy the data files to any computer or computer network used by individuals who have purchased this book.

A Tour of a Visual Basic .NET Application

The International Summer Games at Friendsville

Friendsville, your hometown of a half million people, has applied to be the host for a future International Summer Games, and is a finalist for this honor. As part of the continuing application process, every aspect of your city's readiness to host these games—including its ability to provide the required level of information systems support—is being examined carefully. Of course, hundreds of Friendsville's citizens have volunteered to help the Friendsville Organizing Committee (FOC) in any way they can; but until now, you have not found a meaningful way in which you can contribute.

Now, however, you do have just the opportunity you have been looking for. FOC has decided to develop a series of demonstration programs, written in Visual Basic .NET, to show the world that Friendsville is fully capable of providing IT support for the proposed games. You have studied Visual Basic, and now you are ready to apply your VB skills even as you continue to learn more about the rich capabilities of the VB .NET language and the .NET platform.

You will be working with a small team of like-minded, civic-spirited individuals: Hilda Reiner, Rick Sanchez, and Althea Brown. In some cases, you will work alone on a complete application. In other cases, you will incorporate modules written by other members of your team, or access databases available externally.

The applications you will write include all those needed to support the International Summer Games, including housing and dining services for the athletes, scheduling and scoring of competitions, credentials for all participants, and tickets for spectators. In terms of application architecture, you will develop Windows Forms, Web Forms, and Console applications; plus, you will access databases created in Microsoft Access and in the Microsoft Desktop Engine (MSDE), as well as sequential and random files.

On your first day with the Friendsville Games Development Team (FGDT), you and your colleagues, Hilda, Rick, and Althea, quickly realize that you each have different levels of experience with the Visual Basic programming language and the .NET platform. Hilda, with more programming experience than the rest of you, is quickly accepted as the team's lead programmer. As the junior member of FGDT, you will learn how to create, modify, and maintain computer applications written in the newest and most sophisticated development model by Microsoft, Visual Studio .NET.

This overview will give you a glimpse of the type and level of the projects you will be able to create once you have completed this text. Accordingly, the first step in your orientation will be to examine an application program that Hilda has written—one that will provide a sense of the kinds of projects and the level of sophistication that will be expected of you. Hilda's program, VillageHousing, will be used to assign athletes, coaches, judges, officials, and staff to accommodations in the International Village. Based on villager identification and housing inventory data stored in a Microsoft Access database, this application accepts new villagers, displays room availabilities, and facilitates room assignments.

Previewing the VillageHousing Application

The VillageHousing application is stored in the VB.NET\Student\Tut00\ VillageHousing folder. The application consists of one Windows Form with a Microsoft Access database as the back end.

tip

The graphical user interface (GUI) is often referred to as the **front end** of an application, because that is what the user sees, while the database or other data file is termed the **back end**, because it is hidden from the user.

To view the VillageHousing application:

1   Click the **Start** button on the Windows taskbar, click **Run** on the Start menu to open the Run dialog box, and then click **Browse** to open the Browse dialog box.

2   Locate and then open the **VB.NET\Student\Tut00\VillageHousing\bin** folder. Click **VillageHousing.exe** in the list of filenames, and then click **Open**. Click **OK**. After a few moments, Visual Basic .Net displays the VillageHousing application shown in Figure 0-1.

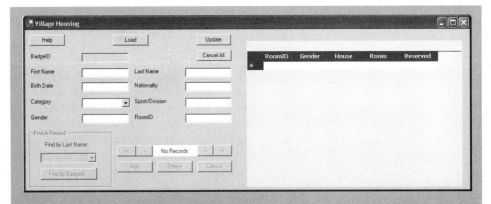

Figure 0-1: Main screen of the VillageHousing application

> **NOTE:** If you do not see the filename extension, your computer is configured to hide file extensions. To display file extensions, open My Computer or Windows Explorer, click Tools on the menu bar, and then click Folder Options. In the Folder Options dialog box, click the View tab. In the Advanced settings frame, uncheck the Hide extensions for known file types check box, and then click OK.

3 Note some of the user-interface features of this application. On the left side, buttons, labels, and text boxes are all neatly aligned. Click the **First Name** text box, and then press **Tab** several times; the focus shifts in a spatially logical pattern (left to right, top to bottom) from control to control throughout the form.

4 Try to click the **BadgeID** text box. You cannot move the focus to this text box because BadgeID has been disabled in the form. Note that the navigation buttons at the lower center of the form are currently disabled.

5 The Help button at the upper left of the form explains how to use the application. Click **Help** to open a Help window outlining basic information on the application. See Figure 0-2.

tip

••••••••••••••••••

▶ BadgeID is what Microsoft Access refers to as an AutoNumber field; if you click the Add button, a new, unique BadgeID is automatically provided. Because the field is disabled for data entry, you cannot enter your own number into that field.

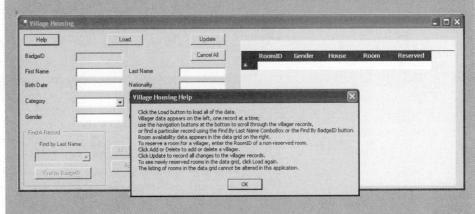

Figure 0-2: Help dialog box for the VillageHousing application

6 Click **OK** to close the VillageHousing Help window.

Now experiment with the application to gain an understanding of what it does.

To experiment with the VillageHousing project:

1   Load the data by clicking the **Load** button, as shown in Figure 0-3.

2   Note that the navigation buttons are now enabled. Scroll through the records of villagers already registered in the database. Click the **arrow** in the Find by Last Name combo box, and click **Able**. The record for Bonnie Able appears. Names are unsorted. Click **Find by BadgeID**, type **10**, and then click **OK**. Ivan Turkovitch's record appears. Click **Find by BadgeID** again, type **70**, and then click **OK**. Note the error message: *That BadgeID is not in the database*. Before clicking **OK**, notice that the last record in the database is displayed; click **OK**, and note that the first record is displayed.

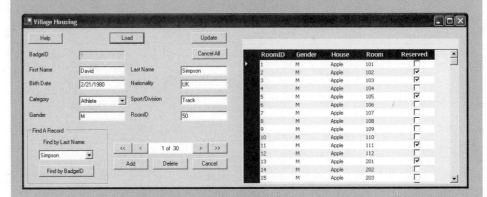

Figure 0-3: Data loaded in the VillageHousing Application

3   Make a room reservation by typing the indicated RoomID for the following villagers (in each case, scroll to the correct **BadgeID**, or click **Find by BadgeID** to get to the correct record; then enter the **RoomID**, and click **Update**):

BadgeID=14, Gerhard Werner, RoomID=**10**

BadgeID=15, Andrea Schmitz, RoomID=**98**

4   Change the RoomID for David Simpson, BadgeID=1, from 50 to **92**.

5   Add the following villagers. Click **Add**, and type into the text boxes, using Tab to move from text box to text box (in each case, changes are not saved until you navigate to a different record or click Update.):

Sally Petersen, 2/10/1969, USA, Athlete, Equestrian, F, RoomID=110

Sven Bjoernsen, 3/16/1980, SWE, Athlete, Track, M, no room

NOTE: As you experiment with this application, note that the software constrains some of the entries to assist the user to enter valid data. The Birth Date text box is defined as a date/time field—so only a valid date may be entered. Category appears as a combo box, and clicking the arrow identifies the possible entries: athlete, judge, staff, official, visitor, or coach. Gender must be entered as M or F. Finally, you must either leave the RoomID field blank (meaning that no room has yet been assigned for this guest) or enter a valid RoomID, that is, a RoomID that exists in the data grid on the right and that has not already been reserved for someone else. Some of these constraints are not checked until the record is saved to the database, either by navigating to a different record or by clicking Update.

6 Locate the villager with BadgeID **15**, and click **Delete**. Then delete **Miguel Jacinto**.

7 Click **Update** to record all of your changes to villager records stored in the database, and then click **Load** again. Note that the changes to the villager records are reflected in the newly reloaded data.

NOTE: The data grid has been formatted to have a pleasant appearance, but the data grid provides only minimal functionality. It lists the rooms in the International Village, showing the RoomID, house, and room number for each room, as well as the designated gender, and a check box indicating whether this room has already been reserved. However, the only way to update the reserved status is to reload the data from the underlying database. This is intentional: the reservations clerks who use this application are allowed to assign or cancel a room reservation, but cannot add or delete rooms in the International Village inventory.

8 Click the **Close** button to close the VillageHousing application.

Although this application includes some fairly sophisticated functionality as described in the previous steps, it is far from complete as a commercial application. Without too much difficulty, a user can make data entry errors that the application does not trap immediately, but that can cause aggravation later. For example, while entering a series of records, the reservations clerk might type a gender other than M or F. This mistake is trapped when Update is clicked, and the error message clearly says that only M or F is accepted—but it won't tell you which record is in violation. Another example is the application does not ensure that a birth date is reasonable or even possible (e.g., a future date is accepted by the system); it only checks that the birth date is a valid date (17/17/1980 would be rejected, because there is no month 17).

As you and your teammates run this application and examine its user-interface features and its functionality, Hilda explains that the Friendsville Games Development Team needs to develop many similar applications: applications designed to be used on only one computer or in a local area network (LAN), applications with only a single Windows Form or perhaps a small number of Windows Forms, and applications that use a fairly simple Microsoft Access database.

As part of your training, you will have the opportunity to create this VillageHousing application yourself in a later tutorial.

Configuring Visual Studio .NET

Visual Studio .NET supports application development in roughly 20 programming languages. Because you will be working in Visual Basic .NET, you should select settings in the Visual Studio .NET **Integrated Development Environment (IDE)** appropriate for a Visual Basic .NET developer. As you become more familiar with the IDE and develop your own programming style and procedures, you will probably want to customize these settings. However, the settings suggested here provide a good starting point and are consistent with instructions, procedural steps, and figures used throughout this text.

To start Visual Studio .NET and customize it for Visual Basic .NET development:

1 Click **Start** on the Windows taskbar, point to **Programs** (**All Programs** in Windows XP), point to **Microsoft Visual Studio .NET**, and then click **Microsoft Visual Studio .NET**. The Microsoft Integrated Development Environment opens. Maximize the Microsoft Visual Studio .NET window, if necessary.

2 In the left pane of the Start Page, click **My Profile**. See Figure 0-4. The My Profile page enables you to set some general parameters for the IDE, indicating, for example, which language you usually develop in, which Windows layout in the IDE you prefer, and which filters to apply to the Help screens that are offered when you search for help on a given topic.

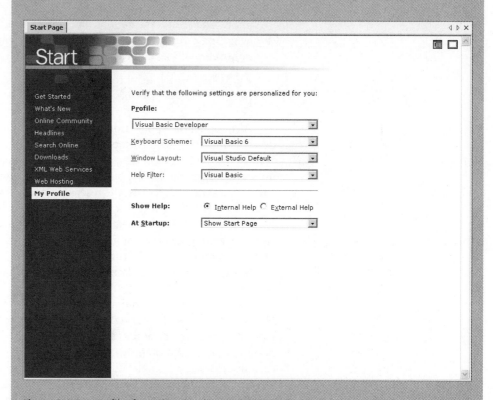

Figure 0-4: My Profile, from the Visual Basic .NET Start Page

3 In the Profile combo box, look at all the options in the drop-down list, and then click **Visual Basic Developer**.

4 In the Keyboard Scheme list box, click **Visual Basic 6**, if necessary.

5 In the Window Layout list box, click **Visual Studio Default**, if necessary.

6 In the Help Filter list box, click **Visual Basic**, if necessary. If you click Visual Basic and Related, the basic Profile scheme changes from Visual Basic Developer to (custom). The Help Filter setting determines which subset of the Visual Studio .NET Help files will be searched or available for all Help functions. Under Show Help, the selection Internal Help (the default) means that Help windows are displayed within the IDE; External Help means that Help windows are displayed in a window outside the IDE. The default selection is fine.

7 In the At Startup list box, you can make whatever choice is most comfortable for you. In this situation, click the default, **Show Start Page**.

The Visual Studio .NET IDE is now set for your use as a developer of Visual Basic .NET applications.

Creating and Opening a Visual Basic .NET Solution and Project

In Visual Studio .NET, a **solution** is a container for one or more projects. A **project**, in turn, consists of a computer program and related components, written in one of the programming languages supported by the Visual Studio .NET platform. The files that constitute a project are stored in the solution container. For the most part, the solutions that you create consist of a single Visual Basic .NET project. Therefore, for practical purposes, the solution and the project refer to the same Visual Basic .NET application. Opening a solution also opens the project in that solution, just as creating a new project also creates a new solution container in which to store the project files.

When starting to use Visual Studio .NET, students sometimes find the terms "solution," "project," and "application" confusing. The following sets of steps are designed to help clarify these terms. You begin by creating a new project and a new solution, closing the new project and solution, and then opening the solution (and noting that you have also opened the project). Then you close the solution again, and open the project (while noting that you have also opened the solution). Also, you create a new (blank) solution, and add a new project to that solution. Therefore you experience several different methods of creating a solution, creating a project, and opening a solution and a project.

To create a new project and solution:

1   Click **Get Started** on the Start Page, and then click **New Project**. The New Project dialog box opens, as shown in Figure 0-5.

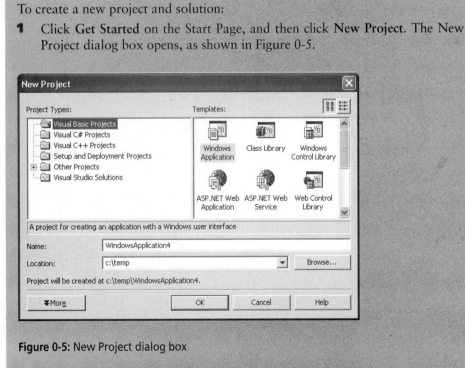

Figure 0-5: New Project dialog box

2   In the New Project dialog box, click **Visual Basic Projects** under Project Types, if necessary.

3   Under Templates, click **Windows Application**, if necessary. When creating a new project, you need to provide a name and location for storing the project and related files.

4 Double-click the **Name** text box to select the default name, and then type **Hello1**.

5 In the Location textbox, type **VB.NET\Student\Tut00**. The New Project dialog box appears as shown in Figure 0-6. Note that Visual Studio informs you that the project will be created at VB.NET\Student\Tut00\Hello1.

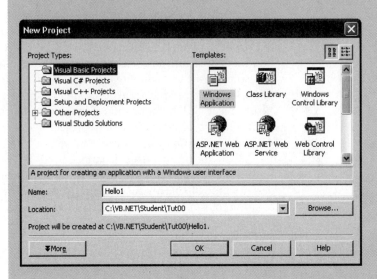

Figure 0-6: Completed New Project dialog box

6 Click **OK** to close the dialog box and finish creating the new project and solution.

The **Solution Explorer** window lists the projects, files, references, and other components that make up a solution. As shown in Figure 0-7, the Solution Explorer window is usually docked in the upper-right corner of the Visual Studio .NET IDE. Notice the following icons in this window and what they represent:

- Solution 'Hello1' (1 project)—Indicates the name of this solution (Hello1) and that it contains one project
- Hello1—Indicates that this is a Visual Basic project
- Form1.vb—Indicates the default name of the first form in a new project

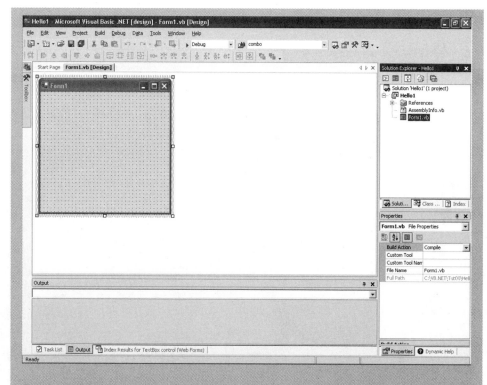

tip

The word "docked" in Microsoft terminology refers to a window that is locked in position along a particular border or in a corner. Most of the "dockable" windows can also "float" anywhere you want them in the IDE. In this text, dockable windows are always docked in their default locations; you can change these settings based on personal preference.

Figure 0-7: Solution Explorer window

7　Next, run the newly created program. To do this, click **Debug | Start** from the main menu. Alternatively, click the ▶ **Start** button. Visual Basic .NET saves the source file, compiles and saves the executable file (you can find it in VB.NET\ Student\Tut00\Hello1\bin\Hello1.exe), and then initiates execution of the program. See Figure 0-8. On the Windows taskbar, note that Form1 is a running program. (The name that appears on the taskbar is the value of the Text property of the active form.)

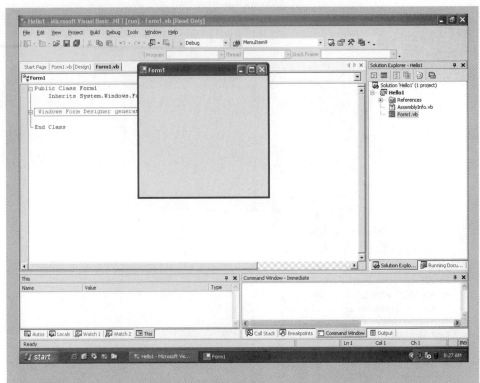

Figure 0-8: Running the Hello1 project

8   Click the **Close** button to end the running application. Note that Form1 no longer appears on the taskbar. Now close the solution.

9   Return to the Visual Studio .NET IDE if necessary, then click **File | Close Solution**. Note that the Solution Explorer window is empty, as shown in Figure 0-9.

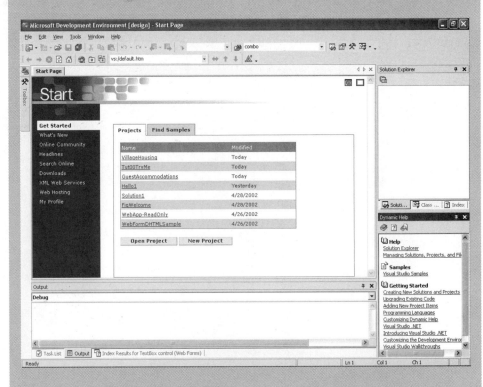

Figure 0-9: Empty Solution Explorer window

You can also open the project by opening the solution using the Open Solution command on the File menu. Try that method next.

To open the solution using the File menu:

1 From the Start Page, click **File** on the menu bar, and then click **Open Solution**. The Open Solution dialog box opens. In the Open Solution dialog box, the folders that appear depend on your previous use of the Open Solution dialog box. If necessary, navigate to the **VB.NET\Student\Tut00 folder**, as shown in Figure 0-10.

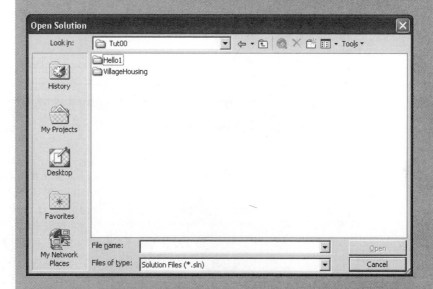

Figure 0-10: Open Solution dialog box

2 Double-click the **Hello1 folder**, and then double-click the solution file **Hello1.sln**. Note that Solution Explorer, which should still be visible on the screen, now lists the same contents as it did earlier when you created the Hello1 project and solution. See that both the solution and the project are listed.

3 Close the solution by clicking **File | Close Solution**. Again, note that Solution Explorer is empty.

You can also open a project directly, without opening its solution. You do this from the Open Project dialog box, which you access using the Open command on the File menu.

To open an existing project:

1 From the Start Page, click the **Open Project** button on the lower center of the page. The Open Project dialog box opens. In the Open Project dialog box, just as in the Open Solution dialog box, the folders that appear depend on your previous use of the Open Project dialog box. If necessary, navigate to the **VB.NET\Student\Tut00** folder, as shown in Figure 0-11.

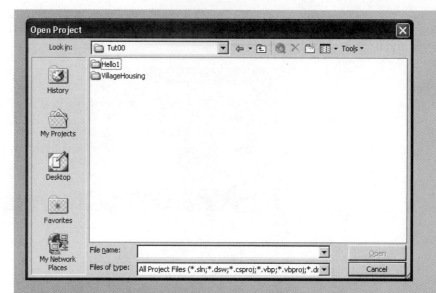

Figure 0-11: Open Project dialog box

2 Double-click the **Hello1** folder, and then double-click the project file **Hello1.vbproj**. Note that the Solution Explorer window now lists the same contents as it did when you created the Hello1 project and solution. If Solution Explorer is not visible, make it visible by clicking its tab or by clicking **View | Solution Explorer**. See that both the solution and the project are listed. Now you can experiment with adding a project to an existing solution.

3 Click **File | Open | Project**. In the Open Project dialog box shown in Figure 0-12, note the two option buttons that enable you to choose between Add to Solution or Close Solution. These option buttons appear in the Open Project dialog box only if a solution is already open. If you choose Add to Solution, the new project you open becomes an additional project in the current solution. If you choose Close Solution, the current solution is closed before another project (and solution) is opened.

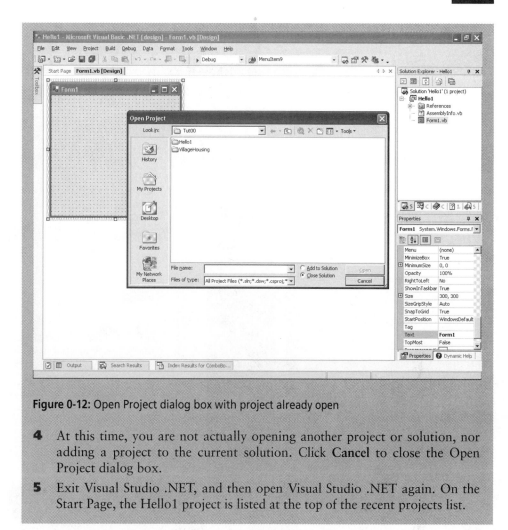

Figure 0-12: Open Project dialog box with project already open

4   At this time, you are not actually opening another project or solution, nor adding a project to the current solution. Click **Cancel** to close the Open Project dialog box.

5   Exit Visual Studio .NET, and then open Visual Studio .NET again. On the Start Page, the Hello1 project is listed at the top of the recent projects list.

In the previous section, you created a new application by creating the Hello1 project. However, you can also create a new application by first creating a blank solution container. This method creates a different folder structure within the solution container than what you saw with the Hello1 project/solution.

Creating a Blank Solution and Adding a New Project

Some developers prefer to start a new application by opening a **blank solution** (that is, a solution containing no project) and then adding a new project to that solution. This approach creates an extra hierarchical level in the folder structure on your computer—unnecessary for a solution containing only one project, but perhaps useful if you plan on creating a solution containing multiple projects. Although you will not be creating a solution with multiple projects in this tutorial, you might like to see how this approach works. Try creating a blank solution, and then adding a new project. Compare the files stored on your hard disk by this method of creating a new project/solution with the method used previously.

To create a blank solution and new project:

1 From the Start Page, click **File | New | Blank Solution.** The New Project dialog box opens, as shown in Figure 0-13. Visual Studio Solutions is selected by default for the Project Types, and Blank Solution is the only available template. Note that this solution will be created in the VB.NET\Student\Tut00\Solution1 folder.

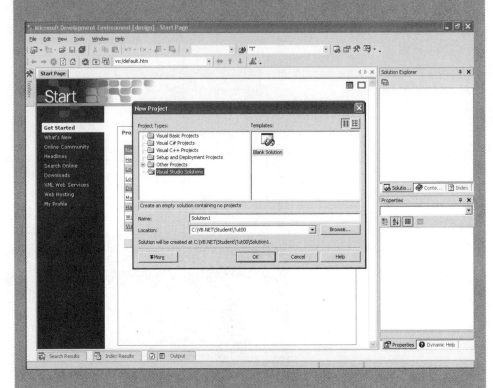

Figure 0-13: Blank Solution in the New Project dialog box

2 Click **OK.** The New Project dialog box closes, and the Solution Explorer window contains the name of the new solution and indicates zero projects, as shown in Figure 0-14. Now you can add a new project to the solution.

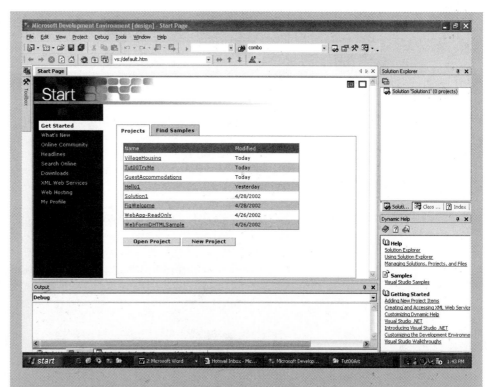

Figure 0-14: Blank Solution in Solution Explorer window

3 Click **File | Add Project | New Project.** The Add New Project dialog box opens, as shown in Figure 0-15. Notice the default project name, WindowsApplication1, and that this new project will be stored in the VB.NET\Student\Tut00\Solution1\WindowsApplication1 folder.

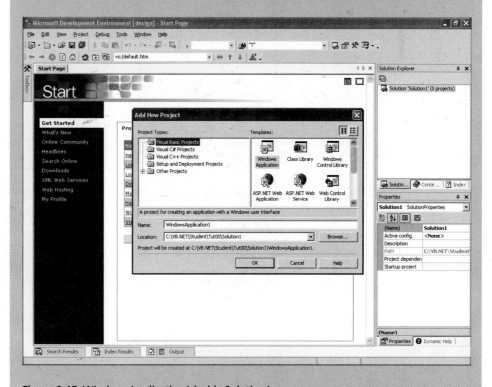

Figure 0-15: WindowsApplication1 inside Solution1

4 Click **OK** to accept the default filename and storage location.

5 Click the **Close** button to exit Visual Studio .NET. The Microsoft Development Environment dialog box opens and asks whether you want to save changes to Solution1.sln. Click **Yes**.

Thus far, you have created two solutions in Visual Studio .NET, each containing one project. You have created these items using two different methods. To better understand the differences between these two methods, you next use Windows Explorer to examine the solutions and their related folders for each project.

To view the solutions in Windows Explorer:

1 Open Windows Explorer and locate the **Tut00** folder on your computer. Click **View | Details**. In the left pane of Windows Explorer, click the **plus box** next to the Tut00 folder, then click the **plus** boxes next to the Hello1 folder and the Solution1 folder. Click the **Hello1** folder, and view its contents. See Figure 0-16.

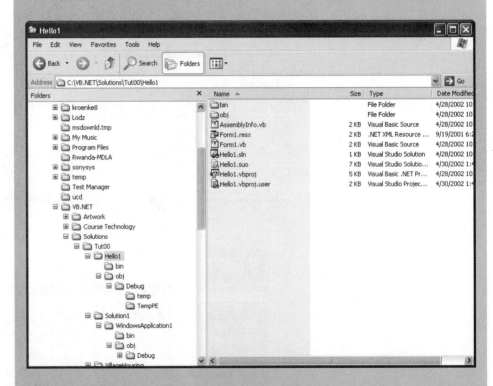

Figure 0-16: Hello1 folder displayed in Windows Explorer

NOTE: If you do not see the file Hello1.suo on your computer, you probably have selected the Do not show hidden files and folders option in Windows Explorer or My Computer. To change this, open Windows Explorer or My Computer. Under Tools, click Folder Options (or Options, in earlier versions of Windows). The Folder Options (or Options) dialog box opens. Click the View tab. In the Advanced settings frame, under Files and Folders, then further under Hidden files and folders, click the option button that reads Show hidden files and folders. Click OK. You should now see the Hello1.suo file. Inside the

Hello1 folder, you find the two files that describe the Hello1 solution, namely Hello1.sln (the solution information file) and Hello1.suo (the solution's user options file). In the same folder, you find the files that make up the Hello1 project: Hello1.vbproj (the project information file), Hello1.vbproj.user (the project's user options file), Form1.vb and Form1.resx (files that describe the form), and AssemblyInfo.vb (the project's assembly instructions). You have a chance to view the content of these files in Exercise 2 at the end of this overview. The Hello1 folder also contains two subfolders, bin and obj. The **bin folder** contains two files, Hello1.exe (the executable program) and Hello1.pdb (the Project Debug Database file, used by the Visual Studio debugger); these files are created each time the project is run from within the IDE. The **obj folder** contains files created during compilation and linking when errors are encountered.

Now you compare the contents of the Hello1 folder with the contents of the Solution1 folder.

2   In the left pane of Windows Explorer, click the **Solution1** folder to display its contents in the right pane. See Figure 0-17.

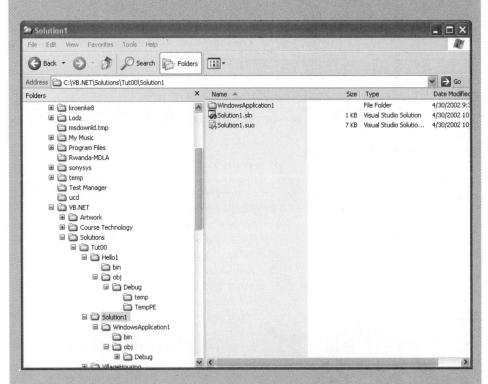

Figure 0-17: Solution1 folder displayed in Windows Explorer

In viewing the contents of the Solution1 folder shown in Figure 0-17 and comparing these contents to the folder contents for the Hello1 folder shown in Figure 0-16, note these two differences:

- The Solution1 folder contains the two solution files you would expect, Solution1.sln and Solution1.suo. However, unlike the Hello1 folder (which contains all the project files), the Solution1 folder contains another subfolder, WindowsApplication1, which in turn contains all the project files. In other words, creating the solution and project with one stroke, as you did for the Hello1 application, results in one less level of subfolders. In general, if you plan on a solution containing only one project, the technique of creating the solution and project together saves one level of complexity and is probably a good idea—this is the approach that has been adopted by the Friendsville Games Development Team. Creating a solution and then creating projects underneath that solution is the alternative approach more appropriate for solutions that contain multiple projects.
- VB.NET\Student\Tut00\Solution1\WindowsApplication1\bin is empty. This is because you have not yet run WindowsApplications1. Doing so would create the .exe and .pdb files, and these files would then be stored in the WindowsApplications1 folder.

You now have completed the Overview. You can either take a break or complete the end-of-lesson exercises.

SUMMARY

- Visual Basic .NET applications can provide solutions for many business information system requirements. Such applications can include a graphical user interface (GUI) running on a local computer, plus (in many instances) a back-end database.
- The Visual Studio .NET Integrated Development Environment (IDE) can be tailored to the needs of a Visual Basic .NET developer through the My Profile page, accessed from the Visual Studio .NET Start Page.
- A Visual Studio .NET solution is a container for one or more Visual Studio .NET projects.
- A solution may contain many projects, and each independent project may be created using a different programming language.
- A solution and project can be created at the same time and treated as a unit when the solution contains only one project.
- A solution can also be created by itself (a blank solution), after which new and existing projects can be added to that solution.

QUESTIONS

1. The first window that opens by default when Visual Studio .NET is launched is called the _____.

2. If the term "front end" refers to an application's GUI, then the term "back end" refers to its _____.

3. The window that lists all of the files in the currently open solution is called _____.

4. The common GUI, windows, programs, and services available to developers in all Visual Studio .NET languages is called the _____.

5. Your personal settings for Visual Studio .NET are recorded in _____.

6. Visual Studio .NET places the executable program in the _____ folder.

7. The filename extension for the solution information file is _____.

8. The filename extension for the project information file is _____.

9. The files stored by the Visual Studio .NET in the bin folder of a project are the _____ and the _____.

10. Both form files and assembly information files have the filename extension _____.

CRITICAL THINKING

At the end of each lesson, reflective questions are intended to provoke you into considering the material you have just read at a deeper level.

1. What is a Windows Forms application?

2. Distinguish between a solution and a project.

3. Why is it important for application developers to view and understand filename extensions?

4. In the Visual Studio .NET IDE, is it useful for a Visual Basic .NET developer to set the Help Filter to Visual Basic? Why or why not?

5. Which default settings for a Visual Basic Developer in My Profile are you most likely to change? Why do you prefer these changes?

6. What kinds of projects can be created in Visual Basic .NET? (Use the New Project dialog box to discover this information.)

EXERCISES

1. In this exercise, you create a blank solution on a floppy disk.
   a. If necessary, start Visual Studio .NET. Create a blank solution called Tut00TryMe, and store it on a floppy disk.
   b. Add a new Visual Basic .NET Windows Form project called TryMe. Change the Form1.vb Text property to Try Me.
   c. Change the BackColor property of the form to blue. Run the application. Exit Visual Studio .NET.
   d. Open My Computer and view the contents of your floppy disk. The Tut00TryMe folder should appear as in Figure 0-18, and the Tut00TryMe\TryMe folder should appear as in Figure 0-19.

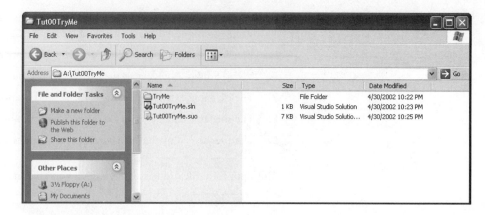

Figure 0-18: A:\Tut00TryMe folder

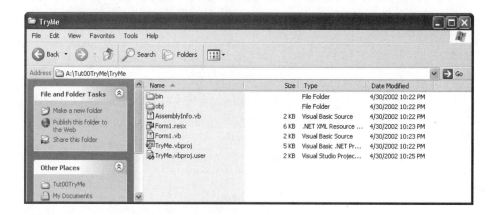

Figure 0-19: A:\Tut00TryMe\TryMe folder

2.   In this exercise, you examine the contents of some of the text files created by Visual Studio .NET. Start by opening Notepad or any text editor, because these files are stored as text. Then, click File | Open. In the Open dialog box, change the setting in the Files of Type combo box to All Files. Navigate to the VB.NET\Student\Tut00\Hello1 folder, and then open AssemblyInfo.vb. In one or two sentences, describe the contents of this file. Repeat this activity for each of the files in the Hello1 folder.

KEY TERMS

- back end
- blank solution
- front end
- Integrated Development Environment (IDE)
- My Profile
- New Project dialog box
- Open Project dialog box
- project
- solution
- Solution Explorer
- Start Page
- Visual Basic .NET file types and folders:
  - executable file (*projectname*.exe)
  - solution information file (*solutionname*.sln)
  - solution's user options file (*solutionname*.suo)
  - project information file (*projectname*.vbproj)
  - project's user options file (*projectname*.vbproj.user)
  - form files (*formname*.vb and *formname*.resx)
  - assembly information file (AssemblyInfo.vb)
  - bin folder
  - obj folder
  - Project Debug Database file (*projectname*.pdb)

The Visual Studio .NET and VB .NET Integrated Development Environment (IDE)

Navigating in the Visual Studio .NET IDE and Developing a Splash Screen

case ▶ Before you can contribute meaningfully to the Friendsville Games Development Team (FGDT), you need to learn your way around the Visual Studio .NET Integrated Development Environment (IDE), the set of windows and tools in which you will find yourself immersed as soon as you begin your first Visual Basic .NET application. Once again, Hilda Reiner has arranged a guided tour for you, Rick Sanchez, and Althea Brown. This tour includes visits to the various windows or screens available in the Visual Studio .NET IDE. If you have had previous experience with the .NET IDE, consider this a refresher. After taking the guided tour, you will develop a splash screen for general use by the FGDT.

Previewing the FIG Welcome Windows Forms Application

The backdrop for your tour of the Integrated Development Environment (IDE) will be your development of the FIG (Friendsville International Games) Welcome "splash screen" application. A **splash screen** is a form that appears momentarily in the foreground and then disappears, usually at application startup, and usually while a complex application is loading in the background. Some organizations always use a splash screen as the startup object for all applications to display the organizational brand name and to provide a consistent look to every application, at least at the start. In the present case, the FGDT proposes to use the FIG Welcome application as the splash screen for all of its projects.

To run the FigWelcome.exe application:

1   Click **Start | Run | Browse**.

2   Navigate to the **FigWelcome.exe** application, located in the VB.NET\Student\ Tut01\FigWelcome\bin folder. Select **FigWelcome.exe**. Click **Open**.

3   In the Run dialog box, click **OK**. FIG Welcome opens, appearing as in Figure 1-1.

Figure 1-1: FIG Welcome, running

Note several items concerning this simple application:

- The background consists of a repeating (or "tiled") image.
- The form has no border, so it cannot be resized or moved at runtime.
- The form has no title bar or control box.
- Controls on the form are limited to two labels and a button.
- On the Windows taskbar, at the bottom of your screen, the name of the running application is "FIG Welcome" with an American flag icon.
- Clicking the Close button terminates the program.

4   Click the **Close** button to close the splash screen.

After completing this lesson, you will be able to:

- Identify the three principle categories of Visual Basic .NET applications: Windows Forms applications, Web Forms applications, and Console applications
- Navigate through the Visual Studio .NET Integrated Development Environment's (IDE) Main menu and toolbars
- Understand the purpose of other major components of the IDE: Code window, Class view, Task List, Output window, Server Explorer, and Help screens
- Identify some of the key differences between Visual Basic .NET and earlier versions of Visual Basic

A Tour of the Integrated Development Environment

Understanding Application Categories

Before building your first application, you should understand the main categories of Visual Basic .NET applications with which you will be working. The FGDT will develop three types of applications (also called "projects" in the .NET documentation): Windows Forms applications, Web Forms applications, and Console applications.

Understanding Visual Basic .NET Windows Forms Applications

Programming a Visual Basic .NET **Windows Forms application** is most similar to traditional Visual Basic programming. The user interface is contained within traditional windows (the kind of interface seen in Microsoft Office) and the application executes entirely on the local machine, although data access could occur over a network. Any application running in a stand-alone environment is a good candidate for development as a Windows Forms application, and many applications running on a local area network also can be implemented in this way. Most business applications in small firms fit this model.

Figure 1-2 shows the Visual Studio Start Page, New Project dialog box. Visual Basic Projects is selected under Project Types, and Windows Application is highlighted under Templates. These are the correct selections to begin creating a new Windows Forms application.

New Project dialog box

Project Types

VB Projects

Templates

Windows Application

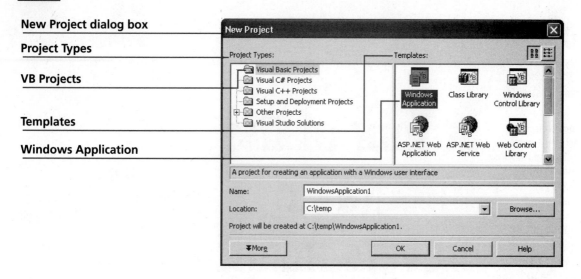

Figure 1-2: Start Page, New Project dialog box, with Windows Application selected

Understanding Visual Basic .NET Web Forms Applications

A Visual Basic .NET **Web Forms application** uses the techniques and protocols of the World Wide Web: the user interface is designed as an HTML or XML document (usually implemented as an Active Server Page (ASP) document). The end user's Web browser renders the HTML/XML/ASP document on the local machine. Meanwhile, the application executes mostly on a server, with little or no actual processing on the client end. Data access occurs over a network through an XML Web service. Although designed to support multiuser applications in an *n*-tier network environment, you can also apply this technology to applications on a stand-alone machine where part of the machine acts as a local host (server), and another part of the machine acts as a client. To render even stand-alone applications scalable and to standardize the user interfaces for both local and networked applications, some developers prefer to develop every application as a Web Forms application. This is a matter of personal preference and local organizational culture. To be a complete developer, you need to become familiar with both Windows Forms applications and Web Forms applications.

Figure 1-3 shows the Visual Studio Start Page, New Project dialog box. Visual Basic Projects is selected under Project Types, and ASP .NET Web Application is highlighted under Templates. These are the settings you need to create a new Web Forms application in VB .NET.

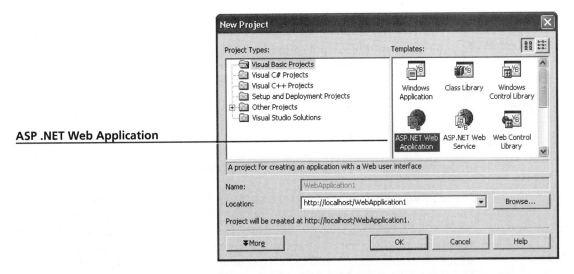

Figure 1-3: New Project dialog box showing the ASP .NET Web application selected

Understanding Visual Basic .NET Console Applications

A Visual Basic .NET **Console application** is a text-only application, which means that it has no graphical user interface (GUI). It is compiled into an executable and run from a command prompt (often referred to as a DOS prompt). Most often, Console applications support system utility functions and are more useful to the systems programmer than to the applications programmer. However, you will find the occasional use for a Console application. You can write a small Console application to experiment with or test a new coding technique, for example, without having to worry about designing a user interface.

Figure 1-4 shows the Visual Studio Start Page, New Project dialog box. Visual Basic Projects is selected under Project Types, and Console Application is highlighted under Templates. These are the correct options to create a new Console application.

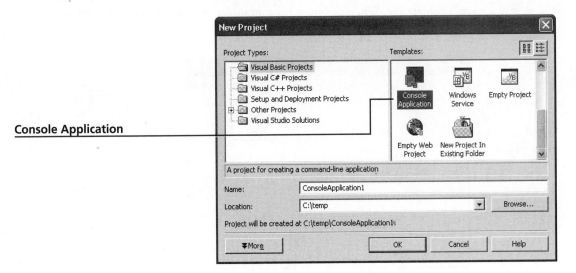

Figure 1-4: New Project dialog box with Console Application selected under Templates

Understanding Other Visual Basic .NET Applications

In addition to the three application categories just described, other templates for Visual Basic .NET projects are available. These include Class Library, Windows Control Library, ASP .NET Web Service, Web Control Library, and Windows Service. These templates will be introduced as you need them. However, the FGDT focuses primarily on Windows Forms applications, Web Forms applications, and Console applications.

Understanding Other Visual Studio .NET Development Tools

Visual Studio .NET offers development tools beyond those available with Visual Basic .NET. The tools available on your computer system may vary depending on which software is installed. A solution may consist of multiple projects. Each project provides a specific type of application written in one of the languages supported within the Visual Studio .NET family, including Visual Basic .NET, Visual C++ .NET, Visual C# .NET, Visual J# .NET, and Crystal Reports, to name just a few.

From the Visual Studio .NET Start Page, when you click New Project, you can browse through the various project types and templates available on your machine.

Understanding the Visual Studio .NET Integrated Development Environment

In this section, you explore the Visual Studio .NET Integrated Development Environment (IDE), while preparing to build the FIG Welcome application at the end of your tour: this is like preparing a sample recipe while touring a famous kitchen; surely, you will enjoy the tour!

Your tour of the IDE uses another simple application already built for you, called Visual Tour, shown running in Figure 1-5. If you care to look at the application during this discussion, it is located in the VB.NET\Student\Tut01\VisualTour folder, where you can open the VisualTour.sln solution or the VisualTour.vbproj project. From the Visual Studio .NET Start Page, you can open either a solution file or a project file. When the solution contains only one project, it doesn't really make a difference which one you open.

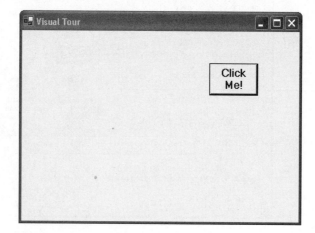

Figure 1-5: Visual Tour application, running

For fun, you can try running this game program, as shown in Figure 1-6, by clicking the Start button or by selecting Debug | Start. If you keep trying, you might be able to click the Click Me! button, at which point you win the game. (If you are not fast enough to click it, the program terminates automatically in 15 seconds.)

click Start inside the Debug menu

Start button

frmTour.vb [Design] tab--opens

frmTour.vb tab--opens

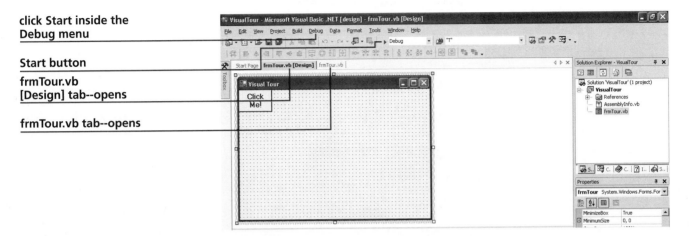

Figure 1-6: IDE showing the VisualTour project

You must be able to switch between the Windows Form Designer view of a form (where you develop the graphical interface) and the Code Editor view of the same form (where you write procedures). To make the form visible in the Form Designer window, you click the frmTour.vb [Design] tab, or frmTour.vb in Solution Explorer, and then click the View Form Designer button at the top of the Solution Explorer window. Alternatively, you can select Designer from the View menu, or press Shift+F7 to open the Form Designer.

To make the form's code visible in the Code Editor window, click the frmTour.vb tab, or click frmTour.vb in Solution Explorer, and then click the View Code button. Alternatively, you can select Code from the View menu, or press F7. As you continue with the tour, you often need to toggle between the Form Designer view and the Code view.

Understanding the IDE Components

The Visual Basic .NET Integrated Development Environment (IDE) consists of multiple components, some of which can be visible or hidden as the occasion warrants. The principle components are the Main menu, toolbars, Form Designer window, Code window, Solution Explorer, Class view, Properties window, Task List, Output window, Toolbox, Server Explorer, and Help screens. You won't need all these components or all the menu selections anytime soon. However, you do need to become acquainted with the items described here.

Understanding the Main Menu

The Main menu provides access to all the items you need in the IDE. This section describes the menu items that you use in this text. Although the Main menu changes depending on the context, Figure 1-7 displays most of the top-level entries. (This is the Main menu that is displayed when you are viewing the Windows Form Designer.)

Figure 1-7: Main menu with Form Designer the active window

Using the File Menu

The following list summarizes the main File menu selections, as shown in Figure 1-8:

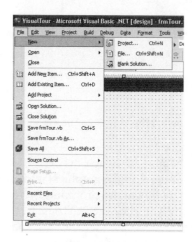

Figure 1-8: File menu with New submenu

- *New*—Opens a new project, file, or blank solution. If you open a new *project*, you must choose between adding this new project to the existing solution or closing the currently open solution. You must also choose which type of project to create. If you open a new *file*, you must choose the type of file to create; it is then added to the current project. If you open a blank *solution*, a new empty solution is created, to which you can then add projects.
- *Open*—Opens an existing project or file, either from your local computer or from the Web. If you open from the Web, you must know the URL of the server, and you must have the appropriate permissions.
- *Close*—Closes the file currently displayed in the main window. This could be a form (in either the Form Designer or the Code Editor) or a Help screen. Closing a file does not remove it from the current project.
- *Add New Item*—Opens the Add New Item dialog box, shown in Figure 1-9, which displays the list of potential new items available here.

Add New Item

Local Project Items

tip
• • • • • • • • • • • • • • •

The Add New Item dialog box is also available from the Project menu.

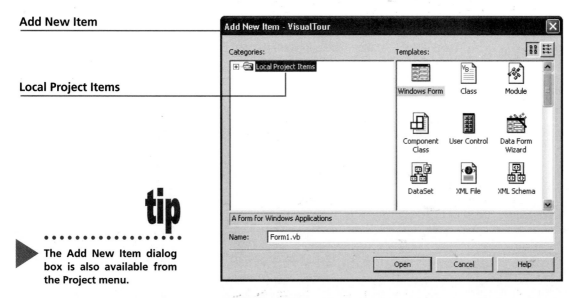

Figure 1-9: Add New Item dialog box showing all Local Project Items

Although you may not use all of these items any time soon, you should understand the kinds of items that you can add to a Visual Basic .NET project. To that end, it's useful to view the list of new items in their appropriate categories. Expanding the list of categories by clicking the plus box next to Local Project Items, and clicking the first category, UI (User Interface items), displays the choices in Figure 1-10. As you can see, these items are all graphical interfaces, that is, forms and controls: the familiar Windows Form, a Data Form Wizard (for accessing a database), or an Inherited Form (more about inheritance in Tutorial 2); a User Control (that is, a control designed by the user), a Custom Control, a Web Custom Control, or an Inherited User Control.

User Interface items

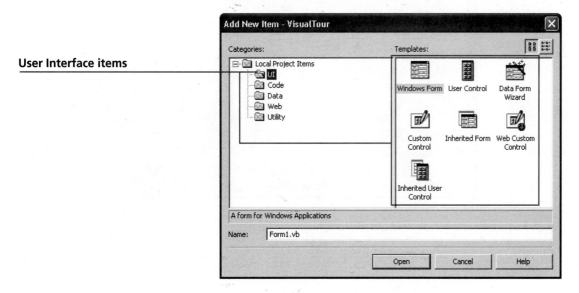

Figure 1-10: Add New Item dialog box—UI (User Interface) items

Clicking the Code folder displays the types of New Items available in that category. Figure 1-11 shows various class files and modules. (You learn about class files in Tutorial 2.)

Selecting the Data category, as shown in Figure 1-12, shows such new items as DataSet, Data Form Wizard, and XML-related components.

Code items

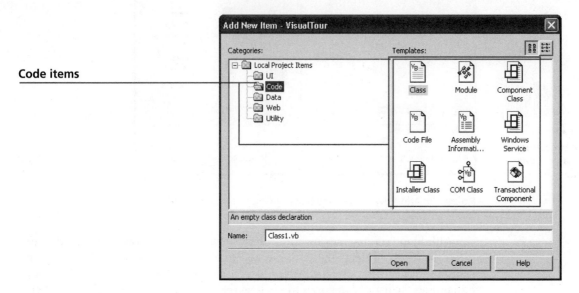

Figure 1-11: Add New Item dialog box—Code items

Data items

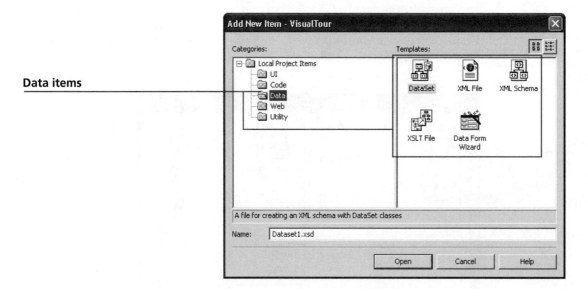

Figure 1-12: Add New Item dialog box—Data items

Figure 1-13 shows the Web category, which includes components related to XML and HTML.

Web items

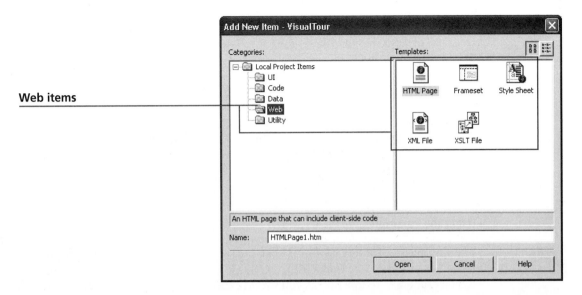

Figure 1-13: Add New Item dialog box—Web items

And finally the Utility category, shown in Figure 1-14, lists a Configuration File, Text File, Crystal Report, and various scripting files. Several of the file types occur under more than one category.

Utility items

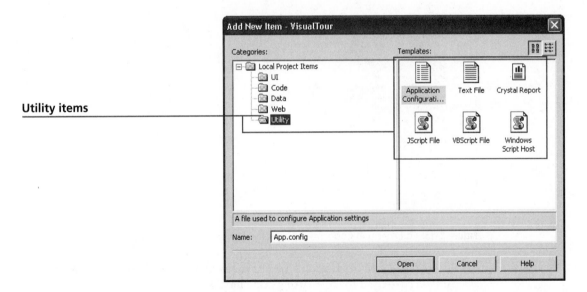

Figure 1-14: Add New Item dialog box—Utility items

The following list continues to discuss the remaining selections on the File menu:

■ *Add Existing Item*—Adds an existing file to the current project. A dialog box lets you select an existing component.

■ *Add Project*—Adds another project to the current solution. As mentioned in the overview, a solution is a container for one or more projects. This menu item allows the developer to add a new or existing project to the current solution.

■ *Open Solution*—Opens a new solution. (The current solution is automatically closed.)

■ *Close Solution*—Closes the current solution.

- *Save, Save As, Save All*—Saves the currently selected component, saves the currently selected component under a different name or in a different location, or saves all components.
- *Source Control*—Not installed in Visual Studio .NET Professional Edition. In the Enterprise Edition, Source Control allows an organization to control multiple versions of software, and to track changes made by each member of a programming team.
- *Page Setup and Print*—Selects settings for printing source code.
- *Recent Files and Projects*—A shortcut for opening the most recently opened files and projects.
- *Exit*—Exits Visual Studio .NET.

Using the Edit Menu

The Edit menu contains very little that is new or different from Microsoft Word or from Visual Basic 6.0. Undo, Redo, Cut, Copy, Paste, Delete, Select All, Find and Replace, and Go To function as you would expect. Cycle Clipboard Ring enables you to paste any items residing on the Windows Clipboard. Additional Edit menu items appear when you change the main window from the Form Designer to the Code Editor. To see these items, you click the Form1.vb tab, select Code from the View menu, or select Form1.vb in Solution Explorer, and then click View Code in Solution Explorer. When you are in Code view, the Edit menu, shown in Figure 1-15, contains these additional selections:

Figure 1-15: Edit menu in Code view

- *Insert File As Text*—Useful if you have saved a block of code as a text file.
- *Advanced*—Used for formatting code blocks.
- *Bookmarks*—Where you place your reminders and locators.
- *Outlining*—Enables you to create an outline for code.
- *IntelliSense*—Provides automatic statement completion and immediate assistance while coding.

Using the View Menu

The View menu, shown in Figure 1-16, contains, among other things, the list of IDE components. If you have closed any of these components, which removes them from the screen, you can open them again from the View menu. Such components include Code (the Code Editor), Designer (the Form Designer), Solution Explorer, Class view, Server Explorer, Properties window, and Toolbox. Of the additional items on the View menu, the following are most useful:

Figure 1-16: View menu providing access to various views and tools

- *Web Browser | Show Browser*—Displays the most recent HTML page (usually a Help screen or the Start Page), and enables you to navigate forward or backwards.
- *Other Windows | Object Browser*—Displays the objects in the active project or the available objects in Visual Studio .NET. As you become more familiar with the .NET Framework, you may find it useful to explore namespaces and classes in the Object Browser. (See Figure 1-17.)
- *Other Windows | Output*—Displays output (error) messages from the most recent compilation.
- *Tab Order*—A toggle for displaying the TabIndex property of every control on the currently displayed form. (To see the Tab Order menu item within the View menu, you need to switch to the Form Designer view.) The TabIndex property determines the tab order, that is, the order in which controls receive focus at runtime, when the user presses Tab. The control with TabIndex 0 receives focus automatically when the form is first displayed. If the user then presses Tab, the control with TabIndex 1 receives focus. Each time the user presses Tab, focus moves to the next control in the Tab Order, based on the TabIndex property—except that any control that cannot receive focus (such as a label or a disabled control) is skipped. In the current Visual Tour application, the Tab Order is unimportant, because frmTour contains only one control. On a data entry form with many fields, this Tab Order toggle switch is useful for assigning the TabIndex property correctly. For example, Figure 1-18 shows the Tab Order view of the VillageHousing application demonstrated in the Overview.

tip

A class is a template for an object, and a namespace contains any number of class definitions. These terms are explained further in Tutorial 2.

Object Browser tab

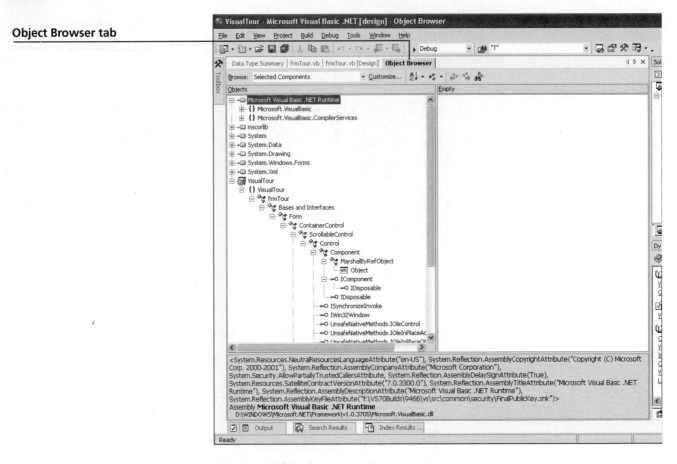

Figure 1-17: Object Browser

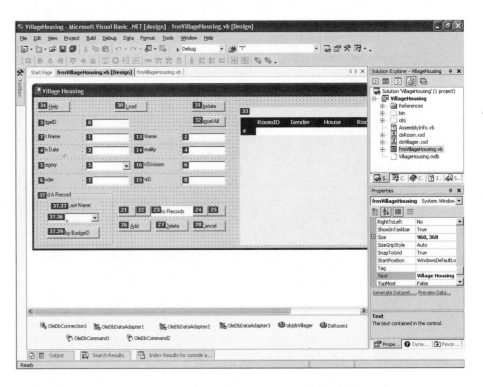

Figure 1-18: Viewing the Tab Order of the Village Housing application

- *Show Tasks*—Navigates among the tasks in the project Task List. On a large project, you may find it useful to make a list of tasks remaining to be done and to track your progress using the Task List. The IDE automatically creates a task to fix each syntax error uncovered during a failed compilation. In addition, you can insert any kind of task into this list, including sending a card for Mother's Day. (See Figure 1-19.) You can also open the Task List by selecting Task List within the Other Windows menu item under the View menu.
- *Toolbars*—Displays a submenu with 24 toolbars, which might seem like overkill. (See Figure 1-20.) If you turn all of them on at once, you won't have any room left on the screen to do any programming; however, from time to time, you might find it useful to open several of these toolbars.

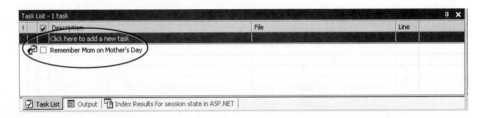

Figure 1-19: Task List

Toolbars

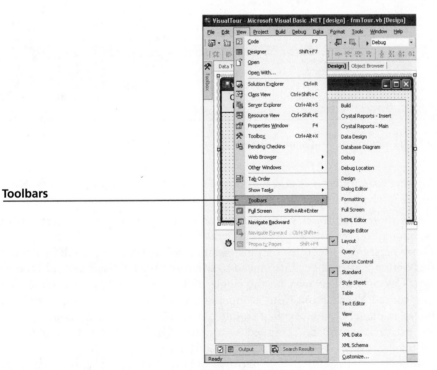

Figure 1-20: Toolbars

- *Full Screen*—Enables you to toggle the main window (Form Designer or Code Editor) between full screen (that is, filling all available screen space except for the Main menu itself) and Normal view (in which the main window occupies the center, but available screen real estate is shared with any other windows that are open).
- *Navigate Backward or Navigate Forward*—Changes the main window display to the previous display (Backward) or returns to the current display (Forward).

■ *Property Pages*—Opens the Property Pages dialog box, which displays certain global settings for a project. The Property Pages dialog box is available only when the name of the project is selected in Solution Explorer. Within the Property Pages, one of the most useful items is the General Properties page within the Common Properties folder, which allows you to modify a project's Startup object, as shown in Figure 1-21.

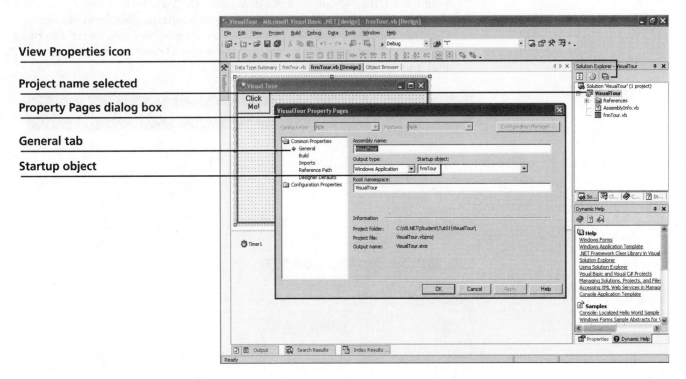

View Properties icon

Project name selected

Property Pages dialog box

General tab

Startup object

Figure 1-21: Property Pages—Common Properties—General

Another useful item is Build within the Common Properties folder, shown in Figure 1-22, where all four options are significant.

■ *Application icon property*—Designates an icon to represent the project while it is running (on the title bar and on the taskbar).

■ *Option Explicit*—Requires that all variables be explicitly declared. By default, this option is turned on. Introduced to Microsoft Visual Basic several versions ago, Option Explicit may be the single most important language refinement that turned Visual Basic from a home hobbyist's toy into a serious programming language. Option Explicit should always be turned on. Without it, a misspelled variable can be compiled as a new variable rather than treated as a mistake, causing unpredictable (and usually erroneous) results.

■ *Option Strict*—Requires that all narrowing conversions be explicitly declared and that late bindings not be allowed. For example, Option Strict would not allow a Single value to be assigned to an Integer variable, unless you use a Cint function, like this: `intMyNumber = CInt(sngMyFloat)`. By default, Option Strict is turned off.

NOTE: The professional programming community is of two minds on this topic: some believe that all narrowing conversions should be explicit, so that the computer programmer is prevented from accidentally truncating an important decimal value. Others feel that implicit type conversions are closely related to encapsulation or information hiding, suggesting that the computer ought to perform this type of conversion without specific programmer intervention. While the jury may still be out on this matter, the Friendsville Games Development Team has decided to accept the Visual Basic .NET default— Option Strict is left off in this text.

■ *Option Compare*—Allows settings of Binary (the default) or Text. This setting determines whether comparisons of string values are case sensitive (binary) or case insensitive (text). For example, with Option Compare Binary, "Bravo" is less than "alpha," that is, "Bravo" comes before "alpha" in the sort order: the ASCII representation of upper case B (66 decimal or 42 hex or 0100 0010 binary) is numerically less than the ASCII representation of lower case "a" (97 decimal or 61 hex or 0110 0001 binary). Again, FGDT follows the default.

Build tab

Options

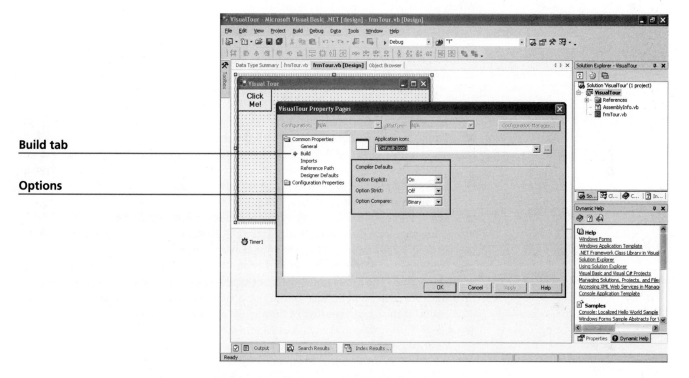

Figure 1-22: Property Pages—Common Properties—Build

Exploring the Project Menu

The first group of Project menu items (Add Windows Form, Add Inherited Form, Add User Control, Add Inherited Control, Add Component, Add Module, and Add Class) are shortcuts to the most common selections in the Add New Item dialog box from the File menu. Under the Project menu, Add New Item and Add Existing Item duplicate selections that are available in the File menu. Exclude From Project removes the currently selected component from the current project. Note that the Exclude From Project menu selection does not destroy the object (by deleting the file that describes that object); rather, it simply removes that object from the current project.

Understanding the Build Menu

This menu is useful when you need to compile a solution without executing it. You do not need this menu initially.

Understanding the Debug Menu

The windows and settings available from the Debug menu are invaluable in discovering why your code is not executing correctly. A central concept here is the **breakpoint**, a place in your code where program execution is suspended (not terminated), and where you can investigate exactly what is occurring. When execution is suspended, the program is said to be in break mode. The easiest way to set a breakpoint is to click the line of code where you want the break to occur, and press F9. (F9 is a toggle— you can click a line of code that has a breakpoint, and press F9 to remove the breakpoint.) While your program is suspended, you can examine the value of a variable or of an object's property. The Debug menu items change depending on which mode the program is in—design, run, or break. Although the Debug menu offers a total of 33 menu selections, the principle Debug selections and their definitions are as follows:

- *Windows | Breakpoints* (available all the time)—Displays all the breakpoints that have been set in the source code.
- *Windows | Autos* (available during run and break time)—Displays the names and values of all variables in the current and previous statements. The current statement is the statement that would be executed next had the breakpoint not occurred, or that is executed next when execution continues.
- *Windows | Immediate* (available all the time)—Displays a window in which the value of any expression can be immediately calculated and displayed. The keyword Print (or a question mark, which is an abbreviation for Print) is typically used to display values. However, you can also use an assignment statement to change the value of variables.
- *Start* (available only at design time)—Starts execution of the program.
- *Continue* (available only at break time)—Resumes execution after a break.
- *Stop Debugging* (available at run and break times)—Halts execution.
- *Step Into* (available at design and break times)—Executes the next statement.
- *QuickWatch* (available only at break time)—Displays the value of a selected variable. While in break mode, you can also view the value of any variable or property visible in the Code window by simply pointing at it with the cursor.
- *Clear All Breakpoints* (always available if at least one breakpoint exits)—Removes all breakpoints.
- *Disable All Breakpoints* (always available if at least one breakpoint exits)—Turns all breakpoints off temporarily. This is a toggle; once selected, it changes to Enable All Breakpoints.

Exploring the Tools Menu

The Tools menu offers a number of advanced features for adding third-party tools, macros, and sophisticated debugging features within the Visual Studio .NET environment. In addition, the Tools menu lets you customize the look of Visual Basic .NET. The Customize and Options menu selections let you tailor the IDE as you see fit. You do not need this menu for now.

Exploring the Window Menu

This menu is similar to the Window menu in all Microsoft Windows applications. When you are in Code view, you may find the **Split** feature useful, because it enables you to view two separate sections of code simultaneously. The Window menu also lets you switch the main or active window among all open windows.

Exploring the Help Menu

Finally, the Help menu provides access to Visual Basic .NET and Visual Studio .NET Help screens. (See Figure 1-23.) You will find yourself constantly using the following Help menu selections as you learn Visual Basic .NET:

- *Dynamic Help*—Displays, usually in the lower-right corner of the screen, a short list of topics related to whatever you are currently doing in the IDE. F1 also activates Dynamic Help, but only opens one Help screen, whereas the Dynamic Help menu selection offers a more complete list of Help topics.
- *Contents*—Opens the table of contents for the Visual Basic .NET Help collection.
- *Index*—Opens a search frame that enables you to enter a keyword and look for that keyword throughout the Help Collection Index. If the keyword relates to only one Help screen, that screen is displayed in the main window. If the keyword relates to more than one Help screen, the IndexResults window opens at the lower left of the screen, and all the related topics are displayed. Double-clicking one of these topics opens that Help screen in the main window.

Figure 1-23: Help menu

- *Search*—Opens a search frame that enables the user to enter a word and find it anywhere in the Help collection. If the search word relates to only one Help screen, that screen is displayed in the main window. If the search word relates to more than one Help screen, the SearchResults window opens at the lower left of the screen, and all the related topics are displayed. Double-clicking one of these topics opens that Help screen in the main window.

Understanding Other IDE Components

In addition to the Main menu, you need to become familiar with some other principle components of the Visual Studio .NET Integrated Development Environment. This section briefly discusses the main window, toolbars, Class view, Properties window, Output window, Toolbox, and Server Explorer. Several components have already been addressed: Solution Explorer, Task List, Immediate window, and Help screens (Contents, Index, Search, Dynamic Help, IndexResults, and SearchResults). You become more familiar with each of these IDE components through subsequent tutorials and through your own experimentation; the overview in the following sections is meant only as an introduction to the features of the IDE.

Understanding the Main Window

The lion's share of screen space in the Visual Studio .NET IDE is taken up by the main window. Tabs at the top of this screen space identify the open windows. (See Figure 1-24.) The initial choices here are the Start Page, the Code window, the Designer window, and the current Help screen. As additional windows or files are opened, other choices become available. Other IDE components surround the main window. Several of these are new to Visual Basic .NET or require further explanation.

Main Window tabs

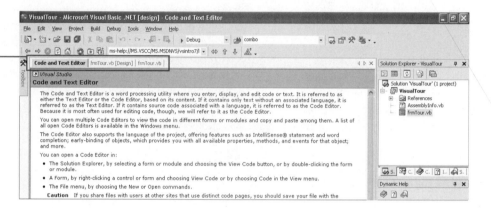

Figure 1-24: Main window tabs

Understanding Toolbars

Toolbars provide a one-click shortcut to menu selections. Although 24 different toolbars are available, the only one almost always visible is the Standard toolbar, shown in Figure 1-25. You can activate other toolbars as needed, and the software automatically activates some of them. Because an unused toolbar wastes valuable screen real estate, you can close any one you do not want to see by clicking the name of the toolbar in the Toolbars submenu on the View menu, or by clicking the toolbar's Close icon, if it has one. Because toolbars duplicate menu selections, none of them are actually necessary.

Figure 1-25: Standard toolbar

Understanding the Class View

The Class view enables you to examine all the symbols used in your application, or available to your application. Classes, as mentioned before, are intimately associated with notions of object-oriented programming, which you and your FGDT colleagues learn about in Tutorial 2 and subsequent tutorials. At the moment, just to get an inkling of what's in store for you, you can take a look at the components of Class view. The Class view becomes available by clicking its icon on the Standard toolbar, or by selecting Class View from the View menu. After clicking the expansion button a few times, the Class view of the VisualTour project looks similar to Figure 1-26. Double-clicking an item in the Class view takes you to an instance of that item in your code or in the Object Browser. You can continue clicking the expansion icon in Class view until you have displayed every namespace, class, object, property, and method that your application does or could use.

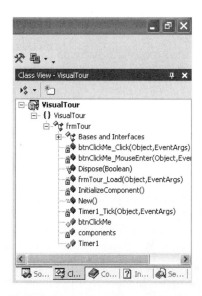

Figure 1-26: Class View of the VisualTour project

Understanding the Properties window

The Properties window displays all the design-time properties of the selected object in the Form Designer. Note the following features:

- Read-only properties are disabled.
- An expansion button appears to the left of group-level properties (properties that can be subdivided or broken down into lower-level properties). For example, you can expand the Location property for a graphical control, causing the Properties window to display its X (horizontal axis) and Y (vertical axis) components individually. Similarly, you can expand the Size property to display its Width and Height components.
- You set some complex properties by clicking an ellipsis (called a "Build button" by Microsoft), which opens a Property Page dialog box. For example, the Font property operates this way: when you click the Font property, the ellipsis appears to the right. Then, when you click the ellipsis, a dialog box opens that lets you set the font name, style, size, and effects.
- When you can select from a list of property setting choices, the Settings box is a combo box with a down arrow that lists the choices.
- The Property window has its own toolbar: clicking the Categories buttons causes properties to be listed by category (Accessibility, Appearance, Behavior, and so on); clicking the Alpha button lists properties alphabetically.

Understanding the Output window

The Output window displays messages to you from the IDE. Most often, you look at this window to see compilation error messages. The Output window is actually divided into a series of panes, each of which receives messages from different portions of the IDE or from other external tools. The panes available to you at any given point in time depend on which part of the IDE you are using.

Understanding the Toolbox

Although you may recognize many items in the Toolbox from previous experiences with Visual Basic 6.0 or with introductory Visual Basic .NET, some of the items in the Toolbox are probably new to you.

The Toolbox is subdivided by tabs, and the particular tabs available depend on the contents of the main window. When you are in Code view, only the Clipboard Ring and the General tabs are visible in the Toolbox. The Clipboard Ring contains items copied onto the Clipboard, and is an enhanced version of the traditional Windows Clipboard. It can contain up to 24 items simultaneously. So, for example, you could copy a number of different sections of code from a form or a project, switch to another form or project, and selectively paste each of the Clipboard items into it. The General tab contains only the Pointer.

When you are in the Windows Form Designer, the visible Toolbox tabs include Data, Components, Windows Forms, and General:

- *Data tab*—Contains a series of nongraphical controls needed for accessing databases; these controls are the subject of detailed treatment in Tutorial 9.
- *Components tab*—Contains controls that you can use with Windows Forms applications and Web Forms applications. For the most part, these controls provide access to events and services that exist outside your application. You do not need any of these items initially.
- *Windows Forms tab*—Lists all the standard graphical controls with which you are familiar, along with (for some of you) a few new ones. You learn to program with all these controls by the time you complete Tutorial 6.

When you are developing a Web Forms application, and you are in the Web Forms Designer, the Toolbox includes a tab for Web Forms controls. A few of these controls are introduced later in this tutorial, but most of them are explored in Tutorial 7.

Understanding Server Explorer

Server Explorer opens and manages data connections to both internal and external databases and related services. This window is discussed in Tutorial 9.

You have now completed Lesson A of Tutorial 1 and the tour of the Visual Studio .NET IDE. You may want to exit Visual Studio at this point. Take a break or complete the end-of-lesson questions and exercises. If you do decide on a break, don't forget to come back and finish these questions and exercises before moving on to Lessons B and C.

SUMMARY

- A Visual Basic .NET Windows Forms application is an application involving a traditional Windows-style user interface and is implemented entirely on a local computer.
- A Visual Basic .NET Web Forms application is an application involving a Web-style interface, usually intended for execution on a server, with the user interface rendered locally on the user's machine by a Web browser.
- A Visual Basic .NET Console application is a local, text-only application that runs from a command prompt.

■ The Visual Basic .NET Integrated Development Environment includes multiple views and windows. The most important for now are the Main menu, Standard toolbar, Windows Form Designer, Code window, Solution Explorer, Toolbox, Properties window, Output window, and Task List.

■ The Visual Basic .NET IDE provides extensive debugging facilities, including breakpoints, tracing (Step Into), and the Immediate window.

■ The Visual Basic .NET IDE also provides an extensive Help system, including various Help screens and windows (Contents, Index, Search, Dynamic Help, IndexResults, and SearchResults), context-sensitive Help (pressing the F1 key), and Web-based assistance.

QUESTIONS

1. The order in which controls receive focus is determined by the _____ property.

2. The measurement scale used in Visual Basic .NET is _____ .

3. In the Properties window, the Location property is broken down into the _____ property and the _____ property.

4. The window that contains a list of project files is called _____ _____ .

5. You can maintain a list of "to do" items in the _____ _____ .

6. The menu selection Add New Item can be found in the _____ menu and in the _____ menu.

7. To return the Main window to the most recent view, click the _____ _____ button.

8. The filename extension for a Visual Basic .NET form is _____ .

9. The Toolbox component that contains up to 24 items copied into it is called the _____ _____ .

CRITICAL THINKING

At the end of each lesson, critical thinking questions are intended to provoke you into considering the material you have just read at a deeper level.

1. What is the Output window used for?

2. Which lower-level elements make up the Font property?

3. Which Help screen is displayed when you press the F1 key while the form is selected in Form Designer?

EXERCISES

1. In this exercise, you start a Windows Forms application and add Button controls, and then reverse the Tab Order of the buttons.

   a. Start a new Windows Forms application called ReverseTab. From the Toolbox, drag a Button control onto the form. Repeat this procedure until you have five buttons arranged from top to bottom on the form. Do not change the default names or the settings of the Text property.

   b. Now reverse the settings of each button's TabIndex property, so that Button5 has a TabIndex of 0, Button4 has a TabIndex of 1, Button3 has a TabIndex of 2, Button2 has a TabIndex of 3, and Button1 has a TabIndex of 4.

   c. Click View | Tab Order to verify that the Tab Order has been reversed.

   d. Click Tab Order again to turn that toggle switch off.

   e. Run the program, and press Tab to move through the five button controls, again verifying that the Tab Order has been reversed.

2. This exercise demonstrates that Visual Studio .NET creates an executable program (an .exe file) when you run a program from within the IDE. Follow these steps:

   a. Run the Visual Tour program from the Windows Start menu. Click Start | Run | Browse. Locate the file VB.NET\Student\Tut01\VisualTour\bin\VisualTour.exe. Select this file, and click Open. Click OK again to execute the application.

   b. Open Visual Studio .NET, and open the VisualTour project.

   c. Make frmTour.vb visible in the Form Designer, if necessary, by selecting frmTour.vb in Solution Explorer, and then clicking the View Designer button 🔲.

   d. Click the Button control (btnClickMe). Click in the Properties window, and change the setting of the Text property to Touch Here.

   e. Run the program from the Windows Start menu again, and note that the button still reads *Click Me*.

   f. Now run the program from the IDE, and note that the button now reads *Touch Here*.

   g. Finally, run the program a third time from the Windows Start menu, and see that the button now reads *Touch Here*. This demonstrates that, when you run the program from inside the IDE, a new executable file is created, containing the revised Text property of btnClickMe.

After completing this lesson, you will be able to:

- Make practical use of the View menu and the Debug menu
- Create controls on a Windows form using the Toolbox
- Develop and implement a splash screen, both as a Windows Forms application and as a Web Forms application

A First Windows Forms Application

The View Menu and the Debug Menu

The tour of the IDE conducted in Lesson A becomes more realistic with some practical, hands-on experimentation. The View menu and the Debug menu especially require some practice.

Experimenting with the View Menu

The purpose of these brief exercises is to review navigating within the View menu (for those previously exposed to Visual Basic .NET), or to introduce it in detail (for those new to this IDE). You will discover many uses for the View menu. Before seeing how it works, you need to close all the open windows in the IDE.

To close all the open windows in the IDE:

1 Click the Solution Explorer **Close** button if it is open. If Solution Explorer is minimized (probably at the top right of your screen), move the cursor over it to restore it, and then close it by clicking its **Close** button.

2 Similarly, click the Class View **Close** button if it is open or minimized.

3 On the left side of your screen, click the Toolbox **Close** button if it is open or minimized, and close the Server Explorer if it is open or minimized.

4 Click, if any of these are open, the Properties window **Close** button (usually at the lower-right side of the screen), the Output window **Close** button, the Task List **Close** button, and the Index Help, Help Contents, and Dynamic Help **Close** buttons.

5 Finally, close the Form Designer as well as the Code window, and remove the Standard toolbar from view by selecting **View | Toolbars**, and toggling **Standard**.

6 If the main window contains a Help screen or the Start Page, close that as well. In short, everything that can be closed should be closed without exiting Visual Studio—so the only visible items are the title bar and the Main menu.

If you have indeed closed every open window in the IDE, you may be surprised to learn that you have not actually closed the files—the VisualTour project is still open and active—rather, you have merely removed all of these windows from view. Next, you reopen the windows or return these items to view, experimenting with different toolbar icons, shortcut keys, and menu selections.

tip

Each of these windows (as well as several others in the IDE) has an Auto Hide feature, indicated by an icon that looks like a pushpin ⊞, ⊞ on the window's title bar. This pushpin is a toggle switch: when the pushpin is vertical ⊞, the window to which it refers is completely visible whenever that window is open—that is, Auto Hide is turned off. When the pushpin is horizontal ⊞, Auto Hide is turned on: the window (when it is open) is visible only while the cursor lingers over it; at other times that window is minimized. The purpose of allowing secondary or supportive windows to be minimized is to conserve screen real estate for the windows you most want to see while you are developing an application, while allowing the secondary window to come into full view whenever you need it.

To reopen the windows in the IDE:

1 Redisplay the Standard toolbar by clicking **View | Toolbars | Standard**.

2 Then, on the Standard toolbar, click the **Solution Explorer** button , **Properties window** button , **Toolbox** button , and **Class View** button .

3 Select **frmTour.vb** in Solution Explorer. Then press **Shift+F7** to open the Form Designer and F7 to open the Code window.

4 Select **Show Tasks** on the View menu, and then click **All** to display the Task (currently empty) List.

5 Select **Full Screen** on the View menu to cause the main IDE editing window— Form Designer or Code window—to fill the entire screen (except for the Main menu, which is always displayed). See Figure 1-27. Return from full screen to Normal view by again selecting **Full Screen** from the View menu, or by pressing the toggle switch **Shift+Alt+Enter**.

Some of the other available windows are discussed when they are needed later.

Figure 1-27: IDE in Full Screen mode

Experimenting with the Debug Menu

The purpose of these exercises is to review the use of the Debug menu (for those previously exposed to Visual Basic .NET) or to introduce it in detail (for those new to this IDE). You will discover the Debug menu most useful for helping you debug your programs.

To experience the Debug menu within the Visual Studio IDE:

1 Open the VisualTour project (if necessary). In Solution Explorer, click **frmTour.vb**, and click the **View Code** button 🔳 to open the Code window (if necessary).

2 At the end of the Private Sub btnClickMe_MouseEnter event procedure, click anywhere on the last line (End Sub), and press **F9**. The line changes to a maroon background, with a maroon ball to the left of the line. This indicates that this line of code is now a breakpoint. When this statement is reached during program execution, execution is suspended and the program enters break mode.

3 Click **Debug** on the Main menu, and note the menu items available at design time. Click **Windows** on the Debug menu, and note the menu items available. (See Figure 1-28.)

4 Next, you examine the Visual Tour application at runtime, but the Timer control terminates the application after only 15 seconds. Therefore, you must disable the Timer. To do so, in Form Designer, click **Timer1** in the tray underneath the form. Then click the **Enabled** property in the Properties window, and set it to **False**.

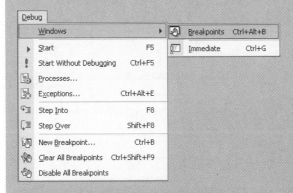

Figure 1-28: Debug menu at Design time

5 Select **Start** from the Debug menu, or click the **Start** button ▶ to initiate execution of the Visual Tour application. While the program is running, click the IDE. Note that you are in run mode and cannot make design changes; as the title bar indicates, frmTour.vb is now a read-only file.

6 Again, select **Debug** on the Main menu, and note the many different menu items available at runtime. Click **Windows** on the Debug menu, and note the menu items available. (See Figure 1-29.)

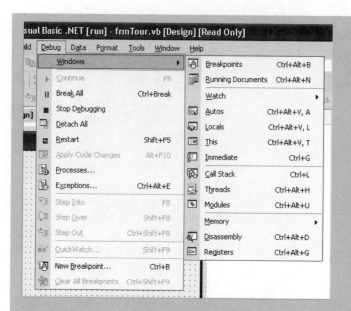

Figure 1-29: Debug menu at runtime

tip

The title bar indicates that you are in break mode. (See Figure 1-30.) The `End Sub` statement appears in yellow, indicating that this is the next statement to be executed when the program continues. The maroon ball with a yellow arrow on the left side of the screen indicates that this is a breakpoint.

7 From the Windows taskbar, click the **Visual Tour** running application. Move the cursor over the **Touch Here** button. Execution is interrupted, and you are returned to the Visual Basic .NET IDE in break mode.

highlighted line marks the next statement to be executed

arrow marks breakpoint

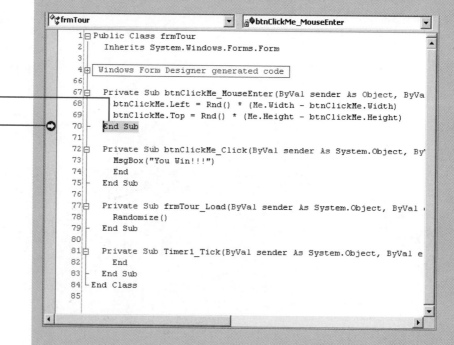

Figure 1-30: Code window in break mode

To continue working with the Debug menu:

1 Click the procedure heading, shown in Figure 1-31, and press the **F9** key. The maroon highlighting indicates that this sets up another breakpoint.

```
Private Sub btnClickMe_MouseEnter(ByVal sender As Object, _
    ByVal e As System.EventArgs) Handles btnClickMe.MouseEnter
```

Figure 1-31: Procedure heading

2 Use your mouse to point at an object and a property. Point at **btnClickMe**, and a ScreenTip appears, stating btnClickMe = {System.Windows.Forms. Button}. Point at the **Height** property of btnClickMe, and the ScreenTip reads btnClickMe.Height=48. While in break mode, pointing at an object causes the object's class to appear in a ScreenTip; pointing at a property causes the property value to appear.

> **NOTE:** A class is a model or template for an object. The class identifies the features and functionality shared by all objects in that class. The characteristics of the class are called attributes. The functionality of the class, that is, the things that objects based on that class are able to do, are called methods. When an object comes into existence, it inherits all the attributes and methods of its base class. The process of creating an object from a class is called instantiation, or creating an instance of the class.

3 Continue executing the program by pressing F5, or by clicking **Continue** on the Debug menu, or by clicking the **Continue** button [▶]. In the running application, move the cursor over the **Touch Here** button again.

4 Now execution is interrupted at the first breakpoint. Move the cursor over the **Left** property in btnClickMe.Left, and make a note of the property value, for example, btnClickMe.Left=244.

5 Click **Step Into** on the Debug menu. This causes one statement to execute, and then returns the program to break mode. Note that the header line for the procedure turns maroon, identifying it as a breakpoint. It is no longer in yellow. Rather, the line that assigns a new value to btnClickMe.Left is yellow, meaning that this is the next line to execute.

6 Point at the **Left** property in btnClickMe.Left. Note that this property value has not changed.

7 Now press F8, the shortcut key for Step Into. Once again, point the cursor at the **Left** property in btnClickMe.Left. Note that this property value changes to, for example, btnClickMe.Left=15.

8 Click **Clear All Breakpoints** on the Debug menu, which removes both of the breakpoints you previously set.

9 Continue executing the program by pressing **F5**, by clicking **Continue** on the Debug menu, or by clicking the **Continue** button [▶]. End this program when you are done examining it.

tip

• • • • • • • • • • • • • • • • •

The **Left** property determines the number of pixels between the left edge of an object and the left edge of the object's container. In Visual Basic 6.0, the default measurement scale for this property and for all dimensions was twips, although you could have chosen a different measurement scale. In Visual Basic .NET, all measurements, except for font sizes, are in pixels.

Creating Controls Using the Toolbox

Lesson B in Tutorial 1 steps you through the construction of three simple programs for the Friendsville Games Development Team, including two Windows Forms applications (the Visual Tour and the Friendsville International Games Welcome Screen that you saw in Lesson A), and one Web Forms application (Web page version of the FIG Welcome project).

Even though the Visual Tour project has been provided to you, try building the project yourself from scratch. The completed form at design time should resemble Figure 1-32.

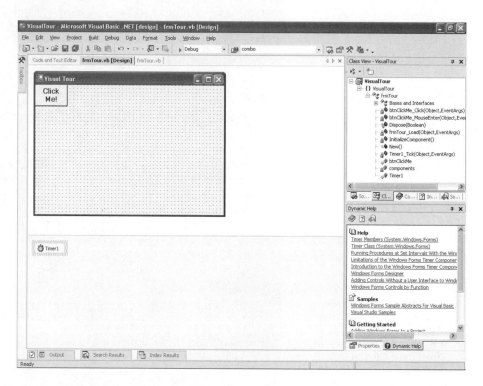

Figure 1-32: Completed frmTour at design time

To start building the MyTour application (your personalized version of Visual Tour):

1　Open **Visual Studio .NET**.

2　From the Start Page, click **New Project**. The New Project dialog box displays a list of available options.

3　In the New Project dialog box, under Project Types, select **Visual Basic Projects** (if necessary), and under Templates, select **Windows Application** (if necessary). The template determines which type of Visual Basic object you want to create.

4　Change the name of the new project to **MyTour**. The default name for each template is not meaningful, so you should change it to something that is meaningful.

5　Modify the location of this new project to **VB.NET\Student\Tut01**, and then click **Open**.

NOTE: Ideally, your projects should be created on your computer's hard drive or a network drive. If you are working in a student lab, and if you have write privileges to a hard drive, you should always create a new project in a folder on the hard drive. Then, after you exit Visual Studio .NET, copy the entire folder containing your project to a floppy disk, assuming you do not have the capability of retaining your work on the hard drive. In this manner, you save a lot of time waiting for compilations—the process of compiling, linking, and executing from a floppy disk is rather tedious.

6   Click **OK**. The MyTour project is created in the location you specified.

Starting with the basic template for the MyTour project, you now customize the graphical user interface (that is, the visual form), and write the code to complete the application.

To continue building MyTour:

1   Right-click **Form1.vb** in Solution Explorer. Click **Rename**, and change the name of the form to **frmMyTour.vb**. Alternatively, you can click **Form1.vb** in Solution Explorer, then click **File Name** in the Properties window, and type **frmMyTour.vb** in the Settings box.

NOTE: The internal form name does not automatically propagate to the external filename. Rather, you must set each name individually—the name of the file in the File Properties (visible in the Properties window when the filename is selected in Solution Explorer), as well as the internal object name of the form (visible in the Properties window when the form is selected in the Form Designer).

2   If necessary, open the **Form Designer** and select the form. Then click inside the Properties window. See Figure 1-33 for a partial listing of the 53 design-time properties of a form.

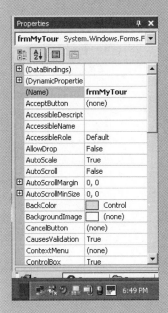

Figure 1-33: Properties window for a form

tip

In earlier Visual Basic releases, the Text property was called the Caption property.

caution

WARNING! You cannot set the Startup object property in the project's Property Pages until after you have renamed the form.

NOTE: Properties can be listed by category by clicking ▦ at the top of the Properties window. The categories include Accessibility, Appearance, Behavior, Configurations, Data, Design, Focus, Layout, Miscellaneous, and Window Style. The properties can also be listed alphabetically by clicking ↓. In the alphabetical listing, the first three entries are not, in fact, alphabetical: DataBindings, DynamicProperties, and Name precede the alphabetical list.

3 Set the Form properties as shown in Figure 1-34.

Property	Setting
Name	frmMyTour
BackColor	Pick a light blue
Size	Width 440 pixels, height 320 pixels
Text	Visual Tour

Figure 1-34: Property settings for the form

4 In Solution Explorer, select the project name **MyTour**. Click the **Properties** icon. When the MyTour Property Pages opens, under Startup object, select **frmMyTour** from the drop-down list, and click **OK**. A project's Startup object is the form or procedure that executes first when the project begins to execute.

5 Open the **Toolbox** at the top left of the screen. Click the **Button** control, and drag it onto the form. Alternatively, you can double-click the **Button** control in the Toolbox, and Visual Basic places the control on the form. See Figure 1-35.

NOTE: You have several options for displaying the Toolbox. First, as noted earlier, you can use the pushpin icons to turn Auto Hide on or off. Next, the initial order of the controls is in decreasing order of frequency of use, so the most common controls are at the head of the list. You can right-click any individual control, and then select Move up or Move down to change its order in the list. You can also sort all the controls alphabetically. In the default List view, all the Windows Forms controls do not fit in the Toolbox window at once, so you need to scroll to find the controls that are hidden. After you become familiar with the icons that represent the controls, or at least most of them, you may want to switch the List view off—again by right-clicking any item, and selecting List view, which is a toggle. When List view is off, all the icons fit in the Toolbox window, and a ScreenTip appears containing the name of each control when you point to it with the cursor, as shown in Figure 1-36. If you want, you can also show all the Toolbox tabs at once, rather than the default display, which shows only those tabs relevant to the current view. If you click Customize Toolbox, a dialog box enables you to add any of dozens of additional controls to the Toolbox, and a Reset button allows you to reset the entire Toolbox to the original default settings.

Figure 1-35: Toolbox with the Button control highlighted

Figure 1-36: Toolbox with the List view turned off

6   With the Button control on the form selected, set the properties in the Button control's Properties window, as shown in Figure 1-37.

Property	Setting
Name	btnClickMe
Font.Size	12 points, bold
Size	Width 75 pixels, height 48 pixels
Text	Click Me!

Figure 1-37: Property settings for the Button control

7 Drag a **Timer** control from the Toolbox onto the form. In the Visual Basic .NET Form Designer, nongraphical controls (controls that are not visible at runtime) appear in a tray underneath the form. Set the timer's **Interval** property to **15000** (15000 milliseconds, or 15 seconds). Set the Timer's **Enabled** property to **True**.

8 This application requires program code in four event procedures. Switch to the Code Editor by clicking **Code** from the View menu. Start with the btnClickMe_MouseEnter event. Open this procedure by clicking **btnClickMe** in the Class Name combo box at the top left of the Code window. See Figure 1-38. Then in the Method Name combo box at the top right of the Code window, click the **MouseEnter** event. At this point, the btnClickMe_MouseEnter event procedure appears in the Code window, and the insertion point is blinking inside that procedure.

Class Name combo box

Method Name combo box

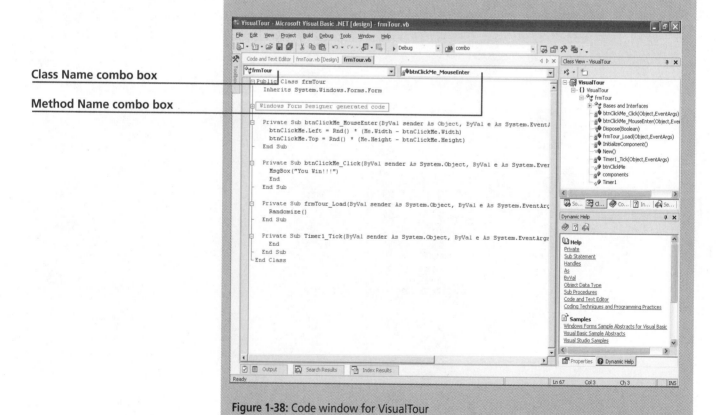

Figure 1-38: Code window for VisualTour

9 Enter the following code in the btnClickMe_MouseEnter procedure:

```
btnClickMe.Left = Rnd() * (Me.Width - btnClickMe.Width)
btnClickMe.Top = Rnd() * (Me.Height - btnClickMe.Height)
```

NOTE: The Rnd() function generates a random fraction less than 1. You experiment with the random number generator in the Console application in Lesson C of this tutorial. For now, notice that the result of this calculation repositions btnClickMe somewhere on the form. Me.Width is the width of the form in pixels (Me always refers to the active form). Hence, the expression Me.Width – btnClickMe.Width is the width of the form less the width of the Button control. Multiply this value times a fractional value (returned by Rnd()), and the result is between 0 and the expression, which is then assigned to btnClickMe.Width. The same logic is used to generate a new value for btnClickMe.Top.

10 Add the lines of code in the following list to the indicated event procedures. Select the object from the Class Name combo box at the top left of the Code window, and select the event from the Method Name combo box at the top right:

- In the btnClickMe_Click event procedure, this code declares victory for the user, and then exits the program:

```
MsgBox("You Win!!!")
End
```

- Open the **frmMyTour_Load** event procedure, by clicking **Base Class Events** (rather than frmMyTour) in the Class Name combo box, and then clicking **Load** in the Method Name combo box. Insert this statement into the frmMyTour_Load event procedure:

```
Randomize()
```

Randomize() improves the performance of the random number generator. (More on the Randomize statement in Lesson C.)

- In the Timer1_Tick event procedure, kill the program when the timer event fires (after 15 seconds):

```
End
```

11 Now run the MyTour application by clicking the **Start** button ▶ or pressing F5. *Voila!* Your first real, albeit quite simple, Visual Basic .NET program! Try to move the cursor over **Click Me**, and click it. If you fail to click the button in time, the program stops in 15 seconds. Aren't you pleased with yourself?

12 Close the project.

Building the FIG Welcome Splash Screen: a Windows Forms Application

Building this application may be slightly more challenging than building MyTour, because the completed program has not been provided to you. But all the steps needed to build this application are included here. Examine the completed form, as shown in Figure 1-39.

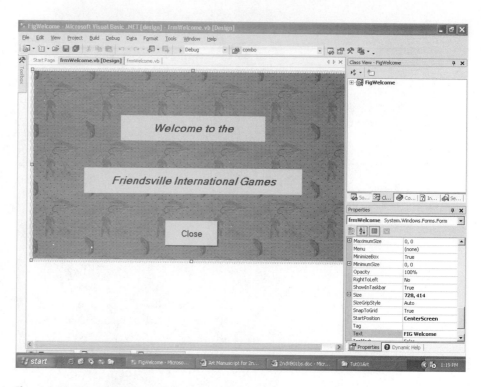

Figure 1-39: Completed frmWelcome

To build the FIG Welcome Splash Screen application:

1   Start a new Windows Forms application called **FigWelcome**. Store this application in the **VB.NET\Student\Tut01** folder.

2   In Solution Explorer, select **Form1.vb**, and change its name (directly in Solution Explorer or in File Properties) to **frmWelcome.vb**. You do this the same way you did it earlier in the MyTour project, and as you will do it in all other projects hereafter.

3   Select the **form** in the Form Designer, and assign the property values, as shown in Figure 1-40.

tip

The Icon property of a form determines which icon appears on the title bar and on the Windows taskbar (along the bottom of the screen) at runtime. No icon appears on the title bar if the ControlBox property is False, or if the FormBorderStyle is set to None. Because the ControlBox property for frmWelcome is set to False, the flag icon appears only in the Windows taskbar.

Property	Setting
Name	frmWelcome
Background Image	Gone Fishing.bmp (from the C:\Windows or C:\WINNT folder)
ControlBox	False
FormBorderStyle	None
Icon	flgusa02.ico (from the Program Files\Microsoft Visual Studio.Net\Common7\Graphics\icons\Flags\ folder)
Size	734, 446
StartPosition	CenterScreen
Text	FIG Welcome

Figure 1-40: Property settings for frmWelcome

▶ If a control is not referenced in code, most programmers leave the default name provided by Visual Basic .NET. If you do change the default name of a label, the correct prefix is lbl.

4 In Solution Explorer, select the project name **FigWelcome**, and click the **Properties** button 🗒 to open the Property Pages for the project. In the General page under the Common Properties tab, reset the Startup object to **frmWelcome**.

5 Place two **Label** controls on the form, as indicated in Figure 1-39. To place a Label control on a form, double-click the **Label** button A in the Toolbox, or select the **control** in the Toolbox and drag it onto the form. Set the **Size** and **Location** roughly as shown. Set the following additional properties.

- Change the Font to **Bold, Italic, 18** points for both labels. Font size is still given in printer's points, even though most other measurements in Visual Studio .NET are given in pixels.
- Change the Text property of the first label to **Welcome to the** and the Text property of the second label to **Friendsville International Games**. The Text property of a Label control was called the Caption property in previous versions of VB.
- Change TextAlign to **MiddleCenter** (the button in the middle of the pop-up). The TextAlign property determines where within the label the text appears.

6 Place a single **Button** control on the form, as indicated in Figure 1-39. Set the **Size** and **Location** roughly as shown. Use the additional settings shown in Figure 1-41.

Property	Setting
Name	btnClose
Font	Bold, 14 points
Text	Close
TextAlign	MiddleCenter

Figure 1-41: Property settings for the Close button

7 Select all three controls on the form. You can do this either by clicking one control, and then pressing **Ctrl** or **Shift** and clicking each of the others; or by clicking anywhere on the form and, while holding the mouse button down, drawing a rectangle on the form that includes all three controls. When all three controls are selected, each displays handles at the corners.

8 With all of the controls selected, click **Format | Center in Form | Horizontally**. All three controls are centered in the form from left to right. Select **Format | Vertical Spacing | Make Equal**. This command equalizes the vertical spacing between controls.

9 While still in the Form Designer, double-click **btnClose**, which opens the Code window for the btnClose_Click event procedure. Type the only statement required in this procedure: **End**.

10 Run the application to verify that it works as advertised. Click the **Close** button to end the application.

11 Back in the IDE, click **File | Close Solution** to close the FigWelcome project.

You now have two Windows Forms applications under your belt.

Building a Web Welcome Splash Screen: a Web Forms Application

Don't panic! You're not really going to learn all about programming Web Forms applications in this first tutorial. Rather, you simply apply what you have learned about the Visual Basic .NET IDE to the creation of a Web Forms version of the FigWelcome Splash Screen application. By doing so, you see how easy it can be to develop and publish a Web page using Visual Basic .NET. The completed application should appear as in Figure 1-42.

Figure 1-42: WebWelcome Web Forms application, running

You do need a modicum of knowledge concerning file structures. Your WebWelcome project will be created on a virtual Web server named http://localhost. The solution file is stored by default in C:\My Documents\Visual Studio Projects\WebWelcome. All of the other files are created in C:\Inetpub\ wwwroot\WebWelcome.

To create the WebWelcome project:

1 Start a New Project. In the New Project dialog box, under Templates for Visual Basic Projects, select **ASP.NET Web Application**. Change the value in the Location box from http://localhost/WebApplication1 to **http://localhost/ WebWelcome**. See Figure 1-43. Click **OK**. The new project opens.

NOTE: A Web Forms application can use a Web form located on any accessible server. If the Web form is on the local machine, it is located on a virtual server called http://localhost. Physically, you can find all the project and Web form files in the Inetpub\ wwwroot\ folder. Visual Studio creates two files for each Web form: an aspx file contains the graphical interface, and an aspx.vb file contains the "Code-Behind" as Microsoft likes to call it.

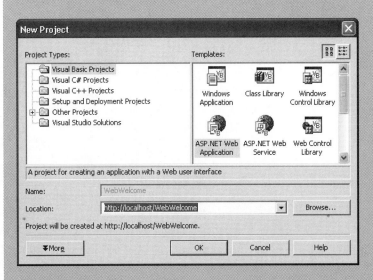

Figure 1-43: New Project dialog box

The Set As Start Page com-mand provides the same functionality as designating the Startup object in a Windows Forms application.

2   In Solution Explorer, change the name of WebForm1.aspx to **WebWelcome.aspx**. Then right-click **WebWelcome.aspx**, and click **Set As start page**. If necessary, click the **WebWelcome.aspx** tab in the main window, so that the blank Web form is displayed.

   NOTE: For compliance with the nomenclature for eXtensible Markup Language (XML) established by the World Wide Web Consortium (W3C), a Web form in Visual Studio .NET is known internally as a document. Every XML docu-ment begins with a document type declaration (DTD), which, in the case of a Visual Basic .NET Web Forms application, identifies this document as a Web form.

3   In the Properties window, set the DOCUMENT properties as shown in Figure 1-44.

Property	Setting
background	GoneFishing.bmp
bgColor	Yellow
pageLayout	GridLayout

Figure 1-44: Property settings for DOCUMENT

4   From the Toolbox, place two **Label** controls on the form, and set the Text property as shown in Figure 1-42. Then, click the **expansion** icon to the left of the Font property, and set the Font subelement properties as shown in Figure 1-45.

Property	Setting
Bold	True
Italic	True
Size	X Large

Figure 1-45: Font property subelement settings

> **NOTE:** The Web Forms Label control, unlike the Windows Forms Label control, has no TextAlign property. Gener-ally this is irrelevant, because the label background color is transparent by default. If you do assign a color to the BackColor property of a label, you should "right-size" the label to fit around the text.

5 Drag a **Hyperlink** control from the Toolbox onto the form, positioned as indicated. Set the Text property to **Click here to visit Course Technology's Website** and set the NavigateUrl property to **http://www.course.com**. Alternatively, you may choose to direct the user to your school's Web site. Size the Hyperlink control to contain your text on one line.

6 Insert an image on your Web form. If the DOCUMENT is currently selected in the Designer, an image can be inserted directly by selecting **Insert | Image**. Alternately, drag an Image control onto the form from the Toolbox. Include the path.

7 In Solution Explorer, click **WebWelcome.aspx**, and, at the top of the Solution Explorer window, click the **View Code** button ▣. The Code window for this Web form opens. Note the filename at the tab on top of the main window: WebWelcome.aspx.vb.

8 Try running the application. When the runtime version appears (compilation and execution take a minute or two), click the **hyperlink** to see that it takes you to the Course Technology Web site (or whichever other Web site you specified). Close the application by closing the browser.

9 Close Visual Studio .NET.

tip

▶ Although the program should execute without difficulty, you may get an error message from the Debugger, indicating that the Web.config file is missing. If this occurs, go to the Debug menu, and select Start Without Debugging.

You have completed this application—perhaps your very first Web Forms project in Visual Basic .NET. And you have completed Lesson B of this tutorial. Before moving on to Lesson C, complete the Questions and Exercises.

SUMMARY

- The conventional prefixes for the objects introduced in this tutorial are `frm` for a Windows form, `web` for a Web form, `btn` for a button, and `lbl` for a label.
- Windows form properties include Name, BackColor, BackgroundImage, ControlBox, FormBorderStyle, Icon, Size, StartPosition, and Text.
- In the Code Editor, the Class Name combo box identifies the objects in the form, whereas the Method Name combo box lists the events and methods available to the currently selected object.
- Web form properties include background, bgcolor, and pagelayout.

■ Controls, properties, and events introduced in this tutorial are summarized in Figure 1-46:

Control	Properties	Events
Button (Windows Forms)	Name, BackColor, Font, Text, TextAlign	Click, MouseEnter
Label (Windows Forms)	Name, BackColor, Font, Text, TextAlign	
Timer (Windows Forms)	Interval, Enabled	Tick
Label (Web Forms)	Font	
Image (Web Forms)	ImageURL	
Hyperlink (Web Forms)	NavigateURL	

Figure 1-46: Controls, properties, and events in tutorial 1

QUESTIONS

1. The statement in code that terminates processing of a Windows Forms application is _____.

2. The time lapse before a timer event fires again is set by the _____ property.

3. The background color of a Windows form is set by the _____ property.

4. The background color of a Web form is set by the _____ property.

5. In a Windows Forms application, the form or procedure executed first at runtime is determined by the _____ _____ property.

6. In a Web Forms application, the form or procedure executed first at runtime is determined by the _____ property.

7. The TabIndex values of all the controls on a form can be viewed at once by turning on the _____ toggle switch from the View menu.

8. Visual Studio .NET saves a Web form in two files, whose filename extensions are _____ and _____.

CRITICAL THINKING

At the end of each lesson, reflective questions are intended to provoke you into considering the material you have just read at a deeper level.

1. In what circumstances do you think a Web Forms application would be preferable to a Windows Forms application?

2. In Visual Basic 6.0, two controls on a form could not have the same TabIndex property, but in Visual Basic .NET, duplicates can occur. What determines the tab order if two controls have the same TabIndex property setting? (The answer can be found in the Visual Basic .NET Help files.)

3. What is the purpose of the Auto Hide feature?

EXERCISES

1. In this exercise, you create your own Welcome screen (Windows Forms application). Include appropriate labels and images. Include a Timer control that closes the application after seven seconds.

2. In this exercise, you create your own Welcome screen (Web Forms application). Include appropriate labels, images, and hyperlinks.

3. In this exercise, you create a Windows Forms application that has a single small Label control positioned at the top left of the form. Make the form's BackColor green. Make the label's BackColor red. Every half second, increase the Width property of the label by 10 pixels, and the Height property by 5 pixels. When the width of the label exceeds the width of the form, use MsgBox to display the message "That's all, Folks!" and end the program. Follow these steps:

   a. Start a new Windows Forms project called Tut01ExB3. Set the form's filename (in Solution Explorer) to frmTut01ExB3.vb, the form's internal name property to frmTut01ExB3, the form's Text property to Growing Label, and the form's BackColor property to green.

   b. From the Toolbox, drag a Label control onto the form. Set its Location property to 0, 0, and its BackColor to red.

   c. From the Toolbox, drag a Timer control onto the form. Set its Interval property to 500 milliseconds (that is, a half second), and set its Enabled property to True.

   d. Double-click Timer1 in the tray below the form. This opens the Timer1_Tick event in the Code window. Insert the code shown in Figure 1-47 into this event procedure.

   e. In the Projects Properties, set frmTut01ExB3 as the Startup object for this project.

```
'the += compound assignment operator adds 10
'to Label1.Width
Label1.Width += 10
Label1.Height += 5   'add 5 to the Height
'Me refers to the current form
If Label1.Width > Me.Width Then
  'prevent the Timer from firing anymore
  Timer1.Enabled = False
  MessageBox.Show("That's all, Folks!")
  End
End If
```

Figure 1-47: Code to insert in Timer1_Tick

4. In this exercise, you add another Timer control to the Visual Tour application. Make Timer2 fire every second. Then, in the Timer2_Tick event, reposition btnClickMe 10 pixels to the right and 5 pixels down. This exercise is similar to Exercise 3. Follow these steps:

   a. In Windows Explorer, create a new folder: VB.NET\Student\Tut01\Tut01ExB4. Copy the contents of the VB.NET\Student\Tut01\VisualTour folder into this new folder. Inside this new folder, rename the solution from VisualTour.sln to Tut01ExB4.sln.

   b. In Visual Studio .NET, open the Tut01ExB4.sln solution. If necessary, display the form in Form Designer.

   c. From the Toolbox, drag a Timer control onto the frmTour. The timer is named Timer2. Set its Interval property to 1000 and its Enabled property to True.

    d.   Double-click Timer2 in the tray below the form. This opens the Timer2_Tick event in the Code window. Insert the code shown in Figure 1-48 into this event procedure:

```
'the += compound assignment operator adds 10 to
'btnClickMe.Left
btnClickMe.Left += 10 'move 10 pixels to the right
btnClickMe.Top += 5    'move 5 pixels down
```

Figure 1-48: Exercise 4: Code to insert in Timer2_Tick

5. In this exercise, you modify the original Visual Tour application so that btnClickMe disappears (Visible property becomes False) and then reappears (Visible property becomes True) every second. This exercise is similar to Exercises 3 and 4. Follow these steps:

    a.   In Windows Explorer, create a new folder: VB.NET\Student\Tut01\Tut01ExB5. Copy the contents of the VB.NET\Student\Tut01\VisualTour folder into this new folder. Inside this new folder, rename the solution from VisualTour.sln to Tut01ExB4.sln.

    b.   In Visual Studio .NET, open the Tut01ExB5.sln solution. If necessary, display the form in Form Designer.

    c.   From the Toolbox, drag a Timer control onto the frmTour. The timer is named Timer2. Set its Interval property to 1000 and its Enabled property to True.

    d.   Double-click Timer2 in the tray below the form. This opens the Timer2_Tick event in the Code window. Insert the code shown in Figure 1-49 into this event procedure:

```
'this code toggles the visibility of btnClickMe
btnClickMe.Visible = Not btnClickMe.Visible
```

Figure 1-49: Exercise 5: Code to insert in Timer2_Tick

Exercises 6 and 7 allow you to both discover the solution to problems on your own and experiment with material that is not explicitly covered in the tutorial.

discovery ▶   6. In this exercise you create a Windows Forms application that has a single small Label control positioned in the middle of the form.

    a.   Make the form's BackColor green. Make the label's BackColor red.

    b.   Every half second, increase the Width property of the label by 10 pixels, and the Height property by 5 pixels. However, reposition the label so that it remains in the middle of the form. *Hint*: The height of the client area of the form (the area under the title bar) is given by Me.ClientRectangle.Height.

    c.   When the width of the label exceeds the width of the form, use MsgBox to display the message "That's all, Folks!" and end the program.

discovery ▶   7. In this exercise, you create a Windows Forms application that displays one small Label control.

    a.   Make the BackColor a contrasting color to the form's BackColor. Position the label at the top left of the form.

    b.   The initial Text property of the label should be "Right." Every half second, move the label 10 pixels to the right.

    c.   When the label hits the right edge of the form, change the Text property to "Down," and begin moving 10 pixels down (rather than to the right) every half second.

    d.   When the label hits the bottom edge of the form, change the Text to "Left," and begin moving left. See the Hint in Exercise 6b. When the label bumps into the left edge of the form, change the Text to "Up" and begin moving up the screen.

After completing this lesson, you will be able to:

- Build a Visual Basic .NET Console application
- Use the Visual Basic .NET random number generator

A First Console Application

Building Random Numbers: a Console Application

Console applications can be helpful to the applications programmer primarily as a way of experimenting with snippets of code, without having to design an entire GUI. When you are not sure how a particular statement, function, method, or class works, this technique can give you the answer you are looking for directly; and it's often a useful addendum to reading about the topic in the Help system.

One such topic presented itself in the Visual Tour application, namely, the Rnd( ) and Randomize( ) functions. In this section, you write a short Console application that demonstrates exactly how random numbers work and are used in Visual Basic .NET (and, actually, in many computer languages).

To write the RandomNumbers Console application:

1 Start a new Console application. To do this, start a new Visual Basic .NET project and, in the New Project dialog box, choose **Console application** under Templates. Call it **RandomNumbers**. Type the code in Figure 1-50 into Sub Main:

```
Dim i As Integer

For i = 1 To 10
  Debug.WriteLine(Rnd)
Next
```

Figure 1-50: Text for the Sub Main procedure

NOTE: Output from a Console application can be sent to the Console object (that is, the DOS window) or to the Debug object. In both cases, the Write ( ) function writes to the specified device, but leaves the print cursor positioned immediately after the last character written. The WriteLine ( ) function writes to the specified device, and then writes a carriage return/linefeed sequence, so that the print cursor ends up positioned at the beginning of the following line.

2 Run the program. You briefly see a DOS window appear and then disappear. Open the **Output** window (usually docked at the lower left of the screen). Increase the size of the Output window by dragging its top border up until it covers about half of the screen. If necessary, use the scrollbar on the right side of the Output window so that you can see all of the results. Note the first few random numbers that are generated. See Figure 1-51.

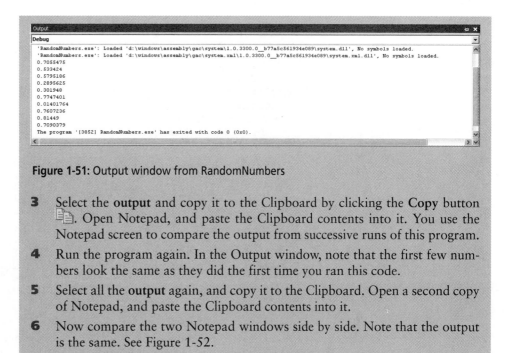

Figure 1-51: Output window from RandomNumbers

3 Select the **output** and copy it to the Clipboard by clicking the **Copy** button. Open Notepad, and paste the Clipboard contents into it. You use the Notepad screen to compare the output from successive runs of this program.

4 Run the program again. In the Output window, note that the first few numbers look the same as they did the first time you ran this code.

5 Select all the **output** again, and copy it to the Clipboard. Open a second copy of Notepad, and paste the Clipboard contents into it.

6 Now compare the two Notepad windows side by side. Note that the output is the same. See Figure 1-52.

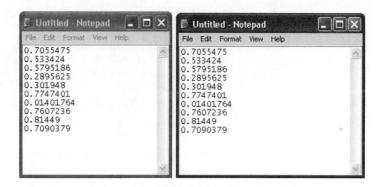

Figure 1-52: Two Notepad windows with same output

You can repeat this procedure a third time, just to prove to yourself that it was no fluke. The fact is that Rnd( ) is really a pseudorandom number generator. If you do not direct it to do otherwise; then every time that it executes, it produces the same sequence of numbers. Rnd( ) produces a random real number n such that $0 <= n < 1$. However, the function works by performing a calculation on the previous number that it produced. This number, called the **random number seed**, is used with the first Rnd( ) function call, and by default the seed is the same whenever a program begins execution.

However, most programs that need a random number generator really want the numbers to be random and totally different each time the program runs. This is the reason for the Randomize( ) function. This function seeds the random number generator based on the setting of the system clock (usually the number of seconds that have elapsed since 1980). Because this setting is different each time a program starts, the sequence of random numbers generated is also different. You will now revise the RandomNumbers Console application to include the Randomize ( ) function, and try it again.

To revise the RandomNumbers application:

1 Insert **Randomize** in the code, as shown in Figure 1-53:

```
Dim i As Integer
Randomize()
For i = 1 To 10
  Debug.WriteLine(Rnd)
Next I
```

Figure 1-53: The Randomize() function

2 Run the program twice, copying and pasting the Output window each time to the two Notepad windows. Compare the results as shown in Figure 1-54.

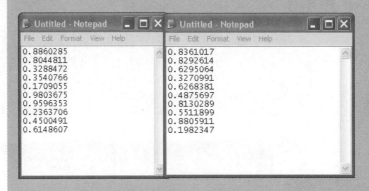

Figure 1-54: Two Notepad windows with different output

3 Save your project and exit Visual Studio .NET

In reality, you don't often want to generate a random number between 0 and 1. Rather, you must convert the fraction returned by Rnd( ) to something more useful. The formula for converting the Rnd( ) return value to an integer within a specified range is

```
Int(Rnd() * (UpperBound — LowerBound + 1) + LowerBound)
```

So, for example, to get a random number from 1 to 10, the formula is

```
Int(Rnd() * (10 — 1 + 1) + 1)
```

Or simply

```
Int(Rnd() * 10 + 1)
```

Try this out with your RandomNumbers program and modify the key line as follows:

```
Debug.WriteLine(Int(Rnd() * 10 + 1))
```

The output from two iterations of the program appears in Figure 1-55.

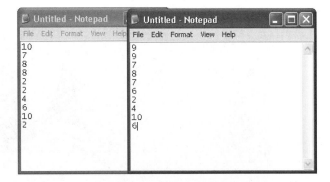

Figure 1-55: Two Notepad windows with different integer results

Finally, you should note that generating the same sequence of random numbers each time a program runs, as Rnd( ) does, by default, is actually a valuable feature in certain applications. For instance, in a scientific experiment, a scientist might want to conduct a series of tests on 100 randomly selected virus samples from a total sample size of 500. By using the feature of Rnd( ) that causes the sequence of random numbers to be repeated at each iteration of the program, the scientist can insure that the same 100 samples are selected every time the program is run. Suppose that the virus samples are in boxes numbered from 0 to 499, represented in Visual Basic by an array of 500 Boolean elements (ablnVirusSample(500)). The code shown in Figure 1-56 randomly selects and then prints the index values of those 100 samples that should be tested, and the same 100 samples will be chosen every time the program runs:

```
Sub Main()
Dim I As Integer
Dim N As Integer
Dim ablnVirusSample(500) As Boolean
'select 100 samples to test
For I = 0 To 99
  Do
    N = Int(Rnd() * 500)
    'but don't select the same sample twice
  Loop Until ablnVirusSample(N) = False
  ablnVirusSample(N) = True
Next I
'print out the index values of the selected samples,
'20 per line
N = 0
For I = 0 To 499
  If ablnVirusSample(I) Then
    N = N + 1
    Console.Write(I)
    Console.Write(" ")
    If N Mod 20 = 0 Then Console.WriteLine()
  End If
Next I
MsgBox("Press any key to Continue")
End Sub
```

Figure 1-56: Code to produce 100 random index values

Running this code in a Console application produces Figure 1-57.

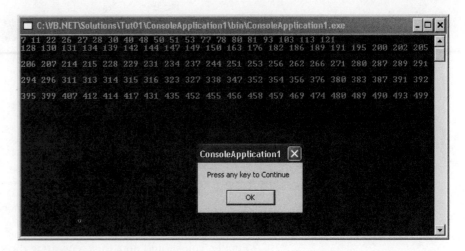

Figure 1-57: Console results—100 randomly selected index values

Other Notes Concerning Console Applications

Console applications are often compiled and subsequently executed from the command prompt (that is, from the Windows Start, Run menu). In this case, output sent to the Console object appears in the command window (sometimes referred to as the DOS window). Also, in this case, output sent to the Debug object is ignored and does not raise an exception (that is, it does not cause an error).

When a Console application requires keyboard input, the ReadLine( ) function is employed. For example, the following solicits a number from the user, reads that number into the variable *x*, and displays the number back to the console. The last two lines, a WriteLine( ) and a blank ReadLine( ) function call, are often used at the bottom of a Console application to prevent the command window from disappearing before the user has had a chance to read the output, as shown in Figure 1-58.

```
Console.WriteLine("Enter a number from 1 to 10")
Dim x As Integer
x = Console.ReadLine()
Console.WriteLine(x)
Console.WriteLine("Press the Enter key to continue")
Console.ReadLine()
```

Figure 1-58: Code to read and display variables

You have now completed Tutorial 1. Complete the questions and exercises that follow before moving on to Tutorial 2.

SUMMARY

■ Console applications are most useful for experimenting with program code.

■ The Rnd ( ) and Randomize ( ) functions provide the capability to generate and manage random numbers. Randomize ( ) guarantees a different sequence of random numbers each time a program runs.

■ Output from a Console application is normally sent to the Console object or to the Debug object.

■ Input in a Console application is obtained from the Console.ReadLine ( ) function.

QUESTIONS

1. The argument of the Int function must be a(n) _____ . The return value from the Int function is always a(n) _____ .

2. For what purpose are console applications most useful?

3. Console applications use the _____ namespace.

4. The _____ function displays output in a Console application.

5. The _____ function reads input into a variable in a Console application.

EXERCISES

1. Write a Console application that displays a 4 × 4 grid of 16 numbers randomly selected from 10 to 99. Leave one space between numbers. Send the output to the Console object. Include a closing message (to prevent the Console from disappearing before one can view the output). The output should look similar to:

```
15 89 44 37
22 11 14 34
67 84 43 22
57 50 24 56
Press any key to continue
```

2. Write a Console application that prompts the user to enter an integer, reads the integer from the keyboard, calculates the sum of all the digits in the integer, and displays the result. For example, if the user types in 1234, the program should display 10 (that is, $1 + 2 + 3 + 4$). Use the Console object for all input and output.

Hint: This problem can be handled through string manipulation or through modulo arithmetic.

For string manipulation, use the Help Index to look up the Str( ), Mid( ), and Len( ) functions. Str( ) returns a string from a numeric argument (but it always leaves a space for the sign of the number), Mid( ) returns a substring from a string. Len( ) returns the length of a string, and the result of $x \mid 10$ is x divided by 10 using integer division—that is, x without its right-hand digit.

For modulo arithmetic, look up the Modulo operator, Mod. For any integer x, the result of the expression x Mod 10 is the right hand digit of x.

3. Write a Console application that prompts the user to enter an integer, reads the integer from the keyboard, and prints the integer out backwards. For example, if the user types in 1234, the program should display 4321. Use the Console object for all input and output. Again, this problem can be handled through string manipulation or modulo arithmetic, using the same hints given in Exercise 2.

Exercises 4 and 5 allow you to discover the solution to problems on your own and experiment with material that is not explicitly covered in the tutorial.

discovery ▶ 4. Write a Console application that displays a 4 × 4 grid of all 16 numbers from 1 to 16. Print a space before each single-digit number. Print a space after every number. Do not permit any number to appear more than once. Use the Console object for all input and output. The output should look similar to the following, but aligned exactly as shown:

```
 4 12 11  5
10  1  3 13
 2  7 14 16
15  6  9  8
```

discovery ▶ 5. Modify the Console application in Exercise 4 so that the application displays an n × n grid rather than a 4 × 4 grid. Solicit $n < 10$ from the user. Use the Console object for all input and output.

KEY TERMS

- application icon
- attribute
- Auto Hide
- BackgroundImage property
- break mode
- Button control
- class
- Click event
- Console application
- current statement
- Document type (Web Form)
- FormBorderStyle property
- Height property
- inheritance
- instance/instantiation
- Interval property
- Label control
- Left property
- Location property
- method
- MouseEnter event
- object
- Option Compare
- Option Explicit
- Option Strict
- property
- Property Pages
- Randomize statement

- Rnd() function
- Size property
- splash screen
- StepInto method
- TabIndex property
- Tab Order view
- Text property
- Tick event
- Timer control
- Top property
- Web Forms application
- Width property
- Windows Forms application
- X, Y properties

Coding of Windows Forms Applications, and the Transition to Objects

Creating a Dining Hall Seat Assigner Windows Forms Application

case ▶ Athletes in the International Village will be given random seat assignments in the dining halls to encourage the development of international friendships. A Windows Forms application is needed that displays a list of randomly generated seating assignments. The application requires no data inputs at all. Output must be displayed in a window, and the user must also have the option of sending the output to a printer or storing it in a sequential file. The Friendsville Games Development Team (FGDT) has been asked to develop this application.

The Friendsville International Village has five dining halls, called North, South, East, West, and Harmony. Each dining hall has 17 tables (lettered A through Q), with 11 numbered seats at each table. The program generates a random list of seat assignments for each date, but the listing for any given date is always the same. In addition to displaying the randomly generated seat assignments on the screen, the program must send a list of seat assignments to a printer, for distribution to the athletes. In addition, the output must be able to be captured in a text file, from which, for example, the data can be retrieved and printed on another computer that does not have the Dining Hall Seat Assigner application.

Previewing the Dining.exe Application

Before creating the Dining Hall Seat Assigner application, you first preview the running program.

To run the completed Dining application:

1 From the Run dialog box on the Start menu, locate and launch **Dining.exe**, located in the VB.NET\Student\Tut02\Dining\bin folder. Note the MainMenu control, the DateTimePicker control, and the ListBox control. See Figure 2-1.

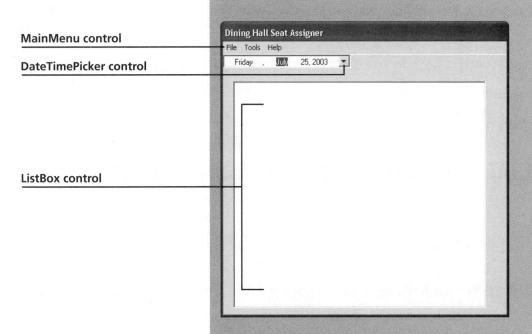

Figure 2-1: Dining application, opening screen

NOTE: Notice the absence of a ControlBox control on the main form and on the About form. The Maximize, Minimize, and Close buttons that normally appear on the right side of the title bar, as well as the control menu normally available by clicking an icon on the left side of the title bar, are missing. Note that the forms in this application always appear in the center of the screen, regardless of your equipment.

2 Click **Help | Instructions** to find out how to use the application. Read the instructions, and click **OK**. Click **Help | About** to display the About form. Then click **OK** to close the form and return to the main form.

3 Click the **DateTimePicker** drop-down arrow, and click **June 1, 2004**, as shown in Figure 2-2. Then click **Tools | Assign Seats** to generate the seating list, an example of which is shown in Figure 2-3. Manually make a list of the first few seat assignments. Then select a different date, and generate a new list of seat assignments. Note that the new list is different from the first list you generated. Now select the same date you started with, and generate a list of seat assignments a third time. Note that this list matches the first list you generated. The same list of assignments is always generated for the same date.

Figure 2-2: DateTimePicker control

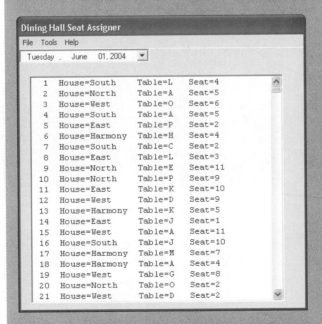

Figure 2-3: Seat assignments for June 1, 2004

NOTE: In the File menu, the two menu items that provide for external output are Save Seats in File, and Print Seats. These selections are enabled only when seat assignments appear in the list box. They are initially disabled (their Enabled property is set to False at design time). After seats are assigned, these two selections are enabled. If a new date is selected in the DateTimePicker control, the list box is cleared, and these two menu selections are once again disabled.

4　Click **File | Save Seats in File**. The Save File As dialog box (see Figure 2-4) lets you choose a filename and location. If you do not specify otherwise, the filename is SeatsFor20040601.txt—the date of the seating—and the location is the folder where the .exe file resides. Click **Save** to accept these default settings. The contents of the list box are saved in the specified file.

Figure 2-4: Save As dialog box

5　Open **Notepad** to view the contents of the file and verify that the seating assignments were saved in the file. Close **Notepad**.

6　Click **File | Print Seats** to activate a PrintPreviewDialog control, as shown in Figure 2-5. This control opens a new window that displays a report inside a PrintDocument control. You might need to maximize the dialog box to read the report. From the screen version of the report (called a print preview), you can click the Print icon to send the report to the printer. Click **Close** to close the print preview and return to the list.

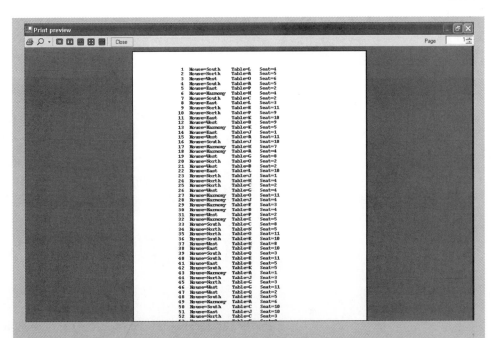

Figure 2-5: Print preview dialog control

7 You can alter the default page layout and printer options by using the corresponding menu items on the File menu. Click **File | Page Setup** to activate the PageSetupDialog control, then click **OK**. Click **File | Printer Setup** to open the PrintDialog control. Both of these are standard dialog boxes used in many Windows software applications. Click **OK** to exit the Printer Setup dialog box.

8 Click **File | Exit** to close the Dining Hall Seat Assigner application when you have finished experimenting with it.

After completing this lesson, you will be able to:

- Understand the basic concepts involved in object-oriented programming (OOP)
- Understand the meaning of the .NET Framework
- Understand the elements of coding in Visual Basic .NET

Object-Oriented Programming Fundamentals

Before studying the specific components of the Dining application itself, you should familiarize yourself with some of the fundamental notions of coding in Visual Basic .NET. If you have programmed before in Visual Basic .NET, this will be a review of material you already know; but if your previous experience is limited to Visual Basic 6.0, you might find this material new.

The topics addressed in this section include object-oriented programming, the .NET Framework, and the syntax and semantics of Visual Basic .NET program code.

Understanding Object-Oriented Programming

In the world of computer programming, an **object** is any named set of data structures and underlying code. Visual Basic .NET is an object-oriented language, designed with and for **object-oriented programming** (**OOP**). To state that Visual Basic .NET was designed *with* OOP means that the components of the language itself are predominantly objects. To state that Visual Basic .NET is designed *for* OOP means that the facilities are present for programmers to create object-oriented programs.

Visual Basic 6.0 was sometimes referred to as a pseudo-object language or as a partially object-oriented language. Visual Basic 6.0 offered numerous graphical objects (forms and controls, for instance) that could be used for designing an application's user interface. These objects had **properties** (descriptors of the object), **methods** (actions that the object could perform), and **events** (occurrences external to the object, but to which the object could respond). These familiar graphical objects also exist in Visual Basic .NET, with relatively few changes.

Visual Basic 6.0 also used objects minimally in program code, but many programmers used them rarely or not at all. By contrast, the program code for Visual Basic .NET is heavily dependent on objects, so this is the area in which you will experience the greatest impact of the new Visual Studio .NET paradigm; thus, it behooves you to review the principles of object-oriented languages.

The basic terms of OOP include these: object, member, member type, property, field, method, event, raising and handling an event, class, instance, encapsulation, information hiding, accessibility, scope, inheritance, base class, derived class, interface, implementation, overloading, and polymorphism (or overriding). The following sections make sense out of these terms to serve as your introduction to OOP by focusing on a graphical object with which you are already familiar: the Button object.

Understanding Objects

The advantage of programming with objects is that, after you create an object, you can reuse it wherever you need it, and you don't need to refer to all of its components in order to use it. A reference to the name of the object suffices to access all of that object's functionality.

Consider the Windows Forms Button object in Visual Basic .NET (called a Command button in Visual Basic 6.0). This object always appears as a rectangle with a narrow border that makes the edge appear raised and that appears to have a light source above and to the left of the button and a shadow along its bottom and right edges. At runtime, when the user clicks a button, the button appears to be depressed, and it retains this appearance until the user releases the mouse. Clicking the button at runtime raises (or generates) the Click event for that button. (You must then write code that handles the Click event; this code is also called an **event handler**.) The features and behaviors described here are transparent to the programmer—you do not see the underlying code that makes a button appear and behave as it does. Furthermore, you do not need to specify any of these elements. Rather, the button, to the Visual Basic programmer, is simply an object that comes ready to be used and reused in any application.

Understanding Encapsulation and Information Hiding

The terms encapsulation and information hiding are closely related. **Encapsulation** means "to make complete unto itself." An encapsulated object exposes to the outside world only those elements of its structure and operations needed by itself or by the outside world to deal with the object. All other elements of the encapsulated object are hidden from the outside world. Often, the hidden elements constitute the majority of the object's parts. Further, an encapsulated object can be treated as a unit; a reference to the name of the encapsulated object automatically includes all of its elements, those that are externally visible and those that are hidden from view. For example, a human being can be considered an encapsulated object—some of its body parts and functions are visible, but most are strictly internal and hidden; yet, the entire human being can be given a name and treated as a whole.

In OOP, an encapsulated program element contains all the parts necessary to accomplish something. But only those parts needed by other program elements to use it are exposed. Typically, *what* the element does is exposed, while *how* the element does it is hidden. This notion is useful in dealing with many elements of computer programming, not just graphical objects such as a Button control. For instance, when you call a function to calculate the square root of a number, you want only the resulting square root to be returned by the function; you do not need, or even want to see, the underlying code that performs the calculation. This is important because human beings have a limited attention span: there is a finite limit to the amount of complexity we can deal with at any one time. So, programmer productivity is dependent on **information hiding**, on the fact that the programming language performs much of its lower-level, detail work out of sight and without the programmer's direct awareness. The encapsulated, internal data and code of an object is called its **implementation**.

An object also has an external appearance, called the **interface**, which consists of all aspects of the object accessible to the outside world. The Button object, for example, has 32 design-time properties (BackColor, Enabled, TabIndex, Visible, and so on) that appear in the Properties window in the IDE, partially displayed in Figure 2-6. These properties are part of the Button object's interface.

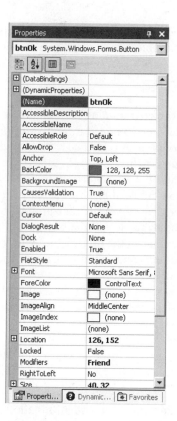

Figure 2-6: Button properties at design time (partial listing)

Understanding Classes

Another important OOP concept is the notion of a class. A **class** is to an object what a blueprint is to a house. The class is a template for the creation of an object. The class defines all the features and functionality inherent in objects built upon that template—the data structures and underlying code, the implementation and the interface that constitute the object. The structure of Visual Basic .NET is built upon classes. For example, the Toolbox actually contains control classes, not the controls themselves. When you click the Button control in the Windows Forms tab of the Toolbox and then drag the button onto a form, you are creating an object (initially called Button1) based upon the definition of the Button class. The process of creating an object from a class is called **instantiation**, and Button1 is also referred to as an **instance** of the Button class. Consider the notion of a human being, which can be looked upon as a class: Alice is an instance of that class. "Human being" has no earthly existence; it is simply a template for the 5 billion instances that presently occupy our planet.

A class can be constructed on the basis of another class that already exists. In this case, the new class **inherits** all the features and functionality of the class upon which it is based. To continue the human analogy, a human can be male or female. A male inherits all the features and functionality of a human, but then adds unique masculine characteristics. The original class is called the **base class,** and the new class created from it is called the **derived class.** For example, Visual Basic .NET has a generic class for all Windows Forms controls, called the Control class. This class defines the features and functionality common to all Windows Forms controls. Based on the Control class, Visual Basic .NET also has a ButtonBase class. The ButtonBase class inherits from the Control class, and further defines the features and functionality common to the Button, CheckBox, and RadioButton controls. The Button class is derived from the ButtonBase class, and so the Button class inherits all the features and functionality of the Control class as well as the ButtonBase class, and further defines the special features and functionality of the Button control. In reality, the hierarchy of classes above the Button class goes higher than the Control class, as you can see in Figure 2-7.

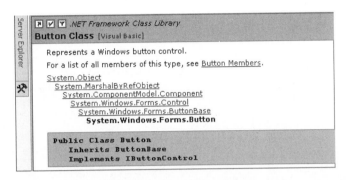

Figure 2-7: Button class: hierarchy of base classes

Understanding Class Members

The elements or components that make up a class and that can be seen by a programmer are called **members**. Class members may include any of these member types: constructors, properties, methods, events, fields, and even other objects. Of these, from your previous experience with Visual Basic 6.0 or Visual Basic .NET, you should already be familiar with properties, methods, and events.

> **NOTE:** A class also includes a great deal of code that normally is completely hidden from the application programmer. For example, the Button class must include the code necessary to render the object on your form, that is, to draw its borders, position and size it on the form, and position its Text property.

The constructor member initializes a new instance of the class and is automatically invoked by the New keyword. Some classes contain fields. For instance, a database table is often imported into a Visual Basic .NET project as a Dataset object, which contains individual fields, identified by name or by index (position). A class also often contains other objects. For example, Visual Basic .NET graphical controls have a Size property, but Size is also an object in its own right, having Width and Height properties.

To continue the Button class example: the Visual Studio .NET Help screen for the Button control (Windows Forms) has a link to a Help screen called Button Members. You may be surprised to find a rather daunting list of 294 members! A partial listing is shown in Figure 2-8. A brief definition of each member is given in the list of all members, with a link to the details concerning that member. For instance, under Public Properties for the Button class, you can find the BackColor property. According to the Help screen, "BackColor (inherited from Control) gets or sets the background color for the control." Clicking the word BackColor in the Button Members list takes you to another Help screen that provides more detailed information about this property.

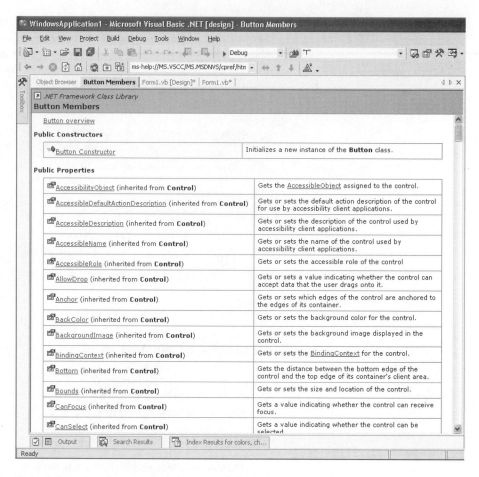

Figure 2-8: Button class members (partial listing)

Understanding Accessibility (Access Type)

The list of 294 Button class members is subdivided by member type and **accessibility** (also called **access type**)—the portion of code within which the member is visible to other code components. For the Windows Forms Button class, the member groupings include public constructors (the methods that "construct" or instantiate a new object), public properties, public methods, public events, protected properties, and protected methods.

Visual Basic .NET supports five levels of accessibility: Public, Protected, Friend, Protected Friend, and Private:

- **Public** access is the most permissive; public entities have no access restrictions.
- **Private** access is the most restrictive; private entities are accessible only within the context in which they are declared.
- **Protected, Friend,** and **Protected Friend** access types are all less permissive than public, but more permissive than private:
  - A class member declared as Protected limits access to the class in which it is declared and to any derived class.
  - An entity declared with the Friend modifier limits access to the program in which the entity is declared.
  - The combination Protected Friend provides access to the union of protected access plus friend access. See Figure 2-9.

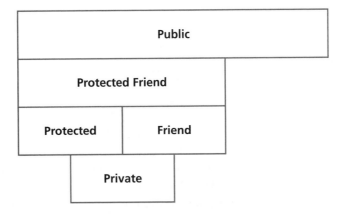

Figure 2-9: Access levels supported in Visual Basic .NET

Although limiting the accessibility of various program elements is not, strictly speaking, only the result of OOP, it is a preferred method for implementing an important aspect of information hiding, a critical component of OOP.

Understanding Scope, Object References, Shared Members, and Qualified Names

The accessibility or access level of an entity is also related to its scope. The **scope** of an entity (such as a variable, an object, or a procedure) is the portion of code in which the entity is available (accessible) and in which the programmer can reference the name of the entity without qualification. For example, imagine a project in which Form1 contains a control called Button1. Button1's scope is Form1. Any code within Form1 can refer to Button1, and Visual Basic .NET interprets this reference as referring to Button1 in Form1. However, imagine now that Form2 is added to this project, and Form2 contains a control named Label2. Code within Form1 cannot refer to Label2 as a stand-alone object name; such an unqualified reference would refer to a control named Label2 on Form1, or be considered out of context and cause a syntax error. For example, this statement appearing in Form1 (assuming Form1 contains no object named Label2) causes an error:

```
Label2.Text = "Friendsville"  'error
```

Actually, referring to Label2 from within Form1 is somewhat more complicated than simply qualifying the name Label2. For example, the following statement also causes an error, even though the name Label2 has been qualified by including a reference to the form in which it occurs:

```
Form2.Label2.Text = "Friendsville"  'error
```

The error message is Reference to a non-shared member requires an object reference. This message, which you may encounter more than once, requires a bit of explanation.

Consider the fact that the definition of a form is actually a class, not an object. (The very first line of code for a form states Public Class *<formname>*.) Hence, the class must be instantiated before it can be referenced. The one exception to this rule is that the definition of a class may include a member (such as an object or property) declared as **Shared**. In such a case, you do not need to instantiate an object before referencing the shared member, because only one copy of the shared member is needed (because all objects based on the class share that member).

At runtime, Visual Basic .NET automatically instantiates the startup object, but any other object not included in the startup object must be instantiated in code.

tip

A name is said to be qualified when the higher-level name of which it is a part is included in the reference. Take, for example, the name Left. Used by itself in the code of a form, this word refers to the Left property of the form—how far the left edge of the form is from the left edge of its container. If you want to refer to the Left() function, which returns a specified number of characters from the left side of a string, then the word Left must be qualified. Specifically, you must refer to Microsoft. VisualBasic.Left().

Therefore, to refer to Form2's Label2 object from within Form1, you must first create an instance of Form2, named frm in the following example. Then, the instance name qualifies the reference to Label2. The complete reference looks like this:

```
Dim frm As New Form2
frm.Label2.Text = "Friendsville"
```

The Dim statement declares an instance of Form2 and calls it frm. (The New keyword always calls the class constructor method.) The second statement references Label2, but the name Label2 is qualified by the name of the form within which it occurs. The qualified name is required by the rules pertaining to scope.

Returning to the discussion with which this section began, scope is actually determined by a combination of three things at the time a program entity is declared:

- The region (block, procedure, module, class, or structure) of the program in which the program entity is declared
- The namespace containing the entity's declaration
- The entity's accessibility

Visual Basic .NET supports four scope levels:

- **Block scope** describes a program element available only within the block in which it is declared. For example, the scope of the variable M in Figure 2-10 is the If...End If statement block in which it is declared.

```
Private Sub Button1_Click(ByVal sender As System.Object, ByVal e As _
    System.EventArgs) Handles Button1.Click
    Dim X As String = "Sample"
    Static Y As Single = 0.0
    If Button1.Left = 0 Then
        Dim M As Integer
        M = 10
        Text1.Text = M
    End IF
    M = 15 ' This statement causes a syntax error (scope violation)
End Sub
```

block scope

Figure 2-10: Block scope example

- **Procedure scope** describes a variable that is declared inside a procedure, but not inside a block within that procedure, thus making the variable available throughout the procedure. In the preceding procedure shown in Figure 2-10, the variables X and Y have procedure scope. Note that in Figure 2-10, M continues to exist as long as the procedure is executing, but any reference to M outside the If statement block is illegal. This could be important if a block is executed multiple times within a procedure—variables declared inside the block are not reinitialized each time the block is executed. The **lifetime** of the variable X, like M, is the period in which the Button1_Click event procedure is executing; both of these variables cease to exist (their storage space is returned to the heap) after the program executes the End Sub statement at the end of the Button1_Click procedure. The static variable Y also has procedure scope, but its lifetime persists as long as the program is running. Upon subsequent visits to the Button1_Click procedure, Y has the same value that it had at the end of the previous execution of the procedure. Because all entities declared within a procedure are local to that procedure (whether declared with the Dim or the Static keyword), the accessibility keywords (Public, Private, Protected, and Friend) are not permitted in these declarations.

- **Module scope** describes an entity that is available throughout the module, class, or structure in which it is declared. Module scope applies to entities declared at the module level—that is, outside any procedure or block within the module, class, or structure—with Dim (that is, without specifying accessibility) or with Private access. A module-level Dim declaration is interpreted as Private access.
- **Namespace scope** describes an entity that is available throughout the namespace in which it is declared. (If a project does not contain any namespaces, defined by the Namespace keyword, the entire project is considered one namespace, and namespace scope is equivalent to project scope.) Namespace scope applies to entities declared at the module level with the Public or Friend keyword.

Understanding Polymorphism

The final aspect of OOP to be mentioned here is **polymorphism**, the ability of a derived class to alter (override) a property or method from its base class. The advantage of polymorphism is that you can create multiple classes with identically named but functionally different properties or methods; at runtime, application programs can call these methods interchangeably. Visual Basic .NET offers a robust implementation of polymorphism, allowing you to use two approaches to achieving it—inheritance and interfacing. You have an opportunity to use both of these approaches in Tutorial 5.

Understanding the Advantages of OOP

Consider the enormous power and efficiency of the notion of a class. If your program uses 10 buttons (10 instances of the Button class), all code that implements this class needs to be stored only once; only the values of individual property settings need to be stored for each button instance.

Furthermore, you can treat any object in your application as a new base class and instantiate other new objects (or classes) on the basis of that class, even including the application itself. This feature makes your code truly reusable. At a corporate or organizational level, developers are encouraged to extend the built-in .NET classes by creating new classes conforming to certain standards and adding them to the class libraries available throughout an organization.

Consider the difference in programmer workload in the following scenario: your organization decides to create a standard corporate logo with animation and with several user-assignable properties, and the powers-that-be mandate that this animated logo be included in every application developed by the company. Without OOP, developers would make a copy of the visual logo, set its properties, copy the animation routines, and then insert all of these into their applications. With OOP, the animated corporate logo is a class (CorpLogo) imported into each application a programmer develops. So far, there is little difference. But a year later, the organization is bought out, and as a result the corporate logo and animation change. Without OOP, considerable programmer effort is needed to copy the new logo, properties, and animation into every application that uses it. And more programmer effort is needed to test it in each application into which it is imported. With OOP, the revised CorpLogo automatically replaces the earlier version as soon as each application is recompiled.

tip

When you begin writing object-oriented programs in Visual Basic .NET, the scope and accessibility rules of the .NET paradigm may seem restrictive to you—certainly, they will cause many false starts and error messages. The temptation is strong, especially when writing the relatively simple academic exercises in a textbook, to revert to traditional procedure-oriented programming, which on the surface seems simpler, more straightforward, and more likely to succeed at getting the immediate task accomplished. However, while the OOP learning curve is initially steeper, OOP ultimately lets you scale much higher mountains. By the time you finish a semester of programming with objects, you will wonder why you ever considered any other approach at all.

Introducing the .NET Framework

Much of the Visual Basic .NET object orientation is achieved through the Visual Studio .NET Framework, which consists of two components: the Common Language Runtime (CLR) and the .NET Framework Class Library.

Understanding the Common Language Runtime

The **Common Language Runtime** (**CLR**) manages code execution at runtime, providing services needed by all languages, such as memory management, garbage collection, thread management, type safety, and code security. Languages that serve as a CLR host (such as Visual Basic .NET) place the appropriate metadata into their object programs, which is then used by the CLR to carry out its tasks. The CLR operates behind the scenes, so you don't see much of it directly as a developer. But you will note some of its benefits: cross-language and cross-platform functionality, better runtime performance, and a much more pronounced object orientation to the whole language than has been the case in earlier versions of Visual Basic.

Using the .NET Framework Class Library

The key to making the CLR scheme work is the **.NET Framework Class Library**, a collection of over 6000 reusable types, classes, and interfaces, which describe the foundation set of objects available to developers in all the Visual Studio .NET languages. Entities in the .NET Framework Class Library are grouped into a hierarchical set of namespaces, each of which can be imported into the developer's application as needed.

All the namespaces in the .NET Framework shipped with Visual Studio .NET begin with the words "System" or "Microsoft." The **System namespaces** define commonly used entities (fundamental and base classes, referenced types, interfaces, events, and event handlers) that are used by developers in any language. The **Microsoft namespaces** are language-specific. Microsoft Corporation recommends that user-defined namespaces begin with the name of the organization that creates it, and that all created namespaces be managed so as to avoid naming conflicts.

Some of the most important System namespaces in the .NET Framework Class Library are shown in Figure 2-11:

Namespace	Definition	Sample classes
System.Collections	Defines various object collections	SortedList, Queue
System.ComponentModel	Implements the behavior of components and controls at design time and at runtime	Component, ComponentCollection, ComponentConverter, ByteConverter, CharConverter

Figure 2-11: Important namespaces

Namespace	Definition	Sample classes
System.Data, System.Data.Common, System.Data.OleDB, and System.Data.SqlClient	Implement the classes needed for access to databases in the ADO.NET architecture, presented in Tutorial 9	Constraint, DataRelation, DataColumn, DataRow, DataTable
System.Drawing	Implements the classes that provide basic graphics functionality	Bitmap, Font, Icon, Brush, Pen, Image
System.IO	Implements the classes used for input/output with data streams and traditional files	BinaryReader, File, FileStream, IOException, Path, FileSystemInfo, FileSystemWatcher
System.Net	Defines the common interface needed for the use of network protocols	AuthenticationManager, Authorization, Cookie, CookieException, DNS, DNSPermission, IPAddress, WebRequest, WebResponse
System.Security	Provides base classes for permissions	PermissionSet, SecurityElement, SecurityManager
System.Text	Provides base classes for handling text in various formats	ASCIIEncoding, Encoder, Decoder, StringBuilder, UnicodeEncoding
System.Web, System.Web.UI.HtmlControls, and System.Web.UI.WebControls	Support browser/server communication, providing classes and interfaces that allow Web pages to display HTML controls and Web controls	HttpApplication, HttpCookie, HttpException, HttpRequest, HttpResponse, HttpUtility, HttpWriter
System.Windows.Forms	Provides classes that implement all controls used in Windows applications	Control, ButtonBase, Button, ComboBox, CheckBox, CheckedListBox, Clipboard, Cursor, DateTimePicker, Label, TextBox
System.Xml	Defines classes for use in XML processing	XmlAttribute, XmlDataDocument, XmlDeclaration

Figure 2-11: Important namespaces (continued)

Within the Microsoft namespace, the namespaces you are most likely to use are those in Microsoft.VisualBasic. However, nothing prevents you from using a namespace defined in Microsoft.Csharp, Microsoft.Jscript, Microsoft.Vsa, or Microsoft.Win32.

Collections of namespaces are implemented through a number of fully compiled **assemblies** (also called dynamic link library (.dll) files). Only the assemblies associated with referenced namespaces are included in an application's executable. This makes for smaller and faster loading executables. But it also means that you must ensure that the appropriate references appear in the source code. The list of references for any project appears in Solution Explorer—it is the first item under the project name.

The most common assemblies needed by each type of application (Windows Forms, Web Forms, or Console) are automatically included in the list of references. For instance, in a new Windows Forms application, you can click the expand button to expand the References listing in Solution Explorer. System, System.Data, System.Drawing, and System.Windows.Forms are all included. See Figure 2-12.

Figure 2-12: Expanded references listing for a new Windows Forms application

User-defined namespaces and classes are implemented in assembly files, which are then added to a class library. Again, you must ensure that the appropriate references to needed assemblies are added to your application. You can do this by right-clicking the References object in Solution Explorer, and then clicking Add Reference.

You need to familiarize yourself with the structure and contents of the .NET Framework Class Library—certainly not all at once, but over time, as you use it, and as you need it. You are encouraged to browse through the Help screens that describe the library. For example, Figure 2-13 displays the Class Library overview topic, "Introduction to the .NET Framework Class Library in Visual Studio." Then, in the second paragraph of that topic, under Namespaces, "Class Library" is a link to descriptions of some of the namespaces.

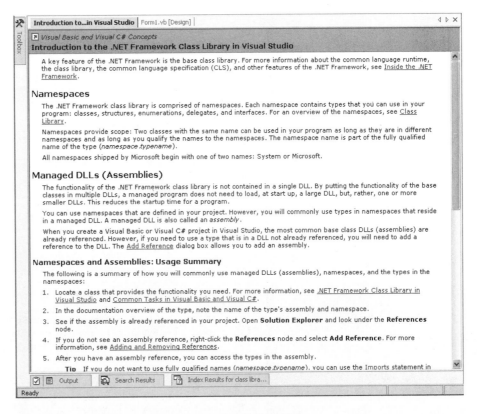

Figure 2-13: Introduction to the .NET Framework Class Library

Coding Windows Forms Applications in Visual Basic .NET

All of this discussion concerning OOP and the .NET Framework Class Library is necessary background for understanding the elements that you find in the Code window of a Windows Forms application.

Loading the Hashing Application

For purposes of the following discussion concerning Visual Basic .NET OOP coding techniques, you use a short sample program named Hashing, which also happens to be one of the intermediate steps in developing the Dining Hall Seat Assigner application in Lesson B of this tutorial. In Lesson B, you examine the logic of the Hashing program. Here in Lesson A, you look at the elements of coding as they relate to OOP and the .NET Framework namespaces.

To view the Hashing program code:

1   In Visual Studio .NET, open the **Hashing.sln** solution located in the VB.NET\Student\Tut02\Hashing folder. Click **Form1.vb** in Solution Explorer, and click the **View Code** button 🔲 to open the Code Editor. Position the insertion point at the top of the code, on line 1. See Figure 2-14.

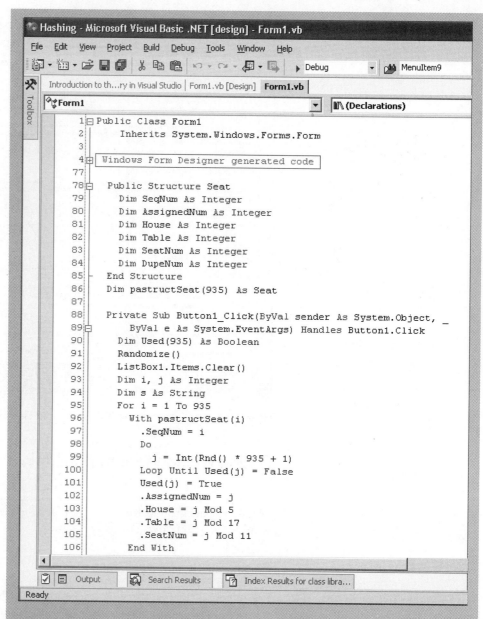

Figure 2-14: Hashing.vb code window

NOTE: The first two lines of code in Figure 2-14 indicate that Form1 is a new class, its accessibility level is Public (accessible throughout the program), and its initial functionality is derived from the Form class defined in the System.Windows. Forms namespace. Note the syntax: Inherits System.Windows.Forms.Form. This is considered a fully qualified name. The keyword Inherits always refers to a base class; the keyword Imports (not shown in the present example) always refers to a namespace.

2   To facilitate this discussion, you will configure the Visual Basic .NET Code Editor to display line numbers. To do this, click **Tools | Options**. In the Options dialog box, click **Text Editor** in the Options list on the left, click **Basic** under Text Editor, and click **General** under Basic. Then on the right, under Display, click the **Line numbers** check box. Click **OK**. See Figure 2-15.

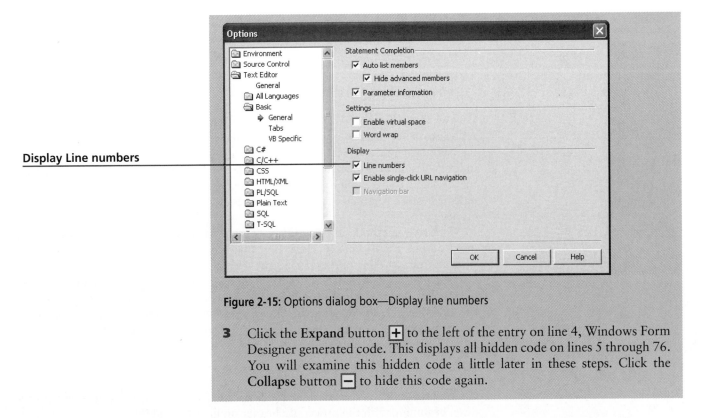

Figure 2-15: Options dialog box—Display line numbers

Display Line numbers

3 Click the **Expand** button ⊞ to the left of the entry on line 4, Windows Form Designer generated code. This displays all hidden code on lines 5 through 76. You will examine this hidden code a little later in these steps. Click the **Collapse** button ⊟ to hide this code again.

You now examine the user-written code in the Hashing program.

Understanding the Structure Statement

The **Structure** statement declares a user-defined data structure, consisting of one or more elements. These elements may be constants, variables, properties, methods, arrays, or other predefined structures. The declaration of elements within a Structure statement ends with End Structure.

In the Hashing program, the first section of user-written code is the declaration of a structure called Seat on lines 78 through 85, as shown in Figure 2-16:

```
Public Structure Seat
    Dim SeqNum As Integer
    Dim AssignedNum As Integer
    Dim House As Integer
    Dim Table As Integer
    Dim SeatNum As Integer
    Dim DupeNum As Integer
End Structure
```

Figure 2-16: Declaration of Public Structure Seat

The keyword Structure replaces the keyword Type in Visual Basic 6.0. Internally, the syntax of the Structure/End Structure statement block matches the syntax of the old Type/End Type statement block. However, the Type/End Type statement needed to appear in a code module; by contrast, the Structure statement block can appear in any code region. The Structure statement is also more flexible, since it can include property and method declarations in addition to constants and variables. The default access type is Public, but more restricted access levels can also be specified in the declaration.

Exploring Structure Variables and Arrays

Following the Structure Seat declaration, the statement Dim `pastructSeat(935)` `As Seat` on line 87 creates an array of 936 elements (instances) of type Seat. The naming convention pastructSeat should be read as "public array of Seat structures." The index values of array elements in Visual Basic .NET always begin with 0 and end with the declared upper bound. So in this case, pastructSeat contains pastructSeat(0), pastructSeat(1), pastructSeat(2), ..., pastructSeat(935), resulting in a total of 936 array elements.

The only methods automatically defined for a structure are assignment and input/output to a random data file. So, you can write a statement such as `pastructSeat(i) = pastructSeat(j)`.

The integers declared inside the structure constitute the properties, or attributes, of the class. Using dot notation, you can access these properties. To continue with this example, you could assign the House at element "j" to the House at element "i" with this code: `pastructSeat(i).House = pastructSeat(j).House`.

Exploring the Event Procedures

Continuing with the user-written code, the next block of code is an event procedure, beginning with the procedure header on lines 89 and 90:

```
Private Sub Button1_Click(ByVal sender As _
    System.Object, ByVal e As System.EventArgs) _
    Handles Button1.Click
```

Several comments pertain to this syntax, which seems a bit more complex than the procedure headers in Visual Basic 6.0.

First, note that accessibility is set to Private (the default value), meaning that this procedure can be called only from within Form1. (If you need to call an event procedure from another form, you must change its accessibility to Public Shared.)

Next, Visual Basic .NET event procedures generally come with two built-in parameters: the first of these is the identification of the *sender* (the object that calls this procedure to be executed). The sender is identified, because a single event procedure can be invoked by multiple events coming from multiple controls, and it might be important to know which object invoked the procedure. The events that this procedure is assigned to handle are listed after the keyword Handles. In this case, the Button1_Click event procedure is only designed to handle the Button1.Click event. The capacity of a single procedure to handle events coming from multiple controls is one of the ways in which Visual Basic .NET provides the functionality previously provided by control arrays, which are no longer supported.

The second built-in parameter in the procedure header is e As System.EventArgs. This entry is a placeholder for those events that must pass **state information** (or other data associated with an event) to the event handler. By default, the System.EventArgs class has no data at all, so "e" is often empty.

The rest of the user-written code in the Button1_Click event procedure is standard sequential logic.

Exploring the Windows Form Designer Generated Code

At this point, you return to the expanded entry beginning on line 4 to examine the hidden code.

> To examine the hidden code in Hashing:
>
> **1**　Expand the Windows Form Designer generated code by again clicking the plus sign next to the heading.
>
> The Windows Form Designer generates the code in this region automatically, and it should not be necessary (nor is it advisable) to modify any of this code yourself. Rather, if changes need to be made, you should fix the design in the Windows Form Designer, and then see that the appropriate changes are propagated here. However, examining this code is quite instructive, especially concerning OOP and the .NET Framework. You study each portion of the Windows Form Designer generated code in the following sections.

The New() Method—the Default Object Constructor

The automatically generated code starts with the Form class member that constructs the instance, line 6 to 14, shown in Figure 2-17.

```
Public Sub New()
      MyBase.New()

      'This call is required by the Windows Form Designer.
      InitializeComponent()

      'Add any initialization after the InitializeComponent() call

End Sub
```

Figure 2-17: New() constructor

Note the keyword New and the InitializeComponent() call. Accessibility of the form is Public, as you would expect, because you must be able to instantiate the form from any location in the program. The MyBase keyword always refers to the base class from inside a derived class. In this case, MyBase is System.Windows.Forms. Form. So, MyBase.New() calls the base class's constructor member in order to instantiate (create) the new form. InitializeComponent() is the local procedure (created by the Windows Form Designer) that performs all necessary initialization routines for components of the new form, such as creating controls and setting properties. If your application needs an additional initialization procedure, you would call it right after the InitializeComponent() call.

The Dispose() Method—the Default Object Destructor

Next, the code includes destructor instructions (to release resources when the program stops executing), which only execute if the normal destruct and garbage collection processes are aborted. These occupy lines 16 through 24 and are shown in Figure 2-18.

```
'Form overrides dispose to clean up the component list.
  Protected Overloads Overrides Sub Dispose(ByVal disposing _
        As Boolean)
      If disposing Then
          If Not (components Is Nothing) Then
              components.Dispose()
          End If
      End If
      MyBase.Dispose(disposing)
  End Sub
```

Figure 2-18: Dispose() destructor

Access to the Dispose() destructor code is Protected, meaning that it is only available to class members. The keyword Overloads identifies a procedure that duplicates another member with the same name but with a different argument list. Overrides indicates a procedure that replaces an identically named procedure in the base class. Both overloading and overriding are discussed in Tutorial 6. If it is necessary to clean up the component list when the form is being disposed, then this procedure calls Components.Dispose(). This can occur, for example, if an End statement in a form is executed while other forms in the application are still executing.

Enabling Event Handlers

The next three statements in the Windows Form Designer generated code enable event handlers for each control class that will appear on Form1:

```
Friend WithEvents Button1 As System.Windows.
Forms.Button
Friend WithEvents ListBox1 As System.Windows.Forms.
ListBox
Friend WithEvents ListBox2 As System.Windows.Forms.
ListBox
```

Friend access means that the object is accessible throughout this program and in any other form, class, or module that is part of the same assembly. WithEvents means that the Handles keyword can be used to assign a particular event handler to handle a particular event associated with this object. Note again the use of fully qualified names for each control class (for example, System.Windows.Forms.Button).

Components—the Container for Controls

Although the Form1 class now has enabled event handlers for its control classes, the controls themselves have not yet been created and associated with Form1. That comes next. First, the following statement declares a private object called components, derived from the Container class.

```
Private components As System.ComponentModel.Container
```

The components declaration enables the creation of controls within the class.

The InitializeComponent() Procedure

Next, the first section of the InitializeComponent() procedure, lines 32 to 40, creates the controls as components of Me, that is, of Form1. See Figure 2-19.

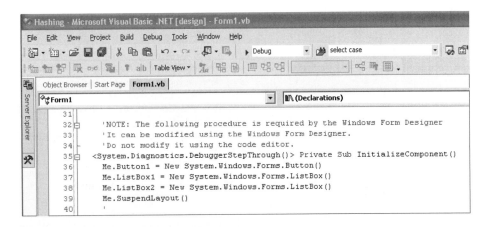

Figure 2-19: InitializeComponent() procedure

The prefix <System.Diagnostics.DebuggerStepThrough()> tells the Source Code debugger not to stop while running this code; it has no effect on the executable module. The New keyword instantiates each object by calling the constructor for that object's class. Finally, the SuspendLayout() method temporarily suspends the layout for the form, which prevents the form from being continually redrawn as the property setting of each control is processed. The code after the SuspendLayout() method sets individual control property settings.

The InitializeComponent() procedure then continues with the nondefault property settings of each control on the form. For example, Figure 2-20 shows the property settings for Button1.

```
41    'Button1
42    '
43    Me.Button1.Location = New System.Drawing.Point(200, 16)
44    Me.Button1.Name = "Button1"
45    Me.Button1.Size = New System.Drawing.Size(64, 24)
46    Me.Button1.TabIndex = 0
47    Me.Button1.Text = "Button1"
```

Figure 2-20: Property settings for Button1, set in InitializeComponent()

This code sets the Location property of Button1 as a New Point object with the X, Y coordinates 200, 16 (recall that these measurements are in pixels) and its Size property as a New Size object 64 pixels wide and 24 pixels high. Normally, a programmer does not directly modify any of this code, but you could just as an experiment. If you type a new value for the Button1 Text property, that new value appears on the button when you view the form in Form Designer.

In the property settings for ListBox1, the default Font property was changed, and so this property appears in the InitializeComponent() procedure at line 51. See Figure 2-21.

```
49    'ListBox1
50    '
51    Me.ListBox1.Font = New System.Drawing.Font _
52      ("Courier New", 8.25!, System.Drawing.FontStyle.Regular, _
53      System.Drawing.GraphicsUnit.Point, CType(0, Byte))
54    Me.ListBox1.ItemHeight = 14
55    Me.ListBox1.Location = New System.Drawing.Point(16, 56)
56    Me.ListBox1.Name = "ListBox1"
57    Me.ListBox1.Size = New System.Drawing.Size(416, 494)
58    Me.ListBox1.TabIndex = 1
```

Figure 2-21: Property settings for ListBox1

Following the property settings for all the controls on the form, the property settings for Form1 itself appear on lines 67 through 75. (See Figure 2-22.) Recall that Me is always a self-reference to the form in which it occurs.

```
67    'Form1
68    '
69    Me.AutoScaleBaseSize = New System.Drawing.Size(5, 13)
70    Me.ClientSize = New System.Drawing.Size(464, 574)
71    Me.Controls.AddRange(New System.Windows.Forms.Control() _
72      {Me.ListBox2, Me.ListBox1, Me.Button1})
73    Me.Name = "Form1"
74    Me.Text = "Form1"
75    Me.ResumeLayout(False)
```

Figure 2-22: Property settings for Form1

The AutoScaleBaseSize property indicates the size that will be used for autoscaling at runtime. This is a reference point concerning the size of the GUI on the computer used to create the form, so that the form's size can be automatically adjusted for the screen size of the computer on which the application runs. The ClientSize property is the size of the entire form, minus the title bar and borders. The Controls.AddRange method actually places the newly created controls on the form. The ResumeLayout() method allows the completion of the form layout, previously suspended in line 39 (recall Figure 2-19).

Hashing Application—Additional Coding Notes

The following are a few additional notes on coding the Hashing application.

- *Dot notation throughout Visual Basic .NET*—In general, Visual Basic .NET has adopted the convention of using a period to separate parts of a long name or reference, moving from the general to the specific. Thus, you see code such as that shown on lines 71 and 72 of Figure 2-22:

```
71  Me.Controls.AddRange(New System.Windows.Forms.
Control() _
72  {Me.ListBox2, Me.ListBox1, Me.Button1})
```

As you work on other Visual Basic .NET applications, expand the Windows Form Designer generated code region from time to time, and try to correlate the code with the settings and selections you make in the Form Designer. This can help you to understand how Visual Basic .NET implements object-oriented programming, how the .NET Framework's namespaces and classes assist in this process, and, therefore, how the entire package works together to achieve the desired functionality of your applications.

■ *With. . . End With structure*—This syntax is useful when a long structure name is used repeatedly in a block of code. In lines 124 through 130, by using With pastructSeat(i), the program avoids having to repeat the name pastructSeat(i) six times. See Figure 2-23.

```
123     For i = 1 To 935
124        With pastructSeat(i)
125           s = .SeqNum.ToString & _
126              " AssignedNum=" & .AssignedNum.ToString & _
127              " House=" & .House.ToString & _
128              " Table=" & .Table.ToString & " Seat=" & .SeatNum & _
129              " Dupe=" & .DupeNum.ToString
130        End With
131        ListBox1.Items.Add(s)
132     Next
```

Figure 2-23: With . . . End With structure

■ *ListBox syntax*—The Items property has a Clear() method, which empties the ListBox control, and an Add() method, which adds one item to the ListBox control. Because the contents of a list box must be a string, the ToString method is used where needed to convert an integer to a string before inserting it in the list box.

To hide the Windows Form Designer generated code:

1 Click the **Collapse** button 🔲 for the Windows Form Designer generated code region again.

2 Click the **Save All** button 🔳.

3 Close the **Hashing** solution.

This completes the InitializeComponent() procedure and Windows Form Designer generated code region.

You have completed Lesson A. Take a break, or complete the end-of-lesson questions and exercises. If you decide on a break, don't forget to come back and finish these questions and exercises before moving on to Lesson B.

SUMMARY

■ Visual Basic .NET is an object-oriented language. Effective programming in this language requires the use of objects, classes, inheritance, encapsulation, and limitations on accessibility and scope.

■ A major advantage of OOP is the enhanced opportunities for software reuse. Classes and objects that have been tested and accepted can be reutilized in other applications without additional testing.

■ The Visual Studio .NET Framework provides numerous namespaces and classes to serve as the foundation for Visual Basic .NET programs. Namespaces provided by Microsoft begin with the words "System" or "Microsoft." System namespaces are common to many languages, whereas most Microsoft namespaces are language-specific.

■ Encapsulation is achieved through limitations on accessibility and scope. Visual Basic .NET provides five levels of access (Public, Protected, Friend, Protected Friend, and Private) and four levels of scope (block, procedure, module, and namespace).

■ Variable arrays are declared with an upper bound. Because the lower bound of every array is 0, the number of elements in an array is the upper bound + 1.

■ User-defined data types in Visual Basic .NET are declared with the Structure statement at the module level and are Public by default.

QUESTIONS

1. The notion that an object is "complete unto itself" is called _____.

2. The process of creating an object from a class is called _____.

3. The class upon which another class is modeled is known as the _____ _____.

4. The class taken from another class is called a(n) _____ _____.

5. To use the classes and types in a particular namespace, you _____ the namespace into the program.

6. The idea that an object or a class may offer the same functionality as a class upon which it is based is called _____.

7. The ability of a class to modify an inherited property or method is called _____.

8. Write the declaration of an array X of 10 integers at the module level, with Friend access.

9. User-defined data types are declared in Visual Basic .NET with the _____ statement.

10. The prefix pastruct in the declaration pastructSeat(935) means _____.

11. Blueprint is to building as _____ is to object.

CRITICAL THINKING

At the end of each lesson, critical thinking questions are intended to provoke you into considering the material you have just read at a deeper level.

1. Distinguish between a class and a structure. (This is trickier than it sounds. Feel free to use the Help screens to assist you in finding the answer.)

2. What is the longest namespace name you can find? Consider the fully qualified name, such as Microsoft.VisualBasic or System.Windows.Forms.

3. Consider the notion of table (that is, dining room table, kitchen table, etc.) as a class. Starting with the class table, construct a complete analogy of the OOP model. That is, invent other classes and objects, and use them to describe the notions of property, method, base class, derived class, encapsulation, and polymorphism.

EXERCISES

1. In this exercise, you create a new Console application. Code the declaration for a user-defined structure called PersonnelStruct. The structure should contain an employee number, employee name, and employee wage rate. Then declare a variable PersonnelRec to be of type PersonnelStruct. Assign the values 123, Jane Wong, and $18.75 to the components of PersonnelRec. Then use WriteLine statements to print the structure and contents of PersonnelRec. The output is shown in Figure 2-24.

```
Structure of PersonnelRec:
    EmpNum As Integer
    EmpName As String
    EmpWageRate As Decimal
Contents of PersonnelRec:
    EmpNum = 123
    EmpName = "Jane Wong"
    EmpWageRate = 18.75
```

Figure 2-24: Sample output for Exercise 1

   a. If necessary, start Visual Studio .NET. Open a new project based on the Visual Basic .NET Console Application template in the VB.NET\Student\Tut02 folder called Personnel.
   b. Declare a public structure at the module level (that is, prior to Sub Main) named PersonnelStruct. Declare three elements inside this structure: EmpNum, an integer; EmpName, a 20-byte, fixed-length string; and EmpWageRate, a decimal.
   c. Declare a variable named PersonnelRec of type PersonnelStruct.
   d. Inside Sub Main(), assign values to the components of PersonnelRec. Specifically, assign 123 to EmpNum, Jane Wong to EmpName, and 18.75 to EmpWageRate.
   e. Also inside Sub Main(), use WriteLine statements to produce a nicely formatted listing of PersonnelRec.
   f. Skip a line, display Press the Enter key to continue, and wait for user input before ending the program.

2. In this exercise, you create a Windows Forms application that allows you to demonstrate your understanding of the Windows Form Designer generated code.
   a. Create a new Windows Forms Application called Tut02Code in the VB.NET\Student\Tut02 folder.
   b. Set these form properties:
       ■ Change the Name property to frmTut02Code.
       ■ Change the BackColor property to LightBlue.
       ■ Change the Text property to Windows Form Designer generated code.
   c. Add a button, a text box, a label, and a list box to the form, as shown in Figure 2-25.

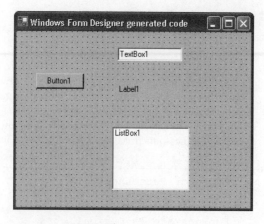

Figure 2-25: Design of frmTut02Code

    d.   Open the Code window, and expand the Windows Form Designer generated code. Copy the entire region into a Word document. Save this Word document as AnnotatedTut02Code.

    e.   In the Word document, insert a comment at the end of each statement of the Windows Form Designer generated code, explaining the purpose and function of that statement.

After completing this lesson, you will be able to:

■ Understand the application logic and coding of the Hashing application

■ Develop a detailed plan for converting a prototype into a production application

■ Add a MainMenu control

■ Add a DateTimePicker control

■ Adjust form properties, object names, and identifiers

■ Move code from Button1_Click() to mnuToolsAssignSeats_Click()

■ Delete unnecessary items

■ Generate a unique seat assignment list for each date

The Basics of Coding

Understanding Hashing Application Logic and Coding

This lesson steps you through the construction of the Dining Hall Seat Assigner application for the Friendsville Games Development Team. The Hashing application provides some underlying logic and sample code that can help you build the Dining application. Your first task is to examine the Hashing application carefully, as that program has already been written for you. Next, you compare the requirements for the Dining application with the existing Hashing application; their differences point to the list of tasks needed to convert Hashing into Dining. In Lesson B, you then complete half the tasks needed to effect this conversion, leaving the other half for Lesson C.

Recall that the Friendsville International Village has five dining halls, with 17 dining tables in each dining hall, and 11 seats at each table. Thus, the dining halls can accommodate 935 guests at one sitting (5 * 17 * 11). The objective is to randomly assign these 935 seats. Although many different techniques can accomplish this purpose, the one proposed here is relatively straightforward. It depends on the fact that the numbers 5, 17, and 11 are all prime numbers. Therefore, no number lower than 935 will be an exact multiple of all three of these prime numbers. As a corollary to this fact, applying the modulus operator to any number from 1 to 935 always results in a unique set of remainders for the divisors 5, 17, and 11. For example, the number 55 is evenly divisible by 5 and by 11 (in each case, the remainder after division = 0), while 55 Mod 17 = 4. At 110, the next number evenly divisible by both 5 and 11, 110 Mod 17 = 8. For each multiple of 55, that multiple Mod 17 is some number from 0 to 16, but it will not twice be the same number. Because these facts may not be intuitively obvious, the Hashing program, among other things, proves it.

The Hashing program randomly selects a number from 1 to 935 and assigns that number to each element of a 935 element array. The algorithm ensures that no randomly selected number is used more than once. After a previously unused random number has been selected, that number is deconstructed (using the Mod operator) into a unique seat assignment (consisting of a house number, table number, and seat number). Then an element-by-element comparison is made to ensure that each seat assignment is unique, and the seat assignments are displayed in a list box. Here are the details of the logic:

At the module level, the Hashing program declares Structure Seat and creates the pastructSeat array in lines 78 through 86. See Figure 2-26.

The rest of the action takes place in the Button1_Click event procedure. The key code block, shown in Figure 2-27, uses a For loop to step through the seating sequence numbers 1 through 935, and randomly assigns a number (the AssignedNum field) to each sequence number. An array of Boolean values called Used(935) identifies which assigned numbers have already been used, and prevents any randomly selected number from being used twice. When a number not previously selected is found, this AssignedNum is recorded in the pastructSeat array, and it is also deconstructed into a house (numbered 0–4), table (numbered 0–16), and seat (numbered 0–10). All of this activity takes place between lines 96 through 108.

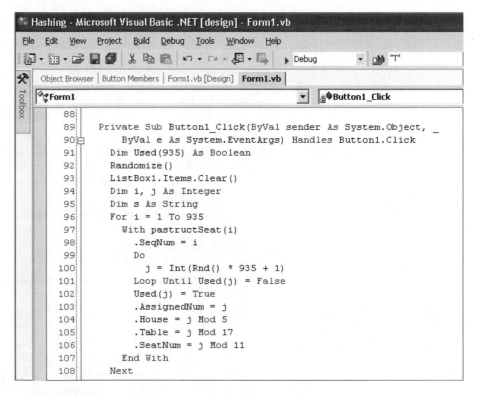

```
1  Public Class Form1
2      Inherits System.Windows.Forms.Form
3
4      Windows Form Designer generated code
77
78     Public Structure Seat
79        Dim SeqNum As Integer
80        Dim AssignedNum As Integer
81        Dim House As Integer
82        Dim Table As Integer
83        Dim SeatNum As Integer
84        Dim DupeNum As Integer
85     End Structure
86
87     Dim pastructSeat(935) As Seat
88
```

Figure 2-26: Module-level declarations in the Hashing program

```
88
89     Private Sub Button1_Click(ByVal sender As System.Object, _
90         ByVal e As System.EventArgs) Handles Button1.Click
91     Dim Used(935) As Boolean
92     Randomize()
93     ListBox1.Items.Clear()
94     Dim i, j As Integer
95     Dim s As String
96     For i = 1 To 935
97        With pastructSeat(i)
98           .SeqNum = i
99           Do
100             j = Int(Rnd() * 935 + 1)
101          Loop Until Used(j) = False
102          Used(j) = True
103          .AssignedNum = j
104          .House = j Mod 5
105          .Table = j Mod 17
106          .SeatNum = j Mod 11
107       End With
108    Next
```

Figure 2-27: Generating random seat assignments

Next, another For loop in lines 109 through 119, as shown in Figure 2-28, compares each element in pastructSeat to every other element in pastructSeat. If any duplicate entry is discovered, the duplicate number is noted in the pastructSeat array, and the duplicate entry is also displayed in ListBox2.

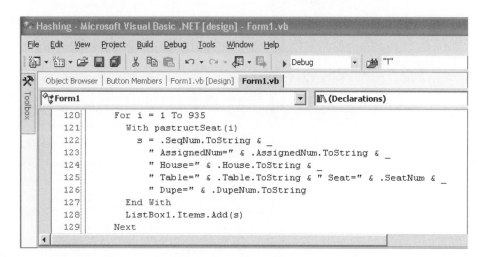

```
109         'search for duplicates
110         For i = 1 To 934
111           For j = i + 1 To 935
112             If pastructSeat(i).House = pastructSeat(j).House And _
113                 pastructSeat(i).Table = pastructSeat(j).Table And _
114                 pastructSeat(i).SeatNum = pastructSeat(j).SeatNum Then
115                 pastructSeat(j).DupeNum = i
116                 ListBox2.Items.Add(i.ToString & "   " & j.ToString)
117             End If
118           Next
119         Next
```

Figure 2-28: Ensuring the absence of duplicates

Finally, in lines 120 to 129, as shown in Figure 2-29, the elements in pastructSeat along with appropriate captions are displayed in ListBox1.

```
120         For i = 1 To 935
121           With pastructSeat(i)
122             s = .SeqNum.ToString & _
123                 " AssignedNum=" & .AssignedNum.ToString & _
124                 " House=" & .House.ToString & _
125                 " Table=" & .Table.ToString & " Seat=" & .SeatNum & _
126                 " Dupe=" & .DupeNum.ToString
127           End With
128           ListBox1.Items.Add(s)
129         Next
```

Figure 2-29: Displaying seat assignments in the list box

NOTE: The name of the Hashing program suggests that it is or uses a hash code or a hashing algorithm, and in a sense it does. That term is sometimes used in the particular context of a unique code associated with a particular software assembly. That type of hash code is based on a mathematical formula applied to the binary representation of a program, and it operates in such a way that even an extremely minor change to the assembly results in a major change to the resulting hash code. The present application, however, is close enough to the notion of a hashing algorithm to merit the term.

Running the Hashing Application

Next, you will run the Hashing program and examine its output. You should fully comprehend how the logic of this program works.

To run and examine the Hashing application:

1 If necessary, start **Visual Studio .NET**, and open the **Hashing** solution in the VB.NET\Student\Tut02\Hashing folder.

2 Click the **Start** button ▶ to run the program. Click **Button1** to generate the random seat assignments. Figure 2-30 displays sample output (your listing of seat assignments will be different). Scroll through ListBox1 to verify that it contains all 935 sequence numbers. Note that the AssignedNum field appears to be in random order. ListBox2 in the upper-left corner of the form is empty, meaning that the program discovered no duplicate assignments.

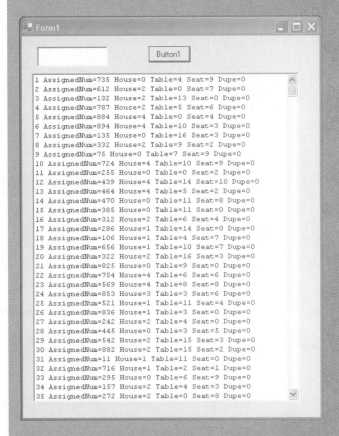

Figure 2-30: Hashing program sample output

3 Click **Button1** again, and note that the seats are assigned in a different order, but ListBox2 is still empty. In fact, click **Button1** as often as you like. This provides fairly good evidence that the assignment scheme works correctly, that all 935 seat assignments have been made, and that no duplicates exist.

4 Exit the running application, returning you to the IDE.

NOTE: The scheme employed here for obtaining unique combinations of numbers is based, as noted earlier, on the fact that all three numerical components (the number of houses, tables per house, and seats per table) are prime numbers. This scheme can be employed with minor modifications, however, even if the component numbers are not prime. For example, if there were eight seats per table, the program would still use 11 as the divisor for the seat number, because 11 is the lowest prime that is >= 8; then, using an If statement, any seat assignment > 8 would be filtered out.

Converting a Prototype into a Production Application

The Hashing application that you have been working with provides the core logic needed to make dining hall seating assignments, although a number of features in the Dining application are missing from the Hashing application. Nevertheless, you will begin with the Hashing application, and make appropriate modifications to that program to turn it into the finished Dining application.

First, you need a list of the things in the Dining application that the Hashing application is missing, as well as a list of the things in the Hashing application that need not be carried over to the Dining application. One method of developing such a list is to run the two programs side by side, and visually note the differences. This leads you to develop your list of tasks, which you can then load into the Task List in the IDE.

This Task List organizes the remaining discussion in Tutorial 2. After you complete these tasks, you will have created the final Dining Hall Seat Assigner application. The conversion of the Hashing application into the Dining application is a practical exercise. You will encounter many occasions in business programming in which a prototype has been created (either by you or by someone else), and you want to build on the prototype to create a production application. Lessons B and C in this tutorial give you experience in doing precisely that.

To develop the Task List for converting the Hashing application to the Dining application:

1 In Visual Studio .NET, run the **Hashing** program again, and click **Button1**. Position the running application (**Form1**) on the right half of the screen, leaving room for the Dining application on the left. Click **Start** on the Windows taskbar. Click **Run** and navigate to **VB.NET\Student\Tut02\Dining\bin**. Click **Dining.exe** to open it, and position the Dining Hall Seat Assigner form on the left half of the screen. In the Dining application, click **Tools | Assign Seats**. See Figure 2-31.

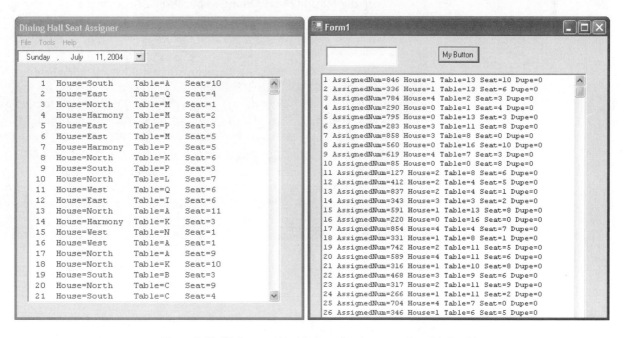

Figure 2-31: Dining and Hashing applications, running side by side

Because your programming assignment is to convert the Hashing application on the right into the Dining application on the left, you should note the following differences between the two applications, and mentally note the items in Hashing that need to be completed or modified:

- The MainMenu control needs to be added to Hashing.
- The DateTimePicker control needs to be added to Hashing.
- Clicking Tools | Assign Seats in Dining is similar to clicking Button1 in Hashing.
- The large list box has analogous but slightly different output in the two applications: from the Hashing application, the AssignedNum and Dupe values are not needed in Dining, because you are now convinced that the seat assignment algorithm produces no duplicates. Hashing's numeric values have been converted: House is a number (0–4) in Hashing, but is a string (North, South, East, West, Harmony) in Dining; Table is a number (0–16) in Hashing, but is a letter (A–Q) in Dining; and Seat is a number in the range 0–10 in Hashing, but in the range 1–11 in Dining. Further, the output in Dining is formatted and spaced so the columns are properly aligned.
- Dining, but not Hashing, provides optional output to a printer or to a sequential file.
- The Dining application generates a unique but consistent set of seating assignments for each date. This notion was not addressed in Hashing.
- The Dining application offers a Help menu with instructions and an About form.
- The Dining application does not have a control box, or Maximize, Minimize, and Close buttons on the Title bar.
- ListBox2 in Hashing (which was programmed to display duplicate seating assignments, but which was never used, because there are no duplicates possible) is not needed in Dining.
- The Hashing application uses default object names (Form1, ListBox1, ListBox2), which should be changed to more meaningful names in the Dining application.

2 Close the **Hashing** and **Dining** applications. Back in the IDE, also close the **Hashing** solution. Next, you will make a copy of the existing Hashing application, and rename it. This copy will be the foundation for your own Dining application.

3 In Windows Explorer, create a new Tut02 subfolder called **MyDining** and copy the contents of the **Tut02\Hashing** folder into it. (Copying the contents of Hashing to a new folder allows you to preserve the Hashing program as is; all of your changes will be made to the copy rather than to the original.) In Visual Studio .NET, open the new **Hashing** solution located in the MyDining folder.

4 In Solution Explorer, right-click 🏁 **Solution 'Hashing' (1 project)**, click **Rename**, and change the name of the solution to **MyDining**. Similarly, right-click **Hashing** 📳, click **Rename**, and change the name of the project to **MyDining**. Then right-click **Form1.vb** 🖽, select **Rename**, and change the name of the form to **frmDining.vb**. See Figure 2-32.

Figure 2-32: Solution Explorer after the names have been changed

5   From the list of differences between Hashing and Dining in Step 2, the Task List is easy to develop. From the View menu, select **Show Tasks | All**. The Task List window opens. Type the Task List into the IDE, as shown in Figure 2-33. Just click the sentence that reads **Click here to add a new task**. When you type this list, include the task number, beginning with **01**.

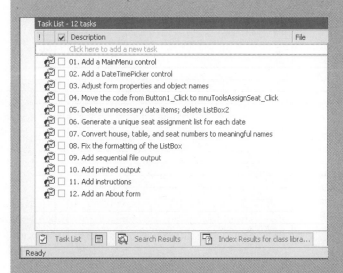

Figure 2-33: Task List in MyDining application

NOTE: You need to include a task number in the description of each task in the Task List, so that the list is displayed in the correct order when sorted by the description field. As each task is completed, you can either check its status check box, or delete the task from the Task List.

6   At this point, as you begin modifying the MyDining (formerly Hashing) application, your screen should appear approximately as in Figure 2-34. Unless you have a huge monitor, open the **Toolbox**, but keep it hidden at the top left. (Recall the Auto Hide pushpin, explained in Tutorial 1.) The Task

List, Search Results, and Index Results tabs should be visible at the bottom of the screen, but these windows should also be hidden. The upper-right panel should contain tabs for Solution Explorer, Help Contents, and Help Index, with the most recently clicked window on top. The lower-right panel should display tabs for the Properties window and Dynamic Help, again with the most recently selected window visible.

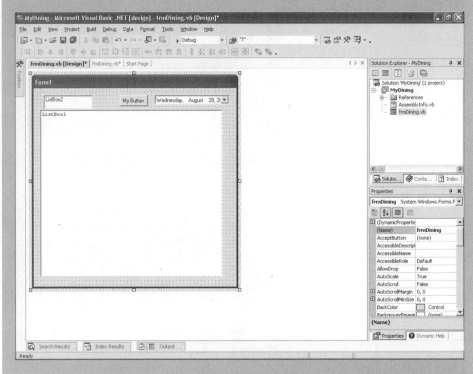

Figure 2-34: The Visual Studio .NET IDE as MyDining modifications are about to begin

NOTE: Be careful; it's possible to inadvertently close needed windows in the IDE, or open and enlarge windows that then consume too much screen real estate.

7   Finally, the main window should be filled with the Form Designer, the Code window, or a Help screen—again, the most recently selected of these three should be displayed. Open **frmDining** in the Windows Form Designer, if necessary. Task 1 begins with the Form Designer on top.

tip

If any window that should be displayed is not, open it from the View menu. Remember that you can click the pushpin toggle switch to change Auto Hide on or off for most of these windows, and they can also be resized to take up just as much space as you desire. Most can also be docked along any border or left floating.

Adding a MainMenu Control (Task 01)

This task involves placing a MainMenu control on the form, inserting the appropriate menu items, setting properties for certain menu items, and renaming the menu items from their default names.

tip

You can also add a MainMenu control by double-clicking the tool in the Toolbox.

To add a MainMenu control:

1 If necessary, click the **frmDining.vb [Design]** tab at the top of the main window to display the Windows Form Designer. In the Toolbox, click the **MainMenu** control, and drag it onto the form. The Form Designer displays the MainMenu1 control in a tray underneath the form (reducing the portion of the window devoted to the GUI). At the top left of the form, the words "Type Here" are displayed.

2 On the form's menu bar, click **Type Here**, type **&File**, and then press **Enter**. Note the following features:

- Type Here text boxes appear below and to the right of the currently selected menu item. Clicking below enables you to enter the next item in the drop-down menu. Clicking to the right enables you to enter another root level item (if you are currently at the top level) or to insert a submenu item (if you are currently at a level below the root level).
- After you press Enter, the Type Here box under File is highlighted.
- The character following & (F in this case) appears as an underscored character in the resulting menu (that is, <u>F</u>). At runtime, this entry (<u>F</u>ile) is available by pressing the Alt key plus the underscored character (Alt+F) to reach the File menu.

NOTE: On some platforms, the underscore does not appear until you press Alt. To see the effect on your computer, run Dining.exe. If the F in File is not underscored, press the Alt key; the underscore should appear.

3 In the **Type Here** box under File, type **&Save Seats in File**. This becomes the first menu item under the File menu. Press **Enter**. Type the remaining File menu items in similar fashion: **Page Se&tup**, **Printer Set&up**, **&Print Seats**, and **E&xit**. See Figure 2-35.

Figure 2-35: File menu

4 In the same fashion, insert one item for the **Tools** menu and two items for the **Help** menu, as shown in Figures 2-36 and 2-37. Be sure to press **Enter** after typing each entry.

Figure 2-36: Tools menu

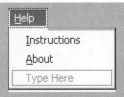

Figure 2-37: Help menu

5 On the File menu, click **Save Seats in File**. In the Properties window, set the Enabled property for this menu item to **False** to disable it. Click **Print Seats**. In the Properties window, set the Enabled property for this menu item to **False** to disable it. (These items should be enabled only after seats have been assigned.)

6 Traditionally, a separator bar separates the Exit menu selection from the items above it. To insert a separator bar, right-click **Exit**, and click **Insert Separator**.

7 By default, Visual Basic .NET assigns internal names to each menu item as MenuItem1, MenuItem2, MenuItem3, and so on. You should change the internal name of each menu item to a meaningful name by clicking **File**. Then right-click, and select **Edit Names**. This is a toggle switch—you remain in Edit Names mode until you turn the switch off by selecting Edit Names again. Type over **MenuItem1** with **mnuFile**, **MenuItem2** with **mnuFileSaveSeats**, **MenuItem3** with **mnuFilePageSetup**, **MenuItem4** with **mnuFilePrinterSetup**, **MenuItem5** with **mnuFilePrintSeats**, and **MenuItem6** with **mnuFileExit**. Note the convention for the names of menu items: the prefix mnu, the root level item (in this case, File, Tools, or Help), and the menu item itself. Figure 2-38 shows the menu item names for the File menu.

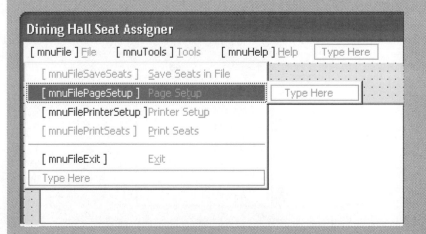

Figure 2-38: Menu item names for the File menu

8 Replace the default names in the Tools and Help menus in similar fashion. The correct menu item names are shown in Figures 2-39 and 2-40.

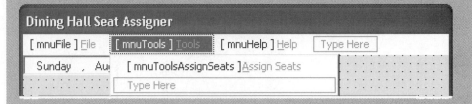

Figure 2-39: Menu item names for the Tools menu

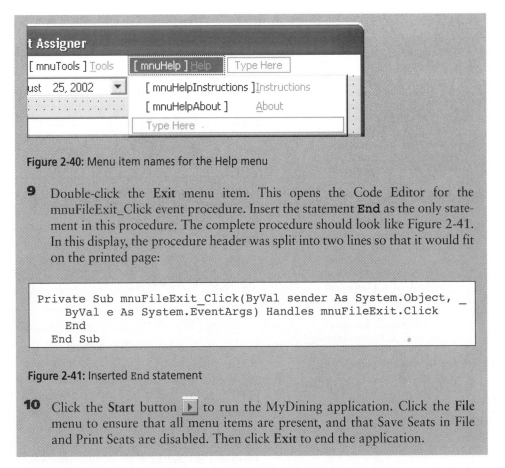

Figure 2-40: Menu item names for the Help menu

9 Double-click the **Exit** menu item. This opens the Code Editor for the mnuFileExit_Click event procedure. Insert the statement **End** as the only statement in this procedure. The complete procedure should look like Figure 2-41. In this display, the procedure header was split into two lines so that it would fit on the printed page:

```
Private Sub mnuFileExit_Click(ByVal sender As System.Object, _
    ByVal e As System.EventArgs) Handles mnuFileExit.Click
    End
End Sub
```

Figure 2-41: Inserted End statement

10 Click the **Start** button ▶ to run the MyDining application. Click the **File** menu to ensure that all menu items are present, and that Save Seats in File and Print Seats are disabled. Then click **Exit** to end the application.

Adding a DateTimePicker Control (Task 02)

When you add the DateTimePicker control, you give the user of the MyDining application the ability to determine the date.

To add a DateTimePicker control:

1 In Form Designer, drag the **DateTimePicker** control from the Toolbox onto the form, and place it and size it appropriately.

2 Run the newly created **MyDining** application to see that it works. Click the **drop-down arrow** to display a calendar, click a **date**, and note that your selected date appears in the control.

NOTE: At runtime, the selected date is available in the DateTimePicker.Value property.

3 Click **File** and then click **Exit** to close the application and return to the IDE.

tip

What do you do if you drag a control onto a form and accidentally put it in the wrong location? In such a case, you simply drag the control to a better location, and resize it as needed. But what if the IDE will not let you drag or resize it? Then perhaps Lock controls has been activated. Lock controls is a toggle switch in the Format menu—the purpose is to prevent the inadvertent repositioning or resizing of controls on a form that has been completed. In the current instance, the author activated Lock controls when the Hashing application was completed. You need to turn the toggle off before you can move or resize any controls on frmDining.

The Hashing program was written to help develop the logic of making randomly selected seat assignments; it was not intended as a permanent addition to the FGDT's repertoire of production applications. You will often find yourself writing short programs (sometimes Console applications) to help you develop an algorithm or to figure out how some code works. If you subsequently decide to use such code in a production application, then you need to convert the code for purposes of internal documentation and to follow the programming conventions and style guidelines of your organization.

Adjusting Form Properties, Object Names, and Identifiers (Task 03)

Several properties of frmDining and its controls need to be modified. By way of summary, frmDining's Text property needs to be changed; the StartPosition should be set to CenterScreen, and the ControlBox should be removed. Also, ListBox1 should have a more meaningful name. Control names as well as variable names should follow standard naming conventions, and the use of constants can make your program more intelligible.

NOTE: The default names of controls and other objects are acceptable when a form can be expected to have only one such control. For example, most forms have only one menu, so MainMenu1 is fine. You will see other examples of this principle in the present application, such as PageSetup1, PrinterSetup1, and PrintDocument1. However, more descriptive names should be employed when multiple controls exist (or might exist in the future).

Navigating Lines of Code

In this and subsequent tasks, you often need to find specific procedures or navigate to specific lines of code. Several techniques can help you do that:

- In almost all cases, the Windows Form Designer generated code should be collapsed. This reduces the total code through which you need to search.
- To find an existing procedure, press Ctrl+F (the Find key), type the procedure name, and press Enter. This usually places the cursor at the beginning of the procedure. If the procedure you are looking for is also called by another procedure, the Find operation may place the cursor on the procedure call rather than the procedure declaration. In this case, repeat the Find operation until the cursor is at the top of the procedure you want.
- Similarly, use the Find operation to find a variable or constant or any other segment of code—but realize that Find may need to be repeated many times to locate the desired line of code, because a variable or constant might occur many times in the program.
- To create an event procedure that does not already exist, select the object that triggers the event from the Class Name combo box at the top left of the Code Editor; then select the event from the Method Name combo box at the top right of the Code Editor. This opens the event procedure you need, and places the insertion point at the blank line between the procedure header and the End Sub statement.
- Another way to create or navigate to an existing event procedure, is to double-click the control that triggers the event in the Form Designer. However, this always creates (or navigates to an existing) default event procedure, such as the Click event for a Button control. If you need some other procedure for that control (such as a Button's MouseDown, DoubleClick, or KeyPress event), then using the Class Name and Method Name combo boxes is the best approach. (If you do create an event procedure that you don't need using the double-click method, you should delete it.)
- To create a user-defined procedure or function, simply place the insertion point on a blank line outside any existing procedure or function but before the End Class statement (the last line of code in a form), and type your own procedure header, such as Private Sub MyProcedure() or Private Function MyFunction(ByVal vintNum As Integer) As Boolean.

Also, as you write the code for this and subsequent programs throughout this book, do not be surprised if your line numbers do not always match those displayed in the text. The line numbers are affected by line continuation characters inserted for textbook legibility, comment lines, and blank lines.

When the ControlBox property is False, you should provide some method of ending the program. For a splash screen, this might be a Timer control that automatically shuts down the form. Or, as in the present case, you might program an Exit menu item to terminate the application. If you run a program whose form has no control box, and if you have no other means of ending the application, press Ctrl+Alt+Delete, open the Task Manager, select the application you want to terminate, and select End Task.

To adjust the form properties, object names, and other identifiers:

1 If necessary, click **frmDining.vb [Design]**, to display the Windows Form Designer. Select the **form** (not any control). In the Properties window, set the **ControlBox** property to **False**. This removes the control box from the upper-left corner of the form, removes the Maximize, Minimize, and Close buttons from the upper-right corner of the form, and removes the Control menu from the Taskbar at runtime.

2 Change the form's Text property from the default **Form1** to **Dining Hall Seat Assigner**.

3 Set the form's **StartPosition** property to **CenterScreen**.

4 Open the Code Editor by clicking the **frmDining.vb*** tab at the top of the main window. Press **Ctrl+H**, which activates the Replace dialog box. In the Find what box, type **ListBox1**. In the Replace with box, type **lstSeats**. Click the **Search hidden text** check box. Click **Replace All**. A message box tells you that 13 occurrences were replaced. Click **OK**. The default name ListBox1 has been replaced with a more meaningful name, lstSeats. Click **Close**.

5 Press **Ctrl+F** to activate the Find feature of Visual Studio .NET, and use it to locate **Public Structure**. Close the Find dialog box. In the Public Structure Seat declaration, change **Seat** to **structSeat**. `struct` is the appropriate prefix for the name of a user-defined structure.

6 After the user-defined structure Seat has been changed to structSeat, this change must be propagated to any variable of that type. Therefore, right after the End Structure statement, highlight the declaration

```
Dim pastructSeat(935) As Seat
```

and replace this with

```
Public pastructSeat (935) As structSeat
```

7 Next, you will declare constants for NUMHOUSES, NUMTABLESPERHOUSE, NUMSEATSPERTABLE, and NUMSEATS at the module level, that is, immediately after the Windows Form Designer generated code. Note that, by convention, constants are written in all caps. Type these four Const (that is, Constant) declarations, as shown in Figure 2-42, after the Windows Form Designer generated code. As a result, with the Windows Form Designer generated code collapsed, frmDining's Code window should begin, as shown in Figure 2-42.

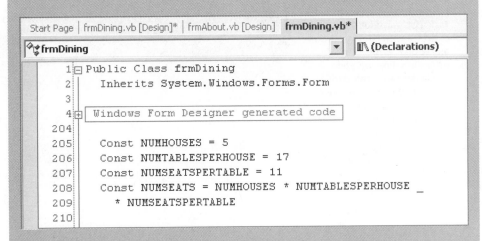

Figure 2-42: First few lines of frmDining, with declaration of constants

8   Use the constant, rather than the literal number, wherever the code calls for that value. For example, the declaration of the constant NUMSEATS uses the previously defined constants NUMHOUSES, NUMTABLESPERHOUSE, and NUMSEATSPERTBLE in its assignment. In the Button1_Click procedure, the house number is generated by the expression j Mod 5; using the constant for NUMHOUSES, change this expression to j Mod NUMHOUSES. In the table assignment, replace 17 with NUMTABLESPERHOUSE. Similarly, change the seat number assignment expression from j Mod 11 to j Mod NUMSEATSPERTABLE. And you can use another universal Find and Replace to replace the six occurrences of 935 with the constant NUMSEATS.

9   In the Button1_Click procedure, change the name of the Boolean array from Used to blnUsedSeats. The conventional prefix for a Boolean variable is bln, and UsedSeats is a more meaningful name than Used. The Seats array is referenced three times in Button1_Click—the declaration and then two more times. You must change each reference to blnUsedSeats.

10   Also in the Button1_Click procedure, change the name of the string variable "s" to strSeat. The variable "s" also occurs three times, so you have three places to make this change. (Be careful! If you use Replace All, you will inadvertently change every instance of "s" to strSeat.) Again, str is the conventional prefix for a string variable, and Seat describes what the string contains.

11   To ensure that you have not introduced any syntax errors into your code, run the **MyDining** program again, and click **Button1** to see the seat assignments. Then click **File | Exit** to return to the IDE.

Moving the Code from Button1_Click to mnuToolsAssignSeats_Click (Task 04)

In the Dining application, seat assignments are generated by selecting Tools | Assign Seats. In Hashing, seat assignments were generated by clicking Button1. Therefore, as part of the conversion from Hashing to Dining, the code in Button1_Click must be moved to mnuToolsAssignSeats_Click.

To move the code from Button1_Click to mnuToolsAssignSeats:

1   Select all of the code within the **Button1_Click** procedure. Do not include the header Private Sub Button1_Click(...) or the End Sub in the selection. See Figure 2-43.

```
Private Sub Button1_Click(ByVal sender As System.Object, _
    ByVal e As System.EventArgs) Handles Button1.Click

Dim blnUsedSeats(NUMSEATS) As Boolean
Randomize()
LstSeat.Items.Clear()
Dim i, j As Integer
Dim strSeat As String
For i = 1 To NUMSEATS
  With pastructSeat(i)
    .SeqNum = i
    Do
      j = Int(Rnd() * NUMSEATS + 1)
    Loop Until blnUsedSeats(j) = False
    blnUsedSeats(j) = True
    .AssignedNum = j
    .House = j Mod NUMHOUSES
    .Table = j Mod NUMTABLESPERHOUSE
    .SeatNum = j Mod NUMSEATSPERTABLE
  End With
Next
'search for duplicates
For i = 1 To 934
  For j = i + 1 To NUMSEATS
    If pastructSeat(i).House = pastructSeat(j).House And _
       pastructSeat(i).Table = pastructSeat(j).Table And _
       pastructSeat(i).SeatNum = pastructSeat(j).SeatNum Then
       pastructSeat(j).DupeNum = i
       ListBox2.Items.Add(i.ToString & "  " & j.ToString)
    End If
  Next
Next
For i = 1 To NUMSEATS
  With pastructSeat(i)
    strSeat = .SeqNum.ToString & _
      " AssignedNum=" & .AssignedNum.ToString & _
      " House=" & .House.ToString & _
      " Table=" & .Table.ToString & " Seat=" & .SeatNum & _
      " Dupe=" & .DupeNum.ToString
  End With
  LstSeat.Items.Add(strSeat)
Next

End Sub
```

move this code

Figure 2-43: Code to be moved from Button1_Click to mnuToolsAssignSeats_Click

2   Press **Shift+Delete**. This deletes the code from the Button1_Click procedure and places that code on the Windows Clipboard.

3   In the Object combo box at the top left, click **mnuToolsAssignSeats**.

4   In the Event combo box at the top right, select **Click**. This opens the mnuToolsAssignSeats_Click procedure and positions the cursor after the header for this procedure.

5   Press **Shift+Insert**. This inserts the code from the Windows Clipboard.

6   Run the **MyDining** program again, click **Tools | Assign Seats** to see the seat assignments, and click **File | Exit**.

tip

· · · · · · · · · · · · · · ·

▶ If the menu selections are still titled MenuItem1, MenuItem2, MenuItem3, and so on, the Edit Names operation did not work correctly. Sometimes an inadvertent mouse-click causes Visual Studio .NET to change the names of menu items back to the default names. In this case, the best work-around is to return to the Form Designer, click Tools in the Dining menu control, and double-click Assign Seats. This opens the appropriate procedure in the Code Editor.

Deleting Unnecessary Items (Task 05)

Several items from Hashing are no longer needed and should be cleaned up before you proceed. ListBox2 displays the details of duplicate seat assignments, but of course there aren't any, so ListBox2 is not necessary. The AssignedNum element of structSeat was used to display the random-selected integer, subsequently deconstructed into a unique seat assignment. In the Dining application, this intermediate value is not needed, so AssignedNum can be deleted from the program. The DupeNum element of structSeat was intended to identify duplicates and is no longer needed. Finally, Button1's function was moved to mnuToolsAssignSeats, so Button1 and its Click event procedure can be removed.

To delete unnecessary items:

1 In the Form Designer, delete **ListBox2**. To do this, select **ListBox2**, and press **Delete**. You must also delete the reference to ListBox2 in the mnuToolsAssignSeats_Click procedure by deleting the following line of code:

```
ListBox2.Items.Add(i.ToString & "  " & j.ToString)
```

2 In the Code Editor, in the mnuToolsAssignSeats_Click procedure, use the Find operation (by pressing **Ctrl+F**) to locate and then delete the lines involving AssignedNum, namely:

```
.AssignedNum = j
" AssignedNum=" & .AssignedNum.ToString & _
```

See Figure 2-44.

3 In the Code Editor, in the mnuToolsAssignSeats_Click procedure, delete the entire section of code involving the search for duplicates. See Figure 2-44.

```vb
Private Sub mnuToolsAssignSeats_Click(ByVal sender As System.Object, _
    ByVal e As System.EventArgs) Handles mnuToolsAssignSeats.Click
  Dim blnUsedSeats(NUMSEATS) As Boolean
  Randomize()
  LstSeat.Items.Clear()
  Dim i, j As Integer
  Dim strSeat As String
  For i = 1 To NUMSEATS
    With pastructSeat(i)
      .SeqNum = i
      Do
        j = Int(Rnd() * NUMSEATS + 1)
      Loop Until blnUsedSeats(j) = False
      blnUsedSeats(j) = True
      .AssignedNum = j
      .House = j Mod NUMHOUSES
      .Table = j Mod NUMTABLESPERHOUSE
      .SeatNum = j Mod NUMSEATSPERTABLE
    End With
  Next

  'search for duplicates
  For i = 1 To 934
    For j = i + 1 To NUMSEATS
      If pastructSeat(i).House = pastructSeat(j).House And _
        pastructSeat(i).Table = pastructSeat(j).Table And _
        pastructSeat(i).SeatNum = pastructSeat(j).SeatNum Then
        pastructSeat(j).DupeNum = i
        ListBox2.Items.Add(i.ToString & "  " & j.ToString)
      End If
    Next
  Next

  For i = 1 To NUMSEATS
    With pastructSeat(i)
      strSeat = .SeqNum.ToString & _
        " AssignedNum=" & .AssignedNum.ToString & _
        " House=" & .House.ToString & _
        " Table=" & .Table.ToString & " Seat=" & .SeatNum & _
        " Dupe=" & .DupeNum.ToString
    End With
    LstSeat.Items.Add(strSeat)
  Next
End Sub
```

delete line → `.AssignedNum = j`

delete lines → (the 'search for duplicates block)

delete line → `" AssignedNum=" & .AssignedNum.ToString & _`

delete line → `" Dupe=" & .DupeNum.ToString`

Figure 2-44: Code to be deleted in mnuToolsAssignSeats_Click

4 Use the Find operation to locate **Structure structSeat,** and delete the declaration for **DupeNum.** You must also delete:

```
Dupe=" & .DupeNum.ToString
```

along with the & _ from the line above it.

5 Use the Find operation to locate the **Button1_Click** procedure, and delete this procedure (only the header and End Sub remain at this point).

6 Switch to the Form Designer by clicking the **frmDining.vb[Design]*** tab, click **Button1** in the Form Designer, and press **Delete.**

7 Run the **MyDining** program again, click **Tools | Assign Seats** to see the seat assignments, and then click **File | Exit.**

Generating a Unique Seat Assignment List for Each Date (Task 06)

The key to generating a unique seat assignment list for a particular date is another feature of the Visual Basic .NET Rnd() function, which you learned about at length in Tutorial 1: when the argument of Rnd() is a negative number, that negative number is used as the seed for computing Rnd()'s return value. For any given initial seed, Rnd() returns the same series of random numbers, because the number returned by Rnd() is always used as the seed for the next Rnd() call. Hence, you can use the selected date as the negative seed for Rnd(), and all subsequent calls to Rnd() (with no argument) generate the same sequence of random numbers for any given date.

This operation also uses the DatePart() function, which returns a portion of a date value. In this case, the program uses the day of the year returned from the DateTimePicker control, with a minus sign in front of it to make it a negative number.

To generate a unique seat assignment list for each date:

1   Navigate to the **mnuToolsAssignSeats_Click** procedure; insert the following code immediately after the variable declarations and before the For loop:

```
Rnd(-DatePart(DateInterval.DayOfYear, DateTimePicker1. _
    Value))
```

Note that the DatePart function has two arguments: DateInterval, which is an enumeration (a listing of constants that stand for integers), and the date value. The result of this statement is that the random number generator is reseeded based on the particular date selected in the DateTimePicker control.

2   To see seat assignments for different dates, the contents of lstSeats should be cleared before a new set of seat assignments is made. Therefore, insert the following statement immediately after the statement you entered in the preceding step:

```
lstSeats.Items.Clear()
```

3   When a user selects a new date in the DateTimePicker control, the list of seat assignments previously generated (if any) is no longer accurate for the new date. So in this case also, the list box should be cleared. Insert the following line of code in the DateTimePicker1_TextChanged event procedure:

```
lstSeats.Items.Clear()
```

4   Run the **MyDining** program again. Click **Tools | Assign Seats** to see the seat assignments. Change the date in the DateTimePicker control, click **Tools | Assign Seats** again. Click **File | Exit**.

You started with 12 tasks, and half of them are now done. Sounds like it's time for a break. Some questions and exercises follow, which should be completed before moving on to Lesson C.

SUMMARY

■   A prototype application is converted to a production application by adding missing or incomplete elements and by applying organizational programming standards and style guidelines.

- A Task List can assist in managing programmer work effort.
- A MainMenu control provides not only menu items readily available to the user, but also click events immediately accessible to the programmer.
- The DateTimePicker control provides a robust date selection facility.
- Initializing Rnd() with a negative random number seed results in a consistent sequence of random numbers for any given seed.
- Visual Basic .NET offers multiple functions for manipulation and parsing of dates, including DatePart(), Year(), Month(), and Day().

QUESTIONS

1. A Task List entered into the IDE can consist of:
   a. tasks entered automatically by the compiler (Build errors)
   b. tasks entered by the programmer
   c. both a and b
   d. neither a nor b

2. When entering menu items, an underscored character is entered by:
   a. a preceding &
   b. a following &
   c. an underscore
   d. Shift+W, followed by the underscore

3. When entering menu item names, the prefix mnu is:
   a. required by the compiler
   b. required by the compiler for any name not supplied as a default name
   c. conventional
   d. none of the above

4. If the Task List has items in it, then _____.
   a. it must be displayed at all times
   b. it must be open at all times, but the window may be autohidden
   c. it may be open or closed, displayed, or autohidden
   d. it can only be displayed in alphabetical order

5. If Rnd(-3) returns a value x in a certain program, then Rnd(-3) _____.
   a. always returns x in the same program
   b. returns x in any program
   c. initiates the same random number sequence every time it is run
   d. is all of the above

6. A listing of named constants to which integer values are assigned is called an _____ and is declared with the _____ statement.

7. To reseed the random number generator based on the day of the month rather than the day of the year, the statement

   ```
   Rnd(-DatePart(DateInterval.DayOfYear, DateTimePicker1.Value))
   ```

   must be changed to _____. (*Hint*: Look up the DateInterval Enumeration in the Help Index.)

EXERCISES

1. In this exercise, you modify the Hashing application to add a second button whose Click event also triggers execution of Button1_Click. To do this:
   a. Drag a new Button control onto the form.
   b. Modify the Handles clause of the Button1_Click event header by adding Button2.Click to the list of events handled by that procedure.

2. In this exercise, you modify the Hashing application, so that only eight seats per table are assigned. (*Hint*: Of the many approaches to this problem, here is one fairly good one: start by examining all the elements of the Boolean array Used(). It should still have elements numbered from 0 to 935, because, as noted earlier, you still need to use the prime number 11 as a factor. If an index number Mod 11 is greater than 7, set the corresponding element in Used() to True, but do not generate a seat assignment. In this way, those potential AssignedNums that would result in an illegal seat number will not be assigned. Then pastructSeat can have an upper bound of 680, and, with compensating modifications to the loop control variables, the program should work just fine. Put your thinking cap on, and try to come up with a better solution!)

3. In this exercise, you create a new Windows Forms application named Colorful Menu, and make the form change colors at the click of a menu item.
   a. Start a new Windows Forms application. Name the solution and the project ColorfulMenu.
   b. Rename the form frmColors.vb, and the internal form name frmColors.
   c. Add a Label control to the form, named lblColor.
   d. Add a MainMenu control. Insert the following menu:

   File
         Exit
   Color
     Red
     Blue
     Green
     White
     Black

   e. Change the names of the menu items, following the scheme suggested in this tutorial—for example, mnuFile, mnuFileExit, mnuColor, mnuColorRed, and so on.
   f. In the Code window, program the mnuFileExit_Click procedure to end the program.
   g. Program the menu selection for each color to set the BackColor property of the form to the corresponding color. At the same time, display the name of the BackColor property value in lblColor. For example, the following is the code for mnuColorRed_Click():

   ```
   Private Sub mnuColorRed_Click(ByVal sender As System.
   Object, _
   ByVal e As System.EventArgs) Handles mnuColorRed.Click
   Me.BackColor = Color.Red
   lblColor.Text = Me.BackColor.ToString
   End Sub
   ```

Exercise 4 is a Discovery Exercise. Discovery Exercises, which may include topics that are not covered in this lesson, allow you to discover the solutions to problems on your own.

discovery ▶ 4   In this exercise, you build on Exercise 3 to use an enumeration of interface colors. To do this:

    a. Add a declaration of an enumeration at the module level of frmColors. You can copy this declaration from the Visual Studio .NET Help screen for the Enum statement, shown in Figure 2-45.

```
Public Enum InterfaceColors
   MistyRose    = &HE1E4FF&
   SlateGray    = &H908070&
   DodgerBlue   = &HFF901E&
   DeepSkyBlue  = &HFFBF00&
   SpringGreen  = &H7FFF00&
   ForestGreen  = &H228B22&
   Goldenrod    = &H20A5DA&
   Firebrick    = &H2222B2&
End Enum
```

Figure 2-45: Declaration of an enumeration

b. Add another root-level entry in the main menu, called Interface Colors. Add the color names in the enumeration as menu items under the Interface Colors root-level entry. Change the root-level entry Colors to Basic Colors.

c. In the Click event procedures for the interface color menu items, set the BackColor property of the form to the interface color using the enumeration, and set lblColor to display the name of the interface color. For example, in mnuInterfaceColorsMistyRose_Click, use these statements:

```
Me.BackColor = System.Drawing.ColorTranslator.FromWin32 _
(InterfaceColors.MistyRose)
lblColor.Text = "Misty Rose"
```

After completing this lesson, you will be able to:

- Convert house, table, and seat numbers to meaningful names
- Format the list box
- Add sequential file output to an application
- Add printed output to an application
- Add help instructions
- Add an About form to an application

Completion of the Dining Hall Seat Assigner Windows Forms Application

Converting House, Table, and Seat Numbers to Meaningful Names (Task 07)

Recall that you were working on the Dining Hall Seat Assigner application at the end of Lesson B. Looking at the Task List, you can see that Tasks 7 through 12 remain.

The first task here, converting a house number from 0 to 4 into the name of the house (North, South, East, West, or Harmony), can be approached in several different ways. The first and most obvious, but perhaps the least elegant, is a series of five If statements, as shown in Figure 2-46.

```
IntHouse = j Mod NUMHOUSES
If intHouse = 0 Then pastructSeat(i).House = "North"
If intHouse = 1 Then pastructSeat(i).House = "South"
If intHouse = 2 Then pastructSeat(i).House = "East"
If intHouse = 3 Then pastructSeat(i).House = "West"
If intHouse = 4 Then pastructSeat(i).House = "Harmony"
```

Figure 2-46: Example of brute force programming

Imagine the code using this method if you had 30 houses instead of five. This is why that approach is considered inelegant; some even refer to it as "brute force programming."

A much better method is to create a string array containing the string values of House names corresponding to the integers 0 through 4. (Note in the following code how an array can be initialized in Visual Basic .NET.) Then, pastructSeat.House is copied from the array at the index corresponding to j Mod NUMHOUSES:

```
Dim astrHouse() = {"North", "South", "East", "West", "Harmony"}
pastructSeat(i).House = astrHouse(j Mod NUMHOUSES)
```

Another alternative method is to use a Select Case structure, as shown in Figure 2-47.

```
Select Case j Mod NUMHOUSES
   Case 0: pastructSeat(i).House = "North"
   Case 1: pastructSeat(i).House = "South"
   Case 2: pastructSeat(i).House = "East"
   Case 3: pastructSeat(i).House = "West"
   Case 4: pastructSeat(i).House = "Harmony"
End Select
```

Figure 2-47: Select Case structure

This is more elegant than a series of If statements, but still somewhat lengthy, especially if there are 30 houses.

You can easily accomplish the conversion of table numbers (0 through 16) to table letters (A through Q) by adding the ASCII value of the letter A, that is, 65, to the table number, and then using the Chr() function to return the ASCII character corresponding to the sum.

```
pastructSeat(i).Table = Chr((j Mod NUMTABLESPERHOUSE)
+ 65)
```

Finally, to obtain the correct seat number (1 through 11), add 1 to the number previously computed (0 through 10).

To convert house numbers to house names, table numbers to table letters, and seat numbers 0-10 to seat numbers 1-11:

1 If you are not currently in Visual Studio .NET, open it and open the **MyDining** application that you are in the process of building.

2 In the Code Editor for frmDining, in the declaration Public Structure structSeat, change the declaration of **House** from an Integer to a **String**, and change the declaration of **Table** from an Integer to a **Char**. After all the changes to structSeat have been made, the completed declaration appears as in Figure 2-48.

```
Public Structure structSeat
   Public SeqNum As Integer
   Public House As String
   Public Table As Char
   Public SeatNum As Integer
 End Structure
```

Figure 2-48: Declaration of structSeat

3 In the mnuToolsAssignSeats_Click procedure, declare and initialize the array of house names by adding the following to the declaration of local variables at the top of the procedure:

```
Dim astrHouse() As String = _
{"North", "South", "East", "West", "Harmony"}
```

4 Rewrite the computation of pastructSeat components, as follows:

```
.SeqNum = i + 1
.House = astrHouse(j Mod NUMHOUSES)
.Table = Chr((j Mod NUMTABLESPERHOUSE) + 65)
.SeatNum = j Mod NUMSEATSPERTABLE + 1
```

At this point, the top half of the mnuToolsAssignSeats_Click procedure should look like Figure 2-49.

```
Private Sub mnuToolsAssignSeats_Click(ByVal sender As System.Object, _
   ByVal e As System.EventArgs) Handles mnuToolsAssignSeats.Click
      Dim blnUsedSeats(NUMSEATS) As Boolean
      Dim strSeat As String
      Dim i, j As Integer
      Dim astrHouse() As String = {"North", "South", "East", "West", "Harmony"}
      Rnd(-DatePart(DateInterval.DayOfYear, DateTimePicker1.Value))
      lstSeats.Items.Clear()
      For i = 0 To NUMSEATS - 1
        Do
          j = Int(Rnd() * NUMSEATS)
        Loop Until blnUsedSeats(j) = False
        blnUsedSeats(j) = True
        With pastructSeat(i)
          .SeqNum = i + 1
          .House = astrHouse(j Mod NUMHOUSES)
          .Table = Chr((j Mod NUMTABLESPERHOUSE) + 65)
          .SeatNum = j Mod NUMSEATSPERTABLE + 1
```

Figure 2-49: Top half of mnuToolsAssignSeats_Click procedure

5 Run the **MyDining** program again. Click **Tools | Assign Seats**. The program does not run correctly until the next task is completed, because the output to lstSeats expects a house number (not a string) and a table number (not a character).

Fixing the Formatting of the List Box (Task 08)

After completing Task 7, you realize that the output to the list box (lstSeats) needs modification to accommodate a house name (a string) rather than a house number, and a table letter (a char value) rather than a table number. But in addition, the display in the original Hashing application was unformatted—that is, the output was not neatly aligned in columns. In the Dining application, the listing of seat assignments appears in a nicely edited and aligned set of columns. In this task, you format the list box to display correctly.

To format list box items:

1 So that the list box contents appear in even columns, you must use a nonproportional font. Therefore, in the Form Designer, change the Font property of lstSeats to **Courier New**, if necessary. To do this, click **lstSeats** in Form Designer. In the Properties window, click the **ellipsis** in the settings box for the Font property. In the Font dialog box, select **Courier New** for the Font, **Regular** for Font style, and **10** for Size. Click **OK**.

2 strSeat was constructed in Task 07, but was not properly formatted. Modify the format of strSeat by formatting each of its seven concatenated string elements, as follows:

- Right-justify the sequence number in three positions. Insert the following code:

```
Microsoft.VisualBasic.Right(" " & CStr(.SeqNum), 3)
```

- Add the string " House=", including the leading space. The & is the string concatenation operator, so that precedes each of the remaining six portions of the string you are constructing. Add the following code:

```
& " House="
```

- Add the house name in a consistent eight-character wide field, left justified. To accomplish this, add the following code:

```
& Microsoft.VisualBasic.Left(.House & "        ", 8)
```

- Add the string " Table=", including the leading space. To accomplish this, add the following code:

```
& " Table="
```

- Add the table letter. To accomplish this, add the following code:

```
& .Table
```

- Add the string "   Seat=". Note the three leading spaces, and add the following code:

```
& "   Seat="
```

- Add the seat number, converted to a string. To accomplish this, add the following code:

```
& CStr(.SeatNum)
```

NOTE: In Figure 2-50, the Left and the Right functions are used to obtain a consistent portion of a string. Left(str, 5) returns the left five characters of str, but the result is shorter than five characters if str is shorter than five characters. Left(str & "   ", 5) returns five characters, regardless of the length of str. Also note that the Left and the Right function names can refer to the properties of an object. To clear up the possible confusion, the function names are fully qualified by the namespace in which they are declared, namely Microsoft.VisualBasic.

3 Insert the resulting code, replacing the original formatting instruction. After these changes, the lower half of mnuToolsAssignSeats_Click appears as in Figure 2-50.

```
        strSeat = Microsoft.VisualBasic.Right(" " & CStr(.SeqNum), 3) & _
            " House=" & Microsoft.VisualBasic.Left(.House & "        ", 8) & _
            " Table=" & .Table & "   Seat=" & CStr(.SeatNum)
    End With
    lstSeats.Items.Add(strSeat)
  Next
End Sub
```

Figure 2-50: Lower half of the mnuToolsAssignSeats_Click procedure

4 Run the **MyDining** program again. Click **Tools | Assign Seats** to see the seat assignments and see how nicely the output is displayed. Click **File | Exit.**

Adding Sequential File Output (Task 09)

Assume that the International Village at the Friendsville International Games will have a computer workstation and printer in each house and in each dining hall. The Dining Hall Seat Assigner program might be executed on one central machine, generating the seat assignments for all of the athletes, and outputting the list of seat assignments to a text file. The text file subsequently may be copied to a floppy disk and delivered (or electronically transmitted) to each house and dining hall in the village. Therefore, the Dining Hall Seat Assigner program must be able to send the list of seat assignments (that is, the contents of lstSeats) to an output sequential file.

This task has three parts:

■ Construct a fixed-length string representing the date for seat assignments. This string is offered to the user as the filename for saving the seat assignments.

■ Provide a standard Save File As dialog box, for the user to select the file location and either accept or modify the proffered filename.

■ Open the output file, write the contents of lstSeats to that file, and close the file.

tip

You can choose **mnuFileSaveSeats** from the Class Name combo box in the Code Editor, and then choose the Click event from the Method Name combo box.

To add sequential file output:

1 Double-click **mnuFileSaveSeats_Click** in the Form Designer to open the mnuFileSaveSeats_Click procedure.

2 The first part of this task is to construct a filename that includes the date for which seat assignments are being saved, something like "SeatsForYYYYMMDD." The basic elements are available in the Year(), Month(), and Day() functions, which return the appropriate integer value from any date, in this case from the Value property of DateTimePicker1. (The call to the Day() function needs to be fully qualified with the Microsoft.VisualBasic namespace.) The value returned from each of these functions is an integer, but you want to concatenate them into a string, so you should declare string variables to hold the return values strYear, strMonth, and strDay. To get a fixed-length date string, a 0 must be prefixed on any single digit month or day. For example, December is represented as "12" and March as "03." Finally, add SeatsFor as a prefix, and .txt as a suffix.

Here is the completed code to construct the filename. Enter the code shown in Figure 2-51 at the beginning of the mnuFileSaveSeats_Click procedure.

```
Dim strDate As String 'to be constructed in the format yyyymmdd
Dim strYear, strMonth, strDay As String 'components of strDate
Dim strFileName As String 'name of textfile, including strDate
strYear = Year(DateTimePicker1.Value)
strMonth = Month(DateTimePicker1.Value)
If Len(strMonth) = 1 Then strMonth = "0" & strMonth
strDay = Microsoft.VisualBasic.Day(DateTimePicker1.Value)
If Len(strDay) = 1 Then strDay = "0" & strDay
strDate = strYear & strMonth & strDay
strFileName = "SeatsFor" & strDate & ".txt"
```

Figure 2-51: mnuFileSaveSeats_Click ( ) procedure

3 In the Form Designer, drop a **SaveFileDialog** control onto the form. SaveFileDialog1 appears in the tray underneath the form, along with the MainMenu control.

4 Back in the mnuFileSaveSeats_Click procedure, you add code (right after the code you entered in Step 2) to set the appropriate properties of SaveFileDialog1, and then you display the dialog box. Assign the filename you have constructed to the dialog's Filename property, of course. In this exercise, you set the Filter and FilterIndex properties. To do this, insert the code shown in Figure 2-52.

NOTE: Then, you may choose to set other properties, as you see fit. You could also assign values to the CheckFileExists, CheckPathExists, DefaultExt, or InitialDirectory properties. (Look up each of these in the Help Index to see what they mean and how they are used.)

```
SaveFileDialog1.FileName = strFileName
SaveFileDialog1.Filter = _
  "txt files (*.txt)|*.txt|All files (*.*)|*.*"
SaveFileDialog1.FilterIndex = 1
SaveFileDialog1.ShowDialog()
```

Figure 2-52: Assigning properties and displaying SaveFileDialog1

5 The last part of this task is to write the contents of lstSeats to the selected file. The FileOpen function has three arguments: a filenumber, which is subsequently used to refer to this file as long as it remains open; the name of the file; and the OpenMode enumeration, which specifies whether the file is being opened for input, output, append, or random access. Because you are writing records to the file, you open the file in Output mode. The WriteLine function, which sends output to a sequential file, has two arguments: the filenumber and the text to be written. The FileClose function has only the filenumber as its argument. The lines of code shown in Figure 2-53 complete the mnuFileSaveSeats procedure. Add these lines after the code you inserted in Step 4.

```
FileOpen(1, SaveFileDialog1.FileName, OpenMode.Output)
Dim i As Integer
For i = 0 To lstSeats.Items.Count - 1
  WriteLine(1, lstSeats.Items(i))
Next
FileClose(1)
```

Figure 2-53: Writing records to the file

6 Run the **MyDining** program. Click **Tools | Assign Seats** to see the seat assignments. Save Seats in File is still disabled. When seats have been assigned, this menu item should be enabled (along with the Print Seats menu item). And when a new date is selected (so that lstSeats is cleared), these two menu items should again be disabled. To accomplish this, add these two statements at the end of mnuToolsAssignSeats_Click:

```
mnuFileSaveSeats.Enabled = True
mnuFilePrintSeats.Enabled = True
```

> And add these two statements to DateTimePicker1_TextChanged:
>
> ```
> mnuFileSaveSeats.Enabled = False
> mnuFilePrintSeats.Enabled = False
> ```
>
> **7** Now run the **MyDining** program. Click **Tools | Assign Seats**. Click **File | Save Seats in File**. Pick a folder to save the text file, and click **OK**. Use Notepad to open the text file, and verify that the operation worked.

Adding Printed Output (Task 10)

This task gives you a chance to work with controls and functionality related to printing. The Printer object used in Visual Basic 6.0 to format and send output to a printer has been replaced by the PrintDocument component.

To specify what to print on each page, you use the graphics methods of the PrintDocument_PrintPage event, especially the DrawString method for printing text. You are responsible for keeping track of line numbers (so that the program knows when a page is full) and for telling the program whether any additional pages remain to be printed. In the present application, this means that the program must also keep track of the current position within lstSeats, using a variable that points to the next item to be printed. Printing can involve many more options and refinements than the basic approach shown here, but this is sufficient to get you started.

The Printers collection in Visual Basic 6.0 has been replaced by the PrintDialog control, which offers a standard Windows Print dialog box. The new PageSetupDialog control provides a standard Windows Page Setup dialog box. Finally, print preview is newly available in Visual Basic .NET with the PrintPreviewDialog control.

> To add printed output:
>
> **1** In Form Designer, drag the **PrintDocument, PageSetupDialog, PrintDialog,** and **PrintPreviewDialog** controls from the Toolbox and drop them onto the form (they are also placed in the tray underneath the form). (Do not use the PrintPreviewControl for this exercise.) Visual Basic .NET assigns default names of PrintDocument1, PageSetupDialog1, PrintDialog1, and PrintPreviewDialog1 to these controls. The default names are acceptable, because only one instance of each control appears on the form, and confusion is not likely to occur by allowing the default names to stand. At this point, all of the controls needed for the Dining application have been added to the form and to the tray underneath the form. The completed graphical form and controls should appear as shown in Figure 2-54.

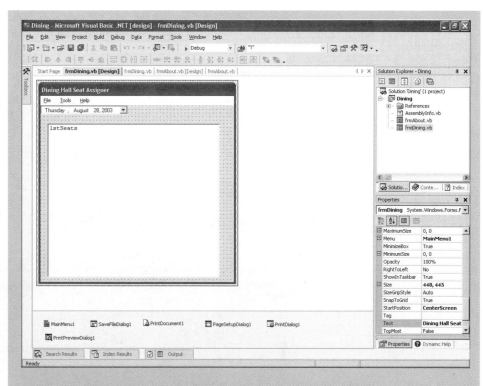

Figure 2-54: Completed frmDining, with controls in the tray underneath

2   In the Properties list, set the Document property of the PageSetupDialog, PrintDialog, and PrintPreviewDialog controls to **PrintDocument1**.

3   In the Code Editor, add a module-level integer variable to point to the next item in lstSeats. Although module-level variables can actually be added anywhere outside a function or procedure, by convention they are always added at the top of a module or class. So in this case, insert the following declaration immediately after the module-level variable you declared previously (the prefix "mint" indicates a module-level integer variable):

```
Public pastructSeat(NUMSEATS) As structSeat
Public mintSeatCtr As Integer
```

4   The main printing logic occurs in the PrintDocument1_PrintPage() procedure. The parameter e As System.Drawing.Printing.PrintPageEventArgs identifies what to print on each line and how to print it. Each time this procedure is invoked, it prints one page. Insert the procedure shown in Figure 2-55.

NOTE: These are the complete page-printing procedures, which you can adapt as necessary for other printing requirements in other applications. You may want to note this page for future reference.

```
Private Sub PrintDocument1_PrintPage(ByVal sender As System.Object, _
    ByVal e As System.Drawing.Printing.PrintPageEventArgs) _
    Handles PrintDocument1.PrintPage
  Dim intLineCtr As Integer
  For intLineCtr = 0 To 54
    e.Graphics.DrawString(lstSeats.Items.Item(mintSeatCtr), _
      New Font("Courier New", 12, FontStyle.Bold), _
      Brushes.Black, 150, 50 + intLineCtr * 17)
    mintSeatCtr += 1
    If mintSeatCtr = NUMSEATS Then Exit For
  Next intLineCtr
  If mintSeatCtr < NUMSEATS Then
    e.HasMorePages = True
  Else
    e.HasMorePages = False
  End If
End Sub
```

Figure 2-55: PrintDocument1_PrintPage( ) procedure

5 To call the PrintPage event procedure, the user clicks the Print icon in PrintPreview. To call PrintPreview, insert the following code into mnuFilePrintSeats_Click. The first line ensures that each new print job starts with the first seat assignment in lstSeats:

```
mintSeatCtr = 0
PrintPreviewDialog1.ShowDialog()
```

6 To activate the PageSetupDialog control, insert the following code into mnuFilePageSetup_Click:

```
PageSetupDialog1.ShowDialog()
```

7 To activate the PrintDialog control (for setting up printers), insert the following code into mnuFilePrinterSetup_Click:

```
PrintDialog1.ShowDialog()
```

8 Run the **MyDining** program. Click **Tools | Assign Seats**. Click **File | Page Setup**. Note the options that you can alter. Click **Cancel** in the Page Setup dialog box. Click **File | Printer Setup**. Note the options that you can alter. Click **Cancel** in the Print dialog box. Click **File | Print Seats**. Maximize the Print Preview dialog box. Scroll through the seating assignments. Click **Print** if you want to waste 17 sheets of paper; otherwise, click **Cancel**. Click **File | Exit** to return to the IDE.

Adding Instructions (Task 11)

After the Dining Hall Seat Assigner application is complete, the actual user of the application may be unfamiliar with the application and how it works. As is the case with most commercial applications, you need to provide a set of instructions to guide the user in using the software correctly.

To add instructions for the use of the application:

1 In Form Designer, double-click **mnuHelpInstructions** to open the Code Editor for this menu item, or open it using the Class Name and Method Name combo boxes. The basic technique here is to create a local string variable, concatenate the text of each line of Help instructions, and add a carriage return or linefeed sequence (vbCrLf) following each line of text. Then, use the string in a MessageBox statement. Figure 2-56 provides a suggested set of Help instructions and the MessageBox statement. Insert this code into mnuHelpInstructions_Click().

```
Dim s As String
s = "Pick the date for which a seat assignment list is desired. "
s &= "Then select Tools | Assign Seats." & vbCrLf
s &= vbCrLf & "File | Save Seats to a File, and File | Print " _
    & "Seats are only available"
s &= vbCrLf & "when a list of seats appears on the screen." _
    & vbCrLf
s &= vbCrLf & "File | Page Setup and File | Printer Setup allow " _
    & "you to specify page and printer options."
s &= vbCrLf & vbCrLf & "Select File | Exit to close the " _
    & "application." & vbCrLf
s &= vbCrLf & "Note that the seat assignment list for any " _
    & "given date is fixed."
s &= vbCrLf & "A different list is produced for each date, but " _
    & "the same list will"
s &= vbCrLf & "be produced every time for the same date."
MessageBox.Show(s, "Dining Hall Seat Assigner - Instructions")
```

Figure 2-56: Help instructions

2 Run the **MyDining** program to ensure that the Help system works. Click **Help | Instructions**. The output should appear as in Figure 2-57.

Figure 2-57: Instructions for the MyDining application

3 Click **File | Exit** to return to the IDE.

Adding an About Form (Task 12)

In most business applications, an about form serves two purposes. First, it identifies authorship and ownership of the application. Credit is often given to the programmers who created it, and a copyright notice identifies the person or organization that owns the software. Second, it assists in software version control, since it usually identifies the release number and revision number of the program. You will now add an about form to the MyDining application. The completed form should appear as in Figure 2-58.

Figure 2-58: About form for the MyDining application

To add an About form:

1 In the MyDining project, click **File | Add New Item | Windows Form**.

2 Set the following properties for the form:

- Set **Name** to **frmAbout**.
- Set **BackColor** to **Blue**.
- Set **ControlBox** to **False**.
- Set **StartPosition** to **CenterScreen**.
- Set **Text** to **About Dining Hall Seat Assigner**.

3 Add a Label control, size and position Label1 as shown in Figure 2-58, and set the following properties:

- Set **BorderStyle** to **Fixed 3D**.
- Set **Font** to **Microsoft Sans Serif, 10 pt., Bold**.
- Set **Text** to **Dining Hall Seat Assigner 1.0**.

4 Add a Label control, size and position Label2 as shown in Figure 2-58, and set the **Text** property to **Copyright 2003 Friendsville Organizing Committee**.

5 Add a Button control to the form as shown in Figure 2-58. Set its **Name** property to **btnOk** and its **Text** property to **Ok**.

6 Add a PictureBox control to the form, as shown in Figure 2-58. Set its **Image** property to **Misc33.ico**, and its **SizeMode** property to **StretchImage**.

NOTE: Note that the image in the PictureBox control is one of the icons shipped with Visual Studio .NET. You can find the file Misc33.ico in the Microsoft Visual Studio .NET\Common7\Graphics\Icons\Misc\ folder, or on the Web at the Microsoft site.

7 The only code needed on the About form is in btnOk_Click(), where the form is closed. Into that procedure, type the statement:

```
Me.Dispose ()
```

8 Click frmDining.vb, and insert the following code into mnuHelpAbout_Click:

```
Dim frm As New frmAbout()
frm.ShowDialog()
```

NOTE: In Visual Basic 6.0, you could have written frmAbout.Show, but that causes this syntax error in Visual Basic .NET: Reference to a non-shared member requires an object reference. This makes sense, if you think about the definition of a form as a class whose internals are encapsulated. You cannot directly access the methods of the class. Rather, you need to instantiate an object based on the class (the Dim statement), and then invoke the ShowDialog() method of that object.

9 Run the program again, and try all of its functions. Your MyDining application is finished, as suggested by Figure 2-59. (Recall that, as you complete a task in the Task List, you can either delete it, or click its check box to indicate that it is complete, causing a line to be drawn through it.)

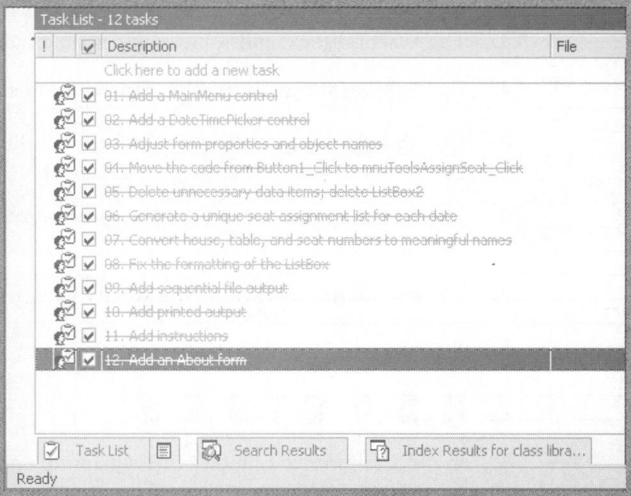

Figure 2-59: Completed Task List

You now have completed Tutorial 2. You can take a break, or continue with the end of the chapter exercises.

SUMMARY

- The SaveFileDialog control provides a standard Windows Save File dialog box for soliciting user options concerning a file to be saved.
- FileOpen(), WriteLine(), and FileClose() functions support sequential file output operations.
- Enumerations and Select Case structures provide interesting approaches to converting numbers into strings.

■ Left(), Right(), and Day() functions (and many others) must be qualified with the Microsoft.VisualBasic namespace.

■ To create neatly aligned columnar output, use fixed-length fields and a nonproportional font.

■ An application may contain multiple forms. Interform references must be object references.

■ Several controls support printed output:

   ■ The PrintDocument component identifies what is to be printed on each page of output.

   ■ The PrintPreviewDialog control prints a screen version of a PrintDocument.

   ■ The PageSetupDialog control provides a standard Windows Page Setup dialog box, for user selection of various page options.

   ■ The PrintDialog control provides a standard Windows Printer Setup dialog box so the user can select a printer.

QUESTIONS

1. The function that opens a file is _____.

2. Within the function that opens a file, the value of the Mode Enumeration must be one of the following: _____, Binary, _____, _____, or Random.

3. The function that sends output to a sequential file is _____.

4. User options for an output file can be obtained using the _____ control.

5. User options for the appearance of printed output can be obtained using the _____ control.

6. The user can select a printer to receive printed output by using the _____ control.

7. The control through which you specify what is printed is the _____ control.

EXERCISES

1. In this exercise, you modify the MyDining application to accommodate a sixth house named "Guest House." You must ensure that no duplicate seat assignments are made, and that no assignments are made to nonexistent houses. The trick here is that six is not a prime number. Therefore, you must calculate NUMSEATS on the basis of seven houses. But then, when constructing strSeat, do not use any seat assigned to house #7. (The rest of the code from MyDining is unchanged.)

2. In this exercise, you write a Windows Forms application to print mailing labels for athletes in the International Village. Follow these steps:

   a. The form must contain a series of text boxes that solicit name and address information from the user.

   b. A menu provides these selections: E_xit, _Verify User Input, and _Print Labels. The Print Labels menu selection should be disabled until user input has been successfully verified.

   c. The Verify User Input menu selection should enable the Print Labels menu selection if all mandatory text boxes are not empty, or provide an error message if mandatory data is missing.

   d. After it has been enabled, the Print Labels menu selection should print five copies of the mailing address on one page, separated by three blank lines.

   e. Include a PrintPreviewDialog control, so that the mailing labels can be printed first to the screen and then, at user discretion, to paper.

3. In this exercise, you write a Windows Forms application to create a randomly selected breakfast menu for the International Village Dining Halls. The menu should be different for each of the five houses in the International Village, but it should be the same every morning for a given house. Breakfast consists of the following:

   - Juice: orange, pineapple, passion fruit, or apple (select randomly)
   - Cereal and milk
   - Main course: pancakes, waffles, scrambled eggs, or cereal (select randomly)
   - Meat supplement: ham, bacon, or sausage (select randomly)
   - Toast or croissant (select randomly)
   - Coffee/tea

   Use a single list box for all five menus. In the list box, display the house name (North, South, East, West, Harmony) followed by the menu.

4. In this exercise, you write a Console application to randomly select 200 integers from 1 to 200. Then display to the screen the integers from 1 to 200, indicating the number of times each was selected; after a user prompt to continue, display to the screen the integers that were selected more than once.

Exercises 5, 6, and 7 are Discovery Exercises. Discovery Exercises, which may include topics not covered in this lesson, allow you to discover the solution to problems on your own.

discovery ▶ 5. In this exercise, you write a Windows Forms application that accepts as input a text file containing seat assignments (as created by the Dining application), and then displays these seating assignments in a list box.

discovery ▶ 6. In this exercise, you write a Console application that accepts as input a text file containing seat assignments (as created by the Dining application), and then prints these seating assignments to the screen. The screen display should print 23 lines at a time, display "Press the Enter key to continue," and then continue printing seat assignments after the user presses Enter.

discovery ▶ 7. In this exercise, you write a Web Forms application that duplicates the functionality of MyDining. This application should produce screen output only (printed and sequential file output are not required).

K E Y   T E R M S

- accessibility
- Add method
- Append mode
- AutoScaleBaseSize property
- base class
- CheckFileExists property
- CheckPathExists property
- Chr() function
- class
- class library
- Clear method
- ClientSize property
- Common Language Runtime (CLR)
- component
- constant declaration (Const)
- container

- ControlBox property
- DatePart() function
- DateInterval enumeration
- DateTimePicker control
- Day() function
- DefaultExt property
- derived class
- Dispose method
- Enabled property
- encapsulation
- enumeration
- event
- field
- FileClose function
- Filename property
- FileOpen function
- Filter property
- FilterIndex property
- handle an event
- implementation
- Imports
- information hiding
- inheritance, Inherits
- InitialDirectory property
- InitializeComponent
- Input mode
- Input function
- InputString function
- instance, instantiation
- interface
- Items property
- Left() function
- lifetime
- LineInput function
- ListBox control
- Location property
- Lock Controls command
- MainMenu control
- member
- member type
- MessageBox class
- method
- Microsoft.VisualBasic namespace
- Month() function
- MyBase
- namespace
- .NET Framework
- New
- object
- object-oriented programming (OOP)
- OpenMode enumeration
- Output mode
- Overloads

- Overrides
- PageSetupDialog control
- Point object
- polymorphism
- PrintDialog control
- PrintDocument component
- PrintPreviewDialog control
- property
- qualified name
- Raise an event
- #Region directive
- ResumeLayout() method
- Right() function
- SaveFileDialog control
- scope
- Shared
- ShowDialog method
- Startup object
- Structure
- SuspendLayout method
- System namespace
- TextChanged event
- ToString method
- Year() function

Visual Basic .NET Fundamentals

Software Security at the Friendsville International Games

case ▶ The Friendsville Games Development Team is in agreement that security is a significant issue and that FGDT-developed software must incorporate appropriate security controls. Accordingly, the team has determined that two programs are needed to support software security for Windows applications. One program, called Logon, is invoked during startup by all Windows applications developed by the FGDT. Logon asks the user to provide a logon name and password before the user is permitted to use an application. The other program, called LogonManager, manages the user logons by allowing new users to request permission to log on, existing users to edit user information, and the system supervisor to control this process. Both programs use a random-access data file called Users that contains information concerning users.

The creation of the complete version of these two applications occupies Tutorials 3 and 4 together. In Tutorial 3, you create the overall structure for the LogonManager program as well as some of its functionality. The fundamental design concept involves a Multiple Document Interface (MDI) form and a series of new Windows Forms controls. In Tutorial 4, you complete the LogonManager application and also create the Logon application.

Previewing the LogonManager Application

The LogonManager project is a Multiple Document Interface (MDI) application. A **Multiple Document Interface (MDI) application** consists of an MDI form (or **parent** form) that serves as a container for one or more **child** forms. The child forms always exist within the boundaries of the MDI form. You are probably familiar with many such programs, such as Microsoft Excel. When Excel is running, you can have many worksheets simultaneously open, each in its own window. Each worksheet can fill the entire client area within Excel, or several worksheets can occupy different portions of the available screen space. Resizing, minimizing, maximizing, or closing the Excel container (that is, the parent) has the same effect on all of the open worksheets (that is, the children).

To view the LogonManager application as a new user, follow these steps:

1 Run **LogonManager.exe**, available in the VB.NET\Student\Tut03 folder. The LogonManager main screen (the MDI form) appears. Click **File** on the menu bar, and note that Initialize, Backup, and Restore are disabled. See Figure 3-1.

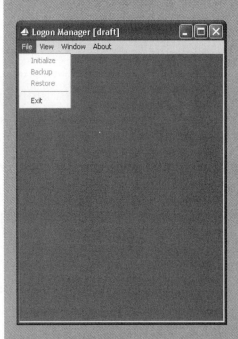

Figure 3-1: LogonManager File menu

2 Click **View | New User**. The New User form appears, and its WindowState property is maximized, that is, it fills all of the parent MDI form.

3 On the Name & Phone tab, type **Geraldine** in the First Name text box, **Springer** in the Last Name text box, enter a number in both the Work Phone and Home Phone text boxes, and designate Geraldine as a **Volunteer** using the Role list arrow. (The Application Date is the system date, and is filled in automatically by the program.) Your form should look similar to Figure 3-2.

Figure 3-2: New User child form, maximized inside the MDI container: Name & Phone tab

4   Click the **Logon Info** tab. Type **gspringer@freestuff.net** in the e-mail address text box, and type **Chicago** in the password and confirm password text boxes. As shown in Figure 3-3, the text that you type in the password and confirm password text boxes appears as asterisks. The program computes the password valid until date, 90 days from the application date.

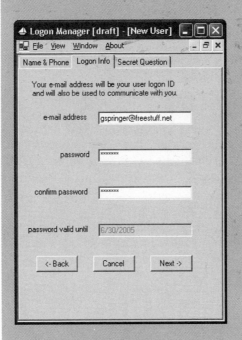

Figure 3-3: New User child form with Logon Info tab showing

5   Click the **Next** button to move to the Secret Question tab, check the **I want to have a secret question** check box, choose **How many cousins do you have?** as your secret question, and type **14** in the Answer text box. See Figure 3-4.

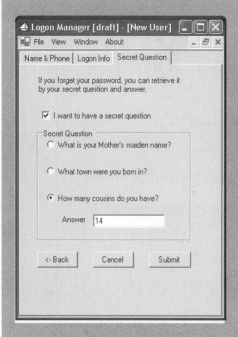

Figure 3-4: New User child form with Secret Question tab showing

6   Click the **Submit** button. This adds a new user request to the list of users, but the user does not have access to anything until the supervisor accepts the new user.

7   Press **Alt+F** to select the File menu, and then press **x** to exit the application.

You now view the LogonManager as the system supervisor.

To view the LogonManager application as supervisor:

1   Run **LogonManager.exe** again.

2   Click **View | Supervisor**. Note that the submenu items are disabled, except for Logon. The supervisor must log on to enable the initially disabled menu items here and in the File menu. Click **Logon** in the Supervisor submenu. A message box appears, telling you that the Logon program is under construction, and that this draft of the LogonManager application assumes a successful supervisor logon; it then enables all supervisor functions. Click **OK**. Click **View | Supervisor**, to verify that all submenu items under Supervisor are enabled. Click **File**, to verify that all File menu items are enabled.

3   Although all menu selections are now enabled, a number of menu selections activate functions you don't develop until Tutorial 4. Therefore, the message *under construction* appears when you select any of those functions in the draft LogonManager application. Click each of the six menu selections that are under construction: in the File menu, click **Backup** and **Restore**; in the View menu, click **Existing User**; and in the Supervisor submenu under the View menu, click **Edit User Info**, **View All Users**, **Reset Expiration Dates**.

4   Click **File | Initialize**. This menu item enables the supervisor to reinitialize the Users file if the file becomes corrupted and no backup is available. This selection

overwrites all previous data in the file. After initialization, the only user is the supervisor, with an initial e-mail address of 1 and the password SUPERVISOR. The program asks whether you absolutely want to initialize the Users file. Click **No** to cancel the file initialization process.

NOTE: If you do initialize the Users file, the original Users file is overwritten. The original file contained user logons for Hilda Reiner, Rick Sanchez, and Althea Brown, in addition to the system supervisor. Restore the original file as follows: In Windows Explorer, navigate to the VB.NET\Student\Tut03 folder. Delete the Users file that you just created. Then rename the Copy of Users file, Users. Then make a new Copy of Users file by clicking Edit | Copy, then Edit | Paste. (You make the backup copy of Users, so that you can restore the original file later in case anything happens to the Users file during development.)

NOTE: In addition to restricting the Initialize, Backup, and Restore functions to the supervisor, a real commercial application would also encrypt the Users file (a topic beyond our scope here).

5   Click **View | Supervisor | Accept New Users**. The form that appears is similar to the New User form you filled out for Geraldine Springer, except that it now has Accept and Reject buttons under the Name & Phone tab, and the Submit button under the Secret Question tab is no longer visible. Click the **Accept** button. The program then reminds the supervisor to send an e-mail message to the new user, stating that the user application has been accepted. Click **OK**.

6   Click **About** on the menu bar to display the About Logon Manager form. Note that this child form occupies only a portion of the space within the parent form. Close the **About** form. Click **View | New User**. Click **About** again; this time the About form is maximized. Click **Window** on the menu bar, and note that all open child forms are listed, with a check mark in front of the active window, the About form. Under the Window menu, click **Cascade**. The child forms are now displayed in overlapping windows, as shown in Figure 3-5. You can open as many additional child forms as you want. Click **File | Exit** to terminate the application.

Figure 3-5: Cascading child forms

After completing this lesson, you will be able to:

- Use primitive data types, naming conventions, and style rules
- Understand and apply the control structures supported in Visual Basic .NET
- Explain the objects and techniques involved in the creation of a Multiple Document Interface (MDI) application
- Understand the purpose and uses of these new Windows Forms controls: TabControl, ComboBox, CheckBox, GroupBox, and RadioButton

Programming Fundamentals and New GUI Objects

Lesson A completes the presentation of Visual Basic .NET programming fundamentals. You have probably been exposed to much of this material in your first Visual Basic course, but some of these ideas are likely to be new. In addition, you should find it useful to see this information consolidated and summarized in one place. Lesson A also discusses the practical techniques needed to create the LogonManager application—MDI forms, and several new Windows Forms controls.

Using Primitive Data Types, Naming Conventions, and Style Rules

This section provides a consolidated reference covering all of the Visual Basic .NET data types, as well as a consistent set of naming conventions and style rules. You will not use all of this information in any single application; this applies to the LogonManager application in this tutorial, as well. However, you have probably encountered most of this information before on a piecemeal basis, introduced in various chapters throughout any introductory programming text on Visual Basic .NET.

Data Types

A computer programming language uses data as one of its fundamental building blocks. Data can be stored in files or databases, and data can occur within a computer program in one of three forms: a literal, a constant, or a variable. Further, a programming language is designed to support specific types of data. Each of these may be a base type included in the computer hardware, or an extension implemented within the language through software. For example, the computer hardware can store an integer in two, four, or eight bytes; it can also store a single character in one byte. A programming language may offer data types that correspond to each of these. But the language also offers data types that are extensions of the data types available in the underlying computer, and these additional data types are implemented through software extensions. For example, a String or a Date-Time data type fits this category.

A **literal** has the face value of each occurrence: 1, 345.678, and SALLY are all literals. The data type for each of these literals is an Integer (1), a floating-point number (345.678) called a Single or a Double in Visual Basic, and a String (SALLY). A **constant** is assigned a literal value that does not change, for example, DAYSINWEEK could be declared as a constant with the literal value 7. The data type of a literal is determined by its value. In most programming languages, the data type of a constant is also inferred from its assigned value, although some languages allow the programmer to specify the data type of a constant. A **variable** is a symbolic reference to an address (or block of addresses) in memory, and the values stored in that memory block can change during program execution. In most programming languages, the data type of a variable is declared by the programmer along with the name of the variable, although in some languages, such as FORTRAN, variable declarations are not required. Because the BASIC language (Visual Basic's predecessor) was derived from FORTRAN, variable declarations in BASIC were optional as well. In Visual Basic, the programmer can require variable declarations through the Option Explicit statement, and indeed you should always do so.

Programming languages are sometimes classified as being strongly typed, weakly typed, or somewhere in between. In a strongly typed language, the programmer must explicitly declare the data type of every variable (and perhaps every constant). In addition, data of one type must be explicitly converted to another type before it can be used as the converted type. For example, a strongly typed language, such as Pascal, does not permit a floating-point variable to be assigned to an integer variable, unless the programmer explicitly calls the function that converts a floating-point variable to an integer. In a weakly typed language, such as C, all kinds of implicit type conversions take place without programmer intervention. For example, in C you can add an integer (such as 1) to a Char value (such as A) and treat the result as either a Char (B) or an Integer (66, the ASCII value that represents B). In previous releases, Visual Basic was a relatively weakly typed language along the sliding scale from weak to strong, but Visual Basic .NET is skewed in the opposite direction. Although you can still assign a Single data type to an integer without an explicit type conversion, many other type conversions are not automatic, especially those involving object variables and references. This helps explain why experienced Visual Basic 6.0 programmers encounter so many syntax errors when they first start programming in Visual Basic .NET.

For reasons of cross-language compatibility, several data types were added or changed in Visual Basic .NET. The prefixes in Figure 3-6 are used by many Visual Basic .NET programmers when declaring variables. A prefix is not required by the programming language; it is merely a convention for making programs easier to read and maintain.[1]

---

[1] This naming convention is called "Hungarian notation," named in reference to its inventor, Dr. Charles Simonyi, who is from Hungary, and who was the chief architect for Microsoft in the early days of DOS.

Data type	Prefix	Storage	Value range [default]
Boolean	bln	2 bytes	True or [False]
Byte	byt	1 byte	[0] to 255 (unsigned)
Char	c	2 bytes	[0] to 65535 (unsigned)
Date	dte	8 bytes	[0:00:00 on January 1, 0001] through 11:59:59 p.m. on December 31, 9999
Decimal	dec	16 bytes	[0] +/- 28 significant digits, with or without a decimal point (replaces the Currency data type)
Double	dbl	8 bytes	Double precision floating point; [0] +/- 18 significant digits E +/- 308
Integer	int	4 bytes	[0] +/- 9 digits
Long	lng	8 bytes	[0] +/- 18 digits
Object	obj	4 bytes	Any type
Short	sht	2 bytes	[0] -32768 to +32767
Single	sng	4 bytes	Single precision floating point; [0] +/- 6 significant digits E +/- 38
String	str	System dependent	[Nothing] 0 to approx. 2 billion characters

Figure 3-6: Visual Basic .NET variables and name prefixes

Naming Conventions

Naming conventions facilitate program readability, understandability, and maintainability. Many independent programmers and most organizations follow some set of naming conventions and style rules. More important than any individual rule is the consistent application of a set of agreed upon rules. The FGDT naming conventions offered here and demonstrated throughout this text are used by many programmers and are, in any case, typical of the types of rules adopted by computer programming shops.

Using Meaningful Names

All programmer-supplied names must be meaningful. This includes names for variables, constants, controls, forms, procedures, properties, methods, functions, modules, classes, structures, components, and other objects. Following these naming conventions goes a long way toward making your programs understandable. Naming conventions are most important on large projects and on team-programming projects.

Naming Variables

Variable names are mixed case and consist of a prefix and a meaningful name. The prefix contains the following:

- The first letter indicates scope: *p* is a public variable, *m* is a module-level variable, *st* is a static local variable, and no scope prefix indicates a dynamic local variable. For parameters, *v* indicates ByVal, and *r* indicates ByRef. Note that the inherent or the assigned access level (Public, Protected, Friend, Protected Friend, or Private) also affects scope.

- The letter "a" indicates an array.
- Data type is indicated by a prefix from the table of data types shown in Figure 3-6. For user-defined data types (structures), the abbreviation "struct" is used.

A meaningful name is a noun or noun phrase, with each word having an initial capital letter. The following are variable declarations that conform with these conventions:

- *Dim mdecInterestRate As Decimal*—A module-level decimal
- *Public pastructUser*—A public array of structures
- *Static stintLineCtr*—A static integer
- *Dim strMessage*—A dynamic local string
- *[in a parameter list] rbln*—A Boolean passed ByRef

Naming Constants

The names of constants are in all uppercase letters. Consider the following declarations:

- `Const DAYSINWEEK = 7`
- `Const SALESTAXRATE = 0.05`

Naming Functions

Function and method names start with a verb as shown in the following examples. The argument or parameter list appears in parentheses after the name, or blank parentheses appear if no arguments or parameters are given:

- Private Function GetNextRecord()
- Public Sub FindLastName()
- Protected Sub EnableDisableTextboxes(vbln As Boolean)

Naming Classes

Class and property names begin with a noun. Consider the following examples:

- Public Class Student
- Public Class AcademicProgram

Naming Controls

Controls have a prefix indicating the control's class. Controls that are not referenced in code may retain their default names, assigned by the software, such as Label1, Panel1, and so on. It is also common practice to use the default name when a control is the only one of its class to appear on a form, such as MainMenu1, Timer1, PageSetupDialog1, or PrintPreviewDialog1. But you should change the name of other controls and objects used in code. Figure 3-7 provides an alphabetical list of Windows Forms controls classes, prefixes, and sample instances.

Class	Prefix	Sample
Button	btn	btnClose
CheckBox	chk	chkReadOnly
CheckedListBox	clb	clbActivities
ColorDialog	clrdlg	clrdlgBackground
ComboBox	cbo	cboEmployeeCategory

Figure 3-7: Visual Basic .NET control classes and their prefixes

Class	Prefix	Sample
ContextMenu	cmnu	cmnuOptions
CrystalReportViewer	crv	crvSummaryRpts
DataGrid	dgr	dgrReservations
DateTimePicker	dtp	dtpArrivalDate
DomainUpDown	dud	dudTopics
ErrorProvider	erp	erpMyForm
FontDialog	fntdlg	fntdlgMessageBox
GroupBox	grp	grpStudentYear
HelpProvider	hlp	hlpMyForm
HScrollBar	hsc	hscZoom
ImageList	iml	imlFlags
Label	lbl	lblTeamName
LinkLabel	llb	llbHomePage
ListBox	lst	lstStateOrProvince
ListView	lv	lvFiles
MainMenu	mmnu	mmnuChildForm
MonthCalendar	mnth	mnthDateRange
NotifyIcon	noti	notiAlarm
NumericUpDown	nud	nudVolume
OpenFileDialog	ofdlg	ofdlgUsers
PageSetupDialog	psdlg	psdlgSummaryRpt
Panel	pan	panStudentYear
PictureBox	pic	picLogo
PrintDialog	pdlg	pdlgSelectPrinter
PrintDocument	doc	docSummaryReport
PrintPreviewControl	ppctrl	ppctrlSummaryReport
PrintPreviewDialog	ppdlg	ppdlgSummaryReport
ProgressBar	prog	progPercentComplete
RadioButton	rad	radBirthplace
RichTextBox	rtb	rtbMessage
SaveFileDialog	sfdlg	sfdlgUsers
Splitter	spl	splListWindow
StatusBar	stat	statMdiMain
TabControl	tab	tabUserInfo
TextBox	txt	txtFirstName

Figure 3-7: Visual Basic .NET control classes and their prefixes (continued)

Class	Prefix	Sample
Timer	tmr	tmrRefreshStatus
ToolBar	tbr	tbrChildForm
ToolTip	tt	ttCancelBtn
TrackBar	trb	trbMarkupPercentage
TreeView	tv	tvFolders
VScrollBar	vsc	vscZoom

Figure 3-7: Visual Basic .NET control classes and their prefixes (continued)

Other types of programming elements also have prefix abbreviations. Some of the more common ones are shown in Figure 3-8.

Element	Prefix	Sample
Class	cls	clsMyClass
Component	comp	compLogon
Control	ctrl	ctrlNewBox
Form	frm	frmWelcome
MDI Form	mdi	mdiMain
Module	mod or bas	modSplash, basSplash
Object	obj	objAnyObject
Structure	struct	structUser

Figure 3-8: Other Visual Basic .NET objects and their prefixes

Web Forms controls also have standard prefixes; these will be presented in Tutorial 7.

Coding Conventions and Style Rules

The purpose of coding conventions and style rules in a programming language is to increase code readability, and, therefore, make it easier to revise and debug. Every programming shop has its own conventions. Some of the more common conventions are discussed in the following sections.

Using Indentation
Use indentation to visually identify groups of related statements. Provided that the option is turned on, the Visual Basic .NET Code Editor enforces this style rule for you. To enable indentation in the Visual Basic .NET IDE, you click Tools I Options.

In the Options dialog box, click Text Editor | Basic | VB Specific. All three of the following check boxes should be checked:

- *Automatic insertion of end constructs*—This option helps to ensure valid syntax by automatically creating a Next statement after you enter a For statement, an End If statement after you enter an If statement, an End Sub after you enter a Sub statement, and so forth.
- *Pretty listing (reformatting) of code*—This option automatically creates the proper indentation for every statement. (It is almost, but not quite, perfect; occasionally, you may find that you must adjust the indentation yourself.)
- *Enter outlining mode when files open*—This option is related to code outlining, that is, marking regions of code so that they can be expanded and collapsed.

Declaring Variables at the Lowest Level

Declare variables at the lowest or most restrictive level that you can, consistent with the requirements of program logic. If a variable is needed only inside a procedure, declare it inside that procedure. If a variable is needed only in one form, declare it at form level in that form. If a variable is needed only inside a standard module, declare it as a Private variable inside that module. Public variables in a standard module are accessible throughout the module's containing namespace, which makes them dangerous, so they should only be employed after the greatest circumspection.

Using Constants

Use constants rather than numeric values when possible. Constants improve program readability and also facilitate program maintenance. For example, in a program that computes taxes for a retail business, declare and then use SALESTAXRATE as a constant rather than using the actual sales tax percentage throughout your program. Then, if the sales tax rate changes in the future, you need to make the corresponding change in code only once.

Writing Code That Is Easy to Read

Try to write code that is easy to read, follow, and understand. Computer programs can do clever, surprising, and tricky things, but your code should not be tricky or surprising, especially to the programmer who must maintain it. Add comments to identify blocks of code (such as "Print headers" or "Search for a match"), and use comments where needed to help elucidate anything that the maintenance programmer—even yourself—needs to know.

Control Structures and Structured Programming

As with the preceding section on Windows Forms elements, you are not likely to need all of the information in this section on control structures all in one program. However, control structures constitute a subject of repeated interest in any introductory programming course, and so it seems appropriate to include here a consolidated summary of all the control structures supported in Visual Basic .NET.

A **control structure** is a method of controlling the execution sequence of instructions at runtime. You are probably familiar with most of these control structures, so consider this a quick review. Error-handling control structures may be new to you, but these will be covered in depth in Tutorial 11. Because Visual Basic .NET control structures are designed with structured programming in mind, the summary of control structures will be clearer following a brief discussion of structured programming.

Structured Programming

Beginning in the mid-1960s, structured programming became popular as programmers discovered the high cost of trying to maintain *un*structured programs, especially programs that made liberal use of the GoTo statement, and programs that contained long, unbroken sections of logic—hundreds, sometimes thousands of lines of code. Critics referred to such programs as "spaghetti code," because following the logic train was like trying to follow a single strand of spaghetti in a bowl.

Although structured programming means different things to different people, the general principles are fairly well agreed upon. Furthermore, most modern programmers (who never learned any other way of writing code) recognize the basic ingredients of structured programming as one of the developmental steps in the direction of object-oriented programming. Structured programs have the following characteristics:

- Control structures are limited to sequence, selection, and iteration, with unlimited nesting of these three types of structures. Most specifically, an unconditional branch (a GoTo statement) is not allowed. The control structures permitted in structured programming are explained later in this section.
- Every procedure has a single entry point and a single exit point. Purists extend this principle to statement blocks, forbidding, for example, the use of an Exit For statement.
- Using **stepwise refinement**, programs are broken down logically or functionally into relatively small blocks of code (25 to 50 statements at most). These blocks of code, called procedures, functions, or modules, are invoked by a procedure or function call, which transfers control only temporarily from the calling routine. Control always returns to the calling routine after the called procedure finishes executing. Thus, by examining the call stack during debugging, you can discover how execution reached a certain point. This traceability greatly assists in program testing, debugging, and verification, while facilitating maintainability and reusability.
- Variables are declared at the lowest possible level, and global variables are used minimally, if at all.

When stepwise refinement has been followed as a program development approach, the related technique of stubbing can be usefully employed. When you begin coding an application, it is useful to build stub units. Early in development, a **stub** is a placeholder for a section of code that will be developed later. The stub allows you to test the main program logic and the overall program flow before writing the detailed code.

The **stubbing** technique also permits you to keep working when you reach a stumbling block—either a section of code that you don't know how to write, or a section to be written by another member of the team who has not yet completed that task. In either case, you can draw a box around that section, insert a stub as a placeholder, and continue working around the stumbling block, putting off the solution to another day. Because of this practice, programmers sometimes refer to stepwise refinement and stubbing rather facetiously as "organized procrastination."

Although not directly a part of structured programming, the use of strong typing (where available in a programming language) and meaningful programmer-supplied names is encouraged, because these features and practices support the objectives of structured programming. Liberal use of comments throughout a program, especially to explain complex logic or seldom-used techniques, also enhances maintainability and reusability.

Visual Basic .NET Control Structures

Recall that the control structures permitted in structured programming are sequence, selection, and iteration. The syntax and semantics that implement these control structures are discussed here.

The **sequence structure** is one statement after another, as suggested by the flowchart segments in Figure 3-9. The sequence structure also includes the Call statement and other methods of invoking a function or Sub procedure. Sequence is the default control structure of all digital computers, based on the Next sequential instruction feature of the underlying hardware. If the computer is not redirected to a different instruction, it automatically reads and executes the next sequential instruction in the program.

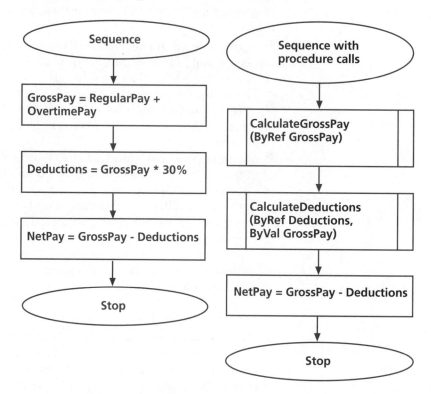

Figure 3-9: The sequence control structure

A **selection structure** provides for the selective execution of one or more imperative statements, depending on a certain condition. The Visual Basic .NET selection structures include the If statement, Select Case statement, Immediate If function, and Try statement. **Iteration structures** provide for the repeated execution of a statement block. The Visual Basic .NET iteration structures include Do, While, For, and For Each loops. This discussion covers these Visual Basic .NET structured selection and iteration control structures.

> **NOTE:** Visual Basic .NET also still supports two unstructured control structures: GoTo and On Error GoTo, but these are not used in structured programming. Some older, unstructured methods (GoSub...Return, Computed GoTo, and Computed GoSub) are no longer supported in this release.

The If Statement

An If statement allows you to specify a condition or test, and if that condition is met, to then execute one or more imperative statements. This is called an If...Then structure: *if* the condition is true, *then* execute the imperative statement. Implicitly, if the condition is false, then the imperative statement is skipped. In the example that follows, when sales (held by the decimal variable decSales) exceed $10,000, then the commission rate (held by the single variable sngRate) is set to 15%. The logic is shown in Figure 3-10.

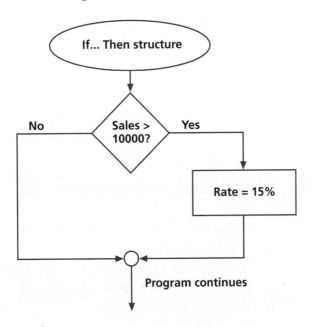

Figure 3-10: If...Then selection control structure

Visual Basic .NET supports both single-line and block formats of this simple If statement, as seen in the Figure 3-10 example:

■ Single-line If...Then

If <condition> Then <statement>

```
If decSales > 10000 Then sngRate = .15
```

■ Block If...Then...End If

If <condition> Then
    Statement1
    [Statement2]...
End If

```
If decSales > 10000 Then
    sngRate = .15
    MsgBox("Commission rate is 15%")
End If
```

An If...Then...Else structure is called for when you want to force a choice between two imperative statements. Using the preceding example, if sales exceed $10,000, then the commission rate is 15%; otherwise, the commission rate is 8%. The logic appears in Figure 3-11.

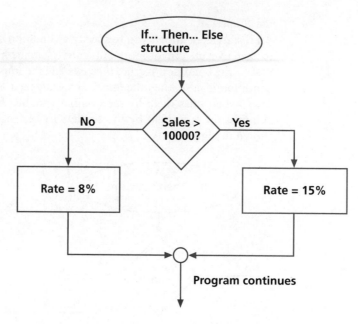

Figure 3-11: If...Then...Else selection control structure

Again, both single-line and block formats are permitted as follows:

■ Single-line If...Then...Else

If <condition> Then <statement> Else <statement>

```
If decSales > 10000 Then sngRate = .15 Else sngRate = .08
```

■ Block If...Then...Else...End If

If <condition> Then
   Statement1
   [Statement2]...
   [StatementN]
Else
   StatementN+1
   [StatementN+2]...
   [StatementM]
End If

```
If decSales > 10000 Then
   sngRate = .15
   MsgBox("Commission rate is 15%")
Else
   sngRate = .08
   MsgBox("Commission rate is 8%")
End If
```

A compound condition tests two or more conditions in the same If clause, separated by one of the logical operators (Or, And, OrElse, AndAlso, and Xor). The model for a compound condition is: *If <conditionA> <logical operator> <conditionB> Then*. (Only the If portion of the If statement is shown in these examples.) The logical operators are defined in the following list, and summarized in the truth table shown in Figure 3-12.

■ *And*—The result is True only when conditionA and conditionB are both True. Both conditions are always tested.

- *Or*—The result is True if at least one of conditionA or conditionB is True. Both conditions are always tested.
- *AndAlso*—The result is True only when conditionA and conditionB are both True. If conditionA evaluates to False, conditionB is not tested, and the operation returns False. This is called a short-circuit compound operator.
- *OrElse*—The result is True if at least one of conditionA or conditionB is True. If conditionA evaluates to True, conditionB is not tested, and the operation returns True. This is also a short-circuit compound operator.
- *Xor*—The result is True only when one and only one of conditionA and conditionB is True. This operator is called the Exclusive Or.

Operator	ConditionA	ConditionB	Result
And	True	True	True
And	True	False	False
And	False	True	False
And	False	False	False
Or	True	True	True
Or	True	False	True
Or	False	True	True
Or	False	False	False
AndAlso	True	True	True
AndAlso	True	False	False
AndAlso	False	(not evaluated)	False
OrElse	True	(not evaluated)	True
OrElse	False	True	True
OrElse	False	False	False
Xor	True	True	False
Xor	True	False	True
Xor	False	True	True
Xor	False	False	False

Figure 3-12: Truth table for Visual Basic .NET logical operators

Here are some examples of compound conditions. The short-circuit operators become obvious if conditionB performs some action in addition to testing a condition, so that you can see whether the action was taken, which indicates whether conditionB was executed at all. For these examples, conditionB is a MsgBox statement.

In the following snippet, both conditions are always evaluated, even when the first result is True, as in this example. If you test this in a program, you see that the message box is generated, even though the truth of 7 being greater than 3 makes the entire If statement True:

```
If 7 > 3 Or MsgBox("Choose yes or no", _
    MsgBoxStyle.YesNo) = MsgBoxResult.Yes Then
```

In the next snippet, because the first condition is True, the second condition is short-circuited (not tested). If you test this in a program, you see that the message box is not generated:

```
If 7 > 3 OrElse MsgBox("Choose yes or no", _
    MsgBoxStyle.YesNo) = MsgBoxResult.Yes Then
```

In the next piece, both conditions are always evaluated, even when the first result is False, as in the following example. If you test this in a program, you see that the message box is generated, despite the fact that conditionA is False.

```
If 7 < 3 And MsgBox("Choose yes or no", _
    MsgBoxStyle.YesNo) = MsgBoxResult.Yes Then
```

And in this last snippet, because the first condition is False, the second condition is short-circuited (not tested). If you test this in a program, you see that the message box is not generated.

```
If 7 < 3 AndAlso MsgBox("Choose yes or no", _
    MsgBoxStyle.YesNo) = MsgBoxResult.Yes Then
```

Select Case

The Select Case structure is useful when the evaluation of a single expression can determine multiple paths. Select Case is used in lieu of a series of simple If statements, or in lieu of a set of nested If statements. Select Case uses the following syntax:

Select Case <expression>
    Case <value>
        Statement(s)
    Case <value>...
        Statement(s)
    Case Else
        Statement(s)
End Select

Execution begins by evaluating *<expression>* and then comparing that value to each Case *<value>*. The first time the result of the comparison is True, the statements in that case are executed, and control then passes to the End Select statement. The *<value>* in Case *<value>* can be a single value, a series of values (comma delimited), or a range of values using the To keyword. You can also use the inequality operator (<>).Case Else is optional—this is the case that is executed if none of the other cases is True. If Case Else is present, it must be the last case in the structure.

The example in Figure 3-13 shows a user-defined function consisting entirely of a Select Case statement. The function accepts an integer parameter and returns a string. The integer passed to the function represents a student score. Within the Select Case statement, the function assigns a student grade to the local variable strGrade. The last statement in the function returns the value of strGrade.

```
Private Function Grade (ByVal vintScore As Integer) As String
  Dim strGrade as String
  Select Case vintScore
    Case 99, 100: strGrade = "A+"
    Case 91 To 98: strGrade = "A"
    Case 90: strGrade = "A-"
    Case > 79: strGrade = "B" 'vintScore is 80-89
    Case > 69: strGrade = "C" 'vintScore is 70-79
    Case > 59: strGrade = "D" 'vintScore is 60-69
    Case Else: strGrade = "F" 'vintScore is <60
  End Select
  Return strGrade
End Sub
```

Figure 3-13: Select Case example, enclosed in a function

Immediate If (IIf)

The IIf function examines *<condition>* and returns *<resultA>* if the condition is True; otherwise, it returns *<resultB>*. It uses the following syntax:

<variable> = IIf(*<condition>*, *<resultA>*, *<resultB>*)

Consider this example:

```
blnPass = IIf(intScore > 59, True, False)
```

If the value of intScore > 59, the function returns True, which is assigned to the Boolean blnPass; otherwise, the function returns False. The IIf function is most useful for shortening otherwise lengthy if-then-else logic in the middle of another function call. For example, if you try the code shown in Figure 3-14 in a Console application, you see that someone with a sex code of M has a wife rather than a husband.

```
Sub Main()
   Dim s As String
   Dim SexCode As String = "M"
   s = InputBox("Please enter the name of your " _
     & IIf(SexCode = "M", "wife", "husband"))
   Console.WriteLine(s)
   Console.ReadLine()
 End Sub
```

Figure 3-14: Immediate If (IIf) function in a Console application

Try...Catch...Finally

This control structure, borrowed from Java, provides a structured programming solution to the problem of error trapping. It is an effective replacement for the unstructured On Error GoTo control structure (which is still supported, but no longer recommended). You will learn about this new control structure in Tutorial 11.

Do Loops

A principle advantage of using a computer program to perform a business function rather than doing it by hand is that the computer can perform the same function over and over again, repeating a series of steps in some kind of loop—an iteration control structure. If you needed to pay only one employee, you would probably calculate the amount and write the check by hand. If you have several employees, you would use a payroll program because you would need to execute the same basic series of steps repeatedly, and an iteration control structure allows you to do this more efficiently than you can by hand.

Iteration control structures come in the form of externally controlled loops and internally controlled loops, and most programming languages support both types. In Visual Basic, Do loops are the principle form of externally controlled loops. An externally controlled loop is one in which the terminator or loop exit strategy is external to the syntactical structure of the loop itself. For example, in a game program, the whole program might be encased in a loop that, at the end of the game, asks the user to play again, yes or no. Exit from the loop depends on user input, not something inherent in the syntax of the loop. Another example is a loop that retrieves data from an input file containing an unknown number of records: input continues until the end-of-file is encountered.

Syntactically, the Visual Basic .NET Do loops are differentiated by being pretest or posttest loops. Further, the test itself can be a While or an Until test. The difference between a pretest and a posttest loop is that a **pretest loop** may never be executed at all, if the exit condition is satisfied before the loop is executed for the first time; whereas a **posttest loop** is always executed at least once, because the exit condition is not tested for the first time until the bottom of the loop is reached. The difference between a While test and an Until test is that a **While test** causes the loop to continue to execute while (as long as) the condition remains True; an **Until test** continues to execute the loop until the condition becomes True (as long as the condition is False). In other words, a While loop exits on a False condition, and an Until loop exits on a True condition.

Consider the general flowchart of a pretest Do While loop shown in Figure 3-15 and the code demonstrating a specific example of this loop shown in Figure 3-16. In this example, the loop is not executed at all if the user enters 0 or a positive value when asked for the first time to enter the number of dependents, in response to the first InputBox function call (prior to the loop). If the user's response is invalid, the user is admonished to enter 0 or a positive number—this occurs inside the loop, and is repeated until the user's response is valid.

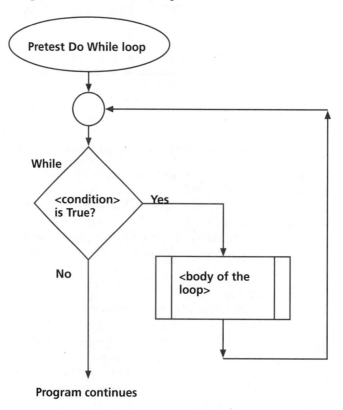

Figure 3-15: Flowchart of a pretest Do While loop

```
intNumDependents = Val(InputBox("Enter number of dependents"))
'Pretest While loop begins here
Do While intNumDependents < 0
  intNumDependents = Val(InputBox("Enter 0 or a positive number"))
Loop
```

Figure 3-16: Example of a pretest Do While loop

In Figure 3-17 you see a flowchart demonstrating the pretest Do Until loop. Figure 3-18 shows a specific example of this loop. The only difference between a pretest While and a pretest Until is the phrasing of the exit condition. You can always express the condition either way.

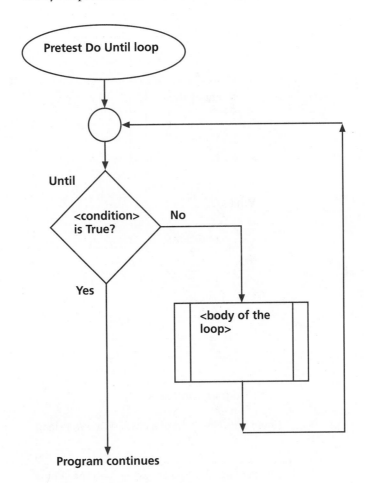

Figure 3-17: Flowchart of a pretest Do Until loop

```
intNumDependents = Val(InputBox("Enter number of dependents"))
 'Pretest Until loop begins here
 Do Until intNumDependents >= 0
   intNumDependents = Val(InputBox("Enter 0 or a positive number"))
 Loop
```

Figure 3-18: Example of a pretest Do Until loop

In a posttest loop, the exit condition is tested at the bottom of the loop rather than at the top. Figures 3-19 and 3-20 show a flowchart and example of the posttest Do While loop. As a result, the body of the loop is always executed at least once—this is the crucial difference between a pretest loop and a posttest loop. After the first execution of the loop, the loop continues to execute while the exit condition is True. In this example, the first time the user is asked to enter the number of dependents occurs within the body of the loop.

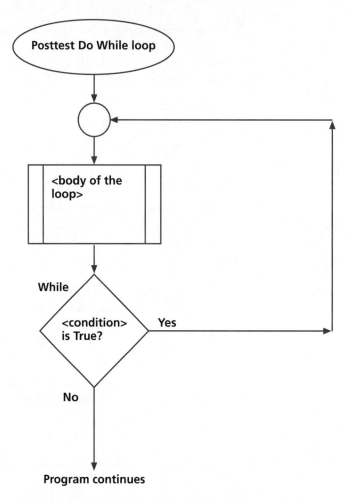

Figure 3-19: Flowchart of a posttest Do While loop

```
'Posttest Do While loop begins here
Do
   intNumDependents = Val(InputBox("Enter number of dependents"))
Loop While intNumDependents < 0
```

Figure 3-20: Example of a posttest Do While loop

The posttest Do Until loop flowchart and example are shown in Figures 3-21 and 3-22, respectively. Again, only the phrasing of the exit condition differentiates the posttest Do Until loop from the posttest Do While loop.

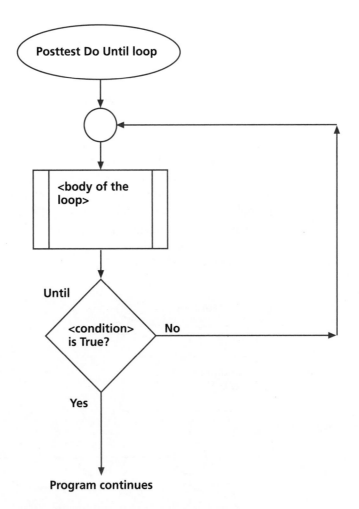

Figure 3-21: Flowchart of a posttest Do Until loop

```
'Posttest Do Until loop begins here
Do
  intNumDependents = Val(InputBox("Enter number of dependents"))
Loop Until intNumDependents >= 0
```

Figure 3-22: Example of a posttest Do Until loop

While Loop

This control structure is a holdover from earlier releases of Visual Basic and performs exactly the same as the While format of the pretest Do loop. The While loop will likely be dropped in future releases, so you should not use it in new code, but you need not change it (at least for now) in existing code. Figure 3-23 displays the rewrite of the Do While...loop using While...End While instead:

```
intNumDependents = Val(InputBox("Enter number of dependents"))
While intNumDependents < 0
  intNumDependents = Val(InputBox("Enter 0 or a positive number"))
End While
```

Figure 3-23: While...End While structure (obsolescent)

For Loop

In addition to the externally controlled Do and While loops, Visual Basic has an internally controlled loop. The difference between these two types of loops is that an externally controlled loop depends on external inputs or events to exit the loop; whereas, an internally controlled loop contains all the elements to initiate, iterate, and exit the loop within its own syntax.

The internally controlled loop in Visual Basic is the For loop. An internally controlled loop requires a loop control variable (LCV), an initial value for the LCV, a limit value for the LCV, a step value (the increment or decrement of the LCV after each iteration of the loop), and a test to determine whether the LCV's limit value has been reached (after which the loop is exited). With the logic of the For loop displayed in Figure 3-24, the syntax of a For loop is as follows:

For <LCV> = <Initial Value> to <Limit Value> [Step <Step Value>]
   Statement(s)
Next [<LCV>]

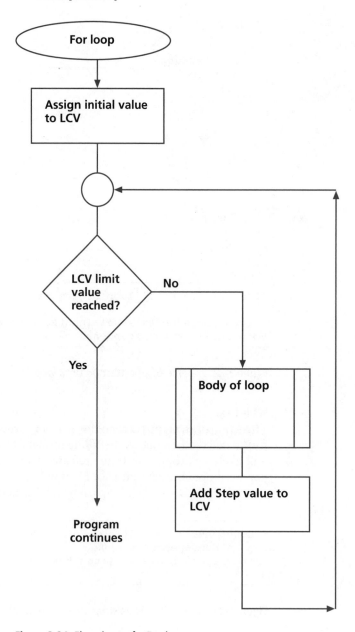

Figure 3-24: Flowchart of a For loop

Figure 3-25 shows a simple For loop, printing line numbers 1 through 10. As this example shows, the Step value can be omitted, in which case Visual Basic assumes that the Step value equals one. (The examples in this section are all given as minuscule Console applications.)

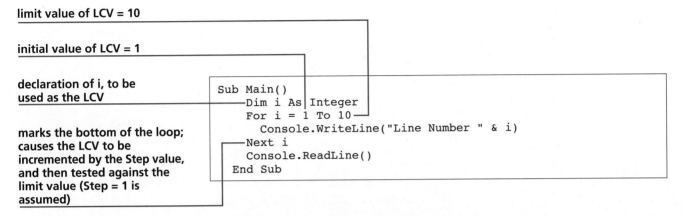

limit value of LCV = 10

initial value of LCV = 1

declaration of i, to be used as the LCV

marks the bottom of the loop; causes the LCV to be incremented by the Step value, and then tested against the limit value (Step = 1 is assumed)

```
Sub Main()
    Dim i As Integer
    For i = 1 To 10
        Console.WriteLine("Line Number " & i)
    Next i
    Console.ReadLine()
End Sub
```

Figure 3-25: A simple For loop, printing numbers 1 to 10

Figure 3-26 demonstrates a For loop with a negative Step value, using it to print a string backwards. The code in Figure 3-26 may require explication, if you are not familiar with the Mid() function. The Mid() function takes three arguments: the name of the string from which the "middle" is to be returned, the beginning position of the return value (where position starts at 1), and the number of characters to be returned.

negative Step value

Mid() function

```
Sub Main()
    Dim s As String = "ABCDEFG"
    Dim i As Integer
    For i = Len(s) To 1 Step -1
        Console.Write(Mid(s, i, 1))
    Next i
    Console.WriteLine()
    Console.ReadLine()
End Sub
```

Figure 3-26: For loop, printing a string backwards

For loops provide the most common method of processing all the elements of an array, as shown in Figure 3-27. (Note the use of the UBound() function, which returns the upper bound or highest index value in the array.)

```
Sub Main()
    Dim s() As String = {"Sam", "Mary", "George", "Barbara", "Tom"}
    Dim i As Integer
    For i = 0 To UBound(s)
        Console.WriteLine(s(i))
    Next i
    Console.WriteLine()
    Console.ReadLine()
End Sub
```

Figure 3-27: Printing the elements of an array

Another common practice is to use a For loop to perform a sequential search of an array, and then exit the loop when a match is found. However, structured-programming purists object to this technique, because it introduces a second exit point from the loop. See Figure 3-28.

Exit For is a second exit point

```
Sub Main()
  Dim s() As String = {"Sam", "Mary", "George", "Barbara", "Tom"}
  Dim i As Integer
  Dim strSearch = "George"
  For i = 0 To UBound(s)
    If s(i) = strSearch Then Exit For
  Next i
  If i > UBound(s) Then
    Console.WriteLine("Search string not found in the array")
  Else
    Console.WriteLine("Search string located at s(" & i & ")")
  End If
  Console.ReadLine()
End Sub
```

Figure 3-28: Using a For loop for a sequential search

If you are a purist, you can still use a For loop to search for an element in an array, but you must introduce another variable to do it, as demonstrated in Figure 3-29.

```
Sub Main()
  Dim s() As String = {"Sam", "Mary", "George", "Barbara", "Tom"}
  Dim i As Integer
  Dim j As Integer = -9
  Dim strSearch = "George"
  For i = 0 To UBound(s)
    If s(i) = strSearch Then j = i
  Next i
  If j = -9 Then
    Console.WriteLine("Search string not found in the array")
  Else
    Console.WriteLine("Search string located at s(" & j & ")")
  End If
  Console.ReadLine()
End Sub
```

Figure 3-29: Alternative sequential search using a For loop

Finally, a Do loop can be as efficient as the Exit For construction, without compromising your structured programming principles. In the version in Figure 3-30, note the short-circuit OrElse, which avoids the comparison of strSearch to s(i) when I > UBound(s) (which causes an IndexOutOfRange exception if allowed to occur). Also note the use of the compound assignment operator in i +=1 (a quicker way of writing i = i + 1). Note the assignment of a series of values to an array variable in Figure 3-30.

```
Sub Main()
  Dim s() As String = {"Sam", "Mary", "George", "Barbara", "Tom"}
  Dim i As Integer = 0
  Dim strSearch = "George"
  Do Until i > UBound(s) OrElse strSearch = s(i)
    i += 1
  Loop
  If i > UBound(s) Then
    Console.WriteLine("Search string not found in the array")
  Else
    Console.WriteLine("Search string located at s(" & i & ")")
  End If
  Console.ReadLine()
End Sub
```

Figure 3-30: Using a Do loop for a sequential search

For Each Loop

For Each is a special form of the For loop that steps through every element in a collection. For example, the For Each loop in Figure 3-31 steps through each control on a form, setting the control's BackColor property to red and its Text property to a sequential number. Note in this example that an object variable must be declared as the type of the collection: in this instance, Controls is the name of the collection, and Control is the type of object in that collection.

```
Dim MyControl As Control
Dim Ctr As Integer
For Each MyControl In Me.Controls
  MyControl.BackColor = Color.Red
  Ctr += 1
  MyControl.Text = Ctr
Next
```

Figure 3-31: For Each loop stepping through a collection

Building Multiple Document Interface Applications

As you saw in the LogonManager executable, an MDI application consists of an MDI form (also called an MDI parent or MDI container in the Visual Basic .NET documentation) and multiple MDI child forms. Figure 3-32 is another example of an MDI application, in this case showing three child forms open and arranged by the user to fill the available space inside the MDI parent.

Remember that the definition of a form is actually a class, as explained in Tutorial 2. Child forms can be multiple instances of the same class, or each child can be an instance of different classes. For example, from the LogonManager main screen, if you click About five times, and then click Window | Cascade, you will see that five copies of the About form (five instances of the child form, but all of the same class) are open. Or you could log on as supervisor, and run New User, About, and Accept New Users concurrently; again, click Window | Cascade to see that all three of these windows are open. In this case, you have multiple forms open, but each is an instance of a different class.

As an analogy, you might say that five copies of the same photograph are five instances of the same class, while five different photographs are instances of five different classes.

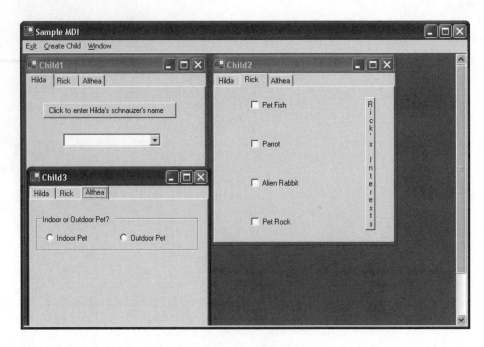

Figure 3-32: Sample MDI application with multiple child forms

The basics of building an MDI application are fairly simple. You designate one form (most often the Startup object) as an MDI form by setting its IsMdiContainer property to True. You add another form (Form2) to the project, which becomes a child form. Because the form is defined as a class, the (parent) MDI form must instantiate a new (child) form2 (Form2Temp), then declare Form2Temp's MdiParent property to be the MDI form itself, and finally show Form2Temp. If data values need to be shared between forms, you declare them as public variables in a module. Creation and manipulation of child forms is usually accomplished through a menu.

In Visual Basic 6.0, an MDI form was a different class than a normal Windows form, and only one MDI form was supported within a project. As a result, setting a regular form's MdiChild property to True automatically made that form a child of the single MdiForm. In Visual Basic .NET, by contrast, a project can have multiple MdiContainer forms, and any form can serve as an MdiContainer by setting its IsMdiContainer property to True. For the child form, the MdiParent property in Visual Basic .NET replaces the MdiChild property in Visual Basic 6.0, because now, rather than simply designating a form as a child (MdiChild offered a True/False property setting), it is necessary to identify which one of many possible forms is the child's parent.

Understanding New Windows Forms Controls

The controls used to create an MDI application in general, and specifically the LogonManager (draft version), that have not yet been discussed include the TabControl, ComboBox, CheckBox, GroupBox, and RadioButton controls. The MDI application can and usually does includes a number of TextBox controls, which you have certainly encountered previously—the TextBox control is essentially unchanged from Visual Basic 6.0. From the running LogonManager application, Figure 3-33 highlights the TabControl control (Name & Phone tab) and the ComboBox control on the New User form. Continuing with the New User form,

Figure 3-34 highlights the CheckBox, GroupBox, and RadioButton controls under the Secret Question tab.

tabs on a TabControl control

TextBox controls

ComboBox control

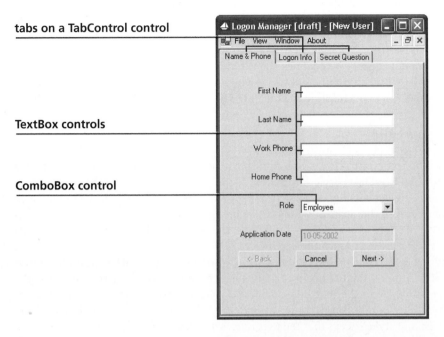

Figure 3-33: LogonManager controls (Name & Phone tab)

CheckBox control

RadioButton controls

GroupBox control

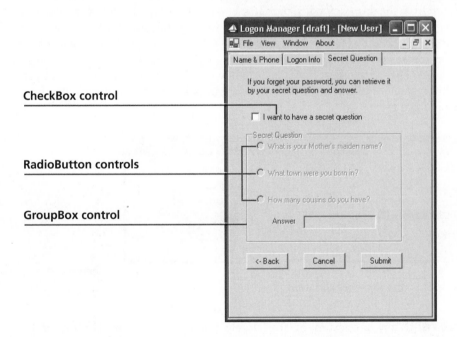

Figure 3-34: More controls in LogonManager (Secret Question tab)

TabControl Control

The purpose of the TabControl control is to conserve screen real estate, as well as to subdivide the user interface into logical segments. A TabControl's principle property is the TabPages Collection; clicking this property's settings box opens the TabPage Collection Editor in a familiar format. At runtime, clicking a tab in the tab control raises the Click event for that tab page (just as clicking a menu item raises the Click event for that menu item).

Other important properties of the TabControl control are Dock and Multiline. The Dock property permits the programmer to align the tab control along one edge of its container, or to fill the container entirely (the default is no docking). In Visual Basic .NET, this new Dock property is a member of many Windows Forms controls. The Multiline property determines the tab display format when the tab page texts are too wide to fit across the control—when Multiline is False (the default), scroll arrows appear; when Multiline is True, tab page texts appear on more than one line.

ComboBox Control

The ComboBox control is a combination list box and text box. In its default style (ComboBox.DropDownStyle.DropDown), the ComboBox control has a text portion that is always visible along with a list arrow that exposes a drop-down list at runtime. Because the drop-down list is usually hidden, the ComboBox control conserves screen space. Also in the default style, the user can select from the drop-down list or type a new entry into the text box.

Two other combo box styles are also available. In ComboBox.Drop DownStyle.Simple, the list portion is always exposed, so no list arrow appears; the user can still type in the text box or make a selection from the list box portion of the control. In ComboBox.DropDownStyle.DropDownList, the control works just like the default style, except that the user must select from the drop-down list—editing of the text portion is not allowed. Samples of the three styles are shown in Figure 3-35. In this figure, the user has clicked the left (DropDown style) combo box and is selecting South from the drop-down list, but the user could have typed a different value into the text box. The middle, Simple combo box always appears as a list box with a text box on top; in this case, the user has typed a new value, "anywhere," into the text box; note the absence of a drop-down arrow. On the right, in the DropDownList combo box, the user has selected East from the drop-down list; in this style, the user is not permitted to type in a new value for the text box, but must select an existing value from the drop-down list.

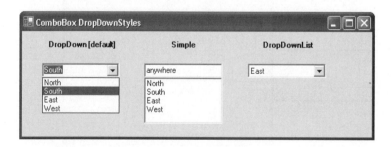

Figure 3-35: Sample ComboBox controls

> **NOTE:** Many properties of the closely related ComboBox, ListBox, and CheckedListBox controls have changed from Visual Basic 6.0 to Visual Basic .NET. See the Help topic, ComboBox Control Changes in Visual Basic .NET for a detailed comparison.

The principle properties of the ComboBox control are Items (another Collection), Items.Count, and SelectedIndex. These three properties replace the List, ListCount, and ListIndex properties in Visual Basic 6.0.

You can add items to a ComboBox control at design time by clicking Items, choosing Collection, and entering strings into the String Collection Editor. Items added in this manner are not visible in the combo box until runtime. At runtime, you can add items by invoking the ComboBox.Items.Add method.

To remove items at runtime, you use the ComboBox.Items.Remove and ComboBox.Items.RemoveAt methods. The difference between these is that the Remove method specifies the item to be removed, whereas RemoveAt specifies the index of the item to be removed. For example, if ComboBox1 contains the items "George," "Sally," "Ann," and "Frank," and if Frank is currently selected, then the statement `ComboBox1.Items.Remove(Combox1.SelectedItem)` removes Frank, `ComboBox1.Items.Remove("Ann")` removes Ann, and `ComboBox1.Items.RemoveAt(0)` removes George.

Items.Count (which is read-only and available only at runtime) indicates the number of items in the list box portion of the control. Items are indexed using a zero-based indexing scheme. An individual item can be accessed at runtime through the SelectedIndex property. The highest SelectedIndex value is one less than the value of Items.Count.

Before any item has been selected, the value of SelectedIndex is -1. Therefore, in your code, you can test the value of ComboBox.SelectedIndex, and if it equals 0, then the user has not yet made a selection from the combo box.

CheckBox Control

The CheckBox control displays an option or condition in its Text property. When the control's Checked property is True, a check mark appears in front of the text. When the Checked property is False, a check mark does not appear. Clicking the check box is a toggle switch, and generates the control's Click event.

Each CheckBox control is independent of other CheckBox controls. That is to say, any number of CheckBox controls on a form or in another container (such as a group box) can be simultaneously True. This feature distinguishes a group of CheckBox controls from a group of RadioButton controls, which offer mutually exclusive choices.

The CheckBox control offers a third possibility, in addition to the Checked property being True or False. The control also has a CheckedState property with three possible settings: Checked (when the Checked property is True), Unchecked (when the Checked property is False), and Indeterminate (when the option is not available). The control also offers a ThreeState property, which is True or False. When the ThreeState property is True, the CheckedState property cycles through the values Checked, Indeterminate, and Unchecked with each mouse click. When the ThreeState property is False, clicking the check box toggles the CheckedState property between Checked and Unchecked, while the CheckedState.Indeterminate setting can only be assigned in code. When the CheckedState property is Indeterminate, the check box appears dimmed, as if it were disabled (but it is not in fact disabled).

GroupBox Control

The GroupBox control in Visual Basic .NET replaces the Frame control in Visual Basic 6.0. The GroupBox control serves as a container for other controls. It also visually segregates one logical grouping of items from another. It can be helpful at design time, because moving a group box from one location to another also moves all of the items within it. Programmatically, the group box and all of its contents can be enabled or disabled, or made visible or invisible, with a single line of code. A GroupBox control is also useful from a user's perspective because it helps the user visually comprehend the logical grouping of items within the box. In one very common implementation, a group box contains a series of RadioButton controls.

RadioButton Control

The RadioButton control in Visual Basic .NET replaces the OptionButton control in Visual Basic 6.0. The functionality is the same, although several properties and methods have changed. Like a CheckBox control, a RadioButton control's Text property states some user-selectable option, and its Checked property has a value of True or False.

Two or more RadioButton controls in the same container present the user with mutually exclusive choices. Only one RadioButton control can have its Checked property True at any given time. Different sets of RadioButton controls on a single form must be placed in separate containers, such as a group box, tab page, or panel.

When a RadioButton, whose Checked property is False, is selected at runtime, the CheckedChanged event is raised, and the Checked property is changed to True. (The CheckedChanged event is also raised when a radio button becomes unchecked because another one has been selected.) Whenever a radio button is selected at runtime, its Click event is raised, regardless of the previous setting of the Checked property. Clicking a radio button that is already True does not change the property to False. The only way to change a radio button to False in the GUI is to click another radio button in the same container.

You now have completed Lesson A. You can stop now and take a break if you prefer, but don't forget to do the end-of-lesson questions and exercises before continuing with Lesson B.

SUMMARY

- All programmer-supplied words should follow certain naming conventions and should in any case be meaningful. Except for a local variable, the first letter of a variable name indicates scope. For a local variable, *st* indicates static, but no prefix indicates a dynamic variable. Next, the letter *a* designates an array. Following this, variables and objects have a three-letter prefix, indicating the class on which the declaration is based. The rest of the name is a meaningful noun phrase, with an initial capital for each word.
- The name of a procedure or function is a mixed-case verb phrase.
- The name of a constant is in all uppercase.
- Structured programming guidelines limit control structures to sequence, selection, and iteration. Structured programming also requires that large code segments be broken into smaller units and controlled through procedure calls. Every procedure or module must have one entry point at the top of the procedure and one exit point at the bottom.
- Large projects and projects involving programmer teams are usually designed using a top-down approach and stepwise refinement. Stubs are placeholders for modules to be developed later in a system development project.
- Selection control structures include the If statement, Select Case, IIf function, and Try statement. Iteration control structures include Do, While, For, and For Each loops.
- In a Multiple Document Interface (MDI) application, one form (the MDI or parent form) serves as a container for one or more child forms. Access to child forms and other MDI functionality is typically controlled through a menu. Open child forms can be listed under a menu item whose WindowList property is set to True. A child form must be instantiated before it can be shown.
- You can enhance a Windows Forms application with TabControl, ComboBox, CheckBox, GroupBox, and RadioButton controls.

Q U E S T I O N S

1. The data type designed to hold currency values is _____.

2. The proper prefix for a variable name for a static array of integers is _____.

3. The proper prefix for a Boolean formal parameter passed ByVal is _____.

4. In Select Case, the default case (executed when none other is True) is _____.

5. The terminator for a Do Until loop is _____.

6. Following conventional naming rules, the name TAXRATE refers to a(n) _____.

7. To declare a form as an MDI form, you set its _____ property to True.

8. Setting the _____ property of a root-level menu item to True causes the Text property of each open child form to appear at the bottom of that menu.

9. A child form's _____ property identifies which MDI form is the container for that child form.

10. Usually, the programmer categorizes and lists user selections in an MDI application by employing a(n) _____ control.

11. The programmer-supplied name of a control should start with a three-letter _____ that indicates the control's _____.

12. Three types of control structures are permitted in structured programming: _____, selection, and _____.

13. The name of a procedure or function should normally be a(n) _____ phrase.

C R I T I C A L   T H I N K I N G

At the end of each lesson, critical thinking questions are intended to provoke you into considering the material you have just read at a deeper level.

1. Some programmers always accept the default names assigned by Visual Basic .NET (TextBox1, Form1, Module1, and so on). Is this or is this not a good idea? Why?

2. Would you prefer a programming language with strong or weak typing? Why?

3. The following statement describes the operation of the Xor operator. Explain this statement in English:

   A Xor B $\equiv$ (A Or B) And Not (A And B)

4. What is the advantage of the compound assignment operator?

EXERCISES

1. Create an MDI application with one small child form. The child form contains no controls. Include a menu with these root entries: Exit, Color, and Window. The Color menu has four selections: Blue, Green, Yellow, and Red. Selecting one of these colors causes a child form in the selected color to appear. The Window menu item offers selections to Cascade, Tile Horizontal, or Tile Vertical, and the Window item's WindowList property is True. To create this application:

    a. Create a new Windows Forms application named Colors in the Tut03 folder. In Solution Explorer, rename the default form filename from Form1.vb to mdiMain.vb. Within the Form Designer, rename Form1 internally as mdiMain, and set its IsMdiContainer property to True.

    b. Designate mdiMain as the Startup object. (Remember that you do this in the Property Pages for the project.)

    c. Drop a MainMenu control onto the form. Type in the specified menu items. Change the default menu item names to meaningful names.

    d. Add another small form to the project named frmChild.

    e. Program the Click events for the menu selections:
        - *Exit*—Terminate the program.
        - *Blue, green, yellow, red*—Instantiate frmChild. Set its BackColor and Text properties to blue, green, yellow, or red, depending on the color selected by the user. Set its mdiParent property to mdiMain. Show the child form.
        - *Cascade, Tile Horizontal, Tile Vertical*—Use the appropriate version of Me.LayoutMdi(MdiLayout.Cascade). (Look up the correct syntax in the Help screens.)

2. Create an MDI application with five child forms to display the various services offered through the Student Union. One child form should display the names and e-mail addresses of six student social clubs. A second child form should display the names and phone numbers of the four workshops offered by the Career Center (Resume Preparation, Interviewing, Career Expectations, and Job Hunting Strategies). A third child form should display the five recreational and physical fitness opportunities available through the Student Union and instruct the user to include the e-mail addresses for these opportunities. A fourth child form should display the names and hours of operation of the Student Union's eating facilities (all-day diner, sandwich shop, pizzeria, and night club). A fifth child form is an About form that lists the name and phone number of the Student Union manager. Design an appropriate menu; child forms are activated by selecting the corresponding menu item.

3. Design an MDI application (this is a paper and pencil exercise at this point; you do not need to create the application in Visual Studio .NET until Lesson B). This application will be a culture and geography quiz for residents of the International Village. The MDI container has a main menu, which allows the user to select Continents, Languages, or Capitals. The main menu also offers an About menu item, which gives credit to the authors of the application, and an Exit item.

    a. Each child form (frmContinents, frmLanguages, and frmCapitals) has a Question button and an Answer button, a label for the question, a combo box for the user's answer, a label for the result (correct or incorrect), and a Done button. When the user clicks the Question button, the program randomly selects a country (one of the participants in the Friendsville International Games), and displays this country name in the question label. The user then selects the answer from the combo box. When the user clicks the Answer button, the program indicates whether the user's answer is correct or incorrect, and then increments either the number correct or the number incorrect, as appropriate. The user can click Question and then Answer as often as desired. When the user clicks Done, the program uses a message box to display the number of correct answers and the number of incorrect answers. To make the programming of this application more efficient, your design should be based on one frmQuiz child form, which is instantiated as frmContinents, frmLanguages, or frmCapitals, depending on the user's menu selection of the quiz category (Continents, Languages, or Capitals).

b. frmContinents: after the user clicks the Question button and a country has been displayed, the user selects the continent from the combo box.

c. frmLanguages: after the user clicks the Question button and a country has been displayed, the user selects that country's native language from the combo box.

d. frmCapitals: after the user clicks the Question button and a country has been displayed, the user selects the capital of the country from the combo box.

e. When the user clicks Exit (on the MDI form), the program displays the number of questions and the number of correct and incorrect answers in each of the three categories, as well as the total number of questions and correct and incorrect answers in all three categories combined.

4. Create an MDI application that conducts an exit survey of guests in the International Village. This application has a menu and three child forms. The menu should let the user open the first child form, then the second, and then the third, by enabling each menu selection as the previous selection is clicked. The child forms are:

a. My Profile child form:

■ Insert a group box titled Gender. Insert two radio buttons in this group box, for Male and Female.

■ Insert a combo box and label for Villager Category. The combo box should contain the choices Athlete, Coach, Judge, Official, Staff, and Visitor.

■ Insert a group box for Age. Inside this group box, insert radio buttons for < 20, 20-30, 30-45, and >45.

b. My International Village Information child form:

■ Insert a combo box and label for House. The combo box should contain the names of the houses in the International Village, namely, Apple, Blueberry, Cherry, Grapefruit, Orange, Plum, Strawberry, and Tangelo. A label should direct the villager to click the House where the villager resided.

■ Insert a group box titled Floor. Inside this group box, insert radio buttons for Ground floor, Second floor, and Upper floor. A label should direct the villager to click the floor where the villager's room was located.

■ Insert a group box titled Activities - Check all that apply. Inside this box, insert check boxes for the following:
   "I ate most of my dinners in the International Village."
   "I usually ate breakfast in the International Village."
   "I used the game room frequently."
   "I used the TV room frequently."

c. My Opinions child form: Insert three group boxes on this form, titled Food, Accommodations, and Activities. In each group box, ask the villager to provide a rating of Exceeded my expectations, Met my expectations, or Did not meet my expectations. (Obviously, these should be radio buttons inside each group box.)

5. This project builds on Exercise 4. Add the capability to save the user's survey answers in a sequential file. To do this, create a structure in a module to hold the results from each child form: Gender; VillagerCategory; AgeCategory; House; Floor; Booleans for Dinner, Breakfast, GameRoom, and TvRoom; and Opinions (0, 1, or 2) for Food, Accommodations, and Activities. Provide default values for each element, replacing the defaults with the user's actual answers. Your program only needs to save the results from one user's survey, and the output file can be called Survey.txt. You can assume that each user who takes the survey submits a Survey.txt file, and that a separate program—not part of this project—summarizes and consolidates these files.

Exercise 6 allows you to discover the solution to problems on your own and experiment with material that is not covered explicitly in the tutorial.

discovery ▶

6. Create a Windows Forms MDI application called Memo. The single child form is filled with a multi-line RichTextBox control, and can be used to create and save a memo as an RTF file. The user can create as many concurrent child forms as desired. Each open memo form, if saved by the user, is saved under the name Memo plus a sequential number plus .rtf (that is, rich text format). Follow these guidelines to create this application:

   a.   The MDI form has a simple main menu, with one root entry named File, and two menu items under File: New Memo and Exit. When the user clicks New Memo, a new child form is instantiated. Increment a static variable and assign this variable after the word "Memo" to the Text property of the child form (so the first child form is Memo1, the next is Memo2, and so on). Then display the child form. When the user clicks Exit, the application terminates.

   b.   The child form contains a RichTextBox 🖼 control whose Dock property is set to Fill. A RichTextBox control is a more functional version of a TxtBox control with which you are already quite familiar. You will not need the many additional features of a RichTextBox control for this exercise—rather, you only need its SaveFile method, explained presently. By default, a RichTextBox permits multi-line entries, so the user can write a memo that fills the rich text box. Also place a Save button in the upper right corner of the form (on top of the rich text box). When the user clicks this Save button, save the contents of the rich text box in a file named the same as the Text property of the child form (that is, Memo1, Memo2, etc.) plus .rtf. The statement you need to do this is:

```
RichTextBox1.SaveFile(Me.Text & ".rtf")
```

After completing this lesson, you will be able to:

■ Build an MDI application

■ Incorporate the following controls into a Windows Forms application: TabControl, ComboBox, CheckBox, GroupBox, and RadioButton

Building a Sample MDI Application

In this lesson, you build a sample Multiple Document Interface (MDI) application, and you incorporate into that application the controls that are needed for LogonManager.

Creating a Sample MDI Application

The Friendsville Games Development Team has decided to build a sample MDI application as a learning exercise. Just to make it fun and interesting, Hilda, Rick, and Althea have each explained to you their personal interest in pets. Your task is to incorporate their personal pet interests into the GUI of this application.

To create an MDI application:

1 Start a new Windows Forms project in the VB.NET\Student\Tut03 folder. Name the project **SampleMDI**. In Solution Explorer, right-click **Form1**, and rename it **mdiMain.vb**. Click the **form** in Form Designer, and then change the form name in the Properties window to **mdiMain**. Click **project name** (SampleMDI) in Solution Explorer, and then open the **SampleMDI Property Pages** dialog box. On the General tab under Common Properties, change the **Startup object** to **mdiMain**. Set mdiMain's **Text** property to **SampleMDI**. Set the form's IsMdiContainer property to **True**. This makes mdiMain an MDI parent form.

2 From the Toolbox, select a **MainMenu** control and drag it onto mdiMain. Type the following items into the menu, as shown in Figure 3-36. Recall that the ampersand precedes the access key, so the menu entries are **E&xit**, **&Create Child**, **&Window**, and **&Cascade**.

Figure 3-36: mdiMain main menu

3 Right-click any menu item, and click **Edit Names**. Replace the default menu item names (MenuItem1, MenuItem2, and so on) by typing names corresponding to the Text property of each item: **mnuExit, mnuCreateChild, mnuWindow**, and **mnuWindowCascade**. See Figure 3-37. Right-click any menu item, and click **Edit Names** again.

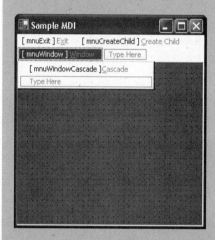

Figure 3-37: Names of mdiMain menu items

4 Click the **Window** menu item, and set its MdiList property to **True**. This tells Visual Basic .NET to maintain a list of all open child forms at runtime. The list appears under the Window menu item, with a check mark in front of the active child.

5 In Solution Explorer, right-click the **SampleMDI** project name; then click **Add | Add Windows Form** to add another form to the project. Name this new form **frmChild**, and set its Text property to **Child**.

Now program the click events for mnuExit_Click(), mnuCreateChild_Click(), and mnuWindowCascade_Click().

tip

The code for establishing the WindowCascade_Click() event is hardly intuitive. The LayoutMdi method replaces the Visual Basic 6.0 Arrange method, and LayoutMdi's argument must be one of the MdiLayout enumeration's values: ArrangeIcons (arrange minimized child forms along the bottom of the form), Cascade (arrange child forms in overlapping windows), TileHorizontal (divide the available space in the MDI form into rows, filling each row with as much of a child form as will fit), and TileVertical (divide the available space in the MDI form into columns, filling each column with as much of a child form as will fit).

6   Open **mdiMain** in the Designer. Double-click **Exit** in the Designer, and then insert **End** in the procedure for mnuExit_Click(). Similarly double-click **CreateChild**, and then insert the code shown in Figure 3-38 to create the mnuCreateChild_Click() event. Finally to create the mnuWindowCascade_Click() event, double-click **WindowCascade**, and then insert `Me.LayoutMdi (MdiLayout.Cascade)`.

```
Dim MyChild As New frmChild() 'instantiate a new child form
MyChild.MdiParent = Me      'designate the new child's parent
MyChild.Show()              'display the new child
```

Figure 3-38: Code for mnuCreateChild_Click()

The qualifier MdiLayout must precede the value. One way of discovering the LayoutMdi method and the MdiLayout namespace and argument values is to begin coding the form name "Me." (Me period). When you type the period, the Visual Basic .NET IntelliSense Autocompletion facility displays a pop-up window, containing properties and methods that are possible in the present context. Eliminate the offerings that are clearly inappropriate, experiment with those that might be correct, and ultimately you will encounter LayoutMdi. After typing Me., you could also press the F1 key to obtain context-sensitive help. Finally, the LayoutMdi method is also mentioned in the Visual Studio .NET Help screens pertaining to MDI applications.

7   Run the **SampleMDI** application, create two child forms, and click **Window | Cascade**. You should see two overlapping child forms within the MDI form, and two instances of the child form listed under the Window menu.

In some cases, you may want to distinguish among similar child forms. One simple method of accomplishing this is to number them.

8   Add the code shown in Figure 3-39 to mnuCreateChild_Click, inserting it right after `Dim MyChild...`.

```
Static intNum As Integer 'declare a static variable
intNum += 1   'compound assignment statement, adds 1 to intNum
MyChild.Text &= intNum 'concatenates the value of intNum
```

Figure 3-39: Additional code in mnuCreateChild_Click()

NOTE: The variable intNum is declared as Static so that it will not be reinitialized every time a new child form is created.

9   Run the **SampleMDI** program again. This time, create four child forms, and click **Window | Cascade**. The result should appear as in Figure 3-40. Then exit the application, and return to the IDE.

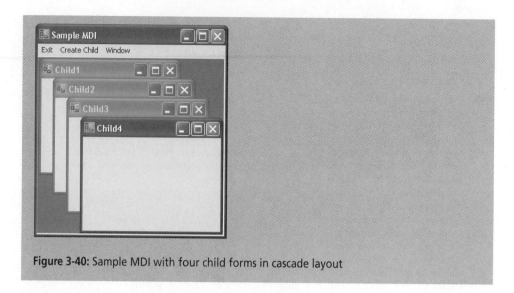

Figure 3-40: Sample MDI with four child forms in cascade layout

Inserting New Controls in the Sample MDI

Recall that the LogonManager application requires the use of the following new controls: TabControl, ComboBox, CheckBox, GroupBox, and RadioButton. In this section, you experiment with these new controls by placing an instance of each in the SampleMDI application.

TabControl Control

In the following steps, you experiment with the TabControl control by placing one on the child form of SampleMDI. Tab controls provide an excellent means of conserving screen space when information can be divided into discrete sets that do not need to be all displayed at once. In this experiment, you display the information concerning each FGDT member's pet interests on one tab page of the tab control.

To add a TabControl control to SampleMDI:

1 Open **frmChild** in the Windows Form Designer.

2 Drag a **TabControl** control ▣ onto the form. Set its Dock property to **Fill** by clicking the Dock property, then clicking the list arrow, and clicking the center rectangle on the container schematic. See Figure 3-41.

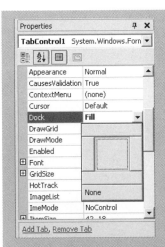

Figure 3-41: Dock property of the TabControl control

3   Click the **TabPages** property; then click the **ellipsis** following Collection to open the TabPage Collection Editor. Click **Add** seven times, adding seven tab pages to the TabPages Collection. Then click **TabPage1** in the Collection Editor, and set the **Text** property to **Hilda**. Similarly, set the **Text** property of TabPage2 to **Rick**, and set the **Text** property of TabPage3 to **Althea**. See Figure 3-42. Click **OK** to exit the TabPage Collection Editor.

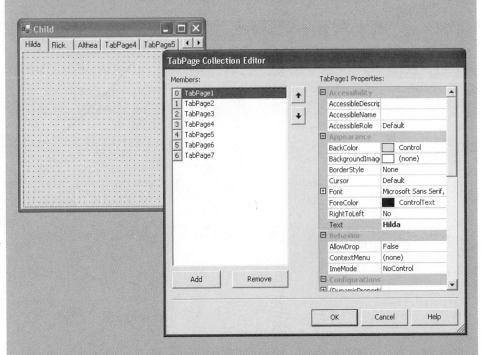

Figure 3-42: Tab control and TabPage Collection Editor

4   Scroll arrows appear on the right side of the tab control's tabs, as shown in Figure 3-43. To remove the scrollbar and display the tabs on multiple lines, click the tab control's **Multiline** property, and then change the property to **True**. Note now that the tab control's tabs are displayed on two lines, as shown in Figure 3-44.

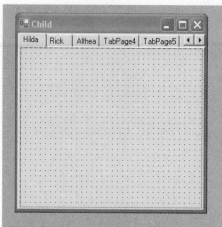

Figure 3-43: Tab control's tabs and scroll arrows (Multiline=False)

Figure 3-44: Tab control's tabs on two lines (Multiline=True)

5 Because seven tab pages are more than enough for SampleMDI, open the **TabPage Collection Editor** again, click **TabPage4**, and click the **Remove** button four times. You should end up with three tab pages. Click **OK**.

6 Run the **SampleMDI** program, enlarge the **MDI form**, and create three child forms. Click a different tab on each form, as shown in Figure 3-45.

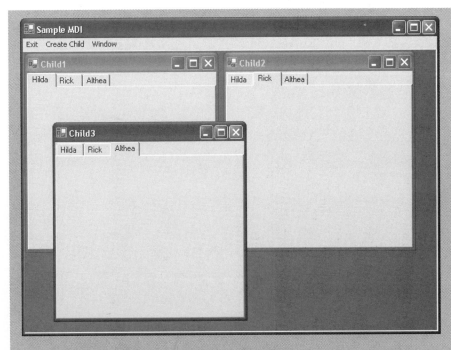

Figure 3-45: SampleMDI, running, with three child forms, each showing a different tab

7 Exit the program, and return to the IDE.

ComboBox Control

To experiment with the ComboBox control, you create a combo box regarding Hilda's pet schnauzer (everyone gets to guess the dog's name), and place this control on the Hilda tab of frmChild. In this case, you use the combo box to display each word of a sentence on a separate line.

To add a ComboBox control to SampleMDI:

1 In the Windows Form Designer for frmChild, drag a **ComboBox** control [icon] onto the form. (Make sure the Hilda tab is selected. Also make sure that TabPage1 is selected, rather than TabControl1.) To set the ComboBox's Text property to an empty string, delete the default value, **ComboBox1**. Change the Name property to **cboHildasDog**.

2 Click the **Items** property; then click the **ellipsis** following Collection to open the String Collection Editor. In the String Collection Editor, enter the following sentence fragment, one word per line: **The name of Hilda's dog is**. See Figure 3-46. Click **OK**.

Figure 3-46: String Collection Editor

3   Run the **SampleMDI** program, create a child form, and click the **list arrow** on the combo box. Note that the list contains the fragment, *The name of Hilda's dog is*, one word per line. Exit the program.

4   Drag a **Button** control [abl] onto frmChild. Set the Button's Name property to **btnDogName**, and the Text property to **Click to enter Hilda's schnauzer's name**. Resize the button to fit the text.

5   Double-click **btnDogName** to open the btnDogName_Click event procedure. Remember that the index of a combo box is base 0, so to select the index number of the last item in the list, you must enter the item count less 1. Enter the code shown in Figure 3-47.

```
Dim s As String = InputBox("Enter name")
cboHildasDog.Items.Add(s)
cboHildasDog.SelectedIndex = cboHildasDog.Items.Count − 1
```

Figure 3-47: Code for the btnDogName_Click() procedure

Note the ComboBox.Items.Add method, ComboBox.SelectedIndex property, and ComboBox.Items.Count property. Assigning a value to SelectedIndex causes the text portion of the combo box to be loaded with the item selected.

6   Run the **SampleMDI** program, create a child form, and click the button to give Hilda's dog a name. Then type the name **Fido**, click **OK**, and then click the **down arrow** in the combo box. SampleMDI should look similar to Figure 3-48.

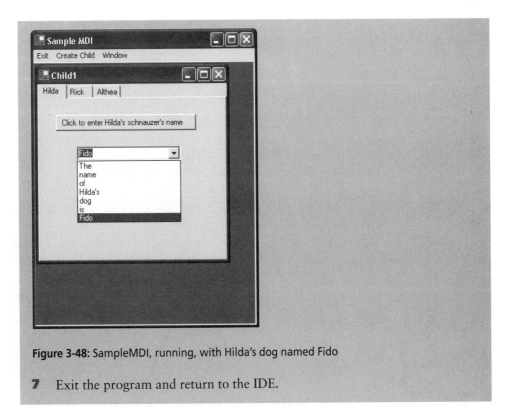

Figure 3-48: SampleMDI, running, with Hilda's dog named Fido

7   Exit the program and return to the IDE.

CheckBox Control

Your next experiment involves the CheckBox control. You place a series of check boxes on Rick's tab page of frmChild's tab control. Rick's pet interests are broader than Hilda's. He may own pet fish, a parrot, an alien rabbit, or a pet rock. He may own none, some, or all of these pets. A message box summarizes these interests.

To add a series of CheckBox controls to SampleMDI:

1   Drag a **CheckBox** control ☑ onto the Rick tab page of TabControl1 on frmChild. TabPage2 should appear at the top of the Properties window. Click the **Copy** button 📋 to copy CheckBox1 to the Clipboard. Click the **Rick TabPage**, and click the **Paste** button 📋 three times.

   NOTE: Copying and pasting a control was one method of creating a control array in Visual Basic 6.0, but Visual Basic .NET does not support control arrays. Therefore, when you paste them, they are assigned default names, which you can then modify.

2   Now you need to arrange the four check boxes. If necessary, open the Layout Toolbar by clicking **View | Toolbars | Layout**. Select the **controls**. Then click **Align Lefts**, which aligns the left side of the check boxes. On the Layout Toolbar, click **Make Vertical Spacing Equal**.

3   Change the Name and Text properties of the four CheckBox controls to what is shown in Figure 3-49.

Old name	New name	Text
CheckBox1	chkPetFish	Pet Fish
CheckBox2	chkParrot	Parrot
CheckBox3	chkAlienRabbit	Alien Rabbit
CheckBox4	chkPetRock	Pet Rock

Figure 3-49: Property settings for the CheckBox controls

4   Drag a **Button** control onto the right side of the tab page, and name it **btnRicksInterests**. Set its Text property to **Rick's Interests**. To make the text run vertically you need to make the control so narrow that that's the only way the software can render it. The completed tab page should appear similar to Figure 3-50.

Figure 3-50: Rick's completed tab page at design time

5   Double-click **btnRicksInterests** to open the Code Editor for the btnRicksInterests_Click event. Insert the code shown in Figure 3-51. Note how the Checked property of each CheckBox control must be examined, and any number of them (from 0 to 4) may be checked. The last If statement specifies the action to take if Rick is uninterested in any of the pet selections offered, and the alternate action to take if Rick expresses interest in one or more of those selections.

```
Dim s As String
If chkPetFish.Checked Then s = "   Pet Fish" & vbCrLf
If chkParrot.Checked Then s &= "   Parrot" & vbCrLf
If chkAlienRabbit.Checked Then s &= "   Alien Rabbit" & vbCrLf
If chkPetRock.Checked Then s &= "   Pet Rock"
If s = Nothing Then
  s = "Rick has no pet interests at all"
Else
  s = "Rick is interested in the following:" & vbCrLf & s
End If
MsgBox(s)
```

Figure 3-51: Code for btnRicksInterests_Click()

6 Run the **SampleMDI** program. Note that mdiMain must be enlarged to accommodate an entire child form. Stop the program, and adjust the **Width** and the **Height** properties (expanded from the **Size** property) of mdiMain so that a child form fits inside mdiMain without the appearance of scrollbars. You can experiment with this to get it right, or take a slightly more scientific approach. To make sure a child form fits inside its MdiParent at runtime, write down the child form's Width and Height properties. Then, look at the MDI form. The child form must fit inside the MDI form's client area, that is, the area beneath the MDI form's menu and inside its left, right, and bottom borders. Make the MDI form large enough to accommodate this.

7 Run the **SampleMDI** program again. Click the **Rick** tab, click any combination of Rick's possible pets (or none of them), and then click the **Rick's Interests** button. Output should appear similar to Figure 3-52, although you may need to alter the size of mdiMain and frmChild to make your program appear precisely as in Figure 3-52.

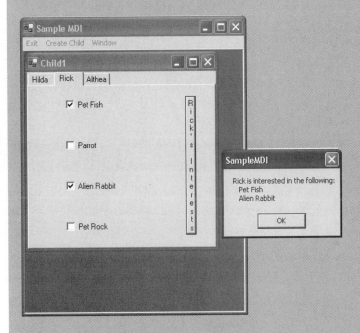

Figure 3-52: SampleMDI, running, showing Rick's tab page, some check boxes checked, and btnRicksInterests clicked, with enlarged mdiMain

GroupBox and RadioButton Controls

In this section, you experiment with the GroupBox and RadioButton controls by placing them on Althea's tab page. Althea's pet interests are every bit as eclectic as Rick's; however, Althea wants to have only one pet, and she has subdivided her choices among small indoor pets and large outdoor pets. When an indoor pet is selected, the outdoor choices are not visible, and vice versa. To support this requirement, you need three group boxes, with a set of RadioButton controls in each.

To add GroupBox and RadioButton controls to SampleMDI:

1 Drag three **GroupBox** controls onto the Althea tab page of TabControl1 of frmChild. Set their **Name, Text,** and **Visible** properties as shown in Figure 3-53.

Old name	New name	Text	Visible
GroupBox1	grpPetType	Indoor or Outdoor Pet?	True
GroupBox2	grpIndoor	Indoor Pets	False
GroupBox3	grpOutdoor	Outdoor Pets	False

Figure 3-53: Properties of the GroupBox controls

2 Draw (do not drag) **RadioButton** controls ⊙ inside each container. Specifically, you need two radio buttons inside grpPetType, three inside grpIndoor, and three inside grpOutdoor. Be careful when drawing each radio button—you must select the radio button from the Toolbox, then click and draw the control inside the group box. An alternate method is to select a RadioButton control you've already created, copy it to the Clipboard, click inside the group box, and then paste it into place.

3 Set the **Name** and **Text** properties of the radio buttons inside each group box as indicated in Figure 3-54.

Container	Name	Text
grpPetType	radIndoor	Indoor Pet
grpPetType	radOutdoor	Outdoor Pet
grpIndoor	radChihuahua	Chihuahua
grpIndoor	radCat	Siamese Cat
grpIndoor	radHampster	Hampster
grpOutdoor	radHusky	Husky
grpOudoor	radTiger	Bengal Tiger
grpOutdoor	radHorse	Race Horse

Figure 3-54: Properties of the RadioButton controls

4 Double-click **radIndoor** to open the Code Editor for the radIndoor_ CheckedChanged event, and insert the following code:
```
grpIndoor.Visible = True
grpOutdoor.Visible = False
```

5 Insert the analogous (but opposite) code for the radOutdoor_CheckedChanged event by double-clicking **radOutdoor** to open the Code Editor and then inserting the following code:
```
grpOutdoor.Visible = True
grpIndoor.Visible = False
```

NOTE: If the user clicks rad1, the rad1_CheckedChanged event fires. If the user then clicks rad2, the rad1_CheckedChanged event fires first, and then the rad2_CheckedChanged event fires. This code works because the radio button that gets clicked fires last. You need to be careful!

---

tip

If you double-click the RadioButton control in the Toolbox, the control is placed on the form, but it is not inside any group box. You can tell whether a RadioButton control (or any other control) is inside a group box or just floating on the form by moving the group box—controls that are inside the group box move along with it.

6 Run the **SampleMDI** program. Maximize the MDI form, and create three child forms, each opened to a different tab page. Your completed application should look similar to Figure 3-55.

7 Exit the program, and exit the **SampleMDI** application.

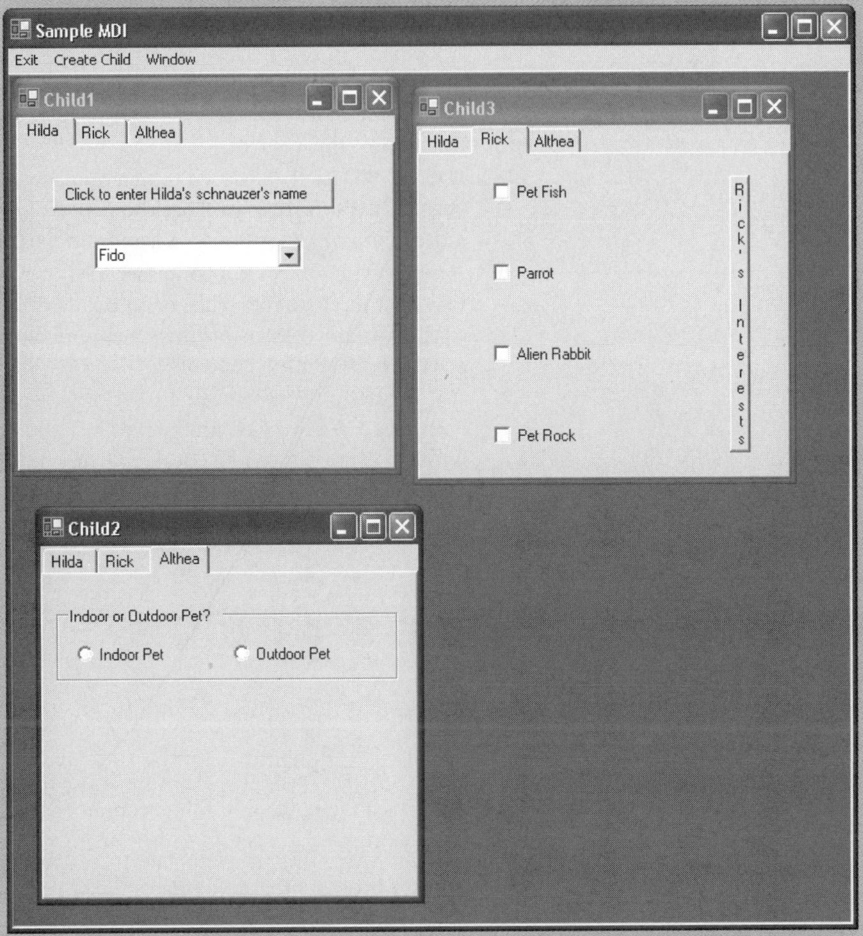

Figure 3-55: Completed SampleMDI running maximized

You now have completed Lesson B. You can stop now and take a break, but don't forget to complete the end-of-lesson questions and exercises before continuing with Lesson C.

S U M M A R Y

- The SampleMDI application demonstrates the features of a Multiple Document Interface application. At runtime, child forms can be instantiated as often as they are needed, yet all child windows are contained inside the parent MDI form, and the entire application can be moved, sized, and terminated as a unit.
- Child forms must be instantiated before they can be displayed using Show() or ShowDialog().

- The TextBox control has not changed materially from Visual Basic 6.0. It is still the principle graphical control for obtaining user input, and its default event is still the TextChanged event. One minor difference is that you must reference the Text property of the TextBox control in order to access it in code.
- A TabControl control is a container control specially designed to save screen real estate by allowing information to be displayed in overlapping tabs. Each tab in turn serves as a container for other controls. Tabs are defined in the TabControl's TabPages Collection.
- A ComboBox control combines the features of a text box and a list box. The text box portion may contain a value selected from the list box portion of the control or typed in by the user. The DropDownStyle property determines the runtime appearance and behavior of this control.
- A CheckBox control is used to determine or display whether a particular option has been selected. A series of CheckBox controls are independent of each other—that is, more than one check box in a group can be checked at the same time.
- A GroupBox control is a container for other controls. It is used to visually separate logical grouping of controls, or to treat a group of controls as a unit (making them all enabled/disabled or visible/invisible, for example). Often a GroupBox control contains a set of RadioButton controls.
- A RadioButton control, like a CheckBox control, determines whether an option has been selected. However, unlike the CheckBox control, only one RadioButton control within a container can be checked at any one time—that is, checking one RadioButton control automatically unchecks all other RadioButton controls within the same container. Radio buttons are therefore used to present options that are mutually exclusive.

QUESTIONS

1. Tab pages can be added to a tab control in the Form Designer by opening the _____.

2. To cause a tab control to fill its container, set its _____ property to _____.

3. The key property that determines the appearance of a ComboBox control is the _____.

4. At design time, items can be added to a ComboBox control by editing the _____.

5. At runtime, the index of the selected item in the list portion of a combo box is identified by the _____ property.

6. At runtime, the number of items in a combo box is given by the _____ property.

7. In Figure 3-48, Hilda's dog is named _____.

8. To create a list of mutually exclusive options inside a group box, use the _____ control.

9. To create a list of options, any number of which can be simultaneously checked, use the _____ control.

10. Container objects introduced in Tutorial 3 include the _____, _____, and _____.

11. When the ThreeState property of a CheckBox control is False, the CheckedState property can only be set to _____ in code.

CRITICAL THINKING

At the end of each lesson, reflective questions are intended to provoke you into considering the material you have just read at a deeper level.

1. Screen real estate can be conserved by using an MDI form plus child forms, or by using tab pages within a tab control. In SampleMDI, both of these techniques were employed. In what circumstances is one of these techniques preferable to the other?

2. For each the following scenarios, would you construct a set of radio buttons, or would you use a set of check boxes instead? Why?
    ■ Selecting the color when buying a new car
    ■ Signing up for extracurricular activities
    ■ Selecting your academic major
    ■ Ordering dessert at a restaurant

EXERCISES

1. Create a Windows Forms application that mimics the functionality of the MDI application described in Exercise 2 at the end of Lesson A by using a TabControl control with five tabs in lieu of the five child forms. Here are the revised specs: create a Windows Forms application with a tab control, docked to fill the form. Place five tab pages on the tab control to display the various services offered through the Student Union. One tab should display the names and e-mail addresses of six student social clubs. A second tab should display the four workshops offered by the Career Center—Resume Preparation, Interviewing, Career Expectations, and Job Hunting Strategies. A third tab should display the five recreational and physical fitness opportunities available through the Student Union. A fourth tab should display the names and hours of operation of the Student Union's eating facilities—all-day diner, sandwich shop, pizzeria, and night club. A fifth tab is an About tab that lists the name and phone number of the Student Union manager.

2. Create a Windows Forms application called Ticket Request. This application solicits information concerning ticket requests for the Friendsville Games Opening and Closing Ceremonies. Use a TabControl control, with these tab pages: 1) Customer name and address, 2) Opening Ceremonies tickets, 3) Closing Ceremonies tickets, and 4) Order Summary. Ticket categories include sky boxes ($1000), reserved box seats ($300), and unreserved grandstand ($150). The user can choose the number of tickets desired in each category. On the Opening and the Closing Ceremonies tab pages, the program should calculate the cost for each category (number of tickets * price), the total number of tickets, and the total cost. On the Order Summary tab page, the program should display the total number of tickets and total cost for Opening Ceremonies tickets, for Closing Ceremonies tickets, and for the sum of Opening plus Closing Ceremonies tickets. Include a $10 handling fee for each order, and the grand total cost of the order.

3. Enhance the Ticket Request application so that it produces a printout of the customer order. (Printing was covered in Tutorial 2.)

4. Create a Windows Forms application with a tab control that could be used for taking orders at the sandwich shops in the International Village. A sandwich order consists of a sandwich selection, a side-order selection, a drink selection, and either fruit or a cookie. The tab control has three tabs. The Sandwich tab (the left tab) lists the five sandwiches available (you can make up the names), using RadioButton controls. The user is expected to select one. The Extras tab (the middle tab) has three GroupBox controls, each of which contains a set of RadioButton controls. The first group box offers french fries,

cole slaw, or chips; the second group box offers milk, bottled water, or soda; and the third group box offers fruit or a cookie. The Order Summary tab (the right tab) contains a ListBox control that displays the user's selections. The ListBox control should be updated whenever the user makes any selection on either of the other two tabs. *Hint*: To update the list box, program the TabControl control's SelectedIndexChanged event.

5. Enhance the Sandwich Shop application in Exercise 4 by putting a button on the Order Summary tab that causes the user's selections (the contents of the list box) to be printed out.

6. Refer to Exercise 3 at the end of Lesson A and implement your design in Visual Basic .NET.

LESSON C

objectives

After completing this lesson, you will be able to:

- Develop a plan for the creation of a fairly complex MDI application
- Create a partially complete, working application

Planning and Building a More Complex MDI Application

Planning the LogonManagerDraft Windows Forms MDI Application

In the course of this tutorial, you have seen examples of all of the individual pieces that make up the LogonManager project. Before building the project, you should develop a plan or overall strategy for your efforts. The basic idea is to start with the big picture, and work your way down to the details, using stepwise refinement. You can start with a big picture presented from a functional standpoint, as in Figure 3-56. Next, each of the items in the list of functions becomes an element or task in a module-oriented hierarchy chart, which is often similar to the application's main menu. Such is the case in the LogonManager application. The stubbing technique allows you to test the partially complete program as you develop it.

Category	Specific function
New user	Apply for a user account
Existing user	Log on Update password
Supervisor	Log on Accept/reject new user requests Edit existing user information Display all users Perform file management functions
File management functions	Initialize Users file Back up Restore
Housekeeping details	Display an About form Exit the application

Figure 3-56: Functional organization of the LogonManager application

The following list outlines the overall plan for building LogonManager:

1. Design structUser, a structure for a record in the random-access Users file.
2. Define the public variables needed for manipulating a record in the Users file and for storing the entire Users file in an array.
3. Start the project and load the defined data structures into a module.
4. Build the MDI form and menu.
5. Program the File | Initialize menu item, which initializes the random-access Users file.
6. Create the mdiMain_Load procedure to load the Users file into an array at startup.
7. Write the menu Click event procedures, but use stubs for those menu items that will not be developed until Tutorial 4. Also insert stubs for the menu items that display the About form (frmAbout) and the New User form (frmUser), developed later in this tutorial. Test the overall logic.
8. Build two empty child forms (frmUser and frmAbout), and connect these to the MDI form by replacing the MDI stubs with calls to the child forms. Test the overall logic.
9. Complete the two child forms that are implemented in the draft application. Use stubs for the Logon functionality. Test the nearly completed application.

You tackle all nine of these tasks in Lesson C. You test and debug the application after completing each step.

Task 1. Designing the Format of the Users File

As the data designer, the question you must ask is, what information does the application sponsor (the Friendsville Organizing Committee) actually need to track concerning the users of its information systems? After much internal discussion, the FGDT, with Althea Brown in the lead, determined that the necessary data items are as follows:

- *Identification*—First and last name, e-mail address (used as the logon), password, home and work phone numbers
- *Status and role*—Active, inactive, new user, or supervisor role
- *Start date*—When the user was first authorized
- *Password expiration date*—Passwords must be changed every 90 days
- *Secret question and answer*—Used to recover a forgotten password

The data structure is declared in a standard module (a code block beginning with the Module statement) so that structUser is accessible throughout the namespace—if the declaration were in a form or component, the structure would only be available in the form or component in which it was declared. In LogonManager, structUser is needed in the MDI form and in the child forms. Althea's actual structure declaration appears in Figure 3-57, and requires a few more words of explanation. This includes the definition of each field, and a description of the possible values that each field may contain.

```
Public Structure structUser
  Public Status As Char
  Public Supervisor As Boolean
  <VBFixedString(25)> Public FirstName As String
  <VBFixedString(25)> Public LastName As String
  <VBFixedString(20)> Public WorkPhone As String
  <VBFixedString(20)> Public HomePhone As String
  <VBFixedString(15)> Public Role As String
  Public StartDate As Date
  <VBFixedString(35)> Public EmailAddress As String
  <VBFixedString(10)> Public Password As String
  Public PasswordExpirationDate As Date
  Public HasSecret As Boolean
  Public Question As Integer
  <VBFixedString(25)> Public Answer As String
End Structure
```

Figure 3-57: Declaration of Structure structUser

- The *Status* field contains three possible values: the value A is for an active record (whether a regular user or a system supervisor), the value I is for an inactive (that is, unused) record, and the value N is for the record of a new user whose application is pending (that is, not yet accepted or rejected by the supervisor).
- *Supervisor* is a Boolean field: when True, this record belongs to someone with supervisor privileges; when False, this is the record of a regular user.
- *<VBFixedString(field length)>* is the new method of declaring a fixed-length string within a structure. This attribute declaration must precede the variable declaration.
- The *Role* field categorizes each user as an employee, contractor, volunteer, visitor, or system supervisor. Selecting system supervisor causes the Supervisor field to be set to True.
- *PasswordExpirationDate* is a Date field. It is computed as 90 days after a new user is approved or an existing user's record is updated. (The exception is that the supervisor's password never expires.)
- *HasSecret* is a Boolean field: when True, the user has elected to designate a secret question and answer; when False, the user has declined to do so.
- *Question* is an integer that corresponds to the secret question selected by the user: 1= "What is your Mother's maiden name?" 2= "What town were you born in?" 3= "How many cousins do you have?" (0 means the user has elected not to have a secret question.)

Task 2. Defining Public Constants and Variables

Manipulating records in a random-access data file is easier if the maximum number of records is known. Because the entire Users file is loaded into an array, the array size should also be a given. (There are ways to program around these restrictions, but the implementation is cleaner and easier if you know the maximum number of users.)

The number of people who need access to FGDT-developed programs is rather small—perhaps 20 or at most 30. For this reason, the maximum number of users tracked by the system is set at 100. This number can be increased with a minor program modification.

The two public variables of type structUser are fairly typical for this kind of application. The first variable (pastructUser(MAXUSERS)) is an array that holds the entire Users file; the second (pstructUserRec) is a simple variable that holds one record. The program also needs a public variable to point to one record within the pastructUser() array; pintRecNum serves this purpose.

These four declarations appear in Figure 3-58. The declarations, like structUser itself, must appear in a standard module.

```
Public Const MAXUSERS = 100
Public pastructUser(MAXUSERS) As structUser
Public pstructUserRec As structUser
Public pintRecNum as Integer
```

Figure 3-58: Declarations of public constants and variables

Task 3. Creating a Partially Complete, Working Application

You now begin coding this application, starting with the standard module, the contents of which have already been created by Althea. This step involves creating a new project and putting Althea's code into a module in that project.

To begin the LogonManagerDraft application:

1 Start a new Windows Forms application named **LogonManagerDraft** in the Tut03 folder.

2 In Solution Explorer, right-click the project name, click **Add | Add Module**. In the Add New Item dialog box, name the module **Module1.vb**.

3 Click **File | Open | File**, and browse to locate **AltheasModule.txt** in the Tut03 folder. Select this item, and click **OK**. Copy the contents of **AltheasModule.txt** into Module1.vb. Close **AltheasModule.txt**.

4 Run the **LogonManagerDraft** program. It should not do anything at this point, but it should compile correctly, and then display an empty Form1. Exit the running application to return to the IDE.

Task 4. Building the MDI Form and Menu

This part of the project mimics the activities you performed when creating the SampleMDI application. If necessary, run the LogonManager application again to refresh your memory as to what the LogonManager's Main menu is supposed to look like. Then create the MDI form and the Main menu.

To create the MDI form and Main menu for LogonManagerDraft:

1 Display the Form Designer for Form1, and set the properties for Form1, as shown in Figure 3-59.

Property	Setting
Name	mdiMain
Text	Logon Manager [draft]
IsMdiContainer	True
StartPosition	CenterScreen
Size	328, 458
Icon	[your choice]

Figure 3-59: Form properties for Form1

tip

Remember the convention for naming menu items: the root-level item consists of the prefix "mnu" followed by the word(s) that appear as the root. In the present menu, the root entries are File, View, Window, and About.

2   Add a **MainMenu** control to mdiMain. Click **Type Here**. Type the menu item text values shown in the right column of Figure 3-60. To enter a separator bar, you can right-click and choose Insert Separator, or you can enter a hyphen in the Type Here box. Disable the menu items that are so identified in Figure 3-60. After all menu item text values have been entered, right-click any part of the Main menu, and click **Edit Names**. Then enter the menu item names shown in the left column of Figure 3-60.

Menu item Name properties	Menu item Text properties
mnuFile	&File
mnuFileInitialize	&Initialize [disabled; i.e., set the Enabled property to False]
mnuFileBackup	&Backup [disabled]
mnuFileRestore	&Restore [disabled]
mnuFileSep1	default name assigned by software
mnuFileExit	E&xit
mnuView	&View
mnuViewNewUser	&New User
mnuViewExistingUser	&Existing User
mnuViewSupervisor	&Supervisor
mnuViewSupervisorLogon	Logon
mnuViewSupervisorAcceptNewUsers	Accept New Users [disabled] [set the RadioCheck property to True]
mnuViewSupervisorEditUserInfo	Edit User Info [disabled]
mnuViewSupervisorViewAllUsers	View All Users [disabled]
mnuViewSupervisorResetExpirationDates	Reset Expiration Dates [disabled]
mnuWindow	&Window [set the MdiList property to True]
mnuWindowCascade	&Cascade
mnuAbout	&About

Figure 3-60: Menu item Name and Text properties

3   Set **mdiMain** as the **Startup object** for the LogonManagerDraft project. Then run the **LogonManagerDraft** application to see that your menu items appear as they should. If you are not sure that your menu items are correct, then run your application side by side with the LogonManager.exe program that has been provided to you, and compare.

Task 5. Initializing the Random-access Users File

At runtime, clicking File | Initialize creates the initial Users file, consisting of one active record for the system supervisor plus 99 inactive records. When the LogonManager application is completed, the file initialization procedure should be used only once, and only by the supervisor, because it wipes out all other existing records. For this reason, the File | Initialize menu selection is disabled at application startup, and is enabled when the supervisor logs on. For now, however, you need to be able to run this procedure during program development. Therefore, you must temporarily enable the menu selection.

The Users file is a random-access file. In Visual Basic .NET, a **random-access data file** has a fixed record length, specified as part of the FileOpen() function call. Each record in the file is identified by an integer record number. Thus, the computer can compute the precise disk location of any individual record by multiplying the record number minus one times the length of one record, and adding the product to the starting point of the file. So, for example, if the record length is 100 bytes, and if the file begins at location 500, then record number 2 begins at location 600, record number 3 at location 700, record number 4 at location 800, and so on. In the FileOpen() function call, you specify the fixed length of one record by using the Len() function, letting Visual Basic perform the record length calculation. After opening the Users file, you initialize one supervisor record and 99 inactive records.

To initialize the Users file:

1 In the Windows Form Designer for mdiMain, on the Main menu for the form itself, select **File | Initialize**, and set this menu item's Enabled property to **True**.

2 Double-click **File | Initialize**, which opens the mnuFileInitialize_Click() procedure. To open the Users file, insert the following code into mnuFileInitialize_Click():

```
FileOpen(1, "Users", OpenMode.Random, OpenAccess.Write, , _
    Len(pstructUserRec))
```

Parameters of the FileOpen() function for a random-access file include the file number (1 in this case), the name of the file, the open mode (Random for a random-access file), access permission (Read, Write, or ReadWrite), share status (Shared by default, and not specified in this case), and the length of one record. The record length here is being calculated by using the Len() function on the structure defined in the code module.

3 Continue coding the mnuFileInitialize_Click() procedure by adding the code shown in Figure 3-61 to create the first record in the Users file for the supervisor.

```
With pstructUserRec
   'initialize the supervisor record
   .Status = "A"c
   .Supervisor = True
   .Role = "System Supv"
   .EmailAddress = 1
   .Password = "SUPERVISOR"
   .PasswordExpirationDate = CDate ("1/1/9999")
   FilePut(1, pstructUserRec, 1)
```

Figure 3-61: Creating the supervisor's record

Note the use of the With construct, which avoids repetition of pstructUserRec as each element of the structure is referenced. (The With construct is terminated by the End With statement, which occurs later in the code.) In the setting of .Status, the *c* in "A"c forces the single character D to be treated as a Char rather than as a string. Obviously, the settings of the e-mail address and password are generic for this text and can be tailored to your own wishes. Also note the FilePut() function, which writes one record to a random-access file. Parameters of FilePut() include the file number, the data to be written to the file, and the record number where the data is written.

4 To create the other 99 inactive records, add the code shown in Figure 3-62 to mnuFileInitialize_Click(). This code also concludes the With...End With construct you initiated in the earlier step, closes the Users file, and confirms to the user that the file has been created.

```
  'initialize inactive records for all other users
  .Status = "I"c
  .Supervisor = False
  .Role = Nothing
  .EmailAddress = Nothing
  .Password = Nothing
  Dim i As Integer
  For i = 2 To MAXUSERS
    FilePut(1, pstructUserRec, i)
  Next
End With
FileClose(1)
MsgBox("File created")
```

Figure 3-62: Creating 99 inactive records

NOTE: With a random-access file, the preferred practice is to create all of the inactive records at the outset. In this way, you can be sure that the disk has room for the entire file. You also guarantee the most efficient processing by having all of the records stored in contiguous locations on disk.

5 To avoid an accident, even one perpetrated by the supervisor, the entire file initialization procedure needs to be prefaced by a positive confirmation that the user (that is, supervisor) really wants to invoke this procedure. One method of doing this is to set all of this code inside an If statement, incorporating a MessageBox() function call that asks the user to confirm his intentions. Add this If statement to your procedure, as shown in Figure 3-63. Remember to include the End If statement before the End Sub statement at the bottom of the procedure.

```
If MessageBox.Show("This action will wipe out any " _
    & "pre-existing file. Are you absolutely positively " _
    & "sure that you want to initialize " _
    & "the Users file?", "Initialization", _
    MessageBoxButtons.YesNo, MessageBoxIcon.Question) _
    = DialogResult.Yes Then
    'BODY OF PROCEDURE
End If
```

Figure 3-63: MessageBox() function call inside an If statement

6 Run the **LogonManagerDraft** program. Click **File | Initialize**. Confirm that you want to create the Users file. You receive the confirmation message, *File created*. Exit the running program.

7 In Notepad, open the **Users** file you just created. It is located in the bin folder. You can read the data items that are stored as ASCII characters. After the first record for the supervisor, only the status code I is visible. Close **Notepad**.

8 Back in the IDE, change the Enabled property of mnuFileInitialize to **False**. (Only the supervisor should be permitted to use this menu item.)

Because you have now built numerous applications in the Visual Studio .NET IDE, future step-by-step instructions will not be so detailed with respect to the menus and features of the IDE.

For purposes of building and testing the LogonManagerDraft application, you can use the Users file that you just created, or the Users file that you accessed when running LogonManager.exe at the beginning of this tutorial. The latter file (located in the VB.NET\Student\Tut03 folder) already contains active records for the members of the FGDT.

Task 6. Loading the Users File into an Array at Startup

At startup, the program should load the Users file into the pastructUsers() array, because this array is used by most of the procedures and child forms. Reading the Users file into the array is also needed when the file is restored or otherwise altered. Therefore, the ReadUsersFile() procedure should be placed in Module1, where any application element can call it.

To load the Users file into the pastructUsers() array:

1   In Solution Explorer, click **Module1**. Click the **View Code** 🔲 button.

2   Add the **ReadUsersFile()** procedure shown in Figure 3-64.

```
Public Sub ReadUsersFile()
  Dim i As Integer
  If System.IO.File.Exists("Users") Then
    FileOpen(1, "Users", OpenMode.Random, OpenAccess.Read,_
        OpenShare.Shared, Len(pstructUserRec))
    For i = 1 To MAXUSERS
      FileGet(1, pastructUser(i), i)
    Next
    FileClose(1)
  Else
    MsgBox("No users file")
  End If
End Sub
```

Figure 3-64: ReadUsersFile() procedure

As you can see, what the code for the ReadUsersFile() procedure does is fairly obvious: after checking to see that the file exists, the procedure opens a random-access file called Users, and reads each record of Users into an element of the pastructUser() array. Note that the syntax of the FileOpen method requires the length of one record as the final parameter when opening the random-access file, as was demonstrated previously. Note also that the FileGet() function retrieves one record from a random-access file. The parameters of FileGet() are the file number (assigned in the FileOpen() function), the destination of the data, and the record number to be retrieved from the file.

3   In the Form Designer for mdiMain, double-click mdiMain's **title bar** to open the mdiMain_Load() event procedure in the Code Editor. Enter the following single line of code, **ReadUsersFile()**, in the mdiMain_Load() procedure to call Sub ReadUsersFile() from Module1, that is, the procedure you just added to Module1.

4   Also add the same line, **ReadUsersFile( )**, as the last line in Sub mnuFileInitialize_Click(), because pastructUser() should be reloaded if the Users file has been reinitialized.

5   Run the **LogonManagerDraft** program to ensure that you have not introduced any syntax errors.

6   Exit the running program, and return to the IDE.

Task 7. Writing the Menu Click Event Procedures

Twelve menu Click event procedures remain to be written in mdiMain.vb (in addition to mnuFileInitialize_Click, already created in Step 3). Some functionality can be programmed directly in mdiMain; the rest of the features require child forms. In this task, you code the simple procedures, and insert stubs for the remainder, including both those developed later in this lesson and those left for Tutorial 4. The menu items with programmable Click events yet to be programmed are these:

- *In the File menu*—mnuFileBackup, mnuFileRestore, and mnuFileExit
- *In the View menu*—mnuViewNewUser, mnuViewExistingUser, mnuViewSupervisorLogon, mnuViewSupervisorAcceptNewUsers, mnuViewSupervisorEditUserInfo, mnuViewSupervisorViewAllUsers, and mnuViewSupervisorResetExpirationDates()
- *In the Window menu*—mnuWindowCascade
- *In the About menu*—mnuAbout

To code the Click events in mdiMain:

1   In the Code window for mdiMain, insert a stub for mnuFileBackup. To do this, double-click **Backup** under the File menu in mdiMain in the Designer. This opens the mnuFileBackup_Click() procedure in the Code Editor. Into this procedure, insert a statement that displays a message to the effect that this module will be developed later, such as the following:

```
MsgBox("This function is under construction", _
     MsgBoxStyle.Exclamation)
```

2   Repeat this procedure for creating a stub for each of the other menu events whose actual implementation is deferred until Tutorial 4—mnuFileRestore_ Click, mnuViewExistingUser_Click, mnuViewSupervisorEditUserInfo_Click, mnuViewSupervisorViewAllUsers_Click, and mnuViewSupervisorResetExpirationDates(). For each of these events, insert a message box indicating that the module is under construction.

NOTE: Remember that you can open the Click event procedure for a menu item either by double-clicking that item in the Form Designer, or by selecting the menu item name from the Class Name combo box in the Code window and then selecting the Click event from the Method Name combo box.

3   The mnuFileExit_Click() event procedure simply ends processing. In this case, you use the End statement rather than discovering all of the instances of open child forms and calling the Dispose method for each. Type **End** into this procedure.

4   The mnuWindowCascade_Click() event procedure arranges open child forms in overlapping windows, as you saw earlier in SampleMDI. Insert the following statement into this procedure:

```
Me.LayoutMdi(System.Windows.Forms.MdiLayout.Cascade)
```

5 The mnuAbout_Click() event procedure displays an About form, yet to be developed. For the moment, just insert this message box statement as a stub:

```
MsgBox("Show an About form")
```

6 The mnuViewNewUser_Click() event procedure displays a child form to collect data concerning a new user, provided that adding another user does not exceed MAXUSERS. At this time, you use a stub to represent the functionality of the child form, but checking for an inactive record can be programmed immediately. Type the code shown in Figure 3-65.

```
Dim i As Integer = 1
Do Until i > MAXUSERS OrElse pastructUser(i).Status = "I"
  i += 1
Loop
If i > MAXUSERS Then
  Dim s As String
  s = "A new user cannot be added at this time (MAXUSERS reached)."
  s &= vbCrLf & "Please notify the system SUPERVISOR!"
  MessageBox.Show(s)
  Exit Sub
End If
```

Figure 3-65: Testing for MAXUSERS

7 Notice the short-circuit OrElse in Figure 3-65: If i > MAXUSERS. You do not want to reference pastructUser(i), because the subscript would be out of range. After this code, insert the following statement in a message box stub: **User form will be displayed to collect info about a New User.**

8 The mnuViewSupervisorLogon_Click() event procedure calls the Logon application (to be developed in Tutorial 4). The Logon program asks the user to provide a logon and password, and also verifies the user's status as a supervisor or a regular user. If the logon is successful, and if the user has supervisor privileges, this procedure goes on to enable all of the initially disabled supervisor functions. For the present, you need to insert a message box statement that explains the future call to Logon, and then you need to enable the supervisor functions. To do this, insert the code shown in Figure 3-66.

```
Private Sub mnuViewSupervisorLogon_Click(ByVal sender As System.Object, _
   ByVal e As System.EventArgs) Handles mnuViewSupervisorLogon.Click
  MsgBox("Supervisor logon should be called here, but the Logon program " _
    & "is under construction. If the supervisor logon is successful, " _
    & "all supervisor functions are enabled. " _
    & "If not successful, an error message is displayed. " _
    & "For the draft LogonManager application, a successful logon is " _
    & "assumed, and all supervisor functions are enabled.")
  mnuFileInitialize.Enabled = True
  mnuFileBackup.Enabled = True
  mnuFileRestore.Enabled = True
  mnuViewSupervisorAcceptNewUsers.Enabled = True
  mnuViewSupervisorEditUserInfo.Enabled = True
  mnuViewSupervisorViewAllUsers.Enabled = True
  mnuViewSupervisorResetExpirationDates.Enabled = True
End Sub
```

Figure 3-66: mnuViewSupervisorLogon_Click() procedure

9 The mnuViewSupervisorAcceptNewUsers_Click() event procedure calls the same User form as mnuViewNewUser_Click(), provided that at least one new user's request is pending. Once again, even though the child form does not yet exist, you can program the search of the pastructUser array to locate a new user record (a record whose Status field = N). Incorporate a stub to represent the display of a child form. To do this, insert the code shown in Figure 3-67 into mnuViewSupervisorAcceptNewUsers_Click().

```
Dim i As Integer = 1
Do Until i > MAXUSERS OrElse pastructUser(i).Status = "N"
  i += 1
Loop
If i > MAXUSERS Then
  MsgBox("No new user requests are pending")
Else
  MsgBox("Display child form")
End If
```

Figure 3-67: mnuViewSupervisorAcceptNewUsers_Click() procedure

10 Test the **LogonManagerDraft** application. Check every menu selection, and then click **File | Exit**.

Task 8. Building Empty Child Forms

The LogonManagerDraft application in this lesson requires two child forms:

■ frmAbout.vb, activated by mnuAbout_Click()
■ frmUser.vb, activated by mnuViewNewUser_Click() and by mnuViewSupervisorAcceptNewUsers_Click()

   NOTE: In Tutorial 4, frmUser.vb will also be activated by mnuViewExistingUser_Click() and by mnuViewSupervisorEditUserInfo_Click(). Also in Tutorial 4, frmViewAll.vb will be activated by mnuViewSupervisorViewAllUsers_Click().

   Your task is to create empty child forms (that is, the GUI without its implementing code), set child form properties, add controls to the child forms, and attach the child forms to the parent, mdiMain.

Create frmAbout.vb
This form provides identification information concerning the Logon Manager application.

To create the About form:

1 Add a **new form** to the LogonManagerDraft project, named **frmAbout.vb**.

2 Set the Text and BackColor properties to **About Logon Manager** and **light yellow** respectively.

3 Add the two **labels** $\boxed{\text{A}}$ as shown in Figure 3-68, and set their size and text properties to match the figure. Add a **PictureBox** control, positioned as shown. Set the Image property to the **sailboat** icon (or another icon of your choosing). The sailboat is located wherever Visual Studio .NET is installed on your computer, in the Microsoft Visual Studio .NET\Common7\Graphics\icons\ Misc folder under the name Misc32.ico.

Figure 3-68: frmAbout in the Form Designer

4   In mdiMain.vb, in the mnuAbout_Click procedure, remove the message box stub you created earlier, and instantiate a New frmAbout. Declare mdiMain (that is, Me) as the MdiParent of the child form, and then display the form. To do this, delete the **MsgBox** you put there before, and insert the code shown in Figure 3-69 instead. The three statements in this procedure are the model for displaying a child form in any MDI application.

```
Dim frmAboutTemp As New frmAbout()
frmAboutTemp.MdiParent = Me
frmAboutTemp.Show()
```

Figure 3-69: mnuAbout_Click() procedure

5   Run the **LogonManagerDraft** application, and to test the About menu item, click the **About** item several times, and then click **Window | Cascade**. Your screen should appear similar to Figure 3-70.

Figure 3-70: Cascading copies of the About form

Create frmUser

The frmUser child form encompasses the core of the LogonManagerDraft application, including more than 40 controls and various property settings for each. Create the GUI and assign properties suggested by Figures 3-71, 3-72, and 3-73. Always name those controls that are referenced in code—in this case, carefully follow the control naming scheme spelled out here. Size and align the controls for a neat, clean appearance. Take your time, and in about an hour, you will have a very nice looking and usable GUI.

tip

If you forget to rename Form1.vb before creating it, then remember to rename both the form file to frmUser.vb in Solution Explorer and the form's Name property to frmUser when the form is open in the Form Designer.

To create the User form:

1 Add a **new form** to the LogonManagerDraft project with the filename **frmUser.vb**. Size **frmUser** to fit in the user area of mdiMain, that is, the area under the toolbar. Set the WindowState property to **Maximized**.

2 Add a **TabControl** control to frmUser, and set its Dock property to **Fill**. Allow the default object name, **TabControl1**, to stand. Add three **tab pages** to the TabPages Collection of TabControl1, named **tabNamePhone**, **tabLogon**, and **tabSecret**. Change the Text properties of the three tab pages.

NOTE: Type the names of controls precisely as indicated here. While you are implementing the graphical design, Hilda is writing the code behind it. Later on, the code segments she is writing will execute correctly only if the object names on your frmUser match the object references in her code.

3 Add three **Button** controls to tabNamePhone as shown in Figure 3-71. Using the naming conventions you learned about earlier in this tutorial, name the three Button controls at the top, **btnAccept**, **btnDelete**, and **btnReject**. These buttons should not be initially visible; their **Visible** property will be set to **True** when the menu item View | Supervisor | Accept New Users is selected. Add four text boxes and one combo box and name these five user-editable fields: **txtFName**, **txtLName**, **txtWorkPhone**, **txtHomePhone**, and **cboRole**. Also add a **text box** for the date called **txtDate**. Set this control's ReadOnly property to **True** so the user cannot edit it. You also need to name the label in front of txtDate, because the words Application Date will need to be changed to Start Date in Tutorial 4. Name this label **lblDate**. Finally, add and name the three buttons at the bottom **btnBack1** (disabled), **btnCancel1**, and **btnNext1**. Add all the labels indicated in Figure 3-71, and set the Text properties of all the buttons as indicated.

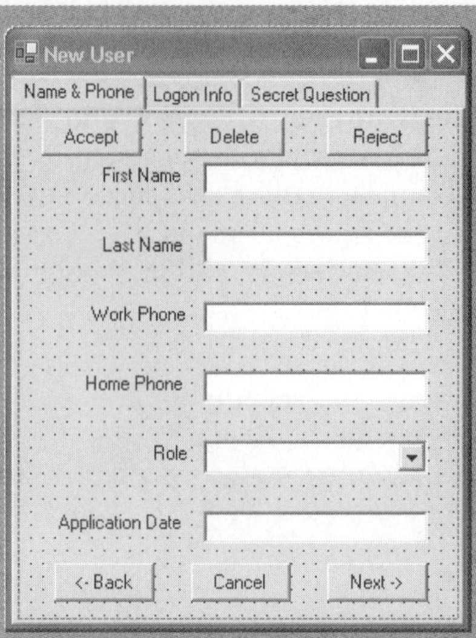

Figure 3-71: tabNamePhone

4   Add the necessary controls to tabLogon as shown in Figure 3-72. Insert the message at the top of the tab page using a label, with the text, **Your e-mail address will be your user logon ID and will also be used to communicate with you.** Name the user-editable fields as follows: **txtEmail, txtPassword, txtConfirm,** and **txtPasswordExpirationDate.** Name the three buttons at the bottom **btnBack2, btnCancel2,** and **btnNext2.** Set the PasswordChar property of txtPassword and txtConfirm to an asterisk (*). Set the ReadOnly property of txtPasswordExpirationDate to **True.** Add all the labels indicated in Figure 3-72, and set the Text properties of all the buttons as indicated.

Figure 3-72: tabLogon

5   Add controls to tabSecret as shown in Figure 3-73. Disable the **GroupBox** control (named grpQuestion). (It is enabled during execution if the user decides to register a secret question.) Use these names for the user-editable controls: **chkSecret** (for the CheckBox control); **radMom, radBirthTown,** and **radCousins** (for the three RadioButton controls); **txtAnswer;** and **btnBack3,**

btnCancel3, and **btnSubmit** (for the three Button controls at the bottom). Set the Text properties of the button controls as indicated in the figure.

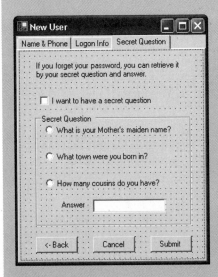

Figure 3-73: tabSecret

6 Run the **LogonManagerDraft** application, and examine your GUI carefully. Make sure that you have included all of the controls, and that each control has been named in accordance with the instructions given.

Next you attach an instance of frmUser to mdiMain in the two places where it is needed in the LogonManagerDraft application, replacing the message box stub inserted there earlier. In each case, the child form's Text property must be assigned, and several other properties also need to be tailored to the specific use of the form. The pintRecNum property identifies the particular user record to be displayed. For a new user, pintRecNum is set to 0. For the Accept New Users menu selection, pintRecNum must be set to the record number of a new user whose application to become a user is pending. Initially, of course, no such new user's record exists. Therefore, to see that the form displays correctly, you temporarily set pintRecNum to 1, the record of the supervisor (the only active record in the Users file after it has been initialized). For both of these procedures, the code has been provided for you in the next two steps and accompanying figures. Examine it carefully, so that you are sure you understand how it works.

7 In mnuViewNewUser_Click(), insert the code shown in Figure 3-74.

```
pintRecNum = 0
Dim frmUserTemp As New frmUser()
frmUserTemp.MdiParent = Me
frmUserTemp.Text = "New User"
frmUserTemp.Show()
```

Figure 3-74: mnuViewNewUser_Click() procedure

8 Replace **mnuViewSupervisorAcceptNewUsers_Click()** with the code shown in Figure 3-75. Note that If and End If are temporarily commented out, and pintRecNum is temporarily set to 1, because you want the code to display the supervisor's record as if this were a new user.

temporarily commented out

temporarily set to 1

temporarily commented out

```
Private Sub mnuViewSupervisorAcceptNewUsers_Click(ByVal _
    sender As System.Object, ByVal e As System.EventArgs) _
    Handles mnuViewSupervisorAcceptNewUsers.Click
    Dim i As Integer = 1
    Do Until i > MAXUSERS OrElse pastructUser(i).Status = "N"
        i += 1
    Loop
    'If Not (i > MAXUSERS) Then
    pintRecNum = 1
    Dim frmUserTemp As New frmUser()
    frmUserTemp.Text = "Supervisor - Accept New User"
    frmUserTemp.MdiParent = Me
    frmUserTemp.btnAccept.Visible = True
    frmUserTemp.btnReject.Visible = True
    frmUserTemp.btnSubmit.Visible = False
    frmUserTemp.Show()
    'End If
End Sub
```

Figure 3-75: mnuViewSupervisorAcceptNewUsers_Click() procedure

9 Run the **LogonManagerDraft** program. Initialize the **Users** file, then click **View | New User** to display frmUser with the appropriate properties. The code behind the GUI has not yet been written, so exit the running program.

10 Run the program again. Click **View | Supervisor | Logon** to obtain supervisor privileges. Then click **View | Supervisor | Accept New Users** to display frmUser with the properties appropriate for this function. (Until the code behind the GUI is written, only the supervisor's record is displayed.) Exit the running program to return to the IDE.

11 Return to the **mnuViewSupervisorAcceptNewUsers_Click()** procedure. Remove the **apostrophe** on the If and End If statements. (This causes the action statements inside the If statement to automatically indent.) Also change the statement just after the If statement to **pintRecNum = i** (the record number of a New User) rather than 1 (the record number of the supervisor).

Task 9. Completing the Child Forms

While you were working on various other portions of the LogonManagerDraft application, Hilda was drafting the code portion of frmUser, and now it is nearly complete—you can paste her code into your program, and then desk check it (that is, step through the code by hand) so that you understand it and to ensure that it does what you want it to do. The frmAbout child form requires no code at all.

frmUser's code

In this section, you first copy the code that Hilda wrote for frmUser. Then you examine each of the procedures in frmUser to make sure that you understand it.

To copy Hilda's code into your form:

1 Insert Hilda's draft code into your frmUser by clicking the **Open File** button 📂 on the toolbar, and opening **Hilda.txt**. Copy the **Hilda.txt code** into the Code Editor for frmUser.vb, right after the Windows Form Designer generated code and before the End Class statement.

Now examine each of the procedures in Hilda's code.

frmUser_Load() This procedure loads the appropriate values into the controls on the form, and then displays the form. If the form is activated for a new user request, just a few items need to be initialized. If the form is activated to accept a new user or edit an existing user, all fields need to be copied from the pastructUser array. Refer to Figure 3-76.

NOTE: Throughout these procedures, the names of the graphical objects that you placed on the form must match the object references in Hilda's code.

```
01   Private Sub frmUser_Load(ByVal sender As System.Object, _
02       ByVal e As System.EventArgs) Handles MyBase.Load
03     cboRole.Items.Add("Employee")
04     cboRole.Items.Add("Contractor")
05     cboRole.Items.Add("Volunteer")
06     cboRole.Items.Add("Visitor")
07     txtPasswordExpirationDate.Text = _
08       DateAdd(DateInterval.Day, 90, Today)
09     If pintRecNum = 0 Then 'new user
10       cboRole.Items.Add("System Supv")
11       cboRole.Text = cboRole.Items(0)
12       txtDate.Text = DateString
13     Else
14       With pastructUser(pintRecNum)
15         txtFName.Text = Trim(.FirstName)
16         txtLName.Text = Trim(.LastName)
17         txtWorkPhone.Text = Trim(.WorkPhone)
18         txtHomePhone.Text = Trim(.HomePhone)
19         If .Supervisor = True Then cboRole.Items.Add("System Supv")
20         Select Case Trim(.Role)
21           Case "Employee" : cboRole.Text = cboRole.Items(0)
22           Case "Contractor" : cboRole.Text = cboRole.Items(1)
23           Case "Volunteer" : cboRole.Text = cboRole.Items(2)
24           Case "Visitor" : cboRole.Text = cboRole.Items(3)
25           Case "System Supv" : cboRole.Text = cboRole.Items(4)
26         End Select
27         txtDate.Text = .StartDate.ToString
28         lblDate.Text = "Start Date"
29         txtEmail.Text = Trim(.EmailAddress)
30         txtPassword.Text = Trim(.Password)
31         txtConfirm.Text = Trim(.Password)
32         chkSecret.Checked = .HasSecret
33         Select Case .Question
34           Case 1 : radMom.Checked = True
35           Case 2 : radBirthTown.Checked = True
36           Case 3 : radCousins.Checked = True
37         End Select
38         txtAnswer.Text = Trim(.Answer)
39       End With
40     End If
41     Me.Show()
42     txtFName.Focus()
43   End Sub
```

Figure 3-76: frmUser_Load() procedure

The following is a discussion of the various lines shown in Figure 3-76 (line numbers in this discussion refer to the line numbers in the figure):

■ *Lines 3–6*—The cboRole combo box is loaded with the roles that always appear: Employee, Contractor, Volunteer, and Visitor. Of course, you could load these strings into cboRole in the Designer as well, but this demonstrates how it can be done in code.

- *Lines 7–8*—The password expiration date is set to 90 days from today. Note the use of the DateAdd() function to perform this calculation. The DateAdd() function has three arguments: the interval or unit of time, the number of units to be added, and the date object to which these units are to be added. DateAdd() calculates and returns the sum. (If the syntax of the DateAdd() function does not appear obvious, click DateAdd(), and press F1. Visual Studio .NET's Dynamic Help gives you additional information.)
- *Lines 9–40*—An If...Else statement tailors the form either for a new (empty) user record or for an existing record.
  - *Lines 10–12*—For a new record (`pintRecNum = 0`), the role of System Supv is added to cboRole, the default for cboRole is set to Employee (Item 0), and today's date (DateString, a built-in function) is assigned to txtDate.
  - *Lines 14–39*—For an existing record (`pintRecNum > 0`), data values are copied from pastructUser(pintRecNum) to the user-editable fields in frmUser. In several cases, data values must be trimmed, converted to strings, or decoded.
  - *Lines 20–26 and 33–37*—Select Case blocks are used to set the selection in the combo box to the appropriate role, and to select the appropriate radio button based on the value of Question.
- *Lines 41–42*—Line 41 shows the form itself, so that Line 42, setting focus to txtFName, is executed after the form has been materialized.

To see the effect of lines 41 and 42, temporarily comment them out. Then when you run the program and click View | New User, the blinking insertion point does not appear.

chkSecret_CheckedChanged Whenever the value of chkSecret changes (because the user checks or unchecks it), the grpQuestion group box should be enabled or disabled accordingly. See Figure 3-77.

```
Private Sub chkSecret_CheckedChanged(ByVal sender As System.Object, _
   ByVal e As System.EventArgs) Handles chkSecret.CheckedChanged
  If chkSecret.Checked Then
    grpQuestion.Enabled = True
  Else
    grpQuestion.Enabled = False
  End If
End Sub
```

Figure 3-77: chkSecret_CheckedChanged() procedure

btnCancel1_Click() Note that this procedure, shown in Figure 3-78, handles btnCancel1.Click, btnCancel2.Click, and btnCancel3.Click. When the user clicks any of these three Cancel buttons, this procedure closes the form without saving the user record.

```
Private Sub btnCancel1_Click(ByVal sender As System.Object, _
   ByVal e As System.EventArgs) _
   Handles btnCancel1.Click, btnCancel2.Click, btnCancel3.Click
  Me.Dispose()
End Sub
```

Figure 3-78: btnCancel1_Click() procedure

btnNext1_Click(), btnNext2_Click(), btnBack2_Click(), and btnBack3_Click() These navigation buttons bring the next or the previous tab page into the foreground by setting the SelectedTab property of the appropriate tab page. See Figure 3-79.

```
Private Sub btnNext1_Click(ByVal sender As System.Object, _
    ByVal e As System.EventArgs) Handles btnNext1.Click
  TabControl1.SelectedTab = tabLogon
End Sub

Private Sub btnNext2_Click(ByVal sender As System.Object, _
    ByVal e As System.EventArgs) Handles btnNext2.Click
  TabControl1.SelectedTab = tabSecret
End Sub

Private Sub btnBack2_Click(ByVal sender As System.Object, _
    ByVal e As System.EventArgs) Handles btnBack2.Click
  TabControl1.SelectedTab = tabNamePhone
End Sub

Private Sub btnBack3_Click(ByVal sender As System.Object, _
    ByVal e As System.EventArgs) Handles btnBack3.Click
  TabControl1.SelectedTab = tabLogon
End Sub
```

Figure 3-79: Navigation button Click event procedures

btnSubmit_Click() This fairly lengthy procedure validates each user-provided entry, and notifies the user of any entry that does not pass muster. If all entries pass the edit checks, the SaveRecord() procedure is called. The following list discusses the line numbers shown in Figure 3-80.

- *Lines 3–4*—The user-editable fields are validated. Two variables assist in this process: "s" is a string that holds an error message, and blnFormComplete is a Boolean, initially set to True. As each field is examined, if something is amiss, an error message is appended to "s," and blnFormComplete is set to False.
- *Lines 5–12*—First name and last name are required fields.
- *Lines 13–16*—An entry is required in at least one of the phone number fields.
- *Lines 17–25*—E-mail address and password are required.
- *Lines 26–33*—The password must be from 7 to 10 characters long.
- *Lines 34–41*—txtPassword and txtConfirm must match exactly. Note the use of the String.Compare() function. This function has three arguments: the two strings being compared, and IgnoreCase as a Boolean. In comparing the password and confirmation, you do not want to ignore case, so the third argument is set to False. The String.Compare() function returns –1 if the first string is less than the second, 0 if the two strings are equal, and +1 if the first string is greater than the second. In this case, the user input is acceptable only if the return value is 0, that is, txtPassword and txtConfirm are equal.
- *Lines 42–46*—After all of the validation is done, if blnComplete is True, processing continues with the SaveRecord() procedure; otherwise, the error message is displayed.

```
01  Private Sub btnSubmit_Click(ByVal sender As System.Object, _
02      ByVal e As System.EventArgs) Handles btnSubmit.Click
03    Dim blnFormComplete As Boolean = True
04    Dim s As String = Nothing
05    If txtFName.Text = Nothing Then
06      blnFormComplete = False
07      s &= "Please fill in the.First Name field."
08    End If
09    If txtLName.Text = Nothing Then
10      blnFormComplete = False
11      s &= vbCrLf & "Please fill in the Last Name field."
12    End If
13    If txtWorkPhone.Text = Nothing And txtHomePhone.Text = Nothing Then
14      blnFormComplete = False
15      s &= vbCrLf & "Please fill in at least one phone number field."
16    End If
17    If txtEmail.Text = Nothing Then
18      blnFormComplete = False
19      s &= vbCrLf & "Please fill in your e-mail address " & _
20        " (used as your logon in this system)."
21    End If
22    If txtPassword.Text = Nothing Then
23      blnFormComplete = False
24      s &= vbCrLf & "Please fill in your password (case sensitive)."
25    End If
26    If Len(txtPassword.Text) < 7 Then
27      blnFormComplete = False
28      s &= vbCrLf & "Password must be at least 7 characters long."
29    End If
30    If Len(txtPassword.Text) > 10 Then
31      blnFormComplete = False
32      s &= vbCrLf & "Password cannot be more than 10 characters long."
33    End If
34    If String.Compare(txtPassword.Text, txtConfirm.Text, False) _
35        <> 0 Then
36      blnFormComplete = False
37      s &= vbCrLf & _
38        "Password and Confirm Password fields do not match."
39      txtPassword.Text = Nothing
40      txtConfirm.Text = Nothing
41    End If
42    If blnFormComplete Then
43      SaveRecord()
44    Else
45      MsgBox(s)
46    End If
47  End Sub
```

Figure 3-80: btnSubmit_Click() procedure

SaveRecord() When changes to a user record have been validated, the user record is copied into the pastructUser array. Then, the WriteUsersFile() procedure is called, after which Me.Dispose() closes the form. The following list discusses the line numbers shown in Figure 3-81.

```
01   Private Sub SaveRecord()
02     Dim i As Integer = 1
03     If pintRecNum = 0 Then 'new user
04       Do Until pastructUser(i).Status = "I"
05         i += 1
06       Loop
07     Else 'existing user
08       i = pintRecNum
09     End If
10     With pastructUser(i)
11       If pintRecNum = 0 Then
12         .Status = "N"
13         .Supervisor = IIf(cboRole.Text = "System Supv", True, False)
14       End If
15       .FirstName = txtFName.Text
16       .LastName = txtLName.Text
17       .WorkPhone = txtWorkPhone.Text
18       .HomePhone = txtHomePhone.Text
19       .Role = cboRole.Text
20       .StartDate = CDate(txtDate.Text)
21       .EmailAddress = txtEmail.Text
22       .Password = txtPassword.Text
23       .PasswordExpirationDate = CDate(txtPasswordExpirationDate.Text)
24       .HasSecret = chkSecret.Checked
25       If radMom.Checked Then .Question = 1
26       If radBirthTown.Checked Then .Question = 2
27       If radCousins.Checked Then .Question = 3
28       .Answer = txtAnswer.Text
29     End With
30     WriteUsersFile()
31     Me.Dispose()
32   End Sub
```

Figure 3-81: SaveRecord() procedure

- *Lines 2–9*—To point to a record within pastructUser, *i* is declared:
  - If this is a new record (pintRecNum = 0), the array is searched for a place to put the record, and *i* points to the first inactive record found in the array.
  - Otherwise, *i* is assigned the value of the pintRecNum, which points to the existing record
- *Lines 11–14*—If this is a new record, .Status is set to *N* and .Supervisor is assigned. Note the use of the Immediate If.
- *Lines 15–28*—Values are copied from the frmUser controls to the corresponding elements in pastructUser(i).
- *Line 30*—The WriteUsersFile() function, which writes the array back to the file, is called.
- *Line 31*—The form is closed.

btnAccept_Click() The supervisor accepts a new user by clicking btnAccept. Refer to Figure 3-82. The following list discusses the lines of code shown in Figure 3-82.

```
Private Sub btnAccept_Click(ByVal sender As System.Object, _
    ByVal e As System.EventArgs) Handles btnAccept.Click
  pastructUser(pintRecNum).Status = "A"
  WriteUsersFile()
  MsgBox("Send an e-mail to " & txtEmail.Text & _
    " stating that the user application has been accepted")
  Me.Dispose()
End Sub
```

Figure 3-82: btnAccept_Click() procedure

- .Status in pastructUser(pintRecNum) is changed from *N* (new record) to *A* (active record).
- The array is written back to the file using WriteUsersFile().
- A message reminding the supervisor to e-mail the user is displayed.
- The form is closed.

btnReject_Click() and btnDelete_Click()   The supervisor can reject a new user by clicking btnReject, and the supervisor can delete an existing user by clicking btnDelete. These two brief procedures are displayed in Figure 3-83 and discussed in the following list.

```
Private Sub btnReject_Click(ByVal sender As System.Object, _
    ByVal e As System.EventArgs) Handles btnReject.Click
  pastructUser(pintRecNum).Status = "I"
  WriteUsersFile()
  MsgBox("Send an e-mail to " & txtEmail.Text & _
    " stating that the user application has been rejected")
  Me.Dispose()
End Sub

Private Sub btnDelete_Click(ByVal sender As System.Object, _
    ByVal e As System.EventArgs) Handles btnDelete.Click
  pastructUser(pintRecNum).Status = "I"
  WriteUsersFile()
  MsgBox("Send an e-mail to " & txtEmail.Text & _
    " stating that the user has been deleted")
  Me.Dispose()
End Sub
```

Figure 3-83: Reject and Delete procedures

- .Status in pastructUser(pintRecNum) is changed from *N* (new record) or *A* (active record) to *i* (inactive record).
- The array is written back to the file.
- The form is closed.

WriteUsersFile()   The WriteUsersFile() procedure opens the Users file in Write mode. Using a For loop, it then writes each record in pastructUser() to the Users file. This procedure is displayed in Figure 3-84.

```
Private Sub WriteUsersFile()
  FileOpen(1, "Users", OpenMode.Random, OpenAccess.Write, , _
    Len(pstructUserRec))
  Dim i As Integer
  For i = 1 To MAXUSERS
    FilePut(1, pastructUser(i), i)
  Next
  FileClose(1)
End Sub
```

Figure 3-84: WriteUsersFile() procedure

Test the LogonManagerDraft Application

A programming task is never complete until you test it. You now run the application to ensure that everything in the LogonManagerDraft application that is supposed to work does so.

To test the LogonManagerDraft application:

1 Run the **LogonManagerDraft** application.

2 If you assigned any object names or variable names that differ from those Hilda employed, you will have Name not declared syntax errors to resolve. In this case, examine any syntax errors, checking the object names and variable names in your form. If necessary, modify your object and variable names so they match those referenced in Hilda's code, and test again.

3 Select **View | New User**, and insert yourself as a new user. After filling in the required data, click **Submit**.

4 Log on as **supervisor**, click **View | Supervisor | Accept New Users**, and accept your own pending New User request.

5 Again, test every other menu item. Many of them are still under construction or are only partially functional, and will be completed in Tutorial 4.

6 Exit the **LogonManagerDraft** application, and then exit **Visual Basic .NET**.

You now have completed Tutorial 3. Stop now for a break, or continue with the exercises.

SUMMARY

■ A Visual Basic .NET random-access data file contains fixed-length records, randomly accessible through a sequential record number. For IO operations, fixed-size elements can be created with the <VBFixedString()> attribute in the element declaration. For random-access files, the length of one record is normally specified by using the Len(record) function. Reading and writing records to a random file are accomplished through the FileGet() and FilePut() functions, respectively.

■ DateString() returns today's date as a string. The Today function returns today's date as a date. DateAdd() returns a date computed by adding a time interval to a date.

■ The OrElse short-circuit construct is sometimes used to avoid accessing a nonexisting array element.

■ Use the Items.Add method to add items to a combo box in code. The SelectedIndex property identifies the selected item.

■ The PasswordChar property of a text box hides the contents of the text box.

■ The CheckedChanged event is triggered when the value of the Checked property changes for a CheckBox control or a RadioButton control.

■ An event procedure can handle events for multiple controls.

QUESTIONS

1. Within a structure declaration, what is the correct syntax for the declaration of strMyField as a fixed-length, 30-character string with Protected accessibility?

2. To retrieve a record from a random-access file, you call the _____ function.

3. To write a record to a random-access file, you call the _____ function.

   Assume that you have a user-written function called Twice(ByVal vint As Integer), which returns the value vint * 2. In the following code, how often is Twice() called?

   ```
   If x=10 And x=11 And x=Twice(3) Then...
   ```

   _____ Always   _____ Sometimes   _____ Never

   Assume that you have a user-written function called Twice(ByVal vint As Integer), which returns the value vint * 2. In the following code, how often is Twice() called?

   ```
   If x=10 AndAlso x=11 AndAlso x=Twice(3) Then...
   ```

   _____ Always   _____ Sometimes   _____ Never

4. What statement do you use to remove the selected item from ComboBox1?

5. What statement do you use to remove from ComboBox1 the item whose index = MyIndex?

6. To ensure that a casual observer is not able to read the contents of a text box, the developer must set the _____ property to True.

7. What event is raised when the user clicks a RadioButton control whose Checked property is True?

8. Complete the following event procedure header, so that the KeyPress, MouseDown, and TextChanged events of TextBox1 trigger the procedure:

   ```
   Private Sub MyEvent ((ByVal sender As System.Object, _
       ByVal e As System.EventArgs)
   ```

EXERCISES

1. Create a Windows Forms application with a TabControl to display the Room Service Menu for the kitchens of the International Village and to record the items desired on a particular order. On the left side of the form, place a list box, which will display the food order selections of the customer. Place a tab control to the right of the list box. The tab control contains Breakfast, Lunch, Dinner, and Beverage tab pages. Each of these tab pages contains a combo box that lists the food and beverage items related to that category. When the user selects an item from one of the combo boxes, the program adds that item to the food order list box. When the user selects an item in the list box, that item is removed from the list box.

2. Create a Console application to add records to the Users file. Use the same random access file structure as was used in this tutorial's LogonManagerDraft application. Internally, implement the same structure for a user record. However, do not read the data into an array. Rather, use the file directly for each IO operation. Declare only simple variables of type structUser. Use Write, WriteLine, and ReadLine function calls to get information from the user, and validate each piece of data as it is obtained, returning for corrected data until it is acceptable. When all of the data for a record has been obtained, write only that one record to the file. Your program should not overwrite an active record, but rather search for an empty or inactive record.

3. Starting with your completed LogonManagerDraft application, add the capability to print the record of one new user, adding this capability to frmUser by placing a Print tab on the TabControl control. Arrange the data in two columns, with the field names on the left and the data values neatly aligned in the right-hand column. (The basics of printing were explained in Tutorial 2.) Use a PrintPreview control, so that you can view the report on the screen without actually printing it on paper. The one-page report should look approximately like Figure 3-85.

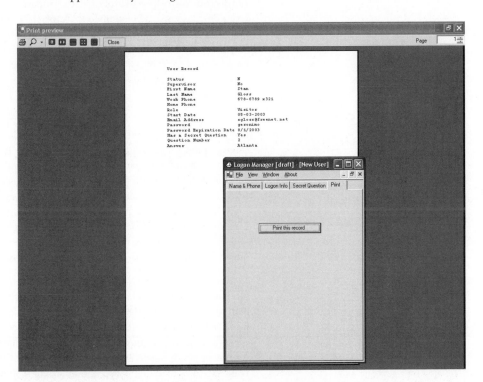

Figure 3-85: New user's record, in PrintPreview

4. Enhance the Ticket Request application, Exercise 2 in Lesson B, so that it saves the customer order in a random access data file called Ticket Order. The customer contact information (name and address) and the number of tickets in each category must be saved; the prices can be reconstructed, so the prices need not be saved.

5. Write a Console application that creates a random-access data file with 26 records and containing, in each record, the record number and the letter of the alphabet whose ordinal position in the alphabet is equal to the record number. That is, record number 1 contains "1 A," record number 2 contains "2 B," and so on, through record 26, which contains "26 Z." Include a structure consisting of an integer and a Char. (*Hint:* within your For/Next loop, you need to convert an integer to a Char with the ChrW function, so that ChrW(65) returns *A.*) Create a second Console application that reads and displays the contents of this random-access file in reverse order.

Exercises 6, 7, and 8 allow you to discover the solution to problems on your own and experiment with material that is not covered explicitly in the tutorial.

discovery ▶ 6. Create a Windows Forms MDI application to allow athletes to register for participation in the Friendsville International Games. Provide a MainMenu control with these items: initialize the file (for 200 athletes), create a new registration, edit an existing registration, view all registrations, and About. The registration form (a child form) should collect contact information (name, address, phone, e-mail), nationality, gender, and sport (track and field, swimming, soccer, etc.). The same registration form should be used to edit an existing registration. Save the information concerning each athlete in an Athletes random-access file. Another child form should contain a list box that displays the record number, the name, nationality, and sport of every athlete who has registered. A third child form should be an About form.

discovery ▶ 7. Create a Web Forms application that duplicates the functionality of Exercise 1 above (the Room Service Menu). Place four DropDownList controls and one ListBox control on a Web page. (The DropDownList Web Forms control is similar to the ComboBox Windows Forms control.) Set the AutoPostBack property to True for all five of these controls (AutoPostBack will be explained in Tutorial 7). In the Page_Load event procedure, load the four DropDownList controls with the breakfast, lunch, dinner, and beverage items, just as you did in Exercise 1—but do this only if IsPostBack is False, that is, the page is being loaded for the first time. Duplicate the rest of Exercise 1's functionality; clicking an item in a DropDownList control should cause the selected item to appear in the ListBox, while clicking an item in the ListBox should cause that item to disappear.

discovery ▶ 8. This project is similar to Exercise 1 above, except that you create an MDI application instead of an application with a tab control to display the Room Service Menu for the International Village's kitchen. The main menu should offer breakfast, lunch, dinner, and beverage menu items, each of which triggers the display of the same child form. The child form has a combo box that lists the various menu selections. When the user selects Breakfast, Lunch, Dinner, or Beverage, the program should instantiate a child form and load the child form's combo box with the appropriate food and beverage items. Dock a ListBox on the left side of the MDI form. When a user selects an item from a child form, add that item to the ListBox on the parent. When the user selects an item in the ListBox on the parent, remove that item from the ListBox.

You may find one aspect of this project to be quite challenging: When the user selects a food item from the combo box on a child form, how do you then add the selected food item to the list box on the parent form? There are actually a number of ways that this can be solved. One of the solutions is as follows: In the combo box's SelectedIndexChanged event procedure, you must search through the collection of controls on the MDI parent form looking for the list box (which you can identify by its Name property). To do this, you create an object ctrl of type Control, and then use a For Each loop to iterate through the controls in the Me.MDIParent.Controls Collection. When you find the list box, you must declare an object of type ListBox, assign the ctrl object to your list box object, and then invoke the Items.Add method for the list box object. The code for this solution will look like Figure 3-86, though obviously your object names might very well be different. You encounter a different solution for this problem in Exercise 1 of Lesson C in Tutorial 4.

```
Private Sub cboMenu_SelectedIndexChanged(ByVal sender As _
    System.Object, ByVal e As System.EventArgs) _
    Handles cboMenu.SelectedIndexChanged
  Dim ctrl As Control
  Dim lst As ListBox
  For Each ctrl In Me.MdiParent.Controls
    If ctrl.Name = "lstOrder" Then
      lst = ctrl
      lst.Items.Add(cboMenu.SelectedItem)
    End If
  Next
End Sub
```

Figure 3-86: cboMenu_SelectedIndexChanged procedure

K E Y   T E R M S

- CheckBox control
- Checked property
- CheckedChanged event
- child form
- collection
- ComboBox control
- Count property
- data types
- DateAdd function
- DatePart function
- DateString function
- Dispose method
- Do loop
- Dock property
- DropDownStyle property
- Exit For
- Exit Sub
- FileGet() method
- FilePut() method
- For Each loop
- For loop
- GoTo statement
- GroupBox control
- IIf function
- IsMdiContainer property
- Items collection
- iteration control structure
- LayoutMdi method
- MDI container
- MdiLayout enumeration
- MdiList property
- MdiParent property
- Module
- Multiline property
- Multiple Document Interface (MDI) application

- On Error GoTo statement
- parameter
- parent form
- RadioButton control
- random-access file
- Remove method
- RemoveAt method
- Select Case statement
- SelectedIndex property
- selection control structure
- sequence control structure
- ShowDialog() method
- stepwise refinement
- String collection
- String.Compare() method
- Structure declaration
- structured programming
- stub (placeholder)
- TabControl control
- TabPages Collection
- Today function
- Trim function
- Try statement
- While loop
- WindowState property

Programming with Objects: Class Libraries and Reusable Code

Previewing the Final Version of the LogonManager Application

case▶ You began the development of the LogonManager application in Tutorial 3. In Tutorial 4, you complete the LogonManager and build the related Logon applications. These projects also introduce you to the concepts of class libraries and reusable code, central to successful object-oriented programming (OOP).

The Logon program is invoked by all Windows applications developed by the Friendsville Games Development Team (FGDT), including LogonManager, whenever system security dictates that application usage be restricted to authorized users. The Logon program asks the user to provide a logon and password before accessing an application. As you already know from Tutorial 3, the LogonManager application manages the user logons: it allows new users to request logon permission, existing users to edit user information, and the system supervisor to control this process. The LogonManager program also calls the Friendsville International Games Welcome splash screen developed in Tutorial 1.

You can see all three programs by running the final version of the LogonManager application, located in the Tut04 folder. This application calls the splash screen and also requests a logon and password (except for a new user). In this preview, you are able to look at the additional functionality of the final version of the LogonManager application that you will create as you work through Tutorial 4.

To view the LogonManager application as an existing user:

1 Run **LogonManager.exe**, available in the VB.NET\Student\Tut04\ LogonManager\bin folder. Note that the FigWelcome splash screen appears for three seconds, and is then replaced by the LogonManager main screen (the MDI form). On the main screen, note the ToolBar control. See Figures 4-1 and 4-2.

Figure 4-1: FigWelcome splash screen

Figure 4-2: LogonManager main screen (MDI form)

2   Click **View | Existing User**, or just click the Existing User icon on the toolbar. This causes the Logon application to execute. See Figure 4-3. The Logon application is an example of a class library, which you learn to create in this tutorial.

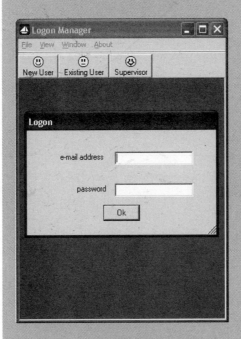

Figure 4-3: Logon screen

3   The Logon form requests an e-mail address and a password. Enter **rick@fgdt.org** as the e-mail address, and **rickfgdt** as the password. Click **Ok**. The Edit User Info form for Rick Sanchez is displayed.

4   Change Rick's Secret Question from his birthplace to the number of his cousins, and then change the Answer to **14**. Click **Submit**.

5   Click the **Existing User** icon on the toolbar. This time, log on as **bspear@cti.com**, and use the password **bspearcti**. Change the password to **pass**, and then submit the change. Note that the password is rejected because it is too short. Change the password to **afternoon**, but in the **Confirm Password** text box, type **AFTERNOON** (all capitals). Note that the password is rejected because the Password and Confirm Password fields do not match. Change the password to **Visual Basic**, and note that the password is rejected because it is too long (it exceeds the 10-character limit). Click **Cancel**, which exits the Edit User Info form without saving any changes.

6   Click the **Existing User** icon on the toolbar again. This time, enter an invalid e-mail address and password (or just click Ok, leaving the e-mail address or the password fields empty). You are prompted to insert the e-mail address and password again. Click **Ok**, then click **Ok** a third time. After the third failed attempt, the message "Logon failure" appears. Click **Ok** to terminate the program.

As you perform these logon steps, you may notice that the Logon program communicates with the LogonManager program. Inside LogonManager, the program needs to know that a user has logged on successfully or not, whether that user is a supervisor, and what the user's record number is in the Users file. All three pieces of information are harvested by the Logon program based on user input and comparisons against the Users file; this information is then passed to LogonManager. As you work through the tutorial, you will learn how to effect this type of communication among application components.

Users who forget their passwords can contact the system supervisor, who can reset a user's password. The system supervisor may want to use the secret question and answer to help verify the user's identity. The supervisor must be able to accept new users, view all the users, reset everyone's password expiration date, and perform other supervisory functions. You now view the LogonManager as the system supervisor.

To view the LogonManager application as supervisor:

1   Run **LogonManager.exe** again.

2   Click the **Supervisor** icon on the toolbar, or click **View | Supervisor | Logon**. The familiar Logon form appears.

3   Enter **1** as the e-mail address and **SUPERVISOR** as the password. Note that all menu selections are now enabled.

4   Click **View | Supervisor | View All Users**. All active records are displayed, and both the parent and child forms are maximized. See Figure 4-4. Note the password expiration dates for all of the users—these were initially set to never expire. Note that Hilda Reiner is record number 2. Also note the record for Geraldine Springer, a new user—the status code is N (for New User). Click the child form's **Close** button to close only the child form.

application's
Restore Down button

child form's
Close button

Figure 4-4: View All Users

5 Click **View | Supervisor | Reset Expiration Dates** to reset the password expiration dates of all users to 90 days from today, then click **Yes**. Click **View | Supervisor | View All Users**, and note that every user's password (except the supervisor's) has been reset. Click the **Restore** button in the upper-right corner of the title bar to return the application to its original size.

6 Click **File** on the menu bar. The Backup and Restore menu items perform their customary functions. Click **Backup** now, and save the **Users.bak** file in a location of your choice. Click **Yes** to replace the existing Users.bak file; click **OK** after the file is backed up successfully. Click **File | Initialize**. The supervisor can use the Initialize menu item to reinitialize the Users file, if for some reason the file becomes corrupted and no backup is available. This selection overwrites all previous data in the file. After initialization, the only user is the supervisor, with an initial e-mail address of 1, the password SUPERVISOR, and a password expiration date of 1/1/9999. Click **Yes** to begin the file initialization process. Click **View | Supervisor | View All Users** in order to verify that the Users file now contains only one active record. Click **File | Restore**, and follow the screen instructions to restore the Users file from the backup copy you created moments ago. Once again, select **View | Supervisor | View All Users** to verify that all user records have been restored. Click the **Restore** button on the title bar to return the form to its normal size.

NOTE: In addition to restricting the initialize, backup, and restore functions to the supervisor, a real commercial application would also encrypt the Users file (a topic beyond our scope here).

7 Click **View | Supervisor**. Note that the Supervisor submenu includes a radio button in front of the **Accept New Users** item, indicating that at least one new user application awaits disposition by the supervisor. Click **Accept New Users**.

8 Click **View | Supervisor | Edit User Info**. You are prompted to insert the record number of the user you want to edit. Enter **2** and click **OK**. You can make any change to Hilda Reiner's record that you want to make. Note that the Password and Confirm Password fields display only asterisks. Even the system supervisor is not permitted to view a user's current password, although the supervisor can change it.

9 Click **About** on the menu bar to display the About Logon Manager form.

10 Click **Window** on the menu bar, and note that all open child forms are listed, with a check mark in front of the active window. On the Window menu, click **Cascade**. Note that the child forms are displayed in overlapping windows, as shown in Figure 4-5. You can open as many additional child forms as you want. Click **File | Exit** to terminate the application.

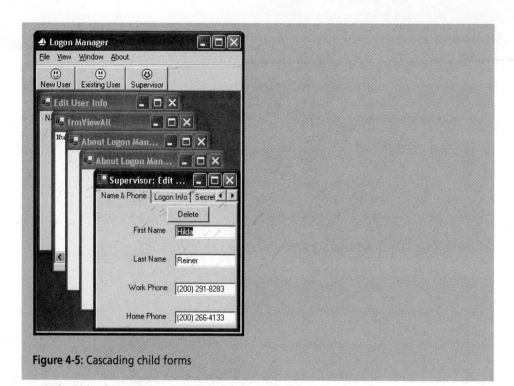

Figure 4-5: Cascading child forms

Code Containers and Class Libraries

Lesson A contains a review of the various Visual Basic .NET elements that serve as containers for declarations, functions, and procedures. These elements include classes, forms, components, modules, structures, and namespaces. You also examine the notion of a class library, and discover how a class library helps you develop reusable code.

Understanding Classes, Forms, Components, Modules, Structures, and Namespaces

One of the principles of structured programming previously discussed is that large programs should be subdivided into smaller, meaningful logical—or functional—units. All of these elements—classes, forms, components, modules, structures, and namespaces—serve as containers for blocks of code, for declarations of constants and variables, and for the definition of properties, events, methods, functions, and procedures.

Class

A class is a blueprint for an object. A **class** defines the properties, fields, methods, and events that go into an object. An **object** is an instance of a class. A class is a **reference type**, meaning that a class does not maintain its own data. Rather, data values reside in an object, which references the class definitions. A class can inherit from another class, and a class is both inheritable and reusable, as you saw with the Button control example in Tutorial 2. A class encapsulates information about itself, limiting access to its internal functionality. Because an object instance must be created from a class, every class must contain a constructor (a method that instantiates an object based on the class) and a destructor (a method that destroys all traces of an object and performs "garbage collection" in main memory).

Form

A **form** is one type of class. It has a graphical component and a code component. A form may be a Windows form or a Web form. A Windows form may serve as a container for other forms, in which case the container is called an MDI form or a parent form, while the forms it contains are called child forms. Generally, a form's declarations are available only internally. Because a form is a class, it must be instantiated as an object before it can be used. This is why the form definition contains a constructor

tip
Web forms are covered in greater detail in Tutorial 7.

tip

• • • • • • • • • • • • • • • •

Visual Basic 6.0 automatically instantiated a form and declared a global variable with the same name as the form. So, for example, if you created a form called frmMyForm, then Visual Basic 6.0 created an instance of frmMyForm and also created a variable called frmMyForm, which you could reference in code. Visual Basic .NET does not automatically instantiate a form or create the global variable. In a Visual Basic .NET Windows Forms application, only the startup form is automatically instantiated; all other forms must be instantiated programmatically.

(New) and an InitializeComponent() method, which are invoked when the form is loaded. This is also why, when your code needs to call another form, that additional form must be created using the New keyword.

The code portion of a Windows form is loaded at the same time and on the same computer as the GUI. The statements that render the graphical controls on the Windows form are all included in the InitializeComponent() method, called by Sub New().

By contrast, even though a Web form class file still defines a class, a Web form need not be instantiated in code. Rather, the Web form is loaded by following a link to its URL. The GUI is loaded on the client's browser, while the code is loaded on the server (a separate, though perhaps virtual, computer). The controls on the form are rendered through the browser, so they are not mentioned in the InitializeComponent() method in the Web form's code. The first time the Web page is visited, the Page_Init() event is triggered, which calls InitializeComponent(). As you will see in Tutorial 7, the GUI and the code for a Web form are stored in separate files because they run on separate computers.

Component

A **component** is a class that conforms to a certain standard for interacting with other components. A component may or may not contain a graphical element; a component always contains a code element. A component can provide an easy way to communicate between projects in a solution: this is how you will use a component later in this tutorial, when you need to establish communication between the Logon project and the LogonManager project. After a component class has been instantiated, its methods are available. For example, assume that OldProject has a class called Component1, which in turn has a procedure called BeamMeUp(ByVal vstrPerson As String). Assume further that a reference to OldProject has been added to the References in Solution Explorer under NewProject. The following code in NewProject can invoke that procedure:

```
Dim MyComponent As New OldProject.Component1()
MyComponent.BeamMeUp("Scotty")
```

Visual Studio .NET supports the Component Object Model (COM), which is a standard for the development of cross-language and cross-platform components. Originally designed for application within the C++ and Java worlds, COM has been extended throughout the languages supported by Visual Studio .NET, including Visual C++ .NET, Visual Basic .NET, C# .NET, and J++ .NET. Components based on COM include certain standardized application program interfaces (APIs), providing true interoperability. Prewritten COM-based components can be added to any Visual Studio .NET project through the Customize Toolbox command. On your machine, if you examine the COM tab in the Customize Toolbox dialog box, you find a list of COM components that have been installed on your computer.

Module

A **module** (also called a **standard module**) is a reference type, consisting of declarations and procedures only. A module is similar to a class in terms of serving as a container for code, but it is unlike a class in several important respects: it can be neither instantiated nor inherited, nor can it be nested inside another structure. A module is like a form in that it has a code component, but unlike a form in that it has no graphical component (design or object view).

You use modules whenever you build a Console application; modules are the basic building blocks of such an application. Modules also occur regularly in many Windows and Web Forms applications.

By default, a module's variables and procedures are shared. Only one copy of a module's data exists (rather than a separate copy for each instance, as is the case with a form). A module's public variables and procedures are accessible and scoped to the namespace that contains the module (rather than just to the module itself). Taken together, these features mean that a module's data values can be globally accessible throughout a project and can be referenced without qualification. However, global variables are easily misused, and, therefore, should only be declared when absolutely necessary.

Structure

A **structure** is an expansion of the user-defined type in previous releases of Visual Basic. A structure can contain different kinds of data items, each with its own accessibility (Public, Private, Friend, and so on). A structure can also contain properties, methods, and events. A structure is a **value type**, meaning that each variable based on a structure contains its own data. A structure is declared at the module or class level, that is, not inside any procedure. The declaration in Figure 4-6, for example, defines the structure structLogonPassword containing Friend, Public, and Private elements, and then declares a Public variable of type structLogonPassword.

```
Module Module1
  Public Structure structLogonPassword
    Friend UserNum As Integer
    <VBFixedString(20)> Public Logon As String
    <VBFixedString(20)> Private Password As String
  End Structure
  Public pstructMyLogonPassword As structLogonPassword
End Module
```

Figure 4-6: Declaration of structLogonPassword

Note that a structure declared within a class (such as a form or a component) is accessible only within that class, whereas a structure declared in a module with public accessibility is accessible globally.

Namespace

A **namespace** organizes the list of names (classes, structures, objects, and so on) that occur in an assembly. An **assembly** is the package that results from compilation. You have seen how the .NET Framework is organized into namespaces. Your own code is organized into namespaces as well. When a program is compiled, Visual Studio .NET creates a single namespace with the same name as the project and puts this namespace definition at the head of the assembly. An assembly can also contain lower-level namespaces, which can in turn contain additional namespaces, so that an entire hierarchy of namespaces is declared, just as the .NET Framework contains a namespace hierarchy. The reason for subdividing a large project into namespaces is to avoid name collisions, which occur when different parts of a project each create program elements with the same name. This problem is more likely to occur when many programmers are working simultaneously on different parts of a project.

Although you need not define lower-level namespaces in a project the size of LogonManager, you should be aware of the definition of the term "namespace" (which occurs often in the Visual Basic .NET documentation). For example, a public variable declared in a module is accessible throughout the containing namespace, which means, in effect, that the variable is available anywhere in your project.

Compiling a Project into a Class Library

A **class library** defines a class, which can then be incorporated into any project simply by including the class library in the project's list of references. Thus a class library is a great way for programmers to create truly reusable objects. You developed FigWelcome as a Windows Forms application in Tutorial 1. So that any FGDT-developed application may call it as a splash screen, this application needs to be compiled and stored in a class library. In addition, the original application needs to be modified: it should run only for three seconds, and then disappear. You will convert FigWelcome into a class library in Lesson B. Before getting to the work of compiling and importing, you need to become more familiar with class libraries, dynamic link libraries, and how they are meant to function once they're imported into applications.

You can take any Windows Forms project and convert it into a class library. You only need to tell the Visual Basic .NET compiler that the output from compilation is a class library rather than an executable program. (You do this on the General tab of the Property Pages for the project, where you tell the compiler that the Output type is a class library rather than a Windows application.) A class library compiles to a DLL file (dynamic link library), rather than an .exe (executable) file. A DLL file cannot be executed directly; rather, it must be called from inside another running program, often referred to as the client.

The output from the compiler is known as an assembly (whether in the form of a dynamic link library or an executable). As mentioned in the discussion of namespaces earlier in this tutorial, the compiler places a namespace declaration at the head of the assembly, using the same name as the name of the project. After you have compiled your project into a class library, the executable project (or client) that calls this library must identify both the class library's DLL file and its namespace name.

In Solution Explorer, the References list identifies files that may be referenced in a project. To make the class library available to the client, you must add the DLL file in the client's References list in Solution Explorer. This action makes all of the namespaces (usually only one) in the DLL available to any component of the client program. For example, you might create a class library project called MyLib containing a form called MyForm. You might also create a Windows Forms application called MyClient, and want to use MyForm from MyLib in the MyClient application. To accomplish this, you add a reference to MyLib in the references list for MyClient. This allows you to instantiate MyForm anywhere in the MyClient project.

Taking this concept a step further, a form or module in MyClient could import MyLib: this would allow any name in MyLib (including, for example, MyForm) to be referenced without qualification.

Creating Efficiency Using Class Libraries

American firms spend about 80% of their software budget maintaining existing software rather than creating new software. So, anything that can be done to reduce that heavy maintenance cost is potentially well worth the investment. If you have a form or module that is used by five client programs, and the form or module needs to be modified, then the modification must be incorporated separately in each of those clients. If on the other hand, the common form or module is a class library project, then you only need to change it once. The five clients must be recompiled, of course, to reference the new assembly; but no other change to the clients is required. As you can see, facilitating software maintenance is the number one reason for creating class library projects.

You have completed Lesson A. You can stop now and take a break, but don't forget to do the end-of-lesson questions and exercises that follow.

SUMMARY

- Visual Basic .NET features robust elements for subdividing code into classes, forms, components, modules, structures, and namespaces.
- A class is a template or blueprint for an object. A class is a reference type that defines the properties, fields, methods, and events of objects instantiated from that class.
- A form is a class that has both a graphical representation and a code segment. Like all classes, a form must be instantiated.
- A component is a class that is designed for interaction with other components, and is useful for such purposes as passing parameters between projects.
- A module, also a reference type, contains code only (no graphical component), and its data values are shared.
- A structure is a value type that defines fields, properties, methods, and events at the module level. Variables, each containing their own data values, are then declared based on the user-defined structure.
- A namespace defines a list of names (classes, structures, other namespaces, etc.) within an assembly.
- A class library defines a reusable program. It compiles to a dynamic link library (DLL)—rather than a load module or executable (EXE)—and it must be called from an external program. To call the class library, the external program includes a reference to the namespace containing the DLL, instantiates the startup form for that project, and then shows the form. An optional Imports statement permits references to names within the class library to be used without qualification.

QUESTIONS

1. The user-defined type from Visual Basic 6.0 has been replaced by the _____ statement in Visual Basic .NET.

2. A special class that conforms to certain standards for interfacing with other classes is known as a(n) _____.

3. A(n) _____ defines a class with both a GUI and a code segment.

4. A standard _____ contains only code and can be neither instantiated nor inherited.

5. A reusable project that compiles to a DLL is called a(n) _____.

6. A library collection of declared names is called a(n) _____.

7. A(n) _____ type holds data values in its own memory allocation, whereas a _____ type holds only a pointer to data values stored elsewhere.

8. After a namespace has been added to a project's _____, the _____ statement can be used to make all the names in that namespace available without qualification.

9. A fundamental programming construct that can be inherited, instantiated, and nested is called a(n) _____.

CRITICAL THINKING

At the end of each lesson, reflective questions are intended to provoke you into considering the material you have just read at a deeper level.

1. In what situation would you want to declare your own namespaces?

2. If XYZ Corp. creates 30 of its own classes and wants to add them to its .NET Framework class library, where should they be added? What root namespace should be used?

3. Describe the difference between reference types and value types, and give a practical example of this difference.

EXERCISES

1. Create a Console application containing a Structure definition for structSport. The elements of this structure include a four-letter abbreviation of the name of the sport, the full name of the sport, the name of the country that invented the sport, the year the sport was invented, and the number of countries participating in that sport in the Friendsville International Games. Also, declare a private array of this structure capable of holding five elements. In Sub Main(), call a procedure that loads three records into the array. Then call another procedure that displays these records. Follow these steps:
   a. Create the Console application named Tut04ExA1. Declare structSport as a private structure at the module level, and define the structure to include strAbbrev, strSportName, strCountry, intYear, and intNumParticipants. Declare the astructSport array(5) to be of type structSport.
   b. In Sub Main(), call the LoadArray() procedure and the DisplayArray() procedure.
   c. In the LoadArray() procedure, use WriteLine() prompts and ReadLine() function calls to obtain user input for three records that you load into the array. Use a Do loop or a For loop.
   d. In the DisplayArray() procedure, use WriteLine() statements inside a For loop to print the contents of the array to the screen.

2. Modify Exercise 1 by putting the LoadArray() and DisplayArray() procedures into a component that you add to the project, which you now name Tut04ExA2. When you are done, Tut04ExA2 has two code elements: Module1, with the structure and array declarations and with Sub Main(), and Component1, with the LoadArray() and DisplayArray() procedures. Note that, in Module1, the array must be declared as public to make it available to Component1; alternatively, you could pass the private array as a parameter in the calls from Sub Main() to the LoadArray() and DisplayArray() procedures in Component1.

3. Modify Exercise 2 by converting it into a Windows Forms application. Keep Module1 and Component1, and keep Sub Main() as the startup object. However, in the LoadArray() procedure, use InputBox function calls to obtain the data from the user, and, in DisplayArray(), use a list box on form1 to display the results.

4. Design Exercise 1 as a Web Forms application. Create the GUI, and write a paragraph describing the issues that must be addressed in order to implement your design. (Your instructor has a Web Forms solution.)

5. Create a Windows Forms application consisting of a form, a module, and a component. In the module, define a public structure consisting of an athlete's name and age, and declare an array of five of these structures. In the component, write one procedure to load data (hard-coded) into the array. Write a second procedure to load the array into a list box object, passed to the procedure ByRef. Write a third procedure to find an athlete's name (passed ByVal) in the array, and display that athlete's age in a message box, or display an error message if the athlete's name cannot be found in the array. In the form, place the list box and three buttons: the Load Array button calls the procedure in the component that loads the array. Clicking this button also enables the other two buttons, initially disabled. The Populate List Box button calls the procedure in the component that loads the array into the list box. The Search button prompts the user (in an InputBox prompt) for an athlete name, and then calls the procedure in the component that searches the array.

6. Rewrite Exercise 5 as a Console application, substituting ReadLine() and WriteLine() function calls for the graphical components. For example, rather than loading a list box, you must print the array contents to the console.

Exercise 7 allows you to both discover the solution to problems on your own and experiment with material that is not covered explicitly in the tutorial.

discovery ▶

7. This exercise deals with nested structures. Create a Windows Forms application. In Form1, declare structAthlete, a structure consisting of the name and age of an athlete. Declare a second structure, structCountryAthlete, consisting of the name of a country and an array of structAthlete. Then declare a third structure, structSportParticipant, consisting of the name of a sport and an array of structCountryAthlete. Declare the necessary variables to hold four athletes in each of five countries in each of three sports. Then load Mary, age 27, from Ghana, in Track, as one athlete in the structure variables you have declared, and display her name, age, country, and sport in labels on the form by referencing the appropriate elements of your variables.

After completing this lesson, you will be able to:

■ Convert a Windows Forms application into a class library

■ Build a class library, and create a solution with multiple projects

■ Incorporate a component into a class library project, and use the component to exchange parameter data with a client program

■ Incorporate the following controls into a Windows Forms application: ImageList, Toolbar, and OpenFileDialog

A Class Library with Passed Parameters

Lesson B shows you how to build a class library application from scratch, including one method of passing parameters between the calling (client) program and the class library program. You are also introduced to three Windows Forms controls needed to complete the final version of the LogonManager application in Lesson C.

Tasks for the FGDT

Rick Sanchez has been given the task of converting the FigWelcome Windows Forms application into a class library. Althea Brown's task is to write the Logon class and compile it into a class library. And you have the task of completing the LogonManager Windows Forms application, with coding assistance from Hilda. Because the completed LogonManager application calls both the FigWelcome and Logon classes, you will want to examine how those classes were created and compiled.

Converting a Windows Forms Application into a Class Library

The FigWelcome Windows Forms application from Tutorial 1 now needs to be compiled and stored in a class library, where any FGDT-developed application can use it. Also, to work as a splash screen, FigWelcome should appear for three seconds and then vanish.

As mentioned earlier, Rick Sanchez was given the task of converting FigWelcome from a Windows application to a class library, and he has completed it. You can find his solution in the RicksWelcome folder in the VB.NET\Student\Tut04 folder. His program works fine, and you can use his version if you prefer later on when building the LogonManager application. However, after completing this task, Rick explained to you and Althea that it was really quite simple and yet a good learning experience, so he suggested that you also build it yourself. These are the steps needed to convert FigWelcome from Tut01 into a reusable splash screen.

To convert FigWelcome from Tut01 into a reusable splash screen:

1 In Windows Explorer, copy the **FigWelcome** folder from the Tut01 folder and paste it into the **Tut04** folder. Then, in Visual Studio .NET, open the FigWelcome solution from the Tut04 folder, and open frmWelcome in the Form Designer.

2   Drop a **Timer** control from the Toolbox onto **frmWelcome** (it will appear in a tray beneath the form), set its **Enabled** property to **True**, set its **Interval** property to **3000** (that is, three seconds), and insert the following statement into the Timer's **Tick** event procedure: `Me.Dispose()`. The IDE at this point appears as in Figure 4-7. Run the **FigWelcome** program to see that it terminates after three seconds.

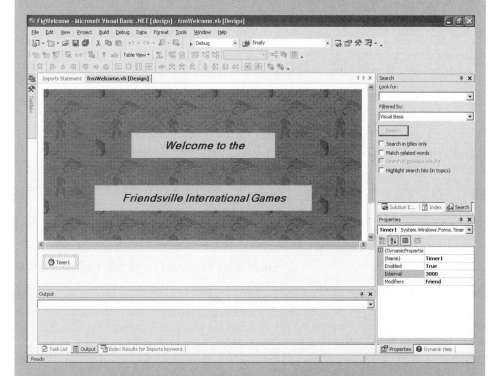

Figure 4-7: frmWelcome in the IDE

> **tip**
> • • • • • • • • • • • • • • • •
> ▶ Make sure that the program terminates on its own before going on to Step 3. If the Close button is removed (your next step), and if the program does not terminate by itself after three seconds, then press Ctrl+Alt+Delete, and end the program from the Windows Task Manager.

NOTE: As a general rule, the proper way to close a form is to use its Dispose method, which releases all resources allocated to that form. This is also the correct way to terminate the processing of a program; that is because when all open forms and modules have been disposed, the program is finished. By contrast, the End statement causes an abrupt and rather rude interruption of processing, leaving the operating system's garbage collector to clean up the main memory and close files. The End statement is bad form, sort of like walking out of the throne room with your back to the emperor. The Dispose method provides a more graceful exit.

3   Delete **btnClose** and the **btnClose_Click** event procedures. Run the **FigWelcome** program again. The program is now ready to be converted into a class library application. In Windows Explorer, in the Tut04\FigWelcome\bin folder, delete **FigWelcome.exe**.

4   Right-click the project name, **FigWelcome** 📘, and click **Properties**. If necessary, navigate through the FigWelcome Property Pages, to the **General tab** of Common Properties, and change the setting in the **Output type** combo box to **Class Library**, as shown in Figure 4-8. Click **OK**.

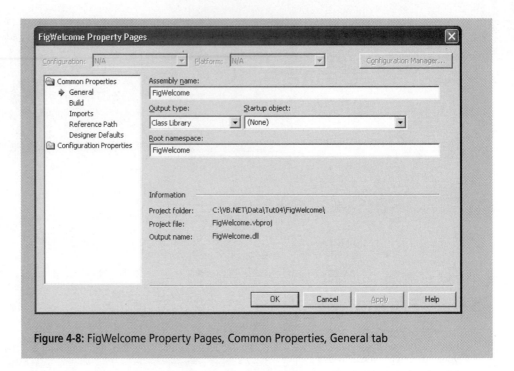

Figure 4-8: FigWelcome Property Pages, Common Properties, General tab

Creating an External Program to Call the Class Library

Because a class library compiles to a DLL rather than to an executable, another external program must start running first, and then this external program (sometimes called the client program) must call the class library. The next task, therefore, is to create a bare-bones external program that calls FigWelcome. After this has been done, it is a simple matter to call the FigWelcome DLL from any other program.

> **NOTE:** If you run the program again at this point, an error message informs you that you cannot directly run a program whose Output type is Class Library. The error message, Figure 4-9, gives you three alternatives for debugging the project; you will use the third of these alternatives, adding an empty project to the FigWelcome solution, and then calling the FigWelcome project from this empty project. (The other two methods are to change it back to a Windows Forms application, because you cannot start a class library project directly, or to tell Visual Studio to start an external project or Web page, which, of course, must include a call to the class library project.)

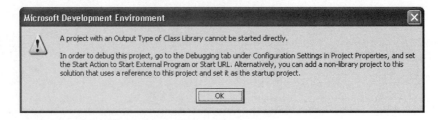

Figure 4-9: Error message—class library project cannot be started directly

To create an external program to call FigWelcome:

1 To add the new, empty project for the purpose of testing FigWelcome as a class library project, right-click **FigWelcome** (the solution name) 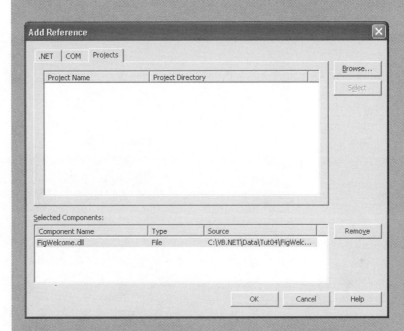, and click **Add | New Project**. Select **Windows Application** in the Templates frame, and name the new project **CallingFigWelcome**. Note that the CallingFigWelcome folder is created under the Tut04 folder.

2 In Solution Explorer, under the CallingFigWelcome project, expand **References**, right-click **References** to see the current References list before you change it, and then click **Add Reference**. In the Add Reference dialog box, click the **Projects** tab. Click the **FigWelcome** project. Click the **Select** button, resulting in the dialog box shown in Figure 4-10. For example, adding a reference to the Project_B namespace inside the References list for Project_A means that Project_A's code can now import the Project_B namespace and use its various elements. Click **OK**.

Figure 4-10: Add Reference dialog box

3 In Solution Explorer, right-click the **CallingFigWelcome** project, which displays the pop-up menu shown in Figure 4-11, and then click the option **Set as Startup Project**. Because the solution has two projects (FigWelcome and CallingFigWelcome), this step is necessary to tell Visual Basic .NET which of these two projects is called upon first to initiate execution at runtime.

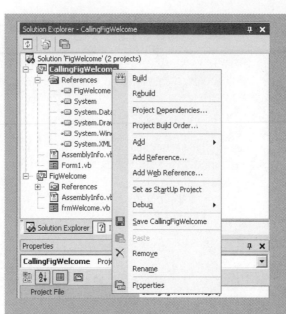

Figure 4-11: Pop-up menu for CallingFigWelcome

4 Open the **Code** window for Form1. Prior to the declaration of Public Class Form1, insert the statement:

```
Imports FigWelcome
```

The Imports statement makes all of the members of the FigWelcome namespace available without qualification in the CallingFigWelcome project. It is never mandatory to use an Imports statement, but it is often convenient to do so, because all the names in the imported namespace can be referenced without the use of qualifiers. The Imports statement can also be used with an alias, as in this example that uses the alias Str:

```
Imports Str = Microsoft.VisualBasic.Strings
```

You could usefully employ this Imports statement in any form that uses the string functions defined by the Microsoft.VisualBasic.Strings namespace. You could then reference Str.Left(*stringname*, *number*) rather than writing out Microsoft.VisualBasic.Left(*stringname*, *number*).

5 Open the **Form Designer**, and double-click the **form**. This opens the Form1_Load event procedure. Insert the following code:

```
Dim MyWelcome As New frmWelcome()
MyWelcome.ShowDialog()
```

Within the CallingFigWelcome project, the preceding Dim statement instantiates MyWelcome as an object of type frmWelcome. The second line then causes the new object MyWelcome to be displayed. If you had not inserted the Imports statement, then the Dim statement would need qualification. That is, it would have to read: `Dim MyWelcome As New FigWelcome.frmWelcome()`.

6 Run the completed **FigWelcome** splash screen application. The difference between Show() and ShowDialog() is that the latter causes the form to be displayed as a modal form—that is, that form must finish executing before the next statement in the calling routine is executed. If you try running the program with the Show() method instead of ShowDialog(), you see that Form1 appears on top of the splash screen before the splash screen has a chance to finish.

tip
· · · · · · · · · · · · · · ·
▶ If you have any difficulties with this application, compare your solution to the RicksWelcome solution. When converting a Windows Forms application into a class library application, the most common problems occur when a necessary, but largely invisible, step is skipped: setting the solution's startup project, setting a project's startup object, adding a reference to the class library's namespace in the References list for the calling application, importing the namespace, or changing an End statement to the Dispose method.

Incorporating FigWelcome into Other Programs

Whenever the splash screen is needed, the FigWelcome project needs to be added to the solution. In the next exercise, you will complete the three necessary steps to achieve this.

To incorporate FigWelcome into other programs:

1 Add a **reference** to the FigWelcome Class Library.

2 Insert the **Imports FigWelcome** statement before the class declaration of the startup form or module in the client application. Although this step is not absolutely necessary, it does allow you to refer to frmWelcome without qualifying it. Also, the Imports statement at the beginning of the form declaration documents the fact that the class library is called within this form.

3 Insert the **Dim** declaration and **ShowDialog**() method shown in Step 5 of the previous exercise into the Sub Main() procedure, the Sub New() procedure (after the InitializeComponent() call), or the Form_Load event procedure of the client. You would insert it into Sub Main() if the startup object for the project is a module. If the startup object is a form, you can insert it in Sub New()—the form's constructor, which executes first—or in the Load event—which executes after Sub New(). You can determine where best to insert this call, as long as you display the splash screen before you display the main form of the application.

Building the Logon Class Library

Althea Brown wrote the Logon class library application. Next you will load it, run it, examine its features carefully, and also build it yourself. Although short, the program provides examples of much of the material covered in this tutorial—material you need to understand in order to complete the LogonManager application.

To incorporate the Logon screen into the various Windows applications of the Friendsville Organizing Committee, the FGDT faces another requirement. How do you pass parameters between the calling (client) program and the called (class library) program? In the case of the LogonManager application, the calling program (LogonManager) should call the Logon program, and should receive an indication that the user successfully logged on (or didn't), an indication that the user is or is not a supervisor, and the user's record number (because this is the only record a nonsupervisor can view or modify). Although this requirement can be handled in a variety of ways, the easiest method is to create a class component that contains the appropriate procedure, including the formal parameters that the called program expects to receive. The calling program then instantiates a new object based on the class component and calls the appropriate procedure.

To study the Logon Class Library application:

1 Open the **Logon** solution that Althea created from the AltheasLogon folder in the Tut04 folder. Note that this solution contains two projects: Logon—the class library—and TryLogon—an empty project that calls the class library (and placed in a folder named AltheasCall).

NOTE: This TryLogon project (as well as the CallingFigWelcome project) includes a Windows form whose default name Form1 is left unchanged. Programmers often leave unchanged the default names of objects that are used only for purposes of compilation, testing, and debugging, and are not part of the finished application. The standard should always be, "Will anyone be confused if I let the default name stand?" When the answer is obviously "No," then it's not worth the trouble to change it. Remember that one of the purposes of this language is to support Rapid Application Development (RAD); you do not want to waste your time documenting things that have no payoff in increased programmer efficiency.

Examine the parts of these projects. Specifically, in the Form1_Load event procedure of the empty TryLogon project, the only bit of functional code is shown in Figure 4-12. This code declares the three parameters passed to Logon: blnLogonOk, a Boolean indicating whether the user logon was successful; blnSupervisor, a Boolean indicating whether the user has supervisor privileges; and intUserName, an integer identifying the user's record number in the Users file. These parameters are all passed ByRef, since TryLogon needs to receive these values back after they are assigned in the Logon program. Note that the actual call is made to Sub Main in MyLogonComponent, declared as an instance of Component1. A message box prints out the values returned by Sub Main in MyLogonComponent.

```
Dim blnLogonOk, blnSupervisor As Boolean
Dim intUserNum As Integer
Dim MyLogonComponent As New Component1()
MyLogonComponent.Main(blnLogonOk, blnSupervisor, intUserNum)
MessageBox.Show("Valid user: " & blnLogonOk.ToString & _
    ControlChars.CrLf & "Record Number: " & intUserNum.ToString _
    & ControlChars.CrLf & "Supervisor: " & blnSupervisor.ToString)
```

Figure 4-12: TryLogon project, Form1_Load event procedure

NOTE: A parameter may be passed to a procedure ByRef or ByVal. When passed ByRef (by reference), the address where the variable is stored in the calling routine is passed to the called routine (function or method). Since the called routine has the address of the variable, any change made to the value of the variable by the called routine changes that value back in the calling routine. When a value is passed ByVal (by value), the value (of the literal, variable, constant, or expression) is passed, rather than an address where that value is stored. As a result, the called routine does not know the address of the source parameter and, therefore, cannot change its value in the calling routine. Rather, the called routine copies the value into an address local to the called routine.

NOTE: The Imports Logon statement appears before the declaration of the Form1 class. Without this declaration at the top, the reference to Component1 in the declaration of MyLogonComponent would need to be qualified.

2 Now examine the three sections of code in the Logon class library itself. This includes Module1, Component1, and frmLogon. Module1, shown in Figure 4-13, must match the Module1 of the LogonManager application. (You will insert the two new public declarations, pblnLogonOk and pblnSupv, in the final version of LogonManager as well.) The Logon program does not need to write to the Users file, but it needs all of the other parts: the maximum

number of users, the structure for a user record, the variables of type structUser, and the procedure to read the Users file. This module was discussed in detail in Tutorial 3.

NOTE: Some programmers routinely change the default names Module1 and Component1 to something more meaningful. Other programmers change these names only when more than one module or component appears in a program, the practice followed by this textbook author. A project's module contains declarations of structures and public variables used throughout the project, and methods that are called from multiple forms. A project typically contains only one such collection of code snippets, and so the term Module1 works well for this purpose. But, you should follow your instructor's guidance in this regard.

```
Module Module1
  Public Const MAXUSERS = 100
  Public Structure structUser
    'Status codes: I = inactive record, A = active, N = new user (pending)
    Public Status As Char
    'A user has supervisor privileges only if .Supervisor is true
    Public Supervisor As Boolean
    <VBFixedString(25)> Public FirstName As String
    <VBFixedString(25)> Public LastName As String
    <VBFixedString(20)> Public WorkPhone As String
    <VBFixedString(20)> Public HomePhone As String
    <VBFixedString(15)> Public Role As String
    Public StartDate As Date
    <VBFixedString(35)> Public EmailAddress As String
    <VBFixedString(10)> Public Password As String
    Public PasswordExpirationDate As Date
    Public HasSecret As Boolean
    Public Question As Integer
    <VBFixedString(25)> Public Answer As String
  End Structure
  Public pastructUser(MAXUSERS) As structUser
  Public pstructUserRec As structUser
  Public pblnLogonOk As Boolean = False    ' new declaration!
  Public pblnSupv As Boolean  ' new declaration!
  Public pintRecNum As Integer

  Public Sub ReadUsersFile()
    Dim i As Integer
    If System.IO.File.Exists("Users") Then
      FileOpen(1, "Users", OpenMode.Random, _
           OpenAccess.Read, OpenShare.Shared, Len(pstructUserRec))
      For i = 1 To MAXUSERS
        FileGet(1, pastructUser(i), i)
      Next
      FileClose(1)
    Else
      MsgBox("No users file")
    End If
  End Sub
End Module
```

Figure 4-13: Module1 in the Logon class library project

3   Now look at Component1, shown in Figure 4-14, which consists of one procedure, Sub Main(), which is called by the calling routine. After reading the Users file into the pastructUser() array, Sub Main displays (modally) an instance of frmLogon (named frmLogonTemp) a maximum of three times. If a logon is successful, three items are returned to the calling routine: the fact that the logon was successful, the supervisor status of the user, and the user record number. (When you are running the program from within the IDE, the calling routine is Form1_Load of TryLogon.) If the logon fails three times, then a Logon Failure message is displayed in Sub Main; also, as a result of the failure, False (as the supervisor privileges) and 0 (as the record number) are returned to the calling routine. When the last statement in procedure Main has been executed, the Logon application terminates.

```
Public Class Component1
    Inherits System.ComponentModel.Component

'Component Designer generated code

  Public Sub Main(ByRef rblnGoodLogon As Boolean, ByRef _
     rblnSupervisor As Boolean, ByRef rintUserNum As Integer)
    ReadUsersFile()
    Dim intTryCount As Integer
    Do
      Dim frmLogonTemp As New frmLogon()
      frmLogonTemp.ShowDialog()
      intTryCount += 1
    Loop Until pblnLogonOk Or intTryCount = 3
    If pblnLogonOk = False Then
      MessageBox.Show("Logon Failure. " & _
        "Please contact the System Supervisor")
    End If
    rblnGoodLogon = pblnLogonOk
    rintUserNum = pintRecNum
    rblnSupervisor = pblnSupv
  End Sub
End Class
```

Figure 4-14: Component1 in the Logon class library project

4   Finally, look at frmLogon, shown in Figure 4-15. You saw the GUI in Figure 4-3. The only procedure is the btnOk_Click event procedure, and the significant portion of that procedure is a For loop that compares the information entered by the user with the records in the pastructUser array.

```
Public Class frmLogon
  Inherits System.Windows.Forms.Form

'Windows Form Designer generated code

  Private Sub btnOk_Click(ByVal sender As System.Object, _
      ByVal e As System.EventArgs) Handles btnOk.Click
    Dim i As Integer
    pblnLogonOk = False
    pblnSupv = False
    pintRecNum = 0
    For i = 1 To MAXUSERS
      With pastructUser(i)
        If .Status = "A" Then
          If .EmailAddress.Trim = txtEmail.Text Then
            If String.Compare(.Password.Trim, txtPassword.Text, _
                False) = 0 Then
              If Today <= .PasswordExpirationDate Then
                pblnLogonOk = True
                pintRecNum = i
                If .Supervisor Then pblnSupv = True
                If DateAdd(DateInterval.Day, 14, Today) > _
                  .PasswordExpirationDate Then
                  MessageBox.Show("Change your password soon. " & _
                    "Current password expires on " & _
                    .PasswordExpirationDate.ToString)
                End If
              Else
                MessageBox.Show("Password has expired")
              End If
            End If
          End If
        End If
      End With
    Next
    Me.Dispose()
  End Sub
End Class
```

A
B
C
D

Figure 4-15: frmLogon in the Logon class library project

Following are notes on some of these methods (letters refer to the letters in Figure 4-15):

   A. The Trim method deletes leading and trailing spaces. Because .EmailAddress is a fixed-length string, it will have trailing spaces, unless the e-mail address is exactly 35 characters long.

   B. The String.Compare method has three arguments: String1, String2, and a Boolean called IgnoreCase. For password verification, IgnoreCase must be False. The String.Compare method returns –1 if String1 < String2, 0 if the strings are equal, and +1 if String1 > String2.

   C. Today is a built-in function that returns today's date.

   D. DateAdd is a built-in function with three arguments: the interval, the amount to be added, and the base date. In the present case, the user receives a warning if the user password is within 14 days of expiration.

5 Run the **TryLogon** application, experiment with various good and bad logon/password combinations, and analyze the results. Recall that the Users file has been preloaded with the authorized logons and passwords shown in Figure 4-16.

Logon	Password	Supervisor status
1	SUPERVISOR	Yes
rick@fgdt.org	rickfgdt	No
hlda@fgdt.org	hildafgdt	No
althea@fgtd.org	altheafgdt	No
bspear@cti.com	bspearcti	No

Figure 4-16: Preloaded logons and passwords in the Users file

Building Logon yourself

As in the case of Rick's FigWelcome, you can use Althea's Logon class library when you complete the LogonManager application, but you will have a much more productive learning experience if you replicate Althea's project yourself. Because the folders provided to you, AltheasLogon and AltheasCall, contain the source code for the completed projects, the step-by-step instructions here provide only an outline of what you need to do. Examine Figures 4-12 through 4-16 carefully in order to build this solution. When necessary, open the completed projects for additional assistance.

To build the Logon class library:

1 Start a new **Windows Forms project** in the VB.NET\Student\Tut04 folder; name it **Logon**. Visual Studio .NET creates the Logon folder and the solution and project files within it. Change the name of Form1.vb to **frmLogon.vb**, and the internal form name from Form1 to **frmLogon**.

2 Build the GUI for frmLogon so that it resembles Figure 4-3. Name the three controls that you must program **txtEmail**, **txtPassword**, and **btnOk**. Remember to set the PasswordChar property of txtPassword to an asterisk.

3 Copy **Module1.vb** from your LogonManagerDraft application in Tutorial 3. All of the data structures and public variables in Logon must be aligned with those in LogonManager, so you should use the same definitions. The ReadUsersFile procedure also must be the same. You can use Windows Explorer to copy **Module1.vb** into the VB.NET\Student\Tut04\Logon folder. Then, in Solution Explorer, right-click the project name, click **Add | Add an Existing Item**, and then add **Module1.vb**.

4 In Solution Explorer, right-click the project name, and click **Add | Add Component**. In the Add New Item dialog box, Component Class is selected. Click **Open**. Component1.vb is added to the project. Carefully enter the code shown in Figure 4-14.

5 Open the **Code Editor** from the btnOk_Click() procedure, and enter the code shown in Figure 4-15. At this point, check for syntax errors by clicking **Build | Build Solution**.

6 Open the **Property Pages** for the Logon project, and change the Output type to a **Class Library**.

7 You need an empty project or an external project to test your Logon Class library project. Right-click the solution name in Solution Explorer, and add another project to this solution. Make the new project a Windows Forms application named **TryLogon**.

8 In Solution Explorer, in the References list for Try Logon, add a **reference** to the Logon class library project. Also in Solution Explorer, right-click the **TryLogon** project name, and designate **TryLogon** as the startup project for this solution.

9 Open the **Code Editor** for Form1. Insert the statement **Imports Logon** before the declaration of Form1. Then, in the Form1_Load() event procedure, insert the code shown in Figure 4-12.

10 Run the **Logon** program, and experiment with various good and bad e-mail address and password combinations, just as you did with Althea's program. Close the application and return to the IDE. Then close the **Logon** solution.

Adding Controls to Complete the LogonManager Application

The controls used in LogonManager that have not yet been discussed include the ToolBar, ImageList, and OpenFileDialog. You can run LogonManager once again to see each of these controls in operation. Figure 4-17 focuses on the ToolBar control on the MDI form. The ToolBar control contains a collection of buttons, and this collection is associated with an ImageList, which in turn contains the three smiley face icons. When you hover the insertion point over a button, you see its ToolTip. The OpenFileDialog is used in the mnuFileRestore_Click() procedure, allowing the system supervisor to select the file from which the Users file is to be restored.

**ToolTip for
New User button**

Figure 4-17: LogonManager controls

Adding a ToolBar Control

A ToolBar control is often used along with a MainMenu control. The ToolBar contains Button controls and/or images that provide shortcuts to some of the most often used menu selections.

Programming the button click events for the buttons on a ToolBar control is similar to programming an event procedure for a control array in Visual Basic 6.0. A single procedure handles the click events for all the buttons, and the individual buttons are differentiated by each button's index value. In Visual Basic .NET, the set of buttons on a ToolBar control is called a collection rather than a control array.

You will now experiment with the ToolBar control by adding one to a new project with a simple menu. As a practical matter, this application's menu is much too simple to require a meaningful toolbar, but it will allow you to see how a ToolBar control works.

To add a ToolBar control to a new application:

1 Start a new Visual Basic .NET Windows application called **SampleToolBar** in the Tut04 folder. Put a **MainMenu control** on Form1 with three entries: **Exit**, **Change Message**, and **Hide Message**. Name these menu items **mnuExit**, **mnuChange**, and **mnuHide** respectively. Drag a large **Label** control onto the form, set its **BackColor** property to **yellow**, its **Text** property to nothing, its **TextAlign** property to **MiddleCenter**, and its **Dock** property to **Top**. At runtime, when the user clicks Change Message, use an InputBox function call to change the contents of the label and to make the label visible. When the user clicks Hide Message, make the label disappear by setting its Visible property to False. When the user clicks Exit, display a message box that says, "That's all, Folks!", and then exits the program. See Figure 4-18. Run the **SampleToolBar** program to ensure that it works. You will then use this simple form to hold a toolbar.

large yellow label
with empty text

Toolbar will be placed
underneath the label

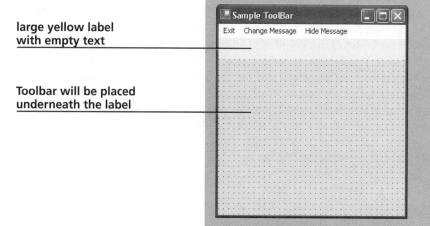

Figure 4-18: SampleToolBar at design time

2 Drag a **ToolBar** control onto the form. If you don't see the ToolBar in the Toolbox, click the down arrow next to the General button to scroll down the list. When you drag a ToolBar control onto a form, by default it docks along the top of the form under the menu and the label, but you can dock it along any side of the form by altering the setting of the Dock property.

3 Click the ToolBar's **Buttons** property, then click the **Collections** setting. This opens the ToolBarButton Collection Editor.

4 In the ToolBarButton Collection Editor, click **Add**. ToolBarButton1 is added. In the properties listing for ToolBarButton1, change the button's **Name** property to **tbrBtnExit**, and change the **Text** property to **Exit**. Type the following message in the **ToolTipText** property: **This terminates the program.**

5 In the ToolBarButton Collection Editor, click **Add** again. ToolBarButton1 is added. In the properties listing for ToolBarButton1, change the button's **Name** property to **tbrBtnChangeLabel**, and change the **Text** property to **Change Message**. Type the following message in the **ToolTipText** property: **Click here to change and show the message.**

6 In the ToolBarButton Collection Editor, click **Add**. ToolBarButton1 is added. Change its **Name** property to **tbrBtnHideLabel**, and change the **Text** property to **Hide Message**. Type the following message in the **ToolTipText** property: **Click here to hide the message.** Figure 4-19 shows the completed ToolBarButton Collection Editor. Click **OK**.

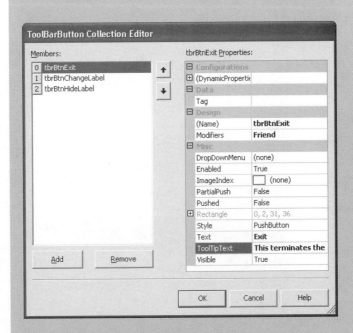

Figure 4-19: ToolBarButton Collection Editor

7   Double-click the **ToolBar** control, which opens the ToolBar1_ButtonClick event procedure in the Code Editor. Insert the code in Figure 4-20 to handle the three buttons (index of 0, 1, and 2) on the toolbar.

```
Private Sub ToolBar1_ButtonClick_1 _
   (ByVal sender As System.Object, ByVal e As _
   System.Windows.Forms.ToolBarButtonClickEventArgs) _
   Handles ToolBar1.ButtonClick
 Const EXIT_SELECTED = 0
 Const CHANGE_SELECTED = 1
 Const HIDE_SELECTED = 2
 Select Case ToolBar1.Buttons.IndexOf(e.Button)
   Case EXIT_SELECTED
     mnuExit_Click(sender, e)
   Case CHANGE_SELECTED
     mnuChange_Click(sender, e)
   Case HIDE_SELECTED
     mnuHide_Click(sender, e)
 End Select
End Sub
```

Figure 4-20: ToolBar1_ButtonClick event procedure

8   Run the **SampleToolBar** program, and click the **Change Message** button. See Figure 4-21. Figure 4-22 shows SampleToolBar, with Label1 changed to "Hello, World!", and the ToolTip over the Change Message button visible.

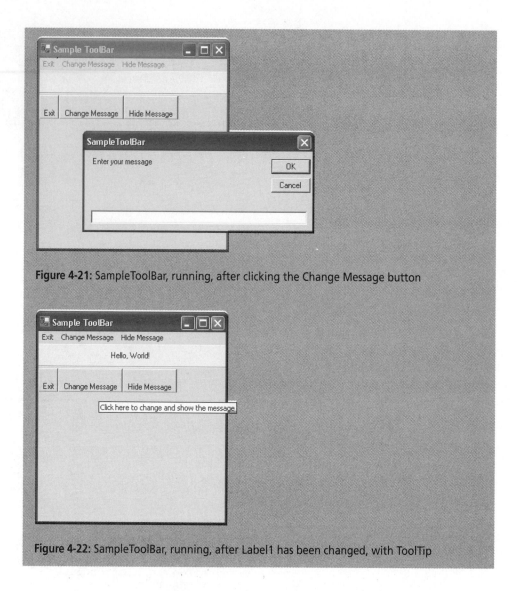

Figure 4-21: SampleToolBar, running, after clicking the Change Message button

Figure 4-22: SampleToolBar, running, after Label1 has been changed, with ToolTip

Adding an ImageList Component

The Visual Basic .NET documentation refers to ImageList as a component rather than a control. An **ImageList** component contains a collection of images (specified through the ImageList's Images property) and can be used in association with any control that has an ImageList property, including the ToolBar, ListView, TreeView, Button, TabControl, CheckBox, RadioButton, and Label controls. Next, you load three images into an ImageList component, and associate these images with the toolbar buttons created earlier.

To add an ImageList to SampleToolBar:

1   Copy and paste three **images** (icons, bitmaps, tifs, or gifs) into the SampleToolBar solutions folder (VB.NET\Student\Tut04\SampleToolBar). Although any image files will do, use the three traffic light icons (red, green, and yellow) **TRFFC10A.ICO, TRFFC10B.ICO,** and **TRFFC10C.ICO** available in the Program Files\Microsoft Visual Studio .NET\Common7\Graphics\icons\Traffic folder.

> **NOTE:** If you do not have access to these icons, you can find a copy of them in the VB.NET\Student\Tut04 folder.

2 Drag an **ImageList** component from the Toolbox onto Form1. ImageList1 appears in the tray underneath the form.

3 Click ImageList1's **Images** property, and then click **Collections** in the settings box. This opens the Image Collection Editor.

4 In the Image Collection Editor, click **Add**. In the Open dialog box, navigate to the **SampleToolBar** folder, and add one of the image files you have copied there. Repeat this process to add the second and third images. Click **OK** to close the Image Collection Editor.

5 Click **ToolBar1**. Set its **ImageList** property to **ImageList1**. Now click ToolBar1's **Buttons Collection** property. In the ToolBarButton Collection Editor, click **tbrBtnExit**. Under tbrBtnExit properties, click **ImageIndex**. Select one of the three images (0, 1, or 2). Repeat this process for **tbrBtnChangeLabel** and **tbrBtnHideLabel**.

6 Run the **SampleToolBar** program to ensure that the images appear properly on the toolbar buttons at runtime. See Figure 4-23.

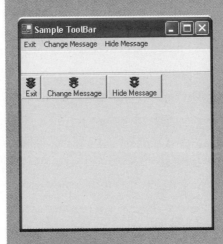

Figure 4-23: SampleToolBar running, with images

Adding an OpenFileDialog Control

The OpenFileDialog control is used by the mnuFileRestore_Click() procedure, which you will program in Lesson C. This control has almost all the same properties, appearance, and behavior as the SaveFileDialog control introduced in Tutorial 2. The only real difference is that its purpose is to designate a file to be opened for input rather than a file to be opened for output.

You have just completed Lesson B. Take a break if you like, but complete the questions and exercises before moving on to Lesson C.

SUMMARY

■ A project compiled into a class library can receive ByVal or ByRef parameters from the calling (client) program. If passed ByRef, the called (server) program can change the values of those parameters and pass them back to the client.

■ One method of passing parameters between programs is through a component class defined in the server program and then instantiated in the client.

■ A ToolBar control is often incorporated into a form, especially an application's main form, and it usually appears under the menu. The toolbar is a container for a collection of button controls that usually provide shortcuts to the most commonly used menu items. Each toolbar button has a ToolTipText property that displays a pop-up message when the insertion point hovers over the button.

■ An ImageList control contains a collection of images. The ImageList itself is not a graphical control, but rather is assigned to any control that has an ImageList property. (Of the controls with which you are already familiar, this includes the ToolBar, TabControl, Button, CheckBox, RadioButton, and Label controls.) The indexes of individual images within the ImageList are then assigned to the ImageIndex property of the receiving control.

■ The OpenFileDialog control allows the user to specify a file to be opened for input.

QUESTIONS

1. To pass a parameter that can be changed by the server, the parameter must be passed _____ .

2. A parameter that cannot be changed by the server should be passed _____ .

3. The principle component of a ToolBar control is its _____ collection.

4. An ImageList control is a(n) _____ for a collection of images.

5. The images in an ImageList control can be many different types of _____ files.

6. To assign a particular image to a toolbar button, the button's _____ property must be set to the _____ of the image within the ImageList control.

7. An effective code container for sharing data between projects is the _____ .

8. The Component Object Model provides a _____ for defining interfaces among different projects.

CRITICAL THINKING

At the end of each lesson, reflective questions are intended to provoke you into considering the material you have just read at a deeper level.

1. In the SampleToolBar program, in the ToolBar1_ButtonClick event, two parameters are passed in each call to a MenuItem's click event. Describe these two parameters.

2. What other methods can you think of for passing variables between projects or between portions of a project?

E X E R C I S E S

1. Create a Windows Forms application. Put a ToolBar control on the form, and put two buttons on the toolbar. Add an ImageList control with two images: a smiley face and a frown. Assign the smiley face to the left toolbar button and the frown to the right toolbar button. Using a Timer control, reverse these images every second. That is, every second the two images should exchange places.

2. Create a Windows Forms application consisting of two projects, a server project (compiled to a class library) and a client project (compiled to an .exe file), with the following functionality:

    a. The server project, called Convert Grader, receives a score (in the form of a Single) and returns a Char, which is the letter-grade equivalent of the score. The score should be received ByVal, the grade ByRef. Inside Convert Grader, convert a grade of 90 or better to an A, 80 to less than 90 to a B, 70 to less than 80 to a C, 60 to less than 70 to a D, and less than 60 to an F. Convert Grader does not have a visible graphical interface.

    b. The client project, called Score, has a text box for obtaining a student score, a button for calling the Convert Grader program, and a label for displaying the letter grade returned by Convert Grader. The user should be instructed to enter the score in the text box. The button should be disabled until the user enters a number into the text box (program the TextChange event to enable the button when the text box gets a numeric value). When the user clicks the button, call the Convert Grader, passing the score from the text box and displaying the letter grade returned by Convert Grader in the label. The GUI for Score appears in Figure 4-24.

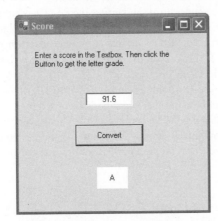

Figure 4-24: Score, running, after calling Grader

3. Create a class library that converts feet into meters, or meters into feet. Create this project, named Tut04ExB3, initially as a Windows Forms application. The form should appear as in Figure 4-25. When the user clicks Convert, the program should convert feet into meters or meters into feet, depending on the settings of the radio buttons. After the program is running, convert it into a class library. Create a small project called TryTut04ExB3 to test the class library project.

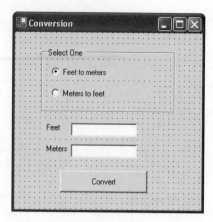

Figure 4-25: frmConvert at design time

4. Create a Windows Forms application consisting of a data file and two projects, a server project (compiled to a class library) and a client project (compiled to an .exe file), with the following functionality:

    a. The data file contains the fastest times (measured in seconds as a floating point value) for each of 10 swimming events.

    b. The server project loads the data file into an array of BestTimes. The calling program passes three parameters to the server project: the event number (ByVal), the new time recorded by a competitor (ByVal), and a message (ByRef). If the time recorded by a new competitor is faster than the time currently in the BestTimes array for that event, the server control returns the message "New Record," records the new time in the BestTimes array, and writes the BestTimes array back to the data file. If the time recorded by a new competitor is not faster than the time currently in the BestTimes array for that event, then a message is returned indicating that the competitor's time was slower than the current best time (which is displayed).

    c. The client program has a form with a button and three text boxes. txtEventNum is used to hold the number (1 thru 10) of a swimming event. txtTime is used to hold the number of seconds recorded by a competitor in the indicated event. Clicking the button causes the client program to make sure that txtEventNum contains an integer from 1 to 10 and txtTime contains a numeric value, and if these criteria are satisfied, call the server program, passing the three text boxes.

After completing this lesson, you will be able to:

- Plan for the completion of the LogonManagerFinal application, including the MDI form, child forms, and calls to two class library projects
- Complete the GUI for mdiMain, incorporating the new ToolBar and ImageList controls
- Complete the menu click event procedures, converting previously created program stubs into working code, modifying frmUser for multiple uses and purposes, and creating frmViewAll
- Incorporate calls to two class library projects, FigWelcome and Logon
- Understand the power of a class library

Class Libraries and Reusable Code

In Lesson C, you complete the LogonManager application begun in Tutorial 3, including mdiMain's menu item click event procedures that were still "under construction" after Tutorial 3, the ToolBar, ImageList, and OpenFileDialog controls introduced in Lesson B, and the child forms. In preparation for these tasks, you should run the two executables and compare them: the LogonManagerDraft application from Tutorial 3 and the LogonManager application from Tutorial 4.

Setting up and Planning the LogonManagerFinal Application

The remainder of Tutorial 4 builds on the LogonManagerDraft application that you created in Tutorial 3. You can either continue to build that application or start anew with the completed LogonManagerDraft application obtained from your instructor.

To set up the LogonManagerFinal application:

1   Create a new folder called **VB.NET\Student\Tut04\LogonManagerFinal**.

2   Into this new folder, copy the contents of either the VB.NET\Student\Tut03\ LogonManagerDraft folder (which you created in Tutorial 3) or the completed LogonManagerDraft application folder you obtain from your instructor. In either case, you now have a folder called LogonManagerFinal, inside of which you have a solution called LogonManagerDraft.sln and a project called LogonManagerDraft.vbproj.

   NOTE: Make sure that you have a copy of the Users file in the LogonManagerFinal\bin folder. For purposes of building and testing the LogonManager application, you can use either the Users file that you created yourself in Tutorial 3, or the Users file that you accessed when running LogonManager.exe at the beginning of this tutorial. If needed, copy one of these two Users files into the Tut04\LogonManagerFinal\bin folder.

3   Click **File | Open Solution**, and open the **LogonManagerDraft.sln** (solution) file. In Solution Explorer, click **Solution 'LogonManagerDraft' (1 project)** . In the Solution Properties window, click the solution name, and change it to **LogonManager**. In Solution Explorer, click the project name, **LogonManagerDraft**. Then in Project Properties, change the name of the project to **LogonManager**.

4   Run the **LogonManager** project from the IDE to make sure that it still works correctly.

> **5**   In Windows Explorer, navigate to the **LogonManagerFinal** folder. Verify that the name of the solution file has been changed to LogonManager.sln, and the name of the project is now LogonManager.vbproj.

You are now ready to work on the final version of LogonManager.

Identifying Tasks to Complete LogonManager

If you run the two executables provided to you—the LogonManagerDraft from Tutorial 3 and LogonManager from Tutorial 4—side by side, you can identify the tasks that still await completion:

- Complete the mdiMain GUI: add ToolBar and ImageList controls, and enhance the application's GUI by placing a RadioCheck in front of the Accept New Users menu item whenever a new user request is pending.
- Write new menu click event procedures for the menu items that were "under construction" at the end of Tutorial 3—mnuFileBackup_Click(), mnuFileRestore_Click(), mnuViewExistingUser_Click, mnuViewSupervisorEditUserInfo_Click(), mnuViewSupervisorViewAllUsers_ Click() (with a new child form), and mnuViewSupervisorResetExpirationDates_Click().
- Incorporate calls to the Logon application in mnuViewExistingUser_Click() and in mnuViewSupervisorLogon_Click().
- Display the splash screen (FigWelcome) at startup.

As you work through this lesson, each of these tasks will be handled in turn.

Completing the mdiMain GUI

As the first step toward completing the LogonManagerFinal application, you need to incorporate ToolBar and ImageList controls into mdiMain. In the following exercise, these controls retain their default names, ToolBar1 and ImageList1, a common programming practice in view of the fact that a form rarely contains more than one toolbar or more than one image list. However, if you did have more than one, then creating meaningful names for each control would be a sound programming practice.

To add an image list and toolbar to mdiMain:

1   Add an **ImageList** control to mdiMain. Add any three icons (.ico files) to its **Images Collection**—these will be the icons added to the buttons on your ToolBar control. You can use the three faces—FACE01 (smile), FACE02 (neutral), and FACE03 (laughing)—shown in Figure 4-26 and located in the Program Files\Microsoft Visual Studio .NET\Common7\Graphics\icons\Misc folder.

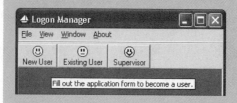

Figure 4-26: Three smileys, with ToolTip for the New User button

2   Add a **ToolBar** control to mdiMain. Set its **ImageList** property to **ImageList1**. In the Buttons property, click **Collection**. In the ToolBarButton Collection Editor, add three **ToolBarButtons**, and set the appropriate **Text** and **ImageIndex** property for each button, as suggested by Figure 4-26. Set the **ToolTipText** property to **Fill out the application form to become a user, Update/verify your user information and change your password**, and **Logon as the system supervisor**, respectively.

3   To open the ToolBar1_ButtonClick event procedure, in mdiMain's Code window, select **ToolBar1** from the Class Name combo box at the top left. Then select **ButtonClick** from the Method Name combo box at the top right.

4   Recall that you can use a Select Case control structure to differentiate among ToolBarButton controls. Add the code shown in Figure 4-27.

```
Private Sub ToolBar1_ButtonClick(ByVal sender As System.Object, _
    ByVal e As System.Windows.Forms.ToolBarButtonClickEventArgs) _
    Handles ToolBar1.ButtonClick
  Const NEWUSER = 0
  Const EXISTINGUSER = 1
  Const SUPERVISOR = 2
  Select Case ToolBar1.Buttons.IndexOf(e.Button)
    Case NEWUSER
      mnuViewNewUser_Click(sender, e)
    Case EXISTINGUSER
      mnuViewExistingUser_Click(sender, e)
    Case SUPERVISOR
      mnuViewSupervisorLogon_Click(sender, e)
  End Select
End Sub
```

Figure 4-27: ToolBar1_ButtonClick() event procedure

5   Run the **LogonManagerFinal** application to see that it still works as it did at the end of Tutorial 3 and to verify that the new toolbar buttons work as advertised.

Implementing a RadioCheck

The system supervisor wants to have a visual indication that a new user request is pending. One method of accomplishing this might be to display a RadioCheck in front of the Accept New Users menu item whenever at least one new user request is awaiting disposition.

When a menu item has a submenu, its click event does not fire when the item is selected. However, a menu item also carries a Select event, which does fire. Therefore, you can program the Select event to either place or erase a RadioCheck in front of the Accept New Users menu item, depending on the presence or absence of at least one N status record in the array. The code to do that is shown in Figure 4-28.

```
Dim i As Integer
Dim blnNewUserPending As Boolean = False
For i = 1 To MAXUSERS
  If pastructUser(i).Status = "N" Then
    blnNewUserPending = True
    Exit For
  End If
Next
mnuViewSupervisorAcceptNewUsers.Checked = blnNewUserPending
```

Figure 4-28: mnuViewSupervisor_Select()

To implement the RadioCheck in front of the Accept New Users menu item:

1 Insert the **mnuViewSupervisor_Select()** procedure shown in Figure 4-28. This code uses a local Boolean variable, blnNewUserPending, initialized to False, to indicate the presence of at least one new user record. When an N record is encountered, the Boolean variable is set to True. After the For loop examines all the elements of the array, you either place or remove the RadioCheck depending on the value of blnNewUserPending. (The RadioCheck's visibility is set by the menu item's Checked property.)

Writing the Click Event Procedures

The new menu click event procedures that need to be written are mnuFileBackup_Click() and mnuFileRestore_Click(), both on the File menu; and mnuViewExistingUser_Click, mnuViewSupervisorEditUserInfo_Click(), mnuViewSupervisorViewAllUsers_Click(), and mnuViewSupervisorResetExpirationDates_Click(), all on the View menu. You will perhaps recall that each of these procedures contained merely a stub in the draft application of Tutorial 3; now it's time to replace the stubs with the real code. In addition, in the mnuViewSupervisorAcceptNewUsers_Click() procedure that you created in Tutorial 3, new code is needed to disable the user-editable controls.

Programming Procedures on the File Menu

The mnuFileBackup_Click() and mnuFileRestore_Click() procedures allow the supervisor to make a backup copy of the Users file, storing that file under a name and in a location chosen by the supervisor, and to restore the Users file from a previous backup.

mnuFileBackup() uses the SaveFileDialog control introduced with the Dining application in Tutorial 2. In this instance, you set the properties of the control in code rather than in the Form Designer. The backup is actually created if the user selects a filename and location and then clicks OK in the Save File dialog box. The backup is created from the records of the pastructUser() array.

In a fashion analogous to the SaveFileDialog control in the backup procedure, the restore procedure uses an OpenFileDialog control. If the supervisor selects a backup file from which to restore and then approves the operation, records are copied from the backup file to the Users file, and then the pastructUser() array is reloaded by calling ReadUsersFile().

To create and test the backup and restore procedures:

1   Begin by dragging a **SaveFileDialog** control and an **OpenFileDialog** control onto mdiMain. They appear in the system tray below the form.

2   Insert the code shown in Figure 4-29 into mnuFileBackup_Click(). This code assigns values to the DefaultExt, Filename, InitialDirectory, Filter, and FilterIndex properties of the SaveFileDialog control.

set properties before opening the dialog box

open the dialog box and continue if the user clicks OK

```
Private Sub mnuFileBackup_Click(ByVal sender As System.Object, _
    ByVal e As System.EventArgs) Handles mnuFileBackup.Click
  SaveFileDialog1.DefaultExt = "bak"
  SaveFileDialog1.FileName = "Users.bak"
  SaveFileDialog1.InitialDirectory = CurDir()
  SaveFileDialog1.Filter = "backup files (*.bak)|*.bak|" & _
    "txt files (*.txt)|*.txt|All files (*.*)|*.*"
  SaveFileDialog1.FilterIndex = 1
  If SaveFileDialog1.ShowDialog() = DialogResult.OK Then
    FileOpen(1, SaveFileDialog1.FileName, OpenMode.Random, _
      OpenAccess.Write, , Len(pstructUserRec))
    Dim i As Integer
    For i = 1 To MAXUSERS
      FilePut(1, pastructUser(i), i)
    Next
    FileClose(1)
    MessageBox.Show("File backed up successfully")
  End If
End Sub
```

Figure 4-29: Code for mnuFileBackup_Click()

The DefaultExt property assigns a default filename extension to the saved file, if the user does not include a filename extension. The Filename property is the name of the file to be saved; it is used as is, if the user does not change it. The InitialDirectory property identifies the folder initially suggested for saving the file, although the user can browse to a different folder.

The Filter property contains zero or more filters for displaying the contents of a folder, and the FilterIndex property indicates which of those filters are applied initially. The filter takes the form "*<filter text1>* | *<filter1>* [| *<filter text2>* | *<filter2>*...]". For example: "Text files (*.txt)|*.txt|All files (*.*)|*.*". The filter index is a 1-based index, and 1 is its default value.

The code in Figure 4-29 then calls the ShowDialog method, which returns a value indicating whether the user has clicked OK or Cancel. If the user clicks OK (DialogResult.OK), the procedure creates the user-selected file in the user-selected folder, copies the contents of the pastructUser array into that file, and notifies the user that the backup was successful.

3   Program the **mnuFileRestore_Click()** procedure, as shown in Figure 4-30.

For the OpenFileDialog control, you set the same properties in code exactly as you did for the SaveFileDialog control. Then, as was the case with the SaveFileDialog, the input/output operation is executed only if the user clicks OK in response to the dialog box. But in this case the I/O operation is a tad more involved: the backup file is opened for input, while the Users file is opened for output. Then, one at a time, records are copied from the backup (input) file (using FileGet) to the pastructUser array, and thence to the Users (output) file (using FilePut).

set properties before
opening the dialog box

open the dialog box and
continue if the user
clicks OK

copy records from the
backup file to the array,
and from the array to
the restore file

```
Private Sub mnuFileRestore_Click(ByVal sender As System.Object, _
    ByVal e As System.EventArgs) Handles mnuFileRestore.Click
    OpenFileDialog1.DefaultExt = "bak"
    OpenFileDialog1.FileName = "Users.bak"
    OpenFileDialog1.InitialDirectory = CurDir()
    OpenFileDialog1.Filter = "backup files (*.bak)|*.bak|" & _
        "txt files (*.txt)|*.txt|All files (*.*)|*.*"
    OpenFileDialog1.FilterIndex = 1
    If OpenFileDialog1.ShowDialog() = DialogResult.OK Then
        FileOpen(1, OpenFileDialog1.FileName, OpenMode.Random, _
            OpenAccess.Read, , Len(pstructUserRec))
        FileOpen(2, "Users", OpenMode.Random, OpenAccess.Write, , _
            Len(pstructUserRec))
        Dim i As Integer
        For i = 1 To MAXUSERS
            FileGet(1, pastructUser(i), i)
            FilePut(2, pastructUser(i), i)
        Next
        FileClose()
        MessageBox.Show("File has been restored")
    End If
End Sub
```

Figure 4-30: Code for mnuFileRestore()_Click

4   Run the **LogonManagerFinal** application. Log on as the **system supervisor** (recall that the supervisor's e-mail address is 1 and the password is SUPERVISOR). Then click **File | Backup**, and save the Users file in the Temp folder as **Users.bak**. Then click **File | Restore**, and restore the Users file you have just backed up. Exit the program and return to the IDE.

Programming Procedures on the View Menu

The mnuViewExistingUser_Click() procedure calls the Logon class library, which determines whether the user is registered in the system, and it also returns the user's record number. The procedure then instantiates a new form based on the frmUser class and displays the form. The code in frmUser retrieves the appropriate user record based on the user's record number returned by Logon.

You incorporate the call to Logon a little later. At the moment, you just want to get the child form working, making the temporary assumption that the user is legitimate and knows the correct user record number.

To (partially) program the remaining stubs in the View menu:

1   Open the **mnuViewExistingUser_Click()** procedure. Insert the code shown in Figure 4-31. This code asks the user for the record number, and then displays a new instance of frmUser.

```
'get value of pintRecNum
pintRecNum = InputBox("The call to Logon goes here. " & _
  "Assume that it works. Enter the user's record number:")
'then instantiate and display an object based on the frmUser class
Dim frmUserTemp As New frmUser()
frmUserTemp.MdiParent = Me
frmUserTemp.Text = "Edit User Info"
frmUserTemp.Show()
```

Figure 4-31: mnuViewExistingUser_Click(), without the call to Logon

The mnuViewSupervisorEditUserInfo_Click() procedure asks for the record number of the user whose record is to be edited, and then displays that user's information using the same multipurpose frmUser that was used for the View | New User, View | Existing User, and View | Supervisor | Accept New Users menus. Except for the fact that this procedure need not ask the user to log on, the code is almost the same as that in mnuViewExistingUser_Click(). (Recall that the supervisor must log on before this procedure is enabled.)

2   Open **mnuViewSupervisorEditUserInfo_Click()**. Type the code shown in Figure 4-32. This code first verifies that the user record number entered by the supervisor represents an active user, and it exits the procedure after issuing an error message if that is not the case. The rest of the procedure instantiates the form and displays it—also making btnDelete visible, since the supervisor can use this form to delete any user.

check for valid user

instantiate the form
and display it

```
pintRecNum = InputBox("Enter record number of existing user")
If pastructUser(pintRecNum).Status = "I" Then
  MsgBox("That record number is inactive", , _
    "Error - Invalid record number")
  Exit Sub
End If
Dim frmUserTemp As New frmUser()
frmUserTemp.Text = "Supervisor: Edit User"
frmUserTemp.MdiParent = Me
frmUserTemp.btnDelete.Visible = True
frmUserTemp.Show()
```

Figure 4-32: mnuViewSupervisorEditUserInfo_Click() procedure

3   Run the **LogonManagerFinal** program to verify that the procedures you have just created work correctly. Exit the program and return to the IDE.

The form frmViewAll displays all of the active records and new (pending) users in the pastructUser() array, and mnuViewSupervisorViewAllUsers_Click() instantiates this new child form and causes it to be displayed. The information appears in a large list box that fills the form, the form is maximized in mdiMain, and mdiMain is maximized to fill the screen, so that there is room to display all or most of the data columns without scrolling.

4   Add a **new form** named **frmViewAll** to the LogonManager project. Set its **WindowState** property to **Maximized**. Add a **ListBox** control, and set its **Dock** property to **Fill**.

5   Insert the code shown in Figure 4-33 into the **frmViewAll_Load()** procedure. This code loads ListBox1 with column headers and then rows from pastructUser(). You might need to experiment to get the spacing to appear as it does in Figure 4-34 when the program is run.

```
Private Sub frmViewAll_Load(ByVal sender As Object, _
    ByVal e As System.EventArgs) Handles MyBase.Load
  Dim i As Integer
  Dim s As String
  s = "Num Status FirstName  LastName   Work Phone          " & _
    "Home Phone          Role        Start    " & _
    "E-mail Address       Expires     Secret Q# Answer"
  ListBox1.Items.Add(s)

  For i = 1 To MAXUSERS
    With pastructUser(i)
      If .Status <> "I" Then
        s = Strings.Right("   " & Str(i), 3) & " "
        s &= .Status & " "
        s &= IIf(.Supervisor, "Supv ", "User ")
        s &= Strings.Left(.FirstName & Space(10), 10) & " "
        s &= Strings.Left(.LastName & Space(10), 10) & " "
        s &= Strings.Left(.WorkPhone & Space(20), 20) & " "
        s &= Strings.Left(.HomePhone & Space(20), 20) & " "
        s &= Strings.Left(.Role & Space(12), 12) & " "
        s &= Strings.Left(Format(.StartDate, "Short Date") & _
          Space(10), 10)
        s &= Strings.Left(.EmailAddress & Space(20), 20) & " "
        s &= Strings.Left(.PasswordExpirationDate & Space(11), 11)
        s &= Strings.Left(.HasSecret.ToString & Space(7), 7)
        s &= .Question.ToString & "   "
        s &= .Answer
        ListBox1.Items.Add(s)
      End If
    End With
  Next
End Sub
```

Figure 4-33: frmViewAll_Load() procedure

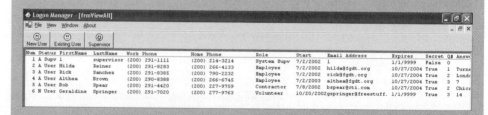

Figure 4-34: View All Users at runtime

6   In **mdiMain**, in **mnuViewSupervisorViewAllUsers_Click**(), insert code shown in Figure 4-35 to maximize mdiMain and show the child form.

```
Dim frmViewAllTemp As New frmViewAll()
Me.WindowState = FormWindowState.Maximized
frmViewAllTemp.MdiParent = Me
frmViewAllTemp.Show()
```

Figure 4-35: Code for mnuViewSupervisorViewAllUsers_Click()

7   Run the **LogonManagerFinal** program, **logon** as the supervisor, and view the child form. Exit the program and return to the IDE.

The mnuViewSupervisorResetExpirationDates_Click procedure gives the system supervisor the ability to reset the password expiration dates of all existing users (except users with system supervisor status) to 90 days from today. (A supervisor's password does not expire.) The code shown in Figure 4-36 first verifies that the supervisor wants to perform this operation. It then steps through the pastructUser array, and for each active record, it resets the PasswordExpirationDate to the date 90 days after today (for regular users) or to January 1, 9999 (for system supervisors). The date 90 days from today is calculated by adding 90 days to the system variable Today, using the DateAdd function.

NOTE: The Users file provided to you contains passwords that never expire for the entire Friendsville Games Development Team. This was done so that the initial file will work whenever you happen to first use it. But, after you select View | Supervisor | Reset Expiration Dates, the passwords for members of the FGDT will in fact expire after 90 days.

8 Type the code into the **mnuViewSupervisorResetExpirationDates_Click()** event procedure shown in Figure 4-36.

```
Private Sub mnuViewSupervisorResetExpirationDates_Click(ByVal _
    sender As System.Object, ByVal e As System.EventArgs) _
    Handles mnuViewSupervisorResetExpirationDates.Click
  If MsgBox("This function resets the password expiration date " & _
      "for all regular users to 90 days from today. Proceed?", _
      MsgBoxStyle.YesNo) = MsgBoxResult.Yes Then
    Dim i As Integer
    For i = 1 To MAXUSERS
      With pastructUser(i)
        If .Status = "A" Then .PasswordExpirationDate = _
          IIf(.Supervisor, CDate("1/1/9999"), _
          DateAdd(DateInterval.Day, 90, Today))
      End With
    Next
    WriteUsersFile()
  End If
End Sub
```

Figure 4-36: Sub mnuViewSupervisorResetExpirationDates_Click()

NOTE: Recall that in Tutorial 3, WriteUsersFile() was a private method in frmUser, but in the code in Figure 4-36, WriteUsersFile() must be called from mdiMain. For this reason, you must move the WriteUsersFile() method from frmUser to Module1, and change its accessibility to Public.

9 Run the **LogonManagerFinal** application again. Log on as the **supervisor**, and click **View | Supervisor | View All Users**. Note the password expiration dates for each active user. Now click **View | Supervisor | Reset Expiration Dates**. Then click **View | Supervisor | View All Users** again, and note the revised password expiration dates for all active users except the supervisor. Exit the application and return to the IDE.

Disabling Controls for Multiple Users and Purposes

One good principle of program design is to prevent users from making changes to data except at those times when changing data is called for. This principle extends also to the supervisor. The idea is to inhibit anyone, even the system supervisor, from harming the data.

When the supervisor is reviewing a new user request, the only indicated action is to accept or reject the request. Therefore, it makes sense to disable all of the other controls on the form.

To disable user-editable controls in frmUser when the Accept New Users menu item has been selected:

1   In frmUser, insert a new procedure called **DisableControls()**. In this procedure, disable all of the user-editable controls on frmUser (TextBoxes, ComboBox, CheckBox, and RadioButtons). The procedure should be public, and it should consist entirely of statements that set the Enabled property of each of these user-input controls to False.

2   In mdiMain, in the **mnuViewSupervisorAcceptNewUsers_Click()** procedure, insert the following statement before showing the child form:

```
frmUserTemp.DisableControls()
```

3   Run the **LogonManagerFinal** program. Create a new user named **Dublin Ireland**, with an e-mail address of **Dublin@fgdt.org**, and the password **dublinfgdt**. His secret question asks for his mother's maiden name, and the answer is **Casey**. Submit the New User.

4   Click **View | Supervisor**. A RadioCheck appears in front of Accept New Users. Log on as the supervisor. Click **Accept New Users**. Dublin Ireland's record appears. Verify that all the user-editable controls have been disabled. Click **Accept**. Click **View | Supervisor**. The RadioCheck no longer appears in front of **Accept New Users**.

5   Exit the application and return to the IDE.

Incorporating Calls to the Logon and FigWelcome Class Library Projects

You have now written all of the new procedures for mdiMain; it is time to turn your attention to the incorporation of the Logon program into LogonManager. The LogonManager application calls Logon to verify a user's e-mail address, password, and supervisor status. The call to FigWelcome is just the opening splash screen. Both calls are to class libraries.

Adding a Call to the Logon Application

The call to the Logon application is needed when an existing user logs on and when a supervisor logs on. Without the call to Logon, anyone could run the LogonManager application and change user passwords, delete users, and create new users. So the call to Logon is necessary to ensure the integrity of the FGDT's logon process.

To insert the Logon application into LogonManager:

1   In Solution Explorer, add a reference to the Logon.dll in the LogonManager's References by right-clicking **References** in Solution Explorer, then clicking **Add Reference**. In the Add Reference dialog box, click the **Projects** tab. Browse to find the **Logon.dll** (in VB.NET\Student\Tut04\Logon\bin), and click **OK**.

2   In the Code window for mdiMain, insert the following statement before the `Public Class mdiMain` statement:

Imports Logon

3   Replace the stub code with a call to the Logon application in the **mnuViewSupervisorLogon_Click()** procedure as shown in Figure 4-37. Recall that execution of the Logon application begins with Sub Main() in Component1, and that it requires three parameters, which indicate (1) whether the logon was successful, (2) whether the user has supervisor privileges, and (3) the user's record number.

```
Dim MyLogon As New Component1()
pintRecNum = 0
MyLogon.Main(pblnLogonOk, pblnSupv, pintRecNum)
If pblnLogonOk = False Then End
If pblnSupv Then
  mnuFileInitialize.Enabled = True
  mnuFileBackup.Enabled = True
  mnuFileRestore.Enabled = True
  mnuViewSupervisorAcceptNewUsers.Enabled = True
  mnuViewSupervisorEditUserInfo.Enabled = True
  mnuViewSupervisorViewAllUsers.Enabled = True
  mnuViewSupervisorResetExpirationDates.Enabled = True
Else
  MsgBox("This user does not have System Supervisor permissions.")
End If
```

Figure 4-37: Code for mnuViewSupervisorLogon_Click()

4   Navigate to **mnuViewExistingUser_Click()**, and add the code shown in Figure 4-38 at the beginning of the procedure, replacing the InputBox function call. In this case, the user need not be a supervisor. The integer returned by Logon (pintRecNum) identifies the user record number.

```
'logon first, and get value of pintRecNum
Dim MyLogon As New Component1()
pintRecNum = 0
MyLogon.Main(pblnLogonOk, pblnSupv, pintRecNum)
If pblnLogonOk = False Then End
```

Figure 4-38: Calling Logon from mnuViewExistingUser_Click()

5   Run the program, checking that the two calls to the Logon application work as advertised. Exit the program and return to the IDE.

Adding the Call to the FigWelcome Splash Screen

Your last task in LogonManager is to call the splash screen at application startup.

The call to display a splash screen can be placed anywhere that causes it to execute before the main application appears on the screen. In this case, you place the call inside the Windows Form Designer generated code.

To insert the FigWelcome splash screen into LogonManager:

1 In Solution Explorer, add a **reference** to the **FigWelcome.dll** in the LogonManager's References. (If you created your own version of the Welcome screen, you can reference that DLL instead.)

2 In the Code window for mdiMain, insert the following statement before the `Public Class mdiMain` declaration:

```
Imports FigWelcome
```

3 Navigate to the Windows Form Designer generated code section, in **Sub New()**, and insert the following after the InitializeComponent() method call:

```
Dim MyWelcome As New frmWelcome()
MyWelcome.ShowDialog()
```

4 Run the **LogonManager** program. The splash screen should appear, then disappear after three seconds, and then the main application should appear. Exit the application, and return to the IDE.

Understanding the Power of a Class Library

Assume that the Friendsville Games Development Team has now developed 20 applications that all call the Logon class library. Assume further that the Friendsville Organizing Committee has determined that every application should display the newly adopted "gone fishing" bitmap as a logo—the image that appears as the background in FigWelcome. To help implement this edict, you have the task of modifying the Logon class library application so that the logon screen includes this bitmap. And this change must be propagated to all of the applications that use the class library.

This exercise should unreservedly demonstrate to you the efficacy of software reuse, of programming with objects, and specifically of building class library applications.

To implement a change to Logon:

1 Open the **Logon** solution, open **frmLogon** in the Form Designer, and set the **BackgroundImage** property to the bitmap file **Gone Fishing.bmp**. Then run the **TryLogon** project, which calls Logon and causes it to compile, updating its DLL. Note the new background of the Logon screen.

2 Run **LogonManager.exe** from the Start menu or from Windows Explorer. Click **View | Existing User** to invoke Logon. Note that it still has its original background. Exit the application.

3 Open **LogonManager** in the IDE, if necessary, and run it from within the IDE. This calls the new DLL for the class library. When Logon is invoked, it appears with the new background. Exit the application, and exit Visual Studio .NET.

4 Now run **LogonManager** once more from the Start menu or from Windows Explorer, and you see the new background in Logon. Exit the application.

If instead of using a class library, frmLogon had been copied into each of the 20 applications that use it, propagating a revised Logon application could become a substantial effort. Since it is a class, propagating a change requires only that each program be recompiled, a much simpler task.

You now have completed Tutorial 4. Stop now for a break, or continue on with the exercises.

S U M M A R Y

- A class library application compiles to a DLL (dynamic link library) file, and so cannot be executed directly.
- To call a class from another application, add a reference to the class's DLL in the calling application.
- To make the members of a class available without qualification, use the Imports statement to import the namespace before the class declaration in the calling application.
- A component can be defined in a class library, and can contain procedures with parameters passed from a calling routine.
- Even a modest-sized program demonstrates the value of top-down planning, a modular approach, and careful adherence to naming conventions. This is especially true in a team programming environment.
- When it comes to program maintenance, the efficiency of OOP becomes obvious. A class library can be updated, and the revised program can be quickly propagated to all of the other programs that use it.

Q U E S T I O N S

1. The output from compiling a class library project is a(n) _____ file.

2. The _____ statement before the class/module/component declaration makes the names defined in a class library available without qualification.

3. To use a class library in a project, you must include it in the _____ list of the client project.

4. The Logon class library includes a(n) _____, which is needed primarily for passing parameters to and from the client project.

5. Today's date is returned by the _____ function.

6. The _____ method returns a string minus any leading or trailing spaces.

7. The tip or hint given in a pop-up when the insertion point hovers over a toolbar button is set by the button's _____ property.

8. Assignment of a value type to a variable creates a copy of the _____ being assigned.

9. Assignment of a reference type to a variable creates a copy of the _____.

E X E R C I S E S

1. Create a Windows Forms MDI application to display the Room Service Menu for the International Village's kitchen. The main menu should offer breakfast, lunch, dinner, snacks, and bar menu items, each of which triggers a child form. Populate the child

forms with ComboBoxes, RadioButtons, CheckBoxes, and ListBoxes arranged as appropriate in GroupBox controls. Each child form should be unique. Figure 4-39, for example, is a suggested frmBreakfast. These controls should all offer food and beverage selections to the user. Dock a ListBox control on the left side of the MDI form. When a user selects an item from a child form, add that item to the list box on the parent. When the user selects an item in the list box on the parent, remove that item from the list box.

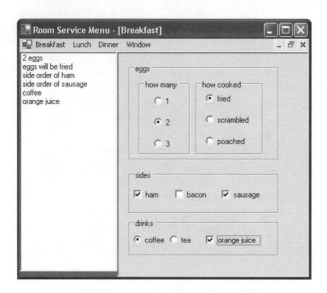

Figure 4-39: frmBreakfast at runtime, inside the MDI form

One aspect of this project might be difficult: How do you communicate from the child form back to its MDI parent? That is, how do you add an item to the list box on the parent within an event procedure in the child form? One method of accomplishing this was mentioned in Exercise 8 of Lesson C in Tutorial 3. Here is another solution. Declare an object of the same type as the parent MDI form, and then assign the parent MDI form to this object. That makes the parent's controls available to the instantiated object, so you can use the list box on the parent form directly. In the sample code shown in Figure 4-40, the CheckedChanged event for a radio button on the breakfast menu is shown. (There are three radio buttons in a group box, for choosing 1, 2, or 3 eggs.) If the user chooses one egg, this event fires. After frm is declared as an object of type mdiRoomSvcMenu (the name of the MDI form), frm is made to point to Me.MdiParent—that is, the actual instance of mdiRoomSvcMenu when the program is running. After this declaration, the parent's list box (lstOrder) can be referenced.

```
Private Sub rad1_CheckedChanged(ByVal sender As _
    System.Object, ByVal e As System.EventArgs) _
    Handles rad1.CheckedChanged
  If rad1.Checked Then
    Dim frm As mdiRoomSvcMenu = Me.MdiParent
    frm.lstOrder.Items.Remove("2 eggs")
    frm.lstOrder.Items.Remove("3 eggs")
    frm.lstOrder.Items.Add("1 egg")
  End If
End Sub
```

Figure 4-40: rad1_CheckedChanged procedure

2. Modify the problem in Exercise 1 as follows: instead of an MDI application and child forms, create TabPage properties on a TabControl control to hold the breakfast, lunch, dinner, and bar items.

3. Create a Console application to add an unlimited number of records to the MyUsers file. Use the same random-access file structure used in this tutorial's Logon and LogonManager applications. Internally, implement the same structure for a user record. However, do not read the data into an array. Rather, use the file directly for each I/O operation. Declare only one simple variable of type structUser. Use InputBox function calls to get information from the user, and validate each piece of data as it is obtained, returning for corrected data until it is acceptable. When all of the data for a record has been obtained, write only that one record to the file. Your program should not overwrite an active record, but rather search for an empty or inactive record.

4. Starting with the completed LogonManager application, add the capability to print all records (one record per page). Add this capability by inserting a Print menu item under the File menu on the MDI form. Only the supervisor has the right to print, so this menu item should be initially disabled, and then enabled when a supervisor logs on. Inactive records should not be printed, so you are actually printing only those records whose status = A or N (that is, Active users and New users whose application is pending). Arrange the data in two columns, with the field names on the left and the data values neatly aligned in the right-hand column. (The basics of printing were explained in Tutorial 2.) From the Dining application in Tutorial 2, recall that the PrintDocument1_PrintPage() procedure prints only one page, and that this procedure is executed repeatedly as long as e.HasMorePages is True. To save on paper, use a PrintPreview control, so that the report prints to the screen. The report should appear approximately like Figure 4-41.

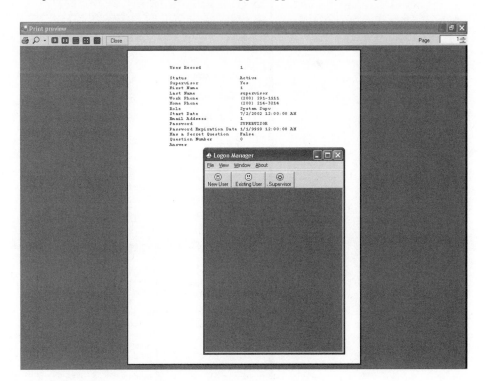

Figure 4-41: Page 1 of a multi-page report of users

Exercises 5 and 6 allow you to both discover the solution to problems on your own and experiment with material that is not covered explicitly in the tutorial.

discovery ▶ 5. Create a Windows Forms MDI application to allow athletes to register for participation in the Friendsville International Games. Provide a ToolBar control in lieu of a MainMenu control. Toolbar buttons should activate child forms that provide these functions: create a new registration, edit an existing registration, view all registrations, and about. The registration form (a child form) should provide an AthleteID (actually the record number in a random-access file). The form should then collect contact information (name, address, phone, e-mail), nationality, sex, and sport. The same registration form should be used to edit an existing registration. Another child form should contain a ListBox control that displays the name, nationality, and sport of every athlete who has registered. A third child form should be an About form. The application should call the FigWelcome splash screen as well as the Logon screen. Save the information concerning each athlete in an Athletes random-access file called Registration.dat. Limit this file to 200 records. Write a routine to initialize the file with 200 inactive records when the application loads, provided the file does not already exist.

discovery ▶ 6. You were asked to design a quiz program in Tutorial 3, Lesson A, Exercise 1 and then you built the quiz program as a Windows application in Tutorial 3, Lesson B, Exercise 6. Now implement the same quiz program as a Web Forms application. The running Web page should appear approximately as in Figure 4-42. A RadioButtonList control contains the three radio buttons named Continents, Languages, and Capitals. You must set the AutoPostBack property of this control to True (AutoPostBack is explained in Tutorial 7).

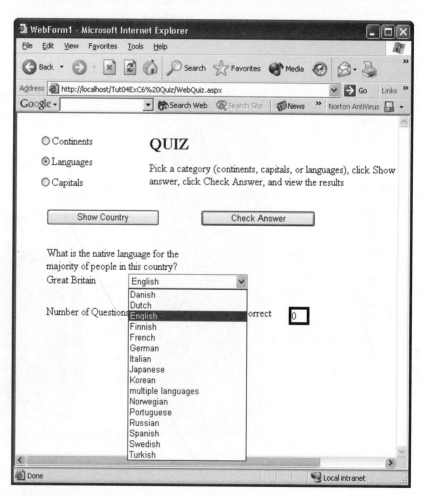

Figure 4-42: Web Quiz, running

KEY TERMS

- ButtonClick event
- Buttons collection
- client application
- Compare() function
- Component class
- DateAdd() function
- ImageIndex property
- ImageList control
- ImageList property
- Images collection
- Imports statement
- OpenFileDialog component
- RadioCheck property
- reference type
- References list
- Select event
- Today function
- ToolBar control
- ToolBarButtons collection
- ToolTips property
- ToolTipText property
- Trim method
- value type

Advanced Windows Forms Controls and Coding

Creating a Basic Model for Competition Scoring

case ▶ One of the principle tasks for the Friendsville Games Development Team (FGDT) is the development of modules for scoring all the competitions. The completed application needs to consist of a series of modules tailored to scoring each event in each sport. Ultimately, competition results must also be recorded in a database. However, the much smaller, immediate task is to demonstrate FGDT's ability to develop the major application later.

The immediate task, therefore, is to develop an overall scheme for this application, encompassing all the sports, plus draft versions of the detail modules for two kinds of competitions: team sports, in which two national teams compete and in which the winner is determined by the most points scored, and individual competitions of up to eight competitors, in which the winner is determined by the fastest time. In Tutorial 6, the Scoring application will be enhanced to include competitions whose winners are determined by longest distance and those competitions whose winners are determined by judging. For competitions among more than two individuals, it will also sort the results into the correct order of finish (1st, 2nd, 3rd, and so on).

Previewing a Draft of the Scoring Application

This draft of the Scoring application provides the basic functionality for scoring individual and team competitions at the Friendsville International Games. It also employs a new user interface and a number of new controls.

To view the completed draft of the Scoring application:

1 Run the completed draft of the **Scoring** application, found in VB.NET\Student\ Tut05\Scoring\bin\Scoring.exe.

2 Expand **Sports** in the TreeView control on the left. Within the Sports category, select **Track**. The Track events appear in the ListView control on the right. See Figure 5-1. Depending on your computer's display characteristics, you may be able to see the Event Date (the right column) without needing to scroll.

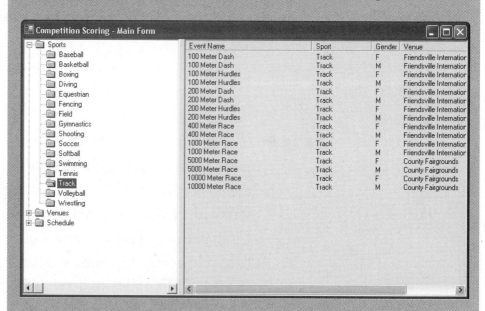

Figure 5-1: Scoring (draft version), main screen, showing track events

This application uses a Windows Explorer-type user interface, which displays event categories on the left and individual events in the selected category on the right (much like Windows Explorer displays folders on the left and folder contents on the right). Double-clicking an event on the right activates the competition-scoring screen for that event. Because many competitions are scored in a similar fashion, standardized forms and controls are developed and then reused as needed.

3 Position the insertion point over the border between the TreeView control (the frame on the left) and the ListView control (the frame on the right). This insertion point positioning activates a Splitter control, changing the insertion point to a double-headed arrow. To resize the TreeView/ListView controls, drag the **Splitter control** to the left, until the Event Date column is visible on the right side of the ListView control, as shown in Figure 5-2. Notice the bottom scroll bar is no longer present as it is no longer needed.

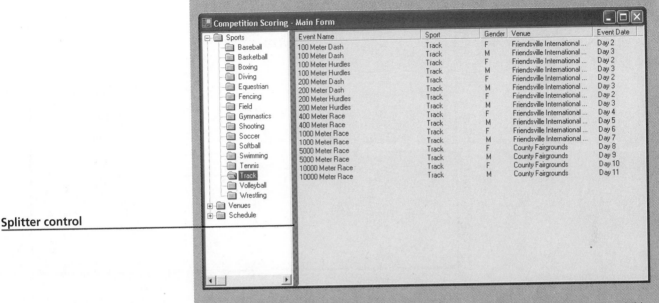

Figure 5-2: Scoring, Main Form, after using the Splitter control to make the Event Date visible

4 Double-click the **Men's 100 Meter Dash** event in the ListView control. The Individual Scoring – Fastest Time form opens. Note that the event header information reflects the Men's 100-Meter Dash event in Track.

5 Click the **Enter Competitors** button. Enter 5 as the number of competitors (the system does not allow fewer than two nor more than eight), and then click **OK.** Enter their names as **Joon, Jan, Harry, Rodrigo,** and **Mikhail.** Using the ComboBox controls, select their nations as **South Korea, Netherlands, Australia, Brazil,** and **Russia** respectively. The form should now appear as in Figure 5-3.

Splitter control

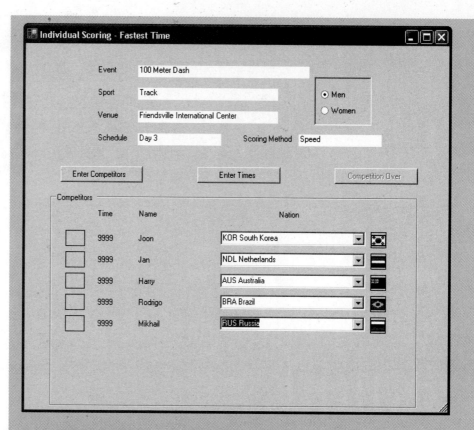

Figure 5-3: Track event – Men's 100 Meter Dash

6 Click the **Enter Times** button, and enter **10.03, 9.82, 9.91, DNF,** and **9.85.** Then click the **Competition Over** button. The Individual Scoring – Fastest Time form indicates that Jan from the Netherlands is the winner, as shown in Figure 5-4. Close that form, which returns you to the main form.

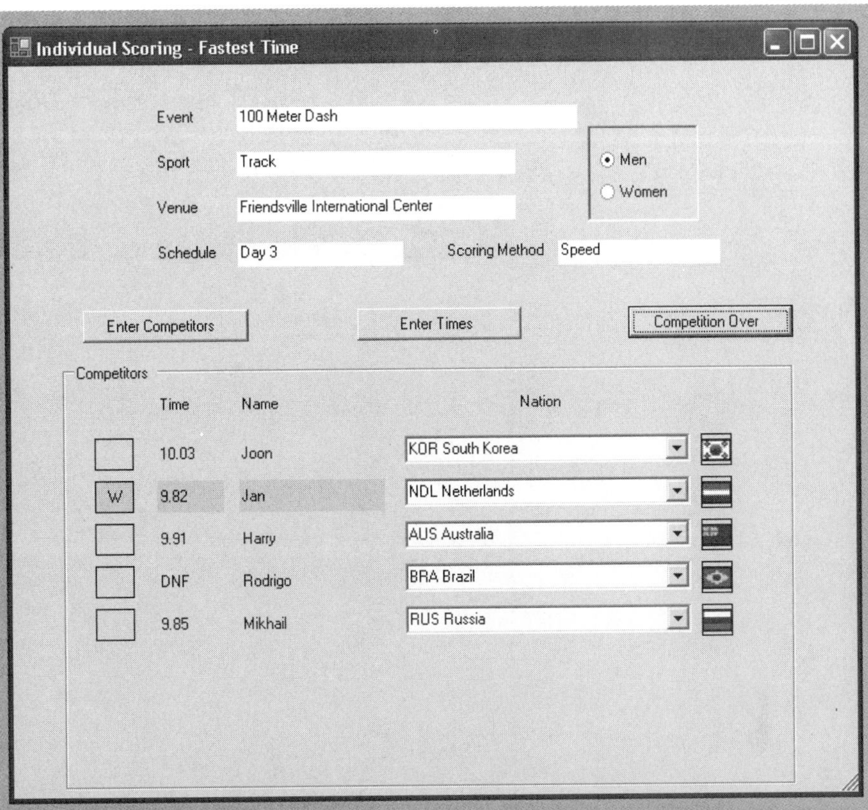

Figure 5-4: Track event – Men's 100 Meter Dash, with the competition complete

7 Click **Soccer** as the sport in the TreeView control, and double-click the women's game between Ireland and Switzerland. Select **Ireland** and **Switzerland** as the two teams in the Nations ComboBox controls. Click the **Add** and **Subtract** buttons as necessary so that Ireland wins the match 3-1. Click **Game Over**. At this point, the screen should appear as in Figure 5-5. Close the form.

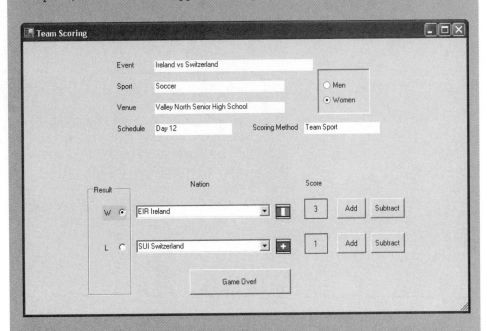

Figure 5-5: Women's soccer, with the Irish victorious

8 Click **Equestrian** as the sport and then double-click **Men's Dressage** as the event. Note that the Individual Scoring – Judges module is still under construction, as shown in Figure 5-6. Close that form. Double-click **Steeplechase**, and the Fastest Time form appears again. Notice that the kind of form presented depends on the scoring method for each event.

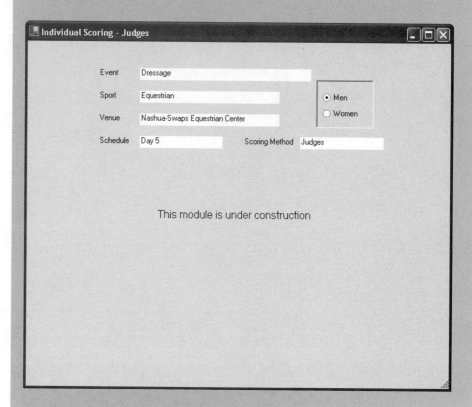

Figure 5-6: Equestrian Men's Dressage, form under construction

9 Click the **main application** (if necessary, drag the Fastest Time form out of the way to expose the Main form). Try to close the **main form**. You cannot close it because the Fastest Time form is still displayed as a modal form (this is done using ShowDialog). A modal form must be closed before any other activity in the main application takes place. Return to the **Fastest Time** form and close it.

10 In the TreeView control, expand **Venues**, and select **Friendsville International Center**. The ListView control now shows all the events scheduled for that venue. Experiment with the other venues. Then expand **Schedule** in the TreeView control, and choose **Day 1**. The ListView control displays all the events scheduled for Day 1 at the Friendsville International Games. Experiment with the other days. Then exit the **Scoring** application.

Explorer-style Interface Concepts

Before creating a draft of the Scoring application, FGDT members must learn the underlying techniques that go into it. Accordingly, Lesson A focuses on the controls and coding techniques that are the building blocks of applications of this type. Lesson B steps you through the creation of Explorer- and Outlook-style user interfaces and user controls, similar to those needed in the Scoring application. You then write your draft of the Scoring application in Lesson C.

Windows Explorer- and Outlook-style Applications

User interfaces in Visual Basic .NET Windows Forms applications fit generally into one of three categories: the single document interface (SDI), the multiple document interface (MDI), or the Explorer-style interface. In a **single document interface**, each form is independent and contains only one document (for example, a text document, spreadsheet, graph, table, or report). For example, Notepad has a single document interface; to open a second document in Notepad, you must close the first document or run a second instance of Notepad. You examined MDI applications in the last two tutorials; multiple documents can be opened simultaneously as child forms under an MDI container form. Microsoft has noted the growing popularity of the Windows Explorer-type interface as well as the closely related Microsoft Outlook-style interface. The **Windows Explorer-style interface** uses two principle controls: a TreeView control and a ListView control. Conventionally, the TreeView control appears on the left side of an application's main form, and it lists general categories, with an expand button that enables the user to expand broad categories into smaller categories. Conventionally, the ListView control appears on the right side of an application's main form, and it lists detailed entries concerning the currently selected category from the TreeView control. Additionally, a Splitter control allows the user to reposition the boundary between the TreeView and ListView controls at runtime. The general format of the Explorer-style GUI is shown in Figure 5-7.

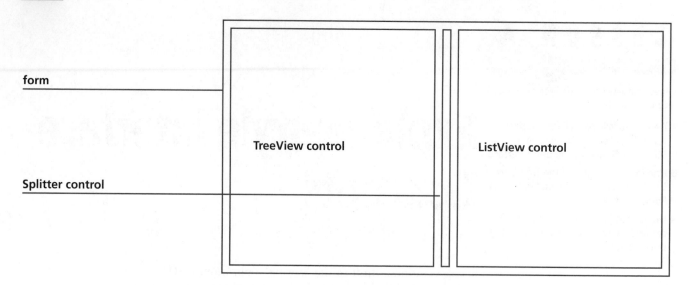

Figure 5-7: General format of the Explorer-style interface

Dozens of applications that fit nicely into this model come immediately to mind. For example, a recipe collection could have three major categories on the left: Type of dish (expandable into Main courses, Side dishes, Snacks, Desserts, Salads, and Soups), Nationality (expandable into American, French, German, Spanish, Chinese, Italian, and Mexican), and Source (expandable into Family recipes, Recipes from cookbooks, and Web links). Selecting a category or subcategory in the tree view causes the recipes in that category to appear in the list view. Selecting an individual recipe in the list view causes that recipe to be displayed. A similar application could guide a user through a music collection or the books in a private library. For another example, a furniture store's catalog could identify furniture categories in the tree view and a list of individual items available for sale in the list view.

A Microsoft **Outlook-style interface** takes this one step further. In addition to the tree view (usually on the left) and a list view (in the upper-right quadrant), this interface contains a third window, often a document of some kind, usually in the lower-right quadrant. In Outlook, this might be a contact or an e-mail message. In the recipe application example described previously, it might be the actual recipe. The Outlook-style interface uses one additional control class, a Panel control, which serves as a container for the ListView control and for the additional window. A Panel control is similar to the GroupBox control introduced in Tutorial 3—it just holds other controls. A second Splitter control allows the user to reposition the boundary between the ListView control and the additional window. The general format of the Outlook-style GUI appears in Figure 5-8.

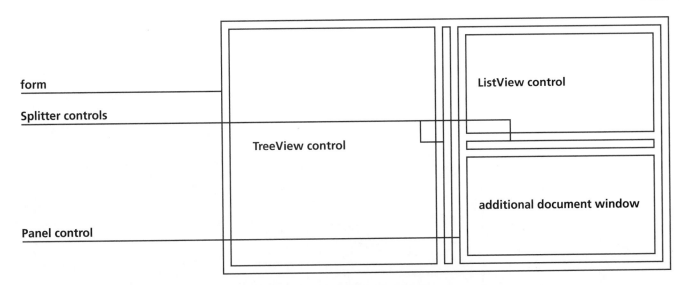

Figure 5-8: General format of an Outlook-style interface

The TreeView, ListView, Splitter, and Panel Controls

Now that you are familiar with the components of the Windows Explorer- and Outlook-style interfaces, you now examine the four controls needed to create these interface-style applications: TreeView, ListView, Splitter, and Panel.

Understanding the TreeView Control

The TreeView control displays a list of items, called **nodes**. The list appears in outline or hierarchical form. Every node in the tree can have lower-level nodes, called **child nodes**, attached to it. A node that has a child is referred to as a **parent node**. Figure 5-9 shows a typical TreeView control.

parent nodes

child nodes

TreeView control

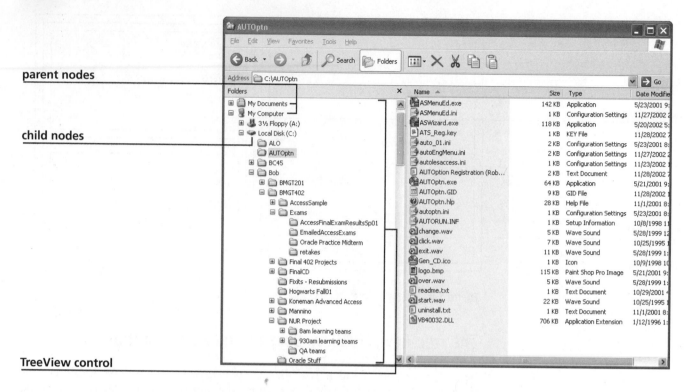

Figure 5-9: TreeView control (from Windows Explorer)

The most important properties of a TreeView control are the Nodes property and the SelectedNode property. The Nodes property is a collection of all of the root-level (or top-level) nodes in the tree view. The SelectedNode property (available only at runtime) determines which node is currently selected.

An icon is typically displayed along with text for each node. The icon to be displayed is determined through the following scheme:

1. You add an ImageList control to the form, just as you did to add images to a ToolBar control in Tutorial 4. You place the desired icons in the Images collection of the ImageList control.

2. In the Properties window for the TreeView control, first assign ImageList1 as the control's ImageList property. Then you assign to the ImageIndex property the index of the icon within the Images collection that should be displayed for all nodes that are not selected. Then, you assign to the SelectedImageIndex the index of the icon that is to be displayed next to the selected node. Thus the tree view's SelectedImageIndex and ImageIndex property settings determine the default icons displayed when a node is selected and not selected. For example, in Windows Explorer's TreeView control, the default icon displayed when a folder is not selected is a closed folder; hence, you can accurately ascertain that the ImageIndex property of the TreeView control contains the index of the closed folder icon in the Images collection of the ImageList control associated with the TreeView control. Similarly, the SelectedImageIndex contains the index of the open folder icon in the Images collection.

3. Finally, you can override the default selections for any particular node by setting the TreeNode.ImageIndex and TreeNode.SelectedImageIndex properties for that node. For example, when a Zip file appears as a node, TreeNode.ImageIndex identifies the index of the image that represents a zipped folder.

Populating and Manipulating the TreeView Control

Sometimes the nodes of a TreeView control are known and can be loaded at design time; this typically occurs when the nodes contain a fixed enumeration, such as the days of the week or the months of the year. Sometimes the nodes are unknown or should only be loaded at runtime; for example, the nodes might contain variable data loaded from a dynamic file. For this reason, you need to understand how to populate the TreeView control from within the IDE as well as programmatically. After the TreeView control has been populated, you need to learn how to manipulate its contents—how your program should react when the user clicks a node, and how your program can detect which node the user clicked.

Populating the tree view at design time You can add nodes to a TreeView control at design time by opening the TreeNode Editor (by clicking the ellipsis in the (Collection) setting of the Nodes property). You can click the Add Root button to add root-level nodes. When any node is selected, the Add Child button adds a node underneath the currently selected node. See Figure 5-10.

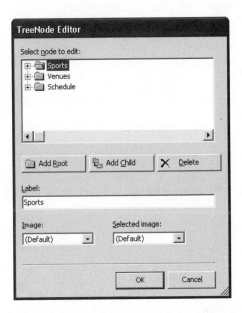

Figure 5-10: TreeNode Collection Editor

The icon displayed with any node can be overridden while in the TreeNode Editor by selecting a particular node and then changing the image in the Image combo box and the Selected image combo box.

Populating the tree view at runtime You can add a new root node at runtime by instantiating a new TreeNode object, and then invoking the Add method of the control's Nodes collection to add that new node instance to the collection. The new node appears below the last existing top-level node. The following code segment shows you how to achieve this:

```
Dim NewNode As New TreeNode("Simple Root Sample")
Tree view1.Nodes.Add(NewNode)
```

You can add a child node under the currently selected node using similar code:

```
Dim MyNode As New TreeNode("Simple Child Sample")
Tree view1.SelectedNode.Nodes.Add(MyNode)
```

Traversing All Nodes of a TreeView Control—Recursion

Often, an application requires a program to visit every node of a TreeView control. For example, you might need to locate a particular node by comparing a search string to the Text property or the Tag property of every existing node. This requires a **recursive method**, that is, a method that calls itself. As each node is visited, that node's children must be visited, and as the first child node is visited, that child's children must also be visited, proceeding through the tree until no more child nodes are left unvisited.

For example, you might want to search through a tree, looking for Baseball. This search requires two procedures: TopLevelSearch steps through the root nodes of the tree view, calling the second procedure (Search4Baseball) and passing two parameters: the root node (n) and a Boolean (FoundBaseball), as shown in Figure 5-11. At the end of this procedure, a message box indicates whether Baseball is in the tree. Note that TopLevelSearch can be invoked from anywhere within the program.

```
Private Sub TopLevelSearch()
  Dim n As TreeNode
  Dim FoundBaseball As Boolean
  For Each n In TreeView1.Nodes
    Search4Baseball(n, FoundBaseball)
  Next
  If FoundBaseball Then
    MsgBox("Baseball is in the tree")
  Else
    MsgBox("Baseball is not in the tree")
  End If
End Sub
```

Figure 5-11: Iterating through the root nodes of a TreeView control

The second procedure, Search4Baseball, shown in Figure 5-12, changes the Boolean parameter to True if the Text property of the current node equals Baseball. It then initiates a search of the current node's child nodes, if any, by calling itself for each of those child nodes. (The logic shown here continues searching through child nodes even after Baseball has been found. You could short-circuit this search by enclosing the For Each loop in Figure 5-12 in an "If Not FB Then" statement.)

```
Private Sub Search4Baseball(ByVal n As TreeNode, ByRef FB As Boolean)
  If n.Text = "Baseball" Then FB = True
  Dim x As TreeNode
  For Each x In n.Nodes
    Search4Baseball(x, FB)
  Next
End Sub
```

Figure 5-12: Search4Baseball

Search4Baseball is a recursive procedure. While TopLevelSearch calls Search4Baseball for each root node, Search4Baseball calls itself for each of the other nodes. If the tree view contains the nodes shown in Figure 5-13, a trace of procedures executed and parameters processed (nodes passed and Booleans returned) would be as shown in Figure 5-14.

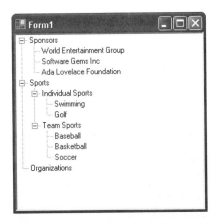

Figure 5-13: Possible nodes in a tree view

Calling procedure	Node passed (ByVal)	Boolean returned (ByRef)
TopLevelSearch	Sponsors	False
Search4Baseball	WorldEntertainment Group	False
Search4Baseball	Software Gems Inc	False
Search4Baseball	Ada Lovelace Foundation	False
TopLevelSearch	Sports	False
Search4Baseball	Individual Sports	False
Search4Baseball	Swimming	False
Search4Baseball	Golf	False
Search4Baseball	Team Sports	False
Search4Baseball	Baseball	True
Search4Baseball	Basketball	True
Search4Baseball	Soccer	True
TopLevelSearch	Organizations	True

Figure 5-14: Trace of procedures executed and nodes processed

Recursion is a powerful concept in computer programming. If you have not encountered it before, then you should study this code carefully. When first introducing recursion, computer-programming texts often show the recursive function Factorial as an example. So, in keeping with that tradition, Figure 5-15 provides the Factorial function in a Console application. The function says that the factorial of any integer *n* is equal to *n* multiplied by the factorial of *n*–1, until *n* becomes 1 (called the base case), at which point the function returns 1.

```
Module Module1
  Sub Main()
    Dim n As Integer
    Console.Write("Enter an integer ")
    n = Console.ReadLine()
    Console.WriteLine(factorial(n))
    Console.ReadLine()
  End Sub
  Function factorial(ByVal n As Integer)
    If n = 1 Then
      Return 1
    Else
      Return n * factorial(n - 1)
    End If
  End Function
End Module
```

Figure 5-15: The Factorial Console application

Understanding the ListView Control

The ListView control has many things in common with the TreeView control. Like the TreeView control, the ListView control displays a list of items and, optionally, an icon next to each item. List view items do not appear as a hierarchy. Rather, list view items appear in one of four views (based on the View property): LargeIcon, SmallIcon, List, or Details. These settings correspond to the settings available in the files pane (right pane) in Windows Explorer. The LargeIcon view displays a large icon to the left of each item's text. The SmallIcon view is the same, but with a small icon. The List view is the same as the SmallIcon view, but all the items appear in one column. The Details view can display multiple columns of information concerning each item. Figure 5-16 provides a snapshot of these four views in Windows Explorer.

SmallIcon view

LargeIcon view

Details view

List view

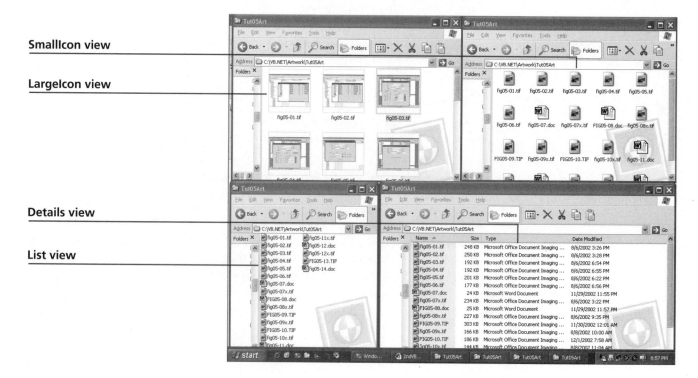

Figure 5-16: The four views in a ListView control (taken from Windows Explorer)

The main property of the ListView control is the Items collection. Items can be added in the Windows Form Designer or in code. In the Windows Form Designer, clicking the ellipsis in the (Collection) setting of the Items property opens the ListViewItem Collection Editor, as shown in Figure 5-17. The Add button adds a ListViewItem, and the Text is assigned in the ListViewItem's Text property.

Figure 5-17: ListViewItem Collection Editor

The icons displayed next to each item in a list view must be contained in two ImageList controls, assigned to the ListView control's LargeImageList and SmallImageList properties. (Of course, nothing prevents you from having only one ImageList control, and then assigning ImageList1 to both the LargeImageList and the SmallImageList properties of the ListView control.) Because individual items in the ListView control have only one ImageIndex property, you must take care to align the images in the two ImageList controls (assuming you do have two image lists). For example, you might have a collection of five images in your imgLittle ImageList control, and another collection of five images in your imgBig ImageList control. You assign imgLittle to the SmallImageList property of ListView1, and imgBig to the LargeImageList property of ListView1. Then, an individual item in ListView1 that has a 0 in its ImageIndex property displays the icon whose index is 0 in imgBig when View.LargeIcon is the current view; that same item displays the icon whose index is 0 in imgSmall in any view other than View.LargeIcon.

Populating a ListView Control

You can also populate a ListView control by inserting ListViewItem objects in code. (A ListViewItem is an item in a list view.) At runtime, identifying and manipulating the selected ListViewItem(s) is also accomplished in code.

One statement adds a ListViewItem to a ListView control. The following code adds an item named My new list view item with an ImageIndex of 2:

```
ListView1.Items.Add("My new List view item", 2)
```

Additional columns of text can be added to a list view item, but these only appear in the Details view. See Figure 5-18 for an example. Within the IDE, the column headers for the ListView control are specified in the ColumnHeader Collection Editor (shown in Figure 5-19), which is accessible through the control's Columns Collection property. The left column displays the text of the ListViewItem itself. Therefore, the first column header should identify the category to which the list view items belong. Subsequent column headers identify the additional information categories. The Add button in the ColumnHeader Collection Editor adds a column header. You can then specify the text, width (in pixels), and alignment for the column header.

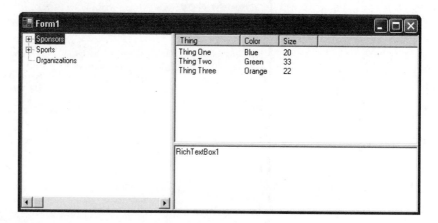

Figure 5-18: A ListView control in Details view

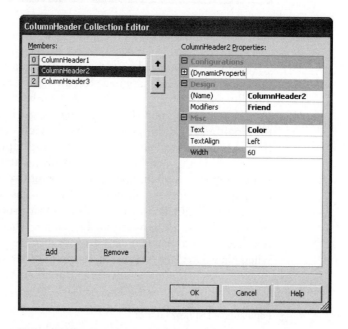

Figure 5-19: ColumnHeader Collection Editor

To accomplish the same thing in code, the Add method of the control's Columns collection is invoked:

```
ListView1.Columns.Add("Color", 60,
HorizontalAlignment.Left)
```

NOTE: If you don't specify column headers, the ListView control displays nothing in Details view.

The additional information (the text that goes into each column after the list view item itself) is referred to as the SubItem collection, which can be added in the IDE or in code. In the IDE, within the ListViewItem Collection Editor, clicking the SubItems Collection property opens the ListViewSubItem Collection Editor. The ListViewItem is automatically listed as the first SubItem in the collection. The Add button allows the programmer to add a subitem corresponding to each column header in the Columns collection. After adding the subitem, you need to specify the Text property. Figure 5-20 shows the SubItem collection for the Thing One list view item.

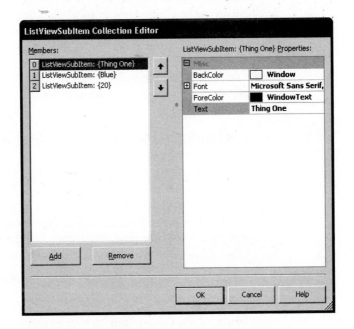

Figure 5-20: ListViewSubItem Collection Editor

To add subitems in code, you must specify the index value of the ListViewItem under which the subItem is to be added. The code looks like this:

```
ListView1.Items(2).SubItems.Add("Orange")
```

In the present example, this code adds the subitem "Orange" to the ListViewItem Thing Three.

Understanding the Splitter Control

The Splitter control permits the user to resize docked controls at runtime. Its most typical application is to allow the user to move the boundary between a TreeView control and a ListView control. Starting with a form containing a TreeView control docked on the left, a Splitter control is added to the form, also docked on the left. This causes the Splitter control to be aligned along the right edge of the TreeView control. Then a ListView control is dropped on the form, and its Dock property is set to Fill. Refer again to Figure 5-7.

When a project is run, the boundary between the tree view and list view, occupied by the invisible Splitter control, becomes a hot spot on the form. When the user hovers the insertion point over this boundary, its shape changes to a double-headed arrow. Then, the user can click and hold the left mouse button and drag the boundary to the left or right.

Understanding the Panel Control

With additional Splitter controls, you can divide the form into smaller and smaller resizable areas. You must take care to include a container control to hold the Splitter and the two docked controls that share the resizable window space.

A container control that serves this purpose well is the Panel control. The Panel control is similar to the GroupBox control discussed in Tutorial 3. The differences are that the Panel control automatically displays scroll bars when the size of the graphical content exceeds the Panel control's display area, and the Panel control does not have a caption.

Continuing with the example of the Splitter control, you might want the right side of the form to be divided into a resizable ListView control on top and a PictureBox control on the bottom. To accomplish this, before adding the ListView control, add a Panel control instead, with its Dock property set to Fill. Then add the ListView control, docked at the top, then the second Splitter, also docked at the top (which positions itself along the bottom edge of the ListView control), and finally the PictureBox control, with its Dock property set to Fill. Look again at Figure 5-8.

Understanding User Controls (Windows Forms)

A **user control** is a control you have defined and created. Visual Basic .NET supports Windows Forms user controls that inherit from an existing Windows Forms control, from the UserControl class, from a previously defined user control, or from the Control class. You learn about these four kinds of user controls in this lesson; you get practice creating some sample controls later in this tutorial.

User Controls Based on an Existing Windows Forms Control

This is the simplest form of a user control. Basically, you modify a Windows Forms control already in the Toolbox to extend its functionality in some way. This type of user control can be useful if an existing Toolbox control already provides most, but not all, of the functionality you need, and you know that you will be able to apply this customized functionality in many instances of the control.

For example, you might have an application that requires users to input numeric data in a series of text boxes, but the data must be entered only once in each text box. As the user completes each text box input, you want to validate the user input as numeric, and then disable the text box (to prevent further input). Now, if your application requires 20 text boxes meeting these specifications, a user control would be a worthy implementation choice. You could build and test your customized ctrlTxtSingleNum control once, place it in the Toolbox along with other controls, and use it in all 20 instances where it is needed. If it turns out that you need to change it in some way, you need to change it only once, build (compile) it again, and the change is automatically propagated to all 20 instances.

You create a control derived from an existing Windows Forms control by creating a Windows Control Library project. By default, such projects inherit from the UserControl class; to base your control on an existing control, you change the inheritance statement to the name of the existing control class, such as

```
Inherits System.Windows.Forms.TextBox
```

You then write any additional methods and expose them by making them public or hide them by keeping them private (the default). You also declare any new properties for the control, describing how the values of any such new properties are obtained and where they are stored (usually in private variables), and also how the values of any new properties are exposed (returned). Figure 5-21 is an example of a property declaration.

```
Private blnValue As Boolean
Property ValidNumber() As Boolean
  Get
    Return blnValue
  End Get
  Set(ByVal Value As Boolean)
    blnValue = Value
  End Set
End Property
```

Figure 5-21: Property declaration example, with a private variable

You then save and build the user control. Because this compiles to a class library rather than an executable, you need a client project to test it. The basic procedures for testing are the same as they are for incorporating the class library project in Tutorial 4. The only difference here is that, after adding a reference to the control's .dll file, you then add your user control to the Toolbox rather than use an Imports statement in code. After the user control is in the Toolbox, you drop it onto a form as you would any other control.

User Control Based on the UserControl Class

The UserControl class provides a container for several controls that you select from the Windows Forms Toolbox. Controls based on this class exhibit all the common properties, methods, and events of the built-in Windows Forms graphical controls: properties such as Location, Size, BackColor, Enabled, and Visible; methods such as BringToFront, GetType, Dispose, GetNextControl, and Hide; and events such as Click, DoubleClick, MouseDown, Enter, and Leave—about 280 such items in all. In structure and function, the UserControl class is a template for a component class that includes a graphical interface.

You create your user control in the User Control Designer, which looks much like the Windows Form Designer. You drag controls from the Toolbox into the User Control Designer, and you write code for the user control and for the individual Windows Forms controls that you have placed inside it.

You can create a user control within a Windows application project, in which case the control can be used anywhere within that project, but not outside it; or you can create an independent Windows Control Library project, in which case any programmer with access to the library can incorporate your user control into any Windows project. The former approach is simpler, but limits the usefulness of the user control to the project in which it is created. The latter approach is slightly more complicated until you get accustomed to doing it, but vastly expands the potential reusability of the control.

From the Project menu, the Add a User Control option adds a user control to the current project. After you have created the control, you build the current project (from the Build menu). The new control then appears in the Toolbox and can be dropped onto any form in the project.

To create a user control as a Windows Control Library, you create a new project of type Windows Control Library. After you have created the control, you save and build the user control, which compiles into a .dll file. A project that uses your user control must include a reference to your user control's .dll file in its References.

After the reference has been added, you can customize the Toolbox, adding this new user control to the Toolbox. After that, you can use your new user control like any other Windows Forms control in the Toolbox.

The properties, events, and methods of the individual Windows Forms controls inside the user control are not normally accessible in code to the projects that inherit the completed user control. That is, the internals of the user control are encapsulated. This prevents, for example, the Timer1_Tick event belonging to a timer component of a user control from conflicting with the Timer1_Tick event of a timer component on the main form of the project. The only exceptions to this rule are those specific internal elements of the user control that have been declared public, and those properties that have been exposed within the user control code through the use of private variables in conjunction with Public Property declarations (Get and Set statements). You see examples of this syntax in Lesson B.

User Controls Based on a Previously Defined User Control

In the discussion of the Button class in Tutorial 2, the System.Windows.Forms. Button class inherits from the System.Windows.Forms.ButtonBase class, which inherits from the System.Windows.Forms.Control class, which inherits from the System.ComponentModel.Component class, which inherits from the System. MarshalByRefObject class, which inherits from the System.Object class. The nesting of derived classes from previously defined base classes can go on indefinitely. The same principle applies to user controls.

After you create a user control and compile it into a Windows Control Library, that .dll is available for the creation of additional user controls that inherit from it. A simple example might be a user control containing an icon and a label representing the Friendsville Games. Another user control might inherit from the first control and add another icon and label representing a particular participating sports federation.

User Controls Based on the Control Class

The three previous types of user controls incorporate existing controls from the Toolbox. Those solutions are appropriate when existing controls provide most of the functionality required by your application. However, some applications require the development of controls unlike any that already exist. Visual Basic .NET supports the development of such controls through the Control class. The Control class provides most of the standard properties, events, and methods of all controls. It provides much of the internal structure needed to operate in its environment—a handle for Windows to keep track of it, message routing, mouse and keyboard events, visual display properties, such as BackColor and Visible, and user-triggered events, such as Click and DoubleClick. It does not include the instructions for painting a graphical control, because it cannot know what the new control is supposed to look like. The developer is responsible for rendering the graphical image of the control, and adding or overriding properties, events, and methods.

Actually creating a new control from scratch is beyond the scope of this text, but you should be aware that it can be done, and also that the existence of the base Control class makes this task feasible for most journeyman programmers.

You have covered a lot of new ground, and you are probably anxious to try out these new concepts as practical applications on your computer. But remember to do the exercises here before continuing with Lesson B.

SUMMARY

- A Windows Explorer-style interface is based on a TreeView control on the left and a ListView control on the right, usually with a Splitter control in between them for resizing during runtime.
- A Microsoft Outlook-style interface is an extension of the Windows Explorer-style interface, in which one of the two panes is further subdivided. The Outlook-style interface uses a Panel control as a container for the pane to be further subdivided and for the inclusion of an additional Splitter control.
- A TreeView control provides a hierarchical listing of items and associated icons, which are often categories of items that may contain lower-level items not shown in the tree view. Often, the node selected in the tree view triggers the listing of the details in a corresponding ListView control.
- A ListView control displays a list of items and associated icons, and may include multiple columns of information in Details view.
- Recursion, the technique of a method calling itself, is a powerful programming tool and is used for traversing all nodes of a TreeView control.
- Visual Basic .NET supports the creation of various kinds of user controls, inheriting from a single existing Windows Form control, from the UserControl class, from a previously created user control, or from the Control class.
- User controls can be compiled into a Windows Control Library and can subsequently be added by reference into the Toolbox of projects that need them.
- Most internals of user controls are hidden from the programs that use them. However, you can add public properties through property declarations and expose methods by making them public.

QUESTIONS

1. A(n) _____ control permits resizing of docked controls at runtime.

2. To build a user control from scratch, you inherit from the _____ class.

3. To build a user control based on the Button control, you inherit from the _____ class.

4. In the IDE, list view items are created in the _____ _____ Editor.

5. Consider this code:

   ```
   ListView1.Items(x).SubItems.Add(y)
   ```

   The variables *x* and *y* represent _____ and _____.

6. The internals of a user control are _____, that is, hidden from view by projects that use the control, except for elements that are specifically _____.

7. By default, the accessibility level of a user control's methods is _____.

8. A container control useful in constructing an Outlook-style interface is the _____ control.

9. The key property of the TreeView control is the _____ _____.

10. A programming technique in which a method calls itself is called _____.

EXERCISES

1. Imagine that you are building the Calculator program (the Windows Accessory, calc.exe). What would be the advantage or disadvantage of creating a special version of the Button control to use throughout that application?

2. Identify the elements of a Windows Explorer-style interface for an application that is used by the clerks selling tickets to the Friendsville International Games. What would the tree view contain? What would the list view contain?

3. Now imagine that you must convert the application in Exercise 2 into an Outlook-style interface. What would the third pane contain?

4. Microsoft Access 2002 is an MDI application. What would the Database Window look like if it were converted to an Explorer-style interface? (You can answer this question by drawing a picture of the window.) Can you combine an Explorer-style interface for the Database Window with other principles of a multiple document interface application? What are the pros and cons of such an arrangement?

5. Describe an Explorer-style interface for the student registration system at your school. What would the tree view contain? What would the list view contain?

6. Describe an Outlook-style interface for displaying the complete schedule of major league baseball for a season. What would the tree view contain? What would the list view contain? What would the third pane contain?

7. Imagine that you are designing the eBay Web site (*www.ebay.com*) as an Outlook-style application. (Obviously, you must temporarily suspend your disbelief to do this, since eBay is a Web Forms and not a Windows Forms application.) How would you structure the necessary elements of the eBay Web site into an Outlook-style application? Again, what would be in the tree view, the list view, and the third pane?

8. Answer the same question as Exercise 7, but use the Course Technology Web site (*www.course.com*) instead of eBay.

9. Organize the menu of your favorite fast-food restaurant into an Explorer-style, touch screen application. Again, what appears in the tree view, and what appears in the list view?

10. Visitors to the Friendsville City Museum can stop at an information kiosk containing a computer with a touch screen. An Outlook-style application on this computer guides the visitor to the museum's exhibits. What would you put in the tree view, the list view, and the third pane?

After completing this lesson, you will be able to:

- Create a Windows Forms application with a Windows Explorer-style user interface
- Create a Windows Forms application with a Microsoft Outlook-style user interface
- Create a user control within a project
- Develop your own controls
- Compile them into a control class library
- Inherit from the UserControl class
- Inherit from other user controls

Explorer-style Interfaces and User Controls

Creating a Windows Explorer-style Graphical Component

You read about the Explorer-style GUI in Lesson A. Now you can build one. This sample project populates a tree view at design time, adding more nodes at runtime. The root nodes represent categories of people at the Friendsville International Games (referees, athletes, and officials), and child nodes represent subcategories under these categories, such as senior and junior referees, and male and female athletes. The project demonstrates how to traverse a tree in code, that is, how to visit each node. Finally, the sample project populates a list view at runtime, inserting into the list view a copy of all tree nodes that have been selected.

To create a Windows Explorer-style GUI:

1. Open **Visual Studio .NET**, and start a new Visual Basic .NET Windows application. Call the project **Sample Windows Explorer style form**. Put this in the **VB.NET\Student\Tut05** folder.

2. Enlarge **Form1** to a width of **600 pixels** and a height of **400 pixels**. (You do this by setting the form's Size property to 600, 400, or by expanding the Size property, and setting the lower level Width property to 600 and the Height property to 400.) Set the form's **Text** property to **Sample Windows Explorer style form**.

3. From the Toolbox, drag a **TreeView control** onto the form. Set its **Dock** property to **Left** and its **Width** property to 300. Click its **Nodes Collection** property, and click the **ellipsis** to open the TreeNode Editor. Add one root node, and name it **My Node**.

4. In the Toolbox, double-click the **Splitter** control. This action adds a Splitter control to the form, with its Dock property set to Left. Visual Basic automatically positions the Splitter along the right side of the TreeView control.

5. Now drag a **ListView control** onto the right side of the form. Set its **Dock** property to **Fill**. The ListView control takes up the remaining space on the form, to the right of the Splitter control.

6. Double-click the form's **Title bar** to open the Form1_Load event procedure in the Code Editor. To show something in the ListView control when you test the GUI, add the following line to this procedure:

```
ListView1.Items.Add("My listviewitem")
```

7. Run the **Sample Windows Explorer style form** application. Drag the **Splitter** control to resize the TreeView and ListView controls, as shown in Figure 5-22. Then close the running application and return to the IDE.

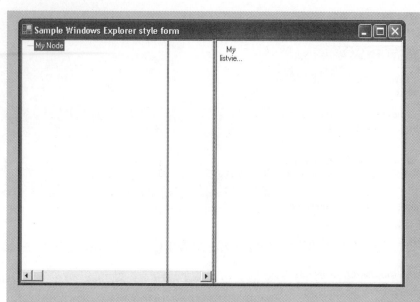

Figure 5-22: Sample Windows Explorer style form, running, showing the Splitter control

Populating the Tree View at Design Time

The nodes in the TreeView control that you create in this sample project are categories and subcategories of people at the Friendsville International Games. Each category (referees, athletes, officials) and subcategory is also associated with an icon. Therefore, you must create both the nodes in the TreeView control, as well as images in an ImageList control. You must assign the ImageList control to the ImageList property of the TreeView control, and then assign the appropriate indexes of individual images to the TreeView control's ImageIndex and SelectedImageIndex properties.

To add images and nodes to the TreeView control in the IDE:

1 Return to the **Windows Form Designer** to continue creating the GUI.

2 From the Toolbox, drop an **ImageList** control on the form. Click the **ellipsis** next to Images Collection in the Properties window to open the Image Collection Editor. Add two icon images from the VS7\Common7\Graphics\ Icons\Office folder: **Folder01.ico** and **Folder02.ico** . (If you do not have a VS7 folder on your computer, look for Program Files\Microsoft Visual Studio .NET instead. If you have neither of these folders, then just copy Folder01.ico and Folder02.ico from VB.NET\Student\Tut05.) You use the closed folder icon as the default image for unselected nodes, and the open folder icon as the default image for selected nodes. Also add the Friendsville Organizing Committee's adopted icon (the sailboat) to the image list: **VS7\ Common7\Graphics\Icons\Misc\MISC32.ico** . (Again, as a backup you can find this icon in VB.NET\Student\Tut05.) In a later step in this sample project, you will assign this icon to the folder representing officials of the Friendsville Organizing Committee.

3 In the Windows Form Designer, click the **TreeView control**. Assign **ImageList1** to the **ImageList** property. Assign 0 (that is, the closed folder icon) to the **ImageIndex** property. Assign 1 (that is, the open folder icon) to the **SelectedImageIndex** property.

4 Click the **ellipsis** next to Nodes Collection in the Properties window, which opens the TreeNode Editor. Delete **My Node**. Click **Add Root**, and type **Referees** as the label. Click **Add Child**, and type **Senior** as the label. Click the **Referees root node**, and click **Add Child** again, and type **Junior** as the label. Click **Add Root**, and type **Athletes** as the label. Continue in this fashion until you have added all of the root and child nodes shown in Figure 5-23. For the Local (FOC) child node, assign the **sailboat icon** as both the **Image** and the **Selected Image**. For all other nodes, leave the Image and Selected Image properties set to the default.

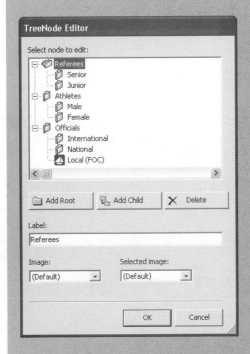

Figure 5-23: TreeNode Editor (lengthened so that all nodes are visible)

5 Run the **Sample Windows Explorer style form** program. Expand each of the three categories (Referees, Athletes, and Officials). Note that the icon changes from a closed to an open folder when a category or subcategory is selected. Note the sailboat icon for the Local (FOC) category.

6 Close the application and return to the IDE.

Populating the Tree View at Runtime

Many applications require root nodes and child nodes that are added to a tree view at runtime. For example, Windows Explorer itself, the model for this type of application, displays each disk drive and each folder on your computer; because these items change dynamically, the tree view is obviously constructed at runtime. Therefore, to use the TreeView control effectively, you need to know how to add nodes programmatically.

In order to acquire this coding skill, assume that, regardless of the number of people categories in the sample Explorer-style project created at design time, one additional category called the Friendsville Boosters must be added at runtime. Further, a Boosters Liaison (a person who liaisons with the Friendsville Boosters Club) must be added as a subcategory to each category, and this new Boosters Liaison subcategory must be numbered. You now add code to make this happen.

To populate a TreeView control at runtime:

1 In the Code Editor, delete the statement in the Form1_Load event procedure that adds a ListViewItem (you deal with the ListView control later, but doing this now cleans up the screen for the present demos).

2 Insert the code shown in Figure 5-24 into the Form1_Load event procedure. (This code is discussed right after you run the application, because the code makes more sense after you see its results.)

```
Line 1    TreeView1.SuspendLayout()
Line 2    Dim newNode As TreeNode = New _
              TreeNode("Friendsville Boosters")
Line 3    TreeView1.Nodes.Add(newNode)
Line 4    Dim n As TreeNode
Line 5    Dim i As Integer
Line 6    For Each n In TreeView1.Nodes
Line 7      TreeView1.SelectedNode = n
Line 8      i += 1
Line 9      newNode = New TreeNode("Boosters Liaison " & i)
Line 10     TreeView1.SelectedNode.Nodes.Add(newNode)
Line 11   Next
Line 12   TreeView1.ResumeLayout()
```

Figure 5-24: Adding tree view nodes at runtime

3 Run the **Sample Windows Explorer style form** application. Expand all of the categories. The result should appear as in Figure 5-25.

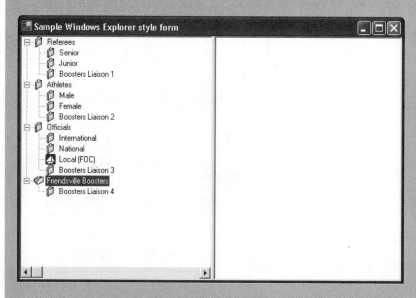

Figure 5-25: Tree view at runtime, with added nodes

4 Quit the application and return to the IDE.

The code in Figure 5-24 accomplishes a lot in just a few lines:

- The first and last lines of this code, the SuspendLayout() and ResumeLayout() methods, are useful whenever you are making multiple changes to the graphical layout of a control. In this case, you are adding multiple items to a ListView control. The purpose is to suspend the graphical layout operation until all the items have been added to the control and then allow the graphics work to be done only once when the layout operation is resumed. You can use the SuspendLayout() and ResumeLayout() methods if you are altering the Size, Location, BackColor, Font, and Dock properties of a control.

- Lines 2 and 3 of the code declare the new Friendsville Boosters tree node and then add this new node as a new root node in the TreeView control. This new root node appears below the last existing root node.

- The rest of this code traverses all the root nodes of TreeView1, adding a child node under each root node. Each child node's text property is Boosters Liaison and a sequential number. To iterate through any collection, you need an object of the type that makes up the collection. In this case, "n" is declared as a TreeNode, the type of object that exists in the TreeView1.Nodes collection.

- To add a child node to any root node, the root node must be selected—hence the first statement inside the For Each loop:

```
TreeView1.SelectedNode = n
```

- After each root node is selected, the new Node object variable is assigned to reference a new instance of a TreeNode, which is then added as a child node under the selected root node.

- This code does not visit the child nodes. That is, a new child node does not appear under Senior, Junior, Male, Female, and so on. To iterate through the children, you need a recursive procedure, discussed in the next section.

Traversing All Nodes of a TreeView Control

You saw one model of a recursive procedure to accomplish tree traversal in Lesson A; now it's time to try it for yourself. You first add another two levels to TreeView1's Nodes collection. Then you insert procedures that add a sequential visit number to the text property of each node as it is visited.

Two procedures are needed: one procedure operates at the level of the TreeView control and accesses the root nodes (similar to the logic of the procedure that adds a child node to each root node). The second procedure is the recursive procedure called by the first procedure. It examines each child node, and then calls itself as it examines the child node of that node (if any). This process continues through all the layers of children until no further child nodes are found.

To process all nodes of the demo TreeView control:

1 In the Nodes Collection for TreeView1, insert additional nodes under the Senior node as shown in Figure 5-26. To do this, click the **Nodes Collection** property to open the TreeNode Editor. In the TreeNode Editor, click **Senior | Add Child**, and type **Internationally Ranked** as the label. Add the remaining nodes shown in Figure 5-26 in the same way.

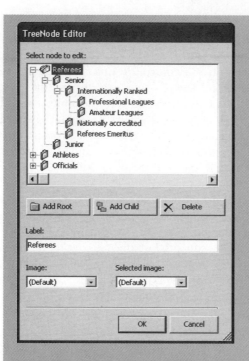

Figure 5-26: TreeNode Editor, with added nodes

2   Place a **Button** control on top of the ListView control. Change its **Text** property to **Iterate all nodes** and its **Name** property to **btnIterate**.

3   Double-click **btnIterate**, and insert the **btnIterate_Click**() procedure shown in Figure 5-27.

```
Dim n As TreeNode
For Each n In TreeView1.Nodes
   ChangeText(n)
Next
```

Figure 5-27: btnIterate_Click()

4   Also insert the new **ChangeText**() procedure, as shown in Figure 5-28. (An explanation of btnIterate_Click() and ChangeText() follows after you run the program.)

```
Private Sub ChangeText(ByVal n As TreeNode)
   Static k As Integer
   k += 1
   n.Text = n.Text & " Visit number: " & k
   Dim aNode As TreeNode
   For Each aNode In n.Nodes
      ChangeText(aNode)
   Next
End Sub
```

Figure 5-28: ChangeText() procedure

5 Run the **Sample Windows Explorer style form** application. Expand all of the nodes. Click the **Iterate all nodes** button. The result should appear as in Figure 5-29. Then close the running application.

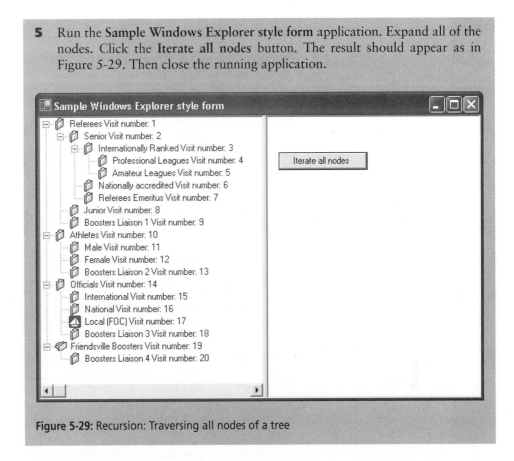

Figure 5-29: Recursion: Traversing all nodes of a tree

Although the code shown in Figures 5-27 and 5-28 is quite brief, understanding how it works is not so simple. Following is a detailed explanation:

- At the time the btnIterate_Click procedure executes, four root nodes exist (Referees, Athletes, Officials, and Friendsville Boosters). Therefore, the For Each loop iterates four times, once for each root node. On each pass through the loop, the root node is passed to the ChangeText() procedure.

- The ChangeText() procedure increments the sequence number "k," and then adds the visit sequence number to the Text property of the node "n" that was just passed into the procedure. Then, for each child node belonging to node "n" (that is, for each node in n's Nodes collection), the ChangeText() procedure calls the ChangeText() procedure, passing to it the child node.

- If a child node has children in turn, ChangeText() is called again. Hence, examine the sequence of procedure calls in this demonstration:

  - btnIterate_Click() begins executing. It calls ChangeText(n), passing the Referees node as the value of "n." (Note that the object passed is the node itself, not just the Text property of the node. So the ChangeText() procedure receives the Referees node, with all of that node's properties and methods.)

  - ChangeText(Referees) begins executing. It appends "Visit number: 1" to the Referees.Text. Next, it identifies the child Nodes collection for Referees, consisting of the nodes Senior, Junior, and Boosters Liaison 1, and it initiates a For Each loop to iterate through those child nodes. For the first node (Senior), the ChangeText(Referees) procedure calls ChangeText(Senior).

  - ChangeText(Senior) begins executing. It appends "Visit number: 2" to Senior. Text. Next, it identifies the child Nodes collection for Senior, consisting of Internationally Ranked, Nationally Accredited, and Referees Emeritus, and it initiates a For Each loop to iterate through those child nodes. For the first node, the Change Text(Senior) procedure calls ChangeText(Internationally Ranked).

■ ChangeText(Internationally Ranked) begins executing. It appends "Visit number: 3" to Internationally Ranked.Text. Next, it identifies the child Nodes collection for Internationally Ranked, consisting of Professional Leagues and Amateur Leagues, and it initiates a For Each loop to iterate through those child nodes. For the first node, the Change Text(Internationally Ranked) procedure calls ChangeText(Professional Leagues).

■ ChangeText(Professional Leagues) begins executing. It appends "Visit number: 4" to Professional Leagues.Text. Next, it identifies the child Nodes collection for Professional Leagues, and finds that Professional Leagues has no children. So the ChangeText(Professional Leagues) procedure finishes processing and returns to its calling routine, ChangeText(Internationally Ranked), where it executes the Next statement, looking for the next aNode in the Professional Leagues.Nodes collection. It finds Amateur Leagues, and so the For Each loop calls ChangeText(Amateur Leagues).

■ ChangeText(Amateur Leagues) begins executing. It appends "Visit number: 5" to Amateur Leagues.Text. Next, it identifies the child Nodes collection for Amateur Leagues, and finds that Amateur Leagues has no children. So the ChangeText(Amateur Leagues) procedure finishes processing and returns to its calling routine, ChangeText(Internationally Ranked), where it executes the Next statement, looking for the next aNode in the Professional Leagues. Nodes collection. It finds that there are no more nodes in that collection. So ChangeText(Internationally Ranked) finishes executing and returns to its calling routine, ChangeText(Senior), where it looks for the next aNode in Senior.Nodes. It finds Nationally Accredited, and so it calls ChangeText (Nationally Accredited).

■ The process continues until all nodes in the entire tree have been processed.

Populating and Manipulating the ListView Control

In many cases the number of potential list view items is some multiple of the number of tree view items, and the list view items are maintained in a data file of some sort. (This is the approach taken in the Scoring application, which you create in Lesson C.) The specific items displayed in the list view depend on which item is selected in the tree view. Typically, the selected node of the tree view (its Text or its Tag property) becomes a search string or a filter for selecting items that will appear in the list view.

In the sample application, you display only the selected node from the TreeView control in the ListView control, adding this line to the list view. In this way, the list view displays a history of all tree view nodes that have been selected. Also, the icon displayed in the list view is the same one that is displayed in the tree view.

To display items in the ListView control:

1   Change the **View** property of ListView1 to **List**.

2   Assign **ImageList1** to the **SmallImageList** property of ListView1.

3   Insert the following statement into the TreeView1_AfterSelect() procedure:

```
ListView1.Items.Add(e.Node.Text, e.Node.ImageIndex)
```

This code adds an item to ListView1. The method contains two arguments: the text of the node, and the index of the image within the SmallImageList assigned to ListView1. Both arguments reference "e," an object of type System.Windows. Forms.TreeViewEventArgs. When the sender is a TreeView control, the event argument identifies the selected node at the time the TreeView control did the sending. In the present case, the same collection of images (contained in ImageList1) has been assigned to both the ImageList property of TreeView1 and the SmallImageList property of ListView1. Therefore, the icon associated with e.Node is the same icon needed in the list view.

4 Run the **Sample Windows Explorer style form** application. Note that the root nodes have all been visited during the Form1_Load procedure. As indicated in Figure 5-30, expand the appropriate nodes as shown; click any tree view node to see that it appears in the list view. Click the **Iterate all nodes** button; then select another node to see that the complete node text, including that which was added programmatically, is copied into the list view. See Figure 5-30.

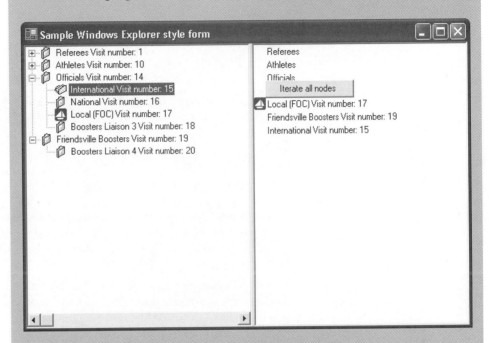

Figure 5-30: ListView control at runtime, populated through code

NOTE: The only icon that appears in the list view is the Sailboat—if you happen to select Local (FOC) as one of the points you visit. Otherwise, the code references only the default value of SelectedImageIndex for each tree view node, and the default value does not propagate forward, unless the tree view node itself is being displayed.

5 Close the application to return to the IDE, and close the solution.

Creating the Microsoft Outlook-style Graphical Component

In this example, you place the TreeView control on the left and divide the right side of the form between the ListView control on top and a PictureBox control below.

To visualize a typical Microsoft Outlook-style application, imagine that the tree view contains the names of athletes at the Friendsville International Games, organized into categories by nationality, and that the list view contains the names of the events in which the selected athlete will compete. When an athlete is selected in the TreeView control, the flag of the athlete's country is loaded into the PictureBox control. When a particular event is selected in the ListView control, a photo of the athlete competing in that event is loaded into the PictureBox control. In the example here, you populate the tree view with the names of several athletes and with each athlete's national flag as the icon assigned from an ImageList. You populate the ListView control with the events that Heidi Gielgud, a Dutch sprinter, runs in; and the PictureBox control gets the flag of the Netherlands. The sample data offers no real functionality, but by manipulating the Splitter controls, you do get a sense of the look and feel of this type of application.

Here is how you create this type of GUI. You will notice that the first four steps are the same as they were for creating a Windows Explorer-style GUI.

To create the Microsoft Outlook-style GUI:

1 In Visual Studio .NET, start a new Windows application project. Call the project **Sample Microsoft Outlook style form**. Put this in the **VB.NET\Student\Tut05** folder.

2 Enlarge **Form1** to a width of **600 pixels** and a height of **400 pixels**. Set the form's **Text** property to **Sample Microsoft Outlook style form**.

3 Place a **TreeView** control on the form. Set its **Dock** property to **Left** and its **Width** property to **200**. Click the **ellipsis** next to Nodes Collection property, and add **root** nodes called **France, Netherlands**, and **Great Britain**. Under the Netherlands root node, add child nodes for Heidi Gielgud and Hans Van Peldt. Add an **ImageList** control to the form, and load the three flag icons into it (found at VS7\Common7\Graphics\icons\Flags\). Then assign **ImageList1** to the **ImageList** property of the TreeView control. Return to the **tree view Nodes collection**, and assign the appropriate flag icon to the **Image** property for each node.

4 In the Toolbox, double-click the **Splitter** control. This action adds a Splitter control to the form, with its Dock property set to Left. Visual Basic automatically positions the Splitter along the right side of the TreeView control.

5 Now add a **Panel** control to the form. Place it in the right half, and set its **Dock** property to **Fill**. The Panel control abuts the Splitter to its left and is used for resizing operations in conjunction with the vertical Splitter control and the TreeView control. The Panel control in turn serves as a container for the other controls to be placed on the right side of the form.

6 Drop a **ListView** control onto the Panel control, and set its **Dock** property to **Top**. It should occupy the upper-right quarter of the form. In the **Items Collection** property, add **ListView items** with the titles of several events for female sprinters: 100 Meter Dash, 100 Meter Hurdles, and 200 Meter Dash.

7 Add another **Splitter** control along the bottom edge of the ListView control, and set its **Dock** property to **Top**.

8 Drag a **PictureBox** control into the lower-right quadrant of the form, and set its **Dock** property to **Fill**. Set its **Image** property to the icon representing the flag of the Netherlands, and set the **SizeMode** property to **StretchImage**.

9 Run the **Sample Microsoft Outlook style form** application, which should look approximately like Figure 5-31. Use both Splitter controls to resize the TreeView, ListView, and PictureBox controls as shown. Close the running application, returning you to the IDE; then close the solution.

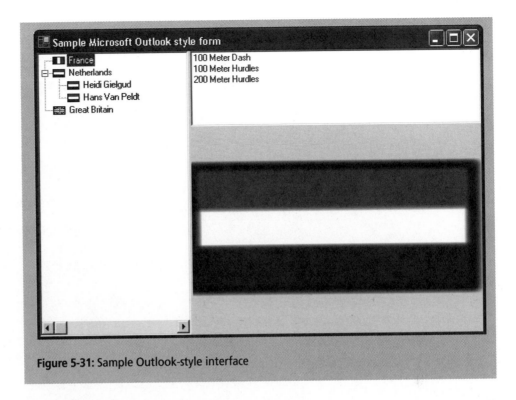

Figure 5-31: Sample Outlook-style interface

Creating User Controls

In this section, you create several versions of the user controls discussed in Lesson A. First, you create an enhanced TextBox control by programming the Leave event for the control. This enhanced text box is compiled as part of the project in which it is created. Second, you rebuild this control as a Windows Control Library. Third, you create a user control based on the UserControl class. And fourth, that new user control is itself inherited by another user control, which is then compiled into a Windows Control Library.

Creating the ctrlTxtSingleNum Enhanced TextBox Control

The ctrlTxtSingleNum control is an enhanced TextBox control designed to accept one-time user input of numeric data. Specifically, once the user enters numeric data and then leaves the text box, the text box is disabled. Otherwise—if nonnumeric data is entered, the invalid data is erased and focus returns to the text box. This functionality is created by programming the Leave event for the control. Because you create this control initially within a project, that project is the only place in which the control can be used.

To create the ctrlTxtSingleNum user control:

1   Start a new Visual Basic .NET Windows application. Put it in the **VB.NET\Student\Tut05** folder. Name the project **NumbersOnlyPlease**.

2   Click **Project | Add User Control**. In the Add New Item – NumbersOnlyPlease dialog box, User Control is already selected. Name this control **ctrlTxtSingleNum.vb**, and then click **Open**.

3   In Solution Explorer, select the code window for ctrlTxtSingleNum.vb. Right after the `Public Class ctrlTxtSingleNum` declaration, change the `Inherits` statement to

`Inherits System.Windows.Forms.TextBox`

NOTE: The Windows Form Designer is no longer available. Visual Basic .NET includes graphic designers for Windows forms, user controls, and Web forms, but it does not have a graphic designer for individual controls. So when you inherit from a Windows Forms control, you lose the graphic designer. The settings of graphic properties of your control will be exactly the same as those of the base class on which your control is based, unless you modify them in code.

4   To set some initial properties for this control, expand the **Windows Form Designer generated code**, and insert these two lines following InitializeComponent() on line 10:

`Me.BackColor = Color.LightBlue`
`Me.Width = 50`

Then collapse the Windows Form Designer generated code.

5   In order to validate the data entered by the user in the enhanced text box, you program the Leave event. The Leave event for a Visual Basic .NET control occurs when focus shifts from this control to another control. To get to the Leave event, click the **down arrow** in the Class Name combo box, and choose (**Base Class Events**). Then click the Method Name **down arrow**, and select **Leave**.

6   Now insert the code shown in Figure 5-32 into the ctrlTxtSingleNum_Leave() event procedure.

```
Private Sub ctrlTxtSingleNum_Leave(ByVal _
    sender As Object, _
    ByVal e As System.EventArgs) Handles MyBase.Leave
  If IsNumeric(Me.Text) Then
    Me.Enabled = False
  Else
    Me.Text = Nothing
    Me.BackColor = Color.Yellow
    Me.Focus()
  End If
End Sub
```

Figure 5-32: ctrlTxtSingleNum_Leave() procedure

7   To make the new control available in the Toolbox, you must save the file containing the user control and build (that is, compile) the project. To do so, click **File | Save**. Click **Build | Build Solution**. Select **Form1** in the Windows Form Designer. Open the **Toolbox**, and notice your new ctrlTxtSingleNum control. Drag three **ctrlTxtSingleNum** controls onto the form. Also place one **Button** control on the form and change the **Text** property to **Done**. Then add **End** to the Done button's code to make it functional.

NOTE: The purpose of the Button control is to have at least one control on the form that can receive focus in addition to the three enhanced text boxes. If you don't include a button, the Leave event from the last ctrlTxtSingleNum control never executes, since there is no other control available to which focus can shift.

8 Run the **NumbersOnlyPlease** application. Test the new control by inputting numeric and nonnumeric data. Close the application.

Adding a Property to Develop the ctrlTxtSingleNum Control

You can declare new properties for a user control. Assume that you want the developer using this control in a project to be able to choose whether the number entered by the user into the control must be positive. (A developer might want to specify that a positive number is required, for example, if a negative number in a particular situation is illogical or illegal—for instance, the number of dependents cannot logically be negative, and a number that is used in finding a square root cannot be negative according to the rules of mathematics.) This Boolean property is to be called PositiveNumRequired, and its default value is True. Although the property is public, its internal representation is carried through a private variable, blnPositiveRequired. Property declarations require `Get` and `Set` statements: The `Get` statement retrieves the value of the property from the private variable, and the `Set` statement stores the property setting in the private variable. This means that, both at design time and at runtime, `Get` executes when you want to look up the value of the PositiveNumRequired property. `Set` executes whenever you assign True or False to that property.

To add a property to ctrlTxtSingleNum:

1 First, you must declare the private local variable that will store the property value. Place the declaration immediately after the `Inherits` statement at the top of the class declaration for ctrlTxtSingleNum, that is, on line 3:

```
Private blnPositiveRequired As Boolean = True
```

2 Next, insert the property declaration header on line 4. This causes the skeleton code for `Get` and `Set` statements to appear:

```
Public Property PositiveNumRequired() As Boolean
```

3 Inside the `Get` statement (on the blank line between `Get` and `End Get`), insert

```
Return blnPositiveRequired
```

This code returns the value of the internal Boolean variable blnPositiveRequired to the public property PositiveNumRequired. Or, to state this another way, the property `Get` statement *gets* the value of the internal variable blnPositiveRequired and *returns* that value to the public property PositiveNumRequired.

4 Inside the `Set` statement, insert

```
blnPositiveRequired = Value
```

This code assigns or *sets* the value of the internal variable blnPositiveRequired based on the value of the public variable PositiveNumRequired. A property `Set` statement always has at least one argument.

5 Finally, to implement the new property's specification internally, you must rewrite the logic of the ctrlTxtSingleNum_Leave() procedure, as shown in Figure 5-33. After modifying the code as shown in the figure, click **Build | Rebuild Solution**, so that the revised user control is available to Form1.

```
Private Sub ctrlTxtSingleNum_Leave(ByVal _
    sender As Object, _
    ByVal e As System.EventArgs) Handles MyBase.Leave
  Dim blnValid As Boolean = False
  If IsNumeric(Me.Text) Then
    If blnPositiveRequired Then
      If Val(Me.Text) > 0 Then
        blnValid = True
      End If
    Else
      blnValid = True
    End If
  End If

  If blnValid Then
    Me.Enabled = False
  Else
    Me.Text = Nothing
    Me.BackColor = Color.Yellow
    Me.Focus()
  End If
End Sub
```

Figure 5-33: Revised ctrlTxtSingleNum_Leave() procedure

6 In Form1, note that PositiveNumRequired now appears in the Properties window for each of the ctrlTxtSingleNum control instances and that the default value is True. Change the value of the middle control to **False,** and run the revised **NumbersOnlyPlease** program. Enter **2** in the top text box; this is accepted by the program, because you entered a positive number. Enter **–2** in the middle text box; this is also accepted because the value you entered is indeed a number, but any positive or negative number is acceptable, because you set PositiveNumRequired to False. Enter **–2** in the third text box; the program rejects this entry, changes the BackColor of the text box to yellow, and returns the focus to that text box, as shown in Figure 5-34. After the user enters a positive value for the third control, the Done button ends the program.

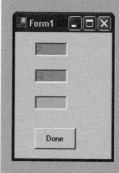

Figure 5-34: Three ctrlTxtSingleNum controls at runtime

Converting ctrlTxtSingleNum into a Windows Control Library

Instead of building a user control within a Windows Forms project, a more useful approach might be to build a Windows Control Library project, compiling the control to a .dll. With a small amount of additional work, ctrlTxtSingleNum can be converted into a class library that can be reused by any other project.

To convert ctrlTxtSingleNum into a Windows Control Library:

1   Start a new Visual Basic .NET project. Choose **Windows Control Library** as the project type. Name the project **ctrlSingleNumLib**, and save it in the **VB.NET\Student\Tut05** folder. In Solution Explorer, change the name of the .vb file from UserControl1.vb to **ctrlSingleNum.vb.**

2   You are now going to copy the code from ctrlTxtSingleNum.vb into ctrlSingleNum.vb. To do this, click **File | Open | File**, browse to **ctrlTxtSingleNum.vb**, and open it. Select all, copy it to the Clipboard, and close that file. Switch to the **Code Editor** for ctrlSingleNum, select all, and paste. Change the class name to **ctrlSingleNum**, and change the name of the **ctrlTxtSingleNum_Leave()** procedure to **ctrlSingleNum_Leave()**. Click **Save All**.

3   Click **Build | Build Solution**, because the .dll file must exist before you can test the control. But testing the control library requires the same steps as testing a class library, such as the ones you worked on in Tutorial 4. That is, you need to create an executable project that imports this control library.

4   In Solution Explorer, right-click the **solution name**, point to **Add**, then click **New Project**. Make this a **Windows Application** project type, name it **TestSingleNum**, and store it under the **ctrlSingleNumLib** folder. In Solution Explorer, right-click the **TestSingleNum** project name, and select **Set as StartUp Project**.

5   In Solution Explorer, right-click **References** under TestSingleNum, and add a reference to the ctrlSingleNum project. In the Add Reference dialog box, click the **Projects** tab, select **ctrlSingleNum**, and then click **OK**.

6   Right-click the **Toolbox**, and select **Customize Toolbox**. In the Customize Toolbox dialog box, click the **.NET Framework Components** tab. Then click **Browse**, and locate the **ctrlSingleNum.dll** file (in the bin folder of the control class project). The ctrlSingleNum control appears in the Components list. Click **OK**.

7   As before, drag three **ctrlSingleNum** controls from the Toolbox onto the form, toggle the **PositiveNumRequired** property on one of them, and test the **ctrlSingleNumLib** application.

You now have a model for building new controls that inherit from existing Windows Forms controls, and for creating new user controls inside a Windows application or in a separate Windows Control Library. One advantage of user controls derived from existing Windows Forms controls, as you will soon see, is that the properties, events, and methods of the base class remain available to additional controls that inherit from them.

Inheriting from the UserControl Class

The UserControl class provides a container for other Windows Forms controls encapsulated within it. You can customize the appearance and behavior of the contained controls, as well as of the user control itself. You can also create properties for the user control.

In this exercise, you create a user control called ctrlReceipt. It provides a text box for the user to enter a currency amount at runtime. It then displays a label for the sales tax computed at five percent, although the percentage can be altered if a different sales tax rate is needed. A third label displays the total amount due. This user control could be used by various Friendsville Games Development Team applications that involve monetary payments that require a receipt—ticket sales, accommodations, meals, and other concessions.

To create ctrlReceipt:

1   Start a new **Windows Control Library** project. Place it in the **VB.NET\Student\Tut05** folder, and name it **ctrlReceipt**. Change the project filename to **ctrlReceipt.vb**. In the Code Editor, change the class name to **ctrlReceipt**. Note that this class inherits from the UserControl class.

2   Open the **User Control Designer**. Build the GUI so that it appears as shown in Figure 5-35. Be sure the three labels on the left have Text properties of **Amount**, **Tax**, and **Total**. Be sure that to the right of these labels there are a **text box** and two more **labels**. Be sure that the control at the top right is a **text box** named **txtAmount**. Beneath this text box, **lblTax** and **lblTotal** need to have a white background and a fixed single border. At the bottom of the control, create **btnCompute**, with Text property **"Compute Tax and Total"**.

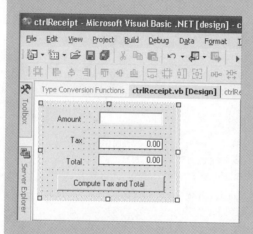

Figure 5-35: ctrlReceipt in the User Control Designer

3   Use the private single variable sngTaxRate along with the public property TaxRate to allow the user to change the default sales tax rate of five percent. Following the model you used in developing ctrlTxtSingleNum, declare

```
Private sngTaxRate As Single = .05
```

4   Then declare a public property called TaxRate, along with the Get and Set statements that copy the value of sngTaxRate to TaxRate, and from TaxRate to sngTaxRate, respectively. Enter the following statement:

```
Public Property TaxRate As Single
```

When you enter this statement Visual Basic .NET automatically creates the skeleton Get and Set statements. Now enter **Return sngTaxRate** inside the Get statement, and **sngTaxRate = Value** inside the Set statement.

5   Write the **btnCompute_Click()** procedure to perform the necessary calculations. Figure 5-36 provides sample code, using obvious object names and formatting the output appropriately.

private variable and public properties

btnCompute_Click() — new code to be added

```vb
Public Class ctrlReceipt
  Inherits System.Windows.Forms.UserControl
  Private sngTaxRate As Single = 0.05
  Public Property TaxRate() As Single
    Get
      Return sngTaxRate
    End Get
    Set(ByVal Value As Single)
      sngTaxRate = Value
    End Set
  End Property

[+] Windows Form Designer Generated Code

  Private Sub btnCompute_Click(ByVal sender As Object, _
      ByVal e As System.EventArgs) Handles btnCompute.Click
    lblTax.Text = Format(txtAmount.Text * sngTaxRate, _
      "currency")
    lblTotal.Text = Format(Val(txtAmount.Text) + _
      lblTax.Text, "currency")
    txtAmount.Text = Format(txtAmount.Text, "currency")
  End Sub
End Class
```

Figure 5-36: btnCompute_Click() (sample code)

6 Click **Save All**, and then build the solution. Once again, you need a client project to test the ctrlReceipt user control. Add a new Windows application project to the **ctrlReceipt** solution, called **TestCtrlReceipt**, and set this as the startup project.

7 Open **Form1** of TestCtrlReceipt in the Windows Form Designer, if necessary. Drag a **ctrlReceipt** user control from the Toolbox onto Form1. This action automatically adds the ctrlReceipt project to the References list for the TestCtrlReceipt project.

NOTE: If you do not see the user control in the Toolbox (it should appear as the last control in the Windows Forms controls tab of the Toolbox), then compile the project again. If you still do not see it, then customize the Toolbox to add ctrlReceipt, as follows: in the Toolbox, right-click and select Customize Toolbox. In the Customize Toolbox dialog box, click the .NET Framework Components tab. Then click Browse, and locate the ctrlReceipt.dll file (in the bin folder of the control class project). The ctrlReceipt control appears in the Components list. Click OK. Finally, drop ctrlReceipt on Form1.

8 Run the **TestCtrlReceipt** application using the default five percent sales tax rate and inputting the amount **7.99**. Figure 5-37 displays sample output. Run the application again, having changed the TaxRate property to something else.

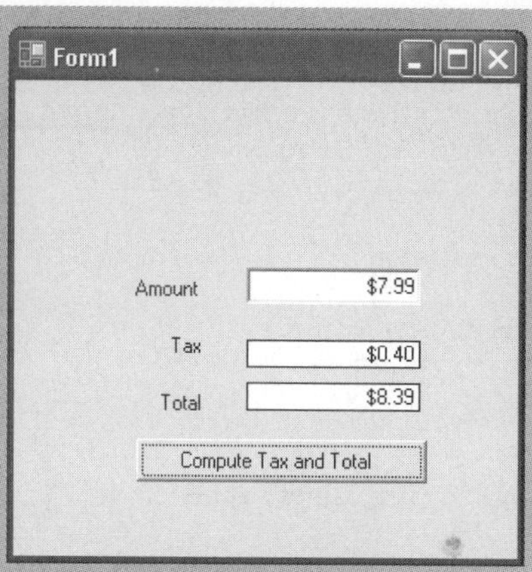

Figure 5-37: TestCtrlRecipt at runtime

Inheriting from Another User Control

Inheritance, as previously mentioned, is an idea that can be extended indefinitely. Consider this one practical example of extending it one level beyond the ctrlReceipt user control you just created. ctrlReceipt could be used by any application that needs to display an amount, tax, and total. You have not tailored the control specifically for the FGDT. As it turns out, every receipt created for the Friendsville Organizing Committee should include the FOC sailboat logo and the FOC name, as well as the purpose of this particular receipt. For this reason, you need to create another user control that uses the existing ctrlReceipt and also incorporates these other elements.

To create the ctrlFocReceipt user control:

1   In Solution Explorer, right-click the **solution** name, and add another **Windows Control Library project** to this solution. Name the new project **ctrlFocReceiptLib**.

2   In Solution Explorer for the new project, name the control **ctrlFocReceipt** and its file **ctrlFocReceipt.vb**. In the User Control Designer, drag a copy of **ctrlReceipt** from the Toolbox onto the control. Add the other additional controls shown in Figure 5-38.

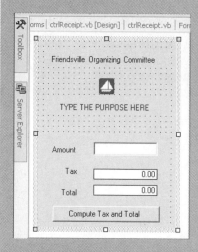

Figure 5-38: ctrlFocReceipt in the User Control Designer

3   The new control, ctrlFocReceipt, must expose two properties for the user programmer: Purpose (to fill lblPurpose) and the TaxRate of the underlying ctrlReceipt. Insert the code shown in Figure 5-39 that declares these two properties and associated private variables.

```
Public Class ctrlFocReceipt
  Inherits System.Windows.Forms.UserControl
  Private sngTaxRate As Single = 0.05
  Public Property TaxRate() As Single
    Get
      Return sngTaxRate
    End Get
    Set(ByVal Value As Single)
      sngTaxRate = Value
      CtrlReceipt1.TaxRate = Value
    End Set
  End Property

  Private strPurpose As String
  Public Property Purpose() As String
    Get
      Return strPurpose
    End Get
    Set(ByVal Value As String)
      strPurpose = Value
      lblPurpose.Text = Value
    End Set
  End Property
```

Figure 5-39: Property declarations for ctrlFocReceipt

4   Click **Save All**, and build the project.

5   To test the new control, add a **Windows application** to the current solution, called **TestCtrlFocReceipt**, and remember to set this as the **startup project**. Add a reference to the **ctrlFocReceiptLib** library, then drop a **ctrlFocReceipt** onto **Form1**. Set the Purpose property to display **Accommodations**, and set the TaxRate property to eight and one half percent for CtrlFocReceipt1. (Note that Visual Basic .NET assigns the default name CtrlFocReceipt1 to the first instance of ctrlFocReceipt on a form.)

6   Run the **TestCtrlFocReceipt** application, inputting **100** for Amount. The output should appear as in Figure 5-40. Close the application and solution.

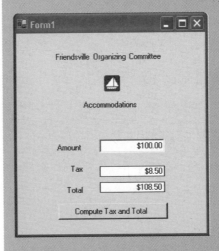

Figure 5-40: TestCtrlFocReceipt at runtime

You have now completed Lesson B. You can take a break now, or keep working; but don't forget to do the exercises here before proceeding with Lesson C.

SUMMARY

- A user control can inherit from any Windows Forms control. You can define additional properties and methods for this user control. You can expose any of these properties or methods by making them public. You can use the Property Get and Set statements to communicate exposed properties to internal, protected variables.

- A user control can be part of a project and compiled with that project. This type of user control can be temporarily added to the Toolbox.

- A user control can be built into a Windows Control Library containing one or more user controls. All of the user controls in a Windows Control Library can be semipermanently added to the Toolbox.

- A Windows Control Library can incorporate a user control from another Windows Control Library.

QUESTIONS

1. By setting the _____ property, you can cause a control to be aligned along one border of its container.

2. The icons displayed next to the nodes of a TreeView control are contained in a(n) _____ control.

3. When a tree view node has been selected, the icon displayed for that node is determined by the _____ property.

4. The _____ method temporarily blocks the repainting of the form.

5. A node with no parent is called a(n) _____ node.

6. In a ListView control, the list of icons displayed next to a list view item in Details view is determined by the _____ property.

EXERCISES

1. Create a user control called ctrlStudentNames that contains a list box and two radio buttons. In the list box, display the first names of 10 students. The radio buttons indicate whether the selected student name is male or female. Also declare a new public property for the control named Male; set this property to True when radMale is checked, and set it to False when radFemale is checked. You can obtain the data (student names and gender of each name) from a text file that you create for this purpose, or you can hard code them into the control. In either case, load them into an array, and declare this array as public (exposing it to developers who import the control). Then write a test project to demonstrate that the control works.

2. Extend the program in Exercise 1. Create a MatchMaker project that uses ctrlStudentNames. When a student name is selected in the list box in ctrlStudentNames,

another list box in the bottom half of the form must display only the names of students of the opposite sex. (*Hint*: Recall that the array in ctrlStudentNames is public and that ctrlStudentNames has a public property named Male.)

3. Create a Windows Explorer-style interface application. Create a text file containing information concerning five nations. The format of this file should be CountryName, followed by CountryInfo. Insert 5 to 10 records for each country. For example, the following might be the entries created for the USA:

   - "USA", "Capital: Washington, DC"
   - "USA", "Population: 280,000,000"
   - "USA", "Continent: North America"
   - "USA", "Political Form: Federal republic"
   - "USA", "Political parties: Republican, Democrat"
   - "USA", "Major trading partners: Canada, Mexico, Japan, EU"
   - "USA", "Longest river: Mississippi"

In this fashion, your data file will end up with 25 to 50 records.

At startup, read through your data file, loading each country name as a root node (but load each country name only once). Then, when a node is selected, clear the ListView control, and then read through the data file again, loading into the list view all of the items that pertain to the selected country.

4. Create a Microsoft Outlook-style interface application. For the data file, TreeView, and ListView controls, follow the specification for the program in Exercise 3. The third window should contain a PictureBox control. Display the flag of the selected country.

5. Create an Explorer-style interface application that contains the menu of your favorite fast-food restaurant. Hard code the information into a series of tables. The tree view nodes are menu categories: breakfast items, entrees, sandwiches, side orders, and drinks. When a node is selected, the list view displays the menu items in the selected category. A subitem displays the price of the item.

6. Create an Outlook-style interface application that extends Exercise 5. The third pane contains a list box, which displays the name and price of each item the user has selected in the list view. The third pane also contains a label that shows the total price for all selected items.

7. Implement your design for the Friendsville City Museum's information kiosk (Exercise 10 at the end of Lesson A).

After completing this lesson, you will be able to:

- Plan a draft of the Scoring application
- Create a draft of the Scoring application
- Assemble prewritten elements
- Build a control library and add it to an application
- Add frmSpeed, the first competition scoring module
- Complete the draft of the Scoring application

Complete an Explorer-style Interface Application with User Controls

Tasks for the FGDT

Development of the draft version of the Scoring application will be a team effort. Hilda, in addition to providing an overall plan for the application and coordinating everyone else's efforts, develops the structure for the Events.txt file, creates the file, and writes the associated code. Rick Sanchez develops user controls, which the other team members can then incorporate in their portions of the application—in fact, if Rick's user controls are compiled into a generally accessible class library, anyone's application will be able to use them by including a reference to the control's DLL file in its References list. Althea's piece involves the "Individual Scoring - Fastest Time" module, which can serve as a model for the other scoring modules. You are responsible for the main form as well as the scoring module for team sports.

Planning a Draft of the Scoring Application

Run the draft of the Scoring application again to refresh your memory concerning its features and elements. Hilda's overall plan is for a Windows Explorer-style user interface on the main form (frmScoreMain). The left pane has a tree view containing the sports, venues, and schedule for the games. The tree view loads in the Windows Form Designer at design time. The right pane contains the list of events in the selected category in Details view; the list view is loaded programmatically after a user makes a selection in the tree view. When the user double-clicks a particular event in the list view, the scoring module for that event is displayed. Four such scoring modules are needed: three individual scoring modules based on distance, speed, and judging; plus one module for recording the scores of team sports events.

Events.txt and Associated Code

Events.txt contains all the events for the Friendsville International Games. Hilda designed the layout for this file, created the actual data file and typed in its contents, and wrote the necessary code to load the data file into an array. You copy this file into an array when the main form loads, where it remains available the whole time the application is running. You use Hilda's layout for this file in Module1.vb.

User Controls

Rick has created three user controls for this application:

- ctrlNation is used for identifying the competing nations in team sports competitions and for identifying the country affiliation of athletes in individual competitions. This control has an associated data file called Nations.txt. Up to this point, Rick has loaded 26 countries into Nations.txt.
- ctrlTeamScore is used in the Team Scoring module. It incorporates ctrlNation plus other elements needed for tracking the team score during the contest.
- ctrlEventHeader, the event header, displays standard header information that appears at runtime at the top of the form for each scoring module. When a list view item is double-clicked, the main form instantiates the appropriate scoring module and calls ctrlEventHeader, passing the event header information to it.

Individual Scoring—Speed

Althea Brown created the only scoring module completed before you begin work on the Team Scoring module. The frmSpeed control provides for the display of the names and country affiliations of two to eight competitors, entering the time for each athlete, and determining the winner (the competitor with the shortest time).

Creating a Draft of the Scoring Application

Because you are creating the main project, you must first initiate that project (the Explorer-style interface); assemble all the elements written by Hilda, Rick, and Althea; complete the main form; and then create the Team Scoring module. You also create stubs for the modules to be completed later (individual scoring based on distance and on judging). Finally, you test and debug the completed application.

Initiating the Main Project

You create a blank solution as a container for the individual projects of this application. You then create the main Windows Forms application within that solution.

To initiate the main project:

1 Click **File | New | Blank Solution**. Name this solution **Scoring (Draft)**, and place it in the **VB.NET\Student\Tut05** folder.

2 In Solution Explorer, right-click **Scoring (Draft)**, and add a new Windows application project called **Scoring**, located under the Scoring (Draft) folder. Right-click **Scoring** and set it as the **startup project**. Change the name of **Form1** to **frmScoreMain**, and the filename to **frmScoreMain.vb**. Click **Scoring**, and open the Property pages for the project. Set the Startup object to **frmScoreMain**.

3 Design the GUI. Place a **TreeView** control on the left (with its Dock property set to Left), a **Splitter control** next to it, and a **ListView** control on the right (with its Dock property set to Fill). Change the form's **Text** property to

Competition Scoring – Main Form. In the Properties window for TreeView1, click the **Nodes Collection** to open the TreeNode Editor. In the TreeNode Editor, add three **Root** nodes (**Sports**, **Venues**, and **Schedule**), and then add the child nodes under each of these, as shown in Figure 5-41.

TreeNodes for frmScoreMain		
Root Node: Sports	**Root Node: Venues**	**Root Node: Schedule**
Baseball	Friendsville International Center (01)	Day 1
Basketball	Memorial Stadium (02)	Day 2
Boxing	Valley Natatorium (03)	Day 3
Diving	Nashua-Swaps Equestrian Center (04)	Day 4
Equestrian	County Fairgrounds (05)	Day 5
Fencing	Friendsville College Gymnasium (06)	Day 6
Field	Municipal Recreation Center (07)	Day 7
Gymnastics	Valley North Senior High School (08)	Day 8
Shooting		Day 9
Soccer		Day 10
Softball		Day 11
Tennis		Day 12
Track		Day 13
Volleyball		Day 14
Wrestling		

Figure 5-41: Tree view nodes in frmScoreMain

4   Add an **ImageList** control. Place a **closed folder icon** and an **open folder icon** in the ImageList's Images Collection. (You can find copies of the closed folder icon and open folder icon in the Tut05 folder.) Back in the TreeView control, assign **ImageList1** to the **ImageList** property. Then assign the index value for the **closed folder** (0) to the **ImageIndex** property, and the index value for the **open folder** (1) to the **SelectedImageIndex** property. If you need additional help adding icons to the ImageList control's Images Collection, see page 246.

5   In the ListView control, set the **View** property to **Details**. Then, in the Columns property, click the ellipsis after (Collection) to open the **ColumnHeader Collection Editor**. (Recall that nothing will show in the Details view if you have not specified the column headers.) In the **ColumnHeader Collection Editor**, enter five column headers, with name, text, and width properties as shown in Figure 5-42.

Name	Text	Width
EventName	Event Name	211
Sport	Sport	100
Gender	Gender	47
Venue	Venue	143
EventDate	Event Date	74

Figure 5-42: Column header properties

6   Click **Save All**. Test the **Scoring** application. The tree view should display its three expandable root nodes. Expand them. The selected node should display an open folder icon; all other nodes should display a closed folder. The list view should display the column headings only. Close the application and return to the IDE.

Assembling Prewritten Elements

You now incorporate the program elements written by other members of the FGDT. You start with Hilda's record layout for Events.txt, then Rick's three user controls, and finally Althea's frmSpeed control.

Events.txt Record Layout and File

The FGDT decided on the information elements needed to describe each event in the Friendsville International Games. The information elements include the sport, the event name, gender, scoring method, venue index, and schedule (day) for the event. Hilda implemented this design by creating the record layout for structEvent and by building the text file.

To add Hilda's record layout and files to the Scoring application:

1   In Solution Explorer, click the project name **Scoring**. Then click **Project | Add Module**. Click **Open** to open the Code Editor for Module1.vb.

2   Click **File | Open | File** to open the file **Hilda.txt**, found in the VB.NET\Student\Tut05 folder and shown in Figure 5-43, and copy its contents into Module1.vb. Close **Hilda.txt**. Save **Module1.vb**.

```
Public Structure structEvent
  <VBFixedString(10)> Public Sport As String
  <VBFixedString(25)> Public EventName As String
  <VBFixedString(1)> Public Gender As String
  <VBFixedString(1)> Public ScoringMethod As String
  Public VenueIndex As Integer
  <VBFixedString(10)> Public Schedule As String
End Structure

Public Const NUMEVENTS = 500
Public pastructEvents(NUMEVENTS) As structEvent
Public pEventRec As structEvent
```

Figure 5-43: Record layout and variables for Events.txt

The layout of structEvent bears a short explanation:

- *Sport*—The name of the sport for each event is needed so that when the user selects a sport in the tree view, your program can search the array of all events and find those related to that sport.
- *EventName*—Description of the event is entered here.
- *Gender*—Establishing the gender for each event is important as part of the event description.

These three elements (sport, event name, and gender) compose the complete event description. For example, "Track, 400-Meter Relay, F" describes the 400-meter relay race in women's track; and "Baseball, Japan vs. USA, M" describes the men's baseball game between Japan and the United States.

- *ScoringMethod*—Important information element, because different scoring modules must be called depending on the method of scoring. TS indicates team scoring for national team events, such as baseball and softball. For individual events, S is for scoring based on speed or fastest time, such as the swimming events; D is for scoring based on distance, such as javelin or shot put; and J is for competition based on judges' scores, such as diving or gymnastics.
- *VenueIndex*—Integer that determines which of eight venues will host the event; the names of these eight venues are loaded into an array, and the VenueIndex is an index into that array. The VenueIndex is necessary in this application so that, when the user selects a particular venue in the tree view, your program can search the array of all events and find those that will be held in that venue.
- *Schedule*—Element that indicates on which day of the Games (Day 1 through Day 14) the event is scheduled. The Schedule is necessary in this application so that, when the user selects a particular day in the tree view, your program can search the array of all events and find those that will be held on that day.

Following the layout of structEvent, Module1 includes three public declarations related to structEvent: the constant NUMEVENTS is the maximum number of events that might be held, and is set at 500. pastructEvents() is a public array of structures of type structEvent—that is, an array that can hold up to 500 events. And pEventRec is a record of type structEvent, that is, a record that can hold one event.

3   Open **Events.txt**, and note that the record layout you saw in Figure 5-43 matches the data in Events.txt, a small portion of which is shown in Figure 5-44. Scroll quickly through the file, so you can get a sense of the contents. So far, 145 events have been scheduled, and Hilda has entered them into Events.txt. At runtime, you will open Events.txt and load the contents of the file into pastructEvents(). After perusing the contents, close **Events.txt**.

```
"General", "Closing Ceremonies", " ", " ", 1, "Day 14"
"Baseball", "USA vs Japan", "M", "TS", 2,"Day 3"
"Softball", "Austria vs Belgium", "F", "TS", 5,"Day 13"
"Softball", "Australia vs Portugal", "F", "TS", 5,"Day 13"
"Track", "100 Meter Dash", "F", "S", 1, "Day 2"
"Track", "100 Meter Dash", "M", "S", 1, "Day 3"
"Diving", "3 Meter Springboard", "F", "J", 3, "Day 12"
"Diving", "10 Meter Springboard", "F", "J", 3, "Day 12"
```

Figure 5-44: Snippet of Events.txt

4 Two of the elements in Module1.vb are coded: ScoringMethod and VenueIndex. Each of these employs a small array to decode the element. Insert the **array declarations** for the pastrScoringMethods() array shown in Figure 5-45 and the pastrVenues() array shown in Figure 5-46 at the end of Module1 before the End Module statement.

```
Public pastrScoringMethods(,) As String = { _
   {"TS", "Team sport"}, _
   {"S", "Speed"}, _
   {"D", "Distance"}, _
   {"J", "Judges"}}
```

Figure 5-45: pastrScoringMethods() array declaration in Module1

```
Public pastrVenues() As String = {"", _
   "Friendsville International Center", _
   "Memorial Stadium", _
   "Valley Natatorium", _
   "Nashua-Swaps Equestrian Center", _
   "County Fairgrounds", _
   "Friendsville College Gymnasium", _
   "Municipal Recreation Center", _
   "Valley North Senior High School"}
```

Figure 5-46: pastrVenues() array declaration in Module1

Small data files whose contents are needed repeatedly in an application can best be loaded into an array. Accessing an array element or searching through an array for an element is much faster than accessing data from disk, whether stored in a traditional file or in a database. In the Scoring application, every time the user selects a node in the tree view, the program must search all of the events that match the node—events in the selected sport node, or events at the selected venue node, or events on the selected day node. Therefore, the most efficient processing approach is to load the entire Events.txt file into an array when frmScoreMain is loaded, and subsequently use this array when searching for events. Thus your next step is to insert the code that loads Events.txt into the pastructEvents() array.

5 A simple loop is all that you need to load Events.txt into the array at the time the application starts up. Open the **Code Editor** for frmScoreMain.vb if necessary, and insert the **frmScoreMain_Load()** procedure shown in Figure 5-47. Note that each iteration of the loop retrieves the values from Events.txt that fill one record in the pastructEvents() array.

```
Private Sub frmScoreMain_Load(ByVal sender As Object, _
    ByVal e As System.EventArgs) Handles MyBase.Load
  Dim i As Integer = 0
  FileOpen(1, "Events.txt", OpenMode.Input)
  Do Until EOF(1)
    With pastructEvents(i)
      Input(1, .Sport)
      Input(1, .EventName)
      Input(1, .Gender)
      Input(1, .ScoringMethod)
      Input(1, .VenueIndex)
      Input(1, .Schedule)
    End With
    i += 1
  Loop
  FileClose(1)
End Sub
```

Figure 5-47: frmScoreMain_Load() event procedure

6 The executable program is created in the bin folder, and the executable must find and open the data files used in the application. For this reason, copy the data file Hilda created, **Events.txt**, into the **Tut05\Scoring (Draft)\Scoring\ bin** folder.

7 Click **Build | Build Solution** to ensure that you have made no syntax errors. (You could also run the application, but it does not do anything yet—so just checking for syntax is good enough for the moment.)

Building a Control Library and Adding It to an Application

Rick's first user control (ctrlNation) is used for team and individual scoring. For team scoring, ctrlNation is incorporated into ctrlTeamScore, whereas for individual scoring, ctrlNation is used in frmSpeed, and later in frmDistance and frmJudge in Tutorial 6.

NOTE: When creating the three user controls for the Scoring application, Rick used the suffix Lib for the project and Windows Control Library name—such as ctrlNationLib—but the suffix was not used for the name of the actual user control—such as ctrlNation. In practice, if a control library contains only one control, then the project/library name and the control name are often the same. If a control library project contains multiple user controls, then the suffix Lib is often used to designate the library, and obviously each control in that library would get a unique name. In the present case, Rick intentionally differentiated the project/library name from the control name so that you could tell which name is being referenced in each instance. Specifically, when you add a reference to a project, you are adding the name of the project/library. When you add a user control to the Toolbox, the control name appears in the Toolbox, the control name is dragged onto a form, and the control name is used in referring to properties, methods, and events of that control.

ctrlNation depends on the existence of the Nations.txt text file, which Rick also created, and it is available in the VB.NET\Student\Tut05 folder. This file contains one record for each country participating in the Friendsville International Games. Each record contains the three-character internationally adopted country abbreviation (USA, FRA, etc.), the name of the country, and an index value indicating the position of this country's flag in the collection of images loaded into an ImageIndex control. Figure 5-48 shows the current contents of Nations.txt. Although at least 100 countries are expected to participate in the Games, Rick has entered only 26 countries into Nations.txt so far.

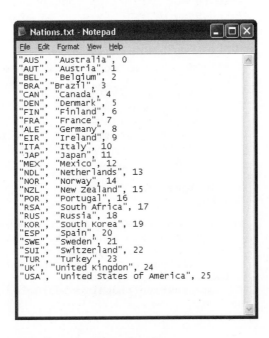

Figure 5-48: Contents of Nations.txt

ctrlNation contains three Windows Forms controls: a combo box is loaded with the names of participating countries from the Nations.txt file, a label is loaded with the flag of the selected country, and an ImageIndex contains all of the flags. Nations.txt also contains an index for each country that corresponds to the location of that country's flag in the ImageIndex control. The entire Nations.txt file, including this index, is loaded into an array when ctrlNation is loaded. Figure 5-49 shows the layout of ctrlNation in the User Control Designer, and Figure 5-50 shows the code for this control.

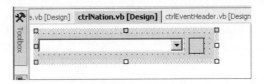

Figure 5-49: ctrlNation in the User Control Designer

```
Public Class ctrlNation
  Inherits System.Windows.Forms.UserControl

+ Windows Form Designer generated code

  Const NUMNATIONS = 100
  Dim mastrNation(NUMNATIONS, 3) As String

  Private Sub ctrlNation_Load(ByVal sender As _
      System.Object, ByVal e As System.EventArgs) _
      Handles MyBase.Load
    Dim i As Integer = 0
    Dim s As String
    FileOpen(1, "Nations.txt", OpenMode.Input)
    Do Until EOF(1)
      Input(1, mastrNation(i, 0))
      Input(1, mastrNation(i, 1))
      Input(1, mastrNation(i, 2))
      s = mastrNation(i, 0) & " " & mastrNation(i, 1)
      cboNation.Items.Add(s)
      i += 1
    Loop
    FileClose(1)
  End Sub

  Private Sub cboNation_SelectedIndexChanged(ByVal _
      sender As System.Object, ByVal e As _
      System.EventArgs) Handles _
      cboNation.SelectedIndexChanged
    lblFlagIcon.ImageIndex = _
      mastrNation(cboNation.SelectedIndex, 2)
  End Sub
End Class
```

Figure 5-50: ctrlNation's code

How to Create the ctrlNationLib Control

Because Rick already created ctrlNationLib, you do not need to replicate the creation of the control (though you are welcome to do so for practice). To create this control, Rick started a new Windows Control Library project and named it ctrlNationLib. He then renamed UserControl1.vb as ctrlNation.vb. In the User Control Designer, he added the three controls shown in Figure 5-49: a ComboBox control which Rick named cboNation, a Label control named lblFlagIcon, and an ImageList control with the default name ImageList1.

cboNation is populated with the country abbreviation and country name from Nations.txt when the ctrlNation control loads, and lblFlagIcon is filled with the selected country's flag icon after the user makes a selection in cboNation. Only ImageIndex1 must be loaded at design time in the GUI. To do this, Rick looked up the icon file representing each country in Nations.txt, and loaded these icon files in alphabetical order (the same order as the records in Nations.txt) into the Images Collection of ImageList1. The flag icons of various nations are available at Program Files\Microsoft Visual Studio .NET\Common7\Graphics\icons\Flags. After designating these flag icons, the Image Collection Editor (lengthened to show all of the flag icons) appears as shown in Figure 5-51. ImageList1 is used to fill lblFlagIcon; therefore, the ImageList property of lblFlagIcon is set to ImageList1.

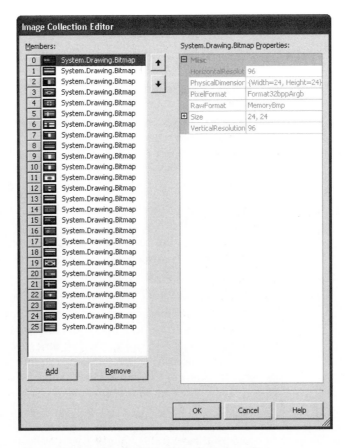

Figure 5-51: Image Collection Editor (lengthened)

The code for ctrlNation, shown in Figure 5-50, is in three pieces: module-level declarations, the control's load procedure—ctrlNation_Load()—and the combo box selection procedure—cboNation_SelectedIndexChanged().

The declarations establish the maximum number of nations as 100, and then declare a two-dimensional array called mastrNation(). mastrNation(100,3) has 100 rows (for up to 100 nations) and three columns. Column 0 contains the country abbreviation, column 1 contains the country name, and column 2 contains the index of the country's flag icon in the ImageIndex images collection.

ctrlNation_Load0 opens Nations.txt, and loads its contents into mastrNation(,). For each record, the procedure also concatenates the country abbreviation with the country name and adds this concatenated string as a new item in cboNation.

cboNation_SelectedIndexChanged() needs only one statement: the correct ImageIndex for the country selected in cboNation is retrieved from the mastrNation(,) array, and this value is assigned as the ImageIndex property of lblFlagIcon.

After creating the GUI and entering the code for ctrlNation, Rick compiled the class library, and then closed the solution.

Though you should understand the construction of ctrlNationLib, and can refer to it when doing the end of lesson exercises here or when constructing your own user controls, in fact the only thing you need to do to make the Scoring application work is to add a reference to it in the Scoring project (Step 3 in the following steps).

To add the ctrlNationLib control library to the Scoring (Draft) application:

1 Copy the **ctrlNation** folder from the VB.NET\Student\Tut05 folder to the Scoring (Draft) folder.

> **NOTE:** You could reference ctrlNationLib in its current location, so copying the folder is not technically required. Copying the folder also interferes with reusability: if you subsequently make a change to the copy of the project, that change is not automatically propagated back to the source. However, you are making the copy here for strictly pedagogical convenience—at the conclusion of this project, all solution components will be included in the Scoring (Draft) folder, where it will be available for further copying and adaptation in Tutorial 6.

2 In Solution Explorer, right-click **Scoring (Draft)** (the solution name), and click **Add | Existing Project**. In the Add Existing Project dialog box, navigate to the ctrlNation folder that you just copied into Scoring (Draft), and click **ctrlNationLib** to add the control library project to the solution.

> **NOTE:** Again, it is not actually necessary to add the control library project to your solution unless you plan on modifying it in some way. In this case, Rick wrote the finished control, and you do not need to modify it. However, in order to use ctrlNation as a model for user controls you develop yourself, you need to be able to see it, and the easiest way to accomplish that is to include the ctrlNationLib project in your solution. Set up in this way, you can open ctrlNation from Solution Explorer, and examine the GUI and associated code. In a real-world application, the owner of a control library might consider the source code proprietary and might not want to make it available to developers. In such a case, you would only have the DLL file, which is all you really need to use for the control in your project. (Well, almost all: this user control needs the Nations.txt file, so you must make that file available as well.)

3 In Solution Explorer, under the Scoring project, right-click **References**, and click **Add Reference**. In the Add Reference dialog box, click the **Projects** tab, and browse to the **ctrlNation** folder in the Scoring (Draft) folder. Select the **ctrlNationLib** project, and click **OK**. Then build the solution. Open the **Toolbox**, and note the presence of the ctrlNation control at the end of the list of Windows Forms controls.

Two different icons can represent a user control in the Toolbox. If you have added a project to your current solution as you just did with the ctrlNationLib project, you can add a reference to that control library project in any other project in the current solution. Also, when you build the solution, the user control is automatically added to the Toolbox, and the icon representing that user control is ▦. If you close the solution and open another solution that does not include this control library project, then that user control does not appear in the Toolbox. You might say, then, that user controls representing internal projects within a solution are temporarily added to the Toolbox.

If, on the other hand, you customize the Toolbox by adding an external DLL as a new .NET Framework component, then any user control within that DLL is placed in the Toolbox and is represented by the ⚙ icon. Thus, this addition to the Toolbox is semipermanent—it stays in the Toolbox until you delete it. Further, if you use such a customized control in a project, then the DLL containing that control is automatically added to the references for that project.

The ctrlTeamScoreLib Control Library and ctrlTeamScore Control

Rick's second user control provides much of the functionality needed for the Team Scoring module, so that later the coding of frmTeam will be quite simple. The original project name for the library containing this user control was TeamScoring, so TeamScoring.dll is the name of the DLL file that the project compiles into, even though Rick subsequently changed the name of the solution to ctrlTeamScoringLib. The only control in this library is ctrlTeamScore, which you will use when you create frmTeam.

The naming of this control library demonstrates a rather odd feature of Visual Basic .NET, of which you should be aware. Three names are involved: TeamScoring is the name of the folder containing the control library project. This was the original project name that Rick assigned when he initiated the project. The original project name stays with the assembly, the namespace, and the DLL file, even if you subsequently change the name of the folder, the solution, and the project.

After initiating the TeamScoring project, Rick changed the name of the solution and the project to ctrlTeamScoringLib. Rick compiled the solution after completing the GUI and code. Now, when you add this control library project to the Scoring (Draft) solution, and then add a reference to this control library project in the References list for the Scoring project, the name that Visual Basic .NET finds and recognizes is ctrlTeamScoreLib. After compilation, ctrlTeamScore appears in the Toolbox, identified by the 🖼 icon.

However, if instead of adding ctrlTeamScoreLib as a project in the Scoring (Draft) solution, you just decided to add ctrlTeamScore as a control in the Toolbox, then you would accomplish this by customizing the Toolbox, clicking the .NET Framework Components tab, and browsing to the file TeamScoring.dll. Adding this DLL file adds ctrlTeamScore as a user control in the Toolbox, identified by the 🖼 icon. If you then created a form in the Scoring project and dragged ctrlTeamScore from the Toolbox onto the form, you would find that a new reference to TeamScoring.dll is automatically added to the References list for the Scoring project.

Because of the way these names are handled by Visual Studio .NET, it behooves you to select the original name of a new control library project very carefully, and then, once having selected the name, to stick with it. This tutorial has used different names for each piece: the original project name, which becomes the original folder, solution, project, namespace, and DLL name. The solution and project names were then changed in Solution Explorer. This was done to help you understand how Visual Studio .NET uses these names.

ctrlTeamScore incorporates an instance of ctrlNation for each team, labels to display the running score, buttons and procedures to add or subtract from each team's score, and a group box with radio buttons to identify the winner when the contest is over. Figures 5-52 and 5-53 display the graphical interface and the code for this control, respectively.

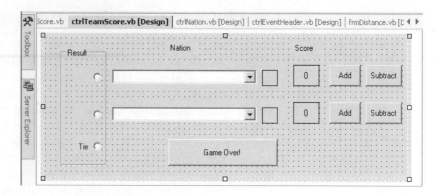

Figure 5-52: ctrlTeamScore [Design]

```vb
Private Sub btnAdd1_Click(ByVal _
    sender As System.Object, _
    ByVal e As System.EventArgs) Handles btnAdd1.Click
  lblScore1.Text += 1
End Sub

Private Sub btnSubtract1_Click(ByVal sender As _
    System.Object, ByVal e As System.EventArgs) _
    Handles btnSubtract1.Click
  lblScore1.Text -= 1
End Sub

Private Sub btnAdd2_Click(ByVal sender As _
    System.Object, ByVal e As System.EventArgs) _
    Handles btnAdd2.Click
  lblScore2.Text += 1
End Sub

Private Sub btnSubtract2_Click(ByVal sender As _
    System.Object, ByVal e As System.EventArgs) _
    Handles btnSubtract2.Click
  lblScore2.Text -= 1
End Sub

Private Sub btnGameOver_Click(ByVal sender As _
    System.Object, ByVal e As System.EventArgs) _
    Handles btnGameOver.Click
  Select Case Val(lblScore1.Text)
    Case Is > Val(lblScore2.Text)
      radTeam2.Text = "L"
      radTeam1.Text = "W"
      radTeam1.BackColor = Color.Yellow
      radTeam1.Checked = True
    Case Is < Val(lblScore2.Text)
      radTeam1.Text = "L"
      radTeam2.Text = "W"
      radTeam2.BackColor = Color.Yellow
      radTeam2.Checked = True
    Case Else
      radTie.Visible = True
      radTie.Checked = True
  End Select
  grpResult.Visible = True
End Sub
End Class
```

Figure 5-53: ctrlTeamScore code

How to Create the ctrlTeamScoreLib Control

Because Rick already created ctrlTeamScoreLib, you do not need to replicate the creation of the control (though you are welcome to do so for practice). To create this control, Rick started a new Windows Control Library project and named it TeamScoring. After initiating the project, he renamed both the solution and the project as ctrlTeamScoreLib. He then renamed UserControl1.vb as ctrlTeamScore.vb.

ctrlTeamScore uses ctrlNation, Rick's first user control developed for this project. Therefore, Rick needed to make ctrlNation available. Rick added ctrlNation to the Toolbox by right-clicking Customize Toolbox, clicking the .NET Framework Components tab, browsing to ctrlNationLib.dll, and clicking OK. He then added the controls shown in Figure 5-49, using the obvious object names: the group box on the left, invisible until Game Over is clicked, is named grpResult. The radio buttons inside the group box are radTeam1 (set to True if Team1 is the winner), radTeam2 (set to True if Team2 is the winner), and radTie (invisible unless the contest ends in a tie). Name and Score have the default names Label1 and Label2. To the right of the group box, the controls on the top row are CtrlNation1 (the default name of the first ctrlNation control added to the project), lblScore1 (Team1's score), btnAdd1, and btnSubtract1. Analogous names were assigned to the bottom row of controls.

The code for ctrlTeamScore, Figure 5-53, contains five click event procedures. Four of these add one to or subtract one from the score for Team1 or Team2. The fifth procedure, btnGameOver_Click(), identifies the winner of the contest.

Rick then compiled the control library. Note that, although the project name is ctrlTeamScoreLib, Visual Studio named the dynamic link library TeamScoring.dll.

These next steps direct you to add Rick's TeamScoring folder to your Scoring (Draft) folder, and to add Rick's user control library to your Scoring application. Follow these steps, or substitute your own ctrlTeamScore user control, if you have created it yourself.

To add the ctrlTeamScoreLib control library to the Scoring (Draft) application:

1 Copy the **TeamScoring** folder from the VB.NET\Student\Tut05 folder to the **Scoring (Draft)** folder.

2 In Solution Explorer, right-click the solution name **Scoring**, click **Add | Existing Project**, navigate to the TeamScoring folder that you just copied into Scoring (Draft), and click **ctrlTeamScoreLib** to add the control library to the solution.

3 In Solution Explorer, under the Scoring project, right-click **References**. Add a reference to the **ctrlTeamScoreLib** project.

4 Compile the solution (by clicking Build | Build Solution). Note that ctrlTeamScore now appears in the Toolbox.

The ctrlEventHeaderLib Control Library and ctrlEventHeader Control

Rick's third user control provides a standardized header display for every scoring module (distance, speed, judging, and team scoring). The control receives event description information from the SetHeaderInfo procedure of the scoring module. (Specific coverage of the SetHeaderInfo procedure will be covered in the next section as part of the frmSpeed module.) The fully decoded information received by the control includes the sport, event name, venue, schedule, scoring method, and gender. ctrlEventHeader then displays this information. Figure 5-54 shows the control's graphical interface. All of the control's code is contained in the load event procedure, as shown in Figure 5-55.

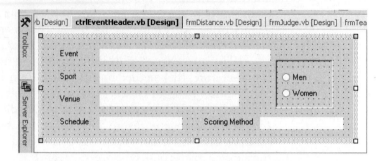

Figure 5-54: ctrlEventHeader [Design]

```
  Public Sub LoadHeaderInfo(ByVal vSport As String, _
    ByVal vEventName As String, _
    ByVal vVenue As String, _
    ByVal vSchedule As String, _
    ByVal vScoringMethod As String, _
    ByVal vGender As String)
    lblSport.Text = vSport
    lblEventName.Text = vEventName
    lblVenue.Text = vVenue
    lblSchedule.Text = vSchedule
    lblScoringMethod.Text = vScoringMethod
    If vGender = "M" Then radMen.Checked = True
    If vGender = "F" Then radWomen.Checked = True
  End Sub
End Class
```

Figure 5-55: ctrlEventHeader code

How to Create the ctrlEventHeader Control

Once again, because Rick already created ctrlEventHeader, you do not need to replicate the creation of the control (though you are welcome to do so for practice). To create this control, Rick started a new Windows Control Library project and named it ctrlEventHeader. After initiating the project, he renamed both the solution and the project as ctrlEventHeaderLib. He then renamed UserControl1.vb as ctrlEventHeader.vb

The control's GUI, Figure 5-54, consists entirely of labels plus a Panel control containing two radio buttons. Default names (Label1, Label2, ..., Label5) are unchanged for Event, Sport, Venue, Schedule, and Scoring Method. For the variable data fields, the BackColor is white, and the names (as you might suspect) are lblEventName, lblSport, lblVenue, lblSchedule, and lblScoringMethod. The Panel control carries the default name, Panel1. The radio buttons inside it are named radMen and radWomen.

Before a form containing ctrlEventHeader is displayed, the control's public LoadHeaderInfo() procedure is called. This procedure, shown in Figure 5-55, simply loads all of the labels and radio buttons with the information passed to the procedure.

Rick then compiled the control library. Note that, although the project name is ctrlEventHeaderLib, Visual Studio named the dynamic link library ctrlEventHeader.dll.

These next steps direct you to add Rick's ctrlEventHeader folder to your Scoring (Draft) folder, and to add Rick's ctrlEventHeaderLib to your Scoring application.

Follow these steps, or substitute your own ctrlEventHeader user control, if you have created it yourself.

> To add the ctrlEventHeaderLib control library to the Scoring (Draft) application:
>
> **1** Copy the **ctrlEventHeader** folder from the VB.NET\Student\Tut05 folder to the **Scoring (Draft)** folder.
>
> **2** In Solution Explorer, right-click the solution name, and click **Add I Existing Project**. Navigate to the **ctrlEventHeader** folder that you just copied into Scoring (Draft), and click **ctrlEventHeaderLib** to add the control library to the solution.
>
> **3** In Solution Explorer, under the Scoring project, right-click **References**. Add a reference to the **ctrlEventHeaderLib** project.
>
> **4** Compile the solution (by clicking Build I Build Solution). Note that ctrlEventHeader now appears in the Toolbox.

Rick's three user controls have now been added to the Scoring (Draft) application. If you look in the Toolbox when frmScoreMain is open in the Designer, you should see these three user controls present: ctrlNation, permanently added to the Toolbox and represented by the 🔧 icon, and ctrlTeamScore and ctrlEventHeader, temporarily added to the Toolbox with the current solution and represented by the 🔲 icon.

Adding frmSpeed, the First Competition Scoring Module

Althea's contribution to the team effort is the individual scoring module for competitions based on speed. frmSpeed is a model for the individual scoring modules for competitions based on distance and on judging, to be developed in Tutorial 6.

Figure 5-56 shows frmSpeed at design time. Note how Rick's user controls are incorporated into the design of this form: ctrlEventHeader is at the top of the form, and grpCompetitors includes eight instances of ctrlNation.

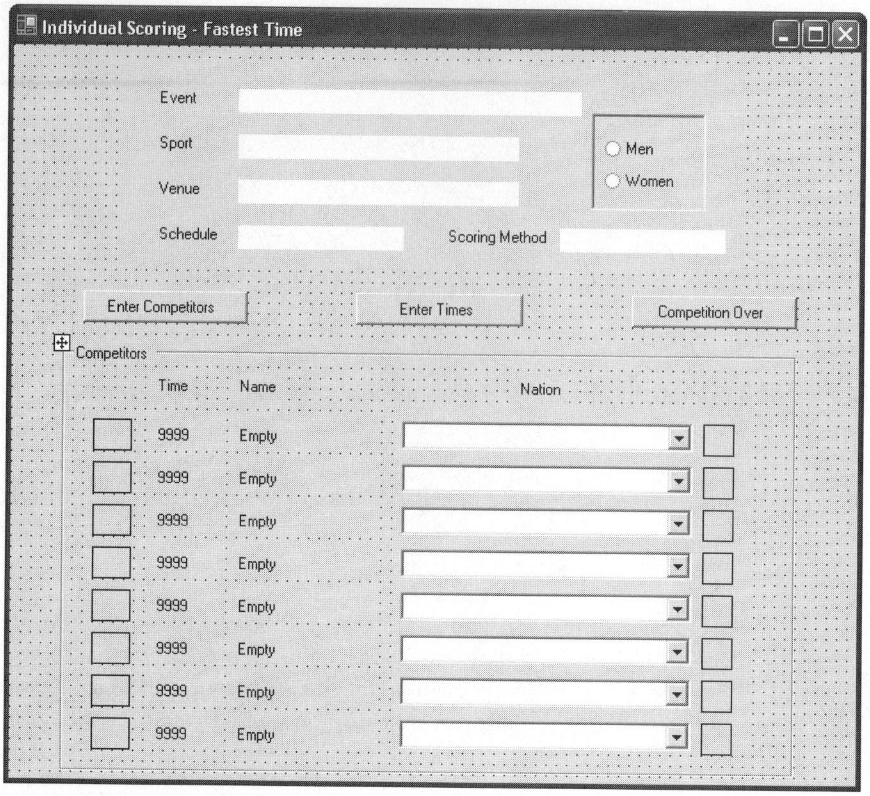

Figure 5-56: frmSpeed at design time

Information for the event header display is passed to the form from frmScoreMain, which calls the SetHeaderInfo procedure before displaying frmSpeed. SetHeaderInfo in turn calls the LoadHeaderInfo method of ctrlEventHeader1. See Figure 5-57. (This code also includes the declaration of mNumCompetitors, a module-level variable needed throughout the form.)

```
Dim mNumCompetitors As Integer

Public Sub SetHeaderInfo(ByVal vSport As String, _
  ByVal vEventName As String, _
  ByVal vVenue As String, ByVal vSchedule As String, _
  ByVal vScoringMethod As String, ByVal vGender As String)

  ctrlEventHeader1.LoadHeaderInfo(vSport, vEventName, _
    vVenue, vSchedule, vScoringMethod, vGender)
End Sub
```

Figure 5-57: SetHeaderInfo method

The grpCompetitors group control contains eight sets of controls, one set for each competitor. These controls and code demonstrate one possible method of handling multiple sets of controls in the absence of control arrays, which were commonly used for this purpose in Visual Basic 6.0 but are not supported in Visual Basic .NET. The method used here is to assign a value to the Tag property of each individual control. The Tag property of a control can contain any data that the programmer wants to associate with the control. In the Windows Form Designer, you can only assign text to the Tag property; but in code, you can assign any kind of object to the Tag property. The labels on the left (lblResult1, lblResult2, ..., lblResult8) are given Tag values of 100, 200, ..., 800. In the next column, the times (lblTime1, lblTime2, ..., lblTime8) are given Tag values of 10, 20, ..., 80. The third column labels (lblName1, lblName2, ..., lblName8) are given Tag values of 1, 2, ..., 8. And the ctrlNation controls in the last column have Tag values of .1, .2, ..., .8. To identify individual controls in code, these Tag properties are searched.

After the initial form is displayed, three buttons beneath the event header control subsequent activity from left to right: Enter Competitors allows the user to enter the names of athletes; Enter Times provides for entering the finishing time for each contestant; and Competition Over triggers a procedure that identifies the winner. The click event procedures for all three of these buttons manipulate the Tag properties of the controls in grpCompetitors.

The controls within grpCompetitors are not visible at startup. Figure 5-58 shows the procedure for entering the competitors' names. As each name is entered, the Tag property is used to identify the correct label to display that name, and also to make the entire row of controls associated with that competitor visible.

```vb
Private Sub btnEnterCompetitors_Click(ByVal sender As _
    System.Object, ByVal e As System.EventArgs) _
    Handles btnEnterCompetitors.Click
  Dim i As Integer
  Dim s As String
  Dim ctrl As Control
  mNumCompetitors = _
    InputBox("Enter the number of competitors (2 to 8)")
  If mNumCompetitors < 2 Or mNumCompetitors > 8 Then
    MsgBox("Invalid number of competitors")
    Exit Sub
  End If
  For i = 1 To mNumCompetitors
    s = InputBox("Enter name " & i)
    For Each ctrl In grpCompetitors.Controls
      If ctrl.Tag = i Then ctrl.Text = s
      If ctrl.Tag = i Or ctrl.Tag = i / 10 Or _
          ctrl.Tag = i * 10 Or ctrl.Tag = i * 100 Then
        ctrl.Visible = True
      End If
    Next
  Next
  btnEnterTimes.Enabled = True
End Sub
```

Figure 5-58: btnEnterCompetitors_Click() procedure

When the user enters the times for each competitor, again the Tag property is examined to identify the correct label to receive each time, as shown in Figure 5-59.

```
Private Sub btnEnterTimes_Click(ByVal sender As _
    System.Object, ByVal e As System.EventArgs) _
    Handles btnEnterTimes.Click
  Dim i As Integer
  Dim s As String
  Dim ctrl As Control
  For i = 1 To mNumCompetitors
    s = InputBox("Enter time for competitor " & i)
    For Each ctrl In grpCompetitors.Controls
      If ctrl.Tag = i * 10 Then ctrl.Text = s
    Next
  Next
  btnCompetitionOver.Enabled = True
End Sub
```

Figure 5-59: btnEnterTimes_Click() procedure

Finally, when the competition is over, Figure 5-60 displays the procedure that identifies the winner and highlights that row in yellow. Again, the tag is used to locate the correct line. (The procedure as written does not provide for a tie; it picks only one winner, namely the first competitor to achieve the fastest time.)

```
Private Sub btnCompetitionOver_Click(ByVal sender _
    As System.Object, ByVal e As System.EventArgs) _
    Handles btnCompetitionOver.Click
  Dim i As Integer
  Dim dblWinningTime As Double = 9999.9
  Dim strWinningTag As String
  Dim ctrl As Control
  For i = 1 To mNumCompetitors
    For Each ctrl In grpCompetitors.Controls
      If ctrl.Tag = i * 10 Then
        If Val(ctrl.Text) > 0 AndAlso _
            Val(ctrl.Text) < dblWinningTime Then
          dblWinningTime = Val(ctrl.Text)
          strWinningTag = ctrl.Tag
        End If
      End If
    Next
  Next
  For Each ctrl In grpCompetitors.Controls
    If ctrl.Tag = strWinningTag Then _
      ctrl.BackColor = Color.Yellow
    If ctrl.Tag = strWinningTag / 10 Then _
      ctrl.BackColor = Color.Yellow
    If ctrl.Tag = strWinningTag * 10 Then
      ctrl.Text = "W"
      ctrl.BackColor = Color.Yellow
    End If
  Next
End Sub
```

Figure 5-60: btnCompetitionOver_Click() procedure

To add frmSpeed to the Scoring (Draft) application:

1 Copy the file **frmSpeed.vb** from the Tut05 folder to the **VB.NET\Student\ Tut05\Scoring (Draft)\Scoring** folder.

2 In Solution Explorer, right-click the **Scoring** project, and click **Add | Add Existing Item**, and select **frmSpeed.vb**.

3 Click **Build | Build Solution** to ensure that you have not introduced any syntax errors.

Completing a Draft of the Scoring Application

Only a few tasks remain to complete the draft version of the Scoring application:

■ Write the code in frmScoreMain that populates the list view when the user selects an item in the tree view.

■ Create frmTeam.

■ Create stubs for frmDistance and frmJudge.

■ Write the code that causes the correct competition-scoring module to appear when the user double-clicks an item in the list view.

Populating the List View

When the user selects a node in the tree view, the Treeview1_AfterSelect() event is fired. You must code the AfterSelect event procedure so that the events related to the selected tree view node are displayed in the list view. This code is partially completed for you in Figure 5-61.

In this procedure, you first assign the appropriate "selected category," based on the text property of the selected node's parent. For example, if the SelectedNode is Baseball, the local variable strSelectedCategory must be set to Sports; if the SelectedNode is Day 4, then strSelectedCategory must be set to Schedule. (If the SelectedNode is a root node, that is, it has no parent, strSelectedNode is assigned a dummy or sentinel value; in this case, the value General was chosen.)

Next, depending on which category was assigned to strSelectedCategory, the SelectedNode's Text property is assigned to the local variable strSearch String, and the pastructEvents() array is searched. For each element "i" of pastructEvents(), if strSearchString matches the corresponding element of pastructEvents(), pastructEvents(i) must be added to the ListView control. To accomplish this, the AddListViewItem() method is called. See Figure 5-62.

```
Private Sub TreeView1_AfterSelect(ByVal _
   sender As System.Object, _
   ByVal e As System.Windows.Forms.TreeViewEventArgs) _
   Handles TreeView1.AfterSelect
 ListView1.Items.Clear()
 Dim i, ItemCtr, intSearchNum As Integer
 Dim strSelectedCategory, strSearchString As String
 If e.Node.Parent Is Nothing Then
   strSelectedCategory = "General"
 Else
   strSelectedCategory = e.Node.Parent.Text
 End If
 Select Case strSelectedCategory
   Case "Sports"
     strSearchString = e.Node.Text
     For i = 0 To NUMEVENTS
       With pastructEvents(i)
         If .Sport = strSearchString Then _
           AddListViewItem(i, ItemCtr)
       End With
     Next
   Case "Venues"
     strSearchString = _
       Microsoft.VisualBasic.Right(e.Node.Text, 4)
     intSearchNum = Val(Mid(strSearchString, 2))
     For i = 0 To NUMEVENTS
       With pastructEvents(i)
         If .VenueIndex = intSearchNum Then _
           AddListViewItem(i, ItemCtr)
       End With
     Next
   Case "Schedule"
     'complete the coding of this case'
 End Select
 'if ListView1 contains no item, then display
 'the message "No events scheduled yet" in ListView1
End Sub
```

Figure 5-61: TreeView1_AfterSelect() procedure (incomplete)

```
Line 1  Private Sub AddListViewItem(ByVal ri As Integer, _
Line 2      ByRef vItemCtr As Integer)
Line 3    With pastructEvents(ri)
Line 4      ListView1.Items.Add(.EventName)
Line 5      ListView1.Items(vItemCtr).SubItems.Add(.Sport)
Line 6-7-8     'add the other SubItems here
Line 9      ListView1.Items(vItemCtr).Tag = ri
Line 10     vItemCtr += 1
Line 11   End With
Line 12 End Sub
```

Figure 5-62: AddListViewItem() procedure (incomplete)

To populate ListView1:

1 In the Code Editor for frmScoreMain, insert the code in Figure 5-61.

2 Complete the **Case "Schedule"** section, modeling your code on the code in the other two cases shown.

3   At the bottom of the procedure, if ItemCtr is zero (that is, no elements have been added to the ListView control), add the message **No events scheduled yet** to **ListView1**. This could happen if the node selected in the tree view is a parent node, or if it is a sport, venue, or day for which no events have yet been scheduled.

4   Also insert the **AddListViewItem**() procedure shown in Figure 5-62. Note the code that adds the .Sport SubItem on line 5. Complete this procedure by adding lines 6 through 8 for the missing subitems (gender, venue, and schedule). When adding a venue subitem, remember that you must use the VenueIndex to retrieve the venue name from the pastrVenues() array.

5   Run the **Scoring (draft)** application to ensure that the list view is populated as it should be. Click a node in the tree view, and note the items that appear in the list view. Then run the original **Scoring** application provided to you, click the same tree view node, and see that the list view contains the same items.

Creating frmTeam

The competition-scoring modules in the Scoring application include both team and individual scoring modules. The draft application already includes frmSpeed, an individual scoring module based on speed or fastest time. Some competitions are based on team scoring, and you now focus on the creation of a module to support that function. The team scoring module, frmTeam, includes ctrlEventHeader, displaying static information concerning the event, and ctrlTeamScore, displaying and recording interactive information concerning this current event.

To add frmTeam to the Scoring (Draft) application:

1   In Solution Explorer, right-click the **Scoring** project, and click **Add | Add Windows Form**. Name the new form **frmTeam**, and its file as **frmTeam.vb**.

2   Set the form's **Text** property to **Team Scoring**, and enlarge the form as needed.

3   From the Toolbox, drop a **ctrlEventHeader** control onto the top half of the form.

   NOTE: If ctrlEventheader does not show up in the Toolbox, then you must add it to the Toolbox. If the ctrlEventHeaderLib project is part of your solution, then compiling that control library project should make the control available in the Toolbox. If this does not work, then try customizing the Toolbox by clicking the .NET Framework Components tab, and browsing for the ctrlEventHeader.dll.

4   From the Toolbox, drop a **ctrlTeamScore** control onto the bottom half of the form. This control allows the user to score the contest.

5   In the Code Editor of frmTeam, insert the **SetHeaderInfo** procedure. Copy this procedure from **frmSpeed**, as shown in Figure 5-57. (The number of competitors—in the first line of code shown in the figure—is not needed for team sports competitions, but the rest of Figure 5-57 is applicable to frmTeam.)

Creating Stubs for frmDistance and frmJudge

You create frmDistance and frmJudge in Tutorial 6. In this tutorial, you complete just the bare outline of these forms—essentially a stub in lieu of the completed form.

To add stubs for the competition scoring modules that will be developed in Tutorial 6:

1 Right-click the **Scoring** project name in Solution Explorer. Click **Add | Add Windows Form**. Name the new form **frmDistance**, and its file **frmDistance.vb**.

2 Drop a **ctrlEventHeader** control onto the top half of the form.

3 Insert a **label** control in the bottom half of the form, with the message **This module is under construction**.

4 Copy the **SetHeaderInfo** procedure from frmSpeed into the Code Editor for frmDistance.

5 Repeat Steps 1 through 4 to create and establish the header information for **frmJudge**.

6 Run the **Scoring** (draft) application to ensure that no syntax errors have been introduced.

Displaying the Competition Scoring Module

You now have created all of the competition scoring modules, at least in stub form. When the user double-clicks an item in ListView1, the appropriate scoring module should be displayed, with the appropriate event header information. Now all that is needed is to add the scoring method (TS for team score, D for distance, S for speed/fastest time, or J for judging) to determine which scoring module is required.

To display the competition scoring module:

1 Program the **ListView1_DoubleClick()** procedure in frmScoreMain, as shown in Figure 5-63.

```
Private Sub ListView1_DoubleClick(ByVal _
    sender As Object, ByVal e As System.EventArgs) _
    Handles ListView1.DoubleClick
  Dim i As Integer
  Dim lv As ListViewItem
  For Each lv In ListView1.SelectedItems
    i = Val(lv.Tag)
    pEventRec = pastructEvents(i)
    With pEventRec
      Select Case .ScoringMethod
        Case "TS" 'team scoring
          Dim frm = New frmTeam()
          frm.setheaderinfo(.Sport, _
            .EventName, pastrVenues(.VenueIndex), _
            .Schedule, "Team Sport", .Gender)
          frm.ShowDialog()
        Case "S" 'speed
          'complete the coding of Case S.
          'then also complete Case D and Case J
        Case Else
          MsgBox("invalid scoring method: " & _
            .ScoringMethod & " at position " & lv.Tag)
      End Select
    End With
  Next
End Sub
```

Figure 5-63: ListView1_DoubleClick() procedure (incomplete)

> **2** The first case shown in Figure 5-63 (with TS for team score) has been written for you. Complete the other cases (S for speed, D for distance, and J for judging), modeled on the TS case.
>
> **3** Run the **Scoring** application. The Scoring (Draft) application is now complete, and all functions should work as they do in the executable provided to you in Scoring.exe at the beginning of this tutorial.

You have now completed Tutorial 5. Stop now for a break, or continue with the exercises.

SUMMARY

- Complex solutions can be assembled from components written independently by various programmers.
- A TreeView control's AfterSelect method can be programmed to populate a ListView control with the items appropriate to the tree view node that was selected.
- You add items to a ListView control with the Add method, and SubItems visible in the Details view are added with the SubItems Add method. An index value points to the correct list view item.
- A ListView control's DoubleClick method can be programmed to execute the appropriate actions, depending on which list view item is clicked.
- One method of identifying and manipulating multiple controls in a control collection is through the Tag property. A For Each loop can examine the Tag property of each control in a particular container, and take the appropriate action.
- A user control can often be reused within an application. In this case, ctrlNation is used in ctrlTeamScore and in frmSpeed (and will be used later in frmDistance and frmJudge). ctrlEventHeader is used in each scoring module as well.
- A change made to a user control is propagated to every application that uses it as soon as the client application is recompiled.

QUESTIONS

1. A _____ solution serves as a container for many projects. In this organization, the folder containing the solution also contains subfolders for each project within that solution.

2. Before anything will show in the Details view of a ListView control, members of the _____ Collection must be specified.

3. When the contents of a short sequential file are needed repeatedly in an application, the most efficient processing approach is to load the file into a(n) _____.

4. The original name of a control library project becomes the name of the _____ file, even if the developer subsequently changes the project name.

5. In an ImageList control, images are loaded into the _____ Collection.

6. Source code that the owner does not want other developers to see or copy is termed _____. When this term applies to commercially available custom controls, the owner usually only makes the DLL file available.

7. Sketch a picture of the icon that represents a temporary addition of a user control to the Toolbox.

8. Sketch a picture of the icon that represents a semipermanent addition of a user control to the Toolbox.

9. To identify a particular control within a series of similar controls within a container, developers sometimes assign a unique value to the _____ property, which can then be examined in a For Each loop.

10. To populate the list view based on the user's selection of a node in the tree view, you must program the TreeView control's _____ event.

11. To trigger some action when the user selects a list view item, developers usually program the ListView control's _____ event.

EXERCISES

1. The Hotel EGG specializes in egg dishes of all kinds, based on a nutritionist's belief that a diet rich in eggs will help the athletes achieve their utmost potential. Create a Windows Forms application with an Explorer-style user interface. In the left pane, use a TreeView control to list the main Hotel EGG Room Service Menu categories: breakfast, lunch, dinner, and bar, plus one more node called Selected Items. Add child nodes under the lunch menu for heart-healthy choices and for a children's menu. Add child nodes under the dinner menu for heart-healthy choices, appetizers, entrees, desserts, and a children's menu. In the right pane, use a ListView control to display the individual menu selections (make up at least four egg-related menu selections for each of the tree view nodes). Then, as items are selected from the list view by the user, add each selected item to the Selected Items folder in the tree view. Hard-code the menu in this application—that is, do not use an external file.

2. Create an Outlook-style application, based on the Nations.txt file. Use an ImageList control (which you can copy from ctrlNation.vb) in conjunction with Nations.txt. In the tree view, list all of the countries, but load them from Nations.txt at runtime. When a country is selected, add that country's name and abbreviation to the list view in Details view, and display that country's flag in a large PictureBox control under the ListView control. In this application, the tree view contains only the country names and is static after the initial load operation. The list view contains the list of all countries that have been selected. And the PictureBox displays the flag of the currently selected country.

3. Write a Windows Forms application with a traditional single document interface. The application displays each of the records in Events.txt, and allows the user to create new records in Events.txt.

4. Write a Windows Forms application with a traditional single document interface. Modify Nations.txt in Notepad, so that the third element in each record is the name of the icon file that represents that country's flag. Then, your Visual Basic .NET application displays each of the records in the revised Nations.txt, including a PictureBox control that displays the country flag.

5. Create a simple four-function calculator, modeled on the Calc.exe accessory in Windows. Like the simple Windows calculator, your calculator has buttons for the digits 0 through 9, a decimal point, a clear button, the four arithmetic operations, and the calculate button. The calculator should appear similar to Figure 5-64.

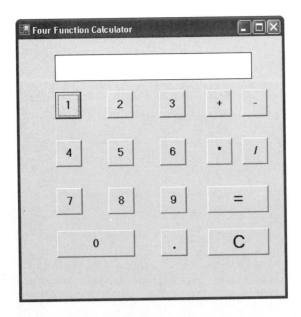

Figure 5-64: Four function calculator

Like most standard calculators, your calculator uses infix notation. That is, the user enters the first operand (by clicking the buttons 0 through 9) into the calculator's display area (lblDisplay), then clicks the operation (+, −, *, or /), then enters the second operand, and then clicks the calculate button (=). The program needs a variable (dblOperand1) to temporarily store the first operand while the user types in the second operand. The program also needs a variable (chrOp) to store a value that indicates which operation (+, −, *, or /) will be performed when the user clicks the calculate (=) button. When the user does click btnCalc, btnCalc_Click() performs the operation indicated by the value of chrOp on dblOperand1 and the second operand, which is sitting in lblDisplay, and then assigns the result of the calculation to lblDisplay.

As part of this project, create a user control (named ctrlOp) that inherits from the Button control—this is the button that the user presses to determine the current arithmetic operation: addition, subtraction, multiplication, or division. This control's Text property determines the arithmetic operation that it sets up: +, −, *, or /. The control has a public click event procedure that receives a Double (dblOperand1, passed ByRef), a Char (chrOp, passed ByRef), and a Label (lblDisplay). When the user clicks the button, that label contains the first operand of the current arithmetic operation, that is, the addend, subtrahend, multiplicand, or dividend. The click event procedure calls a public method in ctrlOp, passing the parameters dblOperand1, chrOp, and lblDisplay. The public method in ctrlOp assigns the contents of lblDisplay to dblOperand1, clears lblDisplay so that the user can enter the second operand, and assigns the button's Text property to chrOp.

6. Create a Windows Control Library project that inherits from the UserControl class. Name the project and the control ctrlSumAvg. The GUI should appear as in Figure 5-65. Expose a new public Boolean property called Sum. In Property Get and Set statements, assign or retrieve the Sum property to or from an internal variable called blnSum, whose default value is False. ctrlSumAvg contains a text box (txtNum), a list box (lstNumbers), two buttons (btnEnter and btnCompute), and two labels—lblOp contains the word "Sum" or the word "Average," and lblResult contains the sum or the average of all the numbers in the list box. At runtime, when the user clicks btnEnter, the number in txtNum should be added to the list box. When btnCompute is clicked, the value in lblResult should be computed, as follows: if blnSum is True, then lblOp should display the word "Sum" and lblResult should display the sum of all the numbers in the list box;

but if blnSum is False, then lblOp should display the word "Average" and lblResult should display the average of all the numbers in the list box. After creating ctrlSumAvg, create a small Test project to test the control.

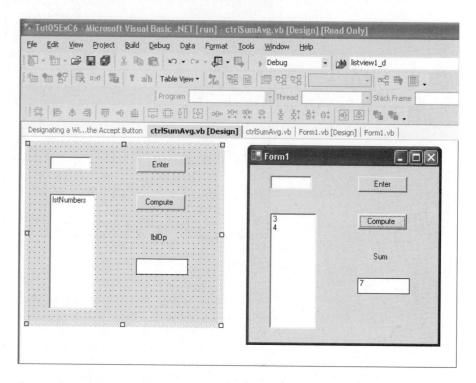

Figure 5-65: ctrlSumAvg at design time, and running in a test program

Exercise 7 allows you to discover the solution to problems on your own and experiment with material that is not covered explicitly in the tutorial.

discovery ▶ 7. Create a Web Forms application that mimics the operation of Exercise 1. Use three list boxes: one for the menu categories, one for the individual items, and one for the selected items. lstCategory contains the following:

- Breakfast Menu
- Lunch – Main
- Lunch – Heart-Healthy Choices
- Lunch – Children's Menu
- Dinner – Appetizers
- Dinner – Entrees
- Dinner – Heart-Healthy Choices
- Dinner – Desserts
- Dinner – Children's Menu

lstItems should contain the menu items available for the currently selected item in lstCategory. lstSelections should contain the list of all individual items that have been selected (that is, the customer's order). *Hint*: You can program the SelectedIndexChanged event for the Web Forms ListBox control, the same way you have done for the Windows Forms ListBox control. However, you must set the AutoPostBack property of the list boxes to True—this property is explained in Tutorial 7.

K E Y   T E R M S

- AfterSelect() event
- child node
- ColumnHeader collection
- Control class
- Details view
- DoubleClick() event
- ImageIndex property
- Items collection (in the ListView control)
- LargeIcon view
- LargeImageList property
- list view
- ListView control
- ListViewItem object
- Microsoft Outlook-style interface
- Nodes collection
- Panel control
- parent node
- recursion, recursive
- procedure
- ResumeLayout() method
- SelectedImageIndex property
- SelectedItems collection (in the ListView control)
- SelectedNode property
- SizeMode property
- SmallIcon view
- SmallImageList property
- Splitter control
- StretchImage
- SubItems collection (in the ListView control)
- SuspendLayout() method
- TreeNode object
- TreeView control
- User Control Designer
- UserControl class
- View property
- Windows Control Library
- Windows Explorer-style interface

More Advanced Windows Forms Controls and Coding

Continuing the Model for Competition Scoring

case ▶ The draft version of the Competition Scoring application was incomplete at the end of Tutorial 5. The complete application requires these additional features and modules:

- Ability to change the start date for the Friendsville International Games
- Ability to change the scheduled day and time for each event
- Construction of the Individual Scoring—Longest Distance module
- Construction of the Individual Scoring—Judges module
- Automatic selection of the nationality and flag icon (in the ctrlNation controls) in team sports
- Ability to select competitors from a list of eligible athletes in individual scoring modules, and with the ctrlNation control corresponding to each competitor automatically selected
- Indication of the results of the first, second, and third-place finishers and so on, in the individual scoring modules, rather than just the winner
- Calls to the FigWelcome and Logon class libraries

Previewing the Scoring Application

After demonstrating the draft of the Scoring application with prospective users, the Friendsville Games Development Team (FGDT) discovered that the schedule for the Friendsville International Games and the individual events need a much more prominent display. For this reason, the Windows Explorer-style interface of the draft application gives way to a Microsoft Outlook-style interface in the final version of this application. Scheduling and rescheduling functionality has been built into a Schedule pane in frmScoreMain, using a MonthCalendar control, a DateTimePicker control, a NumericUpDown control, and a TrackBar control.

Experiment now with the completed application.

To view the completed final version of the Scoring application:

1 Navigate to **VB.NET\Student\Tut06\Scoring06\bin**. Double-click **Scoring.exe** to run the Scoring application.

2 After the splash screen, enter the supervisor's logon (**1** in the e-mail address field, and **SUPERVISOR** in the password field), click **OK**, then click **OK** again; the main screen appears as in Figure 6-1. In the lower-right pane, the schedule for the Games appears. The MonthCalendar control spans two months, because the 14-day Games could occur in two months. The Event ID says Start, and the NumericUpDown control indicates Day 1. The TrackBar control along the bottom of this pane always matches the value of the NumericUpDown control.

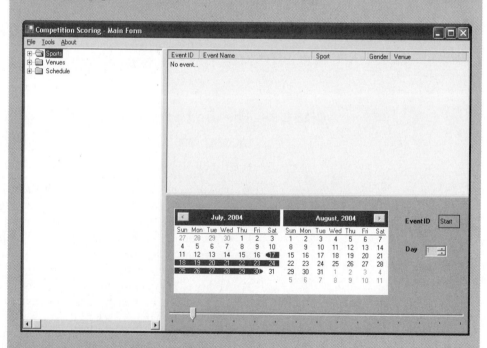

Figure 6-1: Scoring main screen, showing the dates of the Games

3 Change the start date for the Games by selecting **Tools | Change Start Date** from the menu, and then click **Yes** in the Scoring dialog box. (Note that Change Event Date is disabled; this item is available only when an event has been selected in the list view.) When you click Change Start Date, the instructions for selecting a new start date for the Games appear. Click **Yes**, read the instruction, and then click **OK.** You can change the month, day, and year using the MonthCalendar control. Select **June 27, 2004.** Click **Done.** The start date is stored in a data file called StartDate.txt, so any change you make to the start date is retained for subsequent computer runs. After you click Done, the MonthCalendar control highlights the 14 days (June 27 through July 10) on which the Friendsville International Games will take place.

4 Expand **Sports,** and click **Baseball** in the TreeView control on the left. Select **USA vs Japan,** the first scheduled baseball game. Note that the Schedule pane has changed, as shown in Figure 6-2. In the ListView control, a unique Event ID identifies each event. The day of the selected event is also displayed in the Schedule pane. The MonthCalendar control displays the calendar date when this game is scheduled to occur. The NumericUpDown and the TrackBar controls display the day of the Games (1 through 14) for this event, and the time appears in a DateTimePicker control. Note that the DateTimePicker control has been formatted to display only the time of day.

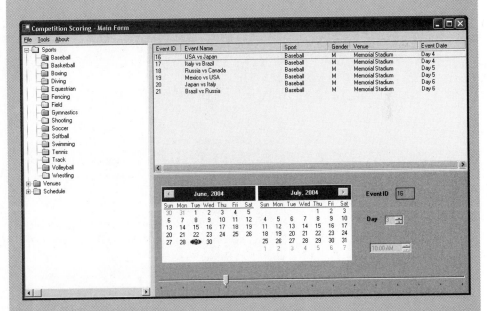

Figure 6-2: Scoring main screen, showing the date and time of a baseball game

5 Change the scheduled time and day for this baseball game. Click **Tools | Change Event Date.** In the NumericUpDown control, select Day **4,** and in the DateTimePicker control, select **9:00 AM.** See Figure 6-3. The MonthCalendar control is not updated until you click Done, but the NumericUpDown, TrackBar, and DateTimePicker controls change immediately. Click **Done.**

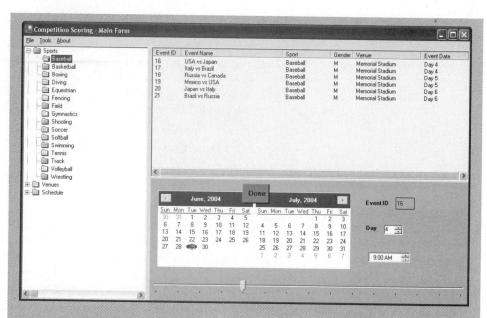

Figure 6-3: Rescheduling a baseball game

6 Click **Swimming** in the tree view. The Tools menu changes: Change Start Date is enabled, and Change Event Date is disabled. Click **Event 47 — Men's 100 Meter Freestyle** in the list view, and note that the Tools menu permits you to change the event date, but not the game's start date.

7 Next, click **Baseball** in the tree view, and double-click the **USA vs. Japan** baseball game to open the Team Scoring module. The contents of the two ctrlNation controls automatically load with the names and flag icons of the two country teams, as shown in Figure 6-4. A method was added to ctrlNation to provide this feature. Events.txt was also modified to include the country codes for the two countries involved in a Team Scoring competition.

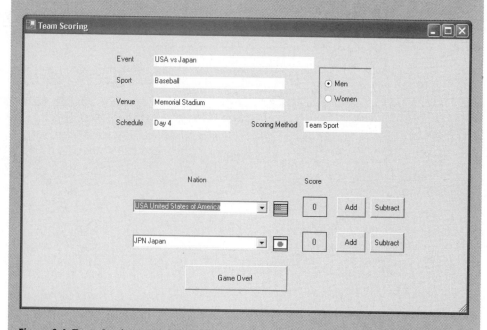

Figure 6-4: Team Scoring module, showing country information loaded automatically

8 Click the **Add** button to add a run for USA. However, the run was actually scored by Japan, so click the **Subtract** button to remove the run from USA, and click the **Add** button to add the run for Japan. Click **Game Over** to highlight the winner. Click the Windows **Close** icon to close the Team Scoring module and return to the main form.

Understanding the Individual Scoring Modules

Of the three necessary individual scoring modules (for competitions based on speed, distance, and judging), only the draft module on speed was created in Tutorial 5. The requirements for the distance and the judging modules are nearly identical to the requirements for the speed module, and so only one common frmCompetition form was created with all of the features common to the three needed modules. Then, using inheritance and polymorphism, this common form was customized to accommodate the unique aspects of the three types of competition. The notions of inheritance and polymorphism are discussed in depth in Lesson A of this tutorial; you use these concepts in building the final version of the Scoring application in Lessons B and C.

Three improvements over the draft of the scoring module are evident in the final version: first, users can select the names of competitors from a combo box, rather than having to type them in individually. Second, as in the Team Scoring module, the country name and flag of each competitor is loaded automatically. Third, the order of finish, from first place to last place, is indicated when the competition is over.

To view the individual scoring modules:

1 Click **Swimming** in the tree view; then in the list view, double-click **Men's 50 Meter Freestyle**, a competition based on speed. This opens the Individual Scoring—Fastest Time module. Click **Enter Competitors**, type 5 in response to the question concerning the number of competitors, and then click **OK**. Five rows appear. Use the drop-down combo boxes to select the names of the competitors—four of them have been chosen in Figure 6-5. If the athlete represents a country whose name and flag are in the system, that information is displayed automatically. If the country is not in the system, the program leaves the country name and flag blank. Also note that only the names of male athletes appear in the combo boxes. Enter the four athletes shown in Figure 6-5; enter **David Simpson** as the fifth competitor.

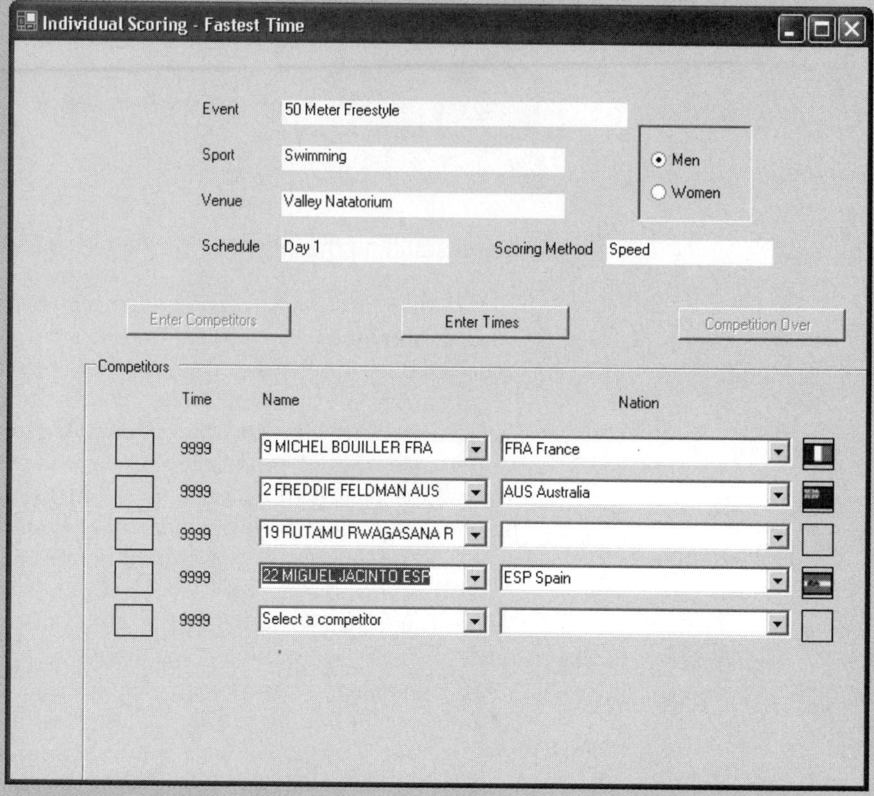

Figure 6-5: Choosing competitors for a swimming event

2 After selecting the competitors, click the **Enter Times** button, and enter the times displayed in Figure 6-6. Then click **Competition Over**. Note in Figure 6-6 that the program correctly identifies the order of finish, including a tie: in this case, a tie for second place.

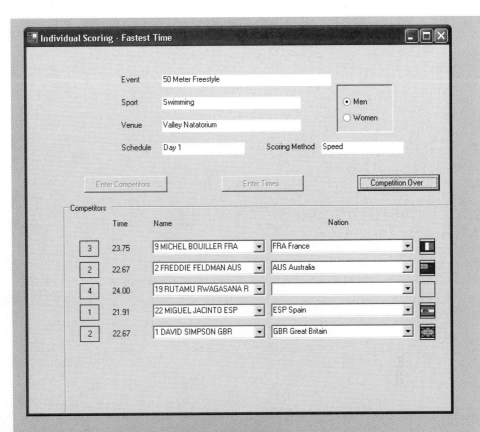

Figure 6-6: Results of the men's 50 Meter Freestyle swim

3 Close the **Individual Scoring—Fastest Time** module, and open an event based on distance. In **Field**, double-click **Women's Long jump**. Click **Enter Competitors**, enter **4** as the number of competitors, and note that the combo boxes display only the names of female athletes. Enter the names of the athletes that appear in Figure 6-7. Click **Enter Distance**, and enter the distances given in the figure. Click **Competition Over**, and note that the program picks the highest number as the winner, rather than the lowest number it picked in swimming. Close the **Individual Scoring—Longest Distance** module event.

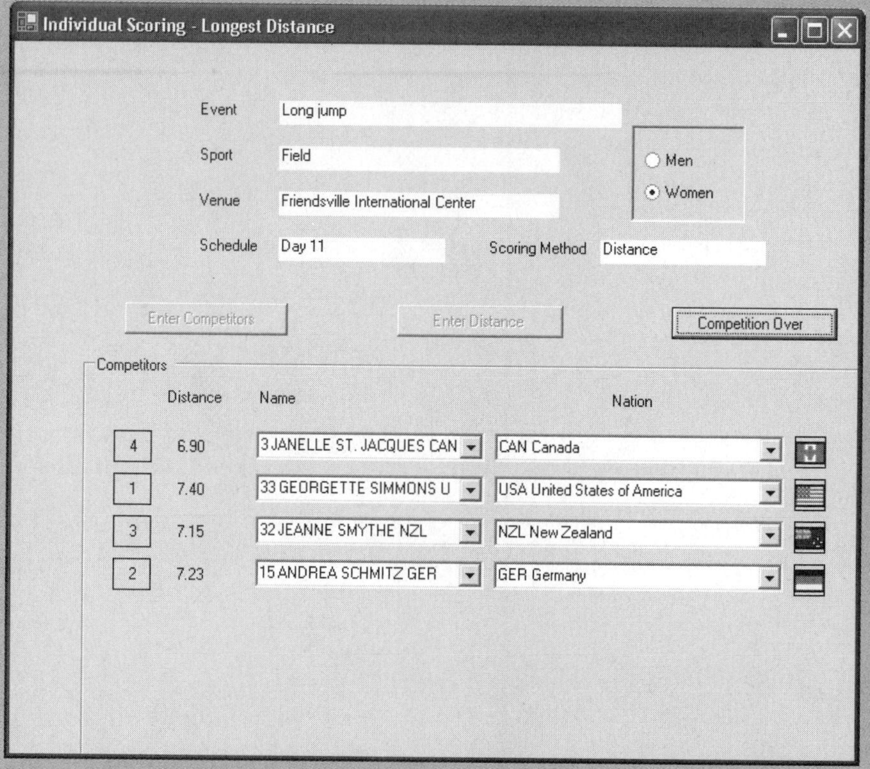

Figure 6-7: Results of the women's Long jump competition

NOTE: Just to give justice to the real winners: the time shown for the men's 50-meter freestyle event is actually the record setting time achieved by Aleksandr Popov in the 1992 Olympics in Barcelona. And the Olympic record holder in women's long jump is Jackie Joyner Kersee, 7.40 meters, at Seoul in 1988.

4 Finally, select an event based on judging—in the Equestrian category, double-click **Women's Dressage.** Click **Enter Competitors.** Enter **4** as the number of competitors. Select the names as before. Click **Enter Scores,** and enter the scores for each competitor. Click **Competition Over.** Again, the results are ordered by total points. The athlete with the highest point total is declared the winner.

The new concepts covered in Lesson A of this chapter include a few more Windows Forms controls, completion of the discussion of object-oriented programming (OOP), more workarounds that substitute for control arrays, and an introduction to sorting an array.

NOTE: Most modern business information systems store their data in databases created and maintained by one of the commercial database management systems rather than in sequential or random access data files. You do need to learn how Visual Basic .NET interfaces with databases. However, your understanding of that topic will be considerably enhanced if you complete the study of object-oriented programming concepts before tackling databases. You get to databases in Tutorial 9. In addition, in the exercises in that tutorial, you have the opportunity to convert the applications in the rest of the text to use databases in lieu of traditional file structures.

After completing this lesson, you will be able to:

■ Understand the MonthCalendar, DateTimePicker, NumericUpDown, and TrackBar Windows Forms controls

■ Discover and apply additional Windows Forms controls, including the ProgressBar, DomainUpDown, StatusBar, ToolTip, RichTextBox, and ContextMenu controls

■ Understand the concepts behind inheritance and polymorphism in Visual Basic .NET, including abstract classes, sealed classes, and the related notions of overloads and shadows

■ Sort tiny arrays (that is, arrays with fewer than 10 elements)

■ Design workarounds for control arrays (no longer supported in Visual Basic .NET)

Advanced Windows Controls, and Inheritance and Polymorphism in OOP

To complete the final version of the Scoring application, you need to understand several new concepts in Visual Basic .NET. Included in this list are such advanced Windows Forms controls as the MonthCalendar control, and sophisticated applications of the DateTimePicker control, NumericUpDown control, and TrackBar control. These four controls are the main ingredients in the new Scheduling pane of the final Scoring application. Several other Windows Forms controls are also discussed in this lesson. Next, you need to complete your understanding of object-oriented programming (OOP), especially inheritance and polymorphism, both of which are used in creating the three individual scoring modules of the final Scoring application. You learn a simple technique for sorting tiny arrays (those with fewer than 10 elements)—a technique used in Lesson C to determine the winner of individual competitions. Finally, you delve into several techniques for manipulating multiple controls of the same type on a form. These techniques compensate for the disappearance of control arrays in Visual Basic .NET, and so they are called workarounds, especially useful when converting Visual Basic 6.0 applications to Visual Basic .NET, but they are also useful when designing new Visual Basic .NET forms. You use these techniques in Lesson C when you must manipulate eight sets of controls of the same type on the form for scoring individual competitions.

Understanding Advanced Windows Forms Controls

The MonthCalendar, DateTimePicker, NumericUpDown, and TrackBar Windows Forms controls are all needed to complete the Scoring application and are introduced in this section. Some of the implementation details for these controls are left for Lesson B when you actually use them in the Scoring application.

Understanding the MonthCalendar Control

The **MonthCalendar control** is a useful alternative to the DateTimePicker control when you need to display a schedule showing multiple dates or months. In the Scoring application, you need to display a two-month calendar, because the 14 days of the Games may span two months. Figure 6-8 is an example of a nine-month calendar display. The number of months displayed in the control is set by the CalendarDimensions property. By default, the current date is displayed and circled. In this case, the current date is the date the figure was created, but you can turn these features off with the Boolean properties ShowToday and ShowTodayCircle. The current date is also selected, but you can change the selection in the IDE or in code using the SelectionRange property. The MaxSelectionCount property, which has the default value of seven, determines the maximum number of dates that can appear in the SelectionRange. Additionally, you can designate certain dates to appear in bold font by setting the BoldedDates property, which is an array of dates. You can show the week number within the year to the left of each row of days by setting the ShowWeekNumber property. You can change the Font, BackColor, ForeColor, TitleBackColor, TitleForeColor, and TrailingForeColor properties to modify the outward appearance of a MonthCalendar control. (The TitleForeColor and TitleBackColor properties refer to the title bar containing the name of the month. The TrailingForeColor property designates the font color for days within months that are not fully displayed in the control.)

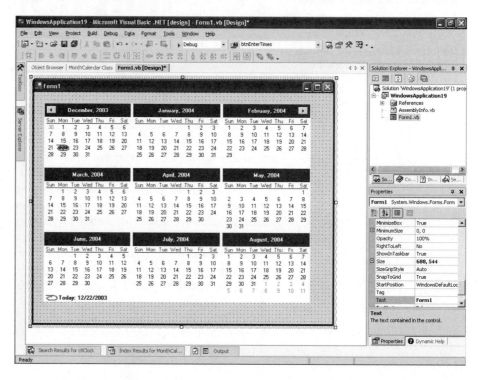

Figure 6-8: MonthCalendar control, showing 3 × 3 calendar dimensions

NOTE: The MonthCalendar control can display only dates that fall between the MinDate and MaxDate properties. However, the MinDate property cannot be set earlier than its default, which is January 1, 1753. (In America and England, the Gregorian calendar was initiated on January 1, 1753.) The MaxDate property cannot be set later than its maximum, December 31, 9998—far enough in the future for all applications except those predicting the next ice age.

Figure 6-9 contains a list of the main properties of this rather complex control.

Property	Definition/Setting
AnnuallyBoldedDates	Bolds an array of dates for each year
BoldedDates	Bolds an array of dates
CalendarDimensions	Displays number of months across (columns) and down (rows) in the control; displays maximum of 12 months; default is 1, 1
FirstDayOfWeek	Designates which day of the week is the leftmost column in the month
MaxSelectionCount	Sets the maximum number of days that can be selected in the SelectionRange; default is 7
MinDate and MaxDate	Set the minimum and the maximum dates permitted in the control; defaults are 1/1/1753 and 12/31/9998
MonthlyBoldedDates	Bolds an array of days that will appear in a month
SelectionRange: SelectionStart and SelectionEnd	Sets the range of dates selected in the control
ShowToday	Shows today's date at the bottom of the control; default is True
ShowTodayCircle	Circles today's date in the month display; default is True
ShowWeekNumbers	Shows the week-of-the-year number (1–52) to the left of each week in the month display; default is False
TitleBackColor	Sets background color of the title area for each month
TitleForeColor	Sets font color of the caption in the title area for each month
TodayDate	Sets the date used by the control as today's date (if not set explicitly, the control uses the system date as today's date)
TodayDateSet	Indicates whether TodayDate has been explicitly set
TrailingForeColor	Determines the font color for the display of days that occur in months not fully displayed

Figure 6-9: Important properties of the MonthCalendar control

Understanding the Formatting of the DateTimePicker Control

Samples of the next three controls to be discussed, the DateTimePicker control, the NumericUpDown control, and the TrackBar control are shown in Figure 6-10.

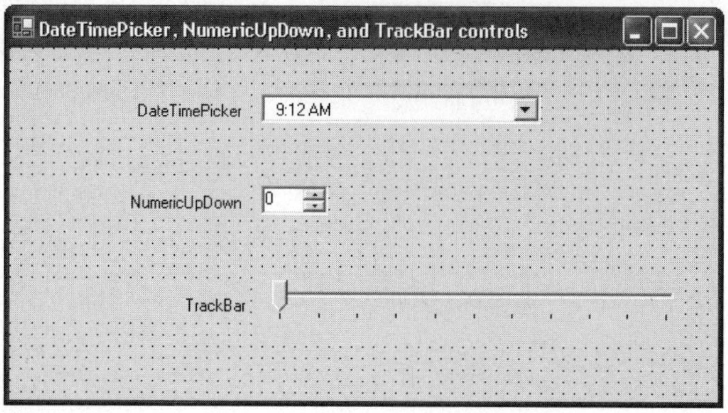

Figure 6-10: Sample DateTimePicker, NumericUpDown, and TrackBar controls

The DateTimePicker control is introduced in the Dining Hall Seat Assigner program in Tutorial 2. In the Scoring application, you use this control only for selecting a time of day.

You set the format of the DateTimePicker display using its Format property. You can use one of the built-in formats: Long (Monday, December 22, 2003), Short (12/22/2003), or Time (8:51:24 AM). You can also design your own format by setting the Format property to Custom and then inserting your format instructions in the CustomFormat property. For example, to display time without seconds, you could use the format h:mm tt, which displays the hour in one or two digits (on a 12-hour clock), the minute in two digits, and either AM or PM. For a 24-hour clock, use H instead of h.

Another interesting property of this control is ShowUpDown. When this property is False (the default), clicking the down arrow displays a month calendar, which it does in the Dining Hall Seat Assigner, and which also looks and acts like the MonthCalendar control. But when you set this property to True, as you will do later in the Scoring application, the control contains an up-down arrow rather than a down arrow, and you can change the value of any element of the displayed date and time by clicking the element you want to change and then clicking the up or the down arrows (or by typing a new value). This feature enables you to restrict the user to changing only those elements of the date/time value that you have chosen to display (based on the format), and prevents the month calendar display when that would be inappropriate.

The main properties of the DateTimePicker control are shown in Figure 6-11.

Property	Definition/Setting
CalendarFont, CalendarForeColor, CalendarMonthBackground, CalendarTitleBackColor, CalendarTitleForeColor, CalendarTrailingForeColor	Determine the display of the month calendar display when the user clicks the dropdown arrow (when the ShowUpDown property is False)
CustomFormat	Is relevant only when the Format property is set to Custom
Format	Determines a predefined format for the control, or allows the user to designate Custom

Figure 6-11: Important properties of the DateTimePicker control

Property	Definition/Setting
MinDate and MaxDate	Set the minimum and the maximum dates permitted in the control; defaults are 1/1/1753 and 12/31/9998
ShowCheckBox	Determines whether a check box appears on the left side of the control
ShowUpDown	Set to False (the default), a down arrow on the right opens a month calendar display; set to True, an up-down arrow is used to change the value of a selected element in the control
Value	Establishes the Date-Time value of the control

Figure 6-11: Important properties of the DateTimePicker control (continued)

In general, the DateTimePicker control is a better choice than the MonthCalendar control when you want users to select only one date. The DateTimePicker control conserves screen real estate, because the month is displayed only when the user clicks the down arrow; also, date validation is easier, because you only have to deal with one date in the control. When you need to enable the user to select multiple dates or a range of dates, use the MonthCalendar.

Understanding the NumericUpDown Control

The **NumericUpDown control** provides a convenient display for a numeric value that the user may need to increase or decrease at runtime. Figure 6-12 shows the most important properties and their definitions, which you can set in the IDE or in code.

Property	Definition	Default
DecimalPlaces	Indicates number of decimal places	0
Hexadecimal	Indicates whether the value is displayed in hexadecimal	False
ThousandsSeparator	Indicates whether a separator (period, comma, space) is displayed after thousands	False
Minimum	Indicates smallest permitted value	0
Maximum	Indicates largest permitted value	100
Value	Indicates current value	0
Increment	Indicates amount by which the value changes when the user clicks the up or down arrow	1

Figure 6-12: Properties of the NumericUpDown control

Understanding the TrackBar Control

The **TrackBar control** provides a visual display and functionality similar to a HorizontalScrollBar control, a fundamental Visual Basic control ever since the first release of the language. In the Scoring application, a TrackBar control provides a graphic representation of the scheduled date of an event, within the 14 days of the Games. Like the horizontal scroll bar, the track bar has a minimum and a maximum value, LargeChange and SmallChange properties, and a Value property. The TickFrequency property determines the number of positions of the track bar pointer from one tick mark to the next. You can set the Value property in the IDE or in code. You can also use the Value property to set other corresponding controls or variables by programming the Scroll event or the ValueChanged event. The principle properties of the TrackBar control are shown in Figure 6-13.

Property	Definition/Setting
LargeChange	Indicates amount added to or subtracted from the Value property when the user clicks the track bar to the right or left of the slider
Minimum and Maximum	Set the smallest and largest values represented on the track bar
Orientation	Sets horizontal (the default) or vertical
SmallChange	Indicates amount added to or subtracted from the Value property when the user drags the slider
TickFrequency	Displays the increment between ticks on the control
TickStyle	Indicates where to display tick marks
Value	Determines the current position of the slider

Figure 6-13: Important properties of the TrackBar control

Discovering Additional Windows Forms Controls

Several more Windows Forms controls deserve mention in this discussion, even though they do not appear in the Scoring application. These controls include the ProgressBar, DomainUpDown, StatusBar, ToolTip, RichTextBox, and ContextMenu controls. Understanding how to use these controls adds more tools to your personal toolbox—it makes you a better programmer, because you have additional techniques that you can call on when needed in a particular application.

Additionally, many other Microsoft and third-party controls are available to the Visual Basic .NET programmer and can be easily added to the Toolbox.

Understanding the ProgressBar Control

Figure 6-14 illustrates a sample of a ProgressBar control and several of the other Windows Forms controls discussed in ensuing paragraphs. This application, named MoreControls and displayed in Figure 6-14, is in the VB.NET\Student\Tut06\ MoreControlsOverloadsShadows folder.

ProgressBar control

RichTextBox control

ContextMenu control

includes a ToolTip (not visible at present)

StatusBar control

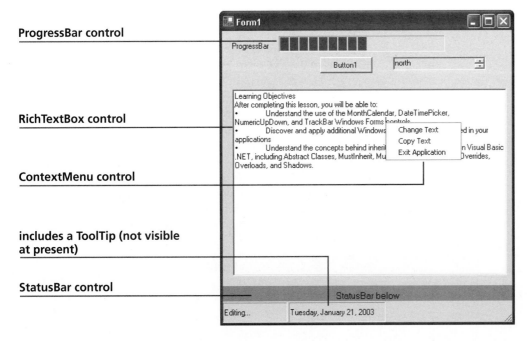

Figure 6-14: Samples of the ProgressBar, StatusBar, ToolTip, ContextMenu, and RichTextBox controls

A **progress bar** can be used in much the same manner as a scroll bar or track bar, but traditionally it is applied to tracking the progress of lengthy background computer operations, such as file copying, printing, or transmitting data. In such operations, the user may think that the program has stopped responding if a long time elapses without a visual indicator that anything is happening. A progress bar can provide a continually updated indicator that an operation is proceeding. For example, a progress bar might display the percentage of files that have been copied, pages that have been printed, or messages that have been transmitted. Typically, the minimum value is zero, and the maximum value represents 100 percent of task completion. The Value property is compared to the Maximum property to determine the percentage of the progress bar display that is filled with boxes. You can change the Value property directly by assigning a new value, or you can call the PerformStep method, which adds the Step property value to the Value property. When the Value property changes, Visual Basic .NET updates the progress bar display. In Figure 6-14, the Value property indicates that the task is half done. The principle properties of the ProgressBar control are displayed in Figure 6-15.

Property	Definition/Setting
Minimum and Maximum	Define the range of the control
Step	Determines the amount by which the Value property is increased when the PerformStep method is executed
Value	Determines the current position of the control

Figure 6-15: Important properties of the ProgressBar control

Understanding the DomainUpDown Control

As you might expect, the **DomainUpDown control** is similar in functionality and appearance to the NumericUpDown control previously discussed. The main difference is that the DomainUpDown control contains a collection of strings, one of which is displayed in the control, whereas the NumericUpDown control contains numbers. You need a different set of properties and methods, however, to load and manipulate the strings in the DomainUpDown control.

The strings can be anything you choose to put there, including numbers. To add or remove items in the Items Collection of the DomainUpDown control at design time, you click Items Collection in the Properties window. This opens the String Collection Editor, where you type in one string per line. In Figure 6-14, the DomainUpDown control contains the collection of strings shown in Figure 6-16. To add or remove items in code, you use the control's Add or Remove method.

Figure 6-16: String Collection Editor

The DomainUpDown control's Sorted property determines whether the items in the control are displayed alphabetically. If Sorted is True, clicking the down arrow in the control displays the next item in ascending alphabetical order. Clicking the up arrow displays the previous item in alphabetical order. If Sorted is False, the items are displayed in the order in which they were entered in the list. The Wrap property determines what happens when you click after the last item or before the first item in the list. If Wrap is True, clicking past the last item displays the first item, and clicking before the first item displays the last item, so the user experiences a continuous scrolling list. Figure 6-17 summarizes the principle properties of the DomainUpDown control.

Property	Definition/Setting
Items	Lists collection of objects in the control
SelectedIndex	Lists index of the currently selected item
SelectedItem	Lists currently selected item
Sorted	Determines whether the items in the collection are maintained in alphabetical order
Wrap	Determines whether the list repeats itself when the user moves up or down past the end of the list

Figure 6-17: Important properties of the DomainUpDown control

Invoking a DomainUpDown control's UpButton or DownButton method in code produces the same results as the user clicking the Up button or the Down button. Thus, you can create a scrolling message, such as a promotion or advertisement. The Scrolling Welcome program in the Tut06 folder is an example. It uses a timer that has a Tick event, which triggers the DomainUpDown control's DownButton event. The DomainUpDown control's Wrap property is set to True, and the Font property is enlarged and set to Bold, Italic. Figure 6-18 shows the form and the String Collection Editor in the IDE.

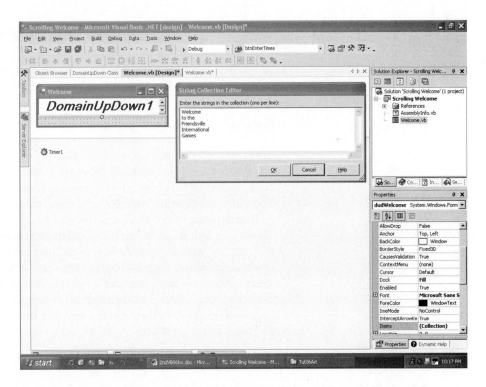

Figure 6-18: DomainUpDown control, appearance on form and String Collection Editor

Understanding the StatusBar Control

The **StatusBar control** is a potentially complex control that is used to display the status of an application. It can contain any number of StatusBarPanel objects, each of which can display text, an image, or programmer-drawn controls, such as a progress bar, track bar, or set of images. Typical Microsoft software packages, such as the Microsoft Office Suite, contain a StatusBar control at the bottom of the window.

You can create StatusBar panel objects in the IDE or in code. The panels are visible only at runtime if the ShowPanels property is set to True (the default is False). In the example in Figure 6-14, the two panels were created in the IDE. "Editing. . ." was assigned as the Text property for StatusBarPanel1. For StatusBarPanel2, the Text and the ToolTipText properties were assigned in the Sub `Form1_Load()` statement, as shown in Figure 6-19. References to individual panels in code use an index (zero based), so that StatusBarPanel2 is referenced as StatusBar1.Panels(1). This index value is available only at runtime. The AutoSize() method is then invoked to conform the size of the panel to its contents.

```
Private Sub Form1_Load(ByVal sender As System.Object, _
    ByVal e As System.EventArgs) Handles MyBase.Load
  StatusBar1.Panels(1).Text = _
    System.DateTime.Today.ToLongDateString
  'the next statement adds a ToolTip to StatusBarPanel2
  '  (see the discussion of the ToolTip control
  '  following the StatusBar control)
  StatusBar1.Panels(1).ToolTipText = _
    System.DateTime.Now.ToShortTimeString
  StatusBar1.Panels(1).AutoSize() = _
    StatusBarPanelAutoSize.Contents
End Sub
```

Figure 6-19: Form1_Load(), assigning properties to StatusBarPanel2

A StatusBar control is often employed to display various status items concerning an application, such as the date, page number, line number, caps lock, and so on.

Understanding the ToolTip Control

ToolTips are small pop-up windows that display text when the user moves the insertion point over a control. Normally, these are used to offer assistance to users while they are entering data or using the information displayed in the control. In many applications, a ToolTip appears when you hover the insertion point over a button on the toolbar. A ToolTip component can be added to any container, such as a form, Panel control, ToolBar, or StatusBar. When the ToolTip component has been added to the container, each control within that container contains a new property called ToolTip on *ToolTip component name*, such as ToolTip on ToolTip1. You can insert ToolTip text for as many controls as you want. In the MoreControls application, a ToolTip was added to StatusBarPanel2 of the StatusBar control programmatically, as shown in Figure 6-19. The ToolTip displays the time of day when the user hovers the cursor over the panel, as shown in Figure 6-20.

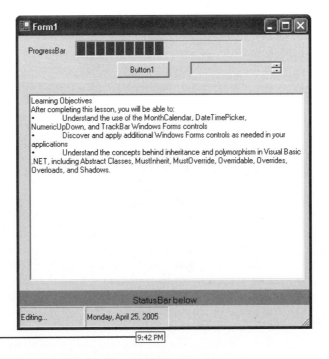

Figure 6-20: ToolTip on StatusBarPanel2

The ToolTip control itself (which appears in the tray underneath the form) has properties that control the display of all ToolTips. See Figure 6-21.

Property	Definition	Default
InitialDelay	Establishes milliseconds that the MousePointer must remain stationary over an object before the ToolTip is displayed	500
AutoPopDelay	Establishes milliseconds that the ToolTip remains visible	5000
ReshowDelay	Establishes milliseconds that transpire before subsequent ToolTips display as the mouse moves to a new ToolTip region	500
AutomaticDelay	Sets the InitialDelay, AutoPopDelay, and ReshowDelay to appropriate values	500
Active	Determines if the ToolTips will be displayed	True
ShowAlways	Determines if the ToolTips will be displayed even when the parent window is not active	False

Figure 6-21: Properties of the ToolTip control

Understanding the RichTextBox Control

The RichTextBox control, shown in Figure 6-14, is a greatly enhanced version of the standard TextBox control. The RichTextBox control provides for the display of formatted text using Rich Text Format (RTF) style and formatting commands. Unlike a standard TextBox control, a **RichTextBox control** allows formatting to be applied to any portion of text selected within the control. For example, a single word or line can be bolded or italicized. You can paste formatted text into the control from the Clipboard (as was done in Figure 6-14) or copy from the control onto the Clipboard. In addition, the RichTextBox.LoadFile method loads the control from an RTF or ASCII file, and the RichTextBox.SaveFile method saves the contents of the control to an RTF or ASCII file.

Armed with a RichTextBox control, your application can demonstrate all the text-formatting functionality of simple word-processing programs, such as WordPad.

Understanding the ContextMenu Component

You can associate a form or control with a **context menu,** a short pop-up menu that appears when the user right-clicks while the cursor hovers over a form or control. In Figure 6-14, a context menu component has been added to the form and associated with the RichTextBox control. In Figure 6-14, the rich text box has been right-clicked, causing the context menu (Change Text, Copy Text, Exit Application) to be displayed.

Commonly, the items in a context menu duplicate items that appear in the form's main menu. To use MainMenu items in a ContextMenu control, the MainMenu control's CloneMenu method must be invoked to make a copy of the MainMenu items. You can also merge menu items and submenu items with the MergeMenu method.

After a ContextMenu component is added to a form, ContextMenuItems can be added to the ContextMenu component in the IDE or programmatically. In the IDE, when the ContextMenu component is selected in the system tray underneath the form, the word *ContextMenu* appears in the menu editor area on the form itself. Then, you can add items using the Menu editor, the same as for a MainMenu control. To add items programmatically, you create each menu item and then add the items to the ContextMenu, as shown in Figure 6-22. This code is part of the Sub Form1_Load event procedure for the sample application shown in Figure 6-19.

```
Dim ItemChange As New MenuItem("Change Text")
Dim ItemCopy As New MenuItem("Copy Text")
Dim ItemExit As New MenuItem("Exit Application")
ContextMenu1.MenuItems.Clear()
ContextMenu1.MenuItems.Add(ItemChange)
ContextMenu1.MenuItems.Add(ItemCopy)
ContextMenu1.MenuItems.Add(ItemExit)
```

Figure 6-22: Adding ContextMenu items programmatically

Understanding Add-ins: Customizing the Toolbox

As initially installed, the Visual Basic .NET Toolbox contains only the most common, general-purpose controls available in the language. However, you can build your own controls and add them to the Toolbox. In addition, Microsoft and dozens of other software manufacturers have created controls that are provided with VB .NET and can be added to the Toolbox. Furthermore, hundreds of special-purpose controls are available for purchase. To see the built-in controls that you can add to the Toolbox, right-click the Toolbox, and choose Customize Toolbox. This displays the Customize Toolbox dialog box, which contains two tabs: COM Components and .NET Framework Components. The COM (that is, Component Object Model) Components tab lists Toolbox-compatible classes and controls that are installed on your computer, manufactured by Microsoft and by many third-party vendors; information given on the tab includes the name of the components, the path on your computer to each component, and the class library to which it belongs. See a sample in Figure 6-23. The .NET Framework Components tab lists members of the .NET Framework, along with the namespace and assembly in which the component is defined. In .NET Framework Components, those items that are checked are already in the Toolbox in the appropriate Toolbox category (Windows Forms, Web Forms, Data, Components, or General); note that this includes user controls. Figure 6-24 shows a portion of the .NET Framework Components tab in the Customize Toolbox dialog box. You can click the check box to the left of desired items under either tab, and then click OK to add those items to the Toolbox.

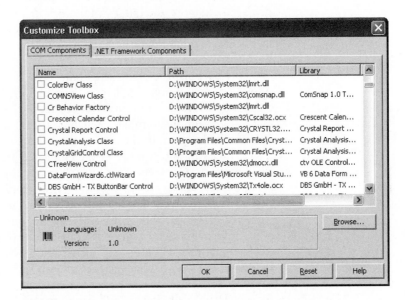

Figure 6-23: COM Components tab in the Customize Toolbox dialog box

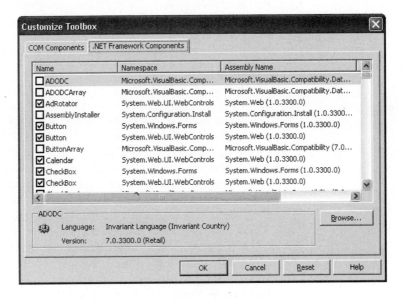

Figure 6-24: .NET Framework Components tab in the Customize Toolbox dialog box

Understanding Inheritance and Polymorphism

You have seen various aspects of the object-oriented programming paradigm in previous tutorials. This section completes the survey of this subject by discussing inheritance and polymorphism. **Inheritance** refers to the ability of a derived class or an instantiated object to inherit the properties, methods, and events of a base class. Visual Basic .NET supports single inheritance only; that is, a derived class or instantiated object can inherit from only one base class. However, that one base class may itself be derived from another base class.

You might think of all Visual Basic .NET classes as a pyramid or tree structure, in which each node inherits from a single parent but each node can have multiple children. For example, the .NET Framework includes a class called Control. Every control in the .NET Framework inherits ultimately from the Control class. As explained in Tutorial 5, the Button class inherits from the ButtonBase class, which inherits from the Control class.

Polymorphism refers to the ability of a derived class or instantiated object to provide its own unique implementation of a method declared or defined in the base class. For example, an EmployeeContacts class might include a method called GetEmployeePhoneNumber, which returns the work phone number of an employee. However, in the case of the security staff, both the work phone and the pager or cell phone number of the employee are needed. Through polymorphism, the EmergencyContacts class, which might inherit from the EmployeeContacts class, contains a special version of the GetEmployeePhoneNumber method, which returns both the work phone and the cell phone instead of just one.

In Visual Basic .NET, the rules for polymorphism require that the base class specifically allows alternative implementations of a method before such polymorphic implementations are permitted. Visual Basic .NET also provides for abstract classes, that is, classes that declare methods that must be implemented in a derived class.

The keywords, attributes, and conceptual definitions of inheritance and polymorphism in Visual Basic .NET are as follows:

- Abstract class (with the keywords MustInherit and MustOverride)
- Sealed class (with the keyword NotInheritable)
- Inheritance (with the keywords Inherits and New)
- Polymorphism (with the keywords Overridable and Overrides)
- Closely related keywords and notions—Overloads and Shadows

Abstract Class

An **abstract class** is a class that cannot be instantiated and must be inherited, because it is incomplete in and of itself. The inherited class must implement those portions of the abstract class that have been declared, but not yet defined. Figure 6-25 provides a simple example of a class called MyAbstractClass. The keyword in the class header that renders the class as abstract is MustInherit. This keyword defines the class as abstract; that is, it can only be inherited and cannot be instantiated directly, because the definition is incomplete. Typically, the abstract class contains standard features inherited by each derived class, suggested here by the Private Sub StandardSub() procedure. Typically, the abstract class also contains unique features that must be implemented by each derived class, suggested here by the Protected MustOverride Sub UniqueSub() procedure declaration. And often, the abstract class contains procedures that may be overridden by the derived class, but do not need to be overridden, suggested here by the Protected Overridable Sub MaybeUniqueMaybeNot() procedure.

Private, Protected, Friend, and Public accessibility levels were discussed in Tutorial 2.

If a class contains a procedure declared with the MustOverride keyword, that class must be declared as abstract; that is, the keyword MustInherit must be included in the class declaration header. Note that a MustOverride procedure contains only the declaration—no body and no End Sub—because the definition of the procedure (the implementation) must be provided by a derived class. Usually, standardized procedures are declared with Private accessibility. Overridable and MustOverride procedures are declared with Protected or Public accessibility. You use Protected if the procedure needs to be visible to only the derived class that provides the implementation. You use Public if the procedure needs to be visible to any component that uses or imports the derived class.

```
Public MustInherit Class MyAbstractClass
  Private Sub StandardSub()
    'code that implements a standardized feature of the class
  End Sub

  Protected MustOverride Sub UniqueSub()
  'the derived class must implement this feature

  Protected Overridable Sub MaybeUniqueMaybeNot1()
    'code that might be standardized, but might be overridden
  End Sub

  Protected Overridable Sub MaybeUniqueMaybeNot2()
    'code that might be standardized, but might be overridden

  End Sub
End Class
```

Figure 6-25: Model for the definition of an abstract class

The Scoring application contains an abstract class called frmCompetition, which you will build in Lesson C. The class contains many elements applicable to all kinds of individual competitions, but it is incomplete in and of itself because it is missing three declarations that are unique to each type of scoring. Therefore, the class is declared as abstract, and any valid class derived from it must provide the missing declarations.

An abstract class usually contains elements that are designed to be inherited without modification. Such properties and methods are typically Private or Protected. However, an abstract class usually also contains Public or Protected methods that are modified or implemented in the inherited class. A method that must be provided by the inherited class is designated with only a header and the keyword MustOverride. Note that the End Sub statement is not provided for a method declared as MustOverride. A method implemented in the abstract class but overridable in a derived class is declared with the keyword Overridable. The sample abstract class provides a Private local method, two Overridable methods, and a MustOverride method.

The definition of a derived class begins with the Inherits keyword, as demonstrated in Figure 6-26. In a class derived from an abstract class, a method that overrides any MustOverridable method declared in the base class must be provided, and a method that overrides a method declared as Overridable in the base class may be provided. In Figure 6-24, the derived class inherits from the base class, provides the required method to fulfill the MustOverride method, overrides one of the two Overridable methods from the base class, and provides its own Private method extending the functionality of the base class.

```
Public Class Form1
  Inherits MyAbstractClass

  Protected Overrides Sub Uniquesub()
    'code here provides the unique implementation
  End Sub

  Protected Overrides Sub MaybeUniqueMaybeNot2()
    'code here replaces the standardized implementation
  End Sub

  Private Sub MyOwn()
    'code here extends the functionality of the base class
  End Sub

End Class
```

Figure 6-26: Model for the definition of a class derived from an abstract class

Instantiation is usually declared with the keyword New. A class can be derived from an abstract class using the keyword Inherits; it cannot be instantiated from an abstract class with the keyword New.

Sealed Class

A **sealed class** is in some ways the exact opposite of an abstract class. A sealed class cannot be inherited; that is, it cannot form the basis for a derived class. A sealed class is declared in Visual Basic .NET with the keyword NotInheritable in the declaration header. The class definition must provide the entire implementation, so the keywords MustOverride and Overridable are not permitted in a sealed class.

Overloading

The **Overloads** keyword declares a method that matches the name of an existing member, but contains a different argument list. For instance, a function that compares two inputs v1 and v2, and returns 1 if v1 is greater than v2, 0 if v1 is equal to v2, and −1 if v2 is greater than v1, might have alternative implementations, depending on whether the input values are numbers or strings. See Figure 6-27 for this example. Sometimes, a method is declared as Overridable so that a derived class is able to overload it. At other times, the base class itself contains overloaded methods.

```
Private Overloads Function Bigger(ByVal v1 As String, _
    ByVal v2 As String) As Integer
  If v1 > v2 Then
    Return 1
  ElseIf v1 = v2 Then
    Return 0
  Else
    Return -1
  End If
End Function

Private Overloads Function Bigger(ByVal v1 As Double, _
    ByVal v2 As Double) As Integer
  If v1 > v2 Then
    Return 1
  ElseIf v1 = v2 Then
    Return 0
  Else
    Return -1
  End If
End Function
```

Figure 6-27: Sample of overloaded methods

Shadowing

Shadowing is another technique related to the notions of overriding and overloading a program element. A program element in a derived class can shadow any program element in its base class. This means that the shadowed element is hidden, and any unqualified reference to the element name refers to the shadowing element rather than the shadowed element. The shadowed element can still be accessed if the element name is qualified. For example, in Figure 6-28, the definition of Form1 includes a structure called structOne, which consists of one numeric element named dbl.structOneInForm1 and is declared as an instance of structOne. Also, the value 8.9 is assigned to dbl. Form2 inherits from Form1, so Form2 has all of Form1's elements, including structOne. However, Form2 contains another declaration of structOne, with the keyword Shadows. The Form2 version of structOne contains a single string element called GivenName. Note that Form2 then contains two instances of structOne: MyOne is an instance of the structOne declared in Form2; whereas MyTwo is an instance of the structOne declared in Form1. As you can see in the MySub() procedure, Frank is assigned to the GivenName element of MyOne, and 4.56 is assigned to the dbl element of MyTwo.

```
Public Class Form1
    Inherits System.Windows.Forms.Form
  Public Structure structOne
    Public dbl As Double
  End Structure
  Dim structOneInForm1 As structOne
  Private Sub SmallSub()
    InForm1.dbl = 8.9
  End Sub
End Class

Public Class Form2
  Inherits Form1
  Private Shadows Structure structOne
    Public GivenName As String
  End Structure
  Dim MyOne As structOne
  Dim MyTwo As Form1.structOne

  Private Sub MySub()
    MyOne.GivenName = "Frank"
    MyTwo.dbl = 4.56
  End Sub
End Class
```

Figure 6-28: Sample of a shadowed program element

Overriding

Overriding requires that the overridden element be declared Overridable, and the overriding element be declared with the Overrides keyword. Overriding also requires that the overriding and the overridden elements have the same calling sequence; that is, the elements must be of the same type (function, sub, or property) and have the same name, same number and type of arguments, and the same type of return value. By contrast, shadowing has none of these requirements, except the same name. A function can shadow a procedure, for instance. In addition, any kind of program element, such as the Structure element in Figure 6-28, can be shadowed.

Microsoft recommends that you use the Shadows keyword whenever you declare a local name that matches an element in your base class. However, the Shadows keyword is not required. If you supply neither Shadows nor Overrides, Shadows is assumed.

Sorting a Tiny Array

Computers spend a significant amount of time sorting and comparing items in lists. Volumes have been written on techniques for making sorting operations efficient. Sorting algorithms vary from the simple to the highly complex, from easy to challenging, and from those generally applicable to any list to those tailored to specific kinds of lists.

One category of list that occurs often in programming is the short list, which requires sorting only a handful of items. For such lists, a simple (and easy-to-code) sorting algorithm is sufficient. The computer compares two items at a time, and if they are in the wrong order, swaps their positions. Many of the more sophisticated sorting routines gain their efficiency through strategies for comparing the correct two items each time. For example, if you need to sort a list of 1000 items, and the item in position 1 before sorting needs to move to position 1000, a sorting algorithm that compares only adjacent items is grossly inefficient, because it takes 999 comparisons and position swaps to move this one item from the first to the last position in the list.

However, if you have only 10 items in the list, this inefficiency is unimportant. In fact, benchmark tests have shown that many of the sorting algorithms that are most efficient on large lists are actually less efficient than the simplest techniques when it comes to sorting tiny lists.

Therefore, it behooves you to have in your programming bag of tricks a simple, handy sort routine applicable to sorting tiny lists, such as the order of finish for the eight runners in the 100 yard dash. The sort routine you learn in this tutorial fits that need, and is appropriate for any array of up to 10 elements. The general algorithm for this routine appears in Figure 6-29, followed by a detailed discussion.

```
Line 1     For i = 0 To NUMELEMENTS - 2
Line 2       If Array(i) > Array(i + 1) Then
Line 3         temp = Array(i)
Line 4         Array(i) = Array(i + 1)
Line 5         Array(i + 1) = temp
Line 6         i = -1
Line 7       End If
Line 8     Next
```

Figure 6-29: Hilda's Simple Sort

This sort routine compares each item in the list to the item that follows it. If the two items being compared, item one and item two, are in the correct order, the algorithm compares the next two items, in this case item two and item three. If the two items are not in the correct order, the algorithm swaps their values, and starts over at the top of the list. In Figure 6-29, in the For loop, "i" varies from 0 to NUMELEMENTS – 2, because arrays in Visual Basic .NET are 0 based (that is, the index of the last element is NUMELEMENTS – 1), and the algorithm compares the element at position "i" with the element at position i + 1, so the last comparison should be made between the element at position NUMELEMENTS – 2 and the element at position NUMELEMENTS – 1. If there are 10 items in the list (that is, NUMELEMENTS = 10, their index numbers are 0 through 9, so the last comparison is between item 8 (that is, NUMELEMENTS – 2) and 9 (that is, NUMELEMENTS – 1). Whenever the items are out of order (the element at position "i" is greater than the element at position i + 1), a swap needs to be made. Three statements (lines 3, 4, and 5 in Figure 6-29) are needed to effect the swap:

- The element at position "i" is copied to temp.
- The element at position i + 1 is copied to the element at position "i".
- temp is copied to the element at position i + 1.
- Finally, "i" is set to –1. Thus, the Next statement at the bottom of the For loop increments "i" from –1 to 0, so the next iteration of the loop starts again comparing the first two array elements.

Understanding Workarounds for Control Arrays

One of the more significant changes in Visual Basic .NET as compared to Visual Basic 6.0 is the absence of control arrays in .NET. In Visual Basic 6.0, a set of controls of the same class and within the same container could be designated as a control array. Controls of a control array shared the same name and the same

tip

If this concept is less than obvious, then perhaps the following analogy can help. You have a purple cup containing juice and a white cup containing milk. If you want to put the juice into the white cup and the milk into the purple cup, what would you do? You would use a third cup, for example, a yellow one. You might pour the juice into the yellow cup, then the milk into the purple cup, then the juice into the white cup.

procedures; they were differentiated by an Index property. Many Visual Basic 6.0 applications were heavily dependent on control arrays. Members of a control array could be traversed with a For loop, and individual controls could be identified by the common name plus their unique index. Converting such applications to Visual Basic .NET is a difficult task, because achieving the same functionality without control arrays may tax your creativity as a programmer.

This section discusses and demonstrates three workarounds for the absence of control arrays in Visual Basic .NET:

1. You can use the Tag property or TabIndex property to identify an individual control or a group of controls, and you can combine this with a For Each loop to iterate through the controls collection looking for the Tag or TabIndex property that you have assigned.

2. You can write a single procedure that handles multiple events, often combined with a Select Case statement that examines the Name property of *sender*. In at least one sense, this second technique represents an improvement over control arrays, because the various controls that share an event handler need not all be of the same type.

3. You can create an array of strings (or of structures) with values that correspond to the Name or Text (or perhaps other) property of each control in the collection. In code, you can treat this array as if it were a control array. When some action or manipulation is required of the actual control corresponding to an element of the array, you use the For Each technique to designate the correct control. But when the action involves only the value of the name or text, you search the array rather than the controls collection.

The demo program ControlArrays2 in the VB.NET\Student\Tut06\ ControlArrays2 folder demonstrates all three of these techniques.

As you can see in Figure 6-30, each row of controls consists of a TextBox control and two Label controls and identifies the name, sex, and age of an athlete in the International Village.

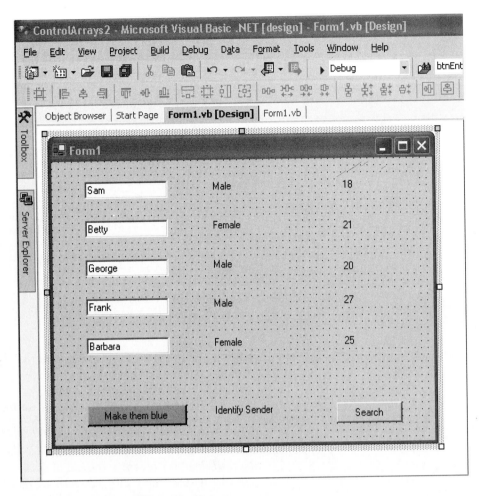

Figure 6-30: ControlArrays2 at design time

ControlArrays2 demonstrates the first workaround (using the Tag property and a For Each loop) as follows: the Tag property of each control identifies the row, starting with row 1. If you were to run the program and click the Make them blue button, you would be prompted to enter a row number. The row of controls you select would change to blue, and all other controls would change to gray. This effect is achieved by the assignment of the Tag property at design time, in combination with a For Each loop that steps through each control in the controls collection, as shown in Figure 6-31.

```
Private Sub btnBlue_Click(ByVal sender As System.Object, _
    ByVal e As System.EventArgs) Handles btnBlue.Click
  Dim c As Char = InputBox _
    ("Enter the row number you wish to turn blue")
  Dim ctrl As Control
  For Each ctrl In Me.Controls
    ctrl.BackColor = IIf(ctrl.Tag = c, Color.LightBlue, _
      Color.LightGray)
  Next
End Sub
```

Figure 6-31: btnBlue_Click() procedure

The second workaround (a procedure that handles multiple events) is demonstrated by the code in Figure 6-32. The Label1_Click() procedure has been programmed to handle the TextChanged event of each TextBox control and the Click event of each Label control on the form. This event procedure also shows how the sender argument can be used to identify the control that triggered the event—in this case, sender. BackColor is referenced in the procedure. If you run the program and either change the text in a text box or click a label, that control's BackColor changes to red.

```
Private Sub Label1_Click(ByVal sender As System.Object, _
    ByVal e As System.EventArgs) Handles Label1.Click, _
    Label10.Click, Label11.Click, Label2.Click, _
    Label3.Click, Label4.Click, Label5.Click, _
    Label6.Click, Label7.Click, Label8.Click, _
    Label9.Click, TextBox1.TextChanged, _
    TextBox2.TextChanged, TextBox3.TextChanged, _
    TextBox4.TextChanged, TextBox5.TextChanged
  sender.backcolor = Color.Red
End Sub
```

Figure 6-32: Label1_Click() procedure

NOTE: All of the event procedures you have encountered in Visual Basic .NET include a Handles phrase that specifies what events from what sources the procedure (an "event handler") can trap (that is, "handle"). For example, if you create a Button1 on a form, the header for the click event procedure is:

```
Private Sub Button1_Click(ByVal sender As System.Object, _
  ByVal e As System.EventArgs) Handles Button1.Click
```

Note the Handles phrase at the end of the header statement. A single event handler can actually handle many different events emanating from many different controls. This is the technique shown in Figure 6-32.

Figure 6-33 demonstrates the third workaround (a parallel array of strings corresponding to the controls that you want to treat as a unit). If you run the program and click the Search button, the message box displays the names and ages of all the males or females, depending on the user's input of M or F. The procedure searches a two-dimensional array named CtrlArray, initialized to contain the name, sex, and age of each athlete—in other words, exactly the same information as appears in the Text property of the controls on the form. You can implement an array that parallels a group of controls by loading the controls from the array, loading the array from the controls, loading the array and the controls from a data file, or hard-coding the array and the controls as was done in ControlArrays2. However, after the controls and corresponding array are initialized, the result is a data structure that you can search and manipulate easily.

```
Dim CtrlArray(,) = {{"Sam", "Male", 18}, _
  {"Betty", "Female", 21}, {"George", "Male", 20}, _
  {"Frank", "Male", 27}, {"Barbara", "Female", 25}}

Private Sub btnSearch_Click(ByVal sender As System.Object, _
    ByVal e As System.EventArgs) Handles btnSearch.Click
  Dim strFound As String
  Dim strSearch As String = UCase(InputBox _
    ("Are you looking for Males (M) or Females (F)?"))
  Dim i As Integer
  For i = 0 To 4
    If Microsoft.VisualBasic.Left(CtrlArray(i, 1), 1) = _
        strSearch Then
      strFound &= "Name: " & CtrlArray(i, 0) & " Age: " & _
        CtrlArray(i, 2) & vbCrLf
    End If
  Next
  MsgBox("Matches found:" & vbCrLf & strFound)
End Sub
```

Figure 6-33: CtrlArray declaration and btnSearch_Click() procedure

Several of these techniques for working with groups of related controls are used in the final Scoring application. All of them are useful in dealing with groups of related controls.

You have now completed Lesson A. You should complete the exercises before continuing with Lesson B, but you can stop now and take a break if you prefer.

SUMMARY

- The MonthCalendar control is useful for picking a range of dates or a list of separate dates spanning one or more months. You can customize the DateTimePicker control to display any date/time format you desire. This control is often preferred when an application calls for the selection of a single date and/or time. The NumericUpDown control enables the user to select a number within a predefined range of numbers. The TrackBar control provides a scrollable indicator of a numeric value between a minimum value and a maximum value.

- The ProgressBar control provides a visual measure of progress toward the accomplishment of some task, such as downloading a file. The DomainUpDown control allows the user to select a string from a predefined list of strings, which may be alphabetically sorted. The StatusBar control is a container control for panels that display the status of an application. The ToolTip control provides a method for offering help to a user when the cursor hovers over a control. The RichTextBox control is a robust version of a TextBox control that supports the rich text-formatting commands. The ContextMenu component provides a short pop-up menu when the user right-clicks a control to which a context menu has been attached.

- Many other Visual Basic .NET controls are available as add-ins or built-ins, by customizing the Toolbox.

- Abstract classes must be inherited; they cannot be instantiated. Sealed classes are the reverse: they can be instantiated, but cannot form the basis of a derived class. Polymorphism is supported by overridable methods and shadowing.

- The simplest sort routine is appropriate for sorting an array of up to 10 elements. This elementary exchange sort iterates through an array, comparing adjacent elements. Whenever two out-of-sequence elements are encountered, their positions are exchanged, and the iteration is reinitiated at the top of the array.

■   Three common techniques for manipulating groups of related controls include the following: (1) using the Tab or TabIndex property to identify each control or group of controls, and iterating through all of the controls with a For Each loop; (2) inserting an event handler that handles multiple events, and examining (with a Select Case construct) the sender that triggers the event; and (3) creating a parallel array that corresponds to the group of controls.

QUESTIONS

1. The _____ property of the MonthCalendar control indicates the start and end dates of the currently selected series of consecutive dates.

2. To let the user select a single date between January 1, 2000, and December 31, 2009, use the _____ control.

3. Which property of the DomainUpDown control indicates whether the first item in the list is displayed when the user tries to scroll past the last item in the list?

4. The step value is given by which property in the NumericUpDown control?

5. Assuming that the default names have been assigned to a series of StatusBarPanel container controls within a StatusBar control, the programmatic reference StatusBarPanel(2) refers to which panel?

6. Who holds the Olympic record in the women's long jump?

7. If a DateTimePicker control's CustomFormat property is set to hh:mm t and the time of day is 3 p.m., what does the control display?

8. The _____ keyword in the class header indicates an abstract class.

9. The _____ keyword in the class header indicates a sealed class.

10. In a derived class, a function is named exactly the same as a sub in its base class. You should include the _____ attribute in the function header.

11. Four functions with the same name provide alternative implementations based on different argument lists. The function headers must all contain the _____ attribute.

12. How many assignment statements are needed to exchange the values assigned to two variables?

CRITICAL THINKING

At the end of each lesson, reflective questions are intended to provoke you into considering the material you have just read at a deeper level.

1. A method that overrides another method must have the same calling sequence as the method being overridden. A method that overloads must have a different calling sequence from the method that it overloads. A method that shadows may have the same or a different calling sequence from the shadowed method. Define calling sequence, and provide an example of overriding, overloading, and shadowing, indicating in each example how the calling sequences are the same or different.

2. HorizontalScrollBar, VerticalScrollBar, TrackBar, and ProgressBar controls provide similar functionality. What types of applications call for one of these controls over another?

3. A simple sorting algorithm has been suggested for sorting tiny arrays—with an upper limit of 10 elements in the array. Is this a reasonable upper limit? As a practical matter, what do you think the size limit should be? How do you know when the array is too large to be sorted efficiently using this simple algorithm?

4. Given an array of three elements containing the values C, B, and A, how many comparisons does the tiny sort routine make to put the array in ascending sequence?

EXERCISES

1. Create an abstract class called MyAbstractForm that inherits from System.Windows. Forms.Form. Place five text boxes on the form, without changing any of their default properties. Include a method called SetBackColor() that must be overridden. Then create two classes derived from MyAbstractForm, naming them MyDerivedRedForm and MyDerivedBlueForm. Make MyDerivedRedForm the Startup object, and place a button on that form that shows MyDerivedBlueForm. In each of these derived classes, program the SetBackColor() method to set the BackColor property of each control on the form to red and to blue, respectively.

2. Create an abstract class based on the UserControl class, and name it MyAbstractUserControl. Place five text boxes on MyAbstractUserControl, without changing any of their default properties. Include a method called SetBackColor() that must be overridden. Then create two classes derived from MyAbstractUserControl, naming them MyDerivedRedUserControl and MyDerivedBlueUserControl. In each of these derived classes, program the SetBackColor() method to set the BackColor property of each control on the user control to red and to blue, respectively. Build the solution, so that these user controls appear in the Toolbox temporarily. Add a startup form to the project called frmImplementMyUserControls. Place one instance of MyDerivedRedUserControl and of MyDerivedBlueUserControl on frmImplementMyUserControls.

3. Create a sealed class called MySealedClass, derived from the UserControl class. Place five labels on the control, without changing any of their default properties. Include a method called GetInput(). Place one button (called btnGetInput) on the control, and call GetInput() in the button click event procedure. In the GetInput() procedure, use an InputBox function call to ask the user for a starting integer, and then load the five labels with a sequence of integers, beginning with the integer supplied by the user in response to the InputBox function call. (For example, if the user enters 10, then the five labels should contain 10, 11, 12, 13, and 14.) Try to create a new class derived from your sealed class, just to prove to yourself that this cannot be done. (*Note*: If you are able to derive from your class, then you have not in fact sealed it.) Add a startup form to the project, and add one instance of MySealedClass to this form. (*Hint*: In GetInput, you can use a For Each loop to iterate through the controls collection, and you can examine each control to see if it is a label by using the TypeOf keyword.) After declaring ctrl, the syntax begins:

```
For Each ctrl In Me.Controls
    If TypeOf ctrl Is Label Then
```

4. Create a class that inherits from the UserControl class. Name this class MyOverridableControl. Design the control to look and act like MySealedClass described in Exercise 3. However, this class is not sealed, and GetInput() must be overridable. Then create a control called OverridesMyOverridableControl, which inherits from MyOverridableControl. In OverridesMyOverridableControl, write a replacement GetInput() procedure, overriding the class's built-in procedure. In this replacement procedure, ask the user for the user's name, and set all five labels to display the user's name. Then, on the startup form, place one instance of MyOverridableControl and one instance of OverridesMyOverridableControl.

5. Create a class that inherits from the UserControl class. Name this control MyOverloadedControl. Place two labels on this control, leaving their default properties unchanged. Write two public overloaded procedures for MyOverloadedControl: SetLabelText(ByVal vdbl As Double) and SetLabelText(ByVal vstr As String). In the first of these procedures, set Label1 to "Double My Number" and set Label2 to double the value of the vdbl parameter. In the second SetLabelText() procedure, set Label1 to "My Name" and set Label2 to display the vstr parameter. Then, on a startup form, place one instance of MyOverloadedControl and two buttons saying Display Number and Display Text. In btnDisplayNumber_Click(), solicit a number from the user with an InputBox function call, and then call MyOverloadedControl1's SetLabelText() procedure, passing the number from the user as a parameter. In btnDisplayText_Click(), solicit the user's name from the user, and call MyOverloadedControl's SetLabelText() procedure, passing the user's name as a parameter.

After completing this lesson, you will be able to:

■ Convert the Scoring application to an Outlook-style interface

■ Incorporate the MonthCalendar, DateTimePicker, NumericUpDown, and TrackBar Windows Forms controls into the Scheduling pane of the Scoring application

■ Modify the layout of Events.txt and structEvent to incorporate an EventID as an identifier or key for each event, change the scheduled start time for each event, and include country codes for scoring events involving national teams

■ Provide the functionality to change the starting dates for the Friendsville International Games

■ Allow the user to change the date and the start time of any specific event

Implementing an Outlook-style Application

Tasks for the FGDT

The other members of the FGDT are beginning to work on another application: recording and reporting the results of all the competitions. Hilda Reiner decided that the draft of the Scoring application written in Tutorial 5 provides a solid basis for you to complete the final version without further assistance from the rest of the team. The only exception to this is that Hilda has prevailed upon another volunteer to construct the sequential data files that this application needs, so these are provided for you. As you begin constructing the final version of the Scoring application, the focus in the first half of this lesson is on the controls and coding of frmScoreMain.

Converting the Scoring Application to an Outlook-style Interface

In this section, you convert the Scoring application from a Windows Explorer-style interface to a Microsoft Outlook-style interface by creating a new Scheduling pane on the main form. You then build the Scheduling pane using the MonthCalendar, DateTimePicker, NumericUpDown, and TrackBar Windows Forms controls. The result will be the same as what you saw in Figures 6-1, 6-2, and 6-3.

> **NOTE:** This lesson assumes that you have successfully completed Tutorial 5, and that you have a working version of the Scoring application as a starting point. To accommodate those who have not completed these tutorials in sequence, a completed version of the Scoring application from Tutorial 5 has been provided to your instructor.

In Tutorial 5, you are introduced to both the Explorer-style user interface and the closely related Outlook-style user interface. The original Scoring application in Tutorial 5 employs the simpler Explorer-style interface. The FGDT has decided to highlight the scheduling aspects of the Scoring application by incorporating schedule information and schedule change functionality on the application's main screen. This can best be accomplished by employing an Outlook-style interface instead.

Conversion of an application from an Explorer-style to an Outlook-style is relatively straightforward, as the following steps demonstrate. Essentially, the right pane, which contained the ListView control in the original Scoring application, is divided into two panes, with the ListView on the upper right and a new pane for scheduling information on the lower right.

To convert Scoring to a Microsoft Outlook-style interface:

1 Copy your completed **Scoring** application from Tutorial 5 into the **VB.NET\ Student\Tut06** folder. Rename the solution folder (but not the solution file) **FinalScoring**. Start Visual Basic .NET, and open the **Scoring** solution from the new FinalScoring folder.

2 Open **frmScoreMain** in the Windows Form Designer, if necessary. Click the **ListView1** control, and change its **Dock** property from Fill to **Top**. This permits another control to be added beneath the ListView control.

3 Click the form, and make the form taller, opening a space underneath the ListView control. On the right side of the form, the space underneath the ListView control is where you build the Scheduling pane. A space does not open underneath the TreeView control on the left because the Dock property of the TreeView control was set originally to Left, meaning that the TreeView control will occupy the entire left border of the form regardless of the height of the form.

4 Click the **ListView** control and then make it shorter, dividing the right side of the form into two roughly equal halves, with the ListView in the top-right pane and an empty pane at the bottom right. With the ListView still selected, click **Edit | Cut** to remove the ListView control and save it on the Windows Clipboard.

NOTE: You must temporarily delete the ListView control, because the Splitter control works correctly only between two controls. In Tutorial 5, you built the Scoring application with the TreeView control on the left and the ListView control on the right, and the Splitter between them. In this tutorial, the TreeView control is still on the left, but the right side will have the ListView control and some other controls in the Scheduling pane. The splitter cannot work with multiple controls on the right. Therefore, you temporarily must cut the ListView control to put another container control on the right.

5 Draw a **Panel control** in the empty pane on the right, and set its **Dock** property to **Fill**. This Panel control now gives the original Splitter control something to bump up against on the right.

6 With the Panel control still selected, click **Edit | Paste** to put the ListView control on the form, above Panel1. Visually, the form looks the same as it did before you cut and pasted the ListView control to the Clipboard, but the Panel control underneath allows the splitter to do its job at runtime.

7 With the ListView control still selected, double-click the **Splitter control** in the Toolbox, and set its **Dock** property to **Top**. This second splitter control allows the user to resize the two panes on the right at runtime, that is, to reallocate the space between the ListView control and the Scheduling pane beneath it.

8 Draw another **Panel control** in the empty space below the ListView control, and set its **Dock** property to **Fill**. Your form should look like Figure 6-1, but without the controls in the Scheduling (lower-right) pane. The Scheduling pane contains a number of separate controls. You need a single container to hold them, and also to bump up against the second splitter above it—this Panel control serves that purpose.

9 Open the **Code Editor** for frmScoreMain. At the end of the header statement for the Sub ListView1_DoubleClick() procedure, add the phrase

```
Handles ListView1.DoubleClick
```

NOTE: At the end of the header statement for the Sub ListView1_DoubleClick() procedure, when you type the keyword Handles, Visual Basic .NET offers a list of objects whose events this procedure might be directed to handle. And when you select or type one of those objects followed by a period, Visual Basic .NET offers a list of events applicable to that object. After you select or type in one such event, if you type a comma and a space, Visual Basic .NET offers the list of objects again. Basically, a single event handler can handle many events.

NOTE: When you cut the ListView control from the form in Step 4, Visual Basic .NET deleted any Handles phrases for that control. As a result, the program still compiles after a control is deleted from a form. However, when you paste the ListView control back onto the form, the Handles phrase is not automatically reinserted, so you must do this yourself manually. This is the rather complicated reason for Step 9.

10 Run the **Scoring** application to ensure that everything still works as it did at the end of Tutorial 5, and to see that you can resize the two right panes on frmScoreMain. The application should appear as in Figure 6-34. Close the application and return to the IDE.

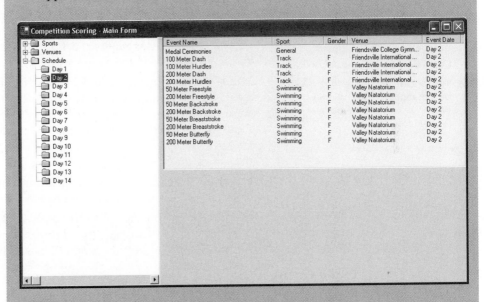

Figure 6-34: Initial conversion of Scoring to MS Outlook-style

Adding Controls to frmScoreMain

The next task is to add the appropriate controls to the Scheduling pane of frmScoreMain. The MonthCalendar control has two purposes: first, it displays the calendar dates for the Friendsville International Games, highlighting all 14 days of the Games. (The user will also have the capability of changing the start date for the

Games.) Second, the MonthCalendar displays the calendar date for an individual event. This date is computed for each event as the (Event Day minus one) plus the StartDate for the Games. A NumericUpDown control displays the Event Day for each event (Day 1 through Day 14), and a DateTimePicker control displays the time for each event. A TrackBar control provides a visual representation of the Event Day. (The user will also have the capability of changing the day and time of an individual event.)

To add controls to the Scheduling pane:

1 Drag a **MonthCalendar** control to Panel2 on frmScoreMain. Expand the **CalendarDimensions** property, and then set the **Width** element to **2**. The default value of the Height element (1) is correct. Set **Enabled** to **False**. You do not want the user to inadvertently change any displayed date(s); only deliberate changes must be allowed. Set the **MaxSelectionCount** property to **14** (the length of the Friendsville International Games). (Recall that the MaxSelectionCount property determines the maximum number of dates that can appear in the SelectionRange, that is, the maximum number of dates from SelectionStart to SelectionEnd, inclusive.) Set the **ShowToday** and **ShowTodayCircle** properties to **False**.

2 As an initial demonstration, expand the **SelectionRange** property of the **MonthCalendar** control. Set the **SelectionStart** date to **July 17, 2004**, and the **SelectionEnd** date to **July 30, 2004**, so that the Games last 14 days.

3 From the Toolbox, drag a **TrackBar** control onto the form, and set its **Dock** property to **Bottom**. It may be necessary to make the form taller so that the TrackBar control fits below the MonthCalendar control. Set its **Minimum** property to **1**, its **Maximum** property to **14** (the number of days in the Games); and set its **Enabled** property to **False** to prevent inadvertent date changes.

4 Widen the form by dragging the **middle-right handle** to the right, so that the form can accommodate an additional column (the Event ID) in the ListView control, as well as the rest of the controls in the Scheduling pane. Then add those controls—the **NumericUpDown** control, the **label** containing the EventID, the **DateTimePicker** control—and their respective labels. Initialize the Text property of lblEventID to **Start**.

5 Name the **NumericUpDown** control **nudDay**. Set its **Minimum** and **Value** properties to **1**, and its **Maximum** to **14**. Set its **Enabled** property to **False**.

6 Name the **DateTimePicker** control **dtpEventTime**. Set its **Visible** and **Enabled** properties to **False**. Set the **Format** property to **Custom**, and the **CustomFormat** property to **h:mm tt**, which displays the hour on the 12-hour clock in one or two digits, the minutes in two digits, and then either a.m. or p.m., for instance, 3:05 P.M.

7 The ListView control is going to need a new left-most column called EventID. To add this column, click **ListView1**, click the **ellipsis** next to the Columns collection, and in the ColumnHeader Collection Editor, click **Add**. Set the **Name** and **Text** properties of the new column to **Event ID**. Click the **up arrows** to move this new column header to the top of the list.

NOTE: As the FGDT's application requirements evolve, it becomes apparent that each competitive event needs a unique, fixed-length identifier, and the field EventID has been chosen for that purpose. Not only is this important for the Scoring application, but also for ticketing and for posting results; a simple identifier for each event is becoming important.

tip

You can also widen the form by changing the Width property in the Properties window.

8 Drag a **MainMenu** control onto frmScoreMain. Add the following three menus and their related submenu items; specifically, on the **File** menu, include **Exit**; on the **Tools** menu, include **Change Start Date** and **Change Event Date**, and add an **About** menu. Name these menu items following the normal naming convention. Change Event Date is initially disabled. If you need a refresher on creating a MainMenu control, this topic is discussed in detail in Tutorial 2.

9 Run the **Scoring** application. The opening screen should appear approximately as shown in Figure 6-35. Close the application. The design of the main screen of the Scoring application is now nearly complete, at least with respect to the GUI. Functionality for some of these new elements comes next.

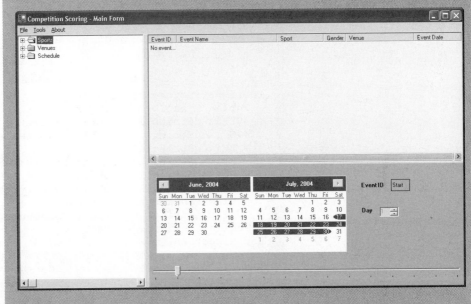

Figure 6-35: Opening screen after GUI modifications

Incorporating an Identifier or Key for Each Event

The final version of the Scoring application requires the use of an EventID to uniquely identify each competition in the Games. This identifier will play a continuing role in these applications. For example, keeping track of results, selling tickets for events, or scheduling athletes for events, can all work more easily if each event has a unique identifier. As soon as the FGDT came to this realization, the decision was made to add the EventID field to the Events.txt file used in Tutorial 5. An EventID functions like a flight number for an airline; it identifies the flight as distinct from all other flights on a given day. The EventID serves a similar purpose. You use the EventID in this and subsequent applications to identify a particular event for scheduling, scoring, recording results, and selling tickets.

As you have already seen in the revised GUI, each event now also has a starting time. The scheduled day and time for each event remains a variable, until such time as the supervisory body casts the schedule in stone. Therefore, this application must allow the user to record schedule changes. The scheduled start time becomes another element in Events.txt.

One other requirement impacts the layout of Events.txt—the need to automatically load the country name and flag for the countries participating in team sports competitions. (This will be covered in Lesson C.) This means that, for events in Events.txt that have a ScoringMethod of TS (team scoring), the country codes for the competing countries must also appear in Events.txt. (The country codes used by the FGDT are the three-character country abbreviations generally used in all international competitions.) To keep the layout of Events.txt standardized for all records, it was also decided that empty strings would be supplied in lieu of country codes for all events that are not TS competitions.

To use the revised Events.txt file and make the necessary coding changes in Scoring:

1   Replace the code in **Module1 structEvent** with the code in Figure 6-36. This changes the structure of the record read in from the file and loaded into the pastructEvents array.

```
Public Structure structEvent
  Public EventID As Integer
  <VBFixedString(10)> Public Sport As String
  <VBFixedString(25)> Public EventName As String
  <VBFixedString(1)> Public Gender As String
  <VBFixedString(2)> Public ScoringMethod As String
  <VBFixedString(3)> Public Country1 As String
  <VBFixedString(3)> Public Country2 As String
  Public VenueIndex As Integer
  <VBFixedString(10)> Public Schedule As String
  Public StartTime As Date
End Structure
```

Figure 6-36: Revised layout of Events.txt

2   Copy the **Events.txt** file from the **VB.NET\Student\Tut06** folder to the **VB.NET\Student\Tut06\FinalScoring\bin** folder.

3   The coding that loads the Events.txt file into an internal array must also be modified. This occurs in the frmScoreMain.vb file in the frmScoreMain_Load() procedure. Substitute the code shown in Figure 6-37 for the corresponding code in the original **frmScoreMain_Load()** procedure. This code adds the statements that input the four new elements in Events.txt, namely, the EventID, Country1, Country2, and StartTime.

```
FileOpen(1, "Events.txt", OpenMode.Input)
Do Until EOF(1)
  With pastructEvents(i)
    Input(1, .EventID)
    Input(1, .Sport)
    Input(1, .EventName)
    Input(1, .Gender)
    Input(1, .ScoringMethod)
    Input(1, .Country1)
    Input(1, .Country2)
    Input(1, .VenueIndex)
    Input(1, .Schedule)
    Input(1, .StartTime)
  End With
  i += 1
Loop
FileClose(1)
pNumEvents = i
```

Figure 6-37: Loading Events.txt into an array

4 The EventID also needs to appear in the ListView control. Therefore, modify the **AddListViewItem()** procedure in frmScoreMain.vb, as shown in Figure 6-38.

```
With pastructEvents(ri)
  ListView1.Items.Add(.EventID)
  ListView1.Items(vItemCtr).SubItems.Add(.EventName)
  ListView1.Items(vItemCtr).SubItems.Add(.Sport)
  ListView1.Items(vItemCtr).SubItems.Add(.Gender)
  ListView1.Items(vItemCtr).SubItems.Add _
    (pastrVenues(.VenueIndex))
  ListView1.Items(vItemCtr).SubItems.Add(.Schedule)
  ListView1.Items(vItemCtr).Tag = ri
  vItemCtr += 1
End With
```

Figure 6-38: AddListViewItem() procedure

Providing Functionality to Change the Start Date for the Games

The start date for the Games is a new element in the final version of the Scoring application. At least until the Friendsville Organizing Committee determines the actual, immutable start date for the Games, the IT team needs to remain flexible—therefore, the StartDate needs to be a variable, and it needs to be stored in an external file where any computer program can use it. You accomplish this by using a data file called StartDate.txt, consisting of one date string. Then, within the program, you load this date from the data file at startup, and you allow the user to change this date through a menu selection.

To incorporate the variable StartDate for the Games:

1 Copy the file **StartDate.txt** from the **VB.NET\Student\Tut06** folder to the **VB.NET\Student\Tut06\FinalScoring\bin** folder.

2   Add the following public variable to the declaration of public variables in **Module1** for the **StartDate**:

```
Public pStartDate As Date
```

3   Insert the code in Figure 6-39 into **frmScoreMain_Load**(). This code enables the Change Start Date menu item, disables the Change Event Date menu item, opens the StartDate text file, and reads its contents pStartDate, and then uses that date to initialize the MonthCalendar control's SelectionStart and SelectionEnd properties.

```
mnuToolsChangeStartDate.Enabled = True
mnuToolsChangeEventDate.Enabled = False
FileOpen(2, "StartDate.txt", OpenMode.Input)
Input(2, pStartDate)
MonthCalendar1.SelectionStart = pStartDate
MonthCalendar1.SelectionEnd = _
  DateAdd(DateInterval.Day, 13, pStartDate)
FileClose(2)
```

Figure 6-39: Loading the Start Date for the Games

4   Place a bright red **Done** button on the form on top of the upper middle of the MonthCalendar control. Name the button **btnDone**, and open the **Properties** list. Set the **Visible** property to **False** so that the user does not see the button at startup. The GUI for frmScoreMain is complete. It should appear at design time, as shown in Figure 6-40.

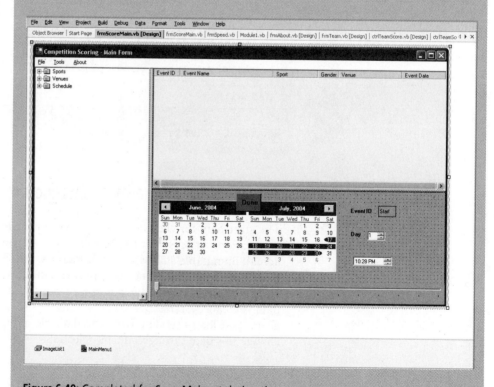

Figure 6-40: Completed frmScoreMain, at design time

5 Program the **mnuToolsChangeStartDate_Click**() procedure to ask the user whether the user wants to change the start date for the Friendsville International Games. If the user answers affirmatively, then give the user instructions on how to change the date in the MonthCalendar control, enable the MonthCalendar control, and make btnDone visible. Enabling the MonthCalendar control allows the user to pick a new start date for the Games. After selecting a new date, the user must click the Done button.

6 When the user clicks the Done button, the new start date is written to the file, and the MonthCalendar control is updated with the new time frame. To implement this, program the **btnDone_Click**() event procedure, as shown in Figure 6-41. Add two more statements to disable the MonthCalendar control and to make the Done button invisible.

```
FileOpen(2, "StartDate.txt", OpenMode.Output)
pStartDate = MonthCalendar1.SelectionStart
Write(2, CStr(pStartDate))
MonthCalendar1.SelectionEnd = _
     DateAdd(DateInterval.Day, 13, pStartDate)
FileClose(2)
```

Figure 6-41: btnDone_Click(), after changing the start date

NOTE: The menu offers two choices under Tools, when the user clicks either, the red Done button appears. You could have two Done buttons programmed separately (named, for example, btnDoneStartDate and btnDoneEventDate), or you could have just one btnDone. You've implemented the latter approach. With a single btnDone, lblEventID determines which function has taken place. When the user is changing the StartDate for the Games, lblEventID contains Start; with any other value in lblEventID, the user is changing an event date.

Displaying and Altering Schedule Data for a Specific Event

When a list view item is selected, three things must happen. First, the selected item's schedule must appear in the Scheduling pane of frmScoreMain. Second, the Change Start Date item on the Tools menu must be disabled. Third, the Change Event Date item on the Tools menu must be enabled. Then, the program must permit the user to change the scheduled day and time of an event.

To display and alter the event day and time:

1 Open the **ListView1_Click**() procedure and code it, as shown in Figure 6-42.

tip

You are programming the Click event here, as distinguished from the DoubleClick event coded in Tutorial 5. The ListView control supports both of these events, and sometimes it is useful to program each event independently. In this case, a single click displays the schedule information for an event and allows a user to change it; whereas a double-click opens the competition scoring module for that event.

```
Private Sub ListView1_Click(ByVal sender As Object, _
    ByVal e As System.EventArgs) Handles ListView1.Click
  Dim lv As ListViewItem
  For Each lv In ListView1.SelectedItems
    pEventRec = pastructEvents(Val(lv.Tag))
    With pEventRec
      lblEventID.Text = .EventID
      nudDay.Value = Val(Mid(.Schedule, 5))
      dtpEventTime.Visible = True
      .StartTime += MonthCalendar1.MinDate
      dtpEventTime.Value = .StartTime
      MonthCalendar1.SelectionStart = _
        DateAdd(DateInterval.Day, nudDay.Value - 1, _
        pStartDate)
      MonthCalendar1.SelectionEnd = _
        DateAdd(DateInterval.Day, nudDay.Value - 1, _
        pStartDate)
    End With
  Next
  mnuToolsChangeStartDate.Enabled = False
  mnuToolsChangeEventDate.Enabled = True
End Sub
```

Figure 6-42: ListView1_Click() event procedure

Most of the code in the ListView1_Click() procedure is fairly obvious—displaying the EventID in lblEventID, the scheduled day of the event in nudDay, and the scheduled date in MonthCalendar1. Displaying the scheduled time of the event in dtpTime is not so obvious, and merits a further explanation.

Even though this DateTimePicker control displays only the time of day due to the custom formatting applied to it, the actual value stored in a DateTimePicker control always includes a date, and that date must fall between the MinDate of January 1, 1753, and the MaxDate of December 31, 9998 (or any more restrictive values you assign to MinDate and MaxDate). To work around this problem, you can add the desired time of day to a date value that falls between the minimum and maximum date (such as MinDate or Today), and then assign the resulting sum to the DateTimePicker control. The code in Figure 6-42 displays this technique by adding .StartTime to MonthCalendar1.MinDate.

Figure 6-43 displays another version of this technique, adding a time of day to Today. In Figure 6-43, the user enters a time of day in response to the prompt, such as "10:00 AM." In the statement that follows, the value returned by the Today function (that is, today's date) is added to the user-entered time of day. The sum is then assigned to a DateTimePicker control.

```
Dim MyTime As Date
MyTime = CDate(InputBox("Enter the desired time of day"))
MyTime += Today
DateTimePicker1.Value = MyTime
```

Figure 6-43: Assigning a time value to a DateTimePicker control

2 The TrackBar control should always mirror the value of the NumericUpDown control (nudDay). In the Code editor, open the **ValueChanged()** event procedure for nudDay, and insert the code shown in Figure 6-44.

```
Private Sub nudDay_ValueChanged(ByVal sender As _
    System.Object, ByVal e As System.EventArgs) _
    Handles nudDay.ValueChanged
  TrackBar1.Value = nudDay.Value
End Sub
```

Figure 6-44: nudDay_ValueChanged() procedure

3 To change its scheduled day or time, the user selects a list view item and then clicks Tools | Change Event Date. To achieve this functionality, program the **mnuToolsChangeEventDate**() procedure to ask the user if he or she wants to change the day or time for this event. If the user answers affirmatively, display instructions for making this change, enable nudDay and dtpEventTime, and make btnDone visible.

4 Clicking the Done button in this case should trigger the code shown in Figure 6-45. Examine this code carefully so that you understand it, but do not insert it yet. This code identifies the correct ListViewItem object and changes its scheduled day and time in the pastructEvents() array, updates the MonthCalendar display, and then writes the entire pastructEvents() array back to the Events.txt file. To the code shown in Figure 6-45, additional code is needed to disable nudDay and dtpEventTime, and make the Done button invisible.

```
Dim i As Integer
Dim lv As ListViewItem
For Each lv In ListView1.SelectedItems
  With pastructEvents(Val(lv.Tag))
    .Schedule = "Day " & nudDay.Value
    .StartTime = Format(dtpEventTime.Value, "h:mm tt")
    MonthCalendar1.SelectionStart = _
      DateAdd(DateInterval.Day, nudDay.Value - 1, _
      pStartDate)
    MonthCalendar1.SelectionEnd = _
      DateAdd(DateInterval.Day, nudDay.Value - 1, _
      pStartDate)
  End With
Next
FileOpen(1, "Events.txt", OpenMode.Output)
For i = 0 To pNumEvents - 1
  With pastructEvents(i)
    Write(1, .EventID)
    Write(1, .Sport)
    Write(1, .EventName)
    Write(1, .Gender)
    Write(1, .ScoringMethod)
    Write(1, .Country1)
    Write(1, .Country2)
    Write(1, .VenueIndex)
    Write(1, .Schedule)
    WriteLine(1, .StartTime)
  End With
Next
FileClose(1)
```

Figure 6-45: btnDone_Click(), after changing an event date/time

5 You have now been given two sets of code for the btnDone_Click() procedure. Your code must determine which code segment to execute based on the value of lblEventID, as explained earlier. Essentially, if lblEventID displays "Start," then the user is changing the start date for the Friendsville International Games; however, if lblEventID displays any other value, the user is changing the day/time of a scheduled event. Because the form contains a single btnDone, you need to implement a selection structure (an If or a Case statement) to distinguish between a change to the start date for the Games and a change to the day/time of an event. The completed btnDone_Click() procedure should appear approximately as shown in Figure 6-46. Replace the initial btnDone_Click() procedure with the code in Figure 6-46.

```
Private Sub btnDone_Click(ByVal sender As System.Object, _
    ByVal e As System.EventArgs) Handles btnDone.Click
  If lblEventID.Text = "Start" Then
    FileOpen(2, "StartDate.txt", OpenMode.Output)
    pStartDate = MonthCalendar1.SelectionStart
    Write(2, CStr(pStartDate))
    MonthCalendar1.SelectionEnd = _
      DateAdd(DateInterval.Day, 13, pStartDate)
    FileClose(2)
  Else 'change event day/time
    Dim i As Integer
    Dim lv As ListViewItem
    For Each lv In ListView1.SelectedItems
      With pastructEvents(Val(lv.Tag))
        .Schedule = "Day " & nudDay.Value
        .StartTime = Format(dtpEventTime.Value, "h:mm tt")
        MonthCalendar1.SelectionStart = _
          DateAdd(DateInterval.Day, _
          nudDay.Value - 1, pStartDate)
        MonthCalendar1.SelectionEnd = _
          DateAdd(DateInterval.Day, _
          nudDay.Value - 1, pStartDate)
      End With
    Next
    FileOpen(1, "Events.txt", OpenMode.Output)
    For i = 0 To pNumEvents - 1
      With pastructEvents(i)
        Write(1, .EventID)
        Write(1, .Sport)
        Write(1, .EventName)
        Write(1, .Gender)
        Write(1, .ScoringMethod)
        Write(1, .Country1)
        Write(1, .Country2)
        Write(1, .VenueIndex)
        Write(1, .Schedule)
        WriteLine(1, .StartTime)
      End With
    Next
    FileClose(1)
  End If
  MonthCalendar1.Enabled = False
  nudDay.Enabled = False
  dtpEventTime.Enabled = False
  btnDone.Visible = False
End Sub
```

Figure 6-46: Completed btnDone_Click() procedure

Final Coding Elements

At this point, you can add a few lines of code to complete what you have implemented thus far.

> To complete the Scoring application:
> **1** Program the About menu selection to display a simple About Scoring form, and program the Exit menu selection to end the application.
> **2** Whenever a tree view item is selected, frmScoreMain_Load() should be invoked again, because the same basic actions are called for. Therefore, insert the call that follows as the first statement in Sub TreeView1_AfterSelect():
>
> ```
> frmScoreMain_Load(sender, e)
> ```
>
> **3** Run the **Scoring** application, try every option, and clean up any odds and ends that you may have overlooked up to this point.

SUMMARY

- Conversion of an existing application from a Windows Explorer-style GUI to an Outlook-style GUI is relatively straightforward. A Panel (or other container) control occupies the right side of the screen and contains the ListView control on top, a second Splitter control is placed below the ListView control, and another container control is placed under the Splitter.
- A number of graphical controls, including the MonthCalendar, DateTimePicker, NumericUpDown, and TrackBar, can be intertwined to support date and time scheduling and manipulation. These controls can interact with the user and with each other to provide robust functionality.
- The DateTimePicker control is preferred for selecting an individual date or time of day. When formatted for time of day, the control must contain a valid date (a date between MinDate and MaxDate).

QUESTIONS

1. A control useful for selecting multiple dates is the _____.

2. A control often preferred for selecting an individual date or time of day is the _____.

3. The _____ property determines how many tick marks appear from one position to the next in a TrackBar control.

4. To set the MonthCalendar control to allow 20 dates to be selected, set the _____ property to 20.

5. In setting the SelectionRange property, if the start date and the number of days to be selected are given, the end date can be computed using the _____ function.

6. In the MonthCalendar control, the property that determines whether the current date appears at the bottom of the control is _____.

7. In a NumericUpDown control, the UpButton method _____ the new value and _____ the control.

8. You can invent your own formatting for the DateTimePicker control by setting the _____ property to Custom and the _____ property to your desired format string.

9. How many months can be displayed in a MonthCalendar control?

10. Which property of the Control class determines the shape of the cursor when the insertion point hovers over the control? (*Hint*: To answer this, you must find a link to the Control class in the System.Windows.Forms Namespace, then read through the members of that class.)

CRITICAL THINKING

At the end of each lesson, reflective questions are intended to provoke you into considering the material you have just read at a deeper level.

1. Consider the btnSearch_Click() procedure discussed in the ControlArrays2 application in this tutorial. How would you modify this procedure, if the requirement were to change the BackColor property of each row of controls that matched strSearch, rather than display the names and ages in a message box?

2. You have seen both a GroupBox control and a Panel control as a container for other controls. The GroupBox control displays text through its Text property, and a Panel control has no Text property. What is the other major difference between them? (*Hint*: To answer this question, place a GroupBox control and a Panel control on a form, place two radio buttons inside each, and then run the program.)

EXERCISES

1. Create an application containing a form with 10 controls of varying types. Create a single event handler that handles one event from each control: a Click event, a TextChanged event, a ValueChanged event, or whatever seems most appropriate for each control. In the event handler, change the BackColor property of the control that triggers the event to yellow, and change the BackColor property of all other controls to white.

   To complete this exercise:
   a. Start a new Visual Basic .NET Windows Forms project. Name the project Tut06BEx1. Rename Form1 as frmHandler.
   b. Place 10 controls on frmHandler—one Button, one TextBox, one RichTextBox, two RadioButtons, one CheckBox, one TreeView, one ListBox, one CheckedListBox, and one Label. Leave the default names on all these controls. Put two nodes into the TreeView control. Put "ListBox1" into the Items collection of the ListBox control, and "CheckedListBox1" into the Items collection of the CheckedListBox control.
   c. Program the Button1_Click() event to change the BackColor of the sender to yellow, and to change the BackColor of all other controls to white. (*Hint*: Use a For Each loop to iterate through the controls collection.)
   d. Notice the Handles clause in the Button1_Click() event header. Insert a comma and space after `Handles Button1.Click`. Then, add one event from each of the other

controls on frmHandler. Use the most obvious events, such as the CheckedChanged event for the RadioButton controls, the AfterSelect event for the TreeView control, the TextChanged event for the TextBox control, and so on.

   e.   Run the program. Perform the action for each control that triggers the event procedure. The control that triggers the event procedure should change to a yellow background color, and all other controls should have a white background color.

2.   Create an application containing a set of 10 text boxes. Initialize these to contain the names of athletes at the Friendsville International Games. (Make sure the user can change these names at runtime.) Place a tall RichTextBox control on the form, along with a Button control named btnSort. When the button is clicked, the following should occur:

   a.   Load the Text properties of the text boxes into an array of strings. To do this, use a For Each loop that iterates through all of the controls on the form. When a text box is encountered, add the Text property of the text box to your string array.

   b.   Sort the array using Hilda's Simple Sort.

   c.   Copy the array into the RichTextBox control, placing each name on a separate line.

3.   Using Notepad, create a small data file called Integers.txt, and place 10 integers into this file, one integer per line. Create a Visual Basic .NET Console application. In this application, load the Integers.txt data file into an array of 10 integers. Sort the array using Hilda's Simple Sort. Display the sorted array in descending numerical order.

4.   Create a Windows Forms application containing a MonthCalendar control with all 12 months of 2005 displayed. Display the week number also. Do not show today's date. Allow the user to select up to 20 dates. When the user selects a date, add the date to a ListBox control.

5.   Create a form containing an HScrollBar, a TrackBar, a ProgressBar, and a NumericUpDown control. For each control, the minimum value must be set to 1 and the maximum to 20. Set the LargeChange property of the TrackBar and ScrollBar controls to 2. When the user changes the value in the ScrollBar, TrackBar, or NumericUpDown control, the values in all four controls must adjust themselves automatically. When any control reaches its maximum value, end the program.

6.   Create a form containing a MonthCalendar control, and experiment with all of its properties. Display four months in the control. Concerning the MonthCalendar control GUI: change the default TitleBackColor, TrailingForeColor, and TitleForeColor properties. Implement a toggle switch to display or not display week numbers. Add toggle switches to display or not display Today's date, and to circle it or not. Let the user determine the range of dates in the control by establishing the MaxSelectionCount property of the MonthCalendar control, and by setting the SelectionStart and SelectionEnd properties.

LESSON C
objectives

After completing this lesson, you will be able to:

- Plan for the remaining tasks in the Scoring application
- Automatically search through and select an item from a combo box based on data selected from an array
- Determine when to use Public (Global) variables
- Build an abstract class and use it in an application
- Create classes that use inheritance and polymorphism

Implementing an Abstract Class

In Lesson C, you complete the final version of the Scoring application. This includes applying the concepts of inheritance and polymorphism to the creation of the three individual scoring modules. You build an abstract class called frmCompetition for this purpose, subsequently deriving the class for each type of individual scoring (speed, distance, and judges) from frmCompetition. The abstract class also involves two other main concepts covered in Tutorial 6: handling groups of related controls, and sorting a tiny array. Finally, you also complete frmTeam and frmScoreMain.

One major improvement to individual competition scoring (compared with the frmSpeed developed in Tutorial 5) is the creation of a list of athletes from which the user selects the competitors for a particular event. A second improvement involves the standardization of the individual scoring modules, based on a new class called frmCompetition. A third improvement is the processing of results at the end of a competition to indicate the order of finish for all competitors.

Planning the Remaining Tasks in the Scoring Application

Although you have done a great deal of work on the final version of Scoring, much of the new functionality specified at the beginning of this tutorial remains to be accomplished. Specifically, the application still needs the following features:

- For events in team sports, the nationality and flag icon (in the ctrlNation controls) should be automatically selected.
- Standardized information about the athletes needs to be stored in a file, and the file needs to be loaded into an array at startup. This array can then be used to populate combo boxes with the names of athletes, from which the users can select competitors for an individual event.
- A new frmCompetition must be created, based on work previously done for frmSpeed. Then, this new frmCompetition becomes the base class for frmSpeed, frmDistance, and frmJudge.
- In all the individual scoring modules, the user should be able to select competitors from a list of eligible athletes, and the ctrlNation control corresponding to each competitor should be automatically selected.
- In all the individual scoring modules, the results should indicate first, second, and third place finishers, and so on, rather than just the winner.
- The FigWelcome and Logon class libraries should be called.

Automatically Searching and Selecting from a Combo Box

In Lesson B, you modified Module1 and frmScoreMain to the revised layout of Events.txt, which includes codes for the two countries involved in Team Scoring competitions. The country codes were added to Events.txt and structEvent so that the correct country name and flag could be automatically displayed in frmTeam. Recall, however, that the internal properties and methods of a user-defined control are not programmatically accessible to the projects that use them. Therefore, ctrlNation itself must be modified to search through its list of nations and display the correct country name and flag. The class frmTeam includes ctrlTeamScore, which in turns contains two instances of ctrlNation, and it is ctrlNation that needs to receive the country codes. Hence, the two country codes (named Country1 and Country2 in the layout of structEvent) must be passed from frmScoreMain to frmTeam, then from frmTeam to ctrlTeamScore and then from ctrlTeamScore individually to ctrlNation1 and ctrlNation2. Finally, in ctrlNation, you must create a method that searches through the available nation codes and, if it finds the right one, assigns the correct country name and flag icon to the constituent controls (a combo box and a label) in ctrlNation. If a competitor's nation does not appear in the list of available nations, this method takes no action, leaving the country and flag areas blank.

To automatically load ctrlNation in Team Scoring events:

1 Replace the call to the **SetHeaderInfo** method in frmScoreMain when the ScoringMethod = "TS," as shown in Figure 6-47. This code replaces the existing Case "TS" code in the ListView1_DoubleClick() procedure. The purpose here is to include the parameters .Country1 and .Country2.

```
Case "TS"
  Dim frm = New frmTeam()
  frm.setheaderinfo(.Sport, .Country1, .Country2, _
    .EventName, pastrVenues(.VenueIndex), .Schedule, _
    "Team Sport", .Gender)
  frm.ShowDialog()
```

Figure 6-47: Revised Case "TS" in ListView1_DoubleClick()

2 Now modify the **SetHeaderInfo** in frmTeam, as shown in Figure 6-48. After modification, the SetHeaderInfo method accepts the new country codes passed to it as vCountry1 and vCountry2, and in turn calls the new SetCountries method of CtrlTeamScore1, passing vCountry1 and vCountry2 to that method.

```
Public Sub SetHeaderInfo(ByVal vSport As String, _
    ByVal vCountry1 As String, ByVal vCountry2 As String, _
    ByVal vEventName As String, _
    ByVal vVenue As String, ByVal vSchedule As String, _
    ByVal vScoringMethod As String, ByVal vGender As String)
  ctrlEventHeader1.LoadHeaderInfo(vSport, vEventName, vVenue, _
    vSchedule, vScoringMethod, vGender)
  CtrlTeamScore1.SetCountries(vCountry1, vCountry2)
End Sub
```

Figure 6-48: Revised SetHeaderInfo method of frmTeam

3 In **ctrlTeamScore**, type the new **SetCountries** method, shown in Figure 6-49. This method accepts the two country codes passed to it as vstrCountry1 and vstrCountry2. It then calls the new SetCountry method for each of the ctrlNation controls within the ctrlTeamScore control, passing one country code to each.

```
Public Sub SetCountries(ByVal vstrCountry1 As String, _
    ByVal vstrCountry2 As String)
  CtrlNation1.SetCountry(vstrCountry1)
  CtrlNation2.SetCountry(vstrCountry2)
End Sub
```

Figure 6-49: New SetCountries method of ctrlTeamScore

4 Finally, you reach ctrlNation, where the country code gets translated into the actual name and flag icon of a country. The new SetCountry method provides for automatic selection of the country name and flag based on the country code passed to the method. However, the revised procedures also allow the control to be used in an application when the country code is not passed to it. To begin this process, open the former **ctrlNation_Load()** procedure and rename it **LoadCboAndArray**, which is what the procedure accomplishes—loading the combo box and the array.

5 Invoke the LoadCboAndArray procedure from inside the SetCountry method and a new ctrlNation_Load() method.

6 Make the changes to the existing code (renaming the Load procedure and creating the new Load procedure), and then insert the SetCountry method shown in Figure 6-50.

```
Public Sub SetCountry(ByVal vstrCountry As String)
  Dim i As Integer, s As String
  LoadCboAndArray()
  For i = 0 To NUMNATIONS - 1
    If mastrNation(i, 0) = vstrCountry Then
      cboNation.SelectedIndex = i
    End If
  Next
End Sub
```

Figure 6-50: SetCountry() method in ctrlNation

7 Run the **Scoring** application, and test a Team Scoring event to see that the country name and flag icon load as they should. Then return to the IDE.

After implementing these changes to Team Scoring, it is also possible to apply the revised ctrlNation to all the individual competitions. If the country code for an athlete is known, it is an easy matter to pass the country code to the ctrlNation control.

Revisiting Public (Global) Variables: Adding Athletes to Module1

The draft version of the Scoring application includes several public variables and constants declared in Module1; the final version introduces several more. As discussed in

Tutorial 2, public variables and constants can present problems due to naming collisions, misinterpretation, scoping problems, and difficulties related to the reuse of software components. In each case, a judgment must be made as to whether a proposed public variable can cause any of these kinds of problems, and whether the convenience of having the public variable outweighs such problems. The decision is often one of judgment. In many cases, the principle should be that a variable needed in only one place should be defined in only that one place, with the most restricted scope possible. This is why a loop control variable, often "i" or "j," is defined in each method that needs such a variable. Even though the variable name is repeated from one method to the next, the variable's purpose and use is distinct in each method, and so it should be a local variable only. When a variable is needed in very few places or when it is needed in a class that could be reused, it should be passed as a parameter to the components that need it. Only when a variable is useful and necessary throughout an application should it be declared as a public variable.

In the present application, these principles result in the list of public structures, arrays, and variables in Module1. In addition to those public declarations previously discussed, the structure and array of athletes must be included. The information needed concerning each athlete is an Athlete ID number (useful, by the way, in many FGDT applications, such as the Dining Hall Seat Assigner and the Village Housing assignments), the first and last names, gender, and country code.

To complete the declaration of public elements and load the array of athletes:

1 Open **Module1** of the Scoring application. Insert the declaration of **structAthlete** immediately after the declaration of structEvent, coding it in accordance with Figure 6-51.

```
Public Structure structAthlete
   Public AthleteID As Integer
   <VBFixedString(20)> Public FName As String
   <VBFixedString(25)> Public LName As String
   <VBFixedString(1)> Public Gender As String
   <VBFixedString(3)> Public Country As String
End Structure
```

Figure 6-51: structAthlete

2 Module1 includes the public declarations of structEvent, structAthlete, the pastrVenues array, the pastrScoringMethods array, and the public constants and variables shown in Figure 6-52. Examine your Module1 declarations carefully, and add those necessary to match those shown in Figure 6-52.

```
Public Const NUMEVENTS = 500 'maximum number of events
Public Const NUMATHLETES = 500 'maximum number of athletes
Public pastructEvents(NUMEVENTS) As structEvent 'array of events
Public pEventRec As structEvent 'one event
'array of athletes
Public pastructAthletes(NUMATHLETES) As structAthlete
'number of competitors in individual competitions
Public pintCompetitors As Integer
Public pStartDate As Date 'start date of the Games
Public pNumEvents As Integer 'actual number of events
Public pNumAthletes As Integer 'actual number of athletes
Public pstrGender As String 'designates an event for Men or for Women
```

Figure 6-52: Global variables and constants in Module1

3   If the Scoring application is designed for use throughout the Games, it makes sense to open a file containing the athletes' information only once when the application starts running, and load this data into a public array. The array is then available for use by each of the scoring modules that needs it. This task is accomplished by the code shown in Figure 6-53. Insert this code into the **frmScoreMain_Load**() procedure.

```
FileOpen(3, "Athletes.txt", OpenMode.Input)
i = 0
Do Until EOF(3)
  With pastructAthletes(i)
    Input(3, .AthleteID)
    Input(3, .FName)
    Input(3, .LName)
    Input(3, .Gender)
    Input(3, .Country)
  End With
  i += 1
Loop
FileClose(3)
pNumAthletes = i
```

Figure 6-53: Loading the Athletes array

4   Based on that sample code, you are in need of the Athletes.txt. Happily, Althea found some time to prepare a sample file—not with all 1000 plus athletes who will compete in the Friendsville International Games, but just a small sample to show how the application works. Copy **Athletes.txt** from **VB.NET\Student\ Tut06** to **VB.NET\Student\Tut06\FinalScoring\bin**.

5   Run the **Scoring** application to ensure that you have not introduced any syntax errors. You will not see the athletes' names until frmCompetition and the classes derived from it are complete.

Building an Abstract Class: frmCompetition

Hilda has determined that the three individual competition scoring methods have requirements so closely aligned that considerable application development time can be saved by creating one model for all three, and then customizing this model as dictated by each scoring method. The new model for all three scoring methods will be an abstract class called frmCompetition, which will be constructed from frmSpeed—the form you created in Tutorial 5. Therefore, the sequence of tasks here is to rename frmSpeed as frmCompetition, modify frmCompetition as needed, and then create a new frmSpeed, frmDistance, and frmJudge as derived classes from frmCompetition.

To create frmCompetition:

1   Open **frmSpeed** in the Windows Form Designer. In the Properties window, change its name from frmSpeed to **frmCompetition**. Right-click the name **frmSpeed.vb** in Solution Explorer, select **Rename**, and type the new filename **frmCompetition.vb**.

NOTE: The main difference in the GUI for frmCompetition compared to the original frmSpeed created in Tutorial 5 is the substitution of combo boxes for labels in the Name column in the Competitors box. The program loads each ComboBox control with the names of the athletes eligible to participate in any competition, that is, male athletes for the men's events and female athletes for the women's events. The user then selects the name of a competitor from a combo box, a big improvement over asking the user to type the name of each competitor.

2 Delete the eight labels (**lblName1, lblName2,** and so on) and replace them with ComboBox controls named **cboName1, cboName2, ..., cboName8.** Set the **Tag** property of each ComboBox to **1, 2, ..., 8,** respectively, and set the **Visible** property for each to **False.** Set the **Text** property for each to **Select a competitor.** The completed GUI should appear as in Figure 6-54.

You can simplify Step 2 by creating the first ComboBox control, setting the Size, Visible, and Text properties, copying the ComboBox control to the Clipboard, and then pasting it onto the form seven times. You then must position all eight controls and individually assign the Tag and Name properties. Alternatively, if you create the eight ComboBox controls first, you can then select all eight and set the Visible and Text properties for all eight simultaneously.

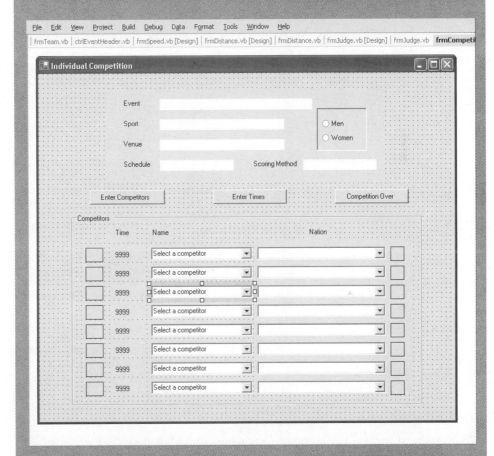

Figure 6-54: frmCompetition at design time

3 Make minor modifications to the GUI: change the **Name** property of **btnEnterTimes** to **btnEnterResults,** and change the Button's **Text** property to **Enter Results.** Within the Competitors group box, the name of the label that serves as a column header for Times should be set to **lblResultsColumnHeader,** and its **Text** property should be **Results.** These changes help make frmCompetition adaptable for all three individual scoring methods. (Recall that the original properties of these controls were tailored to competitions based only on speed.)

4   The next modification involves loading those eight combo boxes with the names of potential competitors. Replace the original **btnEnterCompetitors_Click()** procedure with the procedure shown in Figure 6-55 for loading the names of potential competitors into each combo box. The data source for each athlete's name and country is the pastructAthletes() array loaded at startup. Also, one filter is used, based on gender—only male athletes are loaded into the combo boxes for men's events, and only female athletes for women's events.

```
Private Sub btnEnterCompetitors_Click _
    (ByVal sender As System.Object, ByVal e As _
    System.EventArgs) Handles btnEnterCompetitors.Click
  Dim i As Integer
  Dim s As String
  For i = 0 To pNumAthletes - 1
    With pastructAthletes(i)
      If .Gender = pstrGender Then
        s = CStr(.AthleteID) & " " & .FName & " " & _
        .LName & " " & .Country
        cboName1.Items.Add(s)
        cboName2.Items.Add(s)
        cboName3.Items.Add(s)
        cboName4.Items.Add(s)
        cboName5.Items.Add(s)
        cboName6.Items.Add(s)
        cboName7.Items.Add(s)
        cboName8.Items.Add(s)
      End If
    End With
  Next
  Dim ctrl As Control
  pintCompetitors = InputBox _
    ("Enter the number of competitors (2 to 8)")
  If pintCompetitors < 2 Or pintCompetitors > 8 Then
    MsgBox("Invalid number of competitors")
    Exit Sub
  End If
  For i = 1 To pintCompetitors
    For Each ctrl In grpCompetitors.Controls
      If ctrl.Tag = i Or ctrl.Tag = i / 10 Or ctrl.Tag = _
          i * 10 Or ctrl.Tag = i * 100 Then
        ctrl.Visible = True
      End If
    Next
  Next
  btnEnterResults.Enabled = True
  btnEnterCompetitors.Enabled = False
End Sub
```

Figure 6-55: btnEnterCompetitors_Click() procedure in frmCompetition

5   When a competitor's name is selected, the program should automatically select the name and flag of the country that competitor represents. Selecting a competitor in any combo box triggers the TextChanged event for that combo box. Therefore, you can program the TextChanged event to invoke the SetCountry method of the corresponding ctrlNation control. Figure 6-56 shows this code for the cboName8_TextChanged() event. Insert this code eight times, once for each combo box's TextChanged event, modifying the references to each control name in each procedure.

```
Private Sub cboName8_TextChanged(ByVal sender As Object, _
    ByVal e As System.EventArgs) _
    Handles cboName8.TextChanged
  CtrlNation8.SetCountry(Microsoft.VisualBasic.Right _
    (cboName8.Text, 3))
End Sub
```

Figure 6-56: cboName8_TextChanged() procedure

6 The logic for entering results has not changed, but you just changed the name of the button from btnEnterTimes to btnEnterResults, and therefore you must also change the name of the procedure to **btnEnterResults_Click()**. Further, your code should reflect the generalized nature of the class. Generalize the InputBox prompt in the btnEnterResults_Click() procedure by entering

"Enter the result for competitor #" & i

7 The previous btnCompetitionOver_Click() procedure needs to be replaced completely, because it was designed to select only the winner. The new procedure determines the order of finish, from first to last place. Replace the existing **btnCompetitionOver_Click()** procedure with the code in Figure 6-57.

```
Private Sub btnCompetitionOver_Click(ByVal sender As _
    System.Object, ByVal e As System.EventArgs) _
    Handles btnCompetitionOver.Click
  Dim i As Integer
  Dim asngMeasure(pintCompetitors + 1) As Single
  Dim aintResult(pintCompetitors + 1) As Integer
  Dim ctrl As Control
  For i = 1 To pintCompetitors
    For Each ctrl In grpCompetitors.Controls
      If ctrl.Name = "lblTime" & Trim(i) Then
        asngMeasure(i) = Val(ctrl.Text) * mintSortOrder
      End If
    Next
  Next
  Call AssignWinners(asngMeasure, aintResult)
  For i = 1 To pintCompetitors
    For Each ctrl In grpCompetitors.Controls
      If ctrl.Name = "lblResult" & Trim(i) Then
        ctrl.Text = aintResult(i)
      End If
    Next
  Next
End Sub
```

Figure 6-57: btnCompetitionOver_Click() procedure

This rewritten btnCompetitionOver_Click() procedure declares an array called asngMeasure to hold the raw results of the competition. To obtain the correct order of finish, this array must be sorted. The raw results of the competition are loaded into this array, multiplied by mintSortOrder (1 for ascending, −1 for descending). The value of mintSortOrder is discussed later. Next, the procedure calls AssignWinners (this procedure is located in Module1). The AssignWinners procedure returns the aintResult array, which identifies the final position for each competitor. For example, if there were four competitors with speed times of 50, 44, 47, and 53, aintResult would contain 3, 1, 2, 4. These values are then assigned to the lblResultN controls.

8 Insert the AssignWinners() procedure, called from frmCompetition into Module1, as shown in Figure 6-58. This procedure first copies the values in asngMeasure to a two-dimensional array, in which column 0 contains the raw measures, and column 1 contains the index of each entry from 1 to pintCompetitors. The array is then sorted, using Hilda's Simple Sort, based on the entries in column 0, swapping when needed the contents of both column 0 and of column 1. After the array has been sorted, column 1 is then copied to aintResult, which is returned to the calling member. Figure 6-59 summarizes the steps involved in assigning the order of finish to the lblResultN labels in frmCompetition.

```
Public Sub AssignWinners(ByVal vasngMeasure() As Single, _
    ByRef raintResult() As Integer)
  'copy vasngMeasure to a local, 2-dimensional array. The
  'raw scores (measures) are copied into column 1, and the
  'index values are assigned to column 2
  Dim asngCopy(pintCompetitors + 1, 2) As Single
  Dim i, intPlace As Integer
  For i = 1 To pintCompetitors
    asngCopy(i, 1) = vasngMeasure(i)
    asngCopy(i, 2) = i
  Next
  'sort the array
  Dim temp As Single
  For i = 1 To pintCompetitors - 1
    If asngCopy(i, 1) > asngCopy(i + 1, 1) Then
      temp = asngCopy(i, 1)
      asngCopy(i, 1) = asngCopy(i + 1, 1)
      asngCopy(i + 1, 1) = temp
      temp = asngCopy(i, 2)
      asngCopy(i, 2) = asngCopy(i + 1, 2)
      asngCopy(i + 1, 2) = temp
      i = 0
    End If
  Next
  intPlace = 1
  For i = 1 To pintCompetitors
    raintResult(asngCopy(i, 2)) = intPlace
    If i < pintCompetitors AndAlso _
      asngCopy(i + 1, 1) > asngCopy(i, 1) Then intPlace += 1
  Next
End Sub
```

Figure 6-58: AssignWinners() procedure in Module1

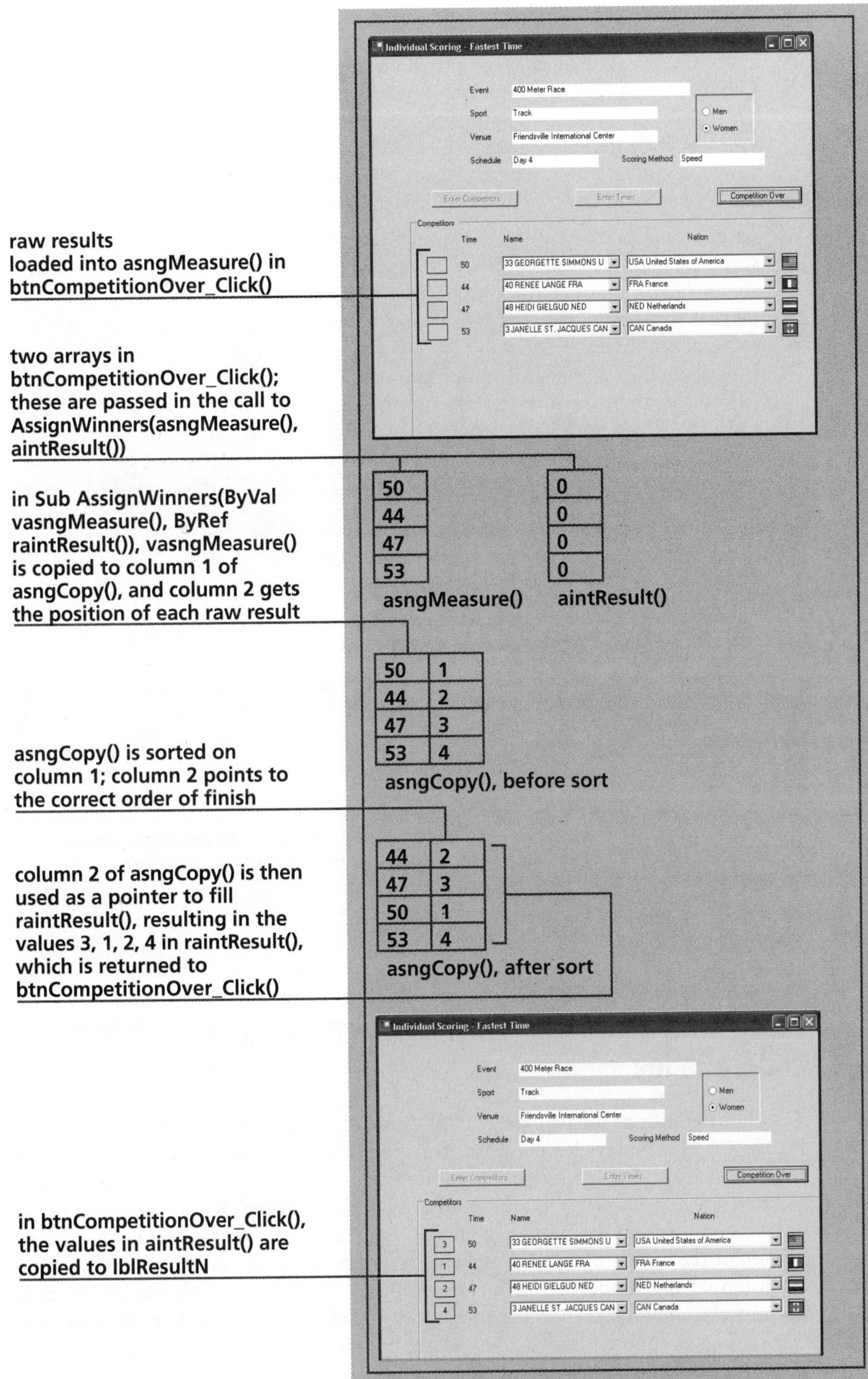

raw results
loaded into asngMeasure() in
btnCompetitionOver_Click()

two arrays in
btnCompetitionOver_Click();
these are passed in the call to
AssignWinners(asngMeasure(),
aintResult())

in Sub AssignWinners(ByVal
vasngMeasure(), ByRef
raintResult()), vasngMeasure()
is copied to column 1 of
asngCopy(), and column 2 gets
the position of each raw result

asngCopy() is sorted on
column 1; column 2 points to
the correct order of finish

column 2 of asngCopy() is then
used as a pointer to fill
raintResult(), resulting in the
values 3, 1, 2, 4 in raintResult(),
which is returned to
btnCompetitionOver_Click()

in btnCompetitionOver_Click(),
the values in aintResult() are
copied to lblResultN

Figure 6-59: Steps in determining the order of finish

9 You should test the program at this point. To see if frmCompetition works correctly, temporarily change the instantiation of frmSpeed in frmScoreMain's ListView1_Doubleclick procedure to instantiate frmCompetition instead. Then run the application, and select an event based on speed, such as a track event. After entering competitors, times, and clicking Competition Over, the result should appear similar to Figure 6-59. After testing, remember to change the reference to frmCompetition back to frmSpeed.

10 Lastly, some elements of frmCompetition must be customized for each type of scoring. To implement this idea, you need to convert frmCompetition to an abstract class, and you must require each derived class to override a procedure that provides the requisite settings. To make frmCompetition an abstract class, insert the code shown in Figure 6-60. Later, in the code for frmSpeed, frmDistance, and frmJudge—as suggested by Figure 6-60—set **lblResultsColumnHeader** to **Time**, **Distance**, or **Score**; you will set the **Text** property of btnEnterResults to **Enter Times**, **Enter Distance**, or **Enter Scores**; and set **mintSortOrder** to 1 for frmSpeed, where the lowest value ranks first, and **–1** for frmDistance and frmJudge—scores where the highest value ranks first.

```
Public MustInherit Class frmCompetition
  Inherits System.Windows.Forms.Form

  'Windows Form Designer generated code
  Public mintSortOrder As Integer = 1

  Private Sub frmCompetition_Load(ByVal sender As _
      System.Object, ByVal e As System.EventArgs) _
      Handles MyBase.Load
    NameObjects()
  End Sub

  Public MustOverride Sub NameObjects()
  'Assign the text properties of lblResultColumnHeader and
  'btnEnterResults, and assign a value to mintSortOrder
```

Figure 6-60: Declarations for an abstract class

Using Inheritance and Polymorphism: frmSpeed, frmDistance, and frmJudge

The class definitions for frmSpeed, frmDistance, and frmJudge are relatively simple. Figure 6-61 provides the code for frmSpeed. You can use this as a model for frmDistance and for frmJudge. One interesting aspect of an abstract class is noteworthy: the graphical interface (if any) of a class derived from an abstract class cannot be viewed in the Windows Form Designer. This is because the Designer must instantiate the object to materialize the view, and by its nature, an abstract class cannot be instantiated. To add or manipulate graphical objects in a class derived from an abstract class, you must enter the statements in code, and assign any nondefault property settings in code. Although you will not be able to view frmSpeed, frmDistance, or frmJudge in the Designer, you can still view frmCompetition.

```
Public Class frmSpeed
  Inherits frmCompetition

  Public Overrides Sub NameObjects()
    lblResultsColumnHeader.Text = "Time"
    btnEnterResults.Text = "Enter Times"
    mintSortOrder = 1 'ascending (fastest time wins)
  End Sub

End Class
```

Figure 6-61: Code for frmSpeed

To create the three individual scoring modules:

1   Add a new **Windows form** to the project. Name this form **frmSpeed** and name the file **frmSpeed.vb**. Using Figure 6-61 as a guide, change the **Inherits** statement to `Inherits frmCompetition`.

2   Note that the name frmSpeed has a squiggly line underneath it, meaning that it has a syntax problem. Point to **frmSpeed** with the insertion point, and read the error message. It tells you that the declaration is incomplete because it must also be an abstract class itself or contain a procedure that overrides NameObjects(). Insert the **NameObjects()** procedure, as shown in Figure 6-61.

3   Click the **Designer**, and note the error message. As mentioned previously, you cannot see frmSpeed in the Designer, because to do so would require the Designer to instantiate frmCompetition, and frmCompetition cannot be instantiated.

NOTE: An abstract class itself (frmCompetition in this case) can be seen in the Designer, but a class derived from an abstract class is not visible in the Designer. If you must change the GUI of a class derived from an abstract class, then you must do so programmatically, usually by typing code into the InitializeComponent() method.

4   In Tutorial 5, you created stub versions of frmDistance and frmJudge, containing only ctrlEventHeader plus a note that the module is under construction. Delete both of these modules now, because you will replace them with new forms derived from frmCompetition.

5   Repeat Steps 1 and 2 to create the new frmDistance. Change the column header to **Distance** and the button text to **Enter Distance**. Change the **mintSortOrder** to −1, that is, descending order.

6   Again, repeat Steps 1 and 2 to create frmJudge, making the column header **Score** and the button text **Enter Scores**. Change the **mintSortOrder** to −1, that is, descending order.

7   Run the **Scoring** application. Everything should now work. The only missing elements are the calls to FigWelcome and Logon at Startup.

Adding FigWelcome and Logon

As announced previously, the Friendsville Organizing Committee wants the standardized FigWelcome splash screen to appear with each production application produced by the FGDT. In addition, secure or limited-access applications require that the user be authorized through the Logon program. Therefore, the final version of

Scoring needs to start with the splash screen and logon. By now, you should be familiar with the procedure for adding these .DLLs to your application.

To add FigWelcome and Logon to the Scoring application:

1 Add the necessary references to the class libraries in the References list for the application.

2 Use the Imports statement to import each library before the class declaration for frmScoreMain.

3 To incorporate FigWelcome and Logon into frmScoreMain, insert the code shown in Figure 6-62 at the top of frmScoreMain_Load().

```
Static blnLogonOk, blnSupervisor As Boolean
Dim intUserNum As Integer
If Not blnLogonOk Then
  Dim frm As New frmWelcome()
  frm.ShowDialog()
  Dim MyLogonComponent As New Component1()
  MyLogonComponent.Main(blnLogonOk, blnSupervisor, _
    intUserNum)
  If blnLogonOk Then
    MsgBox("Valid user: " & blnLogonOk.ToString & _
      vbCrLf & "Record Number: " & _
      intUserNum.ToString & vbCrLf & _
      "Supervisor: " & blnSupervisor.ToString)
  Else
    End
  End If
End If
```

Figure 6-62: Incorporating FigWelcome and Logon

4 Test the completed **Scoring** application to ensure that everything works as intended.

You have now completed Tutorial 6, and the final version of the Scoring application is complete. Stop now for a break, or continue on with the exercises.

SUMMARY

■ Inheritance and polymorphism can greatly simplify complex coding tasks. Variations between implementations can be handled with overrides, overloads, shadows, and related techniques.

■ From an existing control library, you can modify the source, or you can derive from the source and modify the derived class.

■ As coding tasks become more complex, scoping rules and encapsulation become more important: public declarations should be minimized to those few elements (structures, methods, variables, constants) that are really needed throughout the project.

■ The simple sorting algorithm is applicable also to multidimensional lists, provided they are short lists.

QUESTIONS

1. The GUI of an abstract class is visible in the Designer.
   a. True
   b. False

2. The GUI of a class derived from an abstract class is visible in the Designer.
   a. True
   b. False

3. When designing a user control, you expose a method to the client application by declaring _____ accessibility for that method.

4. When designing a user control, you limit a method's exposure to only a class derived from your user control by declaring _____ accessibility for that method.

5. When designing a user control, you limit a method's exposure to only the internal definition of the class in which it is designed by declaring _____ accessibility for that method.

6. An overloaded method has multiple implementations with different _____.

7. If method A overrides method B, the two methods must have the same _____.

8. The _____ keyword declares a sealed class.

9. The _____ keyword declares an abstract class.

10. If a base class contains Public Sub A, and you want to replace this method with Public Function A in a derived class, then you should declare Public Function A with the _____ attribute.

EXERCISES

1. Convert the final Scoring application to a Windows Forms MDI application. Follow these specifications:
   a. Include a menu that essentially replicates the TreeView control in the Scoring application. The menu's root level entries are Exit, Sports, Venues, Schedule, and Window. Clicking Exit ends the application. The submenu under Sports lists the 16 sports in the Friendsville International Games, the submenu under Venues lists the eight venues, and the submenu under Schedule lists the 14 days of the Games. The Window root entry has no submenu, but its MdiList property is set to True.
   b. When a submenu item under Sports, Venues, or Schedule is selected, a child form appears containing a ListView control that displays the list of events for that sport, in that venue, or on that day. This ListView control replicates the functionality of the ListView control in the Scoring application.
   c. When the user double-clicks an item in the child form, a scoring form should be displayed modally. To do this, copy the code for ListView1_DoubleClick() in Scoring. The scoring forms (frmTeam, frmCompetition, frmSpeed, frmDistance, frmJudge) can also be used from the Scoring application.
   d. At startup, incorporate calls to FigWelcome and Logon.
   e. You do not need to replicate the functionality of the third pane in the Outlook-style interface of the final Scoring application.

2. Design and create a random access data file, named Results.dat, to save the results of each team scoring competition, using the EventID as the record key. Include the EventID, country code, and score for each team. Also include a status byte to indicate whether the record is Active (Status = A) or Inactive (Status = I). Write a console application to initialize this file. When you initialize Results.dat, make all of the records inactive, and include enough records for all of the events in Events.txt. (You will use this data file in Exercises 3 and 4.)

3. Modify the final Scoring application, adding the capability to save the results of each team competition in the Results.dat random access data file created in Exercise 2. To do this, include a Save Results button on frmTeam. When the user clicks this button, build the record for Results.dat, including the status (A) and the country code and score for each team. Then write the record to Results.dat. Note that you will need to modify CtrlTeamScore by adding two new procedures, GetScore1() and GetScore2(), because the labels containing the scores are encapsulated within CtrlTeamScore. You will need to retrieve these scores from CtrlTeamScore in order to save them in Results.dat.

4. Modify the application from Exercise 3 to also display the results of previously-reported team competition events. When the user double-clicks a team competition event in the list view, your application should check to see whether the record for that event in Results.dat is active. If the record is active, then frmTeam should display the previously-recorded results. Note that you will need to modify CtrlTeamScore by adding two new procedures, PutScore1() and PutScore2(), because the labels containing the scores are encapsulated within CtrlTeamScore. You will need to send these scores from the Results.dat record to CtrlTeamScore to be displayed in the labels of that control.

5. Add a StatusBar control to the Scoring application. Display today's date in one panel, the record number and total records in a second panel (such as "Record Number: 16/145"), and the EventID in a third panel (such as "Event ID: 16").

6. Add ContextMenu controls to frmScoreMain and frmCompetition in the Scoring application. On frmScoreMain, place a context menu on the TreeView control (with the entries Change Start Date and Exit), the ListView control (with the Entries Change Event Date and Score Event), and the third pane (with the entry Done). On frmCompetition, add a context menu to the entire form with the entries Enter Competitors, Enter Results, Competition Over, and Close. Individual entries in each context menu should be disabled or enabled when it is appropriate to do so, and must provide the functionality suggested by its title. (This involves invoking a menu item or button click event procedure.) Also, the Context MenuItem called "Enter Results" on frmCompetition must be modified in each inherited form to match the button on the form, that is, "Enter Scores" for frmJudge, "Enter Distance" for frmDistance, and "Enter Times" for frmSpeed.

Exercises 7 and 8 allow you to discover the solution to problems on your own and experiment with material that is not covered explicitly in the tutorial.

discovery ▶ 7. Identify each component of the Scoring application that could be a sealed class, and implement your decisions. Explain why each class, form, module, and user control is or is not a possible sealed class.

discovery ▶ 8. Start with a 3 × 3, two-dimensional array of randomly selected integers. Sort the array and display it so that the values appear in ascending numerical order. For example, if the original array contains:

```
4    7    15
27   2    7
1    14   12
```

the final array should appear as:

```
1    2    4
7    7    12
14   15   27
```

KEY TERMS

- abstract class
- Active property
- AutomaticDelay property
- AutoPopDelay property
- AutoSize() method
- base class
- BoldedDates property
- CalendarDimensions property
- CloneMenu() method
- Contents property
- ContextMenu control
- CustomFormat property
- DateTimePicker control
- DecimalPlaces property
- derived class
- DomainUpDown control
- DownButton method
- Handles phrase
- Hexadecimal property
- HorizontalScrollBar control
- Increment property
- inheritance
- InitialDelay property
- LargeChange property
- MaxDate property
- Maximum property
- MinDate property
- Minimum property
- MonthCalendar control
- MustInherit class attribute
- MustOverride procedure attribute
- NotInheritable class attribute
- NumericUpDown control
- Overloads procedure attribute
- Overridable procedure attribute
- Overrides procedure attribute
- Panels collection
- polymorphism
- Popup event
- ProgressBar control
- ReshowDelay property
- RichTextBox control
- sealed class
- SelectionCount property
- SelectionEnd property
- SelectionRange property
- SelectionStart property
- Shadows procedure attribute
- ShowAlways property
- ShowToday property

- ShowTodayCircle property
- ShowWeekNumber property
- SmallChange property
- StatusBar control
- StatusBarPanel object
- ThousandsSeparator property
- TickFrequency property
- TitleBackColor property
- TitleForeColor property
- ToLongDateString method
- ToolTip component
- ToolTipText property
- ToShortTimeString method
- TrackBar control
- TrailingForeColor property
- UpButton method
- ValueChanged event
- VerticalScrollBar control
- Wrap property

Web Forms: Web Pages with Server Controls

The EventSchedule Application

case ▶ The main Visual Basic .NET applications that the Friendsville Games Development Team has built so far are intended for use by the staff of the Friendsville International Games. The Dining Hall Seat Assigner is used by the food services staff; the Competition Scoring application supports the judges, officials, and public information office; LogonManager is used by the FGDT itself to authorize and monitor the use of FIG programs and data. However, the FGDT also needs to develop some applications that will be used by the public, including some that will be accessed over the World Wide Web. In this tutorial, Hilda Reiner (FGDT team leader), Rick Sanchez, Althea Brown, and you turn your attention to Web-based applications intended for the general public.

The first Web application the FGDT team creates allows the public to view the schedule of events for the Friendsville International Games, along with seating diagrams for the various venues and ticket prices for each event. The users of this application will decide which events, sports, venues, or days to view. Therefore, although there is no database access involved, the application does need to interact with a server. For this reason, it needs to be created as an interactive Web Forms application rather than a static HTML Web page. In Tutorial 9 you will learn how to access and update a database in a Windows Forms application, and in Tutorial 10 you will learn how to incorporate and update a database from a Web Forms application.

Previewing the EventSchedule Web Forms Application

Previewing a Web Forms application is not quite as simple as previewing a Windows Forms application, which simply requires you to run the executable on a Windows machine. A Web Forms application actually runs on a different (though virtual) machine—a Web server, running under Internet Information Server (IIS). And, the application is housed in a virtual directory, where it is protected from the local machine, and where it cannot do any damage to the local machine. All of these security features are critical to the proper functioning of a public network such as the Internet, as you shall soon discover.

> **NOTE:** This application must be installed on a computer that is running Internet Information Server (IIS) 5.0 or later. You must have permission to run the installer on the computer, and you must also have IIS permissions. If this is your own computer, just log on as an administrator. If this is not your computer or network, you may need to ask for assistance from the system administrator.

▶ This deployment project deploys the EventSchedule ASP.NET Web Forms application to the FigEvents virtual folder. No source code is included in this install. Another deployment project, which has been made available to your instructor, installs the application to the FIG virtual folder and does include the source code.

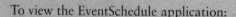

To view the EventSchedule application:

1 Copy all of the files in the DeployEventScheduleWithoutSourcecode Debug folder to your Web server computer. Then run **Setup.exe** in that folder.

2 Start your Web browser. Navigate to **http://localhost/FigEvents**. The opening page of the EventSchedule application appears, as shown in Figure 7-1.

Figure 7-1: EventSchedule opening Web page

3 Under Category, click **Sports**. The Subcategory Baseball appears. Under Events, click the game between the USA and Japan under Baseball Events. The page should now appear as in Figure 7-2. Note how the scoring method is displayed. Note the schedule information: the day of the games, the calendar date, and the time.

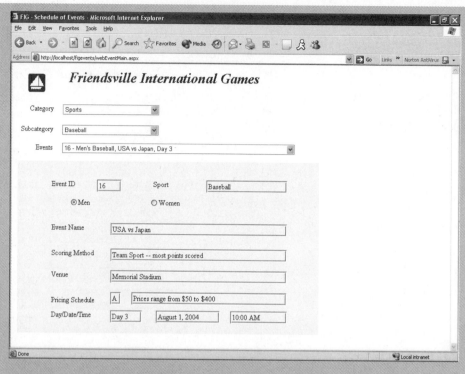

Figure 7-2: Schedule for a baseball game between USA and Japan

4 Under Subcategory, click **Equestrian**. Under Events, select **Women's Equestrian Dressage**, Day 6 under Equestrian Events in the drop-down list. The result should appear as in Figure 7-3.

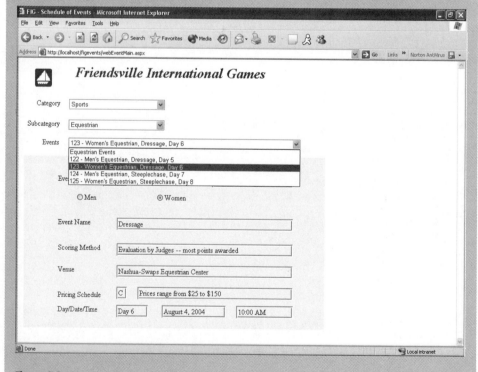

Figure 7-3: Women's Equestrian event—Dressage

5 Under Category, click **Venue Event Schedule**. The Subcategory combo box fills with the names of the venues. Then if you pick a particular venue from the Subcategory drop-down list, the list of events at that venue appears in the Events combo box. Similarly, clicking Days under Category causes the Subcategory drop-down list to fill with the days of the games, and then selecting one of the days causes the Events combo box to fill with all of the events scheduled to take place on that day.

6 Under Category, click **Venue Price Schedule**. A hyperlink appears, as shown in Figure 7-4. Click the **Click for Venue Seating and Prices** hyperlink to see the top of the Venue Seating Diagrams and Pricing Schedules page, as shown in Figure 7-5. This page also explains the seating and pricing schedules: all seats in all venues are color-coded, from red (most expensive seats), to blue, then yellow, and then green. Of course, not all venues have four color categories. Seats for each event are offered in one of three pricing schedules—A, B, and C—depending on the anticipated demand for tickets for each event.

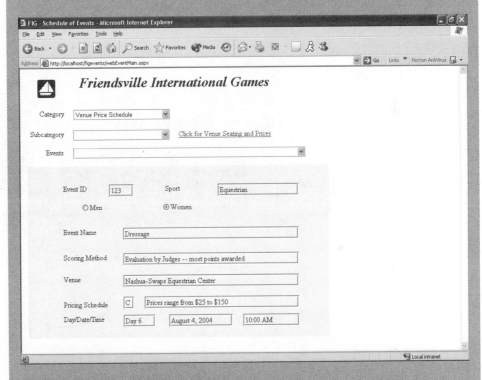

Figure 7-4: Hyperlink to the venue seating diagrams and prices

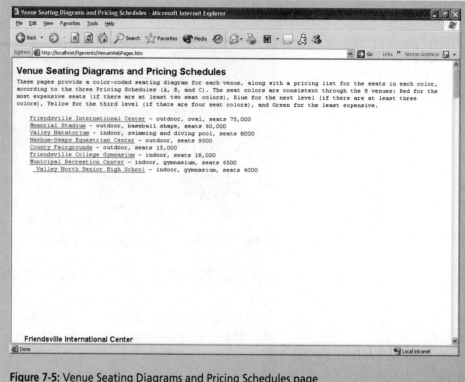

Figure 7-5: Venue Seating Diagrams and Pricing Schedules page

7 Click the **County Fairgrounds** hyperlink to see the seating diagram and price schedules for that venue, as shown in Figure 7-6. Similar displays can be seen for each venue. Click the **Back** button to return to previous pages or back to the main page for the application.

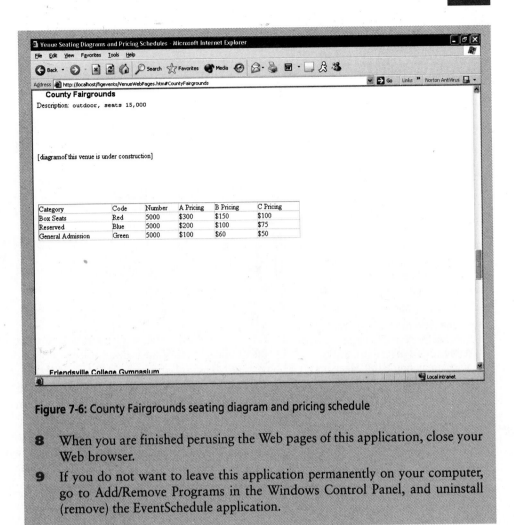

Figure 7-6: County Fairgrounds seating diagram and pricing schedule

8   When you are finished perusing the Web pages of this application, close your Web browser.

9   If you do not want to leave this application permanently on your computer, go to Add/Remove Programs in the Windows Control Panel, and uninstall (remove) the EventSchedule application.

- Understand the background of the Internet, and the notions of packet switching and a stateless medium

- Understand the operating principles of the World Wide Web, especially HTML, Web browser software, HTTP, and the Web's cataloging scheme and search engines

- Understand the features of XML that make it the language of choice for Web-based computer applications

- Define and describe ASP.NET Web Forms applications

- Understand the basic approach to the construction and deployment of Web Forms applications, distinguishing among HTML elements and client controls, HTML server controls, and Web server controls

- Describe the importance of workarounds

The World Wide Web: Environment for Web Forms Applications

Lesson A introduces the basic programming concepts involved in building Web Forms applications. What it does not do is provide a comprehensive introduction to Hypertext Markup Language (HTML), Web pages, and the World Wide Web. These topics are mentioned here in a most cursory fashion, as they really are the subject of another course and deserve far more in-depth coverage than can be provided in one chapter of a book about Visual Basic .NET. But with that caveat, you should be able to follow the discussion and implement the solutions provided in this tutorial, even if you are a novice Web-page developer. Following the Background section, you focus on the Visual Basic .NET computer programming that lies behind a Web Forms application, rather than on the internal coding of the Web page.

Background: Before There Were Web Forms...

Several technical developments laid the foundation for Visual Basic .NET Web Forms applications. First, of course, is the Internet itself, initiated in 1969. Next is the World Wide Web, introduced in 1989. And the third is XML (eXtensible Markup Language), which evolved during the 1990s.

The Internet

The Internet started as ARPANET, a creation of the U.S. Department of Defense's Advanced Research Projects Agency (ARPA). The original idea was to develop a computer network linking the Defense Department's research laboratories and the universities performing defense-related research. From the beginning, two fundamental notions made it possible for ARPANET to grow way beyond its initial purpose: first, the network would have no central computer in control of all of its nodes. (A node is a connection point to a communications network.) In 1969, this was a relatively revolutionary idea. Second, the network would handle only unclassified information. Because the data was not classified, it did not need to be related absolutely to military research, and as a result, participating universities began adapting the network to other educational purposes. Ultimately, the nondefense use of ARPANET overshadowed the defense-related use, and the Department of Defense decided to transfer the responsibility for the network to a civilian agency. Thus, the network was renamed the Internet (that is, a network of networks), and in 1983, the U.S. military introduced its own MILNET to assume the defense-related work of ARPANET. Within a few years, the Internet began to be adapted for commercial purposes, a trend greatly facilitated by the advent of the World Wide Web.

Today's Internet consists of an Internet backbone—mostly fiber-optic cable and communications satellites, plus routers and switches. Well over a million servers are interconnected through the Internet.

You should also appreciate two characteristics of the modern Internet:

- The Internet is a packet-switched network.
- The Internet is stateless.

Packet Switched

A **packet-switched network** is one in which messages are transmitted from node to node in fixed-length message blocks called packets. An individual message, at its origination, is divided into sequentially numbered packets. Each packet consists of a header identifying the origination and destination computers, a date-time stamp, and the packet number, followed by the packet body. When a packet is transmitted, each computer that receives the packet has the task of forwarding the message to another point in the Internet that is closer to its destination. Because this happens in real time and the available transmission paths are often busy, the "path of least resistance" from the origination point to the destination point changes constantly, and is not necessarily the most direct route. Therefore, packets do not necessarily arrive at their destination in the same order as they were sent. The destination computer, when it has received all of the parts of a message, reassembles the original message by putting the packets in the correct sequence. The protocol for accomplishing all of this work is called **Transmission Control Protocol/Internet Protocol**, or **TCP/IP**. TCP involves creating the packets at the origination end and reassembling the packets into the complete message at the destination end; the IP portion involves the method of switching, storing, and forwarding packets from node to node.

Stateless

After a transmission has been completed, the Internet itself forgets about it. That is to say, the Internet does not maintain knowledge concerning the originator, recipient, or contents of messages, nor does it maintain a connection between the originator and the recipient (the server and the client). Another way of explaining this characteristic is that the Internet does not maintain session state. However, if you are using the Internet to purchase books from Course Technology, then both you and the publisher have a keen interest in remembering who you are, what books you have selected, where they should be shipped, and how they are being paid for. For you and Course Technology, these kinds of interactions do need to maintain session state.

A number of protocols and services are devoted to this issue of session state. An in-depth treatment of session state is beyond this text, but you should be aware of this issue, because it helps to explain the structure and behavior of Web forms. For example, you are accustomed to declaring a module-level variable within a Windows Form. You expect that variable to come into existence when the Windows form is loaded and to remain in existence as long as the application is running and the form has not been closed. Because the Internet is a stateless medium, Web forms do not work that way. Rather, every time an event on a Web form forces data to be sent back to the server (called a PostBack event), the code for that Web page is reloaded—and any variable declarations begin anew.

The World Wide Web

Since the mid 1990s, some people have begun to equate the World Wide Web with the Internet, but actually the Web is only one of the services available on the Internet. The others include Telnet (remote computing), Usenet newsgroups, File Transfer Protocol (FTP), Standard Mail Transfer Protocol (SMTP) for e-mail, and Gopher (a text-based menu system)—all of which are considerably older than the Web.

The **World Wide Web** is based on the pioneering work of Tim Berners Lee, who introduced the Web in 1989 as a means for sharing information among the world's nuclear research centers. The basic motivation behind the invention of the Web was the need of nuclear physicists to share research findings and information. A researcher in one locale might suspect that information relevant to his research was available in other research centers around the world, but unless he knew exactly which documents were in exactly which center, he had no way of locating and obtaining those documents. Tim Berners Lee designed the World Wide Web as a solution to this problem. The Web has come to so dominate our thinking about the Internet and about modern business, that for some of us, life without the Web is no longer imaginable, and many seem to think that the Web has been with us for as long as the telephone. It may surprise you to find that in 1993, the World Wide Web consisted of about 50 Web sites.

The Web depends on several facilities, over and above the basic Internet protocols (TCP/IP) described earlier. These are Hypertext Markup Language (HTML), Web browser software, Hypertext Transfer Protocol (HTTP), a cataloging or registration scheme, and search engines.

Hypertext Markup Language (HTML)

Web pages consist of content elements (that is, the text and images that are to be displayed in the Web page) along with HTML tags, which are instructions that dictate how the content elements are to be displayed. In general, **markup languages** are inserted into a text document (that is, they "mark up" the text) in order to describe the data or provide formatting or processing instructions. Many markup languages exist, modeled more or less on the Standard Generalized Markup Language (SGML) developed in the 1960s and 1970s. In the case of **Hypertext Markup Language (HTML)**, the purpose is to describe the presentation of the data, that is, to provide formatting instructions. Figure 7-7 is an example of a simple Web page, and Figure 7-8 is the same page in HTML view. Fundamentally, the purpose of HTML is to provide a standardized method for providing format instructions for a document, a method that can be properly interpreted (or "materialized") by any Web browser, regardless of the platform on which the browser resides.

Figure 7-7: A simple Web page, in normal view

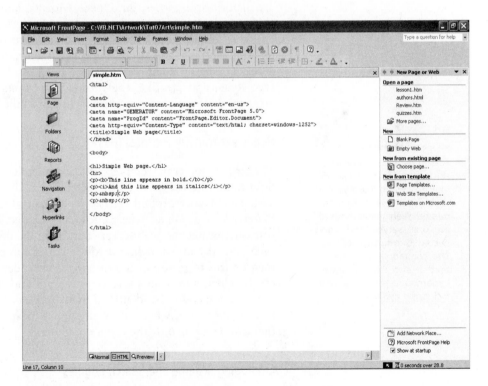

Figure 7-8: A simple Web page, in HTML view

HTML tags are enclosed in angled brackets (< >). Each tag refers to the text that follows the tag. Most tags mark a spot where particular formatting begins, and the same tag preceded by a forward slash marks the end of that formatting. Study Figure 7-8, noting the following tag pairs: <html> and </html> enclose the entire document, indicating that the markup language for this document is HTML. <head> and </head> surround the document header information, providing information about the language (English-US), the software that created the document (Microsoft FrontPage 5.0), and related items. The actual body of the document is enclosed between the <body> and </body> tags. The first line of the body is in Heading 1 style, indicated by the <h1> and </h1> tags. The <hr> tag indicates that a horizontal rule (that is, a divider line) should be inserted. <p> and </p> indicate a paragraph; <b> and </b> enclose bolded text; and <i> and </i> enclose italicized text. Although dozens of additional HTML tags exist, you can get a basic understanding of how HTML tags work without going into much more detail.

Web Browser Software

Web browser software resides on a client, end-user computer. Its main purpose is to properly interpret the markup language tags in a Web page and render the page on the client computer's screen. A Web browser also interprets hypertext—links to other Web pages. The first Web browser from Tim Berners Lee (1989) was rather rudimentary by today's standards. In 1992, Marc Andreesen and friends at the University of Illinois developed Mosaic, a vastly improved browser. Mosaic offered many new tags, allowed text and images to be intermingled on one page, and translated a hypertext link directly into a connection to another Web page. Subsequently, many browsers have come into existence. Internet Explorer and Netscape Navigator are the principle entries, but Opera, Mozilla, and others have also been developed. (Marc Andreesen was a main developer for Netscape Navigator.)

The **Web browser** allows any Web page to be displayed, masking and accommodating differences among operating systems, monitors, and graphics software. To accommodate different screen sizes, screen resolutions, color capabilities, available type fonts, and the like, the browser interprets each formatting instruction and arranges the visual display as best it can, given the capabilities of the client computer.

Hypertext Transfer Protocol (HTTP)

The term "hypertext" refers to text that includes a hidden reference (called a hyperlink) to another Web page, Web site, or location within the current or a different Web page. Hypertext and HTTP are the central features that make the World Wide Web what it is. When a user clicks a hypertext link on a Web page, the browser software locates the Web server containing the destination Web page, retrieves that Web page (by downloading it to the client computer), and opens it. The browser then returns to its job of interpreting and rendering the newly retrieved document on the client computer's screen. To locate and retrieve a Web page, the browser needs only its address, identified by its Internet URL (Uniform Resource Locator). It does not matter where the Web page is located, as long as it resides on a server that can be reached by the client computer.

Cataloging Scheme and Search Engines

To best serve our communications needs, Web servers (and other Internet servers) are identified by words. A **URL address** consists of the Internet service, the domain name, the path to the Web page (if necessary), and the title of the Web page (if necessary).

tip

A Web page is an individual document file that can be materialized in a browser; a Web site is a series of inter-related Web pages housed on one server and connected through hyperlinks. The common term "hypertext" is also taken to mean hypermedia—an image that includes a hyperlink.

The **domain name** correlates to the Internet Protocol (IP) address of the server. The format is shown in these examples:

- *http://www.course.com*—Course Technology's Website; if a URL contains no filename, the browser searches for index.html or Welcome.html. (The filename extension can be .htm.)
- *http://academic.pgcc.edu/~bspear/*—The author's homepage; again, the actual filename is index.html.
- *http://www.inform.umd.edu/EdRes/UgradInfo/UgradStudies/bulletin.html*—The URL includes the path to the document as well as the document name itself.
- *ftp://ftp.microsoft.com*—Microsoft Corporation's File Transfer Protocol site, used for uploading and downloading files.
- *telnet://wam.umd.edu*—This URL defines a telnet address.

The **domain name server** (**DNS**) for a Web server usually consists of www, followed by a meaningful domain name, and the top-level domain (TLD). (If a server's IP address is known, you can always reach it with the numeric address rather than the domain name.)

When the Web was invented, the number of participating servers was small enough so that all extant Web pages could be searched for any information residing on any server. As the Web mushroomed, the matter of naming conventions, registration of DNSs, and identification of Web pages by title and subject became increasingly important. An organization called ICANN (Internet Corporation for Assigned Names and Numbers) was created to handle the matter of naming conventions, registrations, and IP address assignments. Initially, seven generic top-level domains (gTLD) were established, listed in Figure 7-9. In the last few years, some of ICANN's responsibilities have been reassigned to other interest groups, and seven additional generic top-level domains have been established, also shown in Figure 7-9. Every nation participating in the Internet also has a TLD consisting of the country abbreviation (us, uk, fr, it, de, etc.), and it can administer names within that TLD as it sees fit.

Original top-level domains		Additional top-level domains	
.com	Commercial	.aero	Aerospace industry
.edu	U.S. educational institutions	.biz	Business
.gov	U.S. government	.coop	Cooperatives
.int	International institutions	.info	Information services
.mil	U.S. military	.museum	Museums
.net	Network providers	.name	Individual persons
.org	Nongovernmental organizations	.pro	Professional persons

Figure 7-9: The Internet's top-level domains

A Web server hosts any number of Web sites, each of which contains any number of Web pages subdivided into any number of folders and subfolders. Because the World Wide Web now contains millions of Web pages, searching all of the available pages is a formidable, even an impossible, task. Therefore, search engines have been developed that narrow a user's search for relevant Web pages to those that meet certain stated search criteria. A **search engine** is a software program combined with a database, where the database consists of an index of Web pages, and the software program searches through the database looking for matches. Technically, publishing a Web page only involves putting the Web page file(s) on a Web server. To be useful to the public, publishing a Web page also involves registering that page with the major search engines.

eXtensible Markup Language (XML)

As the number of participating servers, users, and applications on the Web grew, many inherent weaknesses in the original HTML scheme became apparent. First, HTML did not support any meaningful interactivity with the user—it only provided a means for a browser to render static Web pages in a standardized fashion regardless of platform. Second, each formatting instruction stood independent of every other instruction, making page modification and maintenance difficult. For instance, if you wanted to change the font color of all headings to red, the only way to accomplish this was to move painstakingly through the document, looking for each heading tag, and adding the appropriate font color tag. Third, the content was confounded with the HTML tags, again making maintenance difficult. And fourth, a Web designer could only use the predefined HTML tags; the software did not permit any new tags to be created by the user.

Several innovations were designed to address these difficulties. Various scripting languages were introduced: CGI Script, JavaScript, VBScript, and JScript. These languages addressed the related issues of interactivity (with users) and the maintenance of session state (between computers). Interactivity requires the use of variables and the updating of databases, so that users can fill out forms, for example, and submit variable information to a database. Scripting languages, as well as full-fledged programming languages such as Java and C++, were used to create applets (small applications that execute on a client machine) and servlets (small applications that execute on the server machine). Both applets and servlets often consist of Java byte code, executed on the destination computer (whether the client or the server) using the operating system's built-in Java virtual machine (JVM).

Although applets gained currency for a few years, for several reasons they have been largely replaced by servlets. The first insurmountable hurdle for applets is that they depend on a common Java virtual machine on each client computer, but the various platform manufacturers could never agree on a single JVM standard, so the dream of true cross-platform portability was never realized. Second, the expectations for applets were probably set too high: proponents talked of applets that would replace personal productivity software on client machines, such as the Microsoft Office suite or Quicken. But downloading an applet that replaces a 10 MB package such as MS Word every time you want to write a memo was not an achievable or realistic goal. Third, applets gave rise to security concerns, because applets intrinsically give access to the client's machine, where nefarious applets might damage the client, interfere with other applications, or surreptitiously harvest private data from the client machine. Because servlets run on the server, they do not make the client machine vulnerable.

The World Wide Web Consortium (W3C) approved enhanced versions of HTML, resulting finally in HTML 4.0, while Microsoft introduced Dynamic HTML (DHTML). These improvements included cascading style sheets (CSS), which allow the Web page designer to design formats (styles) for a Web page, and then to reference the defined style sheet within the Web page itself. This serves the purpose of separating data content from the presentation of the data, and allows subsequent modification of a style in only one place rather than at each occurrence inside a Web page. For example, if the user decided that every Heading 1 should appear in red, then the definition of Heading 1 in the CSS file could include the specification of red as the font color. Then, any reference to Heading 1 in the Web page itself would use the CSS definition and appear in red.

In 1998, all of the early improvements to HTML were subsumed into XML. Adopted by W3C and endorsed by all the major software manufacturers and vendors and embraced by the programming community, **eXtensible Markup Language (XML)** has become the standard on which Web applications are now based. XML may be the most significant improvement to the World Wide Web in the last decade. Today, a Web designer/programmer develops an XML document and associated style sheets. XML Web services include the definition of datasets and specification of processing instructions. In the Microsoft programming world, the foundation technology for implementing XML is Active Server Pages in the .NET Framework (ASP.NET).

Web-based applications are categorized in several ways. First, they can be client-based or server-based. Client-based Web applications are computer programs delivered to a local browser, and executed on the client machine. By contrast, server-based applications execute on the server. Client-based applications include static Web pages, Windows Forms applications distributed to the client machine, and applets executing on the client. Server-based applications include XML documents containing or referencing servlets, applications that run on the server, and applications that update a database accessed through the server. Visual Basic .NET Web Forms applications consist of ASP.NET Web pages plus server-based code.

ASP.NET Web Forms Applications

Although XML is a welcome, standards-based initiative, actually developing XML documents and applications remains a challenging task. This is where Visual Basic .NET Web Forms applications come in. Literally millions of programmers have been exposed to earlier versions of Visual Basic and have learned to develop Windows applications using Visual Basic's straightforward and understandable syntax and programming constructs. With Visual Basic 6.0, some limited support for Web-oriented applications was also provided. Visual Basic .NET extends both the simplicity and robustness of Visual Basic to the World Wide Web. With Visual Basic .NET Web Forms, you design XML applications that consist of ASP.NET documents materialized in a browser, XML Web services that provide data, and ASP.NET code that executes on the Web server.

And you can accomplish all of this without learning to program in XML itself. Almost all of the coding techniques and most of the graphical objects that you have learned concerning Visual Basic .NET Windows Forms also exist for Web Forms. You design the GUI using the Web Form Designer, much the same way as with the Windows Form Designer. Visual Basic .NET saves this as an ASP.NET Web page (.aspx file), translating the graphical design elements into XML. You also write code for this Web page in the Code Editor, the same as you wrote code in the Code Editor for a Windows form. The code (referred to by Microsoft as the CodeBehind module) is saved in an .aspx.vb file.

When you start a new ASP.NET Web application, Visual Basic .NET creates the main Web Forms file (WebForm1.aspx) plus a number of support files, including Global.asax.vb, Styles.css, Web.config, and WebApplication1.vsdisco. From the discussion of Web-based applications up to this point, the role of each of these files becomes readily apparent by examining its code. Although you do not modify any of these support files in the applications introduced in this text, you should nevertheless understand the purpose of each. In the next section of this lesson, you examine the structure of the support files first, and then consider the main Web Forms file.

Web Forms Application Support Files

The optional file **Global.asax.vb** (along with the related Global.asax and Global. asax.resx) provides a common structure for all of the code necessary to maintain session state, if this is needed in your application. The default skeleton form of Global.asax is shown in Figure 7-10. If your application needs specialized code for maintaining session state, this is where you would put it. If your application does not need to maintain session state, then these three support files are unnecessary.

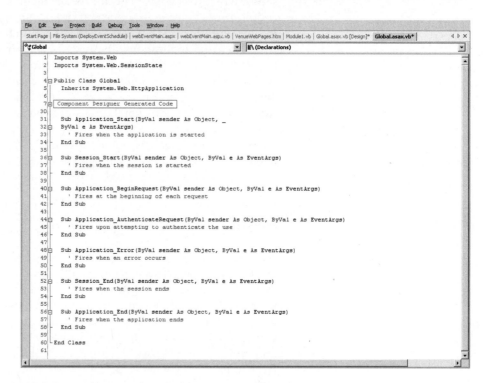

Figure 7-10: Global.asax.vb default skeleton contents

Styles.css provides the cascading style sheet for a Visual Basic .NET Web Forms application. This is in the standard format of any XML cascading style sheet. Styles.css provides default values for all necessary styles, which are used unless overridden on individual Web pages. Figure 7-11 shows the beginning of the default Styles.css created by Visual Basic .NET. You would not normally modify the settings in this file.

Web.config sets the system configuration for the application, including the compilation language, dynamic debugging option, error trapping, authentication, authorization, tracing, session state options, and globalization (8, 16, or 24-bit encoding). The default Web.config file includes comments that explain all of these configuration settings. A portion of this file (without the detailed comments) is shown in Figure 7-12. You can see the entire file, including the comments, by double-clicking it in Solution Explorer.

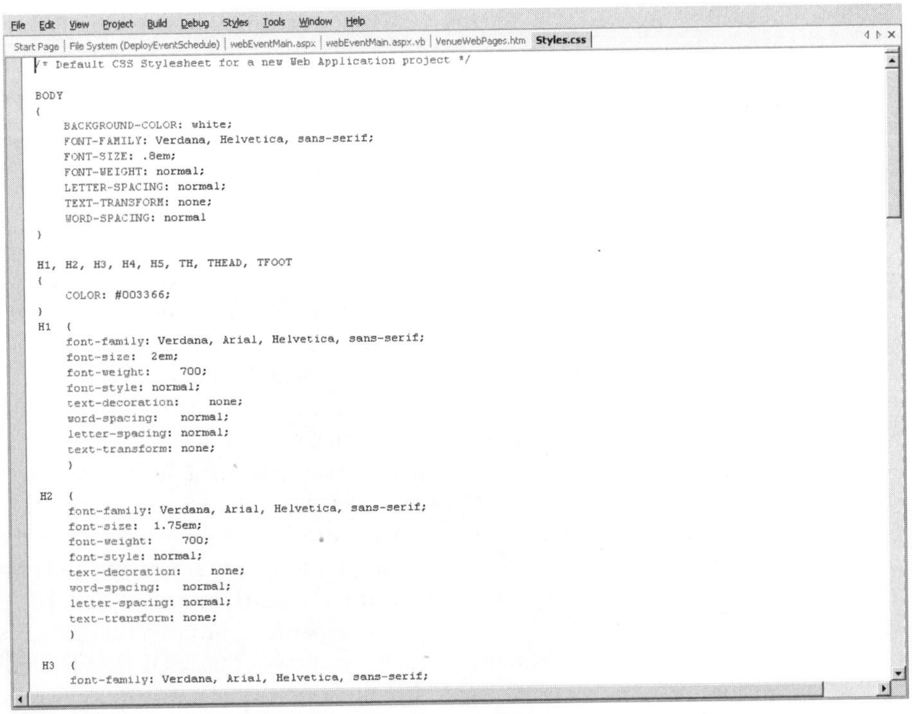

Figure 7-11: Default Styles.css for a Web Forms application

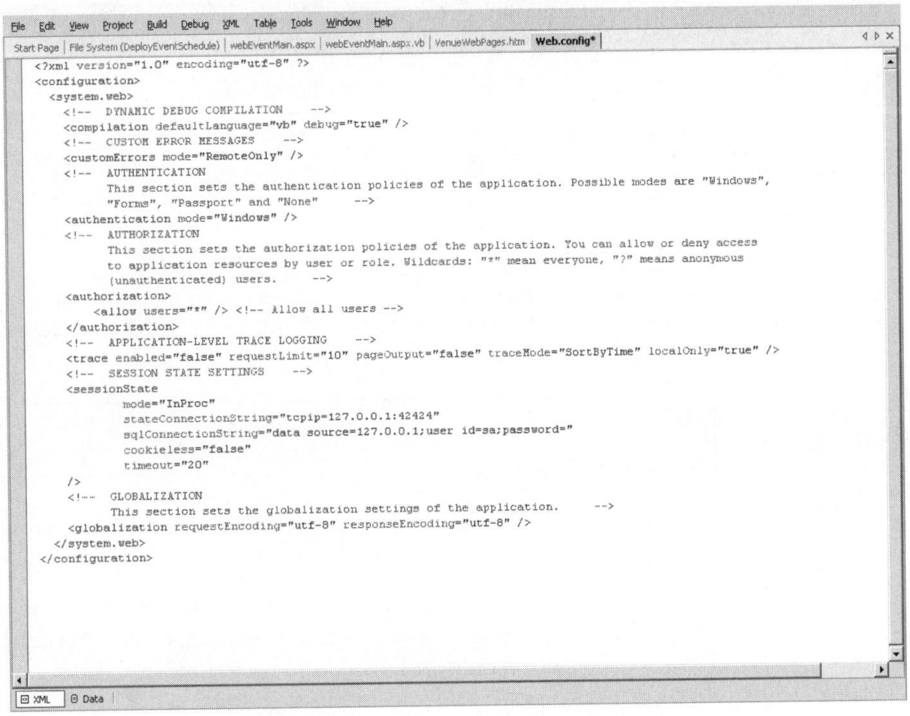

Figure 7-12: Default Web.config for a Visual Basic .NET Web Forms application

If your application includes or uses one or more XML Web services, and if the owner of the Web service wants the public to be able to discover the service, then the file **WebApplication1.vsdisco** serves as a container for links (URLs) to discovery files that describe the XML Web service. A **discovery file** contains the URL of a Web site within which the source code for an XML Web service may be dynamically discovered. XML Web services are discussed more fully in Tutorial 9.

WebForm1—the Web Form Itself

As you know, Console applications consist only of code, contained in modules, Module1 being the default name for the first module (the name Module1 can be altered). The core of a Windows Forms application is contained in Windows Forms, Form1 being the default name of the first form. Form1 is stored in two files: Form1.vb (containing both the GUI and the code) and Form1.resx (an XML resource file, which identifies the files containing XML schemas for datasets used by the form). The main part of a Web Forms application is contained in Web Forms, WebForm1 being the default name of the first Web form. WebForm1 is stored in three files: WebForm1.aspx (which contains the GUI only), WebForm1.aspx.vb (the "CodeBehind" module, containing the code for WebForm1.aspx), and WebForm1.aspx.resx (again, the XML resource file). The reason that the GUI and the code for a Web form are separated into two files is that they are executed on different (sometimes virtual) machines. The GUI is delivered to a client computer and rendered through that client's browser software, whereas the CodeBehind is executed directly on the server. See Figure 7-13 for a summary of project-related files for the three fundamental project types in Visual Basic .NET.

Project type	Console	Windows	Web
GUI	None	Form1.vb	WebForm1.aspx
Code	Module1.vb	Form1.vb	WebForm1.aspx.vb
XML resources	None	Form1.resx	WebForm1.aspx.resx, Web.config, Styles.css
Assembly	AssemblyInfo.vb	AssemblyInfo.vb	AssemblyInfo.vb
Project information	ConsoleApplication1.vbproj, ConsoleApplication1.vbproj.user	WindowsApplication1.vbproj, WindowsApplication1.vbproj.user	WebApplication1.vbproj, WebApplication1.vbproj.webinfo, WebApplication1.vsdisco
Session state information	None	None	Global.asax, Global.asax.vb, Global.asax.resx

Figure 7-13: Summary of project files—default names

As you have already read, one advantage of Web Forms applications for a Visual Basic programmer is that nearly everything you have already learned about Windows Forms is transferable to Visual Basic .NET Web Forms. A few things, however, do require explanation. This includes the basic page layout of the Web Form, HTML controls, and Web Server controls.

If you are unfamiliar with HTML design and scripting, you can refer to the dozens of Help screens concerning HTML in the Visual Studio .NET Framework documentation, or refer to a Web page or XML design text.

HTML Elements

When a Web Form appears in the Web Form Designer, the Toolbox has tabs for HTML elements/controls and for Web Forms controls. Intrinsic HTML elements available under the Toolbox's HTML tab include static text and browser (client) controls that may run client-side script. You can place these on your Web form, and they will work as they always do in any HTML document. HTML elements have attributes that you can set using the Properties window in the IDE.

HTML Server Controls

You can convert some HTML elements into **HTML server controls**, that is, controls associated with code that executes on the server. Most of the attributes of the (former) HTML element map directly to properties of the (new) HTML server control, and are available programmatically, although a few of the property names are different from their counterpart Windows Forms or Web Forms controls. For example, a Text Field HTML element, when converted to an HTML server control, functions similarly to a TextBox control, though it has a Value property instead of a Text property.

Not all HTML elements can become server controls. For example, static text typed into a Web Form is not accessible from the server, nor can most events associated with that text be trapped by server-side code.

If you have an HTML server control and subsequently decide that you do not need any server-side code related to it, you should convert the HTML server control back into a simple HTML element, because HTML server controls use machine resources. Ideally, a Web form should only contain Web server controls and HTML server controls that require server-side code.

Web Server Controls

Visual Basic .NET also offers some 30 Web server controls, available in the Web Form Designer from the Web Forms tab of the Toolbox. Many (but not all) of these Web server controls correspond to similar Windows Forms controls. A few provide functionality that is tailored to Web-based applications. For example, the AdRotator control provides the capability to display randomly selected banner ads or announcements on a Web page. The many validation-related controls result from the fact that a principle use of Web Forms is to collect input data from the user, the validation of input data being of paramount importance to Web developers. Figure 7-14 lists the Web Forms server controls and corresponding Windows Forms controls.

Web Forms server control	Windows Forms control	Purpose
AdRotator	None	Cycles through a series of clickable banner ads
Button	Button	Clickable text button
Calendar	MonthCalendar, DateTimePicker	
CheckBox	CheckBox	

Figure 7-14: Web server controls and corresponding Windows Forms controls

Web Forms server control	Windows Forms control	Purpose
CheckBoxList	CheckedListBox	
CrystalReportViewer	CrystalReportViewer	
DataGrid	DataGrid	
DataList	None	Display rows in a table
DropDownList	ComboBox	
Hyperlink	LinkLabel	
Image	PictureBox	
ImageButton	Button	Clickable picture button
Label	Label	
LinkButton	LinkLabel	Clickable button/ hyperlink
ListBox	ListBox	
Literal	None	Similar to a Label
Panel	Panel	
PlaceHolder	None	Container for controls dynamically added or removed
RadioButton	RadioButton	
RadioButtonList	None	A group of radio buttons
Repeater	None	Container for a list of data items, displayed in custom templates
Table	None	Displays a table, created and manipulated dynamically
TextBox	TextBox	
Timer (under the Component tab)	Timer	
ValidationSummary	None	Displays a summary of errors
XML	None	Reads XML data and writes it to a Web page at this control's location
Validation Web Server controls: The following five controls are used to validate user input on Web Forms pages. They have no counterparts in Windows Forms controls.		
CompareValidator	Compares user's entry to a variable or static value	
RangeValidator	Ensures user's entry falls within a specified range	
RegularExpressionValidator	Ensures user's entry matches a specified pattern	
RequiredFieldValidator	Prevents the user from skipping a required field	
CustomValidator	Allows you to apply your own validation logic	

Figure 7-14: Web server controls and corresponding Windows Forms controls (continued)

Although many of the properties of these Web server controls are the same or similar to the corresponding Windows Forms controls, there are some generic differences with respect to events. These differences often stem from the fact that the Web page is rendered in a browser on a client machine, whereas the code is executed on the server, which is usually a different, and often a remote, machine. Many events that are trapped in a Windows Forms application, triggering any associated code, are not trapped at all in a Web Forms application, because to do so would overburden the network with the transmission of a constant stream of trivial event data from the client to the server, most of which would not trigger any code execution anyway. For example, MouseOver and MouseMove events are not trapped on a Web page. Many other events, which are indeed trapped on the client, are not immediately posted to the server, but rather await the next click event or other event that is posted. This technique is used for most change events—Text_Changed, Value_Changed, and so on. When the user is filling out a typical form, all of the text boxes are filled before the user clicks the "Submit" button, causing the page to be posted to the server where all of the user-entered data items are processed at once. However, you can force a change event to be immediately posted to the server by setting the AutoPostBack property to True.

A Web form may contain HTML elements, HTML server controls, and Web server controls—you can mix and match them as you see fit. From a design standpoint, one type of control might be preferred over the other, depending on such factors as these:

- If the control triggers both client-side and server-side script, then an HTML server control is required.
- Some Web server controls, such as AdRotator and Calendar, as well as container controls, provide functionality not easily replicated with HTML server controls.
- If an HTML-object programming model is preferred, HTML server controls should be used.
- If a Visual Basic .NET programming model is preferred, Web server controls should be used.

One other aspect of HTML coding bears mentioning at this point: the Web Forms you create, including the Web pages you create or employ in a Visual Studio .NET application, should exhibit well-formed HTML. Well-formed HTML is simply HTML that complies with the stricter syntax requirements of XML. You can still use all of the HTML tags with which you may be familiar, but your HTML should conform to XML restrictions. If you create a Web form within the Visual Basic .NET IDE, and if you build your Web form in the Designer in Design view, then the Web form is a fully compliant XML document. If you build your Web form in HTML view, or if you add existing Web pages to your project, then you need to take care that XML syntax is followed.

▶ **For an explanation of the syntax rules, look up "Well-formed HTML" in the Visual Basic .NET Help Index.**

Deployment of Web Forms Applications

A Web Forms application can be deployed on the same server on which it is developed or on a different machine. In either case, you must create a Web Setup project, which prepares all of the files necessary to install the application. **Setup and Deployment Projects**, one of the project types available from the New Project dialog box, allows you to set up a variety of projects. In this tutorial, you will create a setup project for a Web Forms application; in Tutorial 8, you will create a setup project for a Windows Forms application. A setup project produces the executable or .dll, all necessary files for the Common Runtime Library, any necessary data or other resource files, and optionally the source code.

Workarounds

The perfect computer programming language has yet to be invented. Whenever a new language or new version of an extant language is introduced, it takes the world's programmers about five minutes to figure out stuff that the new entrant cannot do at all or cannot do well. Visual Basic .NET is no exception to this general principle. In fact, Microsoft and multiple other software manufacturers are working on new languages and improving new releases of old languages all the time.

Because an existing language may not perform some necessary function at all, or completely or efficiently, programmers often face a programming requirement whose solution is not provided directly by the chosen programming language, or that does not work as advertised. It is at this point that programmers must become truly creative. You have encountered at least one such situation with Visual Basic .NET in earlier tutorials: the lack of control arrays. You also were introduced to several suggested techniques for dealing with this issue.

Whenever you find yourself with a programming requirement whose obvious or straightforward solution is blocked or not supported by the programming language you are using, you look for one or more methods that will let you work around the problem. Sometimes (but not often), you invent an elegant solution. Sometimes you end up extending the programming language beyond its originally intended purpose, proving that the language can do even more than its inventors claimed. And sometimes the solution is quite inelegant, taking more time and more programming than it probably should. Such a solution is politely called a "**workaround**," but sometimes also disdained as an example of "brute force programming." Workarounds are fairly common and therefore fairly important in the real world. It behooves you to learn something about them. This tutorial gives you an example of a fairly complex workaround.

You have now completed Lesson A. You can stop here and take a break if you prefer, but don't forget to do the end-of-lesson questions and exercises before proceeding with Lesson B.

SUMMARY

- The Internet, begun in 1969, is a packet-switched, stateless network of networks. The Internet backbone is mostly fiber-optic cable and satellite transmission media, with routers and switches at interconnection points. A connection point to the Internet is called a node. The principle software supporting end-user machines is TCP/IP. The Internet provides communications services, including HTTP, FTP, Telnet, Gopher, Usenet, and SMTP.

- The World Wide Web, initiated in 1989, provides a standardized and universal means of storing and retrieving information among participating computers called Web servers. Transmission takes place through Hypertext Transfer Protocol (HTTP), which runs over the Internet. Data is stored in Web pages, written originally using Hypertext Markup Language (HTML), but today often written in a more robust language called XML.

- ASP.NET is a Microsoft facility for creating XML documents. Within Visual Basic .NET, Web Forms is the bridge to ASP.NET technology and XML. Web Forms extends the established Visual Basic programming model to the World Wide Web.

- A Web form may contain simple HTML elements and client controls (with client-side script), HTML server controls, and Web server controls. Though some of these controls are unique to Web Forms, most of them mirror Windows Forms controls. The Web form GUI is saved as an XML document file with .aspx as the file type. At runtime, this XML document is delivered to the client machine and materialized through the client's browser.

■   The CodeBehind module of a Web form is stored in a separate file from the GUI, with .aspx.vb as the file type. At runtime, the CodeBehind module executes on the server. Coding of a Web form is quite similar to coding of a Windows form. One principle difference has to do with the need on a Web form to account for the stateless feature of the Internet, as a result of which the code is reloaded on each round-trip to the server.

■   A Web Forms application can be distributed by creating a Web setup project.

QUESTIONS

1. The _____ property determines whether a change event causes the Web form to be immediately reposted to the server.

2. An HTML element's _____ map directly to an HTML server control's _____.

3. Tim Berners Lee is known for the invention of _____.

4. Marc Andreesen is known for the development of _____.

5. XML is an acronym for _____.

6. A Web form's server-side code is often called the _____ module.

7. The Internet is _____, meaning that a message is divided into consecutively numbered, fixed-length blocks, and each block is transmitted separately.

8. The Internet is _____, meaning that the Internet itself does not maintain a connection or the status of a connection.

9. The name of the XML resource file for a Web form named MyWebForm would be _____.

10. A support file that identifies authorization and authentication for a Visual Basic .NET Web Forms application is named _____.

11. A support file that specifies the cascading style sheet default settings for a Visual Basic .NET Web Forms application is named _____.

12. The default name for the main Web page in a Visual Basic .NET Web Forms application is _____.

CRITICAL THINKING

At the end of each lesson, reflective questions are intended to provoke you into considering the material you have just read at a deeper level.

1. Consider the implementation of the Logon application as a Web Forms application. The Windows form contains two text boxes (for the e-mail address and the password) plus a Submit button. As a Web form, would you use HTML server controls (a TextBox control and a Submit button are both available) or Web server controls? Why?

2. The FGDT is considering the development of a Village Security System that would be implemented by the house manager of each house in the International Village. Would you recommend developing this as a Windows Forms or as a Web Forms application? Why would you recommend one over the other?

EXERCISES

The following are paper and pencil exercises for designing Web forms. On each drawing, indicate HTML elements with an H, HTML server controls with HS, and Web server controls with W. Be prepared to explain why you have chosen each category. If you prefer, you can create the GUI in Visual Basic .NET.

1. Design a Web form for displaying and updating the athlete's training schedules while staying in the International Village.

2. Design a Web form for displaying and updating the list of countries participating in the Friendsville International Games, along with the list of sports in which each country is participating, and the number of athletes registered for the Games from each country.

3. Design a Web site (that is, a series of Web forms) for displaying selected results from previous international competitions.

4. Design a Web site (that is, a series of Web forms) for retrieving daily results from the competitions at the Friendsville International Games.

After completing this lesson, you will be able to:

- Design the general scheme for the EventSchedule application
- Build Module1 and the webEventMain Web form for the EventSchedule application
- Add the Venue Seating and Pricing Web page
- Complete and test the EventSchedule application
- Use the HTML server controls and Web server controls from the Toolbox

Building a Web Forms Application

Tasks for the FGDT

In Tutorial 7, the FGDT is back to a total team effort. You are responsible for the main Web form (the GUI) and its associated code (referred to as the CodeBehind module). With a few enhancements, the data structures and public variables designed in the Scoring applications of Tutorials 5 and 6 can be applied to the EventSchedule application. Hilda has assigned herself responsibility for implementing those enhancements. Hilda has given Rick the unenviable task of getting the contents of the Events.txt file into an array in the EventSchedule application. Meanwhile, Althea has been asked to put together the seating diagrams and pricing schedules for all eight venues.

In this lesson you create the EventSchedule Web Forms application. You also experiment with some additional HTML elements, HTML server controls, and Web server controls beyond those used in the EventSchedule application.

General Design for the EventSchedule Application

If necessary, run the EventSchedule application again, to refresh your memory of its contents and features. From an application design standpoint, the program consists of three parts:

1. The contents of Events.txt from Tutorial 6 (with the addition of the pricing schedule for each event) must be available throughout the program; this is best accomplished by loading this information into an array, as was done in Tutorial 6. To demonstrate an alternative approach, a two-dimensional string array is used in Tutorial 7 rather than the structEvent structure and the pastructEvent() array that was used in Tutorials 5 and 6.
2. The webEventMain Web form displays a category, subcategory, list of events in the selected category/subcategory, and one selected event detail. webEventMain is a Visual Basic .NET Web form.
3. VenueWebPages.htm displays the seating and price schedules for each of the eight venues. VenueWebPages.htm is a Web page created in Microsoft Word and is saved as an HTML file.

Building the EventSchedule ASP.NET Web Forms Application

You begin to build the EventSchedule application with a skeleton Web Forms project, and then add Module1 taken from Tutorial 6.

When you develop a Web Forms application, you begin by starting a New Project from the Start Page. You then select Visual Basic Projects from the Project Types frame of the New Project dialog box, and ASP.NET Web application from the Templates frame. The default location for a new Web Forms project is a new folder on the virtual Web server on the local machine (*http://localhost/WebApplication1*), but you are not restricted to this virtual Web server: you can develop a new Web Forms application on any Web server to which you have access and on which you have the requisite permissions; for example, you might have access and permission to be able to use the Internet Information Server on a computer in your school's computer lab. Of course, you can also use your own project name rather than the default name WebApplication1.

The physical storage location of the default virtual server is inetpub\wwwroot\WebApplication1. You must be careful when using the physical storage location directly (for example, by copying files into or out of this folder in Windows Explorer). Because of security restrictions on Web server applications, you should only modify the contents of the virtual folder in conjunction with software that recognizes and has the appropriate permissions on the virtual folder, such as Internet Information Server and Visual Studio .NET.

To begin building the EventSchedule application:

1   From the Visual Studio .NET Start Page, start a **New Project**. In the New Project dialog box, click **Visual Basic Projects** under Project Types, and then click **ASP.NET Web Application** under Templates. In the Location text box, replace **WebApplication1** with **EventSchedule**. Note that the project name will be EventSchedule, and that the project will be created on http://*localhost*, that is, the Web server installed on your local machine. Click **OK**.

2   In Solution Explorer, change the default name of **WebForm1.aspx** to **webEventMain.aspx**. If necessary, set the pageLayout property of the form to GridLayout.

Controls may be placed on a Web form in the same way that they are placed on a Windows form, with absolute positioning of each element within its container. This is called **GridLayout**. You implement GridLayout by setting the PageLayout property of the Web form's DOCUMENT object to GridLayout. With this setting, the ShowGrid and SnapToGrid options are available in the Format menu.

Alternatively, controls may be placed on a Web form using FlowLayout. When the DOCUMENT's PageLayout property is set to **FlowLayout**, elements do not have absolute positioning attributes. Rather, elements appear from top to bottom in the order that they occur, much like they do in a word-processing document.

The main difference between GridLayout and FlowLayout is apparent when you insert or delete an element on a Web form. If you insert an element in GridLayout, the new element appears exactly where you position it, and the position of other elements on the page is not affected. If you insert a new element in the middle of other elements in FlowLayout, the positions of elements that follow the new element are adjusted downward to make room for the new element. You should experiment with GridLayout and FlowLayout to see how each one works.

When the Web Forms Designer is open, two tabs appear in the lower-left corner: Design and HTML. In the Design view, you can add and manipulate graphical elements on the form, and they appear in preview mode as they will at runtime. In HTML view, you can edit the HTML tags and text directly.

3   Begin to build the GUI so that it starts to look similar to Figure 7-15. Adding objects to a Web form follows procedures similar to adding controls to a Windows form. One difference is that the Toolbox contains both a Web Forms tab (for Web server controls and Web Forms components) and HTML (for HTML elements, convertible into HTML server controls).

4   Start by placing an **Image** Web Server control at the top left of the form. Using Windows Explorer, copy the sailboat icon **MISC32.ICO** into the **EventSchedule** folder, located at inetpub\wwwroot\EventSchedule. Then set the Image control's **ImageURL** property by clicking its ellipsis. In the Select Image dialog box, choose **All Files** from the **Files of type** combo box, select **Document Relative** from the **URL type** combo box, and type **MISC32.ICO** in the **URL** text box.

5   Add a **Label** Web Server control to the right of the sailboat. Set the **Text** property of the Label to **Friendsville International Games**, with **Blue ForeColor** and **X-Large** font size.

6   Then drop three **DropDownList** Web server controls at the top of the form: using the ID property, name them **ddlCategory**, **ddlSubcategory**, and **ddlEvent**; and set their **AutoPostBack** properties to **True** (because a user-selected change to any of these controls should trigger an immediate response).

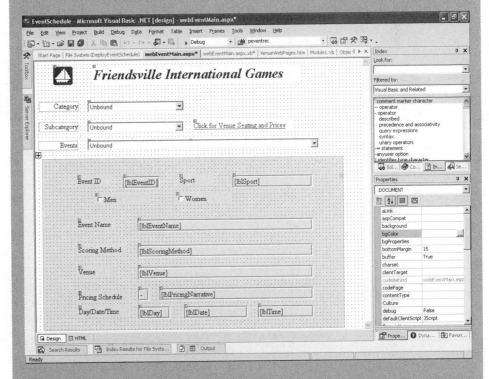

Figure 7-15: webEventMain.aspx at design time

7   To the left of the DropDownList controls in Figure 7-15, add the three labels (**Category, Subcategory, Events**) as HTML elements. (Drag these from the HTML tab of the Toolbox.)

8   To the right of ddlSubcategory, place a **HyperLink** Web server control with the default name **HyperLink1**; set its **Text** property to **Click for Venue Seating and Prices**, and its **Visible** property to **False**.

9 The event detail information is contained in a Grid Layout Panel HTML element covering the lower two-thirds of the form. Place the **Grid Layout Panel** on the form.

10 Create all of the objects within the Grid Layout Panel (except the Men and Women RadioButton controls) as Web server **Labels** using Figure 7-15 as a guide: the static elements have default names and could equally have been HTML elements; the variable data items have meaningful names that appear on the form (lblEventID, lblSport, etc.). (Exception: In Figure 7-15, the name of lblPricingSchedule is not visible. Furthermore, to make lblPricingSchedule as small as it appears in the figure, set its Text property to a hyphen.) For these variable items, set their **BorderStyle** properties to **Groove**. Add two **RadioButton** Web server controls, and name them **radMen** and **radWomen**. When your form is complete, the controls should match the table shown in Figure 7-16.

Name	Type	Properties
Image1	Image Web server control	MISC32.ICO (sailing ship icon)
Label1	Label Web server control	Text: "Friendsville International Games"; Font: Times New Roman, Bold, Italic, X-Large; ForeColor: Blue
Unnamed	HTML Label	"Category"
Unnamed	HTML Label	"Subcategory"
Unnamed	HTML Label	"Events"
ddlCategory	DropDownList Web server control	
ddlSubcategory	DropDownList Web server control	
ddlEvent	DropDownList Web server control	
HyperLink1	HyperLink Web server control	Visible: False; Text: "Click for Venue Seating and Prices"
Unnamed	HTML Grid Layout Panel	Style: bgColor: #ffff99
Label2	Label Web server control	"Event ID"
lblEventID	Label Web server control	Empty text
Label3	Label Web server control	"Sport"
lblSport	Label Web server control	Empty text
Label4	Label Web server control	"Event Name"
radMen	RadioButton Web server control	
radWomen	RadioButton Web server control	

Figure 7-16: Summary of controls on webEventMain

Name	Type	Properties
lblEventName	Label Web server control	Empty text
Label5	Label Web server control	"Scoring Method"
lblScoringMethod	Label Web server control	Empty text
Label6	Label Web server control	"Venue"
lblVenue	Label Web server control	Empty text
Label7	Label Web server control	"Pricing Schedule"
lblPricingSchedule	Label Web server control	- (text = a hyphen)
lblPricingNarrative	Label Web server control	Empty text
Label8	Label Web server control	"Day/Date/Time"
lblDay	Label Web server control	Empty text
lblDate	Label Web server control	Empty text
lblTime	Label Web server control	Empty text

Figure 7-16: Summary of controls on webEventMain (continued)

NOTE: In the Web Form Designer, a Label Web server control displays the Text property of the label, or, if the Text property is empty, it displays the ID (that is, Name) property. The Designer will not permit you to make the label too small to display whatever it is trying to display (Text or ID). Therefore, to make the control small, set the Text property to a hyphen.

Now that you've completed the GUI, the next step is to determine how to load the three DropDownList controls. At runtime, ddlCategory should always display All, Sports, Venue Event Schedule, Venue Price Schedule, and Days. This can be accomplished by loading these items in the Items Collection Editor in the Web Forms Designer, or programmatically through code. In this case, you will load these items programmatically. The other two DropDownList controls contain variable lists, depending on the user selections of category (which determines the subcategory list) and subcategory (which determines the events list), so these two dropdown lists can only be populated programmatically.

To load the DropDownList controls programmatically:

1 Double-click **webEventMain** in the Web Form Designer to open the Page_Load event in the Code Editor, and insert the code shown in Figure 7-17. This code loads ddlCategory. Note the use of the If statement, checking the value of IsPostBack. This check ensures that ddlCategory is loaded only once, not every time the Page_Load event is executed, which occurs when the Web form is initially sent from the server to the client and again every time the page returns from the client machine back to the server (called a PostBack event). The only time you want to load ddlCategory is the very first time the page loads, that is, when IsPostBack is False. Also note that the ddlCategory_ SelectedIndexChanged procedure is invoked when ddlCategory is initially loaded (more on that event procedure in a moment), but because this procedure is not yet written, the call is commented out. Finally, note that the call to LoadEvents() has also been commented out—more about that later in the tutorial as well.

these two procedure calls are commented out for the moment

```
Private Sub Page_Load(ByVal sender As System.Object, _
    ByVal e As System.EventArgs) Handles MyBase.Load
  If Not IsPostBack Then
    'LoadEvents()
    ddlCategory.Items.Add("All")
    ddlCategory.Items.Add("Sports")
    ddlCategory.Items.Add("Venue Event Schedule")
    ddlCategory.Items.Add("Venue Price Schedule")
    ddlCategory.Items.Add("Days")
    'ddlCategory_SelectedIndexChanged(sender, e)
  End If
End Sub
```

Figure 7-17: Page_Load event procedure for webEventMain

Loading ddlSubcategory and ddlEvent both require that the events of the Friendsville International Games (the contents of Events.txt) be available. Loading ddlSubcategory also requires the names of sports and venues. Therefore, at this point in development, the revised Events.txt needs to be available, and Module1.vb from Tutorial 6 with appropriate revisions needs to be incorporated in the EventSchedule project as well. You start with the revised Events.txt.

2   Hilda modified the records in Events.txt to add the PricingSchedule ("A," "B," or "C") at the end of each record. (A small portion of the revised Events.txt appears in Figure 7-18.) Copy **Events.txt** from the VB.NET\Student\Tut07 folder to the project folder, **inetpub\wwwroot\EventSchedule**. Then add this file to the project by right-clicking the project name **EventSchedule** in Solution Explorer, and clicking **Add | Add Existing Item**. In the Add Existing Item dialog box, change the Files of type combo box at the bottom of the dialog box to **All Files (*.*)**, select **Events.txt**, and then click **Open**. Events.txt is added to the EventSchedule project.

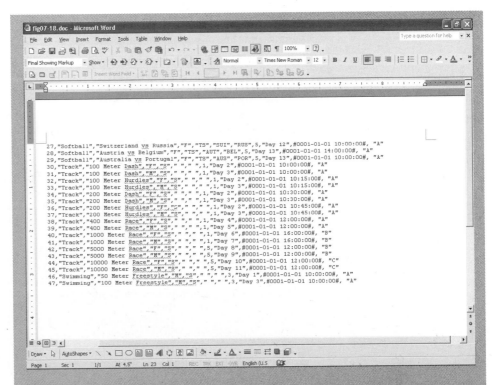

Figure 7-18: Snippet of the revised Events.txt

The next task involves modifications to Module1.vb from Tutorial 6. Hilda also agreed to effect these changes, but they are so simple that you can actually do them yourself with a bit of instruction.

3 A copy of Module1 from the final Scoring application in Tutorial 6 has been placed in VB.NET\Student\Tut07. Copy this version of **Module1.vb** into the project folder, **inetpub\wwwroot\EventSchedule**, and then add this file to your project. Follow the same procedure as adding Events.txt to the project: right-click the project name **EventSchedule** in Solutions Explorer, click **Add │ Add Existing Item**, search for **All Files**, select **Module1.vb**, and then click **Open**.

4 Open **Module1.vb** in the Code Editor, and eliminate the following items that are irrelevant to the EventSchedule project: **structEvent** and **structAthlete** and variables based on those structures, as well as the **AssignWinners()** procedure.

5 Initialize **pStartDate** to **July 30, 2004**, and declare the **AllEvents(NUMEVENTS, 11)** string array to contain all of the contents of Events.txt. The result should appear as in Figure 7-19. (The figure includes comments that explain the contents of each of the 11 columns in AllEvents().) Also add the declaration of pastrSports(), as shown in Figure 7-19.

new array

initialize pStartDate

```
Module Module1
 Public Const NUMEVENTS = 500
 Public AllEvents(NUMEVENTS, 11) As String
 'AllEvents columns: 0=EventID, 1=Sport, 2=EventName, _
 '   3=Gender, 4=ScoringMethod, 5=Country1, _
 '   6=Country2, 7=VenueIndex
 '   8=Schedule (Day), 9=StartTime, 10=PriceSchedule
 Public pStartDate As Date = "July 30, 2004"
 Public pNumEvents As Integer

 Public pastrSports() As String = {16, _
   "Baseball", "Basketball", "Boxing", "Diving", _
   "Equestrian", "Fencing", "Field", "Gymnastics", _
   "Shooting", "Soccer", "Softball", "Swimming", _
   "Tennis", "Track", "Volleyball", "Wrestling"}

 Public pastrVenues() As String = {8, _
   "Friendsville International Center", _
   "Memorial Stadium", _
   "Valley Natatorium", _
   "Nashua-Swaps Equestrian Center", _
   "County Fairgrounds", _
   "Friendsville College Gymnasium", _
   "Municipal Recreation Center", _
   "Valley North Senior High School"}

 Public pastrScoringMethods(,) As String = { _
   {"TS", "Team sport"}, _
   {"S", "Speed"}, _
   {"D", "Distance"}, _
   {"J", "Judges"}}
End Module
```

Figure 7-19: Revised Module1.vb

6 You still need to write the code that loads Events.txt into the AllEvents() array. Place the procedure shown in Figure 7-20 in Module1.vb. Hilda suggests placing this code in Module1.vb, but it could be placed instead in webEventMain.aspx.vb and work equally as well. Then remove the **apostrophe** before LoadEvents() in the Page_Load procedure of webEventMain.aspx.vb, so that the LoadEvents() procedure is invoked.

```
Public Sub LoadEvents()
    Dim i, j As Integer
    FileOpen(1, _
      "http://localhost/EventSchedule/Events.txt", _
      OpenMode.Input)
    Do Until EOF(1)
      i += 1
      For j = 0 To 10
        Input(1, AllEvents(i, j))
      Next
    Loop
    FileClose(1)
    pNumEvents = i
  End Sub
```

Figure 7-20: Sub LoadEvents()

> **NOTE:** The FileOpen() statement specifies *http://localhost/EventSchedule/*, the address of the Web server, as the location in which to look for Events.txt. The reason for specifying the Web server address is that this application is intended to run on a server. Therefore, the file should be available via the URI (Uniform Resource Identifier) of the server.

7 Run the **EventSchedule** application. The error message, shown in Figure 7-21, tells the tale: URI formats are not supported by the FileOpen() statement.

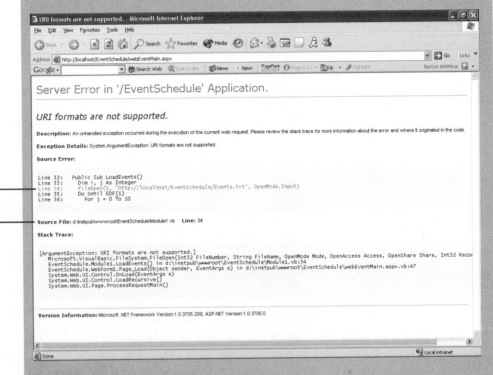

exception (error) generated by this line

source file location

Figure 7-21: Server error: URI formats are not supported

8 To get around this restriction, use a revised procedure by declaring a variable of type URI to hold the Web address, and then use the URI variable in the FileOpen() statement. Replace the existing **FileOpen()** statement with the code shown in Figure 7-22. But this results in the same error, as shown in Figure 7-23.

```
Public Sub LoadEvents()
  Dim i, j As Integer
  Dim myURI As New _
    Uri("http://localhost/EventSchedule/Events.txt")
  FileOpen(1, myURI.ToString, OpenMode.Input)
  Do Until EOF(1)
    i += 1
    For j = 0 To 10
      Input(1, AllEvents(i, j))
    Next
  Loop
  FileClose(1)
  pNumEvents = i
End Sub
```

Figure 7-22: Revised LoadEvents() procedure

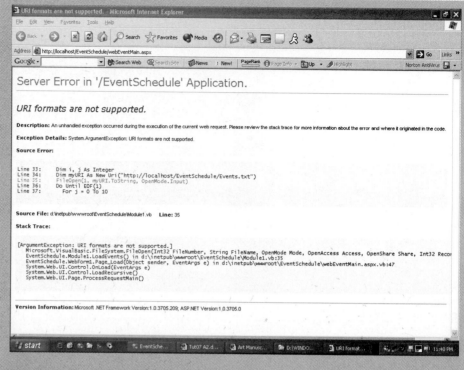

Figure 7-23: Same server error message

9 The server error messages hint at a temporary solution to this problem during application development. Note in Figures 7-21 and 7-23 the address of the source module that raises the exception: *inetpub\wwwroot\EventSchedule\Module1.vb*. The source code is accessible at runtime via its physical address rather than by its virtual Web server address. Although this solution may not suffice for the actual deployment of the EventSchedule application, you may be able to use the physical address of Events.txt for now. (The deployment solution is discussed in Lesson C.) Hence, substitute a third version of **Sub LoadEvents()**, as shown in Figure 7-24, and then run the **EventSchedule** application again.

```
Public Sub LoadEvents()
  Dim i, j As Integer
  FileOpen(1, _
    "d:\inetpub\wwwroot\figeventschedule\Events.txt", _
    OpenMode.Input) 'your disk drive may be different
  Do Until EOF(1)
    i += 1
    For j = 0 To 10
      Input(1, AllEvents(i, j))
    Next
  Loop
  FileClose(1)
  pNumEvents = i
End Sub
```

Figure 7-24: Sub LoadEvents(), third attempt

10 This version of the Sub LoadEvents() procedure produces no error messages, but also does not prove that the AllEvents() array was loaded. To establish that the procedure at least processed all of the records in Events.txt, place a **breakpoint** on the End Sub statement at the end of the LoadEvents() procedure, and run the **EventSchedule** application again. While in break mode, point to pNumEvents. If all of the input data was input, pNumEvents should equal 145. Click **Debug | Stop Debugging**, and remove the **breakpoint**.

▶ Recall that you insert a breakpoint by placing the cursor anywhere in an executable statement and pressing the F9 function key. This is a toggle switch—you can remove the breakpoint the same way.

Complete webEventMain.aspx.vb

webEventMain's coding is nearly complete. Only four procedures are needed: adding one event to the list of events in ddlEvent, and the SelectedIndexChanged event procedure for each of the three drop-down lists. The purpose and identity of each of these procedures is as follows:

1. No matter which category/subcategory is selected by the user, the process of extracting event header information from AllEvents() and placing a concatenated string item into ddlEvent is the same, so it makes sense to construct one procedure to accomplish this task. The procedure you use to do this is titled AddOneEvent().

2. When the user selects Sports, Venue Event Schedule, or Days in ddlCategory, the appropriate string array must be loaded in ddlSubcategory. When the user selects All in ddlCategory, then all events must be listed in ddlEvent. And when the user selects Venue Price Schedule in ddlCategory, then the link to the Venue Web pages must be made visible. All of these actions are triggered by the ddlCategory_SelectedIndexChanged event.

3. When the user selects an item in ddlSubcategory, the filtered list of events that matches the user's selection must be loaded into ddlEvent. Again, these actions are triggered by the DropDownList control's SelectedIndexChanged event.

4. When the user selects an event in ddlEvent, the details concerning that event must be extracted from the AllEvents() array and displayed in the corresponding labels on the Web form. You use the ddlEvent_Selected IndexChanged event to trigger this action.

Remember, the procedures must include resetting or deleting previous selections, and also initializing the controls at startup. You now examine and insert each of these procedures in turn.

To complete the coding of webEventMain:

1 Insert **Sub AddOneEvent()** in webEventMain, as shown in Figure 7-25.

```
Private Sub AddOneEvent(ByVal i As Integer)
  Dim s As String
  s = AllEvents(i, 0) & " - "
  If AllEvents(i, 3) = "M" Then s &= "Men's "
  If AllEvents(i, 3) = "F" Then s &= "Women's "
  s &= AllEvents(i, 1) & ", " 'sport
  s &= AllEvents(i, 2) & ", " 'event name
  s &= AllEvents(i, 8)
  ddlEvent.Items.Add(s)
End Sub
```

Figure 7-25: Sub AddOneEvent()

The purpose of the AddOneEvent() procedure is to load one event into ddlEvent. The procedure is invoked when the category All is selected, or when a particular sport, venue, or day subcategory has been selected. The information loaded into ddlEvent includes the EventID, the gender and name of the sport, the name of the particular event itself, and the day on which the event takes place. The information is extracted from row "i" of AllEvents().

2   Insert **Sub ddlCategory_SelectedIndexChanged**(), as shown in Figure 7-26.

clears the previous items from ddlSubcategory and ddlEvent, and hides HyperLink1

you need to code these Cases yourself as part of Steps 3–5

```
Private Sub ddlCategory_SelectedIndexChanged(ByVal sender _
    As System.Object, ByVal e As System.EventArgs) _
    Handles ddlCategory.SelectedIndexChanged
  Dim i As Integer
  ddlSubcategory.Items.Clear()
  ddlEvent.Items.Clear()
  HyperLink1.Visible = False
  Select Case ddlCategory.SelectedIndex
    Case 0 'All
      ddlEvent.Items.Add("All Events")
      For i = 1 To pNumEvents
        AddOneEvent(i)
      Next
    Case 1 'Sports
      For i = 1 To pastrSports(0)
        ddlSubcategory.Items.Add(pastrSports(i))
      Next
      ddlSubcategory.SelectedIndex = 0
      ddlSubcategory_SelectedIndexChanged(sender, e)
    Case 2 'Venue Event Schedule
        'Type this portion of the procedure yourself.
    Case 3 'Venue Price Schedule
        'Type this portion of the procedure yourself.
    Case 4 'Days
        'Type this portion of the procedure yourself.
  End Select
End Sub
```

Figure 7-26: Sub ddlCategory_SelectedIndexChanged()

At the beginning of this procedure, the subcategory items and event items previously loaded into ddlSubcategory and ddlEvent, respectively, should be cleared, because the newly selected category causes a different set of items to be loaded into these two drop-down lists. In addition, the HyperLink control should be hidden.

The bulk of the procedure is a Select Case construct. Different actions are mandated depending on which item is selected in ddlCategory. One could examine the selected item itself or the index of the selected item, but the index is the more obvious, because the trappable event is the change to the index. Therefore, the Select Case construct examines the five possible values of ddlCategory.SelectedIndex. The actions to be taken in Case 0 and Case 1 have been written for you. You must code Cases 2, 3, and 4 yourself:

Case 0: When the user selects category All (ddlCategory.SelectedIndex = 0), all events need to be loaded into ddlEvent, while ddlSubcategory remains empty. Therefore, for each event *i* in AllEvents, the AddOneEvent(i) procedure is invoked. (Recall that Sub AddOneEvent() adds one event to ddlEvent.)

Case 1: When the user selects category Sports (ddlCategory.SelectedIndex = 1), the names of all the sports in the Friendsville International Games must be loaded into ddlSubcategory. Note that the number of sports in the Games is stored in pastrSports(0). (In Module1, the number of sports was initialized as 16.) After loading the items into ddlSubcategory, the SelectedIndexChanged event for ddlSubcategory needs to be invoked. The reason for doing this is to allow the user to see the Baseball events. If the SelectedIndexChanged event for ddlSubcategory is not called, and if the user then clicks the Baseball subcategory, the SelectedIndexChanged event does not fire, because the default value of the index is 0, and selecting index 0 (that is, Baseball) does not represent a change.

3 Insert the code for Case 2. Model it on the code for Case 1. When the user selects Venue Event Schedule (ddlCategory.SelectedIndex = 2), the action is analogous to selecting Sports, except that the source array is pastrVenues() instead of pastrSports().

4 Insert the one-line statement for Case 3. When the user selects Venue Price Schedule (ddlCategory.SelectedIndex = 3), simply make **HyperLink1** visible.

5 Insert the code for Case 4, modeled on the code for Case 1. When the user selects Days (ddlCategory.SelectedIndex = 4), ddlSubcategory must be loaded with "Day 1," "Day 2," "Day 3," ..., "Day 14." Then invoke the **SelectedIndexChanged** event for ddlSubcategory. Finally, in the Page_Load event procedure, remove the **apostrophe** before the call to ddlCategory_SelectedIndexChanged()—3rd line from the bottom in Figure 7-17.

This completes Sub ddlCategory.SelectedIndexChanged. You next turn your attention to Sub ddlSubcategory.SelectedIndexChanged().

6 Insert **Sub ddlSubcategory.SelectedIndexChanged()**, as shown in Figure 7-27.

you need to add this code to complete the procedure

```
Private Sub ddlSubcategory_SelectedIndexChanged(ByVal _
    sender As System.Object, ByVal e As System.EventArgs) _
    Handles ddlSubcategory.SelectedIndexChanged
  Dim i As Integer
  Select Case ddlCategory.SelectedIndex
    Case 1 'Sports
      ddlEvent.Items.Clear()
      ddlEvent.Items.Add _
        (ddlSubcategory.SelectedItem.Text & " Events")
      For i = 1 To pNumEvents
        'In AllEvents(i, 1), the 1 indicates the Sport column
        If AllEvents(i, 1) = _
            ddlSubcategory.SelectedItem.Text Then
          AddOneEvent(i)
        End If
      Next
    Case 2 'Venue Event Schedule
      ddlEvent.Items.Clear()
      ddlEvent.Items.Add(ddlSubcategory.SelectedItem.Text _
        & " Events")
      For i = 1 To pNumEvents
        'In AllEvents(i, 7), 7 indicates the Venue Index column
        If pastrVenues(AllEvents(i, 7)) = _
            ddlSubcategory.SelectedItem.Text Then
          AddOneEvent(i)
        End If
      Next
    Case 4 'Days
            'Type this portion of the procedure yourself.
  End Select
End Sub
```

Figure 7-27: Sub ddlSubcategory_SelectedIndexChanged()

The requisite action when the user selects a subcategory is dependent again on the category. For example, if the user selects Swimming as a subcategory when Sports is the category, then AllEvents() must be searched for each occurrence of Swimming within the Sport column. When a Swimming event is encountered, that event must be added to ddlEvent using the AddOneEvent() procedure. If the user selects County Fairgrounds as a subcategory when Venue Event Schedule is the category, then AllEvents() must be searched for each occurrence of County Fairgrounds within the Venue column. And if the user selects Day 3 as a subcategory when Days is the category, then AllEvents() must be searched for each occurrence of Day 3 within the Day column. Figure 7-27 is completed for the Sports category and the Venue Event Schedule category, that is, when the index of ddlCategory equals 1 or 2. You need to complete the last case, when the selected category is Days, that is, when the index of ddlCategory equals 4.

Examine Case 1 (Sports) more carefully. After ddlEvent is cleared, a header consisting of "Sports Events" is added to ddlEvent. The subsequent For loop examines the Sport column (that is, column 1) of each row in AllEvents, comparing that value to the name of the sport selected by the user in ddlSubcategory. Whenever these two values match, AddOneEvent() is called to add that event to ddlEvent.

Now examine Case 2 more carefully. This is quite similar to Case 1, except that AllEvents(i, 7) contains the VenueIndex, not the name of the venue. Therefore, the comparison value being sought is the element in pastrVenues() pointed to by AllEvents(i, 7), not the value in AllEvents(i, 7) itself.

7 Insert code for Case 4, which executes when the user has selected the Days category. This code should be modeled directly on Case 1. The only difference is that the day on which an event is scheduled is contained in column 8 of AllEvents() rather than in column 1.

8 Run the **EventsSchedule** application. At this point, the three drop-down lists should load and behave appropriately. You have not yet programmed the selected event in ddlEvent to cause the information concerning that event to load in the lower two thirds of the form. And you have not yet programmed HyperLink1 to take the user to the Venue Seating Diagrams and Pricing Schedule. When you are done looking at the application, close your browser.

9 Turn your attention to ddlEvent. When the user selects a particular event in ddlEvent, then the details concerning that event must be displayed in the controls within the Grid Layout Panel control. Insert the **Sub ddlEvent_ SelectedIndexChanged**() procedure that accomplishes this, as shown in Figure 7-28.

For loop and If—finding a match between EventID and one row in AllEvents()

gender check for women's events (Step 10)

assign a value to lblScoringMethod

assign a value to lblPricingNarrative

```
Private Sub ddlEvent_SelectedIndexChanged(ByVal sender _
    As System.Object, ByVal e As System.EventArgs) _
    Handles ddlEvent.SelectedIndexChanged
  Dim i As Integer
  lblEventID.Text = Val(ddlEvent.SelectedItem.Text)
  For i = 1 To pNumEvents
    If AllEvents(i, 0) = _
        Val(ddlEvent.SelectedItem.Text) Then
      lblSport.Text = AllEvents(i, 1)
      lblEventName.Text = AllEvents(i, 2)
      If AllEvents(i, 3) = "M" Then 'check for a Men's event
        radMen.Checked = True
      Else
        radMen.Checked = False
      End If

      'check for a women's event (code this case yourself)

      lblScoringMethod.Text = ""
      Select Case AllEvents(i, 4) 'scoring method
        Case "TS"
          lblScoringMethod.Text = _
            "Team Sport -- most points scored"
        Case "S"
          'type this case yourself
        Case "D"
          'type this case yourself
        Case "J"
          'type this case yourself
      End Select
      lblVenue.Text = pastrVenues(AllEvents(i, 7))
      lblDay.Text = AllEvents(i, 8)
      lblDate.Text = Format(DateAdd(DateInterval.Day, _
        Val(Microsoft.VisualBasic.Mid(AllEvents(i, 8), _
        5)) - 1, pStartDate), "MMMM d, yyyy")
      lblTime.Text = Format(AllEvents(i, 9), "Short Time")
      lblPricingSchedule.Text = AllEvents(i, 10)
      Select Case lblPricingSchedule.Text
        Case "A"
          lblPricingNarrative.Text = _
            "Prices range from $50 to $400"
        Case "B"
          'type this case yourself
        Case "C"
          'type this case yourself
      End Select
    End If
  Next
End Sub
```

Figure 7-28: Sub ddlEvent_SelectedIndexChanged()

Within Sub ddlEvent_SelectedIndexChanged(), the EventID of the selected item in ddlEvent is used as the search criterion to locate the corresponding row in AllEvents(). The sole purpose of the For loop and the conditional statement within it is to find the correct row in AllEvents() that matches the user-selected event in ddlEvent. You might wonder why a For loop is used to traverse all of the rows in AllEvents(), rather than just using the EventID in the selected item of ddlEvent as an index into AllEvents(). The reason is that, even though right now the 145 events fill AllEvents() in sequence, this might not always be the case. At some future time, some existing events might be dropped, and others might be added, but not in the same sequence. Therefore, because the relationship between an EventID and a row index of AllEvents() is not necessarily fixed for all time, it makes better sense to search through the AllEvents() array looking for the correct EventID.

When the correct row is found, the data items from that row are copied directly or manipulated as needed to fill the labels in webEventMain. This constitutes most of the coding in Figure 7-28. You must code three items yourself in this procedure.

10 Insert your own code where shown in Figure 7-28 to check for a women's event and to set the radio buttons accordingly. Your code should be modeled on the code that check's for a men's event, immediately preceding. Based on the gender, either radMen or radWomen should be True, and the opposite gender should be False. When coding this to check for a women's event, do not make the mistake of assuming that an event not for men must be for women, because some events, such as opening and closing ceremonies and daily medal ceremonies, are not designated for either sex.

11 Insert your own code where shown in Figure 7-28 to assign the appropriate value to the scoring method and the pricing narrative. When the scoring method is S, D, or J, assign an appropriate value to lblScoringMethod, based on the model for the TS scoring method. And when the pricing schedule is B or C, assign an appropriate value to lblPricingNarrative, based on the model for pricing schedule A.

tip

To create your own Web page in Visual Studio .NET as part of another project, just right-click the project name, click Add | Add HTML Page, give the page a name, and click OK. A new HTML page is added to your project. As is the case with a Web form, the HTML Designer offers two views on tabs in the lower-left corner of the page: Design and HTML. The Design tab displays a preview of your Web page as it will appear at runtime, whereas the HTML tab displays the HTML code that constitutes the specification for the page. The Toolbox offers the same HTML elements as you get in a Web form, but it does not offer the Web Forms controls. Also, if you right-click an HTML element that you have added to an HTML page, the shortcut menu does not include "Run as Server Control." This is because an HTML page executes entirely on the client.

Adding VenueWebPages.htm

The EventSchedule application now needs only the Venue Seating Diagrams and Pricing Schedules to be complete. As agreed upon within the FGDT, Althea has been working on this aspect of the project. She created a Web page using Microsoft Word, and then saved it as HTML. This Web page, unlike a Visual Basic .NET Web form, requires no interaction with the server. It contains static text and images and internal links to the sections of the document describing each venue. Though this particular Web page was created using Microsoft Word, you can create a Web page using any word processor, text editor, or Web page creation tool, including FrontPage or Visual Studio .NET.

To add VenueWebPages.htm to the EventSchedule project:

1 Copy **VenueWebPages.htm** (which is available to you in C:\VB.NET\Students\ Tut07) into **inetpub\wwwroot\EventSchedule**.

2 In Solution Explorer, right-click the **EventSchedule** project name, and click **Add | Add Existing Item**. Search for **Web files**, select **VenueWebPages.htm**, and then click **Open**. Visual Basic .NET adds VenueWebPages.htm to the EventSchedule project.

3 In the Designer for webEventMain.aspx, select the **HyperLink1** control. Select the **NavigateUrl** property, click the **ellipsis**, select **VenueWebPages.htm**, and then click **OK**.

4 Run the completed **EventSchedule** application. In the **Category** drop-down list, select **Venue Price Schedule**. This causes the HyperLink1 control to become visible. Click **HyperLink1**, which opens VenueWebPages.htm. Navigate to the various venues for the games, using the internal links within VenueWebPages.htm.

Using HTML Controls on a Web Form

This Web Forms application lets you experiment with additional Web server controls and HTML server controls. As mentioned earlier, the most common Web server controls mimic similar Windows Forms controls, though they provide functionality that is unique to the Web. HTML server controls provide similar functionality to Windows Form controls, but the attributes of HTML elements (which become properties if the HTML element is converted into an HTML server control) are quite a bit different.

To create the Just4Fun Web Forms application:

1 Start a new **Web Forms** application on **http://localhost**. Name the application **Just4Fun.**

2 Rename the main form **webJust4Fun.aspx.**

3 Create the GUI shown in Figure 7-29. Start by creating the objects at the top left of this form: the **HTML Button, HTML Reset Button,** and **HTML Submit Button.** (All of the objects in the top half of the form, down to and including the Horizontal Rule, are HTML elements.) Right-click the **HTML Button (Button1),** and select **Run As Server Control.** (For this short demo, you can allow all of the default IDs and names to stand.)

file field HTML element

text area HTML element

password field HTML element

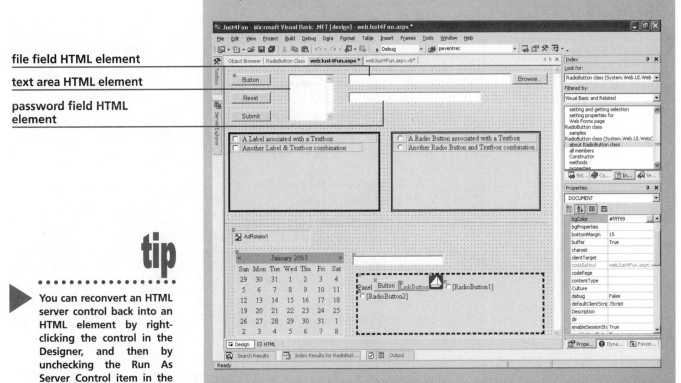

tip

● ● ● ● ● ● ● ● ● ● ● ● ● ● ● ●

You can reconvert an HTML server control back into an HTML element by right-clicking the control in the Designer, and then by unchecking the Run As Server Control item in the shortcut menu. Or, in HTML view, you can remove the runat="server" option from the control's HTML tag. You do not need to delete the ID attribute—and you should not delete it, if there is any client-side script that references that element.

Figure 7-29: webJust4Fun.aspx at design time

To convert any HTML element into an HTML server control, in Web Forms Designer, you drag an HTML element onto the Web form from the HTML tab of the Toolbox. Then, you right-click the element in the Designer, and click Run As Server Control. The Designer responds by giving the HTML element a default ID, such as Text1, and by making events related to this control available in the Code Editor.

An HTML Button control executes whatever client-side script is associated with it (and whatever server-side script as well, if the element has been converted into an HTML server control, as you have done in this case). A Reset Button control reloads the original Web page, erasing any changes the user may have entered on the page. A Submit Button submits the entire page for processing by client-side script.

4   Next, create the following HTML elements to the right of the buttons: a **Text Area**, a **File Field**, and a **Password Field**.

A Text Area HTML element allows the user to enter multiple lines of text. A File Field HTML element allows the user to browse through folders and select a file. Below the File Field element is a Password Field HTML element, which displays a large black dot in place of each character entered at the keyboard.

5   Place two **Flow Layout Panel** HTML elements just above the horizontal rule, and insert the **Horizontal Rule** element. Inside the left Flow Layout Panel, drop two **Checkbox** HTML elements, along with **Labels** associated with each check box. Inside the right Flow Layout Panel, drop two **Radio Button** HTML elements, along with **Labels** associated with each radio button.

As you add objects inside the Flow Layout Panel, each new object occupies the next immediately available space to the right of the last existing element in the container (if no item in the container is currently selected), or to the right of the currently selected item. If insufficient space within the container exists to the right of the last existing or currently selected object, then the new object appears on the next line. Note that the text area or label associated with a Checkbox HTML element or a Radio Button HTML element—unlike the Web Forms and Windows Form counterparts—is a separate HTML element and is not built in to either the Checkbox or Radio Button elements.

The Radio Button HTML elements behave slightly differently from RadioButton Web server controls and RadioButton Windows Forms controls. Radio Button HTML elements and HTML server controls are only in the same group if they have the same ID property. In this case, they are both named rb (for "Radio Button"). RadioButton Web server controls are in the same group if they have the same GroupName property.

This example also demonstrates that a Web Form in grid layout can contain an HTML container element that uses flow layout; the reverse is also true.

6   Now add the Web server controls beneath the Horizontal Rule element in Figure 7-29. This includes **AdRotator**, **Calendar**, **TextBox**, and **Panel** controls. Inside the Panel, drop a **Button**, **LinkButton**, **ImageButton**, and two **RadioButton** Web server controls.

An AdRotator control is associated with another XML document called an AdvertisementFile, which in turn contains a series of banner ads. Whenever the Web form is updated, one of the ads in the AdvertisementFile is randomly selected and is displayed in the AdRotator control.

Under the AdRotator control is a Calendar Web server control. This control offers some but not all of the functionality of the Windows Forms MonthCalendar control. Specifically, you can display only one month at a time, and by setting the SelectionMode property, you allow the user to select no date; only one date; one date or one week; or one date, one week, or one entire month. But you cannot use the control to select various other date ranges, nor to select multiple nonconsecutive dates. Selecting a date triggers the SelectionChanged event.

To the right of the Calendar control are a TextBox Web server control and a Panel Web server control. The TextBox Web server control displays text, as you might expect. The Panel Web server control supports flow layout only. In this case, the Panel control contains three button-type controls, laid out from left to right: a Button Web server control, a LinkButton Web server control, and an ImageButton Web server control. It also contains two RadioButton Web server controls, which share the GroupName grb (group RadioButton).

With all of these controls, the important learning principle is that many different kinds of controls can be incorporated on a Web form and successfully implemented.

7 Insert code to make the Just4Fun application come to life, as suggested by Figure 7-30. At the beginning of this code, note that only Button1 is identified as an HTML server control; the other controls declared in the CodeBehind module are Web server controls. HTML elements are not listed in webJust4Fun.aspx.vb at all. Create procedures for the controls, as shown in Figure 7-30, writing the three lines of code as indicated.

```vb
Public Class WebForm1
    Inherits System.Web.UI.Page
  Protected WithEvents AdRotator1 As _
      System.Web.UI.WebControls.AdRotator
  Protected WithEvents TextBox1 As _
      System.Web.UI.WebControls.TextBox
  Protected WithEvents Button1 As _
      System.Web.UI.HtmlControls.HtmlInputButton
  Protected WithEvents Panel1 As _
      System.Web.UI.WebControls.Panel
  Protected WithEvents Button2 As _
      System.Web.UI.WebControls.Button
  Protected WithEvents ImageButton1 As _
      System.Web.UI.WebControls.ImageButton
  Protected WithEvents LinkButton1 As _
      System.Web.UI.WebControls.LinkButton
  Protected WithEvents Calendar1 As _
      System.Web.UI.WebControls.Calendar

[+] Web Form Designer Generated Code

  Private Sub Page_Load(ByVal sender As System.Object, _
      ByVal e As System.EventArgs) Handles MyBase.Load
    'Put user code to initialize the page here
  End Sub

  Private Sub Calendar1_SelectionChanged(ByVal sender As _
      System.Object, ByVal e As System.EventArgs) _
      Handles Calendar1.SelectionChanged
    TextBox1.Text = Format(Calendar1.SelectedDate, _
      "Long Date")
  End Sub

  Private Sub Button1_ServerClick(ByVal sender As _
      System.Object, ByVal e As System.EventArgs) _
      Handles Button1.ServerClick
    TextBox1.Text = "Button 1 was clicked."
  End Sub

  Private Sub LinkButton1_Click(ByVal sender As _
      System.Object, ByVal e As System.EventArgs) _
      Handles LinkButton1.Click
    LinkButton1.Text = "You clicked the LinkButton."
  End Sub
End Class
```

write these three lines of code

Figure 7-30: webJust4Fun.aspx.vb

8 The only other code needed for this application is the advertisement file and associated .gif images. In Solution Explorer, right-click the **Just4Fun** project name, select **Add | Add New Item**, and in the Add New Item dialog box, click **XML file**. Change the name of the file to **MyAds.xml**, and click **Open**. Follow the precise format of Figure 7-31, substituting your own organizations (employers) or schools, .gif image files, and Web sites for the ones listed in that file (or feel free to use the ones shown here). Save the file. The graphic image files referenced in the advertisement file must be placed in the same folder as the advertisement file. Then specify your .xml file in the AdvertisementFile property of the AdRotator control.

```
<Advertisements>
    <Ad>
            <ImageUrl>newlogo.gif</ImageUrl>
            <NavigateUrl>http://www.course.com</NavigateUrl>
            <AlternateText>Thomson Learning - Course Technology
            </AlternateText>
            <Impressions>80</Impressions>
            <Keyword>Topic1</Keyword>
    </Ad>
    <Ad>
            <ImageUrl>top_logo_03.gif</ImageUrl>
            <NavigateUrl>http://www.pgcc.edu</NavigateUrl>
            <AlternateText>Prince George's Community College
            </AlternateText>
            <Impressions>80</Impressions>
            <Keyword>Topic2</Keyword>
    </Ad>
    <Ad>
            <ImageUrl>umtitle.gif</ImageUrl>
            <NavigateUrl>http://www.umd.edu</NavigateUrl>
            <AlternateText>University of Maryland</AlternateText>
            <Impressions>80</Impressions>
            <Keyword>Topic2</Keyword>
    </Ad>
</Advertisements>
```

Figure 7-31: MyAds.xml

9 Run the **Just4Fun** application. One possible output screen is shown in Figure 7-32. When you have finished viewing it, close your browser, and close the **Just4Fun** solution.

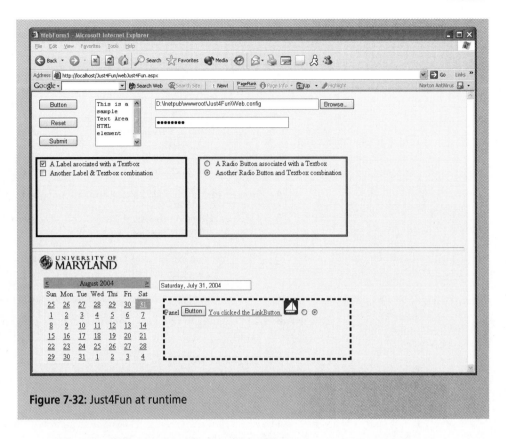

Figure 7-32: Just4Fun at runtime

This completes Lesson B and the development of the EventSchedule Web Forms application. You still need to set up and deploy the application in Lesson C. But before tackling that topic, you should answer the review questions and do the exercises that follow.

SUMMARY

- A Web Forms project has much the same outward appearance as a Windows Forms project: the GUI uses similar controls, properties, events, and methods. One major difference is that the CodeBehind module runs on a server, whereas the GUI is rendered through a Web browser.
- A Web page contains HTML tags and client-side script; a Web Form also contains server controls and server-side script.
- Adding an external data file to a Web Forms application presents problems with file access in the distributed application.
- Change events in a Web form are normally processed following the next click event, but change events can be processed immediately if the AutoPostBack property is set to True.
- One of the Web server controls unlike any Windows Forms control is the AdRotator Web server control, which displays a randomly selected banner ad from a file of advertisements.

QUESTIONS

1. The _____ Windows Forms control is similar to the DropDownList Web Forms control.

2. To convert an HTML element into an HTML server control, _____ the HTML element in the Web Forms Designer, and then select _____.

3. The _____ event is triggered when the user selects a different item in a DropDownList control.

4. In well-formed HTML, every <p> tag must be terminated by a _____ tag.

5. Code executed on the local computer and triggered by an HTML element is called _____ script.

6. The Calendar Web Forms control provides similar functionality to the _____ Windows Forms control.

7. Selecting a new date in a Calendar control triggers the _____ event.

8. To add an item to a DropDownList control programmatically, one employs the _____ method of the _____ collection.

9. The Panel Web Forms control uses _____ layout.

10. To convert an HTML server control back into a simple HTML element, you right-click the control and uncheck _____.

11. The _____ HTML element erases all changes entered by the user and reloads the original Web page.

CRITICAL THINKING

At the end of each lesson, reflective questions are intended to provoke you into considering the material you have just read at a deeper level.

1. Why does a change event, by default, not trigger associated server code immediately? Why must it wait for a click (or similar) event?

2. Why is simple HTML text not available through server code?

3. Why is a Web form (.aspx file) converted automatically to XML? In other words, from Microsoft's standpoint, what is the advantage of XML? Why didn't they choose to implement .aspx files through a native or proprietary file format?

EXERCISES

1. Re-create the Dining Hall Seat Assigner application from Tutorial 2 as a Web Forms application. Do not include the ability to save the seat assignments in a file, nor to print the seat assignments.
   a. Create a new ASP.NET Web application, named webSeatAssigner.
   b. Name the main form webSeats. Design the GUI to match, insofar as possible, the Dining Hall Seat Assigner from Tutorial 2.

    c.   Copy the code from the Dining Hall Seat Assigner in Tutorial 2 and modify it as necessary to accommodate the object names you have created in webSeatAssigner.

2.   Re-create the Logon (not LogonManager) application from Tutorial 3 as an ASP.NET Web application, named webLogon. Handle the Users file the same as you handled Events.txt in the EventSchedule application. Display a successful logon on a Web form called SuccessfulLogon. Show that there is a valid user, the supervisor status, and the record number.

3.   Create a Visual Basic ASP.NET Web Forms application. In the IDE, load the Items Collection of a DropDownList control with 10 integers. Place a Submit Button HTML element on the form, and designate it as a server control. When the user clicks the control at runtime, copy the contents of the DropDownList control into an array of 10 integers. Sort the array in descending numerical order using the sorting algorithm in Tutorial 6. Copy the sorted array to a ListBox Web server control.

    a.   Create a new ASP.NET Web application named webSimpleSort. Name the Web form webSort.

    b.   Add a DropDownList control named ddlInput. In the Items Collection, add 10 items, setting the Text property of each item to an integer value.

    c.   Add a Submit Button HTML element on the form, and convert it into an HTML server control. Name the button btnSubmit.

    d.   Add a ListBox Web server control to the form, named lstNumbersInOrder.

    e.   In the btnSubmit_ServerClick() procedure, load the contents of ddlInput into an Integer array, use the sorting algorithm from Tutorial 6 (Hilda's Simple Sort) to sort the integers in descending numerical order, and then copy the array contents to lstNumbersInOrder.

4.   Create a Web Forms application containing 10 Web server controls of varying types. Create a single event handler that handles one event from each control—a Click event, a TextChanged event, a ValueChanged event, a ScrollChanged event, or whatever seems most appropriate for each control. In the event handler, change the Text property of a Label control to indicate the name of the control that triggered the event handler.

5.   Create a Web Forms application. Place links to the following: your school's main Web site, your instructor's Web page, and your own personal Web page. Insert a TextBox Web server control on the Web form, along with a button control. Prompt the user to enter a URL into the text box. When the user clicks the button control, open the Web page specified in the TextBox control.

6.   Create a Web Forms application named MyAthlete. This application displays a drop-down list of the names of your favorite athlete. When the user selects an athlete from the drop-down list, a HyperLink Web server control displays the name of that athlete's team and is a link to the team's home page, while another HyperLink control displays the name of the sport and is a link to one of the sport's governing bodies. For example, selecting a soccer player who plays for Real Madrid causes one HyperLink control to display Real Madrid and the other HyperLink control to display FIFA.

    a.   Name the Web form on this application webAthlete. Place the DropDownList Web server control on the form. Name it ddlAthlete, and set its AutoPostBack property to True. Create two HyperLink controls on the form: hypTeam and hypSport.

    b.   In the Page_Load event procedure, load ddlAthlete with the names of your favorite athletes, but only if IsPostBack is False. Also load four string arrays, as follows: the name of the team, the URL of the team's home page, the name of the sport, and the URL of one of the sport's governing bodies. Load the first element of each array into the Text property of hypTeam, the NavigateURL property of hypTeam, the Text property of hypSport, and the NavigateURL property of hypSport.

    c.   In ddlAthlete's SelectedIndexChanged procedure, based on the index of the selected athlete, load the corresponding element from each of the four arrays into the appropriate Text and NavigateURL properties of hypTeam and hypSport.

7. Create a Web Forms application that mimics the functionality of frmTeam in the Scoring application from Tutorial 6. Allow the user to select an EventID from a drop-down list, triggering the display of all the items on the form, but limit the user's selection to an EventID for team sports competitions.

8. Create a Web Forms application that mimics the functionality of frmUser in the LogonManager application from Tutorial 4. This project requires a creative solution on your part, because the TabControl Windows Forms control has no counterpart among Web Forms controls.

   NOTE: You will likely install the Users file in the WINDOWS\system32 folder. When writing to the Users file, you may encounter a file permissions error stating that the ASP.NET process is not authorized to write to this file. If this occurs, you must grant write-access to ASP.NET for that file. To do this, open Windows Explorer, navigate to the Users file in the WINDOWS\system32 folder, right-click the file, click Properties, and click the Security tab. (If the Security tab is not visible, click Tools on the menu bar, click Folder Options, and then click the View tab. In the Advanced settings list box, scroll all the way down, and uncheck the option Use simple file sharing (Recommended). After changing this setting, the Security tab is visible in the Properties window for any file.) Within the Security tab, click Add to add the {*machinename*}\ASPNET user. Highlight the ASP.NET account, and check the Write box in the Allow column.

After completing this lesson, you will be able to:

- Build a setup project to deploy the EventSchedule application
- Implement workarounds to make the data in Events.txt available to the deployed Web Forms application
- Deploy the EventSchedule application to a remote machine

Deploying a Web Forms Application

In Lesson C you build the setup project needed to deploy the EventSchedule application, and then you actually deploy it. This lesson also describes two workarounds needed to make the EventSchedule application work on a computer other than the one on which the application is developed.

Building a Web Setup Project to Deploy the EventSchedule Web Forms Application

When you created a distribution version of a Visual Basic 6.0 application, you used the Package and Deployment Wizard, one of the Visual Basic 6.0 Tools programs that shipped with Visual Basic 6.0, but was not part of Visual Basic 6.0 itself. In Visual Basic .NET, this functionality is provided as part of the basic package. With Visual Basic .NET, you create a special **setup project**, which in turn creates all the necessary files for deployment of your application; the setup project is just another kind of Visual Basic project, like a Windows Forms or Web Forms or Console or User Control project. Visual Studio .NET offers both a Setup Project (for deployment of Windows Forms applications) and a Web Setup Project (for deployment of Web Forms applications). This section steps you through the creation of a Web Setup package for the EventSchedule application.

To create the setup project for the EventSchedule application:

1. Open **Visual Studio .NET** and the **EventSchedule** application. In Solution Explorer, right-click the name of the solution, and click **Add | New Project**. In the Add New Project dialog box, click **Setup and Deployment Projects** under Project Types, and then click **Web Setup Project** under Templates. In the Name text box, change **WebSetup1** to **DeployEventSchedule**. See Figure 7-33. Click **OK**. DeployEventSchedule becomes the name of the Web deployment project, and the File System Editor opens.

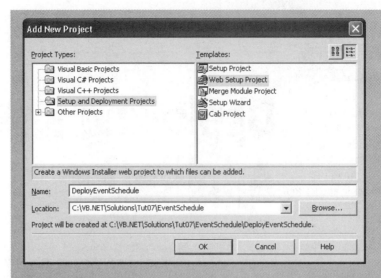

Figure 7-33: Add New Project dialog box, selecting a Web Setup Project

2   With the project name **DeployEventSchedule** selected in Solution Explorer, in the Properties window select the **ProductName** property, and type **EventSchedule**. This is the name of the product that users will see when the application is installed on another server.

3   Next, you must add the output from the EventSchedule Web Forms project to the deployment project. To do this, select the **Web Application folder** in the File System Editor. Then, in the main menu, click **Action | Add | Project Output**. In the Add Project Output Group dialog box, ensure that the **EventSchedule** project is selected; then select **Primary output** and **Content Files**. The primary output is the fully compiled .dll file, in the present case, EventSchedule.dll; Content Files are any other files that are part of the application, such as, in the present case, VenueWebPages.htm. See Figure 7-34. Click **OK**.

tip
••••••••••••••••••
▶ If you want to distribute your source code along with the deployed project, then, in the Add Project Output Group dialog box, select Source Files in addition to Primary output and Content Files.

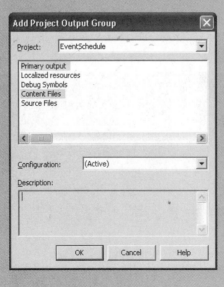

Figure 7-34: Add Project Output Group dialog box

4 Next, you must set the properties for the installer. Select the **Web Application folder** in the File System Editor. In the Properties window, select the **VirtualDirectory** property, and enter **FIG**. Then, still in the Properties window, select the **DefaultDocument** property, and enter **webEventMain.aspx**. The VirtualDirectory property identifies the virtual folder in which the installer places the deployed application, unless the user selects a different folder. The DefaultDocument property identifies a Web application's Start Page.

5 You are now ready to build the Web Setup project. Click **Build | Build DeployEventSchedule**. The output messages should appear as in Figure 7-35. (You can enlarge your Output window if you want to view as much of the screen as is shown in Figure 7-35.)

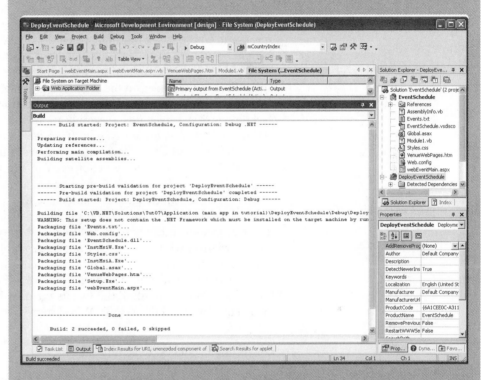

Figure 7-35: Output window following Build | Build WebSetup1

NOTE: The Output files include Events.txt and VenueWebPages.htm, but these files will be treated differently after the installation is complete. The running application will find the Web page in the EventsSchedule virtual folder on the server, but it will not find Events.txt in the same place.

6 To deploy the application to the Web server on your development computer, select the **DeployEventSchedule** project in Solution Explorer, and then click **Install** from the Project menu. The Install Wizard indicates that it is installing EventSchedule. When installation is complete, visit **http://localhost/FIG**, and after a minute the application should load and execute. Close the browser when you are done looking at the application.

If you are distributing this application to a Web server that does not have the .NET Framework installed, then you must obtain and install DotNetRedist.exe before the install can work. DotNetRedist.exe (size approx. 20 MB), the redistributable version of the .NET Framework, is a free download from the Microsoft Web site, and may be distributed with your application.

On the Project menu, you can click Uninstall if you want to uninstall the application.

Because of the problems with locating Events.txt at runtime, deployment to a different computer does not work just yet. (Currently, the FileOpen() method looks for Events.txt in the hard coded location \inetpub\wwwroot\EventSchedule; but Events.txt is not likely to be there on any other computer!) You return to complete this deployment scenario after you fix the problem with the location of Events.txt.

Implementing Workarounds for Events.txt

Workarounds were discussed theoretically in Lesson A. Now it's time to apply this concept practically.

Presently, a problem exists where a sequential file does not seem to be readily accessible from the Web Forms application installed on a remote computer. If you simply add a sequential file to a project, it can be deployed with the application; however, at runtime on the target machine, when the operating system executes the FileOpen() method, if the absolute path has not been hard coded, it looks for the file in the WINDOWS\system32 folder on whatever drive the operating system is installed, rather than in the folder on the Web server where you have installed the application. For example, if the EventSchedule application were installed on the Course Technology Web server, then the application would look for the VenueWebPages.htm file in the *http://www.course.com/FIG folder*; but it would look for Events.txt in C:\WINDOWS\system32 (assuming Windows had been installed on drive C).

This leaves you with two choices. You can design a workaround to load the contents of Events.txt into an appropriate array, by enclosing each data value in Events.txt inside an assignment statement that places the data value in the array. Or, you can deploy Events.txt on the target machine in the WINDOWS\system32 folder or in some other hard coded folder where your program can find it. The second alternative, while viable, may not be desirable, because some developers prefer to avoid placing data files directly on a client machine, and some client machines, for security reasons, avoid accepting such files. Either way, this lesson demonstrates both workarounds: loading the Events.txt data into an array, and then deploying the Events.txt file to the WINDOWS\system32 folder.

Converting Events.txt to LoadEvents.txt

This "Conversion Workaround" involves converting Events.txt into a series of assignment statements that can be included in a procedure, called at startup, that loads the contents of Events.txt into the AllEvents() array. The resulting procedure is quite long and tedious, but you will use an automated procedure to create it. By loading AllEvents() from internal assignment statements, you avoid the external sequential file altogether.

Implementing this idea is not especially difficult, but figuring out how to do it might require some serious brainpower. Rick did most of the conceptual development for you. Follow along closely as you implement the solution.

To convert Events.txt into LoadEvents.txt:

1   Start a new **Visual Basic .NET Console Application** called **ConvertEvents**. Type in Rick's code for the **Sub Main**() procedure, as shown in Figure 7-36.

```
Public Sub Main()
  Dim i, j As Integer
  Dim x As String
  FileOpen(1, "Events.txt", OpenMode.Input)
  FileOpen(2, "LoadEvents.txt", OpenMode.Output)
  Do Until EOF(1)
    For j = 0 To 10
      Input(1, x)
      WriteLine(2, "AllEvents(i," & j & ") = " & x)
    Next
    WriteLine(2, "i +=1")
    i += 1
  Loop
  FileClose(1)
  Console.WriteLine("Number of events = " & CStr(i))
  Console.ReadLine()
End Sub
```

Figure 7-36: Rick's code for Sub Main() in ConvertEvents

This procedure opens Events.txt as input and creates LoadEvents.txt as output. For each line of data in Events.txt (that is, for each event), the procedure creates 12 lines in LoadEvents.txt. The first 11 lines take a data value from Events.txt and make it into an assignment statement of the form "`AllEvents(i, j)=x`," where i is the record or row number, j is the column number, and x is the data value. The 12th line increments i.

2   Run the **ConvertEvents** application—it doesn't do anything yet, because Events.txt is not present, but it does create the bin folder, where you need to put Events.txt.

3   Copy **Events.txt** from the \inetpub\wwwroot\EventSchedule folder to the **ConvertEvents\bin** folder.

4   Run this application again. It should produce the initial LoadEvents.txt file, about 43 KB in size. Open the **LoadEvent.txt** file, and make sure that it looks like Figure 7-37. If it does not, redo your steps up to this point, because it is much easier to fix the Console application that created LoadEvents.txt than to edit the resulting file.

```
"AllEvents(i,0) = 32"
"AllEvents(i,1) = Track"
"AllEvents(i,2) = 100 Meter Hurdles"
"AllEvents(i,3) = F"
"AllEvents(i,4) = S"
"AllEvents(i,5) =   "
"AllEvents(i,6) =   "
"AllEvents(i,7) = 1"
"AllEvents(i,8) = Day 2"
"AllEvents(i,9) = #0001-01-01 10:15:00#"
"AllEvents(i,10) = A"
"i +=1"
"AllEvents(i,0) = 33"
"AllEvents(i,1) = Track"
"AllEvents(i,2) = 100 Meter Hurdles"
"AllEvents(i,3) = M"
"AllEvents(i,4) = S"
"AllEvents(i,5) =   "
"AllEvents(i,6) =   "
"AllEvents(i,7) = 1"
"AllEvents(i,8) = Day 3"
"AllEvents(i,9) = #0001-01-01 10:15:00#"
"AllEvents(i,10) = A"
"i +=1"
```

Figure 7-37: Snippet of LoadEvents.txt

5 Before LoadEvents.txt can be used, several universal edits are needed. Notice that each statement in LoadEvents.txt is a quoted string of the form "xxx=yyy" but the executable code you need in Visual Basic is of the form xxx="yyy". (Notice the placement of the leading quotation mark.) Three Find-and-Replace edits can solve the problem. Open the **Replace** dialog box. In the Find what text box, enter **"All**. Then in the Replace with text box, enter **All**, and then click the **Replace All** button. This takes a minute to execute, because 1595 records must be altered.

6 In the Find what text box, enter **=**, then in the Replace with text box, enter **= "**. Then click the **Replace All** button.

7 In the Find what text box, enter **"i += 1"**, then in the Replace with text box, enter **i += 1**. Then click the **Replace All** button. After these changes, the file should begin with the entries shown in Figure 7-38. Save the revised file as **LoadEvents2.txt**, and close the file.

```
AllEvents(i,0) = "1"
AllEvents(i,1) = "General"
AllEvents(i,2) = "Opening Ceremonies"
AllEvents(i,3) = " "
AllEvents(i,4) = " "
AllEvents(i,5) = " "
AllEvents(i,6) = " "
AllEvents(i,7) = "1"
AllEvents(i,8) = "Day 1"
AllEvents(i,9) = "#0001-01-01 19:00:00#"
AllEvents(i,10) = "A"
i +=1
AllEvents(i,0) = "2"
AllEvents(i,1) = "General"
AllEvents(i,2) = "Medal Ceremonies"
AllEvents(i,3) = " "
AllEvents(i,4) = " "
AllEvents(i,5) = " "
AllEvents(i,6) = " "
AllEvents(i,7) = "6"
AllEvents(i,8) = "Day 2"
AllEvents(i,9) = "#0001-01-01 21:00:00#"
AllEvents(i,10) = "B"
i +=1
AllEvents(i,0) = "3"
AllEvents(i,1) = "General"
AllEvents(i,2) = "Medal Ceremonies"
AllEvents(i,3) = " "
AllEvents(i,4) = " "
AllEvents(i,5) = " "
AllEvents(i,6) = " "
AllEvents(i,7) = "6"
AllEvents(i,8) = "Day 3"
AllEvents(i,9) = "#0001-01-01 21:00:00#"
AllEvents(i,10) = "B"
i +=1
AllEvents(i,0) = "4"
AllEvents(i,1) = "General"
AllEvents(i,2) = "Medal Ceremonies"
```

Figure 7-38: LoadEvents2.txt snippet, after universal Find-and-Replace operations

tip

If this were the final version of the application, you would now remove Events.txt from the EventsSchedule project in Solution Explorer, and then rebuild the deployment project. By doing this, the installer would not attempt to install Events.txt on the client machine. However, in the present case, you still need Events.txt for the second workaround, so do not remove it from the solution.

Completing the Conversion Workaround Implementation
Implementation involves substituting the code in LoadEvents2.txt for the code in the LoadEvents() procedure in Module1 of EventSchedule.

To complete the workaround:

1 Open the **EventSchedule** Web Forms application. Open **Module1**. You are going to reuse the LoadEvents() procedure later in this lesson, so don't erase it—just rename it as **LoadEventsHold**() and leave it there.

2 Start a new **Sub LoadEvents**() procedure in Module1. Open **LoadEvents2.txt**, and copy the contents of the entire file into the new **Sub LoadEvents**() procedure. At the bottom of this procedure, insert the statement **pNumEvents = i**.

3 Run the **EventSchedule** application to ensure that it works correctly. Then return to the IDE.

4 Select the **DeployEventSchedule** project in Solution Explorer. Click **Build |
Build DeployEventSchedule**. The EventSchedule project can now be deployed
to a remote Web server, because the application no longer requires the sequential file. The steps in deploying the compiled application are explained after
the presentation of the second workaround.

Another Workaround Approach: Deploying Events.txt in \WINDOWS\system32

Although the conversion workaround described previously does work and meets the
immediate requirement, it is far from an ideal solution. One significant drawback is
its relative inflexibility: the steps involved in creating the workaround solution need
to be repeated every time new events are added to the Friendsville International
Games. Therefore, even though you might not be too enamored with the idea of
exporting a data file to a user's machine, sometimes that might be the best approach.

In the present case, you go back to the original idea of loading the sequential file
Events.txt directly into the AllEvents() array at startup. But this time, you begin by
discovering where the operating system expects to find the file by default—that is,
with no path specified. Then you revise the instructions to the installer to put it there.

tip

▶ After you have successfully
completed all of these steps,
you can delete the Sub
LoadEventsWorkaround()
procedure.

To discover the default path for a sequential data file and to revise the instructions to the Windows Installer accordingly:

1 Open the **EventSchedule** application and **Module1**. Change the name of Sub
LoadEvents() to **Sub LoadEventsWorkaround()**. Change the name of Sub
LoadEventsHold() to **Sub LoadEvents()**.

2 In the newly renamed Sub LoadEvents, remove the path in the FileOpen
statement. The revised statement should read:

```
FileOpen(1, "Events.txt", OpenMode.Input)
```

3 Run the **EventsSchedule** application. This time, the server error indicates
"File not found." It also indicates where the system looked for the file—on
the disk drive on which the operating system is loaded, in the WINDOWS\
system32 folder. See Figure 7-39. So now the trick is to tell the Windows
Installer to place Events.txt in that folder.

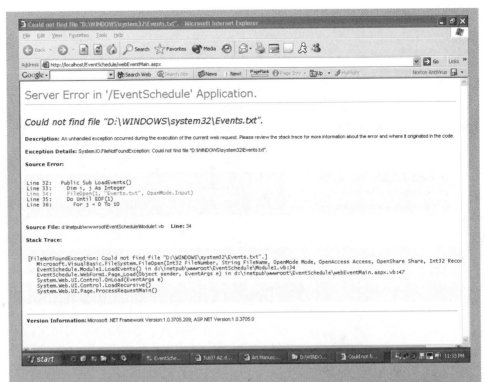

Figure 7-39: Server error—File not found

4 In Solution Explorer, select the **DeployEventSchedule** project and, if necessary, open the **File System Editor**. (You can open the File System Editor by clicking the File System Editor icon in Solution Explorer when a deployment project is selected.) In the File System Editor, click **File System on Target Machine**. Click **Action | Add Special Folder | Windows Folder**. Under File System on Target Machine, select **Windows Folder**. Click **Action | Add | Folder**. A new folder appears. Change its name to **System32**. Select the **System32** folder in the left pane of the File System Editor. Click **Action | Add | File**. Navigate to the **\inetpub\wwwroot\EventSchedule** folder, and select **Events.txt**. Click **Open**. The File System Editor should now appear as in Figure 7-40. Note that these steps cause the installer to install Events.txt to the WINDOWS\system32 folder on whichever drive holds the operating system on the destination machine.

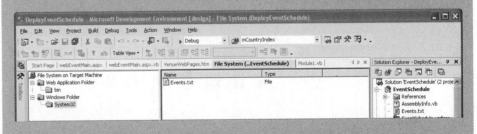

Figure 7-40: File System Editor, showing Events.txt in the System32 folder

After you have successfully completed all of these steps, you can delete the Sub LoadEventsWorkaround() procedure. Again, deleting the procedure is not mandatory—just good housekeeping.

5 Try running the **EventSchedule** application again. It still does not work, because Events.txt is still not in the \WINDOWS\system32 folder. Now select **DeployEventSchedule** in Solution Explorer, and then click **Build | Build DeployEventSchedule**. With DeployEventSchedule still selected in Solution Explorer, click **Project | Install**. Follow the prompts to install the EventSchedule application in the FIG virtual folder (or any other virtual folder you designate).

6 Open your browser, and visit **http://localhost/FIG**. The EventSchedule application loads and runs. Also open **Windows Explorer** and navigate to the \WINDOWS\system32 folder on the disk drive containing your operating system. Notice that Events.txt is present there. Finally, navigate to **\inetpub\wwwroot\FIG**. Note the files that have been installed. webEventMain.aspx is just the XML file for the GUI. In the bin folder, all of the application's code (that is, compiled versions of webEventMain.aspx.vb and Module1.vb) is contained in the dynamic link library, EventSchedule.dll.

Deploy EventSchedule to a Remote Computer

Now that the EventSchedule application is running smoothly, you can complete the tasks needed to deploy to a remote computer.

By default, Windows Installer is located in \documents and settings\ *yourloginname*\My Documents\Visual Studio Projects*solutionfolder*\ *deploymentprojectname*\ *project configuration*\ *deploymentprojectname*. msi. The default *project configuration* is Debug. Therefore, for example, on the author's computer, where the operating system is installed on drive D:, the full path to this file is D:\ documents and settings\ Bob\My Documents\Visual Studio Projects\ EventSchedule\Deploy EventSchedule\Debug\ DeployEventSchedule.msi.

To deploy the EventSchedule application to another Web server:

1 First, locate the Windows Installer that you just built.

2 Copy the *deploymentprojectname*.msi file and all other files and subfolders in the folder to the Web server computer.

3 On the Web server computer, double-click the **Setup.exe** file to run the installer. Follow the prompts until the message "EventSchedule has been successfully installed" appears.

4 Run the **EventSchedule** application by opening your browser and visiting **http://***webservercomputername***/FIG**.

5 If you subsequently want to uninstall the application, open the **Windows Control Panel**, double-click **Add or Remove Programs**, click **EventSchedule**, and then click the **Change/Remove** button.

You now have completed Tutorial 7. Stop now for a break, or continue on with the following exercises.

S U M M A R Y

■ In Visual Studio .NET, Setup and Deployment Projects includes templates for creating the files needed to deploy various kinds of projects. A Web Setup project creates the necessary files for deploying a Visual Basic .NET Web Forms application.

■ Within a setup project, the File System Editor allows the programmer to identify all of the files and folders that an application needs. Typically, this includes the Primary output files from a project (the .exe or .dll), Content Files (such as XML files), and other files (such as traditional data files).

- A workaround is a solution to a programming problem that compensates for a deficiency in the programming language—something missing from the language, a requirement not properly supported, or a software bug. A professional programmer must sometimes resort to a workaround in order to accomplish some programming task.
- The File System Editor allows the developer to designate the folder on the target computer where files will be installed.
- When the setup project is built, the result is a set of files that can be copied to a remote computer. These files include Setup.exe, which runs the installer.
- The target computer must have the .NET Framework installed before running the install program. To install a Web Forms application, the target computer must also be running IIS. And you must have the appropriate permissions to install to the target machine and to install to IIS.

QUESTIONS

1. The default window displayed in the IDE for a deployment project is _____.

2. In which property do you specify the name of the application as it will be known to the target computer?

3. You specify the folder in which the application will be installed on the target server in the _____ property.

4. The primary output of a deployment project compilation is a _____ file.

5. Coding techniques that compensate for stumbling blocks are called _____.

6. The file type of the Microsoft installer is _____.

7. You specify the startup page in a deployment project by setting the _____ property.

8. To uninstall a project on the development computer from within the IDE, click _____.

9. To uninstall a project on a remote computer, select _____ from the Control Panel.

10. By default, a Web Forms application looks for an ancillary file (such as a sequential input file) in the _____ folder.

EXERCISES

1. Create a Web Forms application that displays the price of one ticket at one event of the Friendsville International Games. The start up Web page displays a drop-down list containing information concerning all of the events at the Games—the same information contained in ddlEvent in the EventSchedule application. The page also instructs the user to select an Event from the drop-down list. When the user makes a selection, the program should display a label containing the name of the venue for that event and a small drop-down list containing the names of the seat categories in that venue (such as Box Seats, Reserved, and General Admission). (The seating categories for each of the venues are in VenueWebPages.htm.) The Web page then instructs the user to select a seating category. When the user selects a seating category, the page displays the price of one ticket. (Ticket prices for each seating category and for each price schedule are in VenueWebPages.htm. The pricing schedule for each event is in Events.txt.)

2. Build the Web Setup project to deploy the application created in Exercise 1.

3. Build the Web Setup project to deploy the Web Forms version of the Dining Hall Seat Assigner project (from Exercise 1 in Lesson B).

4. Build a Web Forms application for displaying and updating the list of countries participating in the Friendsville International Games, along with the list of sports in which each country is participating, and the number of athletes registered for the Games from each country.

5. Build the Web Setup project to deploy the application developed in Exercise 4.

Exercises 6 and 7 allow you to both discover the solution to problems on your own and experiment with material that is not covered explicitly in the tutorial.

discovery ▶ 6. Build the Web Setup project to deploy the Web Forms version of the Logon project (from Exercise 2 in Lesson B). How will you deal with the Users file? What are the security issues surrounding deployment of the Users file, and what can be done to satisfy the obvious security concerns? What facilities in Visual Basic .NET might be of assistance here?

discovery ▶ 7. Use the objects introduced in the Just4Fun Web Forms application in this tutorial for a new, more meaningful application whose purpose is to advertise the Friendsville International Games. Use other controls as well. Include at least three instances of user input, validated with the help of one of the validation controls.

KEY TERMS

- AdRotator Web server control
- AutoPostBack property
- brute force programming
- Button HTML element
- ButtonClick event
- Calendar Web server control
- Checkbox HTML element
- CodeBehind module
- CompareValidator Web server control
- CustomValidator Web server control
- DropDownList Web server control
- File Field HTML element
- File System Editor
- Flow Layout Panel HTML element
- FlowLayout attribute setting
- Global.asax file
- Grid Layout Panel HTML element
- GridLayout attribute setting
- Horizontal Rule HTML element
- HTML client controls
- HTML server controls
- HyperLink Web server control
- ImageButton Web server control
- Label HTML element
- Label Web server control

■ LinkButton Web server control
■ PageLayout attribute
■ Panel Web server control
■ Password Field HTML element
■ PostBack event
■ ProductName property
■ Radio Button HTML element
■ RadioButton Web server control
■ RangeValidator Web server control
■ RegularExpressionValidator Web server control
■ RequiredFieldValidator Web server control
■ Reset Button HTML element
■ SelectedIndex property
■ SelectedIndexChanged event
■ SelectionChanged event
■ Setup and Deployment Projects
■ Submit Button HTML element
■ Text Area HTML element
■ Textbox Web server control
■ Transmission Control Protocol/Internet Protocol (TCP/IP)
■ Web Form Designer
■ Web Form file (.aspx, .aspx.vb)
■ Web Forms application
■ Web server controls
■ Web Setup project template
■ workarounds
■ XML resource file (.resx)

Data Structures: Sorts, Binary Searches, Linked Lists, and ISAM Files

The Up Close and Personal Windows Forms Application

case ▶ The Friendsville Games Development Team is developing some applications for the general public that will be distributed on CDs rather than on the Web. In Tutorial 8, the application involves personal details concerning each of the athletes who will be competing in the games. In promoting the Games, the Friendsville Organizing Committee wants to give (or preferably sell) to the public a CD highlighting the lives of the athletes. Of course, at this point, no one knows who the athletes will be, so a boilerplate format is used for the biographical details, and a stick figure is used in place of a photo.

Many organizations develop such applications that are intended for execution on a stand-alone computer, and they must decide whether each such application should be developed as a Windows Forms or a Web Forms application. But the fact is that many potential users do not have a Web server running on their machine, so a Windows Forms application may garner a potentially larger audience, and that is what the FGDT decided to create.

Previewing the Up Close and Personal Application

Although this application may seem quite simple at first, upon closer examination you will find that it contains many new principles and computer-programming techniques.

To view the Up Close and Personal application:

1   Run **UpClose.exe**, available in the VB.NET\Student\Tut08 folder. The Start-up form displays four combo boxes. Initially, all athletes in the data file are displayed, sorted by Athlete ID. Click the **Name** list arrow to see the list of 25 athletes, and note that they are sorted by Athlete ID. Also, note the information displayed for each athlete: Athlete ID, first and last name, and country code. See Figure 8-1.

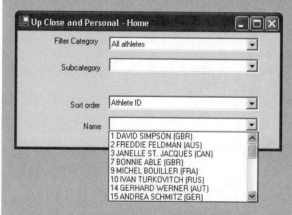

Figure 8-1: Up Close and Personal - Home form

2   Click the **Sort Order** list arrow, click **Lastname, Firstname,** and then click the **Name** list arrow. Do the same for each sorting possibility in the Sort order combo box. (As you discover later, a different sorting algorithm is used to achieve each sort order.) Click **Sort order**, and select **Lastname, Firstname.**

3   To change the selection in the Filter Category and display only the male athletes, click the **Filter Category** list arrow and then select **Male athletes.** Click the **Name** list arrow, and note that only the names of male athletes are shown. Repeat this step for female athletes.

4   To display only those athletes participating in a particular sport, click the **Filter Category** list arrow, and then select **Filter by Sport.** In the subcategory combo box, Baseball apppears by default. Click the **Name** combo box, and note that no names appear. This is because the small sample file of athletes created for this application includes no baseball players. Click the **Subcategory** combo box, and select **Swimming.** Now click the **Name** combo box, and note that six names appear, including a subset of both men and women and that they are sorted by last name, as shown in Figure 8-2.

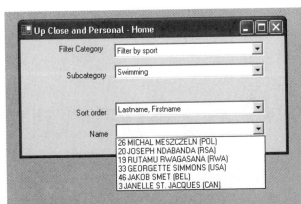

Figure 8-2: Up Close and Personal: swimmers sorted by last name

5   Select **Janelle St. Jacques** from the Name combo box. The information concerning the selected athlete is displayed, as shown in Figure 8-3.

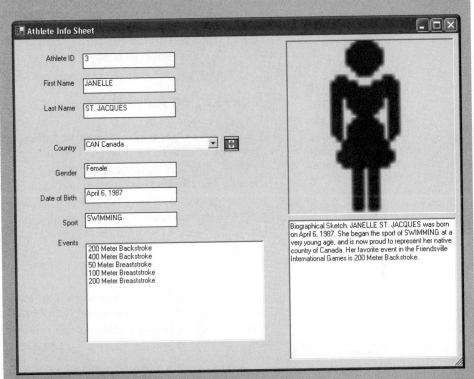

Figure 8-3: Athlete Info Sheet

The Athlete Info Sheet displays essentially the same information for every athlete. A data file of some kind provides the Athlete ID, name, country, date of birth, sport, and events. The biographical information in the sample application is constructed from these same information elements, and the photo is just an icon file representing a man or a woman—but the software must support a unique biographical sketch and a photograph for each athlete. For purposes of demonstration, you construct the sample boilerplate biographies and default "photos," but the application must allow for the inclusion of real biographies and photos later when the names of real athletes are known.

6   Close the **Athlete Info Sheet** and the **Up Close and Personal** application when you have finished experimenting with them.

After completing this lesson, you will be able to:

- Comprehend the main table-sorting algorithms (bubble sort, selection sort, insertion sort, shuttle sort, Shell sort)
- Appreciate a simple file-sorting algorithm
- Understand sequential and binary search techniques
- Construct a linked list
- Understand the structure of pseudo-ISAM files in Visual Basic .NET

tip

Some texts refer to these in-memory data structures as arrays, some as tables, and some as both. In Tutorial 8, array and table are used interchangeably.

Data Structures

Lesson A discusses the concepts behind the coding of the Up Close and Personal Windows Forms application. The unifying theme of this tutorial is data structures, including some of the principle ways that data is manipulated in memory and in files. The new concepts include various table-sorting algorithms, file sorting, sequential and binary searches, linked lists, and Index Sequential Access Method (ISAM) files. These traditional computer science and advanced computer-programming topics give you insights that translate into improved programming skills and also provide a foundation for the discussion of databases in Tutorial 9. With these techniques and skills, you are able to tackle increasingly complex algorithms.

Table-sorting Algorithms

You saw a very simple table-sorting algorithm in Tutorial 6, appropriate for sorting tiny arrays (those with fewer than 10 elements). In the Up Close and Personal application, an array of up to 500 athletes must be sorted, so Hilda's Simple Sort is inappropriate to the task. The 10-element size restriction has nothing to do with whether or not the algorithm works on an array of any size (it works), but rather on the speed of sorting. As the array size increases, the number of comparisons needed to sort the array increases geometrically. Specifically, using Hilda's Simple Sort, an array of 10 elements in reverse order takes 174 comparisons and 45 exchanges to sort into the correct order, but an array of 100 elements takes 166,749 comparisons and 4950 exchanges to sort into the correct order.

Table-sorting algorithms vary from the type that is quite simple to code but rather inefficient in execution to the more complex to code but much more efficient in execution. Some of the principle table-sorting routines are presented conceptually here; you will code them as you develop the Up Close and Personal application in Lesson B.

NOTE: At the outset, it should be noted that table sorts are vastly more efficient than file sorts, because only main memory is involved in table sorts, but disk access is involved in file sorts. A brief discussion of file sort routines follows this section on table sorts.

In the description of each sort, you should assume that the data to be sorted is in an array of integers called List1. (An array of any data type works as well.) You should also assume that the objective in each case is to sort the elements in ascending order. To understand the individual algorithms, it may be useful to take five pencils of different lengths, lay them down in parallel but haphazard order, and then apply each sorting algorithm in this discussion to your "List" of five pencils, moving them around the table until you understand how the algorithm works. After you have seen how to sort a table of individual data items, you then examine the sorting of records (where each row in the table consists of multiple data items).

Bubble Sort or Waterfall Sort

A **bubble sort** or **waterfall sort** is another exchange sort, like the very simple sort covered in Tutorial 6. And like that algorithm, it only compares adjacent elements, that is, List1(i) compared to List1(i+1). It performs reasonably well on medium-sized arrays ranging from 10 to 100 records. The two names of this sort refer to the way the elements move as the table sorting takes place. If you watch the highest-valued elements gravitate toward the bottom of the table, you might call this a waterfall sort; if you focus on the lowest-valued elements, you see them percolate or bubble up toward the top. Regardless of the perspective, the same action is taking place.

The bubble sort, which is the more common name for sorts of this type, uses nested For loops. The outer loop limits the number of comparisons made inside the inner loop. The inner loop passes through the table, comparing adjacent elements and exchanging their values when necessary. Each pass through the table results in one more element resting in its final position, which means that on the next pass one less comparison needs to be made. Figure 8-4 shows the basic code for a bubble sort.

```
Line 1    Public Sub BubbleSortBasic()
Line 2       Dim List1() As Integer = {4, 5, 2, 1, 3}
Line 3       Dim i, j, temp As Integer
Line 4       Dim Numrecs As Integer = _
                List1.GetUpperBound(0) + 1
Line 5       For i = Numrecs - 2 To 0 Step -1
Line 6          For j = 0 To i
Line 7             If List1(j) > List1(j + 1) Then
Line 8                temp = List1(j)
Line 9                List1(j) = List1(j + 1)
Line 10               List1(j + 1) = temp
Line 11            End If
Line 12         Next
Line 13      Next
Line 14   End Sub
```

Figure 8-4: Bubble sort, basic code

In Figure 8-4, line 2 declares the simple List1 array, used throughout the examples in this section. Line 3 declares i, the loop control variable for the outer loop, and j, which controls the inner loop. Line 4 declares and computes the number of elements in the array. The GetUpperBound(n) function returns the highest index value in the dimension n of the referenced array. Because all Visual Basic .NET arrays are zero-based, the number of records is actually the return value of GetUpperBound(0)+1.

Line 5 initiates the outer loop, controlling the total number of comparisons made on each pass through the array. On the first pass, the number of comparisons is Numrecs–2, because the last comparison should be made between the second to last element of the array, that is, List1(Numrecs–2), and the last element of the array, namely, List1((Numrecs–2)+1). After the first pass through the array, the last array element must contain the highest-valued item and is in its final home. Therefore, on the second pass, a comparison with this final element is not necessary. This is why the maximum index of elements to be compared (that is, the variable i) decreases with each iteration of the outer loop.

Line 6 initiates the inner loop, controlled by the loop control variable j. The inner loop iterates as long as j does not exceed i. In each iteration of the inner loop, the value of List1(j) is compared with the following element (line 7), and, if they are out of sequence, the two elements are swapped (lines 8 to 10).

If you suspect that the table may already be sorted or nearly sorted before the sorting operation begins, then it may be useful to halt the sort prematurely when you know that the table has been sorted. For example, you might have an array filled with the number of medals won by each country in the Games so far, sorted in descending numerical order by the number of medals won. After updating the information in the array with the number of new medals awarded today, you want to re-sort the list. Perhaps some countries will move up or down the list because of the new medal count at the end of today's competitions, but the order of countries is not likely to change very much from what it was yesterday. Of course, discovering after each pass through the outer loop whether the array has been sorted bears a small cost: you must expend some resources to check whether the table has been sorted. Figure 8-5 includes this enhancement. This enhancement involves assigning a sentinel value to temp before the initiation of the inner loop. When the inner loop completes, if temp still contains the sentinel value, then the table has been sorted.

enhancement: early exit when table is sorted

```
Line 1    Public Sub BubbleSortEnhanced()
Line 2       Dim List1() As Integer = {4, 5, 2, 1, 3}
Line 3       Dim i, j, temp As Integer
Line 4       Dim Numrecs As Integer = _
                List1.GetUpperBound(0) + 1
Line 5       For i = Numrecs - 2 To 0 Step -1
Line 5A         temp = -9999
Line 6          For j = 0 To i
Line 7             If List1(j) > List1(j + 1) Then
Line 8                temp = List1(j)
Line 9                List1(j) = List1(j + 1)
Line 10               List1(j + 1) = temp
Line 11            End If
Line 12          Next
Line 12A         If temp = -9999 Then Exit For
Line 13       Next
Line 14    End Sub
```

Figure 8-5: Improved bubble sort

Mathematical Explanation of Cost

In terms of cost, the unimproved bubble sort requires $N(N-1)/2$ comparisons. This is because on the first pass through the inner loop, the program makes $N-1$ comparisons: if there are five elements in a table, then on the first pass, four comparisons are made. On each succeeding pass through the inner loop, one fewer comparisons occur, until only one comparison takes place. Hence, for a five-element table, the bubble sort makes a total of $4+3+2+1=10$ comparisons. The formula for the sum of integers from 1 to N is given by $m(m+1)/2$. In this case, $m=4$ (that is, $N-1$), so the number of comparisons is $4*5/2$, which is 10.

When considering the performance of an algorithm, precision in calculations is unnecessary because you are dealing with approximations anyway. To simplify approximations, mathematicians use Big O notation, in which all constants are removed. In this case, if the 1 and 2 are removed from the formula, the result is N^2, which is easier to both remember and calculate than $N(N-1)/2$. The basic idea of Big O notation is that, as N gets larger, the value of the expression increases exponentially (N^2), and the constants 1 and 2 have less and less impact on the result. Hence, when dealing with very large approximations, constants can be ignored without materially affecting the conclusions. Using this notation, the number of comparisons in the unimproved bubble sort is written as $O(N^2)$.

The number of comparisons may be reduced by the enhanced version of the sort. Remember that each exchange takes three assignment statements. The number of exchanges depends on how badly ordered the list is at the start. So, in the worst-case scenario, where the list starts out in reverse order, the number of assignments needed to sort it is $3(N)(N-1)/2$—that is, three assignment statements for every comparison. (Note that this expression also reduces to $O(N^2)$.) An exchange is unnecessary whenever the adjacent elements being compared are already in the correct sequence with respect to each other. Hence, the bubble sort executes more quickly the closer the original list is to being in the correct order.

Selection Sort

A **selection sort** is relatively simple to understand conceptually. It uses two list areas, named here List1 (the original, unsorted array) and List2 (the final, sorted array). The algorithm steps through List1 looking for the smallest value in the list. After passing through the array, the smallest item is then copied to the first position in List2, while in List1 the smallest element is assigned a value larger than any other possible value in List1 so that it is not again selected as the smallest. This process is repeated, identifying the smallest element remaining in List1; when found, this element is copied to the next position in List2, and the smallest element in List1 is assigned a very high value. This continues until all the elements in List1 are copied to List2. At the end of the sort routine, if necessary, List2 is copied back to List1. The selection sort algorithm is displayed in Figure 8-6. Again, you can use pencils to see how this works. You arrange five pencils of varying lengths on one sheet of paper (List1), and lay beside it a second sheet of blank paper (List2). You also need five full-length, new pencils, longer than any of the five pencils you are sorting. Now pass through List1, pointing finally to the shortest pencil. Move that pencil to List2, and in its place, put one of the new pencils. Now repeat the process until List1 contains five new pencils, and List2 contains the original pencils in the correct order.

```
Line 1    Public Sub SelectionSort()
Line 2       Dim List1() As Integer = {4, 5, 2, 1, 3}
Line 3       Dim List2(5) As Integer
Line 4       Dim Numrecs As Integer = _
                List1.GetUpperBound(0) + 1
Line 5       Const HIGHVALUE As Integer = 9999
Line 6       Dim List1Index, LowIndex, List2Index As Integer
Line 7       For List2Index = 0 To Numrecs - 1
Line 8          LowIndex = 0
Line 9          For List1Index = 1 To Numrecs - 1
Line 10            If List1(List1Index) < List1(LowIndex) Then
Line 11               LowIndex = List1Index
Line 12            End If
Line 13         Next
Line 14         List2(List2Index) = List1(LowIndex)
Line 15      Next
Line 16   End Sub
```

Figure 8-6: Selection sort algorithm

The way this code operates is as follows. List1Index (declared at line 6) is a pointer to an element in List1 and is used to control the inner loop, which makes successive passes through List1 (from line 9 to line 13). List2Index (also declared at line 6) is a pointer to an element in List2 and is used to control the outer loop (lines 7 through 15), as the lowest element in List1 after each pass is copied to the next available position in List1 (line 14). LowIndex points to the smallest value in List1 during each pass of the inner loop.

In terms of cost, the selection sort uses twice as much memory as a bubble sort, because of the space needed for List2. But the number of assignment statements executed in a selection sort is only 2N, as compared to a worst case of $O(N^2)$ for the bubble sort. One advantage of a selection sort is its predictability: creation of the sorted List2 from the original List1 takes exactly the same amount of time and comparisons regardless of the order of List1.

Insertion Sort

The **insertion sort** is useful because it is the only sort routine that allows you to sort elements as they are introduced. It is ideal for sorting new items as they come into existence rather than sorting items in a preexisting array. However, you can also use a preexisting array as the source for items to be sorted.

One common application of the insertion sort occurs during sport competitions. In the Women's Equestrian Hurdles event, for example, 30 riders might compete. (A competitor's score in this event is the sum of the number of seconds she takes to go through the course, plus penalty points for knocking down any barriers. The lowest overall score wins.) After the first rider's ride, you can say that she is in the lead. After five riders have ridden, you can list those riders in order, sorted by points scored—and so on. At any stage of the competition, by using an insertion sort, the elements of List2 are maintained in the correct order based on all of the elements submitted to the list *so far*.

The operation of an insertion sort is shown in the algorithm in Figure 8-7. The basic idea of an insertion sort is that each new item is compared, in the Do Until header at line 9, to the final element in the existing list—called here List2(List2Index)—after List2Index has been initialized to List2Count–1 (at line 8), that is, one less than the number of elements in List2. If NewItem is greater than the existing element, then the Do Loop is exited, and NewItem is inserted in the sorted list at position List2Index+1 (at line 13). If NewItem is not greater than the existing item at position List2Index, then that item is moved to position List2Index+1 (at line 10), making room for NewItem. Then List2Index is decremented (at line 11), and the process is repeated until the proper spot for NewItem is encountered. If you reach the first position in List2, that is, List2Index<0 (also tested in the Do Until header at line 9), without discovering the proper insertion point for NewItem, then you break out of the Do Loop anyway and NewItem is inserted at position 0.

```
Line 1     Public Sub InsertionSort()
Line 2        Dim NewItem As Integer
Line 3        Dim List2(50) As Integer
Line 4        Dim List2Count, List2Index As Integer
Line 5        List2Count = 0
Line 6        NewItem = InputBox _
                 ("Enter an integer to be sorted (-9 to quit)")
Line 7        Do Until NewItem = -9 Or List2Count = 50
Line 8           List2Index = List2Count - 1
Line 9           Do Until List2Index < 0 OrElse _
                    NewItem >= List2(List2Index)
Line 10             List2(List2Index + 1) = List2(List2Index)
Line 11             List2Index -= 1
Line 12          Loop
Line 13          List2(List2Index + 1) = NewItem
Line 14          List2Count += 1
Line 15          NewItem = InputBox _
                    ("Enter an integer to be sorted (-9 to quit)")
Line 16       Loop
Line 17    End Sub
```

Figure 8-7: Insertion sort algorithm

In most implementations, the insertion sort is interrupted at various points to display the contents of the sorted array up to that point. For example, in Figure 8-8, a display routine is added to this Console application to display the contents of List2() after every five NewItem insertions.

display routine

```
Public Sub InsertionSort()
  Dim NewItem As Integer
  Dim List2(50) As Integer
  Dim List2Count, List2Index As Integer
  List2Count = 0
  NewItem = InputBox _
    ("Enter an integer to be sorted (-9 to quit)")
  Do Until NewItem = -9 Or List2Count = 50
    List2Index = List2Count - 1
    Do Until List2Index < 0 OrElse _
        NewItem >= List2(List2Index)
      List2(List2Index + 1) = List2(List2Index)
      List2Index -= 1
    Loop
    List2(List2Index + 1) = NewItem
    'display after every 5 new items
    If (List2Count + 1) Mod 5 = 0 Then
      System.Console.WriteLine("List2 when count = " & _
        (List2Count + 1))
      For List2Index = 0 To List2Count
        System.Console.Write(List2(List2Index) & " ")
      Next
      System.Console.WriteLine()
    End If
    List2Count += 1
    NewItem = InputBox _
      ("Enter an integer to be sorted (-9 to quit)")
  Loop
End Sub
```

Figure 8-8: Insertion sort with an added display routine

If the new items presented to the insertion sort come from a preexisting array (List1 in these examples), then the cost of an insertion sort is slightly less than the cost of a selection sort, because comparisons are only made among items that have already been sorted, and because comparisons for each new item end when the proper location in List2 has been ascertained. If the source of NewItem is external, especially if it is manual input after each rider has completed a ride, then the processing cost is irrelevant, because the computer will be waiting on the next rider's score far longer than the user awaits completion of the sorting process.

Shuttle Sort

A **shuttle sort** is another version of an exchange sort. This sort proceeds only once through the array, comparing adjacent elements. When it encounters two elements that need to be reversed, it not only reverses those two elements, but also propagates that exchange backwards through previous elements in the array, until the exchanged element finds its proper place among all of the elements that have been sorted so far. The algorithm is displayed in Figure 8-9.

```
Public Sub ShuttleSort()
  Dim List1() As Integer = {1, 3, 4, 5, 6, 8, 9, 7, 2, 10}
  Dim Numrecs As Integer = _
    List1.GetUpperBound(0) + 1
  Dim i, HoldIndex, temp As Integer
  For i = 0 To Numrecs - 2
    If List1(i) > List1(i + 1) Then
      HoldIndex = i
      Do While i >= 0 AndAlso List1(i) > List1(i + 1)
        temp = List1(i)
        List1(i) = List1(i + 1)
        List1(i + 1) = temp
        i -= 1
      Loop
      i = HoldIndex
    End If
  Next
End Sub
```

Figure 8-9: Shuttle sort algorithm

For example, if the initial array of 10 integers contains {1, 3, 4, 5, 6, 8, 9, 7, 2, 10}, then the shuttle sort compares each pair of elements moving forward (1–3, 3–4, 4–5, 5–6, 6–8, 8–9, 9–7) until it needs to make an exchange at 9-7. At that point, the sort interrupts its forward progress and exchanges elements backwards until element 7 is positioned between 6 and 8. Then it resumes the forward comparison, encountering 9–2. The sort interrupts its forward progress again and propagates the exchange backwards until 2 is positioned between 1 and 3. When the entire list has been traversed, the array is sorted.

The performance of the shuttle sort on completely unordered arrays is not markedly different than that of a bubble sort, but it performs much better than the other sorts introduced thus far if the table is nearly sorted to start with and only a few items need to be correctly repositioned, especially if the items to be repositioned are near the bottom of the original table and need to move up. (The bubble sort can be coded so that it moves the highest value all the way to the bottom on each pass, or the lowest element all the way to the top on each pass, but not both. The shuttle sort is equally efficient in moving elements in either direction.) Another advantage of the shuttle sort is that it gets you halfway to the Shell sort, explained next.

Shell Sort

The **Shell sort** (named after its inventor) was designed to address one of the problems of many of the sorts that preceded it: namely, the fact that many exchange sorts compare and, therefore, exchange only adjacent elements. Therefore, if you have an element at position 999 in a 1000 element array, and that element belongs at position 0, it will take 998 exchange operations (each of which takes three assignment operations) to move that element to its final home. This seems woefully inefficient. The Shell sort algorithm displayed in Figures 8-10 and 8-11 solves this problem.

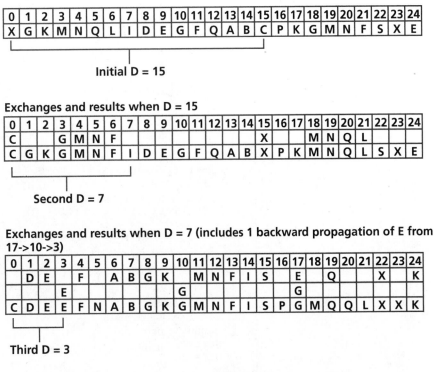

0	1	2	3	4	5	6	7	8	9	10	11	12	13	14	15	16	17	18	19	20	21	22	23	24
X	G	K	M	N	Q	L	I	D	E	G	F	Q	A	B	C	P	K	G	M	N	F	S	X	E

Initial D = 15

Exchanges and results when D = 15

0	1	2	3	4	5	6	7	8	9	10	11	12	13	14	15	16	17	18	19	20	21	22	23	24
C			G	M	N	F									X			M	N	Q	L			
C	G	K	G	M	N	F	I	D	E	G	F	Q	A	B	X	P	K	M	N	Q	L	S	X	E

Second D = 7

Exchanges and results when D = 7 (includes 1 backward propagation of E from 17->10->3)

0	1	2	3	4	5	6	7	8	9	10	11	12	13	14	15	16	17	18	19	20	21	22	23	24
	D	E		F			A	B	G	K		M	N	F	I	S		E		Q			X		K
			E								G							G						
C	D	E	E	F	N	A	B	G	K	G	M	N	F	I	S	P	G	M	Q	Q	L	X	X	K

Third D = 3

Exchanges and results when D = 3 (includes backward propagations of A(3->0), B(4->1), I(11->:8), G(14->11->8), M(15->12), L(18->15->12), and K(21->18->15->12))

0	1	2	3	4	5	6	7	8	9	10	11	12	13	14	15	16	17	18	19	20	21	22	23	24
			A	B	G	E	F	M		F	I		G	G	M		N	L			K			S
A	B		C	D				G			I	K		M	L			M			N			
A	B	E	C	D	G	E	F	G	K	F	I	K	G	M	L	P	N	M	Q	Q	N	X	X	S

Last D = 1

Exchanges and results when D = 1 (includes backward propagations of F(9->8->7), G(12->11->10), M(17->16), N(20->19->18), and S(23->22))

0	1	2	3	4	5	6	7	8	9	10	11	12	13	14	15	16	17	18	19	20	21	22	23	24
		C	D	E	E	F	G		F	I	K	G	K	L	M	N	M	P		N	Q		S	X
							F	G	G	G	I	K				M	N	N	P	Q		S	X	
A	B	C	D	E	E	F	F	G	G	G	I	K	K	L	M	M	N	N	P	Q	Q	S	X	X

Figure 8-10: Schematic of the Shell sort algorithm

```
Public Sub ShellSort()
  Dim List1() As Integer = {11, 3, 4, 5, 6, 8, 9, 7, 2, 10}
  Dim Numrecs As Integer = _
    List1.GetUpperBound(0) + 1
  Dim i, D, HoldIndex, temp As Integer
  'set the initial distance
  D = 2
  Do Until D > Numrecs
    D *= 2
  Loop
  D = D / 2 - 1
  'main body of the Shell sort
  Do Until D = 0
    For i = 0 To (Numrecs - 1) - D
      If List1(i) > List1(i + D) Then
        HoldIndex = i
        Do While i >= 0 AndAlso List1(i) > List1(i + D)
          temp = List1(i)
          List1(i) = List1(i + D)
          List1(i + D) = temp
          i -= D
        Loop
        i = HoldIndex
      End If
    Next
    D /= 2
  Loop
End Sub
```

Figure 8-11: Shell sort algorithm

The Shell sort starts by calculating an optimum distance D between elements to be compared. (A good method for determining the initial D is explained in a moment.) On the first pass through the table, Table(*n*) is compared to Table(*n*+D), and, if these two elements are not in the correct sequence, their values are exchanged. The comparison and swapping continue for n=0, n=1, n=2, and so on, until n+D exceeds the number of elements in the table. This completes the first pass through the table. D is then halved (with the result rounded down, so that half of 15 is 7), and the second pass begins. The process continues until D=0, at which point the table has been sorted.

One more important concept is incorporated into the Shell sort: building on the notion of a shuttle sort, when two elements are swapped, this exchange is propagated backward through the table, that is, comparing Table(*n*) with Table(*n*–D), and swapping them if necessary.

Calculation of the initial D can be optimized by ensuring that D is always an odd number. This increases the likelihood that different elements are compared when D remains rather large, so that an element that needs to move a great distance moves early in the game. If an element does not begin moving until D=1, then it takes just as many exchanges to arrive at its final home as in the shuttle sort. The best way to achieve this optimal initial distance is by calculating the greatest multiple of 2<=N, and then subtracting 1 from that number. So if an array has 100 elements, the initial D should be 63 (64 being the largest multiple of 2<=100). Then, when D is halved on each subsequent pass, it becomes 31, 15, 7, 3, and 1. You can see the disadvantage of an even-numbered D: if D=8, for example, then the same pairs of elements are compared again indirectly when D=4, and again when D=2.

In the example in Figure 8-10, the initial D=15 is calculated as described here. So on the first pass through the table, Table(0) is compared to Table(15), Table(1) is compared with Table(16), ..., and Table(9) is compared with Table(24). Elements that are discovered to be out of sequence are swapped. However, backward propagation usually does not occur on the first pass through the table, because *n*–D is usually less than 0, and a table element with a negative index does not exist. At the end of the first pass, D is halved, becoming 7.

On the second pass, Table(0) is compared to Table(7), Table(1) with Table(8), Table(2) with Table(9), and so on. During this pass, although many swaps take place, only one backward propagation occurs: when Table(17)—K—is compared with Table(24)—E, then E propagates backward to Table(10) and then further to Table(3).

Spend some time examining Figure 8-10 until you feel comfortable with how the Shell sort works (this is not very easy). Then examine the code in Figure 8-11. For such a complex algorithm, the code is less complicated than you might have anticipated.

You have now examined the simple sort suggested by Hilda in Tutorial 6, the bubble or waterfall sort, the improved bubble sort, the selection sort, the insertion sort, the shuttle sort, and the Shell sort. Although each of these routines is capable of sorting any table, each is most useful in certain situations. Figure 8-12 summarizes the applicability of the sort routines you have visited.

The discussion of table-sorting algorithms in this text is not exhaustive. Among the algorithms not covered, the reader is referred to the Quicksort as perhaps the best for very large arrays.

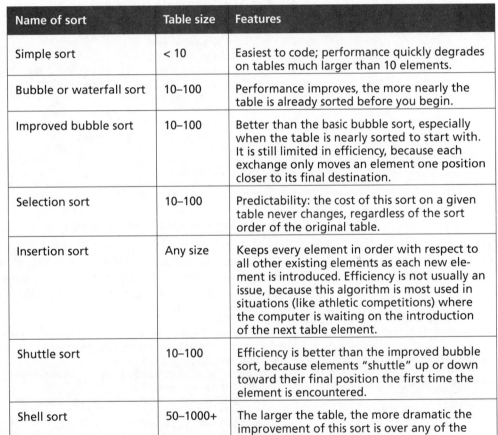

Name of sort	Table size	Features
Simple sort	< 10	Easiest to code; performance quickly degrades on tables much larger than 10 elements.
Bubble or waterfall sort	10–100	Performance improves, the more nearly the table is already sorted before you begin.
Improved bubble sort	10–100	Better than the basic bubble sort, especially when the table is nearly sorted to start with. It is still limited in efficiency, because each exchange only moves an element one position closer to its final destination.
Selection sort	10–100	Predictability: the cost of this sort on a given table never changes, regardless of the sort order of the original table.
Insertion sort	Any size	Keeps every element in order with respect to all other existing elements as each new element is introduced. Efficiency is not usually an issue, because this algorithm is most used in situations (like athletic competitions) where the computer is waiting on the introduction of the next table element.
Shuttle sort	10–100	Efficiency is better than the improved bubble sort, because elements "shuttle" up or down toward their final position the first time the element is encountered.
Shell sort	50–1000+	The larger the table, the more dramatic the improvement of this sort is over any of the other sorts discussed in this text.

Figure 8-12: Summary of sort routines

Sorting of Records

An array may contain multiple dimensions or fields. When an exchange or other assignment needs to be made, you must exchange or assign the entire record (row), not just the sort key. If you do not exchange all of the fields, then it would be as if you took a roster of students, including their names, e-mail addresses, and phone numbers, and then sorted only their names: the name column would end up in the correct alphabetical order, but the e-mail addresses and phone numbers would no longer be associated with the correct names.

For example, consider a list of bowlers with their scores. In this list, column 0 identifies each bowler by a bowler ID number, and column 1 contains that bowler's score. This data can be loaded into a two-dimensional array. The procedure in Figure 8-13 uses a bubble sort to sort the array, with column 1 as the sort key. Note that when an exchange is necessary, the exchange statements are repeated for each column.

```
Public Sub BubbleSortWith2DimensionalArray()
'bowler ID number is in column 0, score is in column 1.
'objective is to sort the bowlers in descending
'order by score (column 1)
  Dim List1(,) As Integer = {{4, 192}, {5, 200}, _
      {2, 144}, {1, 152}, {3, 118}}
  Dim i, j, temp As Integer
  Dim Numrecs As Integer = _
    List1.GetUpperBound(0) + 1
  For i = Numrecs - 2 To 0 Step -1
    For j = 0 To i
      If List1(j, 1) < List1(j + 1, 1) Then
        'swap column 0
        temp = List1(j, 0)
        List1(j, 0) = List1(j + 1, 0)
        List1(j + 1, 0) = temp
        'swap column 1
        temp = List1(j, 1)
        List1(j, 1) = List1(j + 1, 1)
        List1(j + 1, 1) = temp
      End If
    Next
  Next
End Sub
```

Figure 8-13: Bubble sort of a two-dimensional array

Now consider the arrangement of the bowlers' names, ID numbers, and scores contained within a structure. Figure 8-14 is an example of sorting an array of structures, in which the comparison is based on one field of the structure, but the exchange references the entire structure.

```
Public Sub BubbleSortOfStructures()
  Const NUMRECS As Integer = 5
  'assume that structBowler contains BowlerID,
  ' BowlerName, and Score
  Dim aBowlers(NUMRECS) As structBowler

  Dim i, j As Integer
  Dim temp As structBowler
  '(insert statements to initialize the aBowlers() array)

  'sort the array of structures
  For i = NUMRECS - 2 To 0 Step -1
    For j = 0 To i
      If aBowlers(j).Score < aBowlers(j + 1).Score Then
        temp = aBowlers(j)
        aBowlers(j) = aBowlers(j + 1)
        aBowlers(j + 1) = temp
      End If
    Next
  Next
End Sub
```

Figure 8-14: Bubble sort of a structure

A Simple File-sorting Algorithm

Sorting a sequential data file is much slower than sorting a table, for two reasons: the data is on some form of media and must be read into memory, and you cannot jump ahead or backward through the file—so anything like the Shell sort is out of the question. In fact, most table sorts are not feasible for sequential files. As a corollary to this principle, you would correctly conclude that, when you need to sort the records in a file, if that file is small enough to fit into main memory, then by far the fastest approach is to load the entire file into an array, sort the array using any of the algorithms presented here, and then rewrite the array to the file. Having said that, the need for file-sorting methods remains, when the file size renders it impractical to load the entire file into an array.

Many file-sorting algorithms have been developed over the years. The one explained here is a basic model for many similar routines. Whether or not you ever need to write a routine to sort a sequential data file, you should at least understand how such a sort routine works.

This file sort routine has four phases: initialization, partition, merge, and finalization. The routine requires a source file used in initialization and a destination file (which can be the same as the source file, but need not be) used in finalization. The routine also requires three other files, each as large as the source file, which are used as work areas while the sort routine is in progress. These files are named MergeFile, PartitionA, and PartitionB. At various points in the sort routine, MergeFile contains all of the records to be sorted, whereas PartitionA and PartitionB each contain some of the records to be sorted.

In the initialization phase, the work areas for MergeFile, PartitionA, and PartitionB are reserved, and the source file is copied to MergeFile.

Next, the partition and merge phases are executed, and they continue until PartitionB is empty at the end of the partition phase. The operation of the partition and merge phases for a sample file can be followed in Figure 8-15.

```
(Initial) MergeFile: 12, 66, 75, 43, 33, 33, 11, 34, 55, 78, 94, 80

1st pass: Partition Phase:
          PartitionA: 12, 66, 75, 33, 33, 80
          PartitionB: 43, 11, 34, 55, 78, 94
       Merge Phase: MergeFile: 12, 43, 11, 34, 55, 66, 75, 33, 33, 78, 80, 94

2nd pass: Partition Phase:
          PartitionA: 12, 43, 33, 33, 78, 80, 94
          PartitionB: 11, 34, 55, 66, 75
       Merge Phase: MergeFile: 11, 12, 34, 43, 33, 33, 55, 66, 75, 78, 80, 94

3rd pass: Partition Phase:
          PartitionA: 11, 12, 34, 43
          PartitionB: 33, 33, 55, 66, 75, 78, 80, 94
       Merge Phase: MergeFile: 11, 12, 33, 33, 34, 43, 55, 66, 75, 78, 80, 94

4th pass: Partition:
          PartitionA: 11, 12, 33, 33, 34, 43, 55, 66, 75, 78, 80, 94
          PartitionB: (empty)
```

Figure 8-15: Partition and merge phases of a sample file sort

In the partition phase, records are read from MergeFile and partitioned into PartitionA and PartitionB. The first record read from MergeFile is written to PartitionA. If the next record read from MergeFile is greater than or equal to the last record, it is also written to PartitionA. Copying records from MergeFile to PartitionA continues until a record read from MergeFile is less than the last record. When this occurs, the record read from MergeFile is written to PartitionB. The following records read from MergeFile are written to PartitionB, as long as each is greater than or equal to the last record. When this is no longer the case, the output file switches back to PartitionA. Whenever an out-of-sequence record is encountered, the output switches from PartitionA to PartitionB, or from PartitionB to PartitionA. This process continues until MergeFile is exhausted, which ends the partition phase. PartitionA and PartitionB are closed for output and opened for input. MergeFile is closed for input and opened for output (which erases its previous contents).

In the merge phase, a record is read from PartitionA and a record is read from PartitionB, and these two records are compared. The lesser-valued record is written to MergeFile, and another record is then read from whichever file sent the previous record to MergeFile. This process continues until PartitionA and PartitionB are both exhausted. All three files are then closed. This completes one pass of the partition and merge phases.

The partition and merge phases are repeated until the partition phase results in all the records ending up in PartitionA (meaning they are all in sequence), and PartitionB is empty. This triggers the finalization phase of the file sort, in which MergeFile is copied to the destination file.

The Up Close and Personal application in Tutorial 8 does not require you to write a file sort routine; nevertheless, it's useful for any programmer to understand how a file sort can work. You might even want to try your hand at coding one.

Sequential and Binary Search Techniques

Pick a number from 1 to 100, and now consider the following two search strategies in order to find the number that you have picked (assume you picked 78). Strategy 1: is the number 1? (No.) Is it 2? (No.) Is it 3? (No.) Is it 4? (No.) Continue until the answer is yes (in this case upon the 78th question). Now you understand a sequential search. In this case, finding the correct number took 78 questions. Using a sequential search technique for finding any number from 1 to 100 takes a maximum of 100 questions and an average of 50 questions.

Strategy 2: is the number 50? (No.) Is it less than 50? (No.) Because the answer is no, you have eliminated numbers 1 through 50. Hence, the next question can ask about the midpoint of the remaining possibilities. Is it 75? (No.) Is it less than 75? (No.) Again, compute the midpoint of the remaining possibilities. Is it 87? (No.) Is it less than 87? (Yes.) Compute the midpoint between 75 and 87, that is, (75+87)/2, or 81. Is it 81? (No.) Is it less than 81? (Yes.) Compute the midpoint of the remaining possibilities, namely (75+81)/2, or 78. Is it 78? Yes! Now you have an inkling of a binary search. This took a total of five iterations of a loop, where each iteration required three statements: is it equal to N, is it less than N, and a recomputation of the midpoint.

Using a binary search technique, each time you ask *Is it less than N?*, the answer eliminates half of the possibilities, and this is followed by a recomputation of the midpoint of the remaining possibilities, from either the upper half or the lower half of the range of possibilities that existed up to that point. To find a number from 1 to 100 takes a maximum of seven iterations of this loop (because $2^7=128$).

The advantage of a binary search technique becomes even more apparent as the table becomes larger. For example, to search through a table of 1000 values takes a maximum of 1000 questions and an average of 500 questions using a sequential search. But the same table can be searched using a binary search technique with only 10 iterations of the loop (because $2^{10}=1024$), as each iteration of the loop reduces the remaining possible answers by half.

Any array, whether ordered or not, can be searched sequentially. But only an ordered array can be searched using a binary search technique. In a sequential search, every element of the array is compared to the search argument, beginning with the first array element and continuing until the search argument is found or all array elements have been compared. As the example illustrates, in a binary search the index of the middle element in the array is computed (the lowest index plus the highest index plus 1, divided by 2), and then the middle element in the array is compared to the search argument. And, if the middle element does not equal the search argument, then the search is narrowed to either the upper half or lower half of the table—that is, if the search argument is greater than the middle element, then the index of the middle element becomes the new lowest index. However, if the search argument is less than the middle element, then the index of the middle element becomes the highest index. This process is repeated until the search argument is found, or until low equals middle, meaning the search argument is not in the array.

The algorithm for a binary search, as shown in Figure 8-16, is actually shorter than the words needed to explain it. In this example, the alphabet is loaded into an array and is then used for the binary search. But the array can contain any list of values, as long as they are ordered.

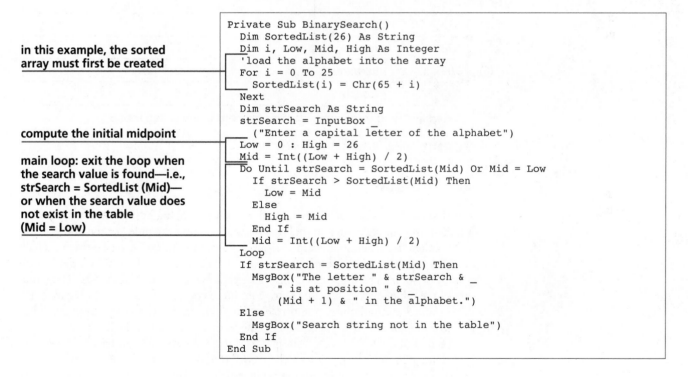

```
Private Sub BinarySearch()
  Dim SortedList(26) As String
  Dim i, Low, Mid, High As Integer
  'load the alphabet into the array
  For i = 0 To 25
    SortedList(i) = Chr(65 + i)
  Next
  Dim strSearch As String
  strSearch = InputBox _
    ("Enter a capital letter of the alphabet")
  Low = 0 : High = 26
  Mid = Int((Low + High) / 2)
  Do Until strSearch = SortedList(Mid) Or Mid = Low
    If strSearch > SortedList(Mid) Then
      Low = Mid
    Else
      High = Mid
    End If
    Mid = Int((Low + High) / 2)
  Loop
  If strSearch = SortedList(Mid) Then
    MsgBox("The letter " & strSearch & _
        " is at position " & _
        (Mid + 1) & " in the alphabet.")
  Else
    MsgBox("Search string not in the table")
  End If
End Sub
```

in this example, the sorted array must first be created

compute the initial midpoint

main loop: exit the loop when the search value is found—i.e., strSearch = SortedList (Mid)— or when the search value does not exist in the table (Mid = Low)

Figure 8-16: Binary search algorithm

Linked Lists

The next in-memory data structure in this lesson is a linked list, which you will implement within a table. Sometimes you encounter a list that must be maintained in its present order, but that must be accessed in a different order. For example, you might have a list of athletes organized by Athlete ID, and you need to keep this list in Athlete ID sequence for whatever reason, but you might want to display that list in alphabetical order by athlete name. A linked list would fit the bill neatly, as shown in Figure 8-17.

Structure of this list:

```
Private Structure structLink
   Dim AthleteID As String
   Dim Name As String
   Dim OtherInfo As String
   Dim Pointer As Integer
End Structure

Dim paLinkedList(8) As structLink
Dim ExternalPtr As Integer = 6
```

Index	AthleteID	Name	(other columns...)	Pointer
(0)	123	Mary		4
(1)	234	Sam		–9 (end of list)
(2)	345	Billy		3
(3)	456	James		7
(4)	567	Sally		1
(5)	678	Josey		0
(6)	789	Barbara		2
(7)	890	Joseph		5

ExternalPtr (which points to the first element in the linked list): 6

Figure 8-17: Sample linked list of athletes

Using a Linked List

You first examine this completed linked list before looking at how to construct one. A linked list consists of an external pointer that contains the index of the first element in the linked list. Then, that element contains a pointer to the second element, which contains a pointer to the third element, and so on. The last element contains a null pointer or some agreed upon sentinel value that marks the end of the list. The structure of the table must include the extra column to contain the pointer. In Figure 8-17, the variable ExternalPointer points to element 6, the first name to appear in an alphabetical listing of athletes. The sentinel value to mark the end of the list is –9.

Using a linked list is fairly simple. You use the external pointer to retrieve the first element in the list, in this case the record for Barbara at index 6 (the value of the external pointer). Then you use the pointer field in Barbara's record to get the next element in the list at index 2 (Billy). Billy's pointer field points to index 3 (James), and James' pointer points to index 7 (Joseph). You continue following the links until Sam's record, whose pointer field marks the end of the list. Sample code to traverse the list in Figure 8-17 is shown in Figure 8-18. This procedure writes the athletes' names in alphabetical order to the Console.

```
Private Sub TraverseTheLinkedList()
  Dim Ptr As Integer = ExternalPtr
  Do Until Ptr = -9
    With paLinkedList(Ptr)
      System.Console.WriteLine(.Name)
      Ptr = .Pointer
    End With
  Loop
End Sub
```

Figure 8-18: Procedure to traverse a linked list

Building a Linked List

Building a linked list is not quite so simple, but the following steps explain exactly how to do it. For this example, assume that you start with the list in Figure 8-19, hoping to end up with the list in Figure 8-17.

```
Private Structure structLink
  Dim AthleteID As String
  Dim Name As String
  Dim OtherInfo As String
End Structure

Dim paOriginalList(8) As structLink
```

AthleteID	Name	(other columns...)
123	Mary	
234	Sam	
345	Billy	
456	James	
567	Sally	
678	Josey	
789	Barbara	
890	Joseph	

Figure 8-19: Original list

To build a linked list, you begin by adding a pointer column to the original table, as well as an external variable to hold the index value of the first element in the list. See Figure 8-20.

Structure of this list:

```
Private Structure structLink
    Dim AthleteID As String
    Dim Name As String
    Dim OtherInfo As String
    Dim Pointer As Integer
End Structure

Dim paOriginalList(8) As structLink
Dim ExternalPtr As Integer
```

Index	AthleteID	Name	(other columns...)	Pointer
(0)	123	Mary		
(1)	234	Sam		
(2)	345	Billy		
(3)	456	James		
(4)	567	Sally		
(5)	678	Josey		
(6)	789	Barbara		
(7)	890	Joseph		

Figure 8-20: Original table with pointer field and external pointer

Next, you create a parallel table to the original table, consisting of three columns: the index, the link field that is the basis for the linked list (such as the name field in the example), and the pointer field, as shown in Figure 8-21. (Sometimes it's easier to copy the entire original table, but that only works if the original table includes a column containing the index value of each row. In any case, these three columns are all that is needed to create the linked list.) When you initially load it, the parallel table is in the same order as the original table. Examine Figure 8-21 as it creates and loads the parallel table.

The next step is to sort the parallel table based on the link field. You can use any table sort technique, but you must remember to exchange the entire record whenever an exchange is needed. See Figure 8-22.

```
Private Structure structParallel
  Dim Index As Integer
  Dim Name As String
  Dim Pointer As Integer
End Structure

Dim paParallelList(8) As structParallel

Private Sub LoadParallelList()
  Dim i As Integer
  For i = 0 To 7
    With paParallelList(i)
      .Index = i
      .Name = paOriginalList(i).Name
    End With
  Next
End Sub
```

Index	Name	Pointer
0	Mary	
1	Sam	
2	Billy	
3	James	
4	Sally	
5	Josey	
6	Barbara	
7	Joseph	

Figure 8-21: Parallel table, with code to load it, in original table order

'use any sort routine to sort the table by name;		
Index	**Name**	**Pointer**
6	Barbara	
2	Billy	
3	James	
7	Joseph	
5	Josey	
0	Mary	
4	Sally	
1	Sam	

Figure 8-22: Parallel table, sorted by link field

When the sort is complete, step through the parallel table, assigning the pointer column. The value in the pointer field is always the original index value (from the original table) of the next element in the parallel table. Then, the original index value of the first element in the parallel table is assigned to the external pointer, and the pointer field of the last element in the parallel table is assigned the sentinel value marking the end of the list. In this case, the sentinel value –9 was chosen. These actions are reflected in Figure 8-23.

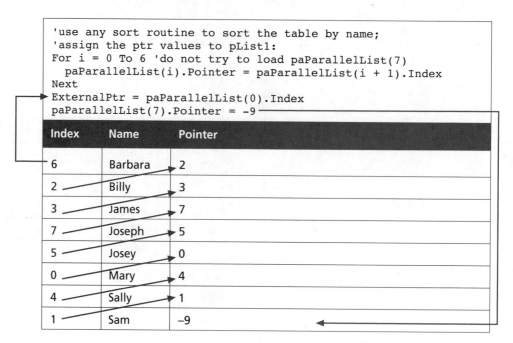

Figure 8-23: Parallel table, sorted by link field and with pointers assigned

Next, you re-sort the parallel table into the order of the original table, as shown in Figure 8-24.

Index	Name	Pointer
0	Mary	4
1	Sam	–9
2	Billy	3
3	James	7
4	Sally	1
5	Josey	0
6	Barbara	2
7	Joseph	5

Figure 8-24: Parallel list, re-sorted into original order

Finally, you copy the pointer field from the parallel table back to the original table, renamed here as paLinkedList(). After these last actions are complete, as shown in Figure 8-25, the parallel table can be discarded.

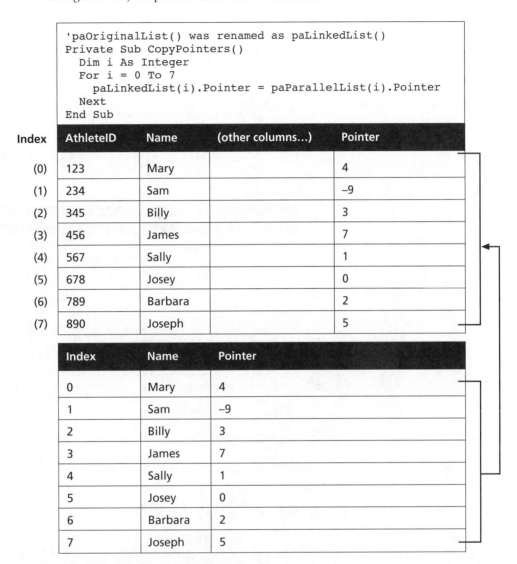

```
'paOriginalList() was renamed as paLinkedList()
Private Sub CopyPointers()
  Dim i As Integer
  For i = 0 To 7
    paLinkedList(i).Pointer = paParallelList(i).Pointer
  Next
End Sub
```

Index	AthleteID	Name	(other columns...)	Pointer
(0)	123	Mary		4
(1)	234	Sam		–9
(2)	345	Billy		3
(3)	456	James		7
(4)	567	Sally		1
(5)	678	Josey		0
(6)	789	Barbara		2
(7)	890	Joseph		5

Index	Name	Pointer
0	Mary	4
1	Sam	–9
2	Billy	3
3	James	7
4	Sally	1
5	Josey	0
6	Barbara	2
7	Joseph	5

Figure 8-25: Completion of the linked list

Inserting a Record into a Linked List

Imagine that a new record for Harry is added to paLinkedList at Index 8, as shown in Figure 8-26. How do you insert him into the links? You follow these steps: traverse the linked list until you identify the record following Harry's record, but always keeping track of the pointer to the current record as well as the pointer to the previous record. This occurs when you reach James. You now want Harry (rather than Billy) to point next to James, so insert Billy's pointer field (3) into Harry's pointer field. And you want Billy to point to Harry, so insert Harry's index (8) into Billy's pointer field.

```
Private Sub InsertIntoTheLinkedList()
  Dim Ptr As Integer = ExternalPtr
  Dim PreviousPtr As Integer = ExternalPtr
  Dim NewIndex As Integer = paLinkedList.GetUpperBound(0)
  If paLinkedList(ExternalPtr).Name < _
      paLinkedList(NewIndex).Name Then
    Do While paLinkedList(Ptr).Name < _
        paLinkedList(NewIndex).Name And Ptr <> -9
      PreviousPtr = Ptr
      Ptr = paLinkedList(Ptr).Pointer
    Loop
    paLinkedList(NewIndex).Pointer = Ptr
    paLinkedList(PreviousPtr).Pointer = NewIndex
  Else 'new record is the first record in the linked list
    paLinkedList(NewIndex).Pointer = ExternalPtr
    ExternalPtr = NewIndex
  End If
End Sub
```

Index	AthleteID	Name	(other columns...)	Pointer
(0)	123	Mary		4
(1)	234	Sam		−9
(2)	345	Billy		was 3, becomes 8
(3)	456	James		7
(4)	567	Sally		1
(5)	678	Josey		0
(6)	789	Barbara		2
(7)	890	Joseph		5
(8)	901	Harry		becomes 3

Figure 8-26: Inserting a record into a linked list

Deleting a Record from a Linked List

To delete a record from a linked list, you traverse the list looking for the record to be deleted, again keeping track of both the pointer to the current record and the pointer to the previous record. When you find the record to be deleted, insert its pointer field into the pointer field of the record that points to this record. The logic for deleting Josey from the linked list is shown in Figure 8-27. Note that, after this code executes, Josey's record is still physically in the table, but you never encounter the record by traversing the links, so it is effectively removed.

```
Private Sub DeleteFromTheLinkedList()
  Dim Ptr As Integer = ExternalPtr
  Dim PreviousPtr As Integer = ExternalPtr
  Dim NewIndex As Integer = _
    paLinkedList.GetUpperBound(0)
  Dim strSearch = InputBox _
    ("Enter name of athlete to be deleted: ")
  If paLinkedList(ExternalPtr).Name = strSearch Then
    'record to be deleted is the first record
    paLinkedList(ExternalPtr).Name = "unused"
    ExternalPtr = paLinkedList(ExternalPtr).Pointer
  Else
    Do Until paLinkedList(Ptr).Name = strSearch _
        Or Ptr = -9
      PreviousPtr = Ptr
      Ptr = paLinkedList(Ptr).Pointer
    Loop
    If paLinkedList(Ptr).Name = strSearch Then
      paLinkedList(PreviousPtr).Pointer = _
        paLinkedList(Ptr).Pointer
      paLinkedList(Ptr).Name = "unused"
    Else
      MessageBox.Show(strSearch & _
        " is not in the linked list")
    End If
  End If
End Sub
```

Index	AthleteID	Name	(other columns...)	Pointer
(0)	123	Mary		4
(1)	234	Sam		-9
(2)	345	Billy		8
(3)	456	James		7
(4)	567	Sally		1
(5)	678	was Josey, becomes unused		0
(6)	789	Barbara		2
(7)	890	Joseph		was 5, becomes 0
(8)	901	Harry		3

Figure 8-27: Deleting a record from a linked list

If necessary, you can also mark the record for deletion, or blank out its fields. If you physically remove the record from the table, all of the links in the linked list are broken, and you have to regenerate the linked list from scratch. Therefore, in some applications, the developer maintains a separate linked list of empty or unused record space within the table, so that, when a new record is to be added, a record is deleted from the linked list of unused records and added to the linked list of active records. This avoids having to build the linked list anew.

Pseudo-ISAM Files in Visual Basic .NET

Most business applications require the storage of information for later use. Up to this point, the Friendsville Games Development Team has used sequential files and random-access files, and beginning in Tutorial 9, database files will be used for this purpose. Data storage in the Up Close and Personal application in Tutorial 8 is based on a concept called an Index Sequential Access Method (ISAM) file. IBM originally introduced ISAM files as an improvement over both sequential and random-access files, combining the two concepts for the many business situations in which random access is often needed, but sequential access might also be needed. For example, the checking account system at a bank requires random-access processing of one customer's record when that customer comes to the bank to make a withdrawal; however, the checking account system requires sequential processing of all the customer records for the purpose of producing monthly checking account statements. ISAMs were invented to fill that need.

Although it is true that the functionality of ISAM files has been largely replaced by database files, you still find the occasional use for the former. This might especially be true for an application like Up Close and Personal, in which the application is intended for distribution to the general public, all of whom cannot be expected to have any particular database software installed on their computers.

This discussion includes a review of sequential and random-access data files, an introduction to the notion of ISAM files, and a summary of the pseudo-ISAM files in Visual Basic .NET. The term *pseudo-ISAM* refers to a file structure that achieves the functionality of the index sequential-access method, even though Visual Basic .NET does not support ISAM files directly. Figure 8-28 depicts the file structures graphically.

Traditional File Structures: Sequential and Random Access

You have already been exposed to two traditional file structures in this text: sequential files and random files. A sequential file contains discrete data items written to the file one after the other. When a sequential file is opened for output or append, the data pointer is positioned at the end of the file, and data is written to the file from that point forward. One advantage of the sequential file structure is that each data item may be of any base data type and any length. You cannot read data from a sequential file when it is opened for output. Closing a sequential file that has been opened for output or to have another item appended to it creates an EOF (end-of-file) mark after the last data item.

When a sequential file is opened for input, the data pointer is positioned at the beginning of the file. Each read operation retrieves one data item from the file and repositions the data pointer following that item. Read operations can continue until the EOF mark is encountered. If you build a sequential data file containing the feeding habits of all the animals in the zoo in alphabetical order, and you want to look up the feeding habits of zebras, you must read about aardvarks and alligators first. That is to say, a sequential file is similar to songs on a cassette tape: there is no way to skip directly to the end of the file and then read the last record, and there is no way to skip around the file. When the sequential file is opened for input, you cannot write data to the file.

tip

A base data type is like a string or an integer or a double, not a structure or array or object.

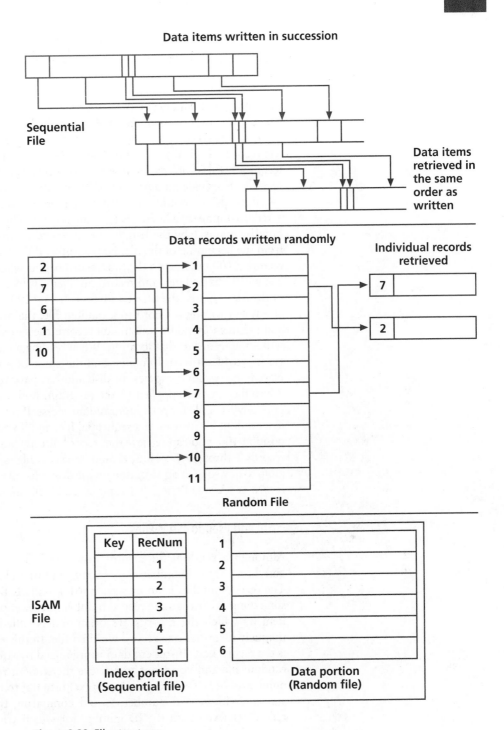

Figure 8-28: File structures

One advantage of sequential file processing is that when you do need to process every data item in a file, this file access method is faster than other methods. The speed comes from the fact that the disk-operating system loads a buffer area before writing to the file, and only writes when the buffer is full or the program closes the file or terminates; and similarly on read operations, the disk-operating system fills the buffer with data items from the file and only returns to read more data after all data items have been extracted from the buffer. Another advantage of a sequential file is its simplicity. For example, in Tutorial 6, you save the start date for the Friendsville

International Games in a sequential file all by itself. Sequential files require no special structures or complicated connections, and the syntax for accessing them is the least complicated of all file access methods.

A random-access data file introduces the notion of fixed-length records rather than individual data items. A record, such as the information concerning a single athlete, consists of a series of data items, such as last name, first name, city of birth, year of birth, and so on. The random-access file consists of the collection of all of the athlete records. Typically, the record layout is defined in a Structure statement, although technically this is not required. An entire record is written to or read from the random-data file in a single input/output (I/O) operation, rather than one data item at a time.

Records in a random file can be written to a specific location in the file based on a record number, which must be an integer. The computer multiplies the record number minus 1 by the length of one record in order to compute an offset address from the beginning of the file. For example, if the fixed-record length of one athlete's record is 100 bytes, then the first record begins where the file begins, the next record begins 100 bytes later, and record number 6 is located 500 bytes after the beginning of the file. That is, the offset address is (6–1)*100=500 bytes.

When writing a record to a random file, the program provides a record number and the memory address of a data record; the system computes the disk address and writes the record to that location. When reading a record from a random file, the program provides a record number and the name of a variable where the record can be placed; the system computes the disk address, retrieves the specified record, and copies it into the variable supplied by the program. Both read and write operations are supported when a file is opened for random access. If the animals' feeding habits are stored in a random file instead of a sequential file, and if you know that the zebra record is at position 100, you can retrieve that record directly without first having to read through records 1 through 99. Thus, a random-access file is more like a music CD—you can jump to any song at any location on the disk. However, unlike the songs on a CD, every record in a Visual Basic .NET random-access file must be the same length.

ISAM and Pseudo-ISAM Files

Although a random file affords quick and direct access to an individual record based on a record number, the user may not often know what the record number is. The record number is an integer, starting with 1. But the file may be organized by something other than the record number, for example, student ID number. The data item by which the records are organized is called the **record key**. A record key uniquely identifies one record within a file. In this example, the student ID number is the record key. If student data is organized by student ID number and stored in a random file and you want to retrieve the student record for the student whose ID number is 441-10-6300, you have no choice but to retrieve the records sequentially, starting with record number 1, and comparing the student ID number of each record retrieved with the ID number for which you are searching, continuing this process until you encounter the record of student 441-10-6300.

ISAM files were invented as a partial solution to this problem. An **Index Sequential Access Method (ISAM) file** actually consists of two portions (two physical files, but only one logical file as far as the programmer is concerned): the data is stored in a random-access file, ordered by a record key field. Then, a separate index file contains a list of all the record keys (column 1) and the record numbers of the associated records (column 2). When the user creates a new record, a new ISAM record is written to the data portion of the file in the correct sequence, and a new entry is also made in the index file. When a record is deleted, the record is not physically removed from the file; rather, a status byte (usually the first element in the record layout) is changed from A for *active* to I for *inactive*. Because the data records are maintained in the proper sequence, the programmer can process all of the records sequentially (which is actually rather fast) in those instances when all of the records might need to be processed, such as printing the monthly statements for all of the customers at the bank. But when only one record needs to be processed, the index file (often small enough to fit entirely in main memory) can be quickly searched, and then just the one data record can be retrieved directly. Figure 8-28 illustrates the relationship between the index and the data portions of an ISAM file.

ISAM files have been implemented on many mainframe computers as part of the operating system. When ISAM files are formally implemented, the programmer is responsible only for maintaining the integrity of the record key field, that is, making sure that the key of each record exists and is unique. The user program supplies a record key for writing or reading a record, and the operating system software takes care of everything else. The actual manipulation of ISAM data and index records is transparent to the programmer—for example, reserving space between records for future growth, repositioning records to permit insertion of a new record in the proper sequence, and updating the data records and index records simultaneously so as to keep them synchronized. (To say that something is *transparent* to the programmer means that the programmer does not see it directly—the ISAM file-processing system takes care of these file maintenance tasks behind the scenes and without direct programmer involvement.) The programmer does not even need to be aware that there are two physical files in existence—from the programmer's perspective, it all appears as one ISAM file.

ISAM technology has not generally been implemented on microcomputers. However, you can gain nearly the same advantages with a pseudo-ISAM file in Visual Basic .NET. Just as with a real ISAM file structure, a **pseudo-ISAM file** on a microcomputer has a data portion and an index portion. The difference is that the programmer (rather than the operating system) is responsible for maintaining both portions, and you do it with two separate files. You build a random-access data file for the data portion of the file, and you build a sequential-access file for the index. In most cases, the index file is small enough to fit entirely into an array in main memory. When retrieving a single record, you search the index array using the record key as the search argument, and when you find the record key, you use the corresponding record number to retrieve the data record from the random file. When you create a new record or delete a record, you make the appropriate change to the index array, and then write the array back to the sequential file. In addition, you must include a routine that recreates the index (the sequential file and corresponding array) in case it becomes corrupted. In this case, you must re-create the index file by reading through every record in the random file, and copying the record key and the record number to the sequential file.

A Sample Pseudo-ISAM File

This section describes a pseudo-ISAM file, including its structure, the contents of sample records, a form for displaying the whole index and one data record, and the associated code. Working through this sample helps to clarify the components and operations of a pseudo-ISAM file.

The purpose of this sample pseudo-ISAM file is to keep track of the thousands of tasks involved in staging the Friendsville International Games. The tasks involve everything from construction to security, from advertising to ticket sales—from soup to nuts, so to speak. The management team wants to be able to record and retrieve any task based on a brief task name, to browse the task names, and to retrieve the complete task description, contact person, and task status. A pseudo-ISAM file for this purpose includes the structures shown in Figure 8-29. A sketch of these file structures, Figure 8-30, helps you visualize how they work.

```
Public Structure structISAM_Data
  'RecStatus = A (active), I (inactive)
  <VBFixedString(1)> Public RecStatus As String
  Public RecNum As Integer
  <VBFixedString(20)> Public TaskName As String
  'TaskStatus = P (planned), I (in progress), F (finished)
  <VBFixedString(1)> Public TaskStatus As String
  <VBFixedString(20)> Public Contact As String
  <VBFixedString(2000)> Public Description As String
End Structure

Public Structure structISAM_Index
  Public RecNum As Integer
  <VBFixedString(20)> Public TaskName As String
End Structure

Public pISAM_DataRec As structISAM_Data
Public paISAM_Index(10000) As structISAM_Index
Public pCboPtr As Integer
```

Figure 8-29: Pseudo-ISAM sample file structures

RecNum	TaskName
1	BldAppleHouse
2	Sec:OpenCerem
3	Sec:CloseCerem
4	I

ISAM index

	Record 1	Record 2	Record 3	Record 4
RecStatus	A	A	A	I
RecNum	1	2	3	4
TaskName	BldAppleHouse	Sec:OpenCerem	Sec:CloseCerem	I
TaskStatus	F	I	P	
Contact	Merrill	Josephson	Josephson	
Description	Build the Apple House in the International Village	Security for the Opening Ceremonies	Security for the Closing Ceremonies	

ISAM data

Figure 8-30: Sketch of pseudo-ISAM files

Notice in the code shown in Figure 8-29 that structISAM_Data describes the data portion of the ISAM file, stored in a file named ISAM_Data and loaded into memory one record at a time into a variable named pISAM_DataRec. The fields (elements) of pISAM_DataRec are as follows:

- *.RecStatus*—The status of the record, either A (active) or I (inactive)
- *.RecNum*—The record number used for writing and reading a random record
- *.TaskName*—The brief name of the task; if the task has not been used, the TaskName also is set to I
- *TaskStatus*—The status of the task; P is for *planned*, I for *in-process*, and F for *finished*
- *Contact*—The contact person for this task
- *Description*—The long description of the specific task

structISAM_Index describes the index file portion of the pseudo-ISAM file, stored in a file named SAM_Index and loaded entirely into memory at start-up into an array named paISAM_Index() with 10,000 elements. Each element of paISAM_Index() contains two fields that correspond to fields of the same name in pISAM_DataRec, namely .RecNum and .TaskName.

At start-up, the sequential index file (ISAM_Index) is loaded into the array, and task names are loaded in cboTaskName. The random-data file (ISAM_Data) is also opened, though no record in ISAM_Data is accessed. See Figure 8-31.

```
Private Sub frmISAM_Load(ByVal sender As Object, _
    ByVal e As System.EventArgs) Handles MyBase.Load
 'routine runs at start-up
 cboTaskName.Items.Clear()
 'open the index file and load it into the array
 FileOpen(1, "ISAM_Index", OpenMode.Input)
 For pCboPtr = 0 To 9999
   Input(1, paISAM_Index(pCboPtr).RecNum)
   Input(1, paISAM_Index(pCboPtr).TaskName)
   cboTaskName.Items.Add(paISAM_Index(pCboPtr).TaskName)
 Next
 cboTaskName.Text = "Select TaskName"
 'close the index file
 FileClose(1)
 'open the data file (remain open during processing)
 FileOpen(2, "ISAM_Data", OpenMode.Random, , _
   Len(pISAM_DataRec))
End Sub
```

Figure 8-31: frmISAM_Load() code

Figure 8-32 suggests a very simple form that could display the key fields of pISAM_DataRec. Note in this form and in the procedures that follow, that the user never sees the RecNum field. The user knows the records only by TaskName. But the computer stores records in the random file by RecNum, and the index provides the bridge between the TaskName field and the RecNum.

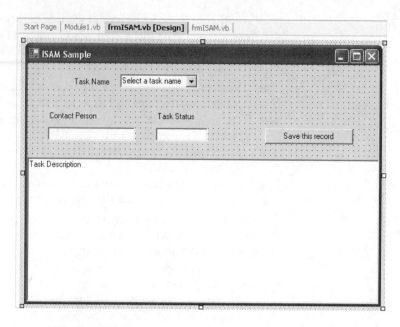

Figure 8-32: frmISAM GUI

During processing, when the user selects a task name from cboTaskName, the corresponding RecNum is retrieved from the paISAM_Index() array, and this RecNum is then used to retrieve the desired record from the random file. This takes place in the cboTaskName_SelectedIndexChanged () procedure, as shown in Figure 8-33.

```
Private Sub cboTaskName_SelectedIndexChanged(ByVal _
    sender As System.Object, ByVal e As System.EventArgs) _
    Handles cboTaskName.SelectedIndexChanged
  'the selected index of cboTaskName identifies
  'the desired record number
  pCboPtr = cboTaskName.SelectedIndex
  FileGet(2, pISAM_DataRec, pCboPtr)
  With pISAM_DataRec
    If .RecStatus = "A" Then
      'load the retrieved record into the form
      txtContact.Text = .Contact
      txtTaskStatus.Text = .TaskStatus
      rtfDescription.Text = .Description
    Else
      rtfDescription.Text = "That record is not active"
    End If
  End With
End Sub
```

Figure 8-33: cboTaskName_SelectedIndexChanged() procedure

Writing a record involves loading the fields of pISAM_DataRec, writing pISAM_DataRec to the random-data file, updating the array to reflect the new index information, and rewriting the entire array back to the sequential index file. This is accomplished in the btnSave_Click() procedure, as shown in Figure 8-34.

```
Private Sub btnSave_Click(ByVal sender As System.Object, _
    ByVal e As System.EventArgs) Handles btnSave.Click
  Dim i As Integer
  'update the array, in case the task name changed
  paISAM_Index(pCboPtr).TaskName = cboTaskName.Text
  'load the data record record from the array and form
  With pISAM_DataRec
    .RecStatus = "A"
    .RecNum = paISAM_Index(pCboPtr).RecNum
    .TaskName = paISAM_Index(pCboPtr).TaskName
    .Contact = txtContact.Text
    .TaskStatus = txtTaskStatus.Text
    .Description = rtfDescription.Text
    FilePut(2, pISAM_DataRec, .RecNum)
  End With
  'rewrite the index file
  FileOpen(1, "ISAM_Index", OpenMode.Output)
  For i = 0 To 9999
    Write(1, paISAM_Index(i).RecNum)
    WriteLine(1, paISAM_Index(i).TaskName)
  Next
  FileClose(1)
End Sub
```

Figure 8-34: btnSave_Click() procedure

If the number of active tasks becomes so large that searching cboTaskName for retrieval of a task becomes too cumbersome, then the entire array can be sorted using one of the sort algorithms previously discussed, and the sorted list can then be searched using a binary search technique. In any case, searching the array in main memory is always faster than searching a file. Thus, the pseudo-ISAM file fulfills its promise of processing very large data files (too large to fit into memory) without giving up too much in terms of processing speed.

Finally, if you find that you must search for records based on another key field (in this case, for instance, you might want to find the tasks for which a particular contact person is responsible), then you can build a secondary index, sorted by the secondary key field. This secondary index can either point to the primary index, or it can be used directly to retrieve records from the random file. For example, in Figure 8-35, column 1 of a secondary index contains the name of the contact person for each task, and column 2 points to the task name (the primary index). To implement this concept, the secondary index is built from the data in the random-access file. Like the primary index based on TaskName, the secondary index is stored in a sequential file, and is loaded into an array at start-up. During processing, the user could select a contact person (perhaps from another combo box). The program would pull up the corresponding TaskName from the secondary index array, then use the TaskName to search the primary index in order to locate the correct record number. Finally, the record number is used to retrieve the appropriate record from the random-data file. The whole point of the secondary index is to speed up data retrieval by searching a small data structure in memory rather than a large data structure on disk.

Secondary index key (Contact)	Primary index key (TaskName)
Clark	ContractFoodSvc
Josephson	Sec:CloseCerem
Josephson	Sec:OpenCerem
Merrill	BldAppleHouse

Figure 8-35: Secondary index

You have now completed Lesson A. This lesson covered a large amount of new material, so you may want to stop now and take a break. In any event, remember to complete the end-of-lesson questions and exercises that follow.

SUMMARY

- The improved bubble sort is an exchange sort that performs reasonably well on medium-sized arrays. Its performance improves if the original table is partially sorted. The selection sort has the advantage of predictability: its processing time is exactly the same regardless of the initial order of elements in the source table. The insertion sort is most useful when the array must be accessed during the same time that elements are being presented to the sort routine, because the array is always in the correct order regardless of the number of elements that have been presented to the array up to that point. The shuttle sort may be the best performing exchange sort, especially on arrays that are nearly in the correct order initially. The Shell sort is the best performer on very large arrays of all those covered in this text. The extra coding needed to implement the Shell sort is well worth the effort.

- For tiny arrays (up to 10 elements), the very simple sorting algorithm introduced in Tutorial 6 is adequate, but its performance deteriorates rapidly for anything much larger. For arrays of up to about 500 elements, reasonable performance can be attained with the improved bubble or waterfall sort, selection sort, insertion sort, or shuttle sort. For very large arrays (over 500 elements), the Shell sort is recommended.

- File sorts operate far more slowly than table sorts. One file sort routine uses three work areas and four phases. In the initialization phase, the source file is copied to a work area. In repeated partition and merge phases, the records in this work area are first distributed to the other two work areas, and then reassembled into one work area, until the file sorting is complete. In the finalization phase, the MergeFile is copied to a destination file.

- A sequential search routine can be used to locate a particular element in any ordered or unordered array. A binary search routine can only be performed on an ordered array. The binary search routine works by locating the midpoint of the range of elements in the array, comparing this element to the search argument, and, if the search argument is not the middle element, then eliminating half of the remaining elements. This process is repeated until the search argument is found.

- A linked list provides a means for accessing the elements of an array in an order other than the physical order of the array elements. An external pointer indicates the first element in the linked list, and a pointer in that record indicates the second element, and so on to the end of the list.

- Visual Basic .NET supports sequential- and random-access files. Sequential-access files contain data items written one after the other, and retrieved in the same sequence. The sequential file is opened for either write or read operations, but not both at the same time. Random-access files support the reading and writing of complete fixed-length data records at random locations based on a record number.

■ Although the operating system does not support ISAM files, you can create pseudo-ISAM files in Visual Basic .NET by combining a sequential file (for the index) and a random file (for the data records), and by performing the various file management tasks yourself. A pseudo-ISAM file may be a good solution for situations in which an application requires rapid retrieval of very large data records from a very large file, based on a record number usually unknown to the user.

QUESTIONS

1. A tiny array is defined as one with fewer than _____ elements.

2. To sort a very large array (greater than 500 elements), the _____ is recommended.

3. A table sort that keeps its elements in order as they are being presented is the _____ sort.

4. Although _____ files are generally not supported on microcomputer operating systems, you can create _____ files in Visual Basic .NET by combining a sequential-access file and a random-access file to achieve similar functionality.

5. How many statements are executed for a bubble sort routine that involves 30 comparisons and 10 exchanges?

6. To begin traversing a linked list, you get the value of the _____, which contains the index of the first element in the list.

7. The pointer field of the last element in a linked list contains a _____.

8. A sort routine that always takes the same execution time no matter what order the elements are in initially is the _____ sort.

9. When a table sort is not practical because of the size of a data file, you must use a _____ routine instead.

10. In a linked list, if record 7's pointer field points to record 9, and record 9 points to record 1, you can delete record 9 from the linked list by assigning _____ to the pointer field of record _____.

CRITICAL THINKING

At the end of each lesson, reflective questions are intended to provoke you into considering the material you have just read at a deeper level.

1. In each iteration of a binary search, you compare the search argument with the array element at the midpoint of the range of possible elements; then, if the array element is not found, you reduce the range by one half, and recalculate the midpoint. For an array of 500 elements, what is the maximum number of iterations needed to locate any element?

2. Some file sort routines use one or more additional work areas during the partition phase. In other words, they partition the MergeFile into PartitionA, PartitionB, and PartitionC. What would be the effect of such a scheme? What is the cost?

3. Explain why you cannot conduct a binary search on a linked list.

EXERCISES

These are all paper and pencil exercises, designed to ensure that you understand the concepts discussed in Lesson A.

1. Draw a table of 10 records of Friendsville International Games athletes. Include an Athlete ID, last name, first name, country, and date of birth. Put the list in numeric order by Athlete ID. When the list is ordered by Athlete ID, make sure that it is not also ordered by last name or by date of birth. Make sure that you do not include a record whose Athlete ID=4.

2. Starting with the result of Exercise 1, modify the table so that it includes a linked list, pointing to all of the athlete records in alphabetical order by last name.

3. Starting with the result of Exercise 2, modify the table so that it also includes a linked list, pointing to all of the records in order by date of birth.

4. Starting with the result of Exercise 3, insert a new record for Athlete ID=4. First, show the table with this new record at the bottom of the table, and update the links. What effect does this have on the original table order? What can you conclude about the use of a linked list for creating and maintaining a table in multiple sort orders?

5. Starting with the result of Exercise 1, use a selection sort that puts these records in order by date of birth. Show the contents of List1 (the original list) and List2 (the result list) after 1 record has been added to List2, after 4 records have been added, and after all 10 records have been added.

6. Starting with the result of Exercise 1, use an insertion sort that places these records in order by date of birth. Assume that the data source is the original table and is called List1, and that the destination table is List2. Show the contents of List2 (the result list) after 1 record has been added to List2, after 4 records have been added, and after all 10 records have been added.

7. Starting with the result of Exercise 1, use a Shell sort that puts these records in order by date of birth. What is the initial D? Show the contents of the table after the first pass. Show the computation of the next D, and the contents of the table after the second pass. Show the computation of the third D, and the contents of the table after the third pass.

8. Assume that the result of Exercise 1 is stored in a sequential file called AthletesByAthleteID. Use the file-sorting algorithm in this lesson to sort the records in this file by date of birth, creating a new file called AthletesByBirthDate. Show the contents of the original MergeFile (that is, a copy of the original table). Show the contents of PartitionA, PartitionB, and the MergeFile for each successive iteration of the partition and merge phases. In addition, show the contents of AthletesByBirthDate at the end.

Implementing Sorting Algorithms

Tasks for the FGDT

Hilda Reiner has assigned the development of this application entirely to you. She did agree to obtain some clerical assistance in constructing the revised Athletes.txt data file, but she asked you to write a program to create the more complex file of athletes' biographies and images. Having now mastered the conceptual material in Lesson A, you create the Up Close and Personal - Home form in Lesson B, and the Athlete Info Sheet in Lesson C. Because this application will be distributed to the public on CDs, you also must develop the deployment package, which is covered in Lesson C.

Creating frmStart and Module1 for the Up Close and Personal Application

Implementing the sorting algorithms you learned about in Lesson A, you begin development of the Up Close and Personal application, focusing on the main form and associated code modules. The main form also includes the requirement to sort pastructAthletes() in a variety of ways. One sorting requirement is also satisfied by the creation of a linked list.

Creating the GUI for frmStart

The initial construction of the Up Close and Personal application involves the GUI for the main form, another version of Module1 that you have seen in several of these tutorials, and event procedures for the main form. The GUI for the main form is quite simple; the interesting thing in this application is the code.

To build the main form GUI for the Up Close and Personal application:

1. Start a new Visual Basic .NET Windows Forms application. Place it in the **VB.NET\Student\Tut08** folder, and name it **UpClose**.

2. Change the name of **Form1** to **frmStart**, and the filename to **frmStart.vb**. Insert the four **labels** and four **combo boxes**. Name the combo boxes **cboCategory**, **cboSubcategory**, **cboOrder**, and **cboName**. Resize the form and insert the controls so that it appears as in Figure 8-36. In the Property Pages for the project, change the Start-up object to **frmStart**.

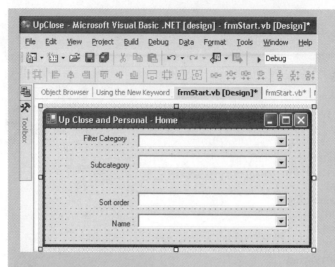

Figure 8-36: GUI for frmStart

Though you have designed many GUIs in this text, you have probably always used the Windows Forms Designer to do so. You should know that forms and controls can also be created in code. You experiment with this Visual Basic .NET feature now by creating one of the labels needed on frmStart.

3   In the Windows Forms Designer, click the **label** on the top left whose text is Filter Category. Now look at the Properties window to determine which properties have been set in code. You notice that in the Properties window, default property settings appear in normal font, whereas nondefault settings are in bold. You need to set most of the properties that appear in bold. You can also open the code window and expand the Windows Form Designer generated code to see all of the properties that have been set. Figure 8-37 lists the properties that you must set in code.

Property	Setting
Name	Label1
Location	40, 8
Size	96, 16
TextAlign	TopRight
Text	Filter Category

Figure 8-37: Nondefault properties of the Filter Category label

4   Delete the selected **label** in the Designer. Now add that same label back into the form by inserting the code shown in Figure 8-38 into the frmStart_Load() procedure. Adjust the Size, Location, and TextAlignment properties as needed to line up with your other controls. Visual Basic .NET provides several avenues for setting the Size (Height and Width) and Location (Left and Top) properties. After declaring the control and setting its properties, the Add method adds this control to the Controls collection for the form.

```
Dim MyNewLabel As New System.Windows.Forms.Label()
With MyNewLabel
  .Left = 40
  .Top = 8
  .Height = 16
  .Width = 96
  .TextAlign = ContentAlignment.MiddleRight
  .Text = "Filter Category"
End With
Me.Controls.Add(MyNewLabel)
```

Figure 8-38: Code for adding the Filter Category label

5 Two of the combo boxes on frmStart have an Items Collection that can be loaded in the Designer. To load them in the Designer, click the **Items Collection** for each control, and type the items as shown in the **String Collection Editor** for each control, in Figures 8-39 and 8-40.

Figure 8-39: String Collection Editor for cboCategory

Figure 8-40: String Collection Editor for cboOrder

NOTE: You could load the item collections for cboCategory and cboOrder in frmStart_Load() instead as you did in Step 4, if you prefer. To load them in code, follow the model for loading cboCategory shown in Figure 8-41, inserting this code in frmStart_Load().

```
cboCategory.Items.Add("All athletes")
cboCategory.Items.Add("Filter by sport")
cboCategory.Items.Add("Filter by country")
cboCategory.Items.Add("Male athletes")
cboCategory.Items.Add("Female athletes")
```

Figure 8-41: Loading cboCategory in code

6   Run the UpClose application to see that the GUI looks correct (especially MyNewLabel).

Developing Module1 for the Up Close and Personal Application

Portions of Module1 from previous tutorials can again be copied into Module1 for the Up Close and Personal application with very little modification. At this point, you may want to run UpClose.exe again to remind yourself of the various structures and data items it uses. The focus in this application is on the athletes themselves, but the program also uses events, sports, and nations.

Compared to the Scoring application in Tutorial 6, the information about athletes in the UpClose application is expanded to include each athlete's date of birth, sport, and events. The application records up to five events for each athlete. Of course, the event information is indicated by storing only the EventID, because the rest of the information concerning each event is available in the Events.txt file. All of this new information (date of birth, sport, and five EventIDs) must be added to Athletes.txt. Althea volunteered to expand Athletes.txt to contain the additional information for a small sample of 25 athletes, which is available to you in the Tut08 folder.

tip

You often encounter real-world programming tasks in which your application needs only a portion of a data file. In this case, the application needs the EventID, Sport, and EventName from the Events.txt file. Nevertheless, the structEvent describes the entire file and, later, LoadEvents() will load the entire file into an array. Using the entire structure and file makes it possible to use a common structure declaration and load routine in every application that accesses the same data file.

To create the initial Module1 for the Up Close and Personal application:

1   Add a new item to the UpClose project, a module, called **Module1.vb**. Insert the definition of **structEvent**, as shown in Figure 8-42. This structure reflects the Events.txt file as you last saw it in Tutorial 7.

```
Public Structure structEvent
  Public EventID As Integer
  <VBFixedString(10)> Public Sport As String
  <VBFixedString(25)> Public EventName As String
  <VBFixedString(1)> Public Gender As String
  <VBFixedString(2)> Public ScoringMethod As String
  <VBFixedString(3)> Public Country1 As String
  <VBFixedString(3)> Public Country2 As String
  Public VenueIndex As Integer
  <VBFixedString(10)> Public Schedule As String
  Public StartTime As Date
  <VBFixedString(1)> Public PricingSchedule As String
End Structure
```

Figure 8-42: structEvent in Module1 of the UpClose project

2   Insert the definition of **structAthlete** into Module1, as shown in Figure 8-43. Note that the definition of structAthlete includes new fields for date of birth (DoB), sport, and events; it also includes a Ptr field because one of the sort algorithms demonstrated in the program employs a linked list.

```
Public Structure structAthlete
  Public AthleteID As Integer
  <VBFixedString(20)> Public FName As String
  <VBFixedString(25)> Public LName As String
  <VBFixedString(1)> Public Gender As String
  <VBFixedString(3)> Public Country As String
  Public DoB As Date
  <VBFixedString(10)> Public Sport As String
  Public Event1 As Integer
  Public Event2 As Integer
  Public Event3 As Integer
  Public Event4 As Integer
  Public Event5 As Integer
  Public RecNum As Integer
  Public Ptr As Integer
End Structure
```

Figure 8-43: Definition of structAthlete in Module1 of the UpClose project

3   Insert the declaration of the **pastrSports()** array, as shown in Figure 8-44. This is the same array declaration you have used in several tutorials.

```
Public pastrSports() As String = {16, _
  "Baseball", "Basketball", "Boxing", "Diving", _
  "Equestrian", "Fencing", "Field", "Gymnastics", _
  "Shooting", "Soccer", "Softball", "Swimming", _
  "Tennis", "Track", "Volleyball", "Wrestling"}
```

Figure 8-44: Declaration of pastrSports() in Module1 of the UpClose project

4   Insert the public declarations of constants and variables as depicted in Figure 8-45. Most of these declarations are familiar to you from previous tutorials, but a few are introduced here for the first time: pList1() is an array of structAthlete. This array holds the records of athletes, which will then be sorted. Based on the selected Filter Category, pList1() contains all or a subset of the athlete records in pastructAthletes(). pList1() is then sorted based on the selected Sort order. pL1Count is a count of the number of records in pList1(). And pintAthlete is an integer variable used to identify one athlete, either by Athlete ID or by an index value.

```
'maximum number of events
Public Const NUMEVENTS = 500
'maximum number of athletes
Public Const NUMATHLETES = 500
'actual number of nations in Nations.txt
Public Const NUMNATIONS = 26

Public pastructEvents(NUMEVENTS) As structEvent
Public pastructAthletes(NUMATHLETES) As structAthlete
'pList1 is the list of names to be sorted & displayed
Public pList1(NUMATHLETES) As structAthlete
'actual number of events
Public pNumEvents As Integer
'actual number of athletes
Public pNumAthletes As Integer
'number of names to be sorted & displayed
Public pL1Count As Integer
'used to identify one athlete
Public pintAthlete As Integer
Public pastrNations(NUMNATIONS, 3)
```

Figure 8-45: Declaration of public constants and variables in Module1 of the UpClose project

5 The last pieces of the initial Module1 code are the three routines needed to load events, nations, and athletes into their respective arrays. Again, the procedures for loading events and for loading nations occurred in previous tutorials, but they are repeated here in Figures 8-46 and 8-47 for your convenience. The procedure for loading athletes, Figure 8-48, is different from the one in earlier tutorials, to reflect the fact that the elements of structAthlete have been expanded. Insert all three of these procedures into your Module1.

```
Public Sub LoadEvents()
  Dim i As Integer
  FileOpen(1, "Events.txt", OpenMode.Input)
  pNumEvents = 0
  Do Until EOF(1)
    With pastructEvents(i)
      Input(1, .EventID)
      Input(1, .Sport)
      Input(1, .EventName)
      Input(1, .Gender)
      Input(1, .ScoringMethod)
      Input(1, .Country1)
      Input(1, .Country2)
      Input(1, .VenueIndex)
      Input(1, .Schedule)
      Input(1, .StartTime)
      Input(1, .PricingSchedule)
    End With
    i += 1
  Loop
  FileClose(1)
  pNumEvents = i
End Sub
```

Figure 8-46: Load routine for pastructEvents()

```
Public Sub LoadNations()
  Dim i, j As Integer
  FileOpen(1, "Nations.txt", OpenMode.Input)
  For j = 0 To NUMNATIONS - 1
    Input(1, pastrNations(j, 0))
    Input(1, pastrNations(j, 1))
    Input(1, pastrNations(j, 2))
  Next
  FileClose(1)

End Sub
```

Figure 8-47: Load routine for pastrNations()

```
Public Sub LoadAthletes()
  Dim i As Integer
  FileOpen(1, "Athletes.txt", OpenMode.Input)
  pNumAthletes = 0
  Do Until EOF(1)
    With pastructAthletes(i)
      Input(1, .AthleteID)
      Input(1, .FName)
      Input(1, .LName)
      Input(1, .Gender)
      Input(1, .Country)
      Input(1, .DoB)
      Input(1, .Sport)
      Input(1, .Event1)
      Input(1, .Event2)
      Input(1, .Event3)
      Input(1, .Event4)
      Input(1, .Event5)
      .RecNum = i
    End With
    i += 1
  Loop
  FileClose(1)
  pNumAthletes = i
End Sub
```

Figure 8-48: Load routine for pastructAthletes()

6   As you have seen in other tutorials, the input files must be accessible to the executable program, and the easiest way to accomplish this is to place these files in the project's bin subfolder. Therefore, copy **Events.txt, Athletes.txt,** and **Nations.txt** from the VB.NET\Student\Tut08 folder to the **VB.NET\Student\ Tut08\UpClose\bin** folder.

7   The initial Module1 is now complete. However, before leaving it, you do want to ensure that you have made no errors in syntax or in structure definitions. Therefore, to call the three subprocedures in Module1, type **LoadEvents(),** **LoadAthletes(),** and **LoadNations()** into the frmStart_Load() procedure of frmStart.

8   Run the **UpClose** application. After you have fixed any errors detected by the software, insert a **breakpoint** at the End Sub statement of Sub frmStart_ Load(). While in break mode, examine the contents of **pNumEvents** and **pNumAthletes**. These should match the actual number of records in those files. Do any other checking you deem appropriate to ensure that your project is operating correctly up to this point, and then clear all **breakpoints**.

Inserting Sub Procedures for frmStart

Besides the Load event for frmStart (most of which code you have already seen), the code in frmStart is concentrated in the four SelectedIndexChanged procedures (one for each combo box). During execution, any change to the selected index of cboCategory, cboSubcategory, or cboOrder causes the following actions, which are all triggered by the SelectedIndexChanged procedure of these three combo boxes:

- If a new index is selected in cboCategory or cboSubcategory, based on the selections in these two controls, the appropriate records are copied from pastructAthletes() to pList1(), and pL1Count is set to the record count of pList1.
- The records in pList1 are sorted based on the setting of cboOrder.
- The records in pList1 are loaded into cboName. This actually requires two different procedures, one to load the records into cboName in the order in which the records appear in pList1, and another to load the records from pList1 into cboName by following the links in the linked list.

NOTE: When programming multiple combo boxes on a form, you must be careful to avoid looping. That is, if selecting an item in ComboBox1 triggers the SelectedIndexChanged procedure for ComboBox2, then you must not allow the SelectedIndexChanged procedure for ComboBox2 to trigger the SelectedIndexChanged procedure of ComboBox1.

When the application opens, the Filter Category is set to All Athletes, which is index 0 in cboCategory. With All Athletes selected, the subcategory field is empty. Also initially, cboOrder is set to sort the athletes by Athlete ID, which is also index 0. In order to trigger the initial sorting of athletes and loading of cboName, the settings of cboCategory and cboOrder must be initialized in frmStart_Load, and one of the SelectedIndexChanged procedures must be invoked.

Finally, when an athlete is selected from cboName, an instance of frmAthlete is displayed—this procedure will be deferred until Lesson C, where you create frmAthlete.

tip

As you know, you can create the header for an event procedure in any of three ways. You can double-click the control in the Designer, which opens the Code Editor and starts the procedure for the most common event associated with the control. You can click the Class Name combo box at the upper left of the Code Editor, and select the control; then, click the Method Name combo box at the top right, and select the event. Or, you can type the procedure header yourself, remembering to insert the standard *sender* and e arguments as well as the Handles clause.

To build the code for frmStart:

1 Open the Code Editor for the **cboCategory_SelectedIndexChanged()** procedure, and type in the code shown in Figure 8-49, adding the missing For loops in Case 0 and Case 1 where indicated.

```
Private Sub cboCategory_SelectedIndexChanged(ByVal _
    sender As _
    System.Object, ByVal e As System.EventArgs) _
    Handles cboCategory.SelectedIndexChanged
  Dim i, j As Integer
  'clear existing items from cboSubcategory,
  '   cboName, and pList1()
  cboSubcategory.Items.Clear()
  cboName.Items.Clear()
  Erase pList1
  ReDim pList1(pNumAthletes)
  Select Case cboCategory.SelectedIndex
    Case 0 'All athletes
      'Use a For loop to copy all the records from
        'pastructAthletes() to pList1()

      pL1Count = pNumAthletes
      cboOrder_SelectedIndexChanged(sender, e)
    Case 1 'Filter by sport
      'Use a For loop to load all the records from
        'pastrSports() into cboSubcategory

      cboSubcategory.SelectedIndex = 0
      cboSubcategory_SelectedIndexChanged(sender, e)
    Case 2 'Filter by country
      For i = 0 To NUMNATIONS - 1
        cboSubcategory.Items.Add(pastrNations(i, 0) & _
          " " & pastrNations(i, 1))
      Next

      cboSubcategory.SelectedIndex = 0
      cboSubcategory_SelectedIndexChanged(sender, e)
    Case 3, 4 'Filter by gender: case 3=Male, case 4=Female
      j = 0
      For i = 0 To pNumAthletes - 1
        If pastructAthletes(i).Gender = _
          IIf(cboCategory.SelectedIndex = _
          3, "M", "F") Then
          pList1(j) = pastructAthletes(i)
          j += 1
        End If
      Next
      pL1Count = j
      cboOrder_SelectedIndexChanged(sender, e)
  End Select
End Sub
```

add For loops in these two cases

Figure 8-49: Sub cboCategory_SelectedIndexChanged()

2 Open the Code Editor for the **cboSubcategory_SelectedIndexChanged**() procedure, and type the code shown in Figure 8-50. Examine the code in Figure 8-50
as you type it in. When you compare cboSubcategory.SelectedItem to
pastructAthletes(i).Sport, you must remember that the Athletes.txt file contains
all uppercase characters, whereas cboSubcategory.SelectedItem does not. To
compare SWIMMING to Swimming, for example, you must convert
cboSubcategory.SelectedItem to all uppercase with the UCase() function. Also,
when you compare cboSubcategory.SelectedItem to pastructAthletes(i).
Country, you must compare only the far-left three characters of cboSubcategory.
SelectedItem to the country code in pastructAthletes(i). You can isolate the far-
left characters of a string with the Microsoft.VisualBasic.Left() function.

```
Private Sub cboSubcategory_SelectedIndexChanged _
    (ByVal sender As _
    System.Object, ByVal e As System.EventArgs) _
    Handles cboSubcategory.SelectedIndexChanged
  Dim i, j As Integer
  Select Case cboCategory.SelectedIndex
    Case 1 'Filter by sport
      For i = 0 To pNumAthletes - 1
        If UCase(cboSubcategory.SelectedItem) = _
            pastructAthletes(i).Sport Then
          pList1(j) = pastructAthletes(i)
          j += 1
        End If
      Next
    Case 2 'Filter by country
      For i = 0 To pNumAthletes - 1
        If Microsoft.VisualBasic.Left _
            (cboSubcategory.SelectedItem, _
            3) = pastructAthletes(i).Country Then
          pList1(j) = pastructAthletes(i)
          j += 1
        End If
      Next
  End Select
  pL1Count = j
  cboOrder_SelectedIndexChanged(sender, e)
End Sub
```

Figure 8-50: Sub cboSubcategory_SelectedIndexChanged()

NOTE: No matter which Filter Category and Subcategory is selected, pL1List() always gets loaded, pL1Count gets assigned, and cboOrder_SelectedIndexChanged gets invoked.

3   Recall that the athletes' names are loaded into cboName either in the physical order of records in pList1() or by following a linked list. This requires separate programmer-supplied procedures, named LoadNames() and LoadLinkedList(). Because the linked list is discussed later, the only procedure you code now is LoadNames(). Type the **LoadNames()** procedure, as shown in Figure 8-51.

```
Private Sub LoadNames()
  Dim i As Integer
  cboName.Items.Clear()
  For i = 0 To pL1Count - 1
    With pList1(i)
      cboName.Items.Add(.AthleteID & " " & .FName & _
        " " & .LName & " (" & .Country & ")")
    End With
  Next
End Sub
```

Figure 8-51: LoadNames() procedure

4   Because cboOrder is used to select the sort order of the athletes' names, and the sorting routines remain to be explained later in this lesson, for now you

want to just call the basic procedure that loads all of the athletes' names into cboName. (You deal with the sort order later.) Therefore, for now, just insert the one line call to **LoadNames()** in **cboOrder_SelectedIndexChanged()**.

5   At start-up, the initial settings of the combo boxes must be established in code, so that cboName will be loaded. To accomplish this, add the code in Figure 8-52 to the frmStart_Load procedure.

```
cboCategory.SelectedIndex = 0
cboOrder.SelectedIndex = 0
cboCategory_SelectedIndexChanged(sender, e)
```

Figure 8-52: Establish initial settings of combo boxes in frmStart_Load()

6   Run the **UpClose** application. cboCategory and cboSubcategory are completely functional. When any item is selected, the filtered names appear as expected in cboName. Notice that cboOrder is not yet functional, so the names always appear in the same order as they are in Athletes.txt.

Creating Four Sort Algorithms for Viewing the Athletes

From Hilda Reiner's viewpoint, one of the educational purposes of the UpClose project is to teach and to demonstrate a series of table-sorting algorithms. You now insert these sort algorithms into the UpClose project. This code is fairly generic and may be of use to other members of the FGDT working on other applications. Therefore, to encourage reusability, you build the sorting routines in a separate module.

NOTE: In Lesson A, much ado was made about choosing the correct sorting algorithm depending on the characteristics of the table to be sorted. Those considerations are not evident in this example. The purpose here is only to give you the opportunity to code the various sort routines, even though all of the routines are being used to sort the same table. So no effort has been made to select the best algorithm for the situation.

To build the SortModule and associated code in frmStart:

1   The first task in this section is to choose the correct sorting algorithm, based on the selection of sort order in cboOrder. After the sorting algorithm is selected, then the individual sorts can be programmed. With this in mind, add a new module to the UpClose project, naming this new module **SortModule.vb,** and then add the code to create the initial SortModule, as shown in Figure 8-53.

```
Module SortModule
  Public Sub ChooseSort(ByVal vintOrder As Integer)
    Select Case vintOrder
      Case 0 'sort by AthleteID
        BubbleSort()
      Case 1 'sort by Lastname, Firstname
        SelectionSort()
      Case 2 'sort by Firstname, Lastname
        InsertionSort()
      Case 3 'sort by country
        ShellSort()
      Case 4 'sort by AthleteID in reverse order
        'LinkedList()
        MsgBox("LinkedList selected")
    End Select
  End Sub

  Private Sub BubbleSort() 'sort on AthleteID
    MsgBox("BubbleSort selected")
  End Sub

  Private Sub SelectionSort() 'sort on Lastname, Firstname
    MsgBox("SelectionSort selected")
  End Sub

  Private Sub InsertionSort() 'sort on Firstname, Lastname
    MsgBox("InsertionSort selected")
  End Sub

  Private Sub ShellSort() 'sort on country abbreviation
    MsgBox("ShellSort selected")
  End Sub
End Module
```

Figure 8-53: Skeleton SortModule.vb

As you can probably ascertain, the ChooseSort() routine is the entry point to this module. It receives an integer parameter, which it uses to select a sort routine. The integer parameter is actually the SelectedIndex property of cboOrder. Therefore, the call to ChooseSort() must be placed in cboOrder_SelectedIndexChanged().

2 Type in the **ChooseSort()** call prior to the call to LoadNames(), and include **cboOrder.SelectedIndex** as the parameter in the procedure call.

3 Run the **UpClose** application. Select each option in cboOrder. Notice that as each option is selected, a message box appears indicating which sort procedure you are in. Remove all of the **MsgBox** statements from the SortModule.

Now you are ready to insert the four sort procedures. Recall that each of these procedures sorts pList1(), which has pL1Count members.

4 Start with the BubbleSort() procedure. Type the **BubbleSort()** procedure, as shown in Figure 8-54, inserting the code for the exchange where indicated. Remember that the exchange must cause the entire record to be swapped, not just the particular field being compared.

```
Private Sub BubbleSort() 'sort on AthleteID
  Dim i, j As Integer
  Dim Temp As structAthlete
  For i = 0 To pL1Count - 2
    Temp.LName = ""
    For j = i + 1 To pL1Count - 1
      If pList1(i).AthleteID > pList1(j).AthleteID Then
          'insert code to exchange pList1(i) with pList1(j)
      End If
    Next
    'sort is complete if no swap was made
    If Temp.LName = "" Then Exit For
  Next
End Sub
```

Figure 8-54: Sub BubbleSort()

5   Next insert the **SelectionSort**(), as shown in Figure 8-55. Recall that in this sort, after the lowest element is copied to List2, that element must be set to a very high value, to ensure that it is not selected again. In this instance, the .LName field is set to "ZZZZZ," a value higher than anyone's name, preventing this element from being selected again as low. When the sort is finished, the sorted records are in List2, and pList1 is corrupted (because the .LName field of each record now equals "ZZZZZ"). Therefore, at the end of the routine, List2() is copied back to pList1().

```
Private Sub SelectionSort() 'sort on Lastname, Firstname
  Dim L1Index, LowIndex, L2Index As Integer
  Dim List2(pL1Count) As structAthlete
  For L2Index = 0 To pL1Count - 1
    LowIndex = 0
    For L1Index = 1 To pL1Count - 1
      If pList1(LowIndex).LName & _
        pList1(LowIndex).FName > _
        pList1(L1Index).LName & pList1(L1Index).FName _
        Then LowIndex = L1Index
    Next
    List2(L2Index) = pList1(LowIndex)
    pList1(LowIndex).LName = "ZZZZZ"
  Next
  For L2Index = 0 To pL1Count - 1
    pList1(L2Index) = List2(L2Index)
  Next
End Sub
```

Figure 8-55: Sub SelectionSort()

NOTE: The parentheses symbols are overloaded in this language. You have certainly observed this earlier, but it is both obvious and somewhat disconcerting in a tutorial dealing with arrays to be sorted, and procedures to do the sorting. In some languages, array dimensions and references are given in brackets, such as pList1[4], whereas procedure parameters are given in parentheses, such as ChooseSort(int). This syntax helps the reader (and the compiler, as a matter of fact) discern which object type is being referenced. Visual Basic .NET unfortunately uses parentheses for both purposes. As a language originally derived from FORTRAN in 1964, BASIC (just like FORTRAN) has suffered from this overloading problem since its inception. There are other examples of the same thing in this language (and also in FORTRAN), notably the equals sign, which is used both for assignment, as in X=5, and for comparison, as in If X=5. Some languages use different operators for these two quite distinct operations, but unfortunately FORTRAN and its derivative languages do not.

6 Insert the code for the **InsertionSort**() procedure, as shown in Figure 8-56. Recall that this sort is most appropriate when the items to be sorted are being introduced from an external source. In this case, you must pretend that pList1 is that external source. As in the case of the selection sort, the final sorted list List2() must be copied back to pList1(), because pList1 is the source of data for the LoadNames() procedure.

```
Private Sub InsertionSort() 'sort on Firstname, Lastname
  Dim L1Index, L2Count, L2Index As Integer
  Dim List2(pL1Count) As structAthlete
  L2Count = 1
  List2(0) = pList1(0)
  L1Index = 1
  Do Until L2Count = pL1Count
    L2Index = L2Count - 1
    Do Until L2Index < 0 OrElse pList1(L1Index).FName & _
        pList1(L1Index).LName >= _
        List2(L2Index).FName & List2(L2Index).LName
      List2(L2Index + 1) = List2(L2Index)
      L2Index -= 1
    Loop
    List2(L2Index + 1) = pList1(L1Index)
    L1Index += 1
    L2Count += 1
  Loop
  'copy List2 back to pList1
  For L2Index = 0 To pL1Count - 1
    pList1(L2Index) = List2(L2Index)
  Next
End Sub
```

Figure 8-56: Sub InsertionSort()

7 Finally, insert the code for **Sub ShellSort**(), as shown in Figure 8-57. Again be sure to insert the code for the exchange where indicated. Remember to swap the entire record.

```
Private Sub ShellSort() 'sort on country abbreviation
  Dim Distance, L1Index, HoldIndex As Integer
  Dim Temp As structAthlete
  'set the initial distance
  Distance = 2
  Do Until Distance > pL1Count
    Distance *= 2
  Loop
  Distance = Distance / 2 - 1
  'main body of the Shell sort
  Do Until Distance = 0
    For L1Index = 0 To (pL1Count - 1) - Distance
      If pList1(L1Index).Country > _
          pList1(L1Index + Distance).Country Then
        HoldIndex = L1Index
        Do While L1Index >= 0 AndAlso _
            pList1(L1Index).Country > _
            pList1(L1Index + Distance).Country
          'insert code to exchange pList1(L1Index) with
          'pList1(L1Index + Distance)

          L1Index -= Distance
        Loop
        L1Index = HoldIndex
      End If
    Next
    Distance /= 2
  Loop
End Sub
```

Figure 8-57: Sub ShellSort()

8 Run the **UpClose** application, and test the various Filter Categories and Sort orders.

Inevitably, you will cause the program to either blow up or to hang. The problem is that several of the sort routines behave badly if they are invoked when there are no items available to sort. To solve this problem, the ChooseSort() routine should only be invoked when the list count is greater than one.

9 Insert the restriction **If pL1Count > 1 Then** in the first line after the header in the cboOrder_SelectedIndexChanged() procedure in frmStart. If necessary, also add an **End If** statement before the **End Sub**.

10 Run the **UpClose** application again and try out a variety of Filter Categories. Everything should work correctly in frmStart, except for the Sort order "Athlete ID – reverse order," which calls upon the linked list, developed next.

Creating a Linked List for Viewing the Athletes in Reverse Order by Athlete ID

A linked list is not the only way that you could display the athletes in reverse order. You could, for example, use a For loop to load cboName with the contents of pList1 from the last element to the first. However, this section does demonstrate an application of a linked list, a data structure the FGDT is likely to encounter more than once. As you may recall, a linked list can be a viable solution anytime you have a table that needs to accessed or traversed in more than one sort order.

As described in detail in Lesson A, the initial activity in creating a linked list is to copy the index and the key field from the original list to an array that also leaves room for the pointer, and to declare the external pointer as well. To do this, you must declare a structure in SortModule to be used for the parallel list in the LinkedList() procedure. Structures cannot be declared within a local procedure, so the structure definition must occur in SortModule at the module level. The external pointer should be available throughout the application: it is assigned a value while the linked list is being created, but it is used whenever the linked list is accessed. It seems logical to place the declaration of pPtr at the end of the list of public constants and variables in Module1. (Some would prefer to place it in SortModule; either location is defensible.) In any case, note that the structLink structure definition, unlike the Public pPtr, is Private. This is done because the structure is used only in SortModule where the linked list is created; no other module of the program needs to have access to it. A program element declared as Private at the module level is available only within that module.

To create the linked list for viewing athletes in reverse order by Athlete ID:

1   Insert the structure definition in SortModule at the module level, as shown in Figure 8-58. Then add the declaration of **Public pPtr As Integer** to the variable declarations in Module1.

```
Private Structure structLink
  Dim RecNum As Integer
  Dim AthleteID As Integer
  Dim Ptr As Integer
End Structure
```

Figure 8-58: Declaration of structLink

2   Although the LinkedList() procedure in Figure 8-59 is rather long, the individual steps are not complicated, and they follow precisely the steps for creating a linked list in Lesson A. Insert the code as shown into the SortModule.

```
Private Sub LinkedList()
  Dim i, j As Integer
  Dim Temp As structLink
  Dim List2(pL1Count) As structLink
  'sort pList1 by AthleteID (to provide a starting point)
  BubbleSort()
  'load the parallel list
  For i = 0 To pL1Count - 1
    With List2(i)
      .RecNum = i
      .AthleteID = pList1(i).AthleteID
    End With
  Next
  'sort the parallel list in reverse order by AthleteID
  For i = 0 To pL1Count - 2
    Temp.AthleteID = Nothing
    For j = i + 1 To pL1Count - 1
      If List2(i).AthleteID < List2(j).AthleteID Then
        Temp = List2(i)
        List2(i) = List2(j)
        List2(j) = Temp
      End If
    Next
    'sort is complete if no swap was made
    If Temp.AthleteID = Nothing Then Exit For
  Next
  'assign the ptr values to List2
  For i = 0 To pL1Count - 2
    List2(i).Ptr = List2(i + 1).RecNum
  Next
  'load the external pointer and the end-of-list sentinel
  pPtr = List2(0).RecNum
  List2(pL1Count - 1).Ptr = -9
  'sort the parallel list by AthleteID (to match pList1)
  For i = 0 To pL1Count - 2
    Temp.AthleteID = Nothing
    For j = i + 1 To pL1Count - 1
      If List2(i).AthleteID > List2(j).AthleteID Then
        Temp = List2(i)
        List2(i) = List2(j)
        List2(j) = Temp
      End If
    Next
    'sort is complete if no swap was made
    If Temp.AthleteID = Nothing Then Exit For
  Next
  'copy the ptr values to pList1
  For i = 0 To pL1Count - 1
    pList1(i).Ptr = List2(i).Ptr
  Next
End Sub
```

Figure 8-59: Sub LinkedList()

3 After the linked list has been created, recall that an alternate procedure is needed to load the athletes into cboName. This is because the LoadNames() procedure loads the names in the physical order of pList1(), whereas loading from the linked list requires that the links be followed. Accordingly, in the cboOrder_SelectedIndexChanged() procedure, you must insert code to choose between LoadNames() and a new procedure called LoadLinkedList(), depending on the value of cboOrder.SelectedIndex: if that index equals 4, then call LoadLinkedList(); otherwise, call LoadNames(). The completed cboOrder_SelectedIndexChanged() procedure appears as in Figure 8-60.

```
Private Sub cboOrder_SelectedIndexChanged(ByVal _
    sender As _
    System.Object, ByVal e As System.EventArgs) _
    Handles cboOrder.SelectedIndexChanged
If pL1Count > 1 Then
    ChooseSort(cboOrder.SelectedIndex)
    If cboOrder.SelectedIndex = 4 Then
        LoadLinkedList()
    Else
        LoadNames()
    End If
End If
End Sub
```

Figure 8-60: cboOrder_SelectedIndexChanged()

4 Insert the **LoadLinkedList()** procedure itself into frmStart, as shown in Figure 8-61. This procedure is modeled on the procedure for traversing a linked list demonstrated in Lesson A.

```
Private Sub LoadLinkedList()
  cboName.Items.Clear()
  Dim Ptr As Integer = pPtr
  Do Until Ptr = -9
    With pList1(Ptr)
      cboName.Items.Add(.AthleteID & " " & .FName & _
        " " & .LName & " (" & .Country & ")")
      Ptr = .Ptr
    End With
  Loop
End Sub
```

Figure 8-61: LoadLinkedList() procedure

5 Run the **UpClose** application. Check that everything related to frmStart is working.

You have completed Lesson B. Take a break or continue with Lesson C. But before you do, first complete the end-of-lesson exercises that follow.

SUMMARY

■ Sorting algorithms for a bubble sort, selection sort, insertion sort, and Shell sort are readily adaptable to any kind of table. Sort operations are facilitated by record structures—an array of records is easier to sort than a two-dimensional array, because assignment statements can be made at the record rather than the individual field level.

- Multiple combo boxes that interact with each other must be carefully programmed to avoid looping. Because items in the combo box are treated as an array in code, you must be careful to avoid references to array elements that do not exit.
- A linked list can be used in lieu of a sort in order to access records in a new logical order without changing their original physical order.

QUESTIONS

1. In the array name pastructAthletes(), what does pastruct stand for?

2. What is the difference between cboOrder_SelectedIndexChanged() and cboOrder.SelectedIndexChanged?

3. What pair of statements allows you to clear the contents of an array (releasing all of its storage locations) and then reallocate new storage locations to the array?

4. In an insertion sort, when a new element is less than any existing element, what condition terminates the search for its proper location in List2?

5. Why is a negative integer a good choice as the sentinel value in a linked list?

6. In the dressage event, after 15 of 30 riders have completed their first ride, you want to display the standings of those 15 riders. Which sort routine is best suited to this task?

7. How would you convert a bubble sort from an ascending to a descending sort routine?

8. The Air Force Space Command tracks some 2000 man-made objects floating around in orbit above the earth. On a real-time basis, these objects are constantly sorted in terms of their potential threat to the United States, based on material, origin, stability, proximity, and other factors. Which of the sort routines is best suited to accomplishing this large sort operation?

9. Given that a selection sort consumes 1000 processing units to sort a badly ordered table, approximately how many processing units would the same selection sort take to sort the same table if it were already sorted before the sort routine starts?

10. You want to use a Shell sort to sort a table of 750 records. What should be the size of the initial D?

EXERCISES

1. Create a Console application that implements a file sort to sort the Athletes.txt file by country. Rather than loading the Athletes.txt file into an array, assume for this exercise that the Athletes.txt file is too large to be loaded into an array. Implement a file sort instead, following these steps:
    a. *Initialization*—Copy Athletes.txt in Windows Explorer to InAthletes.txt, which becomes the source file for your file sort routine. Inside your program, copy InAthletes.txt to MergeFile.txt.
    b. *Partition and merge*—Follow the logic explained in Lesson A, creating PartitionA.txt and PartitionB.txt as the work files created in the partition phase. Use a record counter on PartitionB, incrementing the record counter whenever you write a record to PartitionB. When this record counter equals 0 at the end of the

partition phase, the file has been sorted. Remember to reset the record counter to 0 at the beginning of each partition phase.

c.   *Finalization*—Copy MergeFile.txt to OutAthletes.txt.

2.   Write a Console application to benchmark several sorting routines on a particular computer. In each test, calculate the elapsed time (to the nearest hundredth of a second) to sort the array. Test the sorting of an array of Doubles with (1) the very simple sort from Tutorial 6, (2) a bubble sort, (3) a selection sort, (4) an insertion sort, (5) a shuttle sort, and (6) a Shell sort. Perform these six tests with the arrays in three different original sort orders. In Sort Order Ascending, load the array with 500 numbers (the numbers 1 to 500) in ascending order, so that the array is already sorted before you start. In Sort Order Descending, load the array with 500 numbers in exactly reverse order (500 to 1). In Sort Order Random, load the array with 500 random numbers. Repeat all of the tests with an array of 2000 Doubles, and once again with 5000 Doubles. Thus you conduct 54 tests in all—six sort routines applied to three sort orders and to three array sizes (6 * 3 * 3 = 54). The output should be a table showing the elapsed time for each sort for each condition of each array.

3.   Implement Exercise 2 as a Windows Forms application, in which the user can specify the size and initial order of the array, and then display the results in one or more controls on the form.

4.   Implement Exercise 3 as a Web Forms application.

5.   Create a Windows Forms application containing three narrow list boxes. In the left list box, insert 20 randomly generated integers from 100 to 999. Create a linked list that points to all of these numbers in descending numerical order, and display the pointer values in the middle list box. In the right list box, display the 20 randomly generated numbers in the order of the links by traversing the linked list. The result should appear approximately as in Figure 8-62.

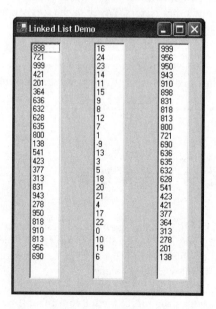

Figure 8-62: Output of Tut05ExB5

Pseudo-ISAM Files and Deploying Windows Applications

Completing the Up Close and Personal Application

In Lesson C, you complete the Up Close and Personal application. This involves three essential tasks: (1) you create the Biographies pseudo-ISAM file for storing biographical information on the athletes; (2) you create frmAthlete, the form that displays an Athlete Info Sheet for a selected athlete (selecting and displaying an individual athlete involves a binary search of all Athlete IDs to locate and display the right row in pastructAthletes(), and also involves retrieving and displaying a record from the Biographies pseudo-ISAM file); and (3) after testing and debugging UpClose, you create a deployment project for the Up Close and Personal application. The deployment project demonstrates the typical procedures used in deploying any Windows Forms application.

Creating a Pseudo-ISAM File

A pseudo-ISAM file, as you learned in Lesson A, consists of a random-access data file plus a sequential-access index file. The index file is typically loaded into an array during processing. The index array is used to look up a record number, and a data record is then retrieved from or written to the random-access file at the location identified by the record number. In the UpClose application, the pseudo-ISAM file stores biographical information concerning each athlete in the Friendsville International Games: the data file contains biographical data, whereas the index contains the Athlete ID and the record number of the associated record.

In many cases, the data record for the random file includes a record key that can also be used as the record number in a random-access file. Such a field is the AthleteID field in Athletes.txt. This field can work as the record number because it is a small positive integer, records in the file are sequenced by this field, and it uniquely identifies one record.

The index portion of the pseudo-ISAM file needs to be in memory, but it need not be a separate array if the information needed is already part of another array. In the present case, the Athlete ID is already part of pastructAthletes(), so you can use that array as the index array for the pseudo-ISAM file.

The random-access portion of this file consists of the Athlete ID (the record key), a free-form text field that can be used to store an athlete's biography, and a field containing the name of a file that stores a picture of an athlete. Of course, this basic file layout could be greatly expanded.

On the Friendsville Games Development Team, the decision was taken to create artificial biographical sketches and substitute an artificial photograph (a stick figure) for the small list of athletes in this demo application. You can construct a bare bones biographical sketch from the information in pastructAthletes(), pastructEvents(), and pastrNations(); add the filename of a stick figure in lieu of the filename of an athlete's photo; and then write this as a record in the pseudo-ISAM file. You might say you will have created a pseudo-ISAM file of pseudo-athletes.

The biographical information is retrieved when frmAthlete is displayed later in this lesson. The first task is to create the pseudo-ISAM file. The code for this task could be placed anywhere—in fact, you could create a separate Console application to accomplish this task. But the most convenient approach is to create the pseudo-ISAM file within the UpClose application, because you already have the three source arrays —(pastructAthletes(), pastructEvents(), and pastrNations()—loaded.

To create the pseudo-ISAM Biographies file:

1 Insert the **file layout** for the random-access data file just after the definition of structAthlete in Module1, as well as the declaration of **pstructBioRec** at the end of the declarations of public constants and variables in Module1, as shown in Figure 8-63. Recall that the pastructAthletes() array serves as the index portion of the random-access file, so you do not need to do anything to create the index.

```
Public Structure structISAM
  Public AthleteID As Integer
  <VBFixedString(1000)> Public Bio As String
  <VBFixedString(50)> Public PicFilename As String
End Structure

'one record in the ISAM file
Public pstructBioRec As structISAM
```

Figure 8-63: structISAM and pstructBioRec declarations

2 Insert the **Sub CreateBioFiles()** procedure (shown in Figure 8-64) in Module1 as well. This code creates a record in the Biographies pseudo-ISAM file for each athlete in pastructAthletes(). For each athlete, the code first constructs a boilerplate biographical sketch from the information in the three source arrays—pastructAthletes(), pastructEvents(), and pastrNations(). It then assigns this sketch to the 1000-character Bio field. It then adds a reference to the filename containing a stick figure of either a man or a woman. Finally, it writes the record to the Biographies file.

```
Public Sub CreateBioFiles()
  Dim i, j As Integer
  Dim s As String
  FileOpen(1, "Biographies", OpenMode.Random, , , _
    Len(pstructBioRec))
  For i = 0 To pNumAthletes - 1
    With pastructAthletes(i)
      s = "Biographical Sketch. "
      s &= .FName & " " & .LName & " was born on " & _
        Format(.DoB, "MMMM d, yyyy") & ". "
      s &= IIf(.Gender = "M", "He ", "She ") & _
              "began the sport of " & .Sport & _
              " at a very young age, "
      For j = 0 To 25
        If .Country = pastrNations(j, 0) Then
          s &= "and is now proud to represent " & _
            IIf(.Gender = "M", "his", "her") & _
            " native country of " & _
            pastrNations(j, 1) & ". "
        End If
      Next
      s &= IIf(.Gender = "M", "His", "Her") & _
        " favorite event in the Friendsville " _
        & "International Games is "
      For j = 0 To pNumEvents - 1
        If .Event1 = pastructEvents(j).EventID Then
          s &= pastructEvents(j).EventName & "."
        End If
      Next
      pstructBioRec.AthleteID = .AthleteID
      pstructBioRec.Bio = s
      pstructBioRec.PicFilename = IIf(.Gender = "M", _
        "misc27.ico", "misc26.ico")
      'insert the statement to write pstructBioRec
    End With
  Next
  FileClose(1)
End Sub
```

Figure 8-64: Sub CreateBioFiles() procedure

3 At least temporarily, insert a call to the CreateBioFiles() procedure in frmStart_ Load(). This call can be disabled or removed after the file has been successfully created.

4 Run the **UpClose** application. After you close the application, look in the bin folder of the UpClose project. Biographies should be a file of about 55 KB in size.

5 To further test your code at this point, write a small Console application to open the Biographies file and display its contents. Remember that the record number is the AthleteID field in Athletes.txt.

Creating frmAthlete, Using a Binary Search, and the Pseudo-ISAM File

Though most of the coding is done, the visual impact of the UpClose application is not yet apparent. That changes here, as you create frmAthlete, which displays an Athlete Info Sheet for a selected athlete.

The code that obtains and displays athlete information for one athlete involves three procedures. First, back in frmStart, the user selects the athlete to be displayed by selecting an athlete name in cboName. Therefore, you must code the cboName_SelectionIndexChanged() procedure to identify the Athlete ID to be displayed, instantiate frmAthlete, and then display the form. Second, in the form load procedure for frmAthlete, a binary search routine is called that locates the correct athlete record in pastructAthletes(). Third, after the correct record is identified, the information from pastructAthletes() and from the Biographies pseudo-ISAM file is retrieved and displayed in the various controls of frmAthlete.

To create frmAthlete:

1 Add a new **Windows** form to the UpClose project. Name this form **frmAthlete** and the file **frmAthlete.vb**. Build the **GUI** shown in Figure 8-65. Control names have been included in this figure, to help you name the controls so that they are consistent with the code in this lesson. (Your form need not display the control names.)

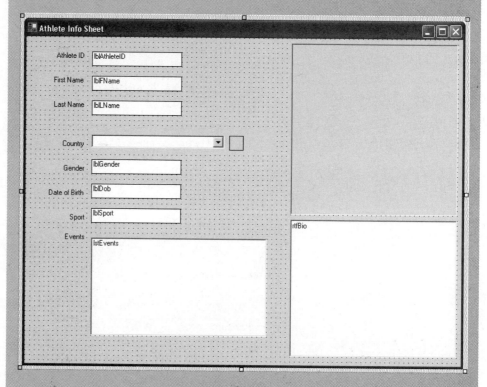

Figure 8-65: frmAthlete at design time, with visible control names

2 Add **ctrlNation** to the Toolbox, and then drop a **ctrlNation** control on the form to the right of the Country label. (If you have forgotten how to add a user control to a project, refer to Tutorial 5 where you learned how to create this control. Recall that you must add a **reference** to the control in the References for the UpClose project, and then customize the **Toolbox** by adding this .NET Framework Component.)

3 Add the **PictureBox** control named **pbxPhoto** in the upper right of the form, a **RichTextBox** control named **rtfBio** in the lower right, and display **Athlete Info Sheet** in the form's title bar.

4 The code associated with frmAthlete includes the cboName_SelectedIndexChanged() procedure in frmStart, the frmAthlete_Load() procedure, and the DoBinarySearch() procedure. Open the **Code Editor** for frmStart, and type in the procedure for **cboName_SelectedIndexChanged()**, as shown in Figure 8-66. This code assigns the Athlete ID number to the pintAthlete public variable. In cboName, each entry consists of the Athlete ID, first name, last name, and country code. Therefore, the Val() function returns the Athlete ID. Now, instantiate **frmAthlete** and show the form instance.

```
Private Sub cboName_SelectedIndexChanged(ByVal sender _
    As System.Object, ByVal e As System.EventArgs) _
    Handles cboName.SelectedIndexChanged
  pintAthlete = Val(cboName.SelectedItem)
  Dim frm As New frmAthlete()
  frm.ShowDialog()
End Sub
```

Figure 8-66: Sub cboName_SelectedIndexChanged() procedure

5 Next, the frmAthlete_Load() procedure calls a procedure named DoBinarySearch(). Type the **DoBinarySearch()** procedure, as shown in Figure 8-67. DoBinarySearch() uses pintAthlete to locate the index value of the selected athlete's record in pastructAthletes(). This code implements the binary search routine explained in Lesson A.

```
Private Sub DoBinarySearch(ByRef rIndex As Integer)
  Dim Low, Mid, High As Integer
  Low = 0
  High = pNumAthletes
  Mid = Int((Low + High) / 2)
  Do Until pastructAthletes(Mid).AthleteID = pintAthlete
    If pintAthlete > pastructAthletes(Mid).AthleteID Then
      Low = Mid
    Else
      High = Mid
    End If
    Mid = Int((Low + High) / 2)
  Loop
  rIndex = Mid
End Sub
```

Figure 8-67: DoBinarySearch() procedure

6 Finally, frmAthlete_Load() assigns values to the controls on the form from pastructAthletes() and from the Biographies file. Type the **frmAthlete_Load()** procedure shown in Figure 8-68.

```
Private Sub frmAthlete_Load(ByVal _
    sender As System.Object, _
    ByVal e As System.EventArgs) Handles MyBase.Load
  Dim Index As Integer
  DoBinarySearch(Index)
  With pastructAthletes(Index)
    lblAthleteID.Text = .AthleteID
    lblFName.Text = .FName
    lblLName.Text = .LName
    CtrlNation1.SetCountry(.Country)
    lblGender.Text = IIf(.Gender = "M", "Male", "Female")
    lblDoB.Text = Format(.DoB, "MMMM d, yyyy")
    lblSport.Text = .Sport
    Dim Events(5) As Integer
    Dim i, j As Integer
    Events(0) = .Event1
    Events(1) = .Event2
    Events(2) = .Event3
    Events(3) = .Event4
    Events(4) = .Event5
    For i = 0 To 4
      If Events(i) > 0 Then
        For j = 0 To pNumEvents - 1
          If Events(i) = pastructEvents(j).EventID Then
            lstEvents.Items.Add _
              (pastructEvents(j).EventName)
          End If
        Next
      End If
    Next
    FileOpen(1, "Biographies", OpenMode.Random, , , _
        Len(pstructBioRec))
    FileGet(1, pstructBioRec, .AthleteID)
    rtfBio.Text = pstructBioRec.Bio
    pbxPhoto.Image = _
      Image.FromFile(pstructBioRec.PicFilename)
    FileClose()
  End With
End Sub
```

Figure 8-68: frmAthlete_Load() procedure

7 Run the UpClose application, trying all of the options from frmStart, and selecting athlete names from cboName.

NOTE: As you have been building UpClose, you have been asked to create multiple small sections of code in disparate locations. Perhaps you would find it useful to see all of the code in one listing. Because you are attempting to learn how to write the code yourself, you are encouraged not to use this listing as a crib, but rather to refer to it only if you have errors in your own code and cannot figure them out. The consolidated code listing appears in Appendix A.

Creating a Deployment Project for a Windows Forms Application

In Tutorial 7, you created a Web Setup project, which creates an installer for a Web Forms application; here you create a Setup project, which creates an installer for a

tip

• • • • • • • • • • • • • • • •

▶ Visual Basic .NET also includes two other types of Setup and Deployment projects, not addressed in this text. A Merge Module project creates an installer for project components that are designed to be shared by many different applications. A Cab project creates a cabinet file to be downloaded to a pre-XML-era Web browser.

Windows Forms application. The steps involved are similar, but you will note some differences. The main practical difference is the destination of the application on the target computer—the installer created by a Web Setup project installs an application in the Virtual Root folder of the target computer's Web server; whereas the installer created by a simple Windows Forms Setup project installs an application in the designated application folder on the target machine.

To create the Setup project for the Up Close and Personal Windows Forms application:

1 In Solution Explorer, right-click the solution name, and click **Add | New Project**. In the New Project dialog box, in the Project Types frame, click **Setup and Deployment Projects**. In the Templates frame, click **Setup Project**. Verify that the project is created in the VB.NET\Student\Tut08 folder; if necessary, browse to the correct folder. In the Name field, type **Up Close Installer**. See Figure 8-69. Click **OK**.

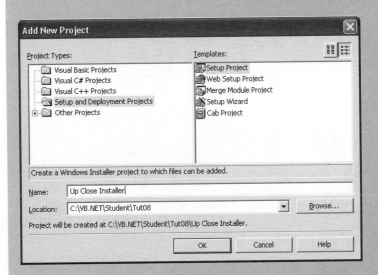

Figure 8-69: Selecting a Setup Project

2 Click **Up Close Installer** in Solution Explorer. In the Properties window, select **ProductName**, and change the setting to **Up Close and Personal**. This is the application name that the user will see in folder names and in the Add/Remove Programs dialog box.

3 Click **Up Close Installer** in Solution Explorer. Click **View | Editor | File System**, or click the File System Editor button at the top left of Solution Explorer.

4 Click **Application Folder** in the left pane of the File System Editor. Click **Action | Add | Project Output**. Ensure that UpClose is selected in the Project combo box. Click **Primary output** in the list box. Click **OK**.

5 Click **Application Folder** in the left pane of the File System Editor. Click **Action | Add | File**. Navigate to the **UpClose\bin** folder. Click **Athletes.txt**. While pressing [Ctrl], also click **Biographies**, **Events.txt**, **Misc26.ico**, **Misc27.ico**, and **Nations.txt**. Click **Open**. The File System Editor should now appear as it does in Figure 8-70.

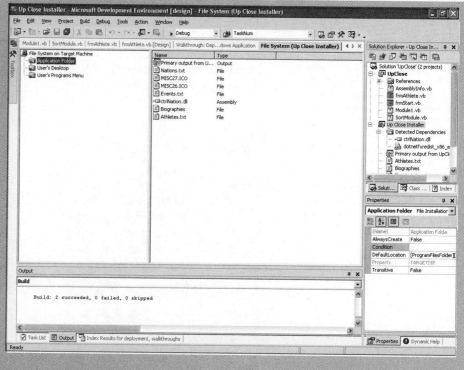

Figure 8-70: File System Editor

tip

As noted in Tutorial 7, Visual Basic .NET applications require certain system files that are part of the .NET Framework. Therefore, to install your application to a machine that does not have the .NET Framework, you must first install Dotnet fx.exe on the target machine. You can obtain Dotnet fx.exe as a free download from the Microsoft Web site, and you can distribute it freely with your application.

6   On the Build menu, click **Up Close Installer**. This builds the installer so that the project is now ready to be installed locally or on another machine.

7   Though this project does not require it, you can make many customizations of the installation program. For example, choose **Up Close Installer** in Solution Explorer, then click **View | Editor | User Interface**. Click the **Start** node under the **Install** node, and then click **Action | Add Dialog**. Note the many features that you can add to the distributed version of your application. If you choose to create any of these additional features, you must click Build | Up Close Installer again to include them in the installer.

8   Click **Project | Install** to install the project on the development machine. Run the **Up Close and Personal** program from its installed location. This ensures that the installer has installed all necessary files to run the application.

9   To install to a different machine, you must copy the built installer to the other machine. In Windows Explorer, navigate to **VB.NET\Student\Tut08\ Up Close Installer\Debug\Up Close Installer.msi**. Copy that file and all other files in that folder to the target computer. This may require a network connection from the development to the target machine, or a CD-R or Zip drive. When the files have been copied to the target machine, run **Setup.exe** on that machine.

You have now completed Tutorial 8. Stop now for a break, or continue on with the following review questions and exercises.

S U M M A R Y

- Pseudo-ISAM files can be used to satisfy large data storage requirements without sacrificing too much in the way of performance. The index portion of the pseudo-ISAM file can be part of any sequential file.
- A binary search algorithm quickly determines the location of an item in a sorted array. The search algorithm is easily adaptable to any array structure.
- Visual Basic .NET provides for deployment of a Windows Forms application with a Setup project, which creates an installer for installing an application on any machine running a Windows operating system. Through multiple options in the Setup project package, you can customize the installer to meet many different application deployment scenarios.

Q U E S T I O N S

1. Using the binary search algorithm given in the text, how do you know when a sought-after item is not in the array?

2. Given a sorted array of 1789 items, how many iterations of the binary search loop are needed to locate one item?

3. In a setup project, the main window in the IDE usually displays the _____.

4. In a setup project, you specify the name of the program to be installed on the target machine by setting the _____ property.

5. In a setup project, you identify the project output from the _____ menu.

E X E R C I S E S

1. Create a Windows Forms application that assists residents in the International Village in understanding and selecting a game from the computers in the game room in each house. Each of the computers in the game room has a number of computer games installed, and additional games are readily available on the Internet. Since villagers come from many countries and may not have the same computer games at home, this application explains something about each game and provides a link to a Web site where additional information can be found. This application requires a pseudo-ISAM file and several sort routines.

   a. The pseudo-ISAM file has an index portion (stored in a sequential file) and a random-access portion (stored in a random-access file). The sequential-access index file for this application, Categories-Games.txt, consists of the game category, the game name, and the record number of the corresponding record in the random access file.

   b. The raw data for the random-access data file is contained in Details.txt and contains the record number, the game description, and the link to a game-related Web site. Before writing the main application for this project, create an appropriate structure and write a small console application to create the random access file (named Games.dat) based on the data in Details.txt.

   c.   The main application for this project contains only one form, frmGame. This form contains the following controls:

- Two radio buttons within a GroupBox control, which allow the user to choose the sort order for displaying the list of games—either by game category or by game name
- A list box containing the name of each game and its game category (sorted either by game category or by game name, based on the currently-selected radio button)
- A RichTextBox control, containing a description of the game currently selected in the list box
- A LinkLabel control, containing a link to a Web site that provides additional information concerning the currently-selected game

   d.   At start-up, load the sequential file into an array. Use an insertion sort to sort the array by game category. Then load the sorted array into the list box.

   e.   If the user changes the sort order to game name, use a bubble sort to put the games in that order. Then empty the list box, and reload it from the newly sorted array.

   f.   If the user subsequently changes the sort order back to game category, use a selection sort to put the games in that order. Then empty the list box, and reload it from the newly sorted array.

   g.   When the user selects a game in the list box, your program must retrieve the record for that game from Games.dat, and then display the game description in the RichTextBox control and set the Web link in the LinkLabel control.

2.   Create a Windows Forms application to display the names of nations competing in the Friendsville International Games along with the number of gold, silver, and bronze medals won by each country. This data is maintained in a separate sequential file that you must create. The program displays the name and medal count in each category, plus the total medals won, for each country. Use an insertion sort while an array of structures is being loaded at start-up, putting the data initially into order by total medals won (descending numeric order). Subsequently, the user selects whether to view the data in order by country (ascending alphabetical order), by gold medals won (descending numeric order), or total medals won (also descending numeric order). Use different sort algorithms to sort the array based on user selection after start-up.

3.   Create a Web Forms version of the project from Exercise 2.

4.   Create a Console application. Read the same sequential data file as is specified in Exercise 2. Load this data into an array, keeping it in descending order by total medals won. Do not load into the array the number of medals in each category; just calculate and load into the array the country name and the total medal count. When you reach the end of the file, display the array, which should show the country name and total medal count, in descending order by total medal count.

5.   Create a Setup Project to deploy the Windows Forms application developed in Exercise 1.

6.   Create a Setup Project to deploy the Windows Forms application developed in Exercise 2.

7.   Create a Web Setup Project to deploy the Web Forms application developed in Exercise 3.

8.   Create a Setup Project to deploy the Console application developed in Exercise 4.

Exercises 9 and 10 allow you to both discover the solution to problems on your own and experiment with material that is not covered explicitly in the tutorial.

discovery ▶   9.   Create a Windows Forms application with a doubly linked list. At start-up, load a sequential file into an array, sorted by athlete last name. Do not change the physical order of records in the array after start-up. The array contains first names and last names of athletes. Use Athletes.txt as the source file for the array, ignoring the data values you do not need in the array. (You must account for them on input, but you do not need to put them into the array.) Then, build a linked list that points to all of the athlete first names in order by first name, but build reverse links at the same time. That is, the reverse link in each record points to the previous first name. (*Hint*: You need two pointer fields and two external pointers.) For the GUI, display the original list, sorted by last name, in a list box. Select one name from the array at start-up, and make this the initial SelectedItem in the list box. Place two buttons with arrows on the form, one arrow pointing to the right and one arrow pointing to the left. When the user clicks the right arrow, select the next name in the array and in the ListBox control using the forward pointer, which will be the next name, alphabetically by first name; when the user clicks the left arrow, select the previous name in the array and in the ListBox control using the backward pointer.

discovery ▶   10.   Build on the application in Exercise 9 by allowing the user to add a new athlete to the array or delete an athlete from the array, and then make all of the necessary modifications to the doubly linked list.

K E Y   T E R M S

- binary search
- bubble sort
- exchange sort
- file sort
- insertion sort
- ISAM file
- linked list
- pseudo-ISAM file
- record key
- selection sort
- sequential search
- Setup project
- Shell sort
- shuttle sort

Data Access with ADO.NET

case ▶ Hilda Reiner, as the team leader and most experienced member of the Friendsville Games Development Team (FGDT), determined from the outset that tackling database access in Visual Basic. NET makes much more sense after learning the basics of Windows Forms, Web Forms, coding principles, and object-oriented programming. But databases are central to modern business information systems. And so from this point forward, you implement solutions using databases rather than traditional file structures. In this tutorial, you build the VillageHousing database application that you previewed in the Overview at the beginning of this text. And in the end-of-lesson exercises, you replace the traditional files used in earlier tutorials with Microsoft Access databases.

Visual Basic .NET supports several data access technologies. This tutorial focuses on the newest and, for many applications, the most useful of these technologies: ADO.NET

Reviewing the Village Housing Application

The Village Housing application is introduced in the Overview at the beginning of this book. This application is used as the basis for your initial tour of a Visual Basic .NET application. In the Overview, you are promised that you will learn how to create the Village Housing application in Tutorial 9. In this preview, you refamiliarize yourself with the entire application and focus specifically on its database aspects.

To preview the VillageHousing application while focusing on its database components:

1 Run **VillageHousing.exe** in the VB.NET\Student\Tut00\VillageHousing\bin folder. Click **Load** to load the database, displaying David Simpson's record on the left and the data grid of all rooms on the right. Click the **Help** button to see the instructions for using the application.

2 Refer to the detailed instructions for previewing this application in the Overview, and experiment with it again. This includes scrolling through the records of the villagers, finding a particular villager's record by name or by BadgeID, making a room reservation for a villager already in the database, adding a new villager, deleting a villager, updating the database, and scrolling through the list of rooms in the data grid.

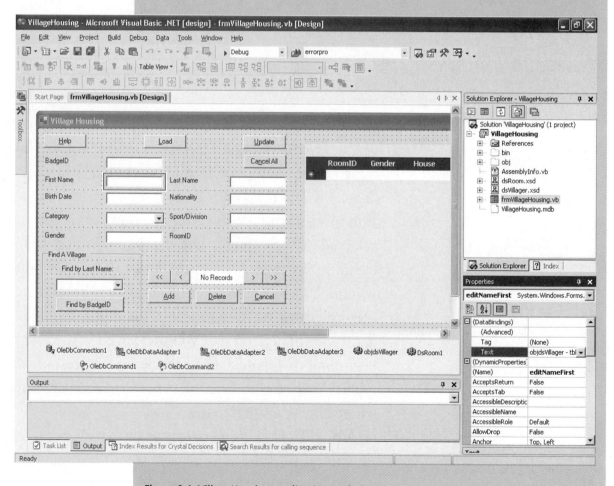

Figure 9-1: VillageHousing application at design time

3 Figure 9-1, frmVillageHousing at design time, displays or suggests many of the database access elements of this application. Look first at the tray underneath the form. OleDbConnection1 is the component that establishes a connection to VillageHousing.mdb, the Microsoft Access database. Every action that uses a database requires a connection to that database. All of the database-related activity of this application uses OleDbConnection1.

4 Next, in Solution Explorer in Figure 9-1, notice the presence of the .xsd classes—dsRoom.xsd and dsVillager.xsd. These classes provide the schema for datasets—collections of data extracted from the underlying database. dsRoom is based on a predefined query in the database, pulling the information needed to load the DataGrid control that you see on the right side of the form. As you discover later, this query selects room information from tblRoom, along with the name of the house in which that room is located—information stored in tblHouse in the database. In the tray underneath the form, you see DsRoom1, an instance of dsRoom.

5 Meanwhile, dsVillager provides the schema for the information concerning each villager, displayed on the left side of the form. This includes the elements of tblVillager, along with the definition of the category for each villager, taken from tblCategory. Unlike dsRoom, dsVillager is created from each table (tblVillager and tblCategory) rather than from a query. This is done so that the dataset can be updated. In the tray underneath the form, you see objdsVillager, an instance of dsVillager.

NOTE: The initial frmVillageHousing form is created using the Data Form Wizard, which automatically names a dataset with the prefix obj (meaning object)—hence the object name objdsVillager. The data grid on the right is added to the form after the Data Form Wizard creates the initial form. But the Windows Form Designer automatically assigns a default name of <dataset name> <sequential number>, so the instance of dsRoom is named DsRoom1.

6 A data adapter is necessary to create a dataset from the underlying database. In the tray underneath the form, you see three data adapters: OleDbDataAdapter1 pulls data from tblVillager and inserts it into objdsVillager; OleDbDataAdapter2 pulls information from tblCategory and adds this information to objdsVillager; and OleDbDataAdapter3 pulls information from a predefined query in the database and uses this information to load DsRoom1.

7 The ADO.NET data model also allows you to execute individual commands directly against a database, rather than using the intermediary of a dataset. In the tray underneath the form, you see two examples of this feature, OleDbCommand1 and OlDbCommand2.

8 Finally, the graphical controls on the form must be bound to individual elements within the datasets. Hence, for example, the Badge ID text box is bound to the BadgeID field in tblVillager in objdsVillager, the First Name text box is bound to the NameFirst element in tblVillager in objdsVillager, and so on. A DataGrid control can be bound to an entire dataset, and so the data grid on the right derives all of its data from DsRoom1.

9 Exit the **VillageHousing** application.

With this brief introduction, you are ready to enter the world of database access within the Visual Studio .NET Framework.

After completing this lesson, you will be able to:

■ Understand fundamental database concepts

■ Implement the relational model

■ Understand ADO.NET data access architecture

■ Work with the specific ADO.NET objects necessary to retrieve and update data from a Microsoft Access database

■ Comprehend the code generated by the Data Form Wizard

Introduction to ADO.NET

Overview of Database Concepts

Lesson A provides an overview of database concepts and then describes the Microsoft ADO.NET data access technology, both the general ADO.NET architecture, as well as the details for accessing a Microsoft Access database. To use ADO.NET technology, you need to learn the detailed objects and services and commands, of course; but you should start with an overview of database concepts. This discussion provides a brief overview of relational databases, data modeling, and relational database design

Relational Databases

The most common model for database management systems (DBMS) in commercial use today is the **relational model**, based on the pioneering work of Dr. E.F. Codd. In this model, based on a branch of mathematics called relational algebra and relational calculus, data is perceived by the user as consisting of a series of one or more tables, consisting of rows and columns. Each table provides information about one entity (person, place, thing, or transaction) or one relationship. Columns in the table represent the characteristics or attributes of the entity, whereas rows represent specific instances of the entity. For example, a Villager table might contain columns for the Badge ID number, last name, first name, sport, country, and so on. Each row in the Villager table provides information concerning one villager, or, in the terminology of a relational DBMS, one villager instance. Figure 9-2 displays the structure of tblVillager, and Figure 9-3 shows the table's contents.

Primary key symbol

Data Type specifies the physical domain of each column (field)

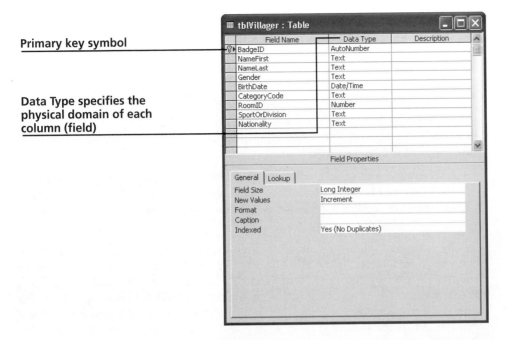

Figure 9-2: Design view of tblVillager in Microsoft Access

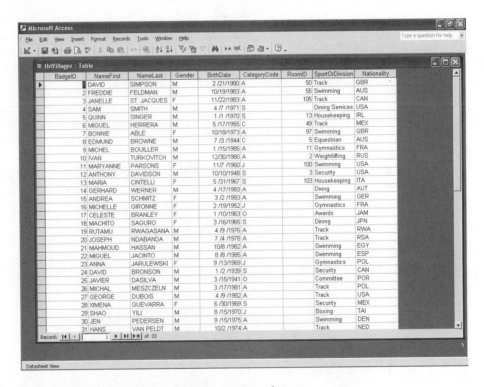

Figure 9-3: Datasheet view of tblVillager in Microsoft Access

Tables in a relational database should follow certain rules established by Dr. Codd. They are as follows:

- Duplicate rows are not permitted.
- Every column name must be unique.

- Column constraints define the domain (the set of possible values) for entries in that column, and each entry must either contain a value from the designated domain or be null.
- The data value in each cell is atomic (that is, no repeating groups, arrays, or structures).
- The order of rows is unimportant; the order of columns is unimportant.

Because duplicate rows are forbidden, it follows that there must be an attribute or a combination of attributes that uniquely identifies a row. This unique row identifier is called the **primary key**.

NOTE: Some of Codd's rules are not strictly enforced by commercial DBMSs. For example, Microsoft Access encourages the designer to assign a primary key, but does not require it. Microsoft Access also permits duplicate rows if there is no designated primary key.

By examining Figure 9-2 and 9-3 carefully, you can see that the structure and contents of tblVillager follow all of Codd's rules. In Figure 9-2, the domain of each column is given by the Data Type (and can be further constrained by the Field Properties at the bottom of the figure), while the BadgeID field is designated as the primary key (indicated in Microsoft Access by the key symbol next to the Field Name). Although the display in Figure 9-3 does show the rows ordered by BadgeID, this is not mandatory—tblVillager is still tblVillager even if the contents are sorted by name, or not sorted at all.

NOTE: The rows of a table constitute a mathematical set, and everything you ever learned about sets is applicable here. The order does not matter: recall that the set {a, b, c} is identical to the set {c, b, a}. Set operations, such as union, intersection, difference, and Cartesian product, are intrinsically included in the notion of relational tables.

NOTE: A note on relational database terminology: you may encounter some programmers who prefer to use the mathematical terms for these concepts. Figure 9-4 provides a cross-reference of equivalent terms.

Common name	Mathematical name
Table	Relation
Column or field name	Attribute
Row	Tuple
Primary key	Key

Figure 9-4: Terminology of relational databases

Data Modeling

A **data model** is a graphical representation of the structure of the data needed to support a particular information requirement. It may be global—an enterprisewide data model—or it may relate to the performance of only one function in one office of an organization. Whatever the scope, the data model is an abstraction of the data requirements that exist in the user's mind.

Several techniques for data modeling have been developed and are in use today. Of these, the most popular technique is the **entity-relationship model**, or E-R model.

Figure 9-5 shows an example of an entity-relationship diagram, whose purpose is to display the entities and relationships between entities for the Village Housing application. A relationship in an E-R diagram is indicated by the diamond shape, and the cardinality of this relationship is represented inside the diamond. In this case, the relationship between villager and room is one to one (1:1), meaning that one villager has at most one room, and one room has at most one villager. Relationships can also be one to many (1:N) or many to many (M:N). For example, a villager has only one category (athlete, staff, official, visitor, etc.), but a category may have many villagers—this is a 1:N relationship, also shown in Figure 9-5. However, an athlete may participate in many events, while each event has many athletes—this is a M:N relationship.

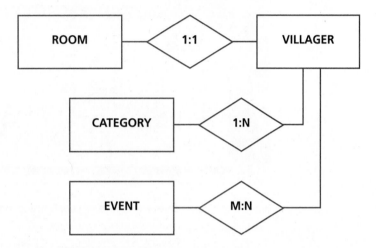

Figure 9-5: Sample E-R diagram

Relational Database Design

Starting from a completed data model, the database designer develops the specific tables, attributes, and relationships needed to implement that model. Often, additional coded elements are identified, which facilitate data entry and enforce standards. For example, in the Village Housing application, the villager's CategoryCode and CountryCode serve this purpose, as does the room's HouseCode. These coded elements require corresponding tables, called **code tables**.

To implement 1:N relationships, the primary key from the table representing the 1 side of the relationship is inserted into the table that represents the N side of the relationship. The key that is so inserted is referred to as a **foreign key**. For instance, to implement the 1:N relationship between tblCategory and tblVillager, the CategoryCode field in tblCategory appears as a foreign key in tblVillager. To implement a 1:1 relationship, the primary key of either table is inserted into the other table as a foreign key. In the 1:1 relationship between rooms and villagers, the primary key of tblRoom (RoomID) is a foreign key in tblVillager. You can see these relationships in Figure 9-6, the Microsoft Access Relationships window for the VillageHousing.mdb database. The one side of the relationship is represented with a 1 and the many side of the relationship is represented with the infinity symbol (∞). (The main database window is also visible in the background.)

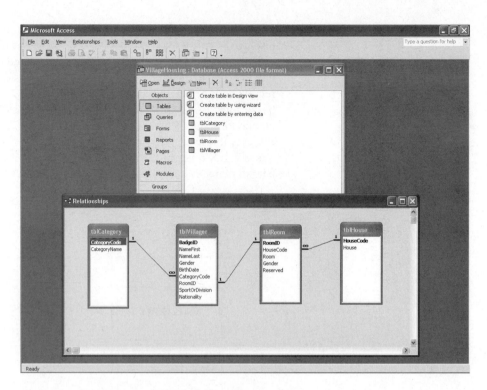

Figure 9-6: Relationships window for VillageHousing.mdb

Figure 9-6 also demonstrates how the DBMS can enforce referential integrity between two tables. For any given relationship, the table that contains the foreign key is referred to as the child table, whereas the table whose primary key is the basis of the relationship is referred to as the parent table. A **referential integrity constraint** on a relationship simply means that, if a value exists in a particular row on the child side of the relationship, then that value must exist in the primary key field on the parent side of the relationship. In most DBMSs, the designer can choose whether or not to enforce referential integrity on any 1:1 or 1:N relationship. Referential integrity is enforced, for example, between tblRoom and tblVillager. To wit: every value entered in the RoomID field of tblVillager must correspond to a RoomID value in tblRoom. This constraint prevents a villager being assigned to a room that does not exist.

M:N relationships cannot be directly represented in a relational database design; to implement a M:N relationship, therefore, you must construct an additional table, called an **intersection table,** to represent the relationship. The primary key of this intersection table is the combined primary keys of the entities participating in the M:N relationship. Each participating entity has a 1:N relationship with the intersection table. For example, Figure 9-7 shows an E-R diagram of athletes and events, which have a M:N relationship. If this diagram were implemented in a relational database design as it is in Figure 9-8, three tables would be required: the intersection table tblAthletesEventsInt shows which athletes are entered into which events, while tblAthletes has a 1:N relationship with the intersection table (because one athlete may enter multiple events), and tblEvents also has a 1:N relationship with the intersection table (because one event has many athletes in it).

Figure 9-7: E-R diagram of athletes and events

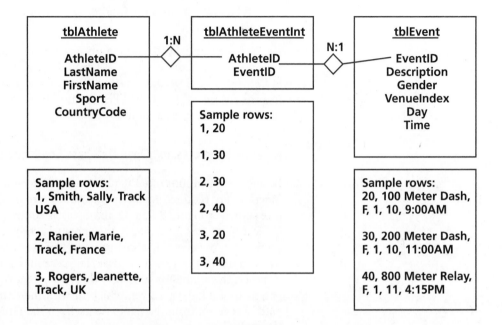

Figure 9-8: Relationships diagram of tblAthletes, tblEvents, and tblAthletesEventsInt, with sample data values

Implementing the Relational Model

Several topics surrounding the implementation of the relational model are most important for programmers who need to access relational databases. These topics include Structured Query Language (SQL); N-tier architecture and Open Database Connectivity (ODBC); security, concurrency control, and resource constraints; and transaction processing. Your appreciation of ADO.NET and your ability to apply this technology effectively will be enhanced by familiarity with these concepts.

Structured Query Language (SQL)

A database management system (DBMS) requires a language to define the structure (or schema) of the data, called the **data definition language (DDL)**, as well as a language for manipulating the data after the structure has been defined, called the **data manipulation language (DML)**. DDL tasks include creating and defining the structure of tables, defining relationships, designating primary and foreign keys, identifying the data type for each column, and defining data constraints (such as uniqueness, domain values, and default values). DML tasks include adding, updating, and deleting records in tables, as well as retrieving and displaying records from one or more tables.

In the 1970s, IBM invented Structured Query Language to handle both DDL and DML tasks. The language has long since been adopted as an ANSI standard. SQL is not a full-fledged programming language, but rather a limited, nonprocedural language used only for DDL and DML tasks in the relational DBMS world. In practice, all commercial DBMSs support SQL for DML tasks, and many also use SQL for DDL tasks. Because SQL has been standardized, SQL commands can be used to manipulate data in almost all commercial DBMSs.

> **NOTE:** A third category of necessary tasks, controlling access to the database, is also recognized, and is commonly known as a data control language (DCL). Many mainframe DBMSs, such as Oracle and IBM's DB2, use SQL for DCL tasks as well.

You can use SQL commands inside your Visual Basic .NET programs to manipulate data stored in a relational database. The key SQL commands are SELECT (to retrieve information from one or more tables), INSERT (to add new records into a table), UPDATE (to modify records in a table), and DELETE (to remove records from a table).

N-tier Architectures and Open Database Connectivity (ODBC)

Business applications often require multiple tiers or layers of software to provide the functionality required by an application. For example, in the typical 3-tier architecture shown in Figure 9-9, a database server controls and manages a centralized database, a Web server manages the network connections to all of the users, and a browser on the client machine provides the user interface and the means for interactive communication with the user. The user may initiate a database request within a browser; this request is passed to the Web server over a network; the request is then passed to a database server, which queries the database. The response follows this path in reverse, from the database itself, to the DBMS, to the Web server, and to the client machine's browser.

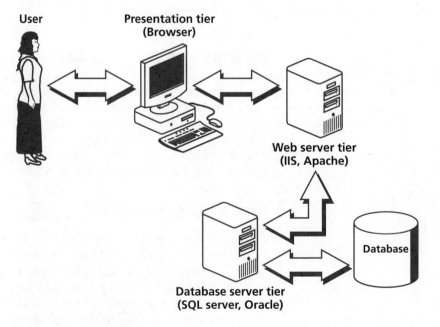

Figure 9-9: 3-tier architecture

Additional software layers are also often involved. For example, business rules may be implemented at any level of an application, security may be added at any level, firewalls may be inserted, or applications may be translated for a local language or culture. In general parlance among database analysts, the database server is referred to as the back end of the application, and the GUI is called the front end. Everything in between is called a middle tier in the architecture.

Database requests could come from multiple application programs written in Visual Basic, C++, Java, PowerBuilder, Delphi, and so on. Database requests can be passed to a database created in MS Access, SQL Server, DB2, Oracle, IMS, ADABAS, MySQL, Informix, and so on. (These are some of the more popular DBMSs.) The application programmer's task is greatly eased if a standardized method exists for correctly translating and parsing all such requests. This standard does exist, created initially by Microsoft, but subsequently adopted by ANSI and implemented to varying degrees by all major vendors. The standard is called the **Open Database Connectivity (ODBC)** protocol. Through ODBC, application programmers can write database requests (essentially SQL statements and calls to prewritten procedures stored in the database) in a standardized fashion. Each application language that supports ODBC contains a Driver Manager. When a connection to a data source is needed, the **Driver Manager** loads the appropriate driver applicable to the data source. Subsequently, the driver parses SQL commands as needed and passes them to the database server, and the driver also translates the results coming back from the database and delivers them to the application program. See Figure 9-10.

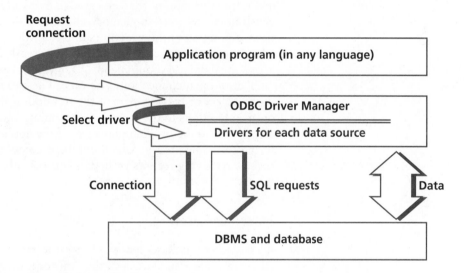

Figure 9-10: ODBC protocol

Security, Concurrency Control, and Resource Constraints

When you design an application program that accesses a multiuser database, you must be aware of several significant additional issues, including security, concurrency control, and resource constraints.

Security is a multilayered issue that really needs to be addressed on a comprehensive basis. For example, it does no good to have an extremely secure centralized database if the passwords needed to access that database are stored in compiled Visual Basic .NET software distributed freely over the Internet or stored in an insecure operating system. If security is compromised at the user level, then the database is essentially unprotected—the database can be penetrated by any person inclined to do so. Security, therefore, is an issue that goes far beyond Visual Basic .NET, although the security available within Visual Basic .NET is certainly a part of it. The most important thing for you to know is that you have the option, by setting the appropriate connection properties, to access a completely public data store (that is, one with no password protection at all); to record a user ID and password in Visual Basic .NET to access a password protected data store; or to tap into the security features of the operating system, the server, and the target DBMS. The final option here is the most secure.

Concurrency control refers to the potential problem caused by multiple users attempting to update or delete a record at the same time. This is the type of problem that occurs when two customers simultaneously purchase the last seat on a particular airline flight, or when an athlete reserves a room in the International Village at exactly the same moment that management removes that room from inventory. Concurrency control is generally an issue that must be handled by the DBMS. However, the application programmer must also be aware that a request to retrieve information from a database or to update information in the database may fail because another user is accessing those records at the same instant. As you will learn in Lesson C, the application program must take concurrency control issues into account. Basically, this means that you write error-handling code that anticipates potential errors when accessing a database, and that provides a gentle recovery from such errors rather than allowing the program to crash.

Resource constraints have been a major issue in the design of both DBMSs and application programs that access databases created in those DBMSs. **Resource constraints** may involve memory allocation, file handlers, and number of connections, among other things. For example, a Microsoft Access database may perform admirably with four concurrent users, but crash or lockup if 1000 users attempt to access the database simultaneously. DBMSs have the capacity for managing a finite number of open connections at a time. The application program can contribute to this problem or become part of the solution: if the application program maintains open connections to the database, consuming scarce resources, then the application contributes to the problem; however, if the application program limits connections to the tiny time slice in which database access is mandated by application logic, such as retrieving records or updating the database, then the application may contribute to the solution to this problem.

Transaction Processing

If a customer purchases a new refrigerator from Sears Roebuck and charges the purchase on his Sears credit card, then this one physical transaction should trigger the following database updates: (1) the purchase is recorded in the customer record (this is true for every customer, whether or not that customer charged the purchase to a Sears credit card); (2) the customer's credit card record must reflect the purchase; (3) the store inventory must be adjusted; (4) the shipping department needs to be notified of the required delivery date for this refrigerator; and (5) the sales associate's commissions table must also be updated. You do not want to update the customer's record, but fail to update the shipping schedule; you do not want to ship the item, but fail to update the inventory records. In brief, the physical transaction—selling a refrigerator—must be reflected in the associated database records either completely, or not at all. If any part of the transaction fails, the whole transaction should fail, and the whole transaction should be resubmitted for reprocessing. The notion that one physical event can trigger multiple changes to the database is referred to as **transaction processing**. When the business rule is that a collection of related database changes should be accomplished together, or none of them should be accomplished, then this collection is often referred to as an **atomic transaction**.

A DBMS usually offers some support for transaction processing. Generally, you are able to mark the beginning of a transaction, commit all pending database changes when all updates are successfully completed, or alternatively roll back (undo) all pending changes if any part of the transaction aborts. At the application program level, you need to be able to take advantage of whatever transaction-processing capability is offered by the DBMS.

Understanding ADO.NET Architecture

The Microsoft architectures for using databases within Visual Basic have evolved through several generations, including Data Access Objects (DAO), Remote Data Objects (RDO), ActiveX Data Objects (ADO), and now ADO.NET. (Though initially developed for Visual C++ rather than Visual Basic, Object Linking and Embedding for Databases (OLE DB) is also part of this evolution.) Each generation built upon the previous generation and introduced new functionality. DAO allowed a Visual Basic program to gain access to a Microsoft Access database on the local machine; RDO facilitated access to remote databases; ADO greatly expanded the number and types (manufacturers) of accessible databases, while providing limited functionality across networks; ADO also made the underlying OLE DB data access technology from the Visual C++ world available to Visual Basic programmers; and ADO.NET provides a common platform throughout Visual Studio .NET for accessing all kinds of data, including both relational and nonrelational data. In addition, ADO.NET is truly scalable in a way that the earlier technologies were not. Visual Studio .NET still supports both ADO and OLE DB, but for the development of new applications, ADO.NET is preferred. In brief, ADO.NET is the new and preferred technology for providing data access within the .NET platform.

ADO.NET and eXtensible Markup Language (XML)

In the last decade, a convergence of technologies has occurred between the World Wide Web and database management systems. In more and more cases, evolving Web-based applications require support from a DBMS, and evolving database applications must be supported on the Web. For example, a university with a sophisticated Web presence may decide to permit online registration, requiring access to a database; or a mail-order firm with a sophisticated database may decide to embark on Internet-based sales. In these cases and thousands like them, the Web and a database must work compatibly, passing data from the database, via the Web to the client, and similarly passing data from the client, via the Web, back to the database.

In the beginning, the World Wide Web, envisioned by Tim Berners Lee, made information (documents) available that were stored in Web pages and delivered by Web servers to any computer on the Web. However, the initial Web did not allow user interaction with a Web page, did not maintain session state, did not collect information from the user, and did not interact with a database. The current commercial incarnation of the Web has the capability of keeping track of each user and recording user inputs.

Tutorial 7 narrates the evolution of the World Wide Web into its current form, most especially the development of XML and its wide adoption by software manufacturers, vendors, and computer programmers. Tutorial 7 notes that database access on the Web is supplied through XML Web services, but no further explanation of those services was given at that point.

tip

See the help topic "Distributed Application Communication" in the Visual Studio Help files for more information on the many uses and approaches to XML Web services.

XML Web services are applications that provide communication between different software applications using standard protocols such as HTTP, XML, XSD, SOAL, and WSDL. XML Web services can be built on various programming models, such as ASP.NET, ATL Server, and .NET Remoting. Though XML Web services are useful for accessing a database, XML Web services have much broader applicability, as this paragraph suggests.

In Visual Studio .NET, XML Web services for accessing a database are constructed using ADO.NET, a common platform for data-related operations. Interestingly, this same platform provides database functionality whether you are building a Windows Forms or a Web Forms application. In the Village Housing project, which is a Windows Forms application, XML Web services provide access to a Microsoft Access database on the local machine. As data moves from the database to your application, it is formatted as XML data. ADO.NET also describes the internal structure of data within an application using XML schemas, using an XML-based protocol called XSD.

Besides being a universally accepted standard, XML also has the advantage of passing fairly easily through firewalls. Many firewalls are configured to allow HTML text to pass, but to block system-level requests—that is, executable code that could potentially damage the receiving machine; XML-formatted data gets around those restrictions and is allowed to pass freely.

You may find it helpful to learn XML, but this is not absolutely necessary to use XML Web services in Visual Studio .NET. The various designers and wizards in ADO.NET create all of the necessary XML coding, and it is generally transparent to the programmer. You can examine the XML coding created by ADO.NET if you so choose, but you do not have to do this, and rarely if ever do you need to modify the XML code directly. If there is one additional language you really should learn in order to make effective use of ADO.NET, that language is SQL rather than XML.

This discussion has mentioned a number of interrelated technologies. Figure 9-11 provides a summary of these terms and definitions.

Technology	Definition
Structured Query Language (SQL)	A standardized language for DDL and DML operations on a relational database
HyperText Markup Language (HTML)	The language for defining a static Web page
eXtensible Markup Language (XML)	Enhanced HTML, provides for interactivity, style sheets, and data structures (schemas)
Open Database Connectivity protocol (ODBC)	The protocol that provides standardized interface definitions between application programs and relational databases
XML Web service	An application that provides communication between two processes, using standard protocols and languages such as HTTP, XML, SOAP, and WSDL
Active Server Pages in the .NET Framework (ASP.NET)	The Microsoft implementation of interactive Web pages in the .NET Framework; ASP.NET Web pages (.aspx files) are constructed in XML, and also provide server-side code, contained in .aspx.vb files
ActiveX Data Objects for the .NET Framework (ADO.NET)	The data access technology for the .NET Framework; ADO.NET objects create XML Web services, which then appear as XML and XSD documents

Figure 9-11: Data access technologies

NOTE: As a point of reference, you may be familiar with other technologies that provide similar functionality to XML Web services. All of these were invented because of the basic inability of a Web server to communicate directly with a database server, requiring some sort of intermediary. For example, ColdFusion (now owned by Macromedia) provides this capability, as does PHP.

ADO.NET Defined

The term *ADO.NET* refers to the collection of data access objects and tools defined in the .NET Framework and Common Language Runtime (CLR). These objects and tools are available to any .NET-managed code application across multiple languages (Visual Basic .NET, Visual C++ .NET, C# .NET, J# .NET, JScript, Visual FoxPro).

ADO.NET offers two data provider models: (1) the OleDb Data Provider supports any data source that is compatible with OLE DB—which in practice means nearly any data source; and (2) the SQL Data Provider provides the most efficient connections to SQL Server. Both of these models use the same fundamental architecture, consisting of these five objects: Connection, DataAdapter, Dataset, Data Command, and DataReader. Except for the DataReader, these objects can all be dropped onto a form from the Data tab of the Toolbox.

The first element in the ADO.NET model is the Connection object, which provides a connection from your application to a data store (usually, but not always, a database). In the most common implementation, a data adapter object briefly opens this connection to obtain data to populate a Dataset object, and to repopulate dataset changes back to the underlying database. After the data burst is transmitted, the data adapter closes the connection until the next time it is needed. The data adapter's methods may include SQL statements and stored procedures in the database. **Datasets**, which are loosely coupled to the data stores, are transmitted and persist across platforms, machines, and applications through XML, and dataset schemas are defined through XSD (an XML-based protocol for describing data structures). The dataset's methods manipulate data on the client side. This configuration of ADO.NET components is shown in Figure 9-12.

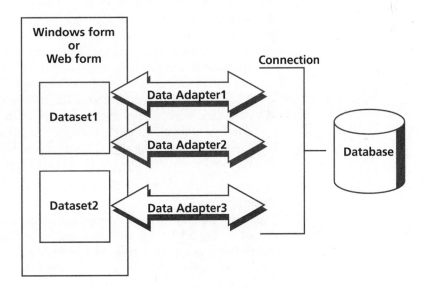

Figure 9-12: ADO.NET configuration with dataset and data adapters

Sometimes tight coupling of the data in your application with data in the underlying database is needed. In such a situation, rather than using data adapters and datasets, you can configure ADO.NET Data Providers to afford direct access to a data store. In this case, data commands and data readers process the database directly on the server side. This type of processing may be valuable for transaction processing and for parameterized queries. A diagram of this type of ADO.NET configuration appears in Figure 9-13.

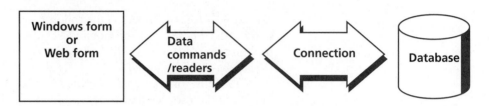

Figure 9-13: ADO.NET configuration with data commands and readers

You have several choices for designing and implementing ADO.NET in your application. Visual Studio provides a number of wizards that step you through the process and automatically configure the requisite elements. You can configure the elements yourself in the Designer, setting the properties of each object manually. Or, you can configure ADO.NET programmatically, which can be quite challenging, but may be necessary if you need to establish the parameters dynamically. In Lesson C, you use a combination of these techniques: you use the Data Form Wizard to design the basic Windows form for data access, and a Data Adapter Configuration Wizard to design additional adapters and datasets. You also use data commands for direct database access. This application does not use data readers.

Data Store

As you've just learned, a Connection object connects your application to a data store. The data store can be any of the following:

- A Microsoft SQL Server 7 or SQL Server 2000 database.
- Any relational database that supports the Open Database Connectivity protocol (ODBC), an industry-standard protocol for interoperability among relational database management systems and applications programming languages that use these DBMSs. Almost all commercial DBMSs do support ODBC, including Microsoft SQL Server, Oracle, DB2, Informix, and so on.
- Any data store accessible through OLE DB. This includes not only relational databases, but also nonrelational data stores such as Excel files, simple text files, ISAM files, hierarchical databases, or graphical and geographical data sources.
- An XML-formatted dataset in the same or another application.

Connection Object

Your application needs a Connection object to transfer data to and from a data store. Visual Studio .NET offers two such objects: an SqlConnection object is optimized for managing a connection to a Microsoft SQL Server 7 or 2000 database; and an OleDbConnection manages a connection to any data store accessible via OLE DB. Both types have similar properties.

The ConnectionString is the most important property of the Connection object. This property contains attribute/value pairs that provide the information necessary to log on and connect to a particular data store. The attribute/value pairs needed for any particular connection depend on the data provider or source, because not all providers require the same attribute/value pairs. In many cases, the components of the ConnectionString are also accessible as individual properties. Visual Basic .NET offers three methods for constructing the ConnectionString: (1) use one of the ADO.NET data access wizards available in the Designer, (2) assign values to the component properties of the ConnectionString, or (3) build the ConnectionString property yourself. If one or more of the required attribute/value pairs for a particular connection is not available as an individual property, then the second method cannot be employed—you must either use a wizard, or construct the ConnectionString yourself. In Lesson C, you will use a wizard to create the initial ConnectionString while developing the VillageHousing application. You then reset the ConnectionString programmatically, so that the running program finds the database no matter where on the computer the application is stored.

As a practical matter, you will usually use a wizard in the Designer to build the ConnectionString. The exception to this approach is when your application must connect to a data store whose connection properties are not known until runtime. In this case, you will most likely still create the connection at design time using the wizard, so that the tables, columns, and constraints are available to you while designing your application. Then, you will change the connection string properties at runtime, based on information stored in a configuration file or provided by the user.

When you create a connection at design time, Visual Studio adds it to the Server Explorer. The Server Explorer is another window normally located along the left side of the screen, in the same location as the Toolbox. Usually, both the Toolbox and Server Explorer have Auto Hide turned on, so only one of these is visible at a time, and then only when it is being actively used. Server Explorer shows all connections and servers that you have created or that are otherwise available in Visual Studio. Once you have created a connection or a server, it remains available in Server Explorer as long as the data store or host server is accessible, even if you open a different solution or close and reopen Visual Studio .NET.

As an example of a ConnectionString, consider the Village Housing application, which connects to VillageHousing.mdb, a Microsoft Access database. The ConnectionString for this Connection object is shown in Figure 9-14.

```
Provider=Microsoft.Jet.OLEDB.4.0;
Password="";
User ID=Admin;
Data Source= C:\VB.NET\Student\Tut00\VillageHousing\VillageHousing.mdb;
Mode=ReadWrite;
Extended Properties="";
Jet OLEDB:System database="";
Jet OLEDB:Registry Path="";
Jet OLEDB:Database Password="";
Jet OLEDB:Engine Type=5;
Jet OLEDB:Database Locking Mode=1;
Jet OLEDB:Global Partial Bulk Ops=2;
Jet OLEDB:Global Bulk Transactions=1;
Jet OLEDB:New Database Password="";
Jet OLEDB:Create System Database=False;
Jet OLEDB:Encrypt Database=False;
Jet OLEDB:Don't Copy Locale on Compact=False;
Jet OLEDB:Compact Without Replica Repair=False;
Jet OLEDB:SFP=False
```

default settings

Figure 9-14: ConnectionString setting

The rather complex ConnectionString shown in Figure 9-14 was built using the Add Connection Wizard. However, this is not as complicated as it appears—most of these are default property settings. The properties that must be specified in this ConnectionString include the data provider (that is, the driver or engine for the database management system), the user ID and password, and the data source (that is, the path and name of the database). The mode must be specified if it is not read/write. There follows a list of extended properties specific to the data provider (Jet OLEDB in this case).

Although the user ID and Password can be set as part of the ConnectionString (as in the present case), this is usually done only for publicly accessible data stores, or in stand-alone Windows Forms applications, because the user ID and Password (along with the rest of the ConnectionString) are compiled and distributed with the application and are therefore not secure. When security considerations warrant it, the safer approach is to obtain the user ID and Password at runtime, and then set these properties through runtime assignments before opening the connection.

Working with Data in ADO.NET

ADO.NET offers two approaches to working with data. In one method, a data adapter is used to populate an in-memory dataset and to return updated data from the dataset to the underlying database. In the second method, you configure a data command to process data directly in the underlying database.

Data Adapters and Datasets

As mentioned earlier, a DBMS can only support a certain number of simultaneous connections. This basic fact limits the scalability of many solutions. That is, an application that works fine with four users may not work with 100 or 1000 users—you cannot "scale the application up." The ADO.NET data adapter provides a partial solution to the challenge of limited connections.

At runtime, the application must call the data adapter's Fill() method. The data adapter establishes a momentary connection to the database using a Connection object. With the connection open, the data adapter populates a dataset, which is an in-memory data store or cache that often looks exactly like the underlying tables. As soon as the dataset has been populated, the data adapter closes the connection. The programmer does not directly create the code to open or close the connection—the open connection and close connection operations are implicit in the data adapter's Fill() method.

After the dataset has been populated, the program works with the data in the dataset—displaying, joining, adding, deleting, and updating records. If the application includes the requirement to update the underlying database, then the application must call up the data adapter's Update() method. When this method is executed, the data adapter again opens the connection, transmits changed records to the database with the appropriate SQL commands, and closes the connection.

Because the data adapter holds the connection only for the time needed to transmit data, the burden on the database server and on the communications network is dramatically reduced. However, you need to be cognizant of the fact that your application may not always be seeing the most current data, because changes that other users make to the database after your dataset has been populated might not be visible to your application until the next time you fill the dataset from the database. Despite this drawback, this approach offers the best performance for many applications.

The data adapter's properties include the commands needed to perform operations against the database. These properties include the SelectCommand (to retrieve data), InsertCommand (to add data), DeleteCommand (to remove data), and

UpdateCommand (to modify data). Each of these four command object properties can contain an SQL statement or a call to a procedure stored in the database. The data adapter's Fill() method uses the setting of the SelectCommand property to retrieve the data from the data source and populate the dataset. The Update() method of the data adapter uses the SQL statements or stored procedures in the InsertCommand, DeleteCommand, and UpdateCommand properties to propagate changes in the original dataset back to the database. The Update() method works by first examining the RowState property for each row in the dataset. The RowState property indicates whether the row is Added, Modified, Deleted, or Unchanged. For each row that is anything other than Unchanged, the Update method calls the appropriate command.

Datasets and XML

A dataset is an in-memory representation of data. It can be constructed from one or more tables, relationships, and/or nonrelational data sources. A dataset contains collections of Tables, Relations, and Constraints:

- A dataset's **Tables collection** contains Table objects based on the DataTable class. Each Table object contains collections of rows and columns.
  - The Rows collection contains instances of the DataRow class. Each row instance has a ChildRelations collection, containing pointers to the child records (if any) related to this row; a ParentRelations collection, containing a pointer to a parent record (if any) related to this row; and a RowState property, indicating whether this record is Added, Modified, Deleted, or Unchanged since the dataset was first populated.
  - A dataset's Columns collection contains Column objects. Each column instance identifies the column's name, the type of XML data that it holds, and a Boolean indicating whether this column is part of the primary key.
- A dataset's Relations collection contains DataRelation objects. Each DataRelation object specifies the relationship between two DataTable objects, based on an element (or collection of elements) in one of the tables corresponding to an element (or collection of elements) in the other table.
- The Constraints collection holds two types of constraints: a uniqueness constraint specifies that the value of a specified column must be unique for each row of a table, and a foreign key constraint specifies the primary key in one table that corresponds to a foreign key in a second table, and also specifies what action to take on the child rows when a parent row is updated or deleted.

When a dataset is filled, the data is transmitted in XML format. When a dataset is persisted or transferred to another component, this also occurs in an XML format. The structure of the dataset is also saved in an XML schema file, named *.xsd. The XML data format and XML schema format are those adopted by the World Wide Web Consortium. The methods of a dataset are saved in *.vb.

Because a dataset is wholly disconnected from the data sources, it can and does provide a standardized model for interaction with application programs. This means that you can develop your application to use a dataset, and you do not need to alter that application because the data source changes from one DBMS to another. Again, XML is the key to this standardized model.

The simplest dataset is just a copy of a table from a database. This dataset includes all of the columns (fields) and rows of the underlying table. It also identifies the primary key, if one exists. Figures 9-15 and 9-16 show the dataset properties and the schema file layout for a very simple dataset, representing the table tblCountry in VillageHousing.mdb. The SQL statement that fills such a dataset is in the form, `select * from [tablename]`, in the present case, `select * from tblCountry`. Using Data Adapter Preview, Figure 9-17 shows the contents of this dataset at design time.

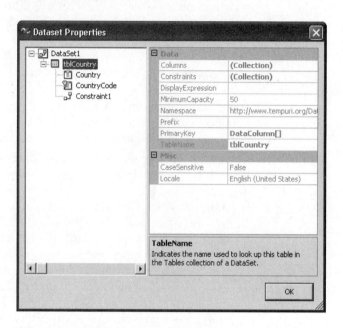

Figure 9-15: Properties of a simple dataset

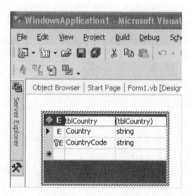

Figure 9-16: Schema of a simple dataset

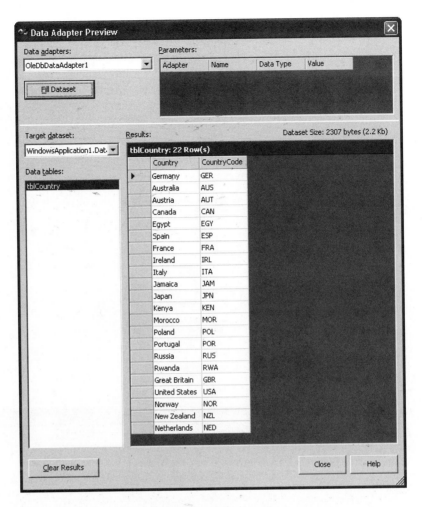

Figure 9-17: Data contents from Data Adapter Preview

A dataset can be configured to contain only filtered rows and/or selected columns from a table. For example, you could build a dataset to contain only the name of the country whose CountryCode is UK. The `select` statement would read, `select Country from tblCountry where CountryCode = 'UK'`. Instead of specifying UK at design time, a parameter can be supplied at runtime as a result of user input. This is referred to as a **parameterized query**. For example, a SelectCommand could contain the query, `select Country from tblCountry where CountryCode = @newcountry`. (Note: in Microsoft Access, the @ parameter is simply a question mark, as in `where CountryCode = ?`.)

A dataset can contain more than one table, and it can store the relationships among those tables, as well as table constraints. By keeping each of the underlying tables separate within the dataset, changes to the data can be propagated back to the database. To create the dataset from multiple tables, you configure a separate data adapter for each source table. You then use the XML Designer to configure the DataRelation object that connects the tables.

Many of the features of a dataset described in this section are visible by examining the schema of a dataset used in the Village Housing application, shown in Figure 9-18. You can see the Table objects and the symbol for the Relation object, the column names and data types, and the primary keys. You can right-click the symbol for the Relation object, choose Edit Relationship, and see the details concerning the relationship between tblVillager and tblCategory, as shown in Figure 9-19. This figure shows a relationship named PersonCat, based on the CategoryCode in tblCategory (the parent table) and CategoryCode in tblVillager (the child table).

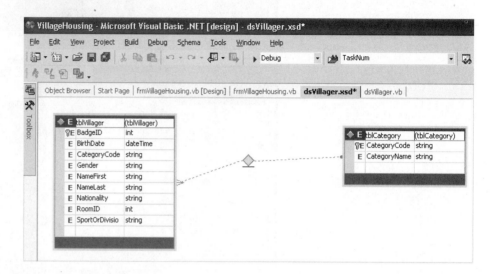

Figure 9-18: dsVillager.xsd

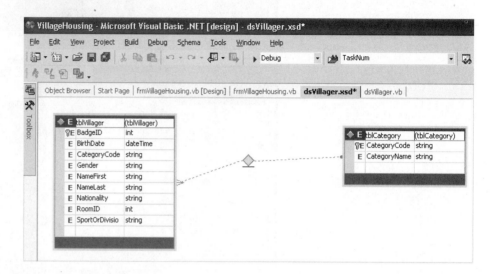

Figure 9-19: Edit Relation dialog box

Data Commands and Data Readers

As you are aware from the preceding discussion, a data adapter creates a dataset, which is a disconnected data store. Although this data access strategy conserves both network and DBMS resources, it is not appropriate for all applications. **Data commands** and **data readers** allow you to remain connected to the database and work with it directly. The available classes are OleDbCommand and OleDbDataReader (for any OLE DB data source), and SqlCommand and SqlDataReader (for databases created in SQL Server).

Although data commands consume more resources, they are more versatile than data adapters and datasets. Like the commands in a data adapter, a data command (OleDbCommand or SqlCommand) consists of an SQL statement or a reference to a stored procedure. Features of data commands include the following:

- Most data commands return an error code, which you can examine to see if the command executed correctly.

- If the data command returns a result set, you can read through it using a data reader (OleDbDataReader or SqlDataReader), which works like a forward-only, read-only cursor. This means that you can use a data reader to read through the rows sequentially, but you cannot jump around among the rows, and you cannot change the data values and send them back to the database.

- In addition to the SELECT, INSERT, UPDATE, and DELETE SQL statements and stored procedures that make up a data adapter's commands, a data command can include data definition language (DDL) SQL statements as well, in order to create or destroy database tables, views, indexes, and relationships. This is the principle feature that makes data commands more versatile than data adapters and datasets: if your application needs to create a table in the database, or create (and store in the database) a particular view of the database, then you must use a data command—data adapters only work with objects that already exist in the database.

- A data command can return database catalog information, or can return data from an SQL Server database in XML format.

- Data commands are often employed to return a scalar value (that is, a single value)—where creating a data adapter and dataset would appear to create unnecessary overhead.

If a data command is expected to return a result set, then you use its ExecuteReader method, and subsequently employ the data reader to examine the result set. If no result set is expected, then you use the data command's ExecuteNonQuery method.

A data command can execute multiple SQL statements or stored procedures, and it can return multiple result sets. For example, you might insert a record into a table, and then select that same record to display inbound controls on a form. This would ensure that the data actually made it into the database, and it would also allow your form to display data values that are provided by the DBMS, such as an autoincrement field or a field with some value computed by a stored procedure.

Transaction processing, explained earlier in this tutorial with the example of purchasing a refrigerator from Sears, is especially amenable to the data command approach. Typically, you would invoke a stored procedure or a series of SQL statements to make the appropriate changes to all relevant tables of a database, and either commit all the changes or roll back the partially completed transaction in the event of failure. To discover whether all parts of the transaction succeeded, you must be connected to the database.

Server Explorer: Design-time Connections

Imagine that you are designing an application that will be distributed to the public and will access a database on the user's computer. At design time, you have no way of knowing where that database will be located. However, if you have a copy of the database schema, then you can open a design time connection to that schema. This makes the entire database structure (tables, columns, relationships, and constraints) available to you at design time, so that you do not have to program these elements in the dark. Server Explorer provides this capability and is a valuable feature of Visual Studio .NET when designing applications that include access to any external data store. You may be planning on using the Connection Wizard or the Data Adapter Wizard, data adapters and datasets designed on your own, data commands configured at design time, or any of these objects created dynamically in code. But if the OLE DB-compliant data source (or even just a template containing the schema for that data source) is available at design time, then you should establish a connection to it at design time, causing it to appear in Server Explorer. This greatly eases the programming tasks in any kind of data access operation. Furthermore, the data stores and schemas identified in Server Explorer remain available to all applications as long as the physical file is available. For example, if Events.txt (used in several tutorials) were converted to a Microsoft Access database, the first connection to that database would appear in Server Explorer. Other applications that needed the same database (or the same database structure) could obtain it from Server Explorer, just by dragging and dropping the database onto a form.

Understanding the Data Form Wizard's Output

You will use the Data Form Wizard in Lesson C to build a skeleton data access application. This wizard is a complete rapid application development tool—for simple data access projects, you may sometimes use the application created by the wizard without further modification. Most often, however, you build on the skeleton created by the wizard. Because you do need to build on it, you need to understand the outputs the wizard creates.

Objects in the Windows Form Designer

Figure 9-20 displays the Windows Form Designer after using the Data Form Wizard to create a form that displays one record at a time in tblVillager. (You will do this yourself in Lesson C.) In sum, the Data Form Wizard creates the GUI that you see in the figure. Each of the text boxes on the form is tied or bound to one field in the dataset. The wizard creates the dataset schema file (dsVillager.xsd) that appears in Solution Explorer as well as the components that appear in the tray underneath the form (objdsVillager, OleDbConnection1, and OleDbDataAdapter1). The wizard also creates (or uses an existing) connection in Server Explorer.

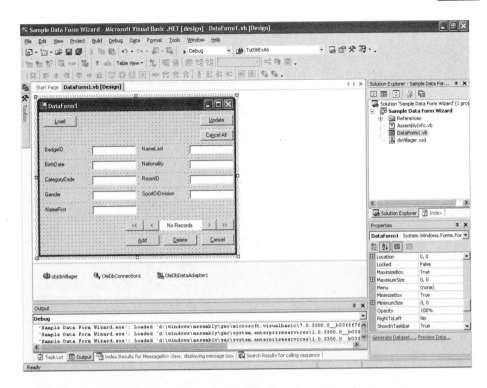

Figure 9-20: frmVillageHousing.vb, created by the Data Form Wizard

First, look at the tray underneath the form, shown in Figure 9-20. There you find OleDbConnection1, OleDbDataAdapter1, and objdsVillager (a dataset object instantiated from the dsVillager dataset class that the wizard created). Look in Solution Explorer and note the file dsVillager.xsd—this is the XML schema definition file for the dataset. You next examine each of these nongraphical components in greater detail: OleDbConnection1, OleDbDataAdapter1, objdsVillager, and dsVillager.xsd.

OleDbConnection1 is in the tray under frmVillageHousing. In the Properties window, the principle property of the connection object is the ConnectionString property. Its contents are displayed in Figure 9-14: the Provider is the Jet engine, the data source is VillageHousing.mdb, and the various security settings are indicated. Creating this connection also resulted in the creation of an object in Server Explorer.

In Server Explorer, with Data Connections expanded, with the ACCESS Database VillageHousing.mdb expanded, and with each of its four table expanded, the result appears as in Figure 9-21. This data connection in Server Explorer remains in Visual Studio .NET as long as VillageHousing.mdb remains accessible in its current location on the computer. You can start a new project, and this data connection is still be available. You can drag any element from this connection onto a form, and Visual Studio creates the connection, data adapter, and dataset in that form to access that data.

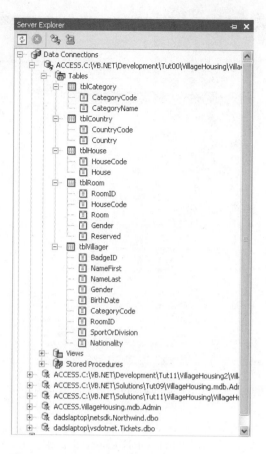

Figure 9-21: Server Explorer, showing connection to VillageHousing.mdb (partially expanded)

Recall that a data adapter in the loosely coupled model of ADO.NET is the intermediary between a data source and a dataset. When the data adapter's Fill() method is invoked, the data adapter opens a connection to the data source, executes the command stored in its SelectCommand property to copy information from the data source into a dataset, and closes the connection. When the data adapter's Update() method is invoked, the data adapter opens the connection, calls the appropriate InsertCommand, DeleteCommand, or UpdateCommand for each new, changed, or deleted row in the dataset, and closes the connection.

OleDbDataAdapter1 (in the tray underneath the form) has several properties and subproperties of interest: SelectCommand, InsertCommand, DeleteCommand, and UpdateCommand. The Properties window for OleDbDataAdapter1 has been enlarged in Figure 9-22, and the SelectCommand property has been expanded. Note that the name of the Select command is OleDbSelectCommand1—this is the name of the command that is invoked automatically by OleDbDataAdapter1's Fill() method. Also note that the Connection property under the SelectCommand property has the setting OleDbConnection1. This is how the adapter knows which connection to open when executing OleDbSelectCommand1. Under the SelectCommand property, note the CommandText element, which contains the SQL Select statement that retrieves all of the information from tblVillager.

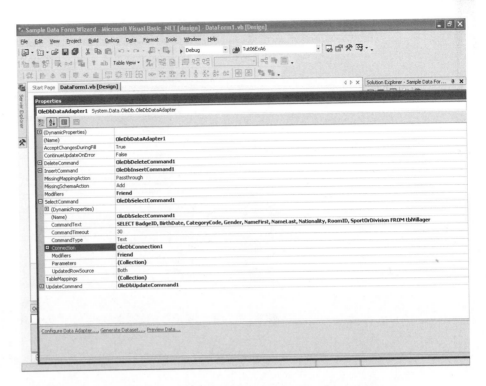

Figure 9-22: OleDbDataAdapter1, showing the SelectCommand property

Figures 9-23 and 9-24 display, respectively, the subproperties under the DeleteCommand property of OleDbDataAdapter1, and under the InsertCommand and UpdateCommand properties of OleDbDataAdapter1. Examine the CommandText properties under the DeleteCommand, InsertCommand, and UpdateCommand properties. These are known as parameterized action queries—that means that the CommandText contains parameters, or variable data supplied at the time of execution. The parameters supplied to the query are taken from the current row of the dataset.

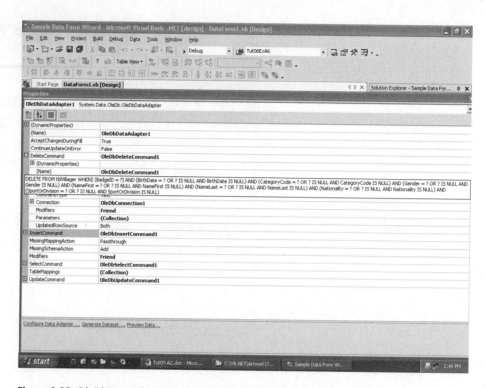

Figure 9-23: OleDbDataAdapter1, showing the DeleteCommand property

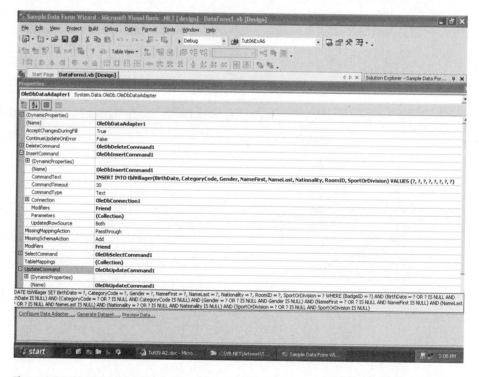

Figure 9-24: OleDbDataAdapter1, showing the InsertCommand and UpdateCommand properties

When the OleDbDataAdapter1 Update() method is invoked, the RowState property of each row in objdsVillager is examined:

- If the RowState equals Added, then the Update() method calls the OleDbDataAdapter1's InsertCommand, and all new data values are taken from that row in the dataset.
- If the RowState equals Modified, then the BadgeID field in the current row of the dataset is used to locate the appropriate record in the database table, and the values of all other fields in that row of the dataset are used to update the corresponding row in the database table.
- If the RowState equals Deleted, then the BadgeID field in the current row of the dataset is used to locate the appropriate record in the database table, and that record is deleted from the database table.
- If the RowState equals Unchanged, then the current row in the dataset is skipped.

Now examine the dataset schema—dsVillager.xsd, which appears in Solution Explorer in Figure 9-20.

The XML schema file for the dsVillager class (dsVillager.xsd) is displayed in the XML Designer, shown in Figure 9-25. The display of tblVillager is lengthened so you can see all of the elements. The elements of the tblVillager are structured as XML elements, not as data types in Microsoft Access. The element types in this table are int, datetime, and string, corresponding to Number, Date, and Text in Microsoft Access. Many other XML element types are available.

tip

To view the dataset schema, you can double-click the XML schema file in Solution Explorer, or you can click the object instantiated from that schema, objdsVillager, in the tray at the bottom of the form and click View Schema at the bottom of the Properties window.

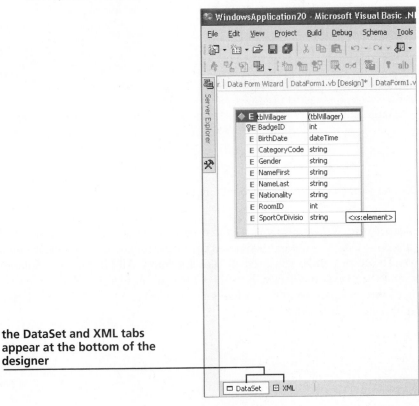

the DataSet and XML tabs appear at the bottom of the designer

Figure 9-25: dsVillager.xsd schema file in the DataSet view

At the bottom of the XML Designer window, two tabs appear, as indicated by Figure 9-25: DataSet and XML. The initial view in Figure 9-25 is the DataSet view. Clicking XML causes the actual XML file to appear, shown in Figure 9-26. Even without training in XML, you can see that this code is written in a markup language and not in Visual Basic .NET.

```xml
<?xml version="1.0" standalone="yes" ?>
<xs:schema id="dsVillager"
targetNamespace="http://www.tempuri.org/dsVillager.xsd"
xmlns:mstns="http://www.tempuri.org/dsVillager.xsd"
xmlns="http://www.tempuri.org/dsVillager.xsd"
xmlns:xs="http://www.w3.org/2001/XMLSchema" xmlns:msdata="urn:schemas-
microsoft-com:xml-msdata" attributeFormDefault="qualified"
elementFormDefault="qualified">
 <xs:element name="dsVillager" msdata:IsDataSet="true">
  <xs:complexType>
   <xs:choice maxOccurs="unbounded">
    <xs:element name="tblVillager">
     <xs:complexType>
      <xs:sequence>
       <xs:element name="BadgeID" msdata:AutoIncrement="true" type="xs:int" />
       <xs:element name="BirthDate" type="xs:dateTime" minOccurs="0" />
       <xs:element name="CategoryCode" type="xs:string" minOccurs="0" />
       <xs:element name="Gender" type="xs:string" minOccurs="0" />
       <xs:element name="NameFirst" type="xs:string" minOccurs="0" />
       <xs:element name="NameLast" type="xs:string" minOccurs="0" />
       <xs:element name="Nationality" type="xs:string" minOccurs="0" />
       <xs:element name="RoomID" type="xs:int" minOccurs="0" />
       <xs:element name="SportOrDivision" type="xs:string" minOccurs="0" />
      </xs:sequence>
     </xs:complexType>
    </xs:element>
   </xs:choice>
  </xs:complexType>
  <xs:unique name="Constraint1" msdata:PrimaryKey="true">
   <xs:selector xpath=".//mstns:tblVillager" />
   <xs:field xpath="mstns:BadgeID" />
  </xs:unique>
 </xs:element>
</xs:schema>
```

Figure 9-26: XML view of XML schema file (dsVillager.xsd)

The Data Form Wizard also creates the code associated with the dataset class. Though it is quite lengthy—about 600 lines of code—examining this code can be quite instructive. To see this code, you need to click the Show All Files icon in Solution Explorer, and then open dsVillager.vb in the Code Editor. Figure 9-27 displays the beginning of this code, showing that it looks like any other Visual Basic .NET class definition file (such as a Windows form).

```
Option Strict Off
Option Explicit On

Imports System
Imports System.Data
Imports System.Runtime.Serialization
Imports System.Xml


<Serializable(), _
 System.ComponentModel.DesignerCategoryAttribute("code"), _
 System.Diagnostics.DebuggerStepThrough(),õ _
 System.ComponentModel.ToolboxItem(true)> _
Public Class dsRoomHouse
    Inherits DataSet

    Private tabletblHouse As tblHouseDataTable

    Private tabletblRoom As tblRoomDataTable

    Private relationHouseToRoom As DataRelation

    Public Sub New()
        MyBase.New
        Me.InitClass
        Dim schemaChangedHandler As _
            System.ComponentModel.CollectionChangeEventHandler _
            = AddressOf Me.SchemaChanged
        AddHandler Me.Tables.CollectionChanged, _
            schemaChangedHandler
        AddHandler Me.Relations.CollectionChanged, _
            schemaChangedHandler
    End Sub
```

Figure 9-27: dsVillager.vb class definition file (excerpt)

Now examine the GUI itself. (Refer back to Figure 9-20.) A Label control and a TextBox control are associated with each column of tblVillager. Button controls at the top of the form allow the user to load the dataset from the database, update the database from the records in the dataset, and cancel all pending changes to the database. Navigation buttons appear near the bottom of the form, along with buttons to add, delete, or cancel changes to an individual record. The Data Form Wizard created all of these controls, assigning the names shown in Figure 9-28.

Control functions	Control names
Controls bound to objdsVillager	lblBadgeID (label), editBadgeID (text box) lblBirthDate, editBirthDate lblCategoryCode, editCategoryCode lblGender, editGender lblNameFirst, editNameFirst lblNameLast, editNameLast lblNationality, editNationality lblRoomID, editRoomID lblSportOrDivision, editSportOrDivision
Controls that affect the whole dataset (at the top of DataForm1)	btnLoad, btnUpdate, btnCancelAll
Navigation controls	btnNavFirst, btnNavPrev, lblNavLocation, btnNavNext, btnLast
Controls that affect only the current record	btnAdd, btnDelete, btnCancel

Figure 9-28: Names of controls on DataForm1

Within the GUI, each Label control gets its Text property from the name of an element in the dataset, and each TextBox control gets its Text property from the value of that element in the current row of the dataset. For example, consider the label and text box associated with Badge ID. The name of the field in the dataset, BadgeID, is the text property of lblBadgeID. The TextBox control is named editBadgeID. In the Properties window, the source of the data displayed in a bound control is specified in the control's DataBindings property settings. The DataBindings.Text property setting for editBadgeID is objdsVillager—tblVillager.BadgeID. Though you may not yet be familiar with this type of property value, it will soon become part of your everyday programming experience. The first part of the setting, objdsVillager, identifies the dataset. Within that dataset, the editBadgeID textbox is bound to the BadgeID field of the tblVillager table. All of the text boxes on this form are similarly bound to a particular field of tblVillager in the objdsVillager dataset. The binding of controls on a form to fields within a dataset causes the values in the current record of that dataset to appear inside the controls.

The Code Behind the Data Form Wizard

The Data Form Wizard creates all of the code in DataForm1.vb, which makes the application fully functional for loading the dataset, displaying and updating records, adding and deleting records, and navigating among the records.

When examining the code in frmVillageHousing.vb, do not worry too much about the specifics—you may not understand all of it. The point here, rather, is twofold: first, even when you have completed the entire project, about 80%–90% of its code will have been automatically created by Visual Basic .NET. Although at some point you do need to understand what it means, you rarely need to create it from scratch. The various wizards and code generators in Visual Basic .NET do most of the work for you. In most cases, professional programmers use the RAD tools of Visual Basic .NET to provide the initial code, and then modify and enhance the automatically generated shell as necessary.

BindingContext and CurrencyManager Objects

Many of the procedures in frmVillageHousing reference the methods and properties of the BindingContext object, which requires a brief explanation. Whenever a form includes controls that are bound to a data source, Visual Studio creates a CurrencyManager object to keep track of the current record to which the control is presently bound. Controls that have the same data source share the same CurrencyManager. Because a form could have multiple data sources, each with its own CurrencyManager object, a supervisor of all CurrencyManagers on the form is needed. The BindingContext object performs this supervisory function. When you need to reference the row of the dataset that you are currently processing, or to which your data-bound controls are currently bound, then you obtain this information from the BindingContext object. Within the dataset itself, the old notion of CurrentRecord no longer obtains, although you may still use the term *current record* to mean the record that your controls are presently displaying. The dataset is one large in-memory data store, and all of its contents are always available. The CurrencyManager (and therefore the BindingContext) acts like a dynamic cursor, with the ability to jump to any position within the data store, as suggested by Figure 9-29.

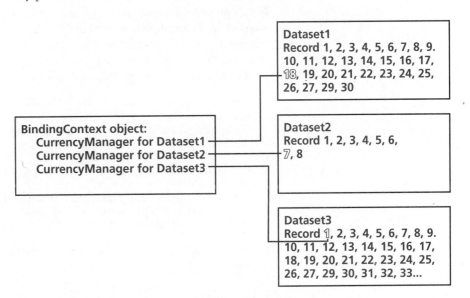

Figure 9-29: BindingContext and CurrencyManager objects

Loading the Dataset

The code created by the Data Form Wizard can be divided into four logical groupings: loading the dataset from the database, updating the database from changes in the dataset, changing one record within the dataset, and navigating between records within the dataset.

The Data Form Wizard breaks down the process of loading the dataset from the database into three levels of procedures in the data form: (1) the btnLoad_Click() procedure calls the LoadDataSet() procedure; (2) the LoadDataSet() procedure calls the FillDataSet() procedure; and (3) the FillDataSet() procedure invokes the data adapter's Fill() method to actually get the data from the database. Each level in this scheme has a specific role to play, explained in this section. The purpose of the overall scheme is to accommodate more complex applications than the simple one you are examining in this lesson, and also to ensure the safety of data access operations, which often can cause errors during processing.

At runtime, clicking btnLoad initiates the actions that load the dataset(s) from the database. The btnLoad_Click() event procedure is shown in Figure 9-30. The first thing you might note about this procedure is the presence of a new programming construct called Try...Catch...Finally...End Try. This construct, borrowed from Java, is useful whenever a program may be doing something that might not work correctly, for whatever reason, including reasons external to the program and not under the developer's control. This construct is covered in depth in Tutorial 11 in the section on error handling. In brief, the Try section includes the statements that you hope will execute correctly; the Catch section provides instructions to the computer on what to do in the event that the code in the Try section causes an Exception (that is, an error); and the optional Finally section (not used in this figure) contains code that must be executed in any event, whether an error occurs or not. Given this explanation, the code in the btnLoad_Click() procedure invokes the LoadDataSet() procedure and the objdsVillager_PositionChanged() procedure. LoadDataSet() is written as a separate procedure so that you can call it from anywhere. It is not dependent on the existence of btnLoad. Some developers might choose to delete btnLoad and instead include a call to LoadDataSet in the New() procedure for the form, or in the click event for a menu item (as you will do yourself in Tutorial 11). The objdsVillager_PositionChanged procedure is invoked whenever any action might require that the display in lblNavLocation be updated. In this case, lblNavLocation displays the message *No Records* upon start-up, but should display *1 of 33* after the records have been loaded.

```
Private Sub btnLoad_Click(ByVal sender As System.Object, _
   ByVal e As System.EventArgs) Handles btnLoad.Click
  Try
    'Attempt to load the dataset.
    Me.LoadDataSet()
  Catch eLoad As System.Exception
    'Add your error handling code here.
    'Display error message, if any.
    System.Windows.Forms.MessageBox.Show(eLoad.Message)
  End Try
  Me.objdsVillager_PositionChanged()
End Sub
```

Figure 9-30: btnLoad_Click() procedure

btnLoad_Click() calls the LoadDataSet() procedure, as shown in Figure 9-31. The LoadDataSet() procedure accomplishes two things in the data-loading scheme: first, recall that a form may display information from more than one dataset. For example, in the VillageHousing application, information on the left side of frmVillageHousing comes from tblVillager and tblCategory (represented in the application by one dataset called dsVillager), while the right side of the form displays information coming from tblRoom and tblHouse (represented in the application by another dataset called dsRoom). The LoadDataSet() procedure includes calls to a FillDataSet() procedure for each dataset needed by the form. Second, within the portion of the LoadDataSet() procedure relating to each dataset, the LoadDataSet() procedure declares a temporary dataset which is then actually filled. After the temporary dataset has been successfully filled, LoadDataSet() empties the contents (if any) of the main dataset, and then merges the temporary dataset with the main dataset. This insulates the main dataset from any errors that might occur during the Fill operation. The following notes explain individual lines in Figure 9-31:

- *Note 1*—Declares the temporary data set objDataSetTemp as an object of type dsVillager. Since this is a reference type, it must point to an object.
- *Note 2*—objDataSetTemp points to a new dsVillager-type object.
- *Note 3*—Calls the FillDataSet procedure, passing the temporary dataset as a parameter. If the operation is successful, the temporary dataset then contains all of the records in tblVillager from the database.
- *Note 4*—If the attempt to fill the dataset fails, this code allows the exception to occur (crashing the program). This is where you insert error-handling code, when that topic is addressed in Tutorial 11.
- *Note 5*—Empties the main dataset on the form, objdsVillager, of all records.
- *Note 6*—Merges records in the temporary dataset objDataSetTemp into the (empty) main dataset objdsVillager. If the attempt to merge records into objdsVillager fails, this code allows the exception to occur, crashing the program.

If a form contains more than one dataset, and if you are using data adapters to fill it, then these steps are repeated for each additional dataset on the form.

```
Public Sub LoadDataSet()
  'Create a new dataset to hold the records
  'returned from the call to FillDataSet.
  'A temporary dataset is used
  'because filling the existing dataset would
  'require the databindings to be rebound.
  Dim objDataSetTemp As _
    Sample_Data_Form_Wizard.dsVillager '(Note 1)
  objDataSetTemp = New _
    Sample_Data_Form_Wizard.dsVillager() '(Note 2)
  Try
    'Attempt to fill the temporary dataset.
    Me.FillDataSet(objDataSetTemp)      '(Note 3)
  Catch eFillDataSet As System.Exception
    'Add your error handling code here.
    Throw eFillDataSet                  '(Note 4)
  End Try
  Try
    'Empty the old records from the dataset.
    objdsVillager.Clear()               '(Note 5)
    'Merge the records into the main dataset.
    objdsVillager.Merge(objDataSetTemp)  '(Note 6)
  Catch eLoadMerge As System.Exception
    'Add your error handling code here.
    Throw eLoadMerge                    '(Note 7)
  End Try
End Sub
```

Figure 9-31: LoadDataSet() procedure

The FillDataSet() procedure, called by LoadDataSet() once for each dataset on the form, is shown in Figure 9-32. FillDataSet() receives the temporary dataset created in LoadDataSet(). Recall that the definition of a dataset includes a reference to the data adapter(s) needed to create it. Therefore, in this case, FillDataSet() can deduce that OleDbDataAdapter1 is the correct adapter needed to fill this temporary dataset, which is an object of type dsVillager. After turning off constraint checking, FillDataSet() calls the OleDbDataAdapter1 Fill method to load the dataset.

```
Public Sub FillDataSet(ByVal dataSet As _
    Sample_Data_Form_Wizard.dsVillager)
  'Turn off constraint checking before the
  'dataset is filled. This allows the adapters
  'to fill the dataset without concern
  'for dependencies between the tables.
  dataSet.EnforceConstraints = False
  Try
    'Attempt to fill the dataset
    'through the OleDbDataAdapter1.
    Me.OleDbDataAdapter1.Fill(dataSet)
  Catch fillException As System.Exception
    'Add your error handling code here.
    Throw fillException
  Finally
    'Turn constraint checking back on.
    dataSet.EnforceConstraints = True
  End Try
End Sub
```

Figure 9-32: FillDataSet() procedure

NOTE: Recall that a dataset may contain data from multiple data sources and that, if the application requires the ability to update those multiple data sources, then each data source must have its own data adapter. For example, in the VillageHousing application, text boxes concerning each villager include all of the elements in tblVillager except CategoryCode, plus the category name from tblCategory. The only way that this data can be made updatable is if one data adapter is used to load the data coming from tblVillager, and a separate data adapter is used to load data coming from tblCategory. (The dataset also requires a relationship to be established between these two dataset tables, mirroring the relationship between the corresponding database tables—but the relationship is internal to the dataset and therefore does not require a data adapter.) In the present case, only one data adapter is needed, because tblVillager in the dataset is an exact copy of tblVillager in the database. This procedure turns off constraint checking, calls the data adapter's Fill method to fill the (temporary) dataset passed to the procedure, and turns constraint checking back on.

Also consider the VillageHousing example in this regard: the value of the CategoryCode in each row of the tblVillager dataset must exist in the CategoryCode field of one record in tblCategory. If tblCategory is loaded first, this presents no problem. But if tblVillager is loaded first, this referential integrity constraint poses a problem. You will find quite a few occurrences of tables that have mutual foreign keys, so that neither table can be loaded first without violating referential integrity constraints until the other table has been loaded. This is the reason that the auto-generated code from the Data Form Wizard turns off constraint checking during the dataset load operation, as indicated in Figure 9-32.

NOTE: The Data Form Wizard may also generate the statements to open the connection before calling the Fill() method and closing the connection thereafter. This is not necessary because the data adapter automatically opens and closes the connection. The program works with or without these statements.

The objdsVillager_PositionChanged() procedure is shown in Figure 9-33. This procedure is invoked whenever the current record could change as a result of some activity. Its function is to display the position of the current record within the dataset. Therefore, objdsVillager_PositionChanged() is called from every event procedure in DataForm1.vb (with the exception of btnCancelAll_Click()).

```
Private Sub objdsVillager_PositionChanged()
  Me.lblNavLocation.Text = _
    (((Me.BindingContext(objdsVillager, _
    "tblVillager").Position + 1).ToString + " of  ") _
    + Me.BindingContext(objdsVillager, _
    "tblVillager").Count.ToString)
End Sub
```

Figure 9-33: objdsVillager_PositionChanged() procedure

Updating the Database

The Data Form Wizard also breaks down the process of updating the database from the dataset into three levels of procedures in the data form: (1) the btnUpdate_Click() procedure calls the UpdateDataSet() procedure; (2) the UpdateDataSet() procedure calls the UpdateDataSource() procedure; and (3) the UpdateDataSource() procedure invokes the data adapter's Update() method to actually send the changed rows back to the database. Each level in this scheme has a specific role to play, explained in this section. Again, the purpose of the overall scheme is to accommodate more complex applications than the simple one you are examining in this lesson, and also to ensure the safety of data access operations.

At runtime, clicking btnUpdate triggers the actions that update the database based on changed rows in the dataset. The logic train is much the same as it is for loading the dataset: btnUpdate_Click(), Figure 9-34, serves only to accommodate a Button control, rather than a menu selection or some other kind of procedure call, and it triggers PositionChanged() as well. Note that this procedure does not throw an exception if an error occurs—rather, it just displays the error message.

```
Private Sub btnUpdate_Click(ByVal sender As System.Object, _
    ByVal e As System.EventArgs) Handles btnUpdate.Click
  Try
    'Attempt to update the datasource.
    Me.UpdateDataSet()
  Catch eUpdate As System.Exception
    'Add your error handling code here.
    'Display error message, if any.
    System.Windows.Forms.MessageBox.Show(eUpdate.Message)
  End Try
  Me.objdsVillager_PositionChanged()
End Sub
```

Figure 9-34: btnUpdate_Click() procedure

UpdateDataSet(), shown in Figure 9-35, creates a temporary dataset to hold all the changes. Then, if there are changes, UpdateDataSet() invokes UpdateDataSource(), which transmits the changed records through the data adapter's Update() method (and which also returns those same records and any errors). When UpdateDataSource(), shown in Figure 9-36, has finished processing, UpdateDataSet() merges the changed records and error messages back into the dataset.

```
Public Sub UpdateDataSet()
  'Create a new dataset to hold the changes
  'that have been made to the main dataset.
  Dim objDataSetChanges As _
    Sample_Data_Form_Wizard.dsVillager = New _
    Sample_Data_Form_Wizard.dsVillager()    '(Note 1)
  'Stop any current edits.
  Me.BindingContext(objdsVillager, _
    "tblVillager").EndCurrentEdit()          '(Note 2)
  'Get the changes that have been made
  'to the main dataset.
  objDataSetChanges = CType(objdsVillager.GetChanges, _
    Sample_Data_Form_Wizard.dsVillager)     '(Note 3)
  'Check to see if any changes have been made.
  If (Not (objDataSetChanges) Is Nothing) Then
    Try
      'There are changes that need to be made,
      'so attempt to update the datasource by
      'calling the update method and passing
      'the dataset and any parameters.
      Me.UpdateDataSource(objDataSetChanges)  '(Note 4)
      objdsVillager.Merge(objDataSetChanges)  '(Note 5)
      objdsVillager.AcceptChanges()           '(Note 6)
    Catch eUpdate As System.Exception
      'Add your error handling code here.
      Throw eUpdate                           '(Note 7)
    End Try
    'Add your code to check the returned dataset
    'for any errors that may have been
    'pushed into the row object's error.
  End If
End Sub
```

Figure 9-35: UpdateDataSet() procedure

```
Public Sub UpdateDataSource(ByVal ChangedRows _
    As Sample_Data_Form_Wizard.dsVillager)   '(Note 8)
  Try
    'The data source only needs to be updated
    'if there are changes pending.
    If (Not (ChangedRows) Is Nothing) Then
      'Attempt to update the data source.
      OleDbDataAdapter1.Update(ChangedRows)  '(Note 9)
    End If
  Catch updateException As System.Exception
    'Add your error handling code here.
    Throw updateException
  End Try
End Sub
```

Figure 9-36: UpdateDataSource() procedure

A few notes help to explain the processing that occurs in UpdateDataSet() and UpdateDataSource():

■ *Note 1*—objDataSetChanges is another temporary dataset of type dsVillager. It holds all of the records in objdsVillager that have been changed—that is, records whose RowState equal Added, Modified, or Deleted. (To understand how this works, you want to remember that each row in the Rows collection of a dataset has a RowState property, indicating whether that row is Added, Modified, Deleted, or Unchanged.)

■ *Note 2*—If the current record contains pending changes, that edit must be ended before the database update processing commences.

■ *Note 3*—The GetChanges method returns all of the rows in a dataset whose RowState equals Added, Modified, or Deleted. Recall that the RowState for each row is also part of the row. The CType() function converts the first argument to the data type of the second argument, and is used by the Data Form Wizard just in case an application happens to have two different but compatible dataset schemas. In this type, all of the records are of type dsVillager, so CType has no material effect. The dataset returned by the GetChanges method is assigned to objDataSetChanges.

■ *Note 4*—If objDataSetChanges is not nothing (meaning it has at least one row in it), then UpdateDataSource() is called, and the dataset objDataSetChanges is passed to that procedure. When that procedure finishes processing, objDataSetChanges contains the changed rows (updated from the database itself), as well as any errors returned from the update process.

■ *Note 5*—The temporary dataset objDataSetChanges is merged into objdsVillager. Records in objDataSetChanges replace corresponding records in objdsVillager.

■ *Note 6*—The AcceptChanges method sets the RowState property of every row to Unchanged. (This method should only be called after GetChanges, Update, and Merge methods have been called, because, after AcceptChanges is executed, you can no longer tell which rows in the dataset have been changed.)

■ *Note 7*—If the update process causes an exception, the exception is thrown again here. Error-handling code can be inserted at this point to prevent the application from blowing up.

■ *Note 8*—The UpdateDataSource() procedure receives the dataset ChangedRows. Each row in this dataset has a RowState of Added, Modified, or Deleted.

■ *Note 9*—The UpdateDataSource() procedure calls the OleDbDataAdapter1 Update method, passing the dataset ChangedRows as a parameter. To understand this processing, think of ChangedRows as an insertion point. As each row is processed, if the RowState is Added, the data adapter's InsertCommand object is executed; if the RowState is Modified, the data adapter's UpdateCommand object is executed; and if the RowState is Deleted, the data adapter's DeleteCommand object is executed. In each case, a row is returned from the database, showing updated values and any errors.

NOTE: Each row of a dataset also contains an Errors collection. If any row in objDataSetChanges causes an error when the row is processed against the underlying database table, that error is returned and noted in that row's Errors collection within objDataSetChanges. In addition, other fields in a row may be changed as a result of updating the underlying table: a record may include a field that is computed from another value stored in the database, and unknown to your application; when this row is returned from the update process, the newly computed field is contained in objDataSetChanges. For all of these reasons, objDataSetChanges may be a different dataset after the call to UpdateDataSource() than it was before the call.

The final procedure to be discussed in this section is btnCancelAll_Click(), shown in Figure 9-37. The user calls this procedure in order to cancel pending changes to the database. The procedure uses the RejectChanges() method of objdsVillager to cancel all pending changes to the database.

```
Private Sub btnCancelAll_Click(ByVal sender As System.Object, _
    ByVal e As System.EventArgs) Handles btnCancelAll.Click
  Me.objdsVillager.RejectChanges()
End Sub
```

Figure 9-37: btnCancelAll_Click()

Changing One Record in the Dataset

btnCancel_Click(), btnDelete_Click(), and btnAdd_Click all affect one record in the existing dataset, as expected. All three procedures, shown in Figure 9-38, reference methods and properties of the BindingContext object, which identifies the target of the action. These three procedures include the following actions:

■ btnCancel_Click uses the CancelCurrentEdit method of the BindingContext object to cancel any edit that is currently pending, to return the row in the dataset to its status before the current edit started, and to set the current record's RowState property to Unchanged.

■ btnDelete_Click() uses the BindingContext object's RemoveAt method to mark the current record for deletion, provided at least one record exists in the dataset. Note that this action does not physically remove the record from the dataset (unlike using the RemoveAt method in a list box, for instance). Rather, the RemoveAt method sets the current record's RowState property to Deleted.

■ btnAdd_Click() completes any pending edit on the current record with the BindingContext's EndCurrentEdit() method, and then calls the BindingContext's AddNew() method, which adds a new, blank record at the end of the dataset and makes that new record the current record.

```
Private Sub btnCancel_Click(ByVal sender As System.Object, _
    ByVal e As System.EventArgs) Handles btnCancel.Click
  Me.BindingContext(objdsVillager, _
    "tblVillager").CancelCurrentEdit()
  Me.objdsVillager_PositionChanged()
End Sub

Private Sub btnDelete_Click(ByVal sender As System.Object, _
    ByVal e As System.EventArgs) Handles btnDelete.Click
  If (Me.BindingContext(objdsVillager, _
      "tblVillager").Count > 0) Then
    Me.BindingContext(objdsVillager, _
      "tblVillager").RemoveAt(Me.BindingContext _
      (objdsVillager, _
      "tblVillager").Position)
    Me.objdsVillager_PositionChanged()
  End If
End Sub

Private Sub btnAdd_Click(ByVal sender As System.Object, _
    ByVal e As System.EventArgs) Handles btnAdd.Click
  Try
    'Clear out the current edits
    Me.BindingContext(objdsVillager, _
      "tblVillager").EndCurrentEdit()
    Me.BindingContext(objdsVillager, _
      "tblVillager").AddNew()
  Catch eEndEdit As System.Exception
    System.Windows.Forms.MessageBox.Show _
      (eEndEdit.Message)
  End Try
  Me.objdsVillager_PositionChanged()
End Sub
```

Figure 9-38: btnCancel_Click(), btnDelete_Click(), and btnAdd_Click() procedures

Navigating from Record to Record in a Dataset

The navigation buttons permit the user to navigate among the records of the dataset. By manipulating the Position property of the BindingContext for objdsVillager, each procedure repositions the current record pointer, as shown in Figure 9-39.

```
Private Sub btnNavFirst_Click(ByVal sender As System.Object, _
    ByVal e As System.EventArgs) Handles btnNavFirst.Click
  Me.BindingContext(objdsVillager, "tblVillager").Position = 0
  Me.objdsVillager_PositionChanged()
End Sub

Private Sub btnLast_Click(ByVal sender As System.Object, _
    ByVal e As System.EventArgs) Handles btnLast.Click
  Me.BindingContext(objdsVillager, "tblVillager").Position = _
    (Me.objdsVillager.Tables("tblVillager").Rows.Count - 1)
  Me.objdsVillager_PositionChanged()
End Sub

Private Sub btnNavPrev_Click(ByVal sender As System.Object, _
    ByVal e As System.EventArgs) Handles btnNavPrev.Click
  Me.BindingContext(objdsVillager, "tblVillager").Position = _
    (Me.BindingContext(objdsVillager, "tblVillager").Position - 1)
  Me.objdsVillager_PositionChanged()
End Sub

Private Sub btnNavNext_Click(ByVal sender As System.Object, _
    ByVal e As System.EventArgs) Handles btnNavNext.Click
  Me.BindingContext(objdsVillager, "tblVillager").Position = _
    (Me.BindingContext(objdsVillager, "tblVillager").Position + 1)
  Me.objdsVillager_PositionChanged()
End Sub
```

Figure 9-39: Navigation button event procedures

You have now completed Lesson A. Take a break or complete the end-of-lesson questions and exercises before continuing to Lesson B.

SUMMARY

- Databases are designed around a data model, an abstraction of the user's information requirements. The entity-relationship data model and E-R diagrams constitute the most widely adopted data-modeling methodology in use today. Relationships between entity classes are categorized based on their maximum cardinality: one-to-one (1:1), one-to-many (1:N), or many-to-many (M:N).

- Most modern commercial database management systems are based on the relational model. In this model, the user perceives data as organized into tables, consisting of rows and columns. The columns represent attributes or characteristics; the rows represent individual records. Each row is individually addressable by its primary key. The rows of a table represent a mathematical set.

- Tables are related to each other through foreign keys. 1:1 and 1:N relationships can be implemented by taking the primary key on the 1 side of a relationship and inserting it as a foreign key on the other (1 or N) side of the relationship. To implement a M:N relationship requires an intersection table.

- Referential integrity constraints are used to ensure that data remains consistent. When a row is inserted into a child table, the value of the foreign key must already exist in the parent table's primary key field.

- Structured Query Language (SQL) is the standard means of communication of the relational database world. SQL standards exist for both the data definition language (DDL) and the data manipulation language (DML). DDL is used to create and modify the schema or structure of a database; DML is used to add, delete, update, and retrieve data records.

- Typical implementations of data-centric applications involve at least three tiers: a database server, a network server, and a client program. With multiple manufacturers involved in each tier, interoperability requires some standards for passing data and database requests. This standard is the Open Database Connectivity protocol, or ODBC.

- Multiuser database applications have many extra challenges, including security, concurrency control, and resource constraints. Security involves protecting data from damage or attack as well as from unauthorized disclosure. Concurrency control involves procedures for handling conflicting concurrent requests from multiple users. Resource constraints address the fact that the resources available to database servers, network servers, and the networks themselves are all limited. One method of conserving resources is to process data in a largely disconnected (loosely coupled) fashion.

- Transaction processing relates to individual physical events that trigger multiple updates to the database. A database system should be able to support transaction processing in such a way that all parts of the transaction are successfully processed, or no part of the transaction is processed. Transaction processing usually requires that the user be directly connected to the database.

- ADO.NET is Microsoft's newest architecture for data access. In Visual Studio .NET, ADO and OLE DB are still supported as well, but ADO.NET is the preferred approach. ADO.NET is closely integrated with eXtensible Markup Language (XML). Data structures are defined by ADO.NET using XML schemas, and data is transmitted in XML format. Because XML is standards-based and nearly everyone has adopted the standard, ADO.NET's dependence on XML makes for nearly universal recognition and acceptance of data and data formats, and also facilitates transmission of data through firewalls.

- ADO.NET offers two data providers, one optimized for use with SQL Server databases, and one for all OLE DB-compliant data sources. Each of these providers offers four objects: a connection, a data adapter, a data command, and a data reader. Each provider can create, feed, and retrieve updated data from a dataset. The SQL Server objects are called SqlConnection, SqlDataAdapter, SqlCommand, and SqlDataReader. The OLE DB objects are called OleDbConnection, OleDbDataAdapter, OleDbCommand, and OleDbDataReader.

- The OleDbConnection object supports connections to both relational (through ODBC) and nonrelational (through OLE DB) data stores. This includes any relational DBMS, plus spreadsheets, text files, and XML-formatted data.

- A dataset is an in-memory data cache, disconnected from the data store. An ADO.NET data adapter uses an ADO.NET connection to access a data store, fills the dataset from the data store, and closes the connection. Later, the data adapter again opens the connection, transmits database updates from the dataset back to the data store, and closes the connection. This approach conserves network and DBMS resources, and makes for faster processing at the user end when not connected to the database.

- A dataset is described in an XML schema (.xsd) file, and the contents are XML elements. Despite this fact, programmers can use ADO.NET datasets and other objects without learning XML, because the various designers and wizards in ADO.NET provide that functionality for the developer.

- ADO.NET also provides command objects and data readers for connected processing. A command object contains one or more SQL statements or invokes one or more procedures stored in the database, and these are processed against the database while a connection remains open. If the command returns a result set from the data store, then an ADO.NET data reader is used to temporarily hold the incoming data and allow the user to scroll through it in a forward-only, read-only fashion.

- Server Explorer maintains permanent information concerning all connections and databases and remote services that have been set up in Visual Studio .NET. These items remain available for use in other projects as long as Visual Studio can still find them.

- The Data Form Wizard is a Rapid Application Development tool that creates the basic template for an application that connects to a database. The wizard assists you in creating a connection, adapter, dataset, and form with all of the necessary controls and code for populating a dataset and sending updates back to the database.

■ The Data Form Wizard and the Data Adapter Configuration Wizard create the XML schemas necessary to ADO.NET, so that you can use these objects without a detailed understanding of XML.

■ Output from using the Data Form Wizard in this lesson includes creation of OleDbConnection1, OleDbDataAdapter1, the dsVillager dataset class, objdsVillager dataset object, a data connection in Server Explorer, the application's main form, and all of the code in that form.

■ The CurrencyManager and BindingContext objects manage all datasets on a form and can be referenced for information about the current position and repositioning within a dataset.

■ Because data access operations sometimes fail, an error-trapping construct call the Try...Catch...Finally...End Try construct is automatically inserted by the Data Form Wizard in code segments that access an external database. (This construct is the subject of more detailed treatment in Tutorial 11.)

■ Layering of application logic is demonstrated. The autogenerated code from the Data Form Wizard includes the code for a button click event, which calls code to load a temporary dataset, which triggers the code to load a dataset from the data source. The same three-level logical structure applies to database updates. Each level performs a precise function. This layering greatly facilitates maintenance and debugging.

QUESTIONS

1. The most popular data model in use today is the _____ data model.

2. An application that involves a database server, a Web server, and a browser is an example of _____ architecture.

3. The protocol that standardizes interaction among relational DBMSs and application programming languages is _____.

4. The ADO.NET object that provides a connection to any OLE DB compliant data source is _____.

5. An attribute or a collection of attributes that uniquely identifies a record in a table is called the _____.

6. Relationships between tables are implemented through the use of _____.

7. In ADO.NET terminology, an in-memory cache for data retrieved from an external data store is called a _____.

8. A forward-only, read-only cursor that allows the user to examine a result set returned by an OleDbCommand object is called a _____.

9. Relationships between entities are categorized based on the number of instances from each entity that may participate in a relationship. This is known as the relationship's _____.

10. When a DBMS requires that a foreign key exist as a primary key in the parent table, this is called a _____ constraint.

11. The object that manages all pointers into datasets on a form is called the _____ object.

12. The method that returns all rows in a dataset whose RowState property is other than Unchanged is _____.

13. The method that completes the processing of pending edits to the current record is _____.

14. The method that cancels pending edits to the current record is _____.

15. The method that cancels all pending changes in the dataset is _____.

EXERCISES

The following are paper-and-pencil exercises that ask you to apply your knowledge of ADO.NET.

1. If your application must connect to an SQL Server database, why would you choose to use the SQL Data Provider in ADO.NET rather than the OLE DB Data Provider? In what circumstances would you choose to use the OLE DB Data Provider instead?

2. The FGDT must develop an application for the dining services staff, to be used for ordering food from various vendors, tracking shipments and payments, and the like. The database is to be stored in one central location, but must be accessed by staff in each of the dining halls. Which approach—data adapters and datasets, or data commands and data readers—would you recommend for this application and why?

3. The FGDT must develop an application for reporting the results of competitions. This application will keep track of each competitor and each event at all eight venues. The database will be stored in one central location, but accessed by staff in each venue. Which approach—data adapters and datasets or data commands and data readers—would you recommend for this application, and why?

After completing this lesson, you will be able to:

- Understand the structure of a Microsoft Access database
- Design tables in a Microsoft Access database for use in a Visual Studio .NET application
- Create relationships between tables in a Microsoft Access database
- Build queries in Microsoft Access that can be called as stored procedures from a Visual Studio .NET application

Microsoft Access

Tasks for the FGDT

In Lesson B, you create MyVillager.mdb, a Microsoft Access database whose structure is an exact copy of the VillageHousing.mdb used in the VillageHousing application. Constructing this database is done in three steps: designing the tables and the properties of the fields within those tables, creating the relationships between tables, and designing the queries that will be called from the VillageHousing application as stored procedures and views. In Lesson C, you create the VillageHousing application, incorporating the ADO.NET Data Providers you learned about in Lesson A and accessing the Microsoft Access database you learn about here in Lesson B.\

Understanding the Microsoft Access Database

Microsoft offers several relational database management systems, including Access and SQL Server. Access is intended primarily as a microcomputer-based DBMS most appropriate for single-user applications. Access can be implemented in a multiuser environment—a workgroup or local area network—but it is not scalable to a large multiuser environment. SQL Server is Microsoft's enterprise-level DBMS, suitable for a large multiuser environment, using multiple servers and thousands of clients. MS Access 2002 includes features that assist users in migrating from MS Access to SQL Server. Visual Studio .NET also includes the Microsoft Desktop Engine (MSDE), which allows you to create or access an SQL Server database.

This section describes the VillageHousing.mdb Microsoft Access database. To accomplish the tasks in this lesson, you should have Microsoft Access or Office XP installed on your computer. If this is not the case, you can follow along with the discussion by examining the figures, but you will not be able to create the database from scratch.

To open the Microsoft Access database to view its broad outlines:

1 Open the **VillageHousing** database, located at VB.NET\Student\Tut09\ VillageHousing.mdb. A snapshot of the database schema is sufficient for this brief tour, so click **Tools | Relationships** to open the Relationships window. Figure 9-40, which you saw earlier, depicts the Relationships window.

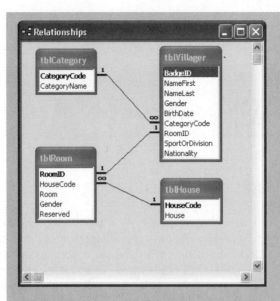

Figure 9-40: Relationships window

The database contains four tables of interest to the VillageHousing application, though two are most important: tblVillager contains information concerning each resident of the International Village and also identifies the room reserved for each resident; tblRoom identifies every room in the village.

> **NOTE:** VillageHousing.mdb contains a fifth table, tblCountry, but this table is not used in the VillageHousing Visual Basic .NET application, so it is ignored in this discussion.

In tblVillager, the primary key is the BadgeID, defined as an AutoNumber field. This means that the (Long) Integer value for the BadgeID field for each new record is provided automatically by Access; it also implies that the user should not be permitted to enter or modify this field.

The CategoryCode identifies the role of each villager: A, C, J, O, S, or V. The corresponding CategoryName appears in tblCategory: A (Athlete), C (Coach), J (Judge), O (Official), S (Staff), or V (Visitor). Keep this relationship in mind as you view the Visual Basic .NET Village Housing application.

The RoomID field in tblVillager is related to the RoomID field (the primary key) in tblRoom. In tblVillager, RoomID is a foreign key, and referential integrity is enforced. This means that a RoomID value entered in a record of tblVillager must already exist in tblRoom; or, to put it more simply, you cannot assign a villager to a nonexistent room, nor can you delete a room if a villager is assigned to it. RoomID in tblVillager is also defined as unique within that table, so you cannot assign more than one villager to a room.

In tblRoom, RoomID is the primary key, and is again an AutoNumber field. Note that the HouseCode field is related to tblHouse in the same way that CategoryCode is related to tblCategory: the HouseCode is a shorthand abbreviation for the name of the house.

2   Close the **Relationships** window.

3 In the Database window, click **Queries**. Three queries are used by the Visual Basic .NET VillageHousing application to build the data that appears in the DataGrid control (the room availability listing):

- *qryCancelReservations*—Sets the Reserved field to No for every record in tblRoom
- *qryUpdateReserved*—Sets the value of the Reserved field in tblRoom to Yes for each RoomID that appears in tblVillager
- *qryHouseRoom*—Retrieves data from tblRoom joined with data from tblHouse; this type of query is called a **table join** because it joins tables together based on a common field

The first two bullets are update queries—that is, they change values stored in the database.

4 You can experiment with the queries in the database by viewing each one in Design view or by running (opening) the query. Double-click each query to run it .Then, while the query results are still open, click **View | Design View** to see the query in the Query Designer, and click **View | SQL View** to see the SQL statement that actually creates the query. Then close the query.

5 You can also view each of the tables in the database. Click **Tables** in the Database window. To open each table in either Design view or Datasheet view, select the table in the Database window, and then click **Design** at the top of the Database window to see the design details of that table, or **Open** at the top of the Database window to see the contents.

Creating a Microsoft Access Database

For review or for practice, creating the VillageHousing database yourself is a useful exercise. You call it MyVillage.mdb, and place it in the VB.NET\Student\Tut09 folder. Even though you create the database yourself, you may still want to use the database provided for you as the data source in your version of the VillageHousing application, because the provided database has been populated with data. The notes in this section help you study VillageHousing.mdb in detail, and guide you in the creation of MyVillage.mdb as an exact copy of VillageHousing.mdb

To create MyVillage.mdb:

1 Open **Microsoft Access**. Click **File | New**. In the frame on the right, click **Blank Database**. In the File New Database dialog box, navigate to **VB.NET\ Student\Tut09**. In the File name text box, type **MyVillager**. Click **Create**. Microsoft Access creates a new database named MyVillager.mdb.

2 In the Database window, double-click **Create table in Design view**. The first table you create is tblVillager. Figure 9-41 shows you tblVillager with the necessary information already typed in. The Design view for a table shows all of the field names in the table, their data types and descriptions, and the primary key. Input the information shown in Figure 9-41. Type the field names as shown. Data types can be typed in or selected from the combo box. Descriptions are optional. Click the **BadgeID** field, and then click the **Primary Key** button.

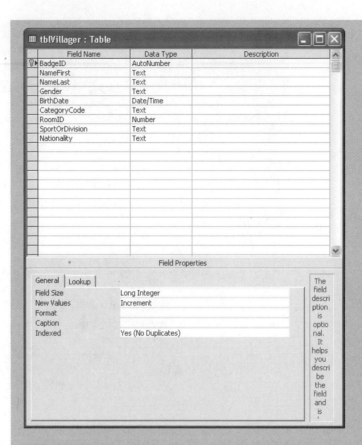

Figure 9-41: tblVillager in Design view, with BadgeID selected

3 In the lower half of the window, Field Properties are displayed for the field that is selected in the top half of the window. In Figure 9-41, the field properties for BadgeID are displayed. To duplicate this table design, you must enter each of the nondefault property settings in the field properties list as each field is selected. (The Indexed property setting for BadgeID is determined by the designation of that field as the primary key; it does not need to be typed in the Field Properties list.) As you can see in Figure 9-41, you do not need to type any nondefault property settings for the BadgeID field.

4 In Figure 9-42, the field properties for the field NameFirst are displayed. Note that the list of field properties depends on the data type of the field, in this case a Text data type. As shown in Figure 9-42, NameFirst has an input mask, a type of constraint on the format of input data. The > sign means that the input characters are converted to uppercase, whereas C indicates any character. Because the field length is 20 characters, there are 20 Cs. The NameFirst field is neither required nor indexed. The nondefault property settings are FieldSize and InputMask: type in these property settings as shown in the figure.

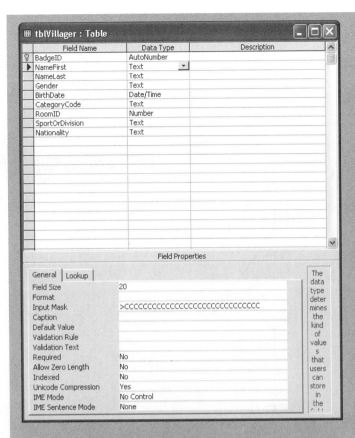

Figure 9-42: tblVillager, with NameFirst selected

> **NOTE:** The default settings are those used most often in most tables. You usually only need to change a few of them.

5   A similar list of field properties exists for each field in the table. Complete the design for tblVillager, including nondefault field properties for each remaining field name. Figure 9-43 provides the remaining field property information. Then save the table, assigning the name **tblVillager**.

Additional field name	Field property	Nondefault setting
NameLast	Field Size Input Mask	25 >CCCCCCCCCCCCCCCCCCCCCCCCC
Gender	Field Size Input Mask Default Value Validation Rule Validation Text	1 >? "M" "M" Or "F" Enter M for male, F for female
BirthDate	Input Mask	99/99/0000;0;_
CategoryCode	Field Size Indexed	1 Yes (Duplicates OK)
RoomID	Field Size Indexed	Long Integer Yes (No Duplicates)
Nationality	Field Size	3

Figure 9-43: Additional fields and nondefault properties in tblVillager

6   Now create **tblRoom** following the same steps you performed in Step 2 of this exercise to create tblVillager. Figure 9-44 shows tblRoom in Design view, from which you can discern all of the field names and data types, the primary key, and the nondefault properties of the primary key. Input all of the **field names, data types,** and **primary key information** for this table following the same steps as you've done previously. Also type in the nondefault settings of the other field names, shown in Figure 9-45.

Figure 9-44: tblRoom in Design view

Additional field name	Field property	Nondefault setting
HouseCode	Field Size Indexed	2 Yes (Duplicates OK)
Room	Field Size Indexed	5 Yes (Duplicates OK)
Gender	(Same as Gender field in tblVillager)	

Figure 9-45: Additional fields and nondefault properties in tblRoom

7   The other two tables, tblCategory and tblHouse, in VillageHousing.mdb are simple lookup tables, consisting of a code (the primary key in column 1) and its definition (in column 2). A lookup table makes it easier to create records in the principle tables, and also saves storage space, because the code is generally an abbreviation for the full item being looked up. Only the Field Size property of the primary key has a nondefault setting in each of these tables. Create and complete these tables based on the information shown in the Design views displayed in Figures 9-46 and 9-47. Close the design window after you have completed each table.

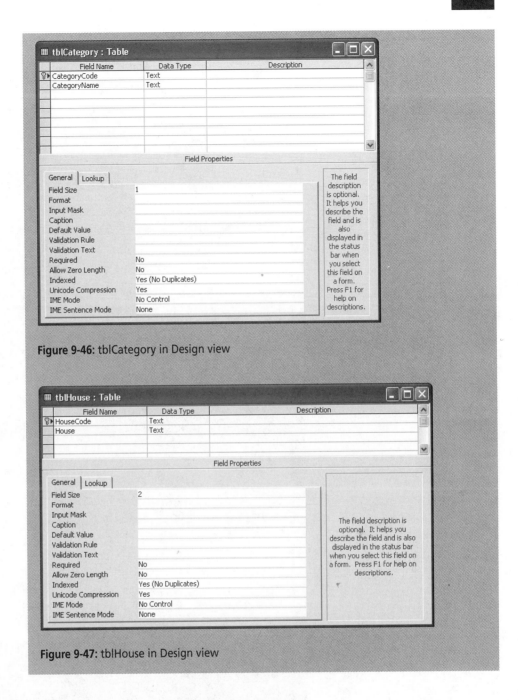

Figure 9-46: tblCategory in Design view

Figure 9-47: tblHouse in Design view

Building Relationships Between Tables

After creating the four tables in MyVillager.mdb, the next step is to build the relationships between tables.

To build table relationships in MyVillager.mdb:

1   Click **Tools | Relationships**. The first time this is done, a dialog box appears, asking you to identify the tables to be added to the Relationships window. If the Relationships window already exists, clicking Tools | Relationships causes

it to open, after which you can add tables. Click **Relationships | Show Table** to open the Show Table dialog box, as shown in Figure 9-48. In this case, add all four tables from the database to the Relationships window by selecting each table name and clicking **Add**. After you have added all four tables to the Relationships window, click **Close**. Expand each table vertically so that all the fields are visible, and arrange all the tables in the window roughly as they appear in Figure 9-49.

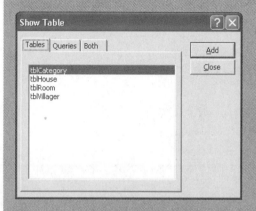

Figure 9-48: Show Table dialog box

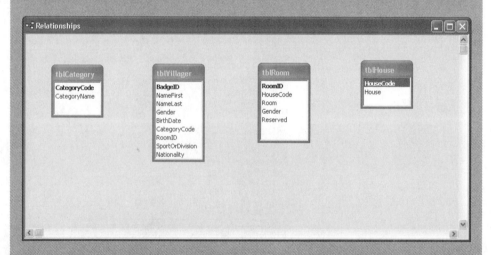

Figure 9-49: Relationships window layout

2 Define the relationship between tblCategory and tblVillager by dragging the **CategoryCode** field from tblCategory to tblVillager. The Edit Relationships window opens, shown in Figure 9-50. In that window, note that MS Access has determined that the Relationship Type is One-To-Many. This is because the CategoryCode is the primary key in tblCategory, meaning a given CategoryCode can occur only once in that table. Because CategoryCode is not the primary key in tblVillager, nor is it constrained to be unique within that table, a given CategoryCode could occur many times in that table. Hence, the program concludes that this is a one-to-many relationship.

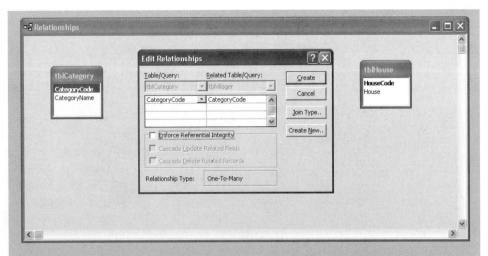

Figure 9-50: Edit Relationships window

3 Click **Enforce Referential Integrity**. As previously explained, this means that when a record is added or updated on the many side of the relationship, that is, in tblVillager, the DBMS checks to see that the CategoryCode in the tblVillager record already exists in tblCategory. The software does not permit a new record in tblVillager if the CategoryCode does not already exist in tblCategory. Click **Cascade Update Related Fields**. This option means that, if the parent record's CategoryCode is changed, all child records are automatically changed as well. For example, if the CategoryCode O for Official were changed to E for Employee, then all of the tblVillager records containing O in the CategoryCode field would be automatically changed to E. Then click **Cascade Delete Related Records**. This option provides that if a record in the parent table, that is, in tblCategory, is deleted, then all child records in tblVillager are likewise deleted. For example, if it were decided that no visitors would be permitted to stay in the International Village, and therefore category V was dropped from tblCategory, then all of the records of visitors in tblVillager would also be removed. Finally, click the **Create** button to finish creating this relationship. The result should appear as in Figure 9-51.

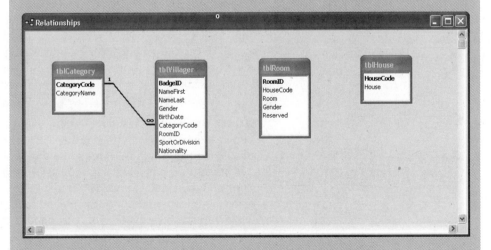

Figure 9-51: Relationships window with one relationship established

4   Next, create the relationship between tblHouse and tblRoom by dragging the **HouseCode** field from tblHouse to tblRoom. This relationship mirrors the relationship you already created between tblCategory and tblVillager, with all of the same recommended settings concerning referential integrity. As such, be sure to establish the same options—**Enforce Referential Integrity**, **Cascade Update Related Fields**, and **Cascade Delete Related Records**. So, if a room is added to tblRoom, its HouseCode must already exist in tblHouse. If a HouseCode in tblHouse changes, the changed code should be propagated to the corresponding records in tblRoom. And if a house is removed from the International Village (dropping its record from tblHouse), then all of its room records should also be removed from tblRoom. Then click the **Create** button.

5   Create the relationship between tblRoom and tblVillager by dragging the **RoomID** from tblRoom to tblVillager. This case is slightly different from the two other relationships you have already established. When looking at the data model at the beginning of this tutorial, you should have noted that the logical relationship between the Villager entity and the Room entity is 1:1—that is, a Room can be assigned to only one Villager, and a Villager can only be assigned to one Room. For this reason, when designing tblVillager, the RoomID field's Indexed property is set to Yes (No Duplicates). This means that a given RoomID can occur in tblVillager only once. The DBMS sees this setting when you create the relationship between tblRoom and tblVillager based on the common RoomID field. Because RoomID is the primary key in the parent table and is unique in the child table, the relationship must be 1:1. With respect to referential integrity, you click **Cascade Update Related Fields**, so that if a RoomID changes in tblRoom, the change is automatically propagated to tblVillager. However, do not click Cascade Delete Related Records, because dropping a room from the International Village should not result in the removal of the villager who was supposed to stay there.

6   When all of the relationships have been established, the Relationships window should appear as in Figure 9-40.

Creating Queries in Microsoft Access

As you can infer from the Database window, an entire application can be created directly in Microsoft Access. The objects available in Access include, in addition to Tables, all of the following: Queries, Forms, Reports, Macros, Modules, and Web pages. However, applications developed only in Access are somewhat limited in scope and in scale—Visual Basic .NET is a far more robust platform from which to develop complete applications.

NOTE: If you have a simple database and a simple GUI, creating the entire application in MS Access may be an effective solution. But as the logic becomes more complex, and the GUI requires more sophisticated controls, and the number of users expands, and the sources of data goes outside the original database, and the application is distributed widely, the simple solution is no longer viable. This is the reason that you need to learn ADO.NET in the Visual Studio .NET Framework—so that you can handle the types of programming tasks encountered daily in the commercial world.

Nevertheless, at least one aspect of the application development functionality of Access can be important to Visual Studio .NET developers: namely, the query capability in Access. (The same, it can safely be said, is true of all relational DBMSs.) You have learned that data commands in ADO.NET can be created either as SQL statements or as stored procedures. This includes direct commands contained in an OleDbCommand or SqlCommand object, or commands contained in a SqlDataAdapter or OleDbDataAdapter object. This is precisely where the stored procedures come in. Some developers find the query design capability of a DBMS to be superior to the query design support within ADO.NET. Therefore, as long as the developer controls the database design, these developers prefer to develop and store the query in the DBMS, and then simply invoke it from ADO.NET. Also, a stored procedure in the database is available to any developer who connects to that database, and if it changes, the change is reflected in all programs that access the database.

Indeed, in the case of the VillageHousing.mdb database and the VillageHousing Visual Basic .NET application, you have control over the whole thing (both the database and the application), so you can implement queries wherever you like. You should learn both approaches—inserting SQL statements directly into your ADO.NET objects (which you do in Lesson C), and creating queries in the DBMS which are then invoked as stored procedures from your ADO.NET objects. Therefore, you develop several queries in Microsoft Access here.

Microsoft Access offers three ways to create a data manipulation language (DML) query: Design view, which employs a GUI known as QBE or Query By Example; SQL view, in which you create the SQL statement yourself; and the Query Wizard, which offers several variations in which you respond to prompts and then let the software create the query for you. Regardless of the methodology used to create a query, the query finally must be translated, parsed, and saved as SQL. In all three of these cases, you can run the query after you have created it, or you can store the query for later execution.

Understanding DML Queries

DML queries fall broadly into two categories: those that retrieve data, called Select queries, and those that change data, called Action queries. Select queries can be based on a single table—called a simple query—or on multiple tables. Multiple table queries can use a subquery (that is, a query within a query) or a table join, in which data is filtered from the Cartesian product of two or more tables. Action queries perform one of three operations: inserting records into a table, deleting records from a table, or updating records in a table.

VillageHousing DML Queries

VillageHousing.mdb contains three queries. The Action queries are invoked as *stored procedures* from the VillageHousing Windows Forms application, whereas the Select query is invoked as a *view*. In Visual Studio .NET, a stored procedure refers to a named component that changes records in the database. Hence, an Action query in Microsoft Access equates to a stored procedure in Visual Studio .NET. In Visual Studio .NET, a view refers to a query that displays a certain record from one or more tables in a database. Hence, a Select query in Microsoft Access equates to a view in Visual Studio .NET.

The first two of these queries resynchronize tblRoom and tblVillager, in order to record new and cancelled room reservations from tblVillager in the Reserved field of tblRoom. These queries are to be executed in sequence: the first query changes the Reserved field of tblRoom to No for every record, after which the second query changes the Reserved field of tblRoom to Yes for any room whose RoomID appears in the RoomID field of a record in tblVillager. These queries are invoked from OleDbCommands in your VillageHousing application, just before the dataset that feeds the DataGrid control is refreshed.

tip
••••••••••••••••
The Cartesian product of two sets consists of every element of one set conjoined (concatenated) with each element of the other set.

The third query is the data source for the DataGrid control in the VillageHousing application. It retrieves every record in tblRoom, with the House Name translated from the HouseCode to the actual house name.

You now create these three queries in MyVillage.mdb.

To view and/or create the queries in VillageHousing.mdb:

1 Click **Queries** in the Database window to open the Queries frame. Double-click **Create query in Design view**.

The first query that you create sets the Reserved field to No for every record in tblRoom.

2 In the Show Table dialog box, click **tblRoom**. Click **Add**. The screen should appear as in Figure 9-52. Click **Close**. By default, the Design view displays a template for a Select Query. Change this to an Update query by clicking **Query | Update Query**.

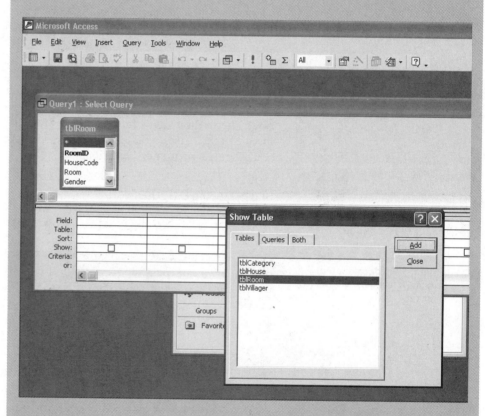

Figure 9-52: QBE template for a Select query with the Show Table dialog box

3 Scroll down the fields in tblRoom, and double-click **Reserved**. This causes the Reserved field to appear in the bottom half of the window. Type **No** in the **Update To** field. The result should appear as in Figure 9-53. Then click the **Run** button ![]. When prompted to update 0 rows, click **Yes**. Click **View | SQL View** to see this query as an SQL statement, shown in Figure 9-54. After this query has been executed, tblRoom shows no reserved rooms. Click the **Save** button ![], and save the query as **qryCancelReservations**.

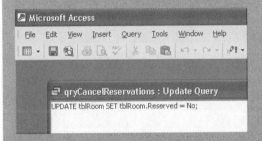

Figure 9-53: Update query in Design view

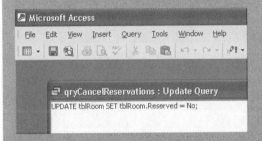

Figure 9-54: Update query in SQL view

The second query that you create sets the Reserved field to Yes for every room that has been reserved by a Villager in tblVillager.

4   Double-click **Create query in Design view.** As before, add tblRoom in the Show Table dialog box, then also add tblVillager from the Show Table dialog box, and then click **Close.** Note that the relationship between tblRoom and tblVillager appears here as well. After you have established a relationship in the Relationships Window in Microsoft Access, Access preserves the relationship in all database operations—queries, forms, reports, and so on.

5   By default, the Design view displays a template for a Select query. Again, change this to an Update query by clicking **Query | Update Query** from the menus. Scroll down the fields in tblRoom, and double-click **Reserved.** This causes the Reserved field to appear in the bottom half of the window. Type **Yes** in the **Update To** field. The result should appear as in Figure 9-55. Then click the **Run** button . When prompted to update 0 rows, click **Yes.** Click **View | SQL View** to see this query as an SQL statement, shown in Figure 9-56. Click the **Save** button , and save the query as **qryUpdateReserved.**

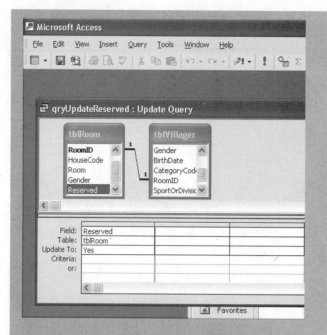

Figure 9-55: qryUpdateReserved in Design view

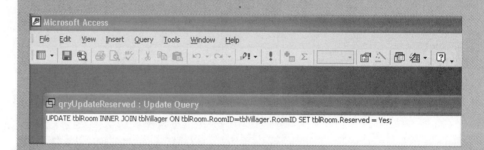

Figure 9-56: qryUpdateReserved in SQL view

Note how the relationship between tblRoom and tblVillager persists in the SQL statement. Before any record is updated, the table join filters the records in the Cartesian product to only those in which the RoomIDs match in the two tables—that is, those rooms in tblRoom that have been assigned to a villager in tblVillager. Therefore, only the records in tblRoom whose RoomID appears in tblVillager have their Reserved field set to Yes. After this query has been executed, all of the RoomIDs in tblVillager show up as Reserved in tblRoom.

NOTE: By the way, the Microsoft Access syntax for a table join is not standard SQL, although a number of commercial products use it. The standard SQL syntax for a join, which is used only for data retrieval operations in standard SQL (that is, Select queries), is shown in Figure 9-57. To update a field in one table based on a value in a second table, a subquery is used instead. The syntax for this query in standard SQL, which also works in Microsoft Access, is shown in Figure 9-58.

```
Select tblRoom.RoomID, tblRoom.Reserved
       from tblRoom, tblVillager
       where tblRoom.RoomID = tblVillager.RoomID".
```

Figure 9-57: Select query using a table join, in standard SQL

```
Update tblRoom
Set tblRoom.Reserved = "Yes"
where tblRoom.RoomID in
(select tblVillager.RoomID from tblVillager)
```

Figure 9-58: Update query using a subquery

The third query that you create for your VillageHousing application is a Select query using a table join. It retrieves every record in tblRoom along with the corresponding House name from tblHouse. For the sake of variety, you create this query using the Microsoft Access Query Design Wizard.

6 In the Queries frame of the Database window, double-click **Create query by using wizard.** In the first dialog box of the wizard, select **tblRoom** from the combo box. Using the **>** arrow, move every field except HouseCode from the list box on the left to the list box on the right. Then select **tblHouse** from the combo box, and use the **>** arrow to move the **House** field from the left list box to the right list box. At this point, the Simple Query Wizard window should appear as in Figure 9-59.

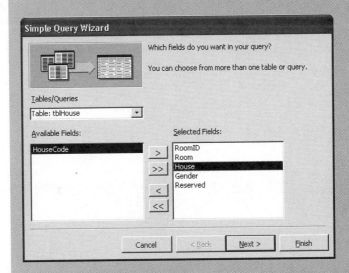

Figure 9-59: Simple Query Wizard

7 Click **Next;** then click **Next** again. Type **qryHouseRoom** as the title of your query, and click **Finish.** Access saves your query and also runs it. Close the query. When you reference this query in Visual Basic .NET, it will be known as a view.

8 MyVillager.mdb and/or your examination of VillageHousing.mdb is now complete. Exit **Microsoft Access** and return to **Visual Studio .NET.**

Lesson C uses the VillageHousing.mdb database provided to you as its data store. You can choose to use MyVillage.mdb instead, but you first have to populate the tables.

You have completed Lesson B, a review and minitutorial for Microsoft Access. Complete the end of lesson questions and exercises that follow before moving on to Lesson C.

SUMMARY

- Microsoft Access offers a GUI designer to create tables, fields, and field properties.

- You must assign a data type to each field. The most common data types are Text, Number, Date-Time, yes-no, and Autonumber.

- You can prescribe the format of each field through an input mask. You can require data to match one of several values by using a validation rule and validation text.

- The primary key of each table should be designated. The primary key can be a single field, or a composite primary key can be constructed from several fields.

- A field may be indexed or not. If it is indexed, duplicates may be either permitted or forbidden. A field may be required (no null values allowed) or not (null values allowed).

- Relationships in Microsoft Access are designed in the Relationships window, by dragging a field from one table to the corresponding field in another table. The related fields must have the same domain (range of legitimate values), but they do not need to have the same name. In the Edit Relationships window, you have the opportunity to establish referential integrity constraints, including cascading updates and deletes.

- Queries in Microsoft Access can retrieve data, called a Select query, or can change data, called an Action query. A Select query may be a simple query, retrieving data from one table, or a more complex query based on multiple tables. Multiple table queries include both subqueries and table joins. When a Select query is stored in the database, it creates what is referred to as a view in Visual Studio .NET. In most cases, a view cannot be updated. Action queries are used to insert, update, or delete records. When an Action query is stored in the database, it is referred to as a stored procedure.

QUESTIONS

1. In Microsoft Access, a field that is supplied by the software and is automatically incremented for each record is called a(n) _____ field.

2. To prescribe the format of input data, you use a(n) _____.

3. The ⬚ symbol identifies the _____.

4. The type of query that retrieves data is known as a(n) _____ query.

5. A query that is contained inside another query is called a _____.

6. A query that combines records from multiple tables to form a Cartesian product and then filters the Cartesian product result is called a _____.

7. In Microsoft Access, a query that changes records in a table is called a(n) _____.

CRITICAL THINKING

At the end of each lesson, reflective questions are intended to provoke you into considering the material you have just read at a deeper level.

1. In what circumstances does Microsoft Access determine that a relationship has one-to-one cardinality?

2. In what circumstances does Microsoft Access determine that a relationship has one-to-many cardinality?

3. If you can develop a complete application in Microsoft Access, what is the advantage of using Visual Basic .NET?

EXERCISES

1. Create a Microsoft Access database that corresponds to the layout of the Users sequential file used in Tutorial 4. Insert 10 records into tblUsers. Create a primary key as an AutoNumber field. Use an appropriate input mask for each field.

2. Create the structure of the Microsoft Access database that corresponds to the layout of the three sequential files used in Tutorial 6: Athletes.txt, Events.txt, and Nations.txt. Put all three files into one database, consisting of tblAthletes, tblEvents, and tblNations. Then add a table for Sports and another table for Venues, based on the contents of the Sports root node and the Venues root node in TreeView1 in frmScoreMain in Tutorial 6. Draw the relationships among these tables: tblSports to tblEvents, tblEvents to tblVenues, tblAthletes, and tblNations. Enforce referential integrity between tblEvents and tblVenues. Then load five records into each of the three tables.

3. Create the structure of a Microsoft Access database that can be used to display ticket prices and availability for all of the events at the Friendsville International Games, based on the information in Tutorial 7.

4. Create the structure of a Microsoft Access database that can replace Tutorial 8's sample pseudo-ISAM file for keeping track of tasks at the Friendsville International Games (p. 495).

ADO.NET in a Windows Application

In Lesson C you build the complete VillageHousing application. You use the ADO.NET designers and wizards to create the necessary data access elements and to bind the controls on the form to these data access elements. You complete the GUI and then complete the coding of frmVillageHousing.vb for those functions not created automatically.

Creating the Form for a Data Access Application

You begin this application by creating the basic form for displaying records from tblVillager. You use a Visual Studio .NET wizard to accomplish this. The Data Form Wizard accomplishes all of the following:

■ Creates a dataset from data you specify, using a new or existing connection to a database, and configures a data adapter to load the dataset and to return changed records to the database

■ Creates bound controls on the form, either in individual text boxes for the purpose of displaying one record at a time, or in a DataGrid control for displaying all of the records in the dataset at once

■ Creates buttons to load the dataset, to add and delete records, to update the database, to cancel pending changes to a record, to cancel all pending changes to the database, and to navigate among the records in the database

You use the wizard to create the initial form for this application, and then use it as a base for further application development.

To start the project and create the GUI for the data access application:

1 Start a new Visual Basic .NET Windows Forms project called **VillageHousing**, placing this project in the **VB.NET\Student\Tut09** folder. In Solution Explorer, delete **Form1**.

2 In Solution Explorer, right-click the project name, then click **Add | Add New Item**. In the Add New Item dialog box, select **Data Form Wizard**, type **frmVillageHousing.vb** as the name of the new item, and click **Open**. The Data Form Wizard opens.

3 Click **Next**. You must type the name of a new dataset. Type **dsVillager**. Click **Next**.

> **tip**
> ●●●●●●●●●●●●●●●
> A database engine is the software that manages the database and that interprets and executes SQL commands.

4   You need a connection to a database. Because you do not yet have a connection to a database, choose **New Connection**; the Data Link Properties dialog box opens.

5   Click the **Provider** tab. Choose the **Microsoft Jet 4.0 OLE DB Provider**. (This is the name of the Access 2000/2002 database engine.) Click **Next**.

6   Navigate to and select **VB.NET\Student\Tut09\VillageHousing.mdb**. Click **Test Connection**, and click **OK** when the message says that this was successful. Click **OK** to exit the Data Link Properties dialog box and return to the Data Form Wizard.

7   In the wizard, click **Next**. Now you are asked to choose the tables or views that you want to be the basis for your dataset. Select **tblVillager**, click the **>** arrow to move tblVillager from the left panel to the right panel, and then click **Next**.

8   From the tables and columns that you just specified for your dataset, you now choose the columns that you want to appear on the Data Form. All of the columns in tblVillager have been preselected, which is fine. Click **Next**.

9   The next window asks you to choose a display style. Recall that the Village Housing application displays the record of one villager at a time. So in this window, click the radio button for **Single record in individual controls**. You are also asked about additional controls on the form, and all options have been preselected; again, this is fine. Click **Finish**. The Data Form Wizard creates the form and all of its controls and code. The result appears as in Figure 9-60.

> **tip**
> ●●●●●●●●●●●●●●●
> The ConnectionString property is difficult to read, because when you click it, it only appears momentarily and then disappears. To see and edit the whole string, click anywhere within the ConnectionString setting, press Ctrl+A (to select the entire string), press Ctrl+Insert (to place the string on the Clipboard), open a new window in Notepad, and press Shift+Insert (to paste the Clipboard contents to the Notepad window). This lets you see the entire ConnectionString property. The result appears as in Figure 9-61. However, as noted in Lesson A, most of these are default property settings. Therefore, if you need to set the ConnectionString property programmatically, the only mandatory components for a Microsoft Access database are the Provider, Data Source, UserID, and Password. (Other data providers may have additional mandatory ConnectionString properties.)

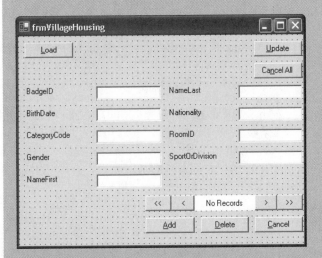

Figure 9-60: frmVillageHousing.vb, created by the Data Form Wizard

10   In Solution Explorer, click the **Project name (VillageHousing)**. Click the **Properties** button. Set **frmVillageHousing** as the **Startup object** for this project. Run the project. Click the **Load** button, and navigate through the records of the database to see that it works as expected. Close the application, and return to the IDE.

Studying the Output from the Data Form Wizard

What has the Data Form Wizard actually created? Quite a lot, as you will now see. The wizard created a set of ADO.NET objects and associated code, the practical counterpoint to the theory you studied in Lesson A. In this section, you briefly review the nongraphical objects first, and then the GUI and code.

To review the nongraphical objects created by the Data Form Wizard:

1 Click **OleDbConnection1** in the tray underneath the form, and then examine the ConnectionString property in the Properties window.

```
Provider=Microsoft.Jet.OLEDB.4.0;
Password="";
User ID=Admin;
Data Source= C:\VB.NET\Student\Tut09\VillageHousing\VillageHousing.mdb;
Mode=ReadWrite;
Extended Properties="";
Jet OLEDB:System database="";
Jet OLEDB:Registry Path="";
Jet OLEDB:Database Password="";
Jet OLEDB:Engine Type=5;
Jet OLEDB:Database Locking Mode=1;
Jet OLEDB:Global Partial Bulk Ops=2;
Jet OLEDB:Global Bulk Transactions=1;
Jet OLEDB:New Database Password="";
Jet OLEDB:Create System Database=False;
Jet OLEDB:Encrypt Database=False;
Jet OLEDB:Don't Copy Locale on Compact=False;
Jet OLEDB:Compact Without Replica Repair=False;
Jet OLEDB:SFP=False
```

default settings

Figure 9-61: ConnectionString property of OleDbConnection1

2 Open **Server Explorer**, and expand the connection to the VillageHousing.mdb Microsoft Access database, if necessary. Expand **Views**, and note that the Select queries appear. Expand **Stored Procedures**, and note that the Action queries appear.

Note that the nongraphical components created by the Data Form Wizard are the same ones discussed in Lesson A, namely, dsVillager.xsd XML dataset schema file in Solution Explorer, and, in the tray underneath the form, OleDbConnection1, OleDbDataAdapter1, and objdsVillager.

Note that the graphical components of frmVillageHousing at this point match the controls discussed in Lesson A: btnLoad, btnUpdate, and btnCancelAll perform their obvious functions. For each field in tblVillager, a matched pair of label and text box controls display the name of the field and the contents of the current record. btnAdd, btnDelete, and btnCancel operate on the current record. And the navigation controls allow the user to move between records.

Note that the code generated by the Data Form Wizard also matches that discussed in Lesson A. Loading the dataset involves the three levels of procedures in btnLoad_Click(), LoadDataSet(), and FillDataSet(). Updating the database involves the three levels of procedures in btnUpdate_Click(), UpdateDataSet(), and UpdateDataSource(). Changes to individual records are handled by btnAdd_Click(), btnDelete_Click(), and btnCancel_Click(). And navigation is handled by btnNavFirst_Click(), btnNavPrev_Click(), btnNavNext_Click(), btnLast_Click(), and objdsVillager_PositionChanged().

tip

All of these objects and procedures are discussed at length in Lesson A. Refer to that lesson if you need a refresher on any aspect of the outputs from the Data Form Wizard.

Adding Data Access Elements to the Form and Completing the GUI

If you return to Figure 9-1 and compare it to the form you've created thus far, you can see that several elements are missing from your frmVillageHousing form. In the completed application:

- Room and House information appears in a DataGrid control on the right side of the form.
- The Load button has moved to the right, and a Help button appears at the top left.
- On the left side of the form, a combo box displays the Category (replacing a text box displaying the CategoryCode).
- editBadgeID, the text box containing the BadgeID, is disabled. This is an Autonumber field in the database, and disabling it prevents users from attempting to change it.
- At the lower left, a group box contains controls that allow the user to search through the Villager records by name or by BadgeID.
- The navigation buttons and the group box are disabled until the Load button has been clicked.
- The label/text box pairs have been rearranged into a more logical sequence, whereas the labels themselves have been altered to conform to English spelling.

To provide this functionality, several ADO.NET data access elements must be added:

- The existing frmVillageHousing displays only the CategoryCode (A, C, J, O, S, or V) in a text box from tblVillager, but the completed application displays the category name that the CategoryCode stands for in a combo box that allows users to select the correct category. The list portion of the combo box contains all of the categories that appear in tblCategory, whereas the text portion of the combo box displays the category name that matches the CategoryCode in the current record. This implies that the dsVillager dataset class must contain data from tblCategory in addition to tblVillager, and it must also contain the relationship between tblCategory and tblVillager based on the common CategoryCode.
- The DataGrid control contains all of the information in tblRoom plus the name of the House extracted from tblHouse based on the common HouseCode in both tables. You could build a dataset for tblRoom, tblHouse, and the relationship between them, the same as you will do for tblVillager, tblCategory, and their relationship. However, to experiment with a different type of dataset, dsRoom will be based on the view called qryHouseRoom, the Select query you created in Microsoft Access.
- Using a view instead of the underlying tables creates another challenge, however, because a view is not updateable. This means that changes made to the data displayed in the data grid cannot be propagated back to the database. Therefore, if you assign a Villager to a room by inserting or changing the RoomID on the left, that information does not change the Reserved status in tblRoom. To correct this problem, you use the two stored procedures that you created in Microsoft Access, assigning each of these to an OleDbCommand, and you invoke the OleDbCommands from btnUpdate. The first of these Action queries, as you may recall, sets the Reserved status to No for every room in tblRoom, whereas the second Action query sets the Reserved status to Yes for each RoomID that appears in tblVillager.

Replacing editCategoryCode with cboCategory

The first of these three tasks is to replace the editCategoryCode text box with a combo box that displays the category of the current record as well as the list of available categories from tblCategory. This task can be usefully subdivided into two tasks: creating the necessary ADO.NET objects to implement the combo box and modifying the GUI.

To create the necessary ADO.NET objects in order to replace editCategoryCode with cboCategory:

1 First create OleDbDataAdapter2, to add tblCategory to the dsVillager dataset. From the Data tab of the Toolbox, drag an **OleDbDataAdapter** onto frmVillageHousing. The Data Adapter Configuration Wizard opens. Click **Next**.

2 Select the connection to **VB.NET\Student\Tut09\VillageHousing.mdb.Admin**, already listed. (Any other connections that exist on your computer are also listed in the combo box.) You could also have chosen to create a new connection for this data adapter. Click **Next**.

3 In the next window, choose the **Use SQL statements** query type, if necessary. Most likely, this is the only option available for an Access database and has been preselected. Click **Next**.

4 In the Generate the SQL statements window, you can type the SQL statement yourself, or you can use the Query Builder. The Query Builder is most useful if you are unfamiliar with SQL. Click **Query Builder**.

5 In the Add Table dialog box, double-click **tblCategory**, and then click **Close**. In the Query Builder, in the tblCategory frame at the top of the window, click the *(**All Columns**) check box. Note that the Query Builder constructs the SQL query, `Select tblCategory.* from tblCategory`. Click **OK**, which returns you to the Data Adapter Configuration Wizard.

6 Click **Advanced Options**. In the Advanced SQL Generation Options screen, click the **Generate Insert, Update, and Delete statements** check box to uncheck it. Your application does not need to make any changes to tblCategory, so these statements are superfluous. Click **OK**. Click **Next**.

7 Click **Finish**. Note that OleDbDataAdapter2 has been added to the tray underneath the form. With OleDbDataAdapter2 selected, click **Generate Dataset** at the bottom of the Properties window. In the Generate Dataset dialog box, verify that the existing dataset VillageHousing.dsVillager is selected, and that tblCategory (OleDbDataAdapter2) is checked. Click **OK**.

8 Click **objdsVillager** in the tray under the form. At the bottom of the Properties window, click **Dataset Properties**. Expand **dsVillager, tblVillager**, and **tblCategory**. Click **Constraint1** under tblCategory, and then expand **Columns** and expand [0] in the list on the right. See Figure 9-62. Examining this figure provides a good understanding of the structure of the dataset. But notice that nowhere in the dataset is the relationship between the tables mentioned, because, although the relationship exists in the database, it does not exist in the dataset whose Data Table objects are derived from the database. Close the **Dataset Properties** dialog box.

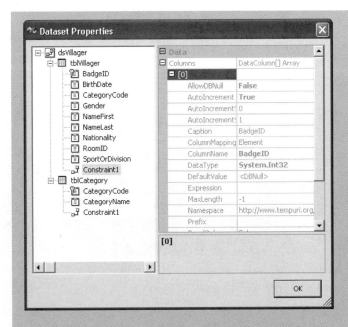

Figure 9-62: Dataset Properties of dsVillager

9 Next, you add the relationship between tblCategory and tblVillager to the
dataset. With objdsVillager selected in the Designer, click **View Schema** at the
bottom of the Properties window. The dsVillager.xsd schema window appears
in the XML Schema Designer. Move the table on the right farther to the right
by dragging the diamond in the upper-left corner of the table window. The
screen should appear as in Figure 9-63. Click either **table**. Then, on the menu
bar, click **Schema | Add | New Relation**. The Edit Relation dialog box opens.
Modify the settings as shown in Figure 9-64 to create the relation. Then click
OK. The schema now appears as in Figure 9-65.

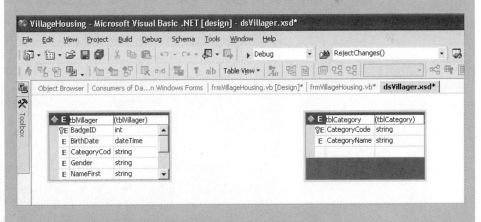

Figure 9-63: dsVillager.xsd schema before adding a data relation

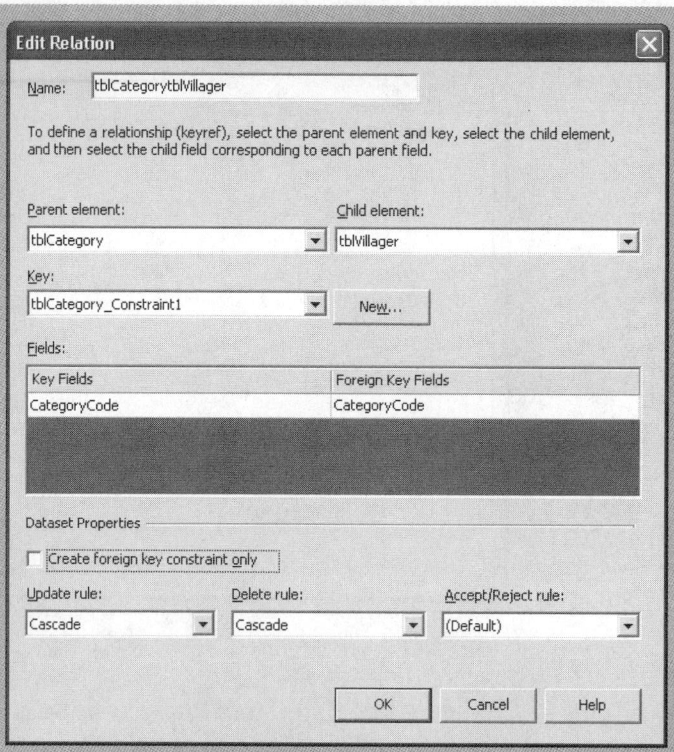

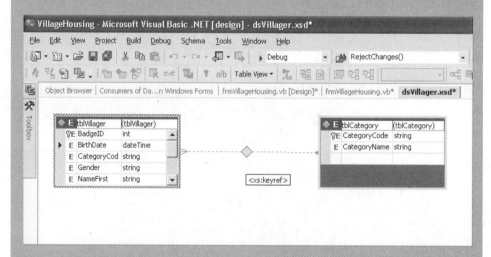

Figure 9-64: Edit Relation dialog box

Figure 9-65: dsVillager.xsd schema with data relation added

10 Run the **VillageHousing** application and click the **Load** button. The error (foreign-key constraint violation) occurs because the code only loads data from OleDbDataAdapter1. As soon as the constraints are reinstated, the dataset is in violation of the constraint. To fix this, locate the **FillDataSet()** procedure in the code for frmVillageHousing.vb. Right after the statement `Me.OleDbDataAdapter1.Fill(dataSet)`, insert the statement:

```
Me.OleDbDataAdapter2.Fill(dataSet)
```

11 Then run the application again, and click the **Load** button. It does not yet do anything new or different, but it raises an exception if you make a mistake.

Now, you modify the GUI to use the new ADO.NET objects you have created.

To replace editCategoryCode with cboCategory on frmVillageHousing:

1   On the left side of the form, a combo box should display the Category (replacing a text box displaying the CategoryCode). Delete **editCategoryCode**, and replace it with a **ComboBox** control named **cboCategory**. This ComboBox control demonstrates a more complex type of binding, because it is actually bound to three different fields in two tables, all in the objdsVillager dataset. A ComboBox control is often used in data-bound applications for this purpose. In the present case, the DropDownList control contains two columns of data, but only one column is visible: the visible column contains the contents of the CategoryName field from tblCategory, and the hidden column contains the contents of the corresponding CategoryCode field in tblCategory.

2   Set the **DataSource** property for cboCategory to **objdsVillager.tblCategory**, that is, the tblCategory table within the dataset.

3   The DisplayMember property indicates which column of the DataSource property the user sees in the ComboBox control. Set the **DisplayMember** property to **CategoryName** (that is, **tblCategory.CategoryName**).

4   The ValueMember property indicates which column of the DataSource the user is actually selecting (unseen). In this case, set the **ValueMember** property to **CategoryCode** (that is, **tblCategory.CategoryCode**).

5   Lastly, the item displayed from the database or selected by the user in the text portion of the ComboBox control must be bound to its proper data store. This is done through the DataBindings.SelectedValue property. Set this property to **objdsVillager—tblVillager.CategoryCode**. Thus the user can select one of the CategoryNames in tblCategory (Athlete, Coach, Judge, Official, Staff, or Visitor) visible in the combo box; meanwhile, the user is really making a selection from the corresponding CategoryCodes in tblCategory (A, C, J, O, S, V); and the selected value is then bound to the CategoryCode field of tblVillager. The properties that you must set for cboCategory are summarized in Figure 9-66.

6   Run the **VillageHousing** application to test cboCategory.

Property	Setting
+(DataBindings)	(expand)
SelectedValue	objdsVillager—tblVillager.CategoryCode
Name	cboCategory
DataSource	objdsVillager—tblCategory
DisplayMember	CategoryName
DropDownStyle	DropDownList
ValueMember	CategoryCode

Figure 9-66: Property settings for cboCategory

Adding the dsRoom Dataset to the Form

The dsRoom dataset is generated by another OleDbDataAdapter and is based on the query qryHouseRoom. You now add these elements to frmVillageHousing.

To add OleDbDataAdapter3 so that the qryHouseRoom view is loaded to the project:

1 In the Windows Form Designer, from the Data tab of the Toolbox, drag another **OleDbDataAdapter** component onto the form. As before, the Data Adapter Configuration Wizard opens. Click **Next**.

2 Select the existing connection to the VillageHousing.mdb database, and click **Next**.

3 **Use SQL statements** has been preselected, so click **Next** again.

4 Click the **Query Builder**. In the Add Table dialog box, click the **Views** tab. Double-click **qryHouseRoom**, and click **Close**. Click the *(All Columns)** check box. Click **OK** to exit the Query Builder. Click **Next**.

5 Note that the Update and Delete statements generated by the wizard do not work, because one cannot determine which columns of the underlying data should be updated or which records should be deleted. This is always the limitation on a view constructed from a table join. Click **Back**. Click **Advanced Options**. Uncheck the **Generate Insert, Update, and Delete statements** check box. Click **OK**. Click **Next**. Note that the warnings have vanished. Click **Finish**.

6 Note that OleDbDtaAdapter3 appears in the tray and is selected. In the Properties window, note that the InsertCommand, DeleteCommand, and UpdateCommand objects are set to none (because this view is not updateable, and because you chose not to attempt to generate insert, delete, and update commands). Expand the **SelectCommand** object, and click the **CommandText** property. Note the contents of the SQL statement, which retrieves every column from the view.

7 At the bottom of the Properties window, click **Generate Dataset**. In the Generate Dataset dialog box, in the Choose a dataset frame, click **New**, and type **dsRoom** as the name of the new dataset. In the Choose which table(s) to add to the dataset frame, verify that **qryHouseRoom (OleDbDataAdapter3)** is selected, and the other two adapters are not selected. Click **OK**. Note that the dataset class dsRoom has been added to Solution Explorer, and DsRoom1, an instance of the class, has been placed in the tray below the form.

8 As explained earlier, synchronization of tblRoom with RoomID assignment changes made in tblVillager requires execution of the two Action queries, qryCancelReservations and qryUpdateReserved. This is needed because dsRoom is based on a view that is not updateable. Therefore, you now add OleDbCommand objects to the form, which invoke those stored procedures. From the Data tab of the Toolbox, drag an **OleDbCommand** object onto the form. OleDbCommand1 appears in the tray beneath the form. In the Properties window, click the **Connection** property, click the **list** arrow, expand **Existing**, and click **OleDbConnection1**. Click the **CommandType** property, and click **StoredProcedure** from the drop-down list. In the CommandText property, type the name of the stored procedure, **qryCancelReservations**. In response to the Regenerate Parameters dialog box, click **Yes**. Repeat these steps to create and configure **OleDbCommand2**, with the CommandText as **qryUpdateReserved**.

9　The final step is to call these new data access elements in code in order to update the database through the Action queries and to load the DsRoom1 dataset. The code to accomplish this is shown in Figure 9-67. Type this code into the tail end of the LoadDataSet() procedure in the frmVillageHousing.vb code window. The code should also be executed when an update is performed. Therefore, insert the following line into btnUpdate_Click(), immediately after the `Me.UpdateDataSet()` statement:

`Me.LoadDataSet()`

```
'Now fill dsRoom
Me.OleDbConnection1.Open()
Me.OleDbCommand2.ExecuteNonQuery()
Me.OleDbCommand1.ExecuteNonQuery()
DsRoom1.Clear()
Me.OleDbDataAdapter3.Fill(DsRoom1)
Me.OleDbConnection1.Close()
```

Figure 9-67: Code for loading DsRoom1

10　Run the **VillageHousing** application to ensure that you have not introduced any syntax errors. However, the new dataset does not appear in a control until you complete the following GUI.

Completing the GUI and Code

Most of the remaining tasks deal only with the GUI.

To complete the GUI and code:

1　Begin by setting the **Size** property of the form to 1000 × 400 pixels. Set the form's **Text** property to **Village Housing**. You may find it easier to work on this large form in Full Screen mode, so select **View | Full Screen** in order to see all or most of the form. Select **View | Toolbox**, so that the controls are available to you to drag onto the form. Press F4 to bring the Properties window into view. Then drag the Properties window to the bottom of the screen. At this point, your screen looks approximately like Figure 9-68. You can now place all of the graphical controls on the form. Click **View | Full Screen** again to return to the normal Visual Studio .NET IDE.

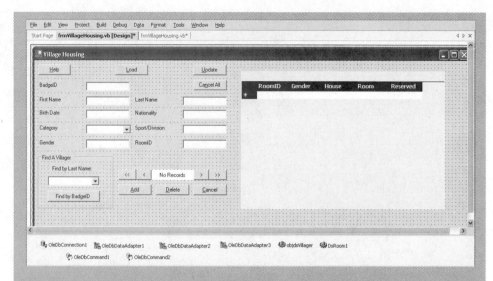

Figure 9-68: frmVillageHousing in Full Screen mode

2 Room and House information must appear in a DataGrid control on the right side of the form. Drop a **DataGrid** control on the form. Position it in the right half of the form, and set the properties shown in Figure 9-69. Run the **VillageHousing** application to see that the DataGrid works correctly.

Property	Setting
Name	dgrdRoom
DataSource	DsRoom1.qryHouseRoom
HeaderBackColor	Maroon
HeaderForeColor	LightGoldenrodYellow

Figure 9-69: Property settings for the DataGrid control

3 Move **btnLoad** to the right. Insert **btnHelp**, and program btnHelp_Click() as shown in Figure 9-70. Run the **VillageHousing** application, and test the **Help** button.

```
Private Sub btnHelp_Click(ByVal sender As System.Object, _
    ByVal e As System.EventArgs) Handles btnHelp.Click
  Dim str As String
  str = "Click the Load button to load all of the data." & vbCrLf
  str &= "Villager data appears on the left, one record at a time;" _
    & vbCrLf
  str &= "use the navigation buttons at the bottom to scroll " & _
    "through the villager records," & vbCrLf
  str &= "or find a particular record using the Find By Last " & _
    "Name combo box or the Find By BadgeID button." & vbCrLf
  str &= "Room availability data appears in the data grid on " & _
    "the right."
  str &= vbCrLf & "To reserve a room for a villager, enter " & _
    "the RoomID of a non-reserved room. " & vbCrLf
  str &= "Click Add or Delete to add or delete a villager." & vbCrLf
  str &= "Click Update to record all changes to the villager " & _
    "records." & vbCrLf
  str &= "The listing of rooms in the data grid cannot be " & _
    "altered in this application."
  MsgBox(str, , "Village Housing Help")
End Sub
```

Figure 9-70: btnHelp_Click() procedure

tip

Remember from working with GroupBox controls, that you must click each contained control in the Toolbox and then draw it inside the group box. If you drag a control to the group box, it's not actually contained within it.

4 Set the **Enabled** property of editBadgeID to **False**. This prevents the user from attempting to change the value of the primary key, which is generated automatically by Access as an AutoNumber field.

5 At the lower left, a group box on frmVillageHousing should contain controls that allow the user to search the Villager records by name or by BadgeID. Drop a **GroupBox** control in the empty space at the lower-left side of the form. Name it **grpFind**, and set the **Text** property to **Find A Villager**. Drop a **Label**, a **ComboBox**, and a **Button** inside grpFind. Set the **Text** property of the Label to **Find by Last Name:** Set the **Name** of the ComboBox to **cboFindByName**, its **DataSource** to **objdsVilager**, its **DisplayMember** to **tblVillager.NameLast**, and its **DropDownStyle** to **DropDownList**. (Nothing else must be done to cboFindByName. When you select a name from the combo box at runtime, the CurrencyManager repositions the dataset to the first record that matches that name.) Run the **VillageHousing** application to see that this works correctly.

6 In grpFind, name the **Button** control **btnFindByBadgeID**, and set its **Text** property to **Find by Badge ID**. Program this control to step through each record in the dataset, stopping when you reach the BadgeID you are looking for, or issuing an error message if you reach the last record without finding a matching record. The code to do this appears in Figure 9-71. Run the **VillageHousing** application. Test this new function by searching for a BadgeID that exists (**BadgeID = 15**), and also for one that does not exist (**BadgeID = 150**).

```
Private Sub btnFindByBadgeID_Click(ByVal sender As Object, _
    ByVal e As System.EventArgs) Handles btnFindByBadgeID.Click
  Dim findBadgeID As Integer = Val(InputBox("Enter BadgeID: "))
  Me.BindingContext(objdsVillager, "tblVillager").Position = 0
  Do Until editBadgeID.Text = findBadgeID Or _
      Me.BindingContext(objdsVillager, "tblVillager").Position _
      = (Me.objdsVillager.Tables("tblVillager").Rows.Count - 1)
    Me.BindingContext(objdsVillager, "tblVillager").Position += 1
  Loop
  Me.objdsVillager_PositionChanged()
  If editBadgeID.Text <> findBadgeID Then
    MsgBox("That BadgeID is not in the database.")
    Me.BindingContext(objdsVillager, "tblVillager").Position = 0
  End If
End Sub
```

Figure 9-71: btnFindByBadgeID_Click() procedure

7   The navigation buttons and the group box should be disabled until the Load button has been clicked. The easiest method of implementing this functionality is to use the Tag property. In the Designer, use the insertion point to select all of the **navigation** controls and the **GroupBox** control. Their common properties appear in the Properties window. Set their **Enabled** property to **False** and their **Tag** property to **Disabled**. Then, to enable these controls when data has been loaded, insert the code shown in Figure 9-72 at the end of the btnLoad_Click() procedure.

```
Dim i As Integer
For i = 0 To Me.Controls.Count - 1
  If Me.Controls(i).Tag = "Disabled" Then _
      Me.Controls(i).Enabled = True
Next
```

Figure 9-72: Code for enabling the navigation controls and the group box

8   The label/text box pairs must be rearranged into a more logical sequence, whereas the labels themselves must be altered to conform to English spelling. Rearrange each **label/text box pair** on the form as shown in Figure 9-73. After you have rearranged all of the controls, select **View | Tab Order**. Then click each control in the correct tab order. Then click **View | Tab Order** again.

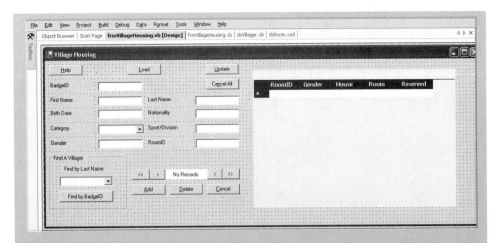

Figure 9-73: Completed GUI for frmVillageHousing

9 The location of the folder for the student data disk on your machine is unknown to the author at the time of writing. The only certainty is that VillageHousing.exe would end up in a \bin folder, and VillageHousing.mdb would end up in the parent folder containing the \bin folder. Therefore, you must insert code in the btnLoad_Click() procedure to locate the database. The code for the entire btnLoad_Click() procedure is shown in Figure 9-74. Make the necessary revisions to your btnLoad_Click() procedure based on Figure 9-74, or just retype the entire procedure as shown.

```
Private Sub btnLoad_Click(ByVal sender As System.Object, _
   ByVal e As System.EventArgs) Handles btnLoad.Click
 Dim strPath As String
 strPath = System.Reflection.Assembly. _
   GetExecutingAssembly.Location
 Dim BeginBin As Integer
 BeginBin = InStr(1, strPath, "\bin")
 strPath = Microsoft.VisualBasic.Left(strPath, _
   BeginBin) & "VillageHousing.mdb"
 OleDbConnection1.ConnectionString = _
   "Provider=Microsoft.Jet.OLEDB.4.0;" & _
   "Password=''; User ID=Admin;Data Source=" & strPath
 Try
   'Attempt to load the dataset.
   Me.LoadDataSet()
 Catch eLoad As System.Exception
   'Add your error handling code here.
   'Display error message, if any.
   System.Windows.Forms.MessageBox.Show(eLoad.Message)
 End Try
 Me.objdsVillager_PositionChanged()
 Dim i As Integer
 For i = 0 To Me.Controls.Count - 1
   If Me.Controls(i).Tag = "Disabled" Then
     Me.Controls(i).Enabled = True
   End If
 Next
End Sub
```

Figure 9-74: btnLoad_Click() procedure

Summary of Data Access Elements

The VillageHousing project now contains the following data access objects: OleDbConnection1, OleDbDataAdapter1, OleDbDataAdapter2, OleDbDataAdapter3, OleDbCommand1, OleDbCommand2, objdsVillager, and DsRoom1. The role played by each of these objects is as follows:

- *OleDbConnection1*—Data access requires, first of all, a connection to a database. An **OleDbConnection** identifies the type of database, its name, its physical location, the username, and the password. In this case, OleDbConnection1 identifies an MS Access database accessed through the JET engine, the filename VillageHousing.mdb, the path, and default security settings.
- *OleDbDataAdapter1, OleDbDataAdapter2, OleDbDataAdapter3*—An **OleDbDataAdapter** is normally associated with a single table or view. Using the data connection, the adapter retrieves data from the specified table or other source, and also sends changes back to the table (insertion of new records, deletion of old records, update of changed records). Thus, a data adapter may contain a number of different commands, such as select, insert, update, and delete. In this case, OleDbDataAdapter1 gets data from tblVillager, and also sends changes back to that table; OleDbDataAdapter2 gets data from tblCategory, and can send changes back to that table; and OleDbDataAdapter3 gets data from qryHouseRoom. OleDbDataAdpater3 cannot send changes back to the database, because a query (view) is not updateable.
- *OleDbCommand1, OleDbCommand2*—These OleDbCommand objects exist for the purpose of executing two update queries: qryCancelReservations and qryUpdateReserved. They exist as command objects rather than as data adapters because they do not actually retrieve any data from the database.
- *objdsVillager, DsRoom1*—These are the datasets used by the application. objdsVillager is filled by OleDbDataAdapter1 and OleDbDataAdapter2, and also maintains the relationship between them through the CategoryCode common to both adapters. DsRoom1 is filled by OleDbDataAdapter3. An important feature of this entire data access scheme is that the dataset, after it is filled, is wholly disconnected from the database. This allows many users to access the data simultaneously, without tying up resources that would be necessary to maintain database connections the entire time an application is running. Only when a command is issued to update the database is another momentary connection established, and after a data burst is transmitted to the database, that connection is closed.

You have now completed Lesson C. Stop now for a break, or continue on with the following exercises.

SUMMARY

- The Microsoft Jet 4.0 OLE DB Provider is the driver for a Microsoft Access or 2002 database. You use an OleDbConnection object to connect to an Access database.
- Through the Query Builder, you can create data adapters and datasets without a detailed knowledge of SQL.
- The XML Designer allows you, again without learning XML, to modify an XML schema to add elements, to incorporate nonrelational data sources, and to create Data Relation objects.
- The DataGrid control can display an entire dataset by setting its DataSource property.

■ The ComboBox control can be bound to two data sources at the same time. One data source is a lookup table or parent table with a column of information easily understandable by humans, and a corresponding column of codes that cross-reference to the second table. The second or child table contains one of these codes. The combo box displays the human-readable data, and also identifies the currently selected item based on the current record in the second table.

QUESTIONS

1. If a ComboBox control is bound to two data sources, the property that identifies the source table for the two columns of data in the control is the _____ property.

2. If a ComboBox control is bound to two data sources, the property that identifies the column of data displayed in the drop-down list is the _____ property.

3. If a ComboBox control is bound to two data sources, the property that identifies the nondisplayed column of code values is the _____ property.

4. If a ComboBox control is bound to two data sources, the property that identifies the currently selected but nondisplayed value is the _____ property.

5. A control that can display an entire table merely by setting its DataSource property is the _____ control.

6. To set the correct tab order for the controls on the form, you should first click _____.

7. A function that locates the place within a string where a substring begins is the _____ function. (*Hint*: Look again at Figure 9-74.)

8. When designing a large form, you can click _____ to allow the Form Designer to occupy the entire screen.

9. If an action query has been assigned to an OleDbCommand, to cause the action query to execute you invoke the _____ method.

10. What information is returned by invoking System.Reflection.Assembly. GetExecutingAssembly.Location?

EXERCISES

1. Create a Visual Basic .NET Windows Forms application that reads the data from the Users sequential file in Tutorial 4, and stores that data in a Microsoft Access database file named Users.mdb. To accomplish this:
   a. Start by designing the Microsoft Access database. This database requires only one table, tblUsers. It should have all of the elements in structUser. Designate the user's e-mail address as the primary key.
   b. In the Visual Basic .NET Windows application, you can use the Data Form Wizard to create the skeleton application. The Data Form Wizard creates one dataset schema, dsUser, with one OleDbDataAdapter and one OleDbConnection.
   c. Add Module1 to the project. In this module, insert the definition of structUser along with the declaration of pUserRec, a public variable of type structUser.
   d. You need to write one new and fairly complex procedure for this project. This procedure should execute btnLoad_Click (in order to open and load the dataset,

even though tblUser is initially empty). The procedure then opens the Users random-access file. Use a loop to read through all of the records in the Users file. Inactive records need not be copied to the Microsoft Access database. But for each record whose status is N or A, you should add a new record to tblUser in the dataset, then assign the elements of pUserRec to the text boxes on the data form, and update the dataset.

    e.   After running your application, open your new Microsoft Access database, and verify that all of the records for active and new users from the Users file now appear in the database.

2.   Building on the results of Exercise 1, modify the Logon application (class library and TryLogon project) from Tutorial 4, using the Microsoft Access database file created in Exercise 1 (Users.mdb) in lieu of the Users random-access file. Rather than using the Data Form Wizard, you will find it easier to start with the completed Logon class library. Add the data access components by employing the Data Adapter Configuration Wizard (automatically invoked when you drop an OleDbDataAdapter onto the form). Then bind each of the three controls on frmLogon to fields in tblUser in the dataset. (Note: You will need to copy Users.mdb to the \bin folders of both the Logon project and the TryLogon project.)

3.   Building on the results of Exercise 1, modify the LogonManager application from Tutorial 4, using the Microsoft Access database file (Users.mdb) created in Exercise 1 in lieu of the Users random-access file. Rather than using the Data Form Wizard, you will find it easier to start with the completed LogonManager application. Add the data access components by employing the Data Adapter Configuration Wizard (automatically invoked when you drop an OleDbDataAdapter onto the form). Then bind each of the controls on frmUser to fields in tblUser in the dataset. To keep this project to a manageable size, do not modify any of the functions that deal with a new user: That is, the New User Toolbar button, View | New User, and View | Supervisor | Accept New Users can be skipped.

4.   Create a Visual Basic .NET Windows Forms application that reads the data from the three sequential files in Tutorial 6 (Athletes.txt, Events.txt, and Nations.txt), and stores that data in a Microsoft Access database file.

    a.   This exercise is similar to Exercise 1, but complicated by the fact that you start with three sequential files rather than one random-access file. Start by designing the Microsoft Access database. Include three tables, named tblAthletes, tblEvents, and tblNations. The fields of tblAthletes should mirror the fields in structAthlete; designate AthleteID as the primary key. The fields of tblEvents should mirror the fields in structEvent; designate EventID as the primary key. tblNations should contain the first two fields in Nations.txt: the CountryCode (make this the primary key), and CountryName.

    b.   Create a Visual Basic .NET Windows Forms MDI application. Use the Data Form Wizard to create three data forms, one for each file. The logic for each form is the logic described in Exercise 1, Steps (b), (c), and (d).

    c.   The MDI form contains a main menu with File menu items for Athletes, Events, Nations, and Exit. Each menu selection should display the corresponding data form. A Windows menu item maintains the WindowList.

    d.   After your program is complete and working, open the Access database and each of its tables to verify that all of the data from the three sequential files now appears in the corresponding database table.

5.   Recreate the Scoring application from Tutorial 6, using the Microsoft Access database file created in Exercise 3 for input in lieu of the three sequential files that were used in that tutorial. Rather than using the Data Form Wizard, you will find it easier to start with the completed Scoring application. Add the data access components by employing the Data Adapter Configuration Wizard (automatically invoked when you drop an OleDbDataAdapter onto the form). Then, in the main form's load event, open the database, load the datasets, and copy the information from each table into the corresponding array in the Scoring application. The rest of the Scoring application should work without modification.

6. Recreate the Dining application from Tutorial 2, but change the sequential file output to a database output. To do this, create the database Seats.mdb, containing one table named tblSeats. tblSeats contains these fields: Date, SeqNum, House, Table, and SeatNum. Date + SeqNum is the primary key. When the user chooses File | Save Seats in File, the program should create 935 records in tblSeats. From the DateTimePicker control, load the date for which seats have been assigned into the date field of tblSeats. Get the sequence number, house, table, and seat number fields from pastructSeat(). Add all 935 rows to the dataset, and then update the underlying database.

Exercise 7 allows you to both discover the solution to problems on your own and experiment with material that is not covered explicitly in the tutorial.

discovery ▶ 7. Enhance Exercise 6, so as to prevent the user from attempting to save seat assignments for a date that has previously been saved in tblSeats.

K E Y   T E R M S

- ADO.NET data access technology
- BindingContext object
- Column object
- Columns collection
- concurrency control
- CurrencyManager object
- data modeling
- data set object
- database management system
- DataGrid control
- DataRelation class
- DataTable class
- DeleteCommand property
- Fill() method
- foreign key
- InsertCommand property
- N-tier architecture
- OleDbCommand object
- OleDbConnection object
- OleDbDataAdapter object
- OleDbDataReader object
- primary key
- relational database management system
- Row object
- Rows collection
- SelectCommand property
- SqlCommand object
- SqlConnection object
- SqlDataAdapter object
- SqlDataReader object
- stored procedure
- Structured Query Language (SQL)
- Table object
- transaction processing
- Update() method
- UpdateCommand property
- XML schema (*.xsd) file

Web Forms with Database Interactivity

The Friendsville International Games Ticket Sales Application

case ▶ The Friendsville Organizing Committee (FOC) has decided to focus their marketing and promotional activities on the Internet, resulting in a large volume of traffic at the Friendsville International Games Web site, www.fig.org. Visitors to that Web site, FOC hopes, will follow the prominent link to the ticket sales Web page. The Friendsville Games Development Team (FGDT) is expected to create a robust, secure, and full-featured, Web-based ticket sales application, through which the public will be able to order and purchase tickets for every scheduled event in the Games.

The preliminary version of this application has been developed and is previewed here. The FGDT's task in this tutorial is to replicate the preliminary FigTickets application. After you re-create this version, you will be prepared to incorporate significant enhancements on your own.

If you are unable to install or run FigTickets, then you should run FigTickets4Windows instead. This Windows Forms version of the application displays the same functionality as FigTickets, with similar screens and application logic. It also uses the same SQL Server database, installed on the local machine and served from there. FigTickets4Windows is discussed in Appendix B.

Of course, in the real world, a Windows Forms application on a local computer would not make much sense for selling tickets to the Friendsville International Games. In terms of the application itself, users today expect a Web-based application that does not require them to download anything onto their local machine. Users are wary about saving cookies on their local machine, much less a complete application, especially one designed only to support retail sales. In terms of the database server, the real database must obviously be centralized—this will not work as a distributed database, in which each user is able to purchase all of the tickets.

Even if you cannot install and run FigTickets in the school's computer lab, you should be able to replicate FigTickets on your own personal computer, if you are the administrator. In this case, you may run FigTickets4Windows for demonstration purposes at school, but then build FigTickets as a Web Forms application on your own machine.

Previewing the FigTickets Web Forms Application

As you step through this application, imagine yourself as a potential customer, reserving and purchasing tickets for the Games over the Web. If you keep this viewpoint in mind, you can both appreciate the preliminary application constructed by the FGDT so far, and get a sense of the enhancements needed later.

NOTE: FigTickets can only be installed on a computer that is running Internet Information Server (IIS). You must have permission to run the installer on the computer, and you must have IIS permissions as well. See the Tutorial 10 note concerning the necessary software and permissions in the "Read This Before You Begin" section of the preface.

To view the FigTickets application:

1 Copy the folder **VB.NET\Student\Tut10\DeployFigTickets** to your Web server computer. Then double-click **WebSetupFigTicketsNoSource.msl** in that folder. Follow the installation instructions, accepting all of the defaults.

2 Before running the completed FigTickets application, the Tickets database must be copied to your computer, and then attached to an instance of SQL Server running on your computer. The folder VB.NET\Student\Tut10\ WebSetupFigTicketsNoSource includes a compressed file named Tickets.zip. Extract the two files in this folder (Tickets.mdf and Tickets_Log.ldf) to the Data folder for the SQL Server instance running on your computer. The most likely path to this folder is C:\Program Files\Microsoft SQL Server\MSSQL$vsdotnet\ Data. The actual folder on your computer may differ from this model. You have now copied the database data (.mdf) and log (.ldf) files to your machine, but these files are not yet attached to SQL Server.

3 To attach the database to an instance of SQL Server, run the osql utility that comes with MSDE. To do this, click **Start | Run**, and type

```
osql —E —S <machinename>\<instancename>
```

where *<machinename>* is the name of your computer and *<instancename>* is the name of the instance of Microsoft SQL Server where you copied the Tickets database. The default instance names for SQL Server are vsdotnet and netsdk, so very likely at least one of these instances exists on your machine. The above command on the author's computer is

```
osql —E —S dadslaptop\vsdotnet
```

If this command is successful, it will open a command (MS-DOS) window, with a line number prompt:

```
1>
```

To attach the Tickets database to this instance of SQL Server, type the following command, beginning at the 1> prompt, substituting the actual path to the database files on your computer, wherever you have placed them. At the end of each line, press Enter, which then prompts you with a new line number:

```
1> exec sp_attach_db @dbname = 'Tickets',
2> @filename1 = 'C:\Program Files\Microsoft SQL
   Server\MSSQL$vsdotnet\Data\Tickets.mdf',
3> @filename2 = 'C:\Program Files\Microsoft SQL
   Server\MSSQL$vsdotnet\Data\Tickets_log.ldf'
4> go
```

NOTE: If you make a mistake while typing, or if you wish to use copy-and-paste, type ed after any line number prompt, press the Enter key, and a text editor will appear. After making your corrections, save and exit the editor to return to the osql facility.

4 Start your Web browser. Navigate to **http://localhost/FigTicketsNoSource**. The server application has no knowledge about the location of the database on the local machine. Therefore, the opening screen initially prompts you to enter the *machinename\instancename* of the SQL Server instance to which the Tickets database is attached. Enter the requested information, and click **Save SQL Server** *machinename\instancename*. The opening page of the FigTickets application then appears as in Figure 10-1 (although the *machinename\instancename* on your computer will be different than the dadslaptop\vsdotnet shown in the figure).

tip
•••••••••••••••••
If you happen to have the full SQL Server package installed on your computer, then you can install the Tickets database with DTS (Data Transformation Services) instead of the osql utility. DTS is much easier to use.

Web address

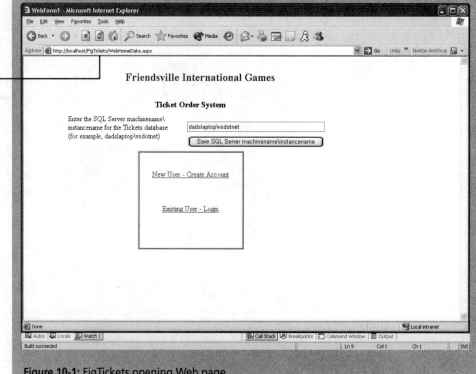

Figure 10-1: FigTickets opening Web page

> **NOTE:** In the application that you create in this tutorial, the opening screen will not prompt the user for the *machinename\instancename* of SQL Server. Rather, you can assume that, in the real-world version of this application, the application developer knows where the database resides, so this information will be hard-coded into the application. Further, the end-user who is ordering tickets to the Friendsville International Games from his home computer has no information about SQL Server.

5 Click **Existing User – Login**. The Login screen appears, as seen in Figure 10-2. Using Hilda Reiner's login information, type **Hilda@fgdt.org** as the e-mail address, and **hildafgdt** as the password. Press **Enter**. The User Account screen appears, containing Hilda's information, as shown in Figure 10-3.

Figure 10-2: Login screen

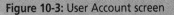

WebUser - Microsoft Internet Explorer

File   Edit   View   Favorites   Tools   Help

Back ·   ·   Search   Favorites   Media

Address   http://localhost/FigTickets/WebUser.aspx

Existing User

E-mail Address	hilda@fgdt.org	Street	109 RIDGEWAY
Password		City	FRIENDSVILLE
First Name	HILDA	State or Province	MARYLAND
Last Name	REINER	Postal Code	21672
		Country	USA
Update Info		Orders	Home

Figure 10-3: User Account screen

tip

If you receive an error message indicating that the login failed or the SqlConnection failed, then you may need to change the security settings in IIS. To do this, you must have administrator privileges on the computer. Open the Control Panel, open Administrative Tools, open Internet Information Services, expand the machinename (local computer), expand Web Sites, right-click Default Web Site, select Properties, and click the Directory Security tab in the Default Web Site Properties window. In the Anonymous access and authentication control frame, click Edit. In the Authentication Methods dialog box, uncheck Anonymous access, uncheck Digest authentication for Windows domain servers, and uncheck Basic authentication (password is sent in clear text). Check Integrated Windows authentication. Click OK to close the Authentication methods dialog box. Click OK to close the Default Web Site Properties window. Close the Internet Information Services window, close Administrative Tools, and close Control Panel. Try running the application again.

6 Click **Orders**. The three orders that Hilda has placed appear. Hilda has already paid for two of these orders. Click **Order Details** for the third order, to view Hilda's three orders along with a list of the tickets that she ordered with OrderID 12, shown in Figure 10-4. Note that the combo box displays the event to which the selected order relates. View Hilda's other orders in the same way.

all of Hilda's orders

tickets in OrderID 12

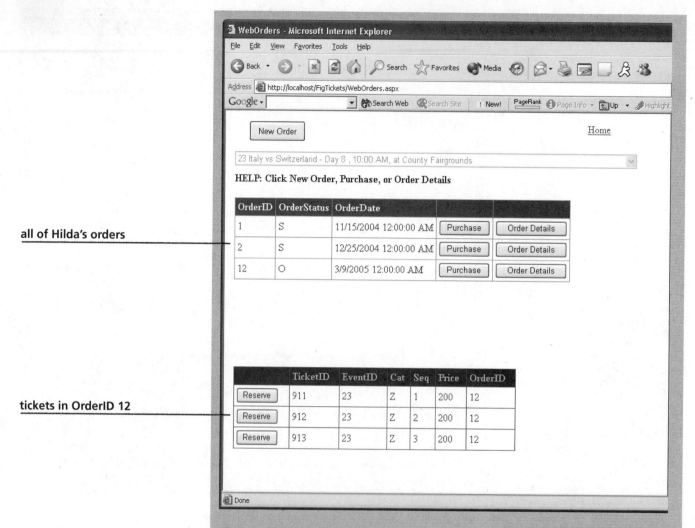

Figure 10-4: Orders placed by Hilda, with details for OrderID 12

7 The FGDT plans on using a Payments Provider to handle credit-card payments over the Web, but this portion of the application has not yet been developed. At the moment, clicking Purchase simply marks the order as paid. Click the **Purchase** button for OrderID 12. Note that OrderStatus changes from O (ordered) to S (sold), and that a Thank You message appears in the Help line, as shown in Figure 10-5.

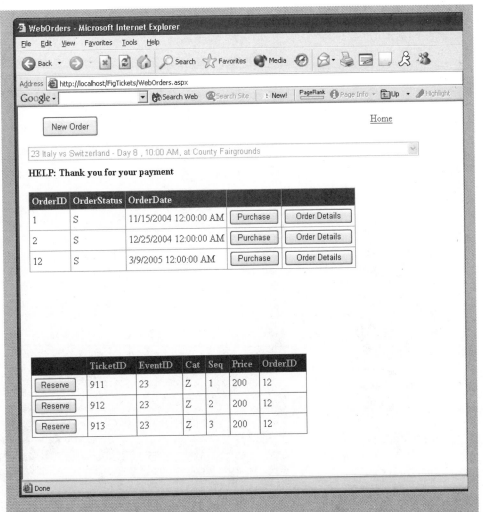

Figure 10-5: Purchase completed for OrderID 12

8 Click **Home.** Note that the home page that appears this time does not prompt you again for the *<machinename>\<instancename>* of the SQL server. This time, click **New User – Create Account.** Enter the information shown in Figure 10-6 for the new user, Mary Dickens. Enter **Boston** for her password. Click **Submit.** The User Account screen for Mary appears.

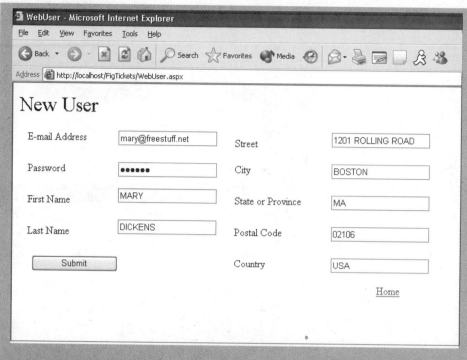

Figure 10-6: New User screen, filled out for Mary Dickens

9 Click **Orders**. On the Orders screen, click **New Order**. From the combo box, select **Event 16 Men's Baseball USA vs. Japan—Day 3, 10:00AM, at Memorial Stadium**. Reserve (by clicking the **Reserve** button) TicketIDs **601, 602, 603, and 604**. Scroll down through all the tickets to see the tickets available for that game. Click **Done**. The Orders screen reappears, updated with the new order, as shown in Figure 10-7. (The OrderID may be different on your screen.)

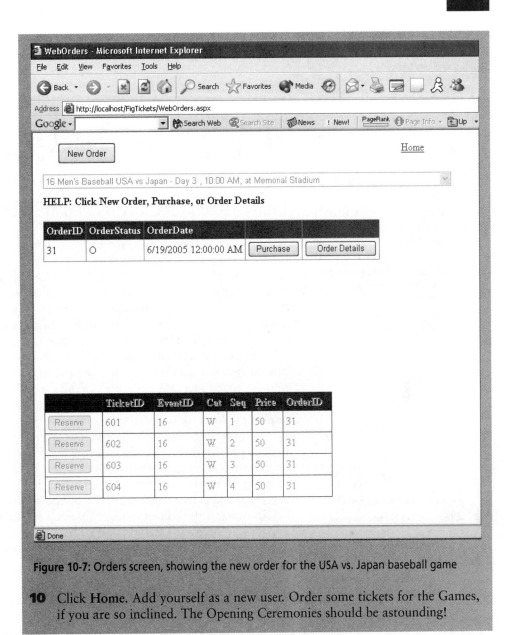

Figure 10-7: Orders screen, showing the new order for the USA vs. Japan baseball game

10 Click **Home**. Add yourself as a new user. Order some tickets for the Games, if you are so inclined. The Opening Ceremonies should be astounding!

After completing this lesson, you will be able to:

- Understand the security models of 3-tier architecture
- Appreciate the capabilities of SQL Server and the Microsoft Desktop Engine
- Understand the Visual Database Tools facility for designing and creating an SQL Server database, including tables, diagrams, relationships, and views
- Use datasets in a Web Forms application to display the sample database

tip

A firewall is a computer program that blocks unauthorized transmissions.

3-tier Architecture

Understanding Security Models in 3-tier (and N-tier) Architecture

Security considerations make interactive database processing on the Web generically different from accessing static Web pages and also different from database processing on a local machine. In Tutorial 9, you read about security and privacy, concurrency control, transaction processing, and 3-tier architecture (client machine or browser, Web server, and database server). The discussion here is intended to deepen your understanding of the most critical security aspects of 3-tier architecture.

Each tier in a multitier architecture must be capable of applying its own security layer. Security has multiple facets. It includes privacy protection, sometimes accomplished through data encryption—the use of a coding scheme to convert the data into an indecipherable collection of bits, requiring the same coding scheme to decrypt the collection of bits back into meaningful information. Physical security implies the need for data backup and recovery procedures. Hardware and software systems at each level must be protected from unauthorized access. Software and data may be protected through the erection of firewalls. Transmitted data must be protected while in transit. Many of these facets of security exist for any type of computer application in any environment. The discussion here focuses on the security aspects of access to a database over a public network.

In general, the security model for each tier can include the three processes of authentication, authorization, and impersonation. A request from a user or a user application initiates these processes, which serve the following functions:

- *Authentication*—The process whereby a user is identified to the system; it answers the question, "Do I know you, and can you prove you are who you say you are?" The information provided by the user is known as credentials. The credentials could be in the form of a username and password, the name of a machine or a network, a user role, or a trusted user certificate—a guarantee from a third party, trusted by both parties to a transaction, that each party to the transaction is legitimate. The credentials provided by the user are then validated against some authority, such as a database containing approved usernames and passwords, or a Windows domain server. (Authentication is not always required; some security models accept "anonymous" or unauthenticated users. For example, many publicly accessible Web sites accept anonymous users.)

- *Authorization*—After the user is authenticated (or if authentication is not required), the next question is whether this user is authorized to conduct the requested activity. For instance, the system may recognize you as an authorized user of the employee database, but still not authorize you to double your salary!

- *Impersonation*—This is an optional process in which a Web application impersonates (or pretends to be) an authorized user, making it possible to provide access to resources over a public network without requiring every user to log on to the Web server. For example, a publicly accessible database may be the type of resource that requires a username and password. To make the database accessible to all users without requiring each user to provide a username and password, the software may use impersonation—automatically making every user appear to be one of the users authorized to access that database. This use of impersonation has essentially the same result as an unauthenticated or anonymous user. However, impersonation is also needed when the Web server implements **connection pooling**—sharing a connection among multiple users in order to conserve connection resources; in this scenario, the Web server impersonates an authorized user on behalf of each actual user (after that user has been authenticated, of course).

Each tier recognizes at least two levels of users (and often many more): administrator and authorized user. An administrator is granted complete or "privileged" access, can call upon all software functions, and can change permissions for everyone else. Authorized users have more limited system privileges. Some security models have different classes of users (called user groups or roles) who are able to access only certain portions of the system. For example, the role of financial analyst may be authorized to access certain financial information, but not personnel data.

The reason for the complexity of the subject of security is that access to a database from a browser over a TCP/IP connection involves at least three tiers, with each tier able to impose its own security restrictions, and the administrator at each tier has many security models to draw from, as suggested by Figure 10-8. Hence, there is no plain and sure way to specify a set of security settings that works in all or even most cases. Rather, each database, network, and workstation combination must be examined to discover what works in that particular case.

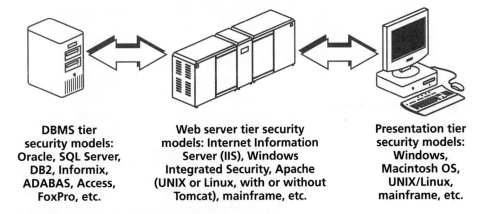

| DBMS tier security models: Oracle, SQL Server, DB2, Informix, ADABAS, Access, FoxPro, etc. | Web server tier security models: Internet Information Server (IIS), Windows Integrated Security, Apache (UNIX or Linux, with or without Tomcat), mainframe, etc. | Presentation tier security models: Windows, Macintosh OS, UNIX/Linux, mainframe, etc. |

Figure 10-8: Security models in 3-tier architecture

> A VPN is a network that acts like a private network totally disconnected from the Internet, but which uses the transmission facilities of the Internet.

Many systems have additional tiers or layers of hardware and software. For example, authentication may be handled on a completely separate server. A virtual private network (VPN) introduces a software layer. A firewall protecting a LAN from the rest of a network becomes an additional tier. And business application logic could be implemented at any level, or interposed as an additional tier, anywhere in the architecture. Again, each of these tiers participates in some way in the security scheme of a system.

Browser or Client Machine Security Using Windows and Internet Explorer

Windows offers a robust security system, through which the system administrator can create and manage user accounts, limit access to certain files or folders, and also designate certain files or folders as shared, either with or without passwords.

Ever since Windows 98, the standard Windows operating system start-up sequence requires a user to log on. Optionally, a password may also be required. In addition, each computer has a name, which must be unique within a local area network. For example, the laptop computer the author is using in writing this book has the name dadslaptop. (You will see this name throughout this tutorial.) To gain access to dadslaptop, the Windows XP Professional operating system requires a user to log on to one of the several Windows user accounts that it recognizes, in this case, one for each family member who uses the machine. The author's username is Bob, with no password required. Windows maintains these names (the machine name, and the username and password) in both encrypted and in-the-clear forms, and is able to pass these names to applications or tiers that need them. For example, an application running on dadslaptop might not recognize the user Bob or might not allow Bob to perform certain administrator functions, unless Bob has been assigned as a system administrator. An application could be configured to accept specific users or specific machines, to prompt the user for a logon and password if the user is not recognized, or to always prompt for a username and password.

> **NOTE:** In an encrypted form, data is coded using an encryption key; someone with access to the encrypted data still cannot decipher it without the decryption key. Data in the clear or in plain text is stored as simple ASCII characters; someone with access to data in this form is able to read it. These security considerations address the situation in which a number of people have access to one machine; the security scheme protects each user's data and applications from other users on the same machine.

Next, the discussion turns to a network situation, in which different people and machines are interconnected.

Working over a Network

When Windows passes credentials over a network connection, they are in this form: machine=IUSR_DADSLAPTOP; user="Bob"; password="pwd". The machine name for any computer is always passed in the form IUSR_*<machinename>*. A blank or unknown username is passed as "Admin" or as "". A blank password is passed as "pwd" or "".

If an application asks for the username and password, these are passed in clear text, which could make them vulnerable. By default, the username and password are passed in clear text, because different operating systems may be participating in the network—you could have Windows, Macintosh, and UNIX/Linux machines all in one network. When Windows passes credentials, if it does not know the environment of every node in the network, its only choice is to pass credentials in the clear.

Therefore, Windows also offers integrated Windows security, in which the username and password are passed as an encrypted token. However, using integrated Windows security requires a domain composed entirely of machines using the Windows operating system.

Network Security—Internet Information Server

The Web server is the central location for Web-based application security. The Web server could be Apache on a UNIX machine, any flavor of Linux, Microsoft Internet Information Server (IIS), Novell NetWare, or some other Web server software. This discussion focuses on IIS—the general concepts are the same with any other Web server package, though some of the specifics would be different.

IIS is fully integrated with Windows security. This means that when IIS requests access to a particular resource resident in a Windows folder, IIS must provide the credentials of an authenticated user—as far as Windows is concerned, IIS is just another process requesting access. However, in publicly available applications on the Internet, all users cannot be expected to provide the same authentications across the board. Therefore, IIS offers a variety of methods to authenticate user credentials, including anonymous access, basic authentication, digest authentication, Windows integrated security, and certificate authentication.

Anonymous Access

Anonymous access is appropriate for publicly accessible applications on the Internet. The Windows machine on which the IIS server is running has an extra Windows user account under the name IUSR_<*machinename*>, where <*machinename*> is the name of the IIS host, such as dadslaptop. When an unknown user sends a request to IIS for access to some resource, IIS impersonates this Windows user account, making the request to Windows under the name <*machinename*>_anonymous, for example, dadslaptop_anonymous.

> **NOTE:** You may have noticed throughout the Visual Studio .NET documentation that many classes have protected members whose names start with the letter I. This convention identifies members that are useful in the definition of interfaces with other classes. The IUSR_<> member is necessary for interfaces within the Windows security domain. (The IUSR interface is part of Windows and not part of the .NET Framework.) Look through the I words in the Visual Studio .NET Help Index to see examples of the many interface specifications in the .NET Framework.

Basic Authentication

Basic authentication is the very simple authentication prescribed by the Worldwide Web Consortium (W3C) and is standard among all Web servers. When basic authentication is prescribed, an unknown user is prompted for a username and password in a standard login dialog. When the user supplies this information to IIS, IIS passes it along to the application. Though widely used, basic authentication is not terribly secure, because the information entered by the user is transmitted to IIS in the clear. It is an acceptable form of security for applications requiring only a medium level of security.

Digest Authentication

Digest authentication works the same as basic authentication, except that the information entered by the user is transmitted to IIS in an encrypted form, providing a more secure process. However, digest authentication is only supported within a Windows domain—so non-Windows users are unable to employ this method.

Integrated Windows Authentication

You have probably encountered integrated Windows authentication, as it is quite common within a local area network of an organization. If a user's credentials have already been authenticated in a Windows network, then IIS is able to use these credentials when it passes a new request to Windows. For example, FGDT members might log on to Windows when they come to work in the morning, and this logon is used to also log on automatically to IIS. Then, for the rest of the day, all of the applications available within FGDT's intranet are accessible to FGDT members without further logons. The information IIS passes is not the username and password, but rather an encrypted token that identifies the user's authentication status. Integrated Windows authentication works well in an intranet, behind a firewall; it does not work well if you must pass through a firewall.

Certificate Authentication

IIS supports the use of digital certificates within the Secure Sockets Layer (SSL). In this scheme, a third party provides a digital certificate to either the user or the Web server, and IIS passes this digital certificate on to the application. The third party is known to both the client and the application and is trusted by both.

Database Security—ASP.NET and SQL Server

A DBMS typically includes authorization services, known as "permissions" in the database world. Although it is possible for the database administrator (DBA) to augment or substitute his own permissions scheme through application logic, most DBAs just use the services offered by the DBMS.

Typically, after a user's credentials have been authenticated by the authorization services, ASP.NET compares these credentials to file system permissions in NTFS (Windows NT File System) or to an XML file that lists authorized users and authorized roles, and lists the permissions that have been granted to each user and to each role.

The DBMS itself—the SQL Server in the present discussion—has a sophisticated internal security scheme, through which the DBA grants permissions. These permissions include the right to retrieve data from a table or a view, insert records, update records, delete records, modify table structures, add tables, remove tables, and grant permissions to other users. The DBA can grant any of these permissions to specified users and to roles, and the roles can then be granted to specified users.

Understanding SQL Server and the Microsoft Desktop Engine

SQL Server is Microsoft's scalable, robust DBMS. It supports complex applications with large databases, forms and reports, sophisticated security schemes and application logic, and operates in a multiuser environment. SQL Server competes with Oracle, Informix, IBM's DB2, and other mainframe relational database management systems.

Microsoft Desktop Engine (MSDE) is a package that ships with Visual Studio .NET Professional Edition, Office XP Professional Edition, and some other Microsoft offerings. MSDE gives application developers access to the SQL Server 7.0 back end. It allows you to create a new database and to manage certain aspects of an SQL Server database, including adding and deleting tables, columns, relationships, and other constraints; designing database diagrams; and creating views and stored procedures. MSDE is a subset of the full SQL Server package.

In this tutorial, you use the MSDE to create two SQL Server databases. The tutorial provides sufficient instruction to accomplish the task at hand, but this is not intended to be a complete treatment of the SQL Server DBMS. The purpose is only to demonstrate how a Visual Basic .NET Web Forms front end communicates with an SQL Server back-end database. The back end could just as well be an Oracle or DB2 database.

Using Visual Database Tools

Visual Database Tools comprise a set of services in Visual Studio .NET that allow you to create and manage an SQL Server 7.0 database, among other things. The easiest way to grasp what Visual Database Tools can do for you is to examine a sample database as it is being created.

Althea Brown, your colleague and friend on the Friendsville Games Development Team, has been experimenting with a very simple SQL Server database and accompanying Web Forms application. Thinking about dining services, seating assignments, and menus in the International Village, she came up with the notion of a simple Web Forms application that would display every athlete's favorite ice cream, so that the Dining Services staff could serve the favorite flavor to each athlete on the night after that athlete's competition. Althea considers even veteran athletes to be kids when eating ice cream, so she decided to name the database KidsFlavors.

In the text and figures in this section, you will see the design and construction of the KidsFlavors database, consisting of two tables:

- *tblFlavor*—The parent table, containing just two columns:
    - pkCode (the primary key, an integer)
    - Flavor (an ice cream flavor, a character string)
- *tblKid*—The child table, containing three columns:
    - pkKid (the primary key, an integer)
    - KidName (the name of an athlete, a character string)
    - Code (an integer, a foreign key referencing tblFlavor)

vuKidsFlavors is a view of this database, consisting of KidName and Flavor—for each KidName, this view displays that athlete's favorite flavor, based on the matching Code from tblKid and pkCode from tblFlavor.

Creating the Database

Althea created the KidsFlavors database in Server Explorer using the Create New SQL Server Database button available through Data Connections. In the Create Database dialog box, shown in Figure 10-9, Althea entered the server name, dadslaptop\vsdotnet, in the Server field; and she entered KidsFlavors in the New Database Name field. She maintained the default radio button selection of Use Windows NT Integrated Security. Had she selected the other radio button, Use SQL Server Authentication, then she would also have to supply a Login Name and Password. (In general, the login name and password technique is less secure, because this information is passed from the user through IIS to the database server as plain text.)

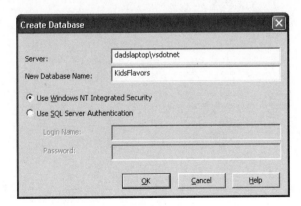

Figure 10-9: Create Database dialog box

Back in Server Explorer, the new database appears under Data Connections as dadslaptop\vsdotnet.KidsFlavors.dbo (dbo stands for database owner). Figure 10-10 shows Server Explorer with this data connection expanded, and shows also the elements of any SQL Server database: Database Diagrams, Tables, Views, Stored Procedures, and Functions.

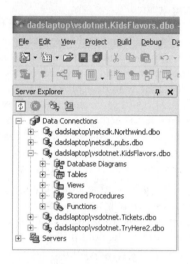

Figure 10-10: Server Explorer with the KidsFlavors database

Designing Tables in the New Database

Althea's next step was to create the first table, using the Visual Database Tools Database Designer. At the top of the Designer, the name of this object is given as dbo.Table1: Table Design (dadslaptop\vsdotnet.KidsFlavors). As shown in Figure 10-11, the elements in this table are pkCode and Flavor. SQL Server, like Access and other DBMSs, offers a variety of data types, but the sample databases in this tutorial use only int (a 4-byte integer), char (a character string with a default length of 10 bytes, but an assignable length that may be set by the dbo), and date (an 8-byte date and time field). In this case, Althea set the Flavor field to a length of 15 bytes. She designated pkCode as the primary key, and she deselected Allow Nulls for the Flavor field, because a row with no Flavor has no meaning. Also in Figure 10-11, the table has been saved under the name tblFlavor.

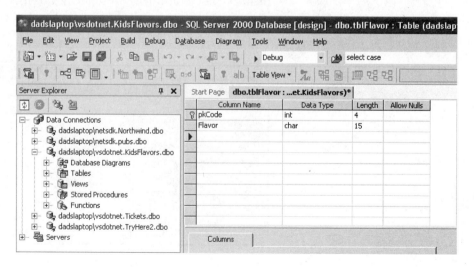

Figure 10-11: Table Designer for tblFlavor

Althea created the other table in the KidsFlavors database in a similar fashion. See Figure 10-12. A structural outline of this two-table database can be seen in Figure 10-13.

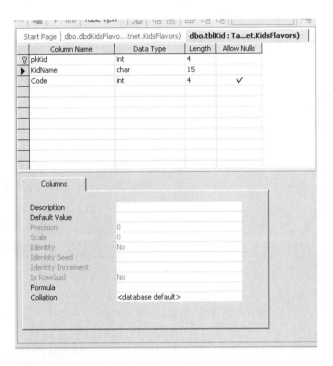

Figure 10-12: Table Designer for tblKid

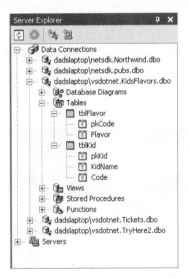

Figure 10-13: Server Explorer, showing the tables and columns in KidsFlavors

Creating Database Diagrams and Establishing Relationships

Before populating the tables of KidsFlavors, Althea thought it was a good idea to establish the relationship between them. In this way, SQL Server can check for referential integrity while data is being added. The easiest way to establish a relationship in Visual Database Tools is by drawing a database diagram. Althea added both tables

tip

••••••••••••••••••

▶ **A DBMS can enforce referential integrity. If two tables have a one-to-many relationship, then the primary key from the one side of the relationship is inserted as a foreign key on the many side of the relationship. The tables exhibit referential integrity if every occurrence of the foreign key (on the many side of the relationship) exists in one record on the one side of the relationship. In the KidsFlavors database, tblKid has an element called Code, a foreign key that points to the primary key in tblFlavor. These two tables exhibit referential integrity if every value for Code in tblKid matches a value of pkCode in tblFlavor.**

to the database diagram shown in Figure 10-14, and saved the diagram under the name dbdKidsFlavor.

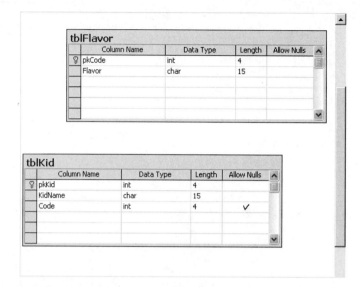

Figure 10-14: dbdKidsFlavor database diagram in ColumnName view

Althea then created the one-to-many relationship between these tables. In the Create Relationship dialog box, this foreign key relationship was named FK_tblKid_ tblFlavor by the Designer software, and is a one-to-many relationship between pkCode in tblFlavor (the primary key table) and Code in tblKid (the foreign key table). As shown in Figure 10-15, Cascade Update Related Fields was checked, so that a change to pkCode would be propagated to the child table. But Cascade Delete Related Records was not checked, because deleting an ice cream flavor should not cause the deletion of athletes who happen to like that flavor. The final database diagram appeared as in Figure 10-16. (This figure shows the ColumnName view of these tables.)

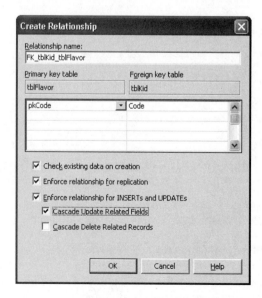

Figure 10-15: Create Relationships dialog box

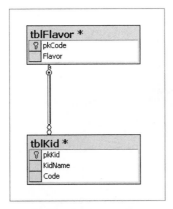

Figure 10-16: dbdKidsFlavors, final diagram

Populating Tables with Visual Database Tools

Althea's next step in using Visual Database Tools was to populate the two tables in the KidsFlavors database. You can open a table using Visual Database Tools, and directly type records into the tables. In Figures 10-17 and 10-18, data has been typed into tblFlavor and tblKid. Because of the referential integrity constraint, tblFlavor must be populated first.

pkCode	Flavor
1	orange
2	strawberry
3	vanilla
4	chocolate

Figure 10-17: tblFlavor with data

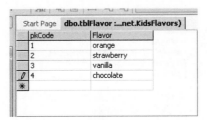

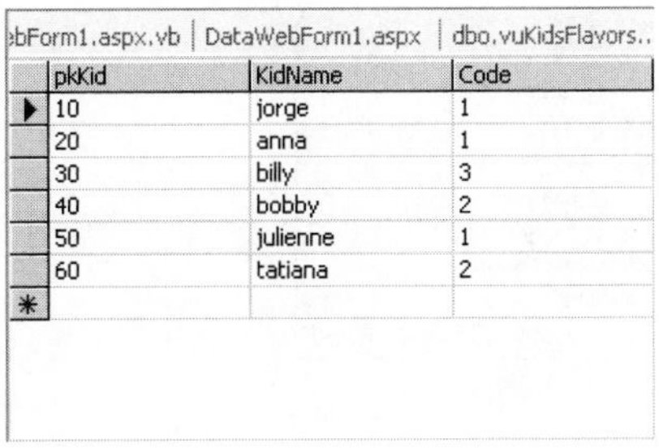

Figure 10-18: tblKid with data

Creating a Database View

The final step in this exercise was to create vuKidsFlavors, a database view created in Server Explorer with Visual Database Tools. The completed View Designer is shown in Figure 10-19. The symbols connecting the two tables show a one-to-many relationship between tblFlavor and tblKid: the diamond shape indicates a relationship, whereas the cardinality of this relationship is indicated by the key symbol on the one side of the relationship (because pkCode is the primary key of tblFlavor) and the infinity symbol on the many side of the relationship (because any given

Code can occur many times in tblKid). The final, fully expanded view of the KidsFlavors database in Server Explorer is shown in Figure 10-20.

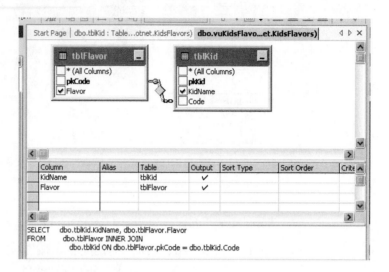

Figure 10-19: vuKidsFlavors

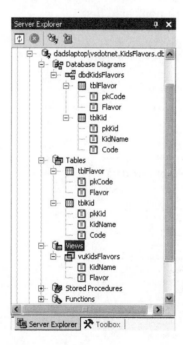

Figure 10-20: Server Explorer with fully expanded KidsFlavors database

Creating a Web Forms Application Using Datasets

You have already been exposed to most of the database theory and Web Forms theory that you need to create a Web Forms application using data adapters and datasets. In addition to the security aspects discussed at the beginning of this lesson, one other item differentiates Web Forms from Windows Forms database applications: data-bound controls in a Web Forms application are not updatable by default. The reason for this is fairly obvious upon careful examination: most data items are retrieved for display only, and the overhead associated with binding every control to every record and data value that is potentially updatable would consume too many page resources. Therefore, the general rule is that bound controls are not automatically updatable, and you must specifically code for the exceptions.

As you learned in Tutorial 9, ASP.NET supports two general approaches to data access. One approach uses data adapters to fill datasets. Insertions, deletions, and changes are then made to the rows in the in-memory dataset, after which these changes are propagated back to the database. The second approach uses data commands that work directly against the database, and data readers that are employed to read the retrieved data for those data commands that return a result set. The main application in Tutorial 9 used data adapters and datasets primarily, with supplementary functions provided through data commands, all in a Windows Forms application. Here, in Tutorial 10, the example you are going to look at in Lesson A employs datasets in a Web Forms application, but does not attempt to update the database. In Lesson C, you will build the main FigTickets application, which uses both datasets and data commands, and does include database updates.

Recall that in Tutorial 9 you used the Data Form Wizard for Windows applications, which can create a form that displays all records in a data grid format, or which displays one record in text boxes along with navigation controls to scroll through the dataset. Both versions are updatable, provided that the underlying dataset is updatable. The Data Form Wizard for Web applications can only provide a form for displaying all records in a data grid, and the data grid is not usually updatable.

Viewing the Sql Server Experiment Web Forms Application

Althea created the Sql Server Experiment application to demonstrate the notion of a Web Forms application accessing an SQL Server database using datasets. The database she used is the KidsFlavors database she created with Visual Database Tools. The sample application contains two forms:

- WebVuKidsFlavors.aspx displays vuKidsFlavors in a DataGrid control. The form was constructed manually, except for the use of the Data Adapter Configuration Wizard. WebVuKidsFlavors also contains a link to DataWebForm1.aspx.
- DataWebForm1.aspx was created with the Data Form Wizard for Web applications. It displays tblKid in a data grid.

Creating Sql Server Experiment and WebVuKidsFlavors

Althea initiated an ASP.NET Web application on *http://localhost* called Sql Server Experiment. With an SqlDataAdapter and the Data Adapter Configuration Wizard, she then created WebVuKidsFlavors.aspx, the first Web form in this application. When creating a new connection for this application, Althea entered in the data link properties shown in Figure 10-21.

At this point, Althea needed to know the name of the database server, in this case dadslaptop\vsdotnet. It may be typed in or selected from the drop-down list. As you may recall, when the KidsFlavors database was created, Windows NT Integrated Security was chosen. This selection must also be made here in item 2. If the server name is correct, then the KidsFlavors database should appear in the drop-down list in the combo box in item 3. Test Connection was employed to ensure that the connection could be established.

> **NOTE:** An important security issue should be noted here. Althea designed KidsFlavors on a local machine, and is now testing the connection on the same machine. Three-tier architecture is not involved at this juncture. Just because you can reach a Windows-protected resource while you are developing an application does not imply that your subsequent application, running on a Web server, will be able to reach that resource at runtime.

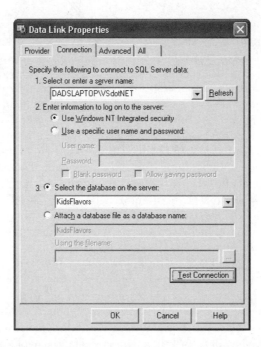

Figure 10-21: Data Link Properties dialog box called from the Data Adapter Configuration Wizard

As Althea followed the prompts in the Data Adapter Configuration Wizard, she chose the Query Builder, and based the query on the view previously stored in the database, called vuKidsFlavors. After choosing (All Columns), the Query Builder appeared as shown in Figure 10-22.

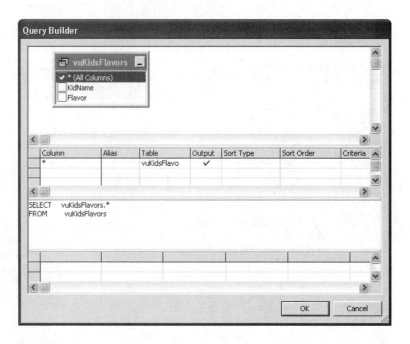

Figure 10-22: Query Builder

View Wizard Results, Figure 10-23, shows that this view cannot be updated. But that's okay, because you only want to display the view. Clicking Finish told the wizard to complete the creation of SqlConnection1 and SqlDataAdapter1.

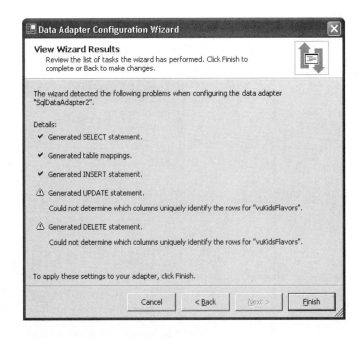

Figure 10-23: View Wizard Results frame

Althea generated the dataset using the Generate Dataset button at the bottom of the Properties window. As a result, dsKidsFlavors.xsd was created as a dataset class, and DsKidsFlavors1 was added to WebVuKidsFlavors.aspx. Figures 10-24 and 10-25 show the schema of dsKidsFlavors and the dataset properties of DsKidsFlavors1, respectively. These views are obtained from the Properties windows when DsKidsFlavors1 is selected in the tray under the form.

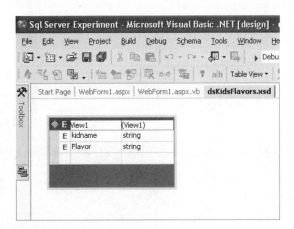

Figure 10-24: Schema of dsKidsFlavors

Althea then wanted to preview the data in DsKidsFlavors1. She was able to preview it through the Preview Data link in the Properties window of SqlDataAdapter1. The result is shown in Figure 10-26.

Figure 10-25: Dataset properties of DsKidsFlavors1

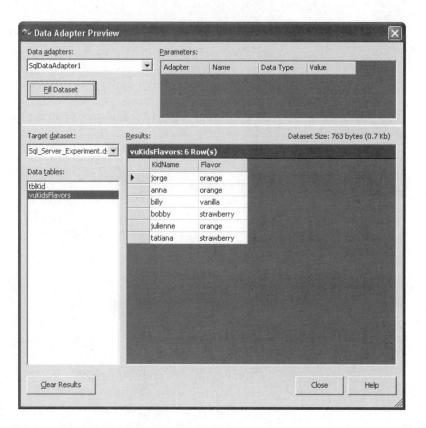

Figure 10-26: Data Adapter Preview window

Adding Controls to the Web Form

Althea added a label, a data grid, and a hyperlink to the form. Properties for these controls were set as shown in Figure 10-27. The completed GUI is shown in Figure 10-28.

Control	Property	Setting
Label1	Text	Kids and Their Flavors
	Font	X-Large
DataGrid1	ID	dgrdVuKidsFlavors
	DataSource	DsKidsFlavors1
	DataMember	vuKidsFlavors
	Font	Medium
	HorizontalAlign	Center
HyperLink1	Text	Kids table
	NavigateURL	(to be set after the DataWebForm is created)

Figure 10-27: Property settings of controls on WebVuKidsFlavors

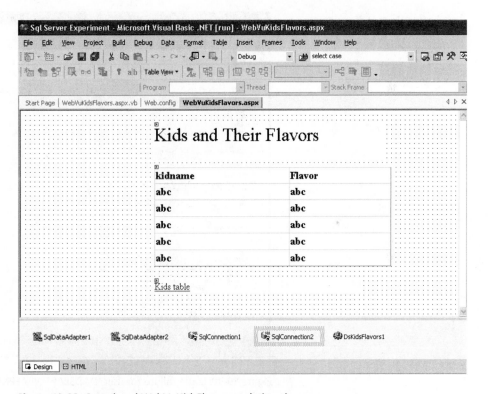

Figure 10-28: Completed WebVuKidsFlavors at design time

The only code needed for this form is shown in Figure 10-29. The Fill() method of a data adapter opens the connection, fills the dataset, and closes the connection. (Several of the Help screens and wizards in the first release of the software suggest that you must separately open and close the connection, but that is not actually necessary.) In Figure 10-29, the statement

```
dgrdVuKidsFlavors.DataBind()
```

binds dgrdVuKidsFlavors to its data source. Even though the DataSource property was set in the designer, the Web Forms version of the DataGrid control requires a separate DataBind() method in code after the dataset has been filled or changed. All of this code is enclosed inside a "If Not IsPostBack" selection statement, which ensures that the dataset is filled only the first time the page is loaded, not after every roundtrip between the client and the server.

```
Private Sub Page_Load(ByVal sender As System.Object, _
    ByVal e As System.EventArgs) Handles MyBase.Load
  If Not IsPostBack Then
    SqlDataAdapter1.Fill(DsKidsFlavors1)
    dgrdVuKidsFlavors.DataBind()
  End If
End Sub
```

Figure 10-29: Page_Load() procedure for WebVuKidsFlavors

Security Settings

When the program was executed for the first time, it generated the error page shown in Figure 10-30, with the message, "Login failed for user 'DADSLAPTOP\ASPNET'." The exception was raised by the attempt to open a connection to the database. As explained in the discussion of security models in 3-tier architecture, the problem here is that Windows does not recognize ASP.NET, and so authentication fails.

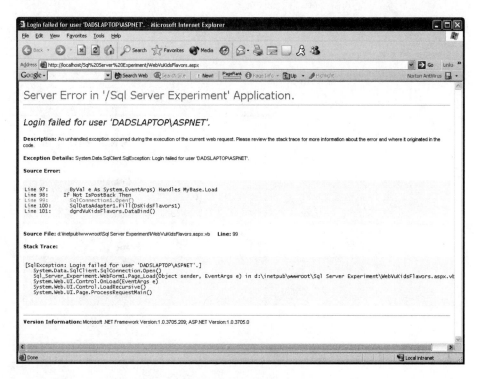

Figure 10-30: Login failure for user 'DADSLAPTOP\ASPNET'

Remember that when Althea was developing the application, making a connection, configuring a data adapter, and previewing the data, she was inside the Windows environment, operating as an authorized Windows user. She was behind the Windows firewall, so to speak. But when the program runs, it has two parts: the Web page is materialized on the local Windows machine, but the server code executes on the Web server named *http://localhost* under IIS. The client issued a call to server code in Page_Load(), and the server issued a call to Windows for access to the database, and that's where the code failed.

The solution to this problem comes in two stages. First, Althea must configure the application to impersonate the user machine. Second, she must tell IIS to use the Windows integrated security settings rather than the username and password scheme when accessing an ASP.NET managed resource.

Impersonation

Impersonation, the process of making the data source believe that a request is coming from an authorized user, is accomplished by inserting the line `<identity impersonate = "true" />` in the Web.config file at line 4, as shown in Figure 10-31. At runtime, IIS applies configuration settings in a hierarchical fashion, with the lowest-level setting taking precedence, overriding any higher-level setting. So, in this case, IIS is instructed to use the credentials of the user machine when passing a resource request to Windows.

```
<?xml version="1.0" encoding="utf-8" ?>
<configuration>
  <system.web>
            <identity impersonate = "true" />
```

Figure 10-31: Web.config file in Sql Server Experiment project

After the change to Web.config was made, Althea ran the program again, resulting in a new error page, shown in Figure 10-32. Now the message is, "Login failure for user 'DADSLAPTOP\IUSR_VAIO'." As you can see, IIS has provided credentials to Windows with the username IUSR_*<machinename>*, but Windows is still rejecting those credentials. Impersonation has worked as far as it can, but you still need to change the security settings for IIS in the Windows environment.

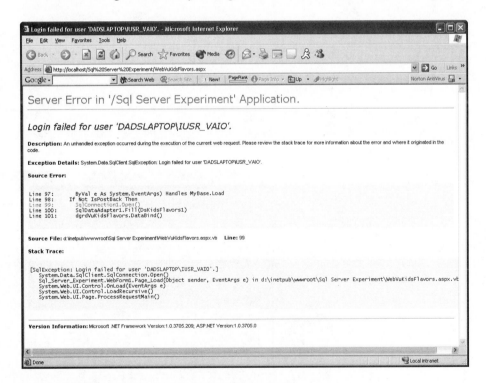

Figure 10-32: Login failure for user 'DADSLAPTOP\IUSR_VAIO'

Internet Information Server Security Settings

Althea then needed to change the IIS security settings to be compatible with the security set in Web.config and in the database. To change the settings, Althea opened the Internet Information Services window in the Administrative Tools of the Control Panel. Figure 10-33 shows the IIS window with all of the Web Forms projects on this machine. One can start or stop the IIS service by clicking the Start or Stop icons. The Default Web Site Properties are displayed in Figure 10-34.

Stop Item button

Start Item button

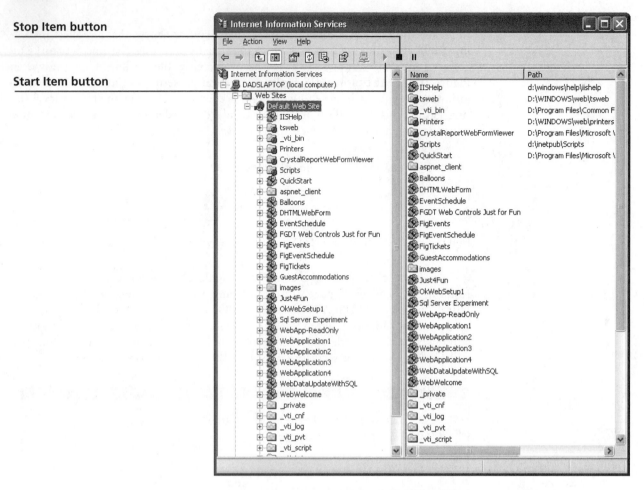

Figure 10-33: Internet Information Services folder

Figure 10-34: Property pages for Default Web Site

Althea accessed the security settings for Default Web Site by clicking the Directory Security tab, which contains the security settings for access to the folders underneath Default Web Site, and she clicked Edit, which opens the Authentication Methods dialog box. Initially, Anonymous access is selected, and the name IUSR_VAIO is visible. Althea unchecked Anonymous access, Digest authentication for Windows domain servers, and Basic authentication (password is sent in clear text), if any of these were checked, and checked only Integrated Windows authentication, as shown in Figure 10-35.

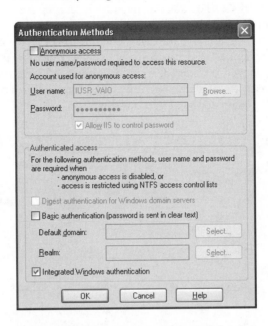

Figure 10-35: Authentication Methods dialog box

This completes the security settings. Running the application results in the display shown in Figure 10-36.

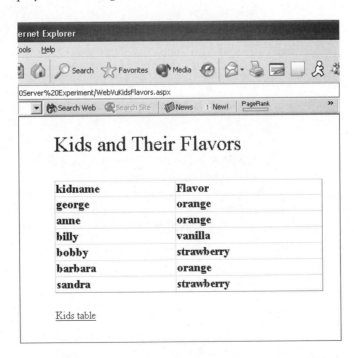

Figure 10-36: Sql Server Experiment at runtime, showing WebVuKidsFlavors

Adding a Data Web Form

Althea created a second form for the Sql Server Experiment, using the Data Form Wizard for ASP.NET applications. In the wizard, she created a new dataset called dsKids, selected the KidsFlavors data connection, and selected all of the columns in tblKid. The wizard created the form shown in Figure 10-37. The wizard instantiates an OleDbConnection and OleDbDataAdapter, even when accessing an SQL Server database. The adapter includes Select, Insert, Update, and Delete OleDbCommand objects, so that it is possible to update the database in code. However, the data grid itself is not updatable by default; in order to implement an update capability, the developer needs to create additional code to identify a row in the dataset that is to be changed or deleted, write the code to change the dataset, propagate those changes back to the database, and rebind the data grid to the dataset. You will do this with the main application in Lesson C.

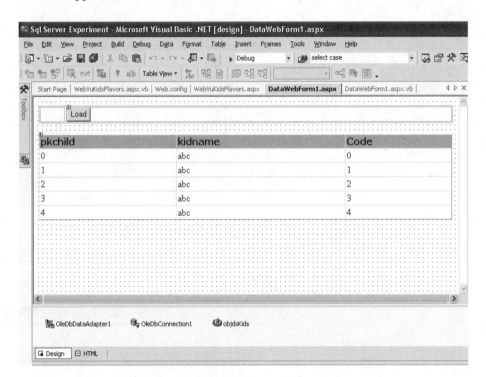

Figure 10-37: DataWebForm1.aspx at design time

Althea then set DataWebForm1.aspx as the NavigateURL property of Hyperlink1 in WebVuKidsFlavors. When the revised application runs, and the Kids table hyperlink is clicked on the opening page, only the Load button appears on DataWebForm1. The reason for this is that a DataGrid control on a Web Form is not rendered at all if it is empty. Clicking the Load button fills the dataset and causes the data grid to appear, as in Figure 10-38.

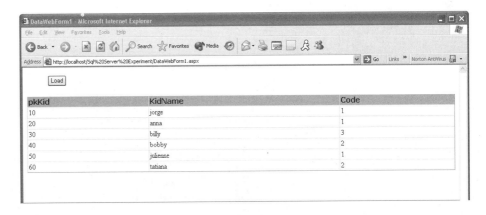

Figure 10-38: DataWebForm1 with filled DataGrid control

You have now completed Lesson A. Don't forget to do the following end-of-lesson questions and exercises.

SUMMARY

- Security considerations make Web-based database processing markedly different from Windows-based processing.
- Each tier—the database server, the Web server, and the client—imposes its own security layer.
- Security elements generally include authentication, authorization, and impersonation.
- Impersonation facilitates anonymous access, but also requires careful application of security measures to protect sensitive data.
- Windows NT Integrated Security provides a highly secure environment, but is only available within a completely Windows domain.
- IIS provides these levels and types of authentication services: anonymous access, basic authentication, digest authentication, integrated Windows authentication, and certificate authentication.
- Authorizations or permissions are usually provided by the DBMS.
- Microsoft Desktop Engine (MSDE) is a package provided with Visual Studio .NET that allows users to create and manage an SQL Server database.
- Visual Database Tools describes a set of database management tools in Visual Studio .NET. These tools allow the developer to view the structure of a variety of data sources, and to manage or create certain types of data sources.
- Database diagrams allow the developer to design tables and table relationships.

QUESTIONS

1. The authentication regime prescribed as a minimum by W3C is called _____.

2. The Web server software available in the Microsoft world is called _____.

3. What three machines (or virtual machines) are included in 3-tier architecture? _____ _____ _____.

4. The subset of SQL Server that ships with Visual Studio .NET is called _____.

5. The process in which a Web server substitutes the credentials of a known machine in lieu of the credentials of an anonymous user is known as _____.

6. After a user is authenticated, the DBMS usually handles the task of _____.

7. The database management tools available in Visual Studio .NET fall under the collective name, _____ Tools.

8. How are usernames and passwords passed in the authentication regime prescribed as a minimum by W3C?

9. How are user credentials passed in Windows integrated security?

10. In Server Explorer, _____ allow the developer to design and draw relationships between tables.

CRITICAL THINKING

At the end of each lesson, reflective questions are intended to provoke you into considering the material you have just read at a deeper level.

1. Considering the choice between basic authentication and digest authentication, when would you choose to use each one? Why?

2. Consider the choice between Microsoft Access and SQL Server. When would you choose to use each one? Why?

EXERCISES

1. Describe the security scheme used in one of the computer labs at your school. What portions of this scheme must a Visual Basic .NET programmer be aware of? What permissions must the programmer have? What provisions must be taken in the Visual Basic .NET programs in order to operate within that security scheme?

2. Describe the security scheme used for administrative computing at your school. Are there different security schemes for student records, human resources, e-mail, and so on? If you were hired to work as a programmer on the student records system, what portions of the security scheme would you need to know? What permissions would you need? What provisions must be taken in your Visual Basic .NET programs in order to operate within that security scheme?

LESSON B
objectives

After completing this lesson, you will be able to:

■ Create a new, or modify an existing, SQL Server database using Visual Database Tools, including the ability to add or modify tables, columns, and constraints

■ Populate an SQL Server database both manually—using Visual Database Tools—and from inside a Windows Forms application

Visual Database Tools

Tasks for the FGDT

The Friendsville Games Development Team studied security issues and Visual Database Tools in Lesson A, along with Server Explorer and the Microsoft Desktop Engine. In Lesson B, you and your FGDT colleagues gain some experience with Visual Database Tools by creating and loading the Tickets database. You create FigTickets, the main application in this tutorial, in Lesson C.

Specifically, Lesson B shows you the details of using Visual Database Tools in Visual Studio .NET. This includes creating an SQL Server database, adding tables, modifying table structures, inserting data, and designing database diagrams. The lesson also includes a Windows Forms application, used to automate the initial population of tables in a database.

Creating a New SQL Server Database

Development of the complete Friendsville International Games Ticket Sales application is a complex and time-consuming task for the Friendsville Games Development Team. Scalable, secure, robust, Web-based, commercial-ready computer applications are among the most challenging and complex project assignments in the software industry today. The complete system calls for a sophisticated SQL Server database and a robust Visual Basic .NET application to match. Such a project would require five or more man-years of development effort.

By comparison, the Tickets SQL Server database and FigTickets Visual Basic .NET application that you develop in Lessons B and C of this tutorial constitute a very modest effort. Nevertheless, these tasks let you experience the basic functionality of this development environment, and encourage you to imagine its potential.

A Note on Installing and Starting MSDE

MSDE is installed by default when Visual Studio .NET is installed, but optionally you can choose not to install it. To run and replicate the applications in this tutorial, you need either the full SQL Server package or MSDE. You also need to be able to identify the instance name of at least one SQL Server instance on the computer you are using, or have that name be accessible to you on a remote server on which you have permissions. At installation time, the administrator can choose an instance name or accept the default. Depending on which package was actually installed on your computer, default instance names may include NetSDK (meaning .NET Software Developers Kit) or vsdotnet (meaning Visual Studio .NET). You may need to ask the system administrator of your local area network to help you identify the server and SQL Server or MSDE instance name. If you are the administrator (for example, if you are using your own personal computer), you can view the list of Services under Administrative Tools in the Control Panel. If you find a service called MSSQLSERVER, then you are running the full SQL Server package, and the instance name is (usually) the same as the machine name. If you find a service whose name begins MSSQL$, then you have MSDE installed, and the instance name is the rest of the word following MSSQL$. For example, on dadslaptop, the list of Services in Administrative Tools includes MSSQL$NetSDK and MSSQL$VSdotNET. Hence, the MSDE servers on dadslaptop are dadslaptop\netsdk and dadslaptop\vsdotnet.

You also need to make sure that SQL Server or MSDE is running. To do so, you must issue the following command from the Run menu:

```
NET START MSSQL$<instance name>
```

If MSDE is already running when you issue this command, nothing troublesome occurs.

In the event that you do not have MSDE or SQL Server installed, you can still follow along with the examples in this tutorial by examining the text and figures carefully, and by replicating the database designs in Microsoft Access.

Designing the Tickets Database

The Tickets database must keep track of the following entity classes: the user (customer) who orders and purchases tickets, the order and sale (which is tied to a particular customer and includes any number of tickets), and the ticket itself. Each ticket must identify details concerning the event and venue. For this reason, the event and venue entities must also be included. Figure 10-39 shows an E-R diagram of the Tickets database.

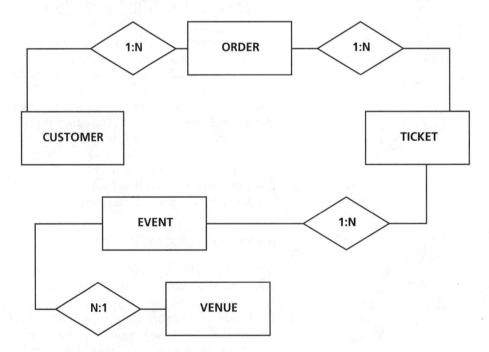

Figure 10-39: E-R diagram for the Tickets database

A common syntax for displaying relational table designs is as follows:

```
'TABLENAME (PrimaryKey, ForeignKey, NonKeyAttribute(s))
```

No spaces are permitted in any of these words. The table name appears in all uppercase, whereas the attributes appear in mixed case, enclosed in parentheses following the table name. The primary key is underscored. Any foreign key is boxed—recall from Tutorial 9 that a foreign key is an attribute in one table that also appears as a primary key in another table. The foreign key implements the relationship between two entities, and is used by the DBMS to enforce referential integrity.

Using this syntax, the design of the necessary tables in the Tickets database appears in Figure 10-40.

```
TBLUSER (Email, Password, LName, FName, Street, City, StateOrProvince,
PostalCode, Country)
TBLORDER (OrderID, OrderStatus, Email, OrderDate)
TBLTICKET (TicketID, EventID, Category, Sequence, Price, OrderID)
TBLEVENT (EventID, Sport, EventName, Gender, ScoringMethod, Country1,
Country2, VenueIndex, Schedule, StartTime, PricingSchedule)
TBLVENUE (VenueIndex, VenueName)
```

Figure 10-40: Table designs for the Tickets database

Notice that tblEvent reflects the contents of Events.txt the last time you encountered it in Tutorial 8, and tblVenue contains the elements of pastrVenue() when you last saw it in Tutorial 7. Although FigTickets does not use absolutely every element in tblEvent, the general design principle of reusability suggests that the FGDT develop one method of storing event information, and use it for all applications that need any event information. Actually, this principle of reusability is one of the main advantages of a database: the use of one common database for all applications throughout an enterprise greatly reduces data redundancy and enhances data consistency.

Most of the domain definitions in this database should be obvious, but several require additional explanation, and are given in Figure 10-41.

Table.Column	Domain definition
tblOrder.OrderStatus	O=Order, S=Sale
tblTicket.Category	Seating category: W, X, Y, or Z
tblTicket.Sequence	Sequential number of tickets within each seating category for each EventID
tblTicket.Price	$50 * (1 or 2 or 3 or 4), based on seating category (W or X or Y or Z)

Figure 10-41: Domain definitions in the Tickets database

The FigTickets application and Tickets database do not support two of the more sophisticated information requirements relating to the public sale of tickets over the Web: first, in a complete ticket sales application, each ticket must be related to a particular gate, section, row, and seat number, based on the physical layout of each venue. Instead, FigTickets includes, for demonstration purposes only, a small tblTickets, with 10 seats in each of four ticket categories (W, X, Y, and Z) for each event, and with a price of $50, $100, $150, or $200 (depending on the seating category). Second, in a complete e-commerce application, a secure payments module is needed for accepting credit-card payments over the Web. In many retail applications, the payments module is outsourced to a company that specializes in that aspect of e-business. In FigTickets, the payments issue is not addressed.

Initializing a New Database and Data Connection

From Server Explorer, you can create a new SQL Server database, as you have seen in Lesson A. You can add tables, columns, and constraints. You can create database diagrams in order to specify relationships. Althea demonstrated these items in Lesson A; in Lesson B, you have the opportunity to implement them yourself. In this lesson, you will also use a Windows Forms application to populate the database.

If Server Explorer is not visible in the Visual Studio .NET IDE, you can make it visible by clicking View | Server Explorer.

If you do not know the name of your database server and do not know how to find it, refer to the "A Note on Installing and Starting MSDE" section earlier in Lesson B.

If the Tickets database already exists on your server (which could occur if you installed the FigTickets application to that server), then name the database MyTickets instead.

To create an SQL Server database called Tickets:

1 Open **Server Explorer**. Right-click **Data Connections**, and then click **Create New SQL Server Database** from the shortcut menu. In the Create Database dialog box, enter the name of your server, and enter **Tickets** as the name of the database. Verify that **Use Windows NT Integrated Security** is selected. The completed dialog box should appear as in Figure 10-42, but with the name of your server instead of dadslaptop\vsdotnet.

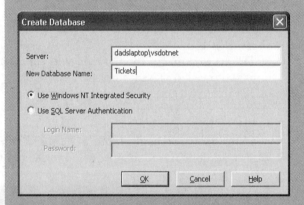

Figure 10-42: Create Database dialog box, creating the Tickets database

2 Click **OK**. After the database has been created, you need to add the five tables that make up this database. Start with tblEvent. Expand **Tickets** in Server Explorer. Then, right-click **Tables**, and click **New Table**. Type in the column names, data types, and lengths shown in Figure 10-43. Designate EventID as the primary key by clicking its row and then clicking the Set Primary Key icon. Using the **File | Save** commands, save this table under the name **tblEvent**.

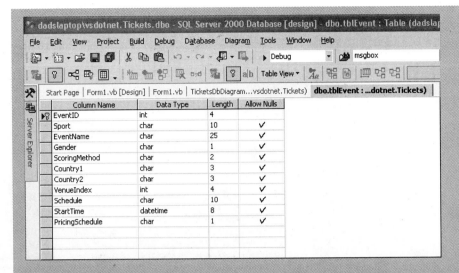

Figure 10-43: Design of tblEvent

3 Add the other four tables to the database in the same fashion, typing in column names, data types, and lengths, assigning the primary key, and saving the table under the specified name, as shown in Figures 10-44, 10-45, 10-46, and 10-47. In some cases, the logical design dictates that Allow Nulls be deselected. For example, in tblUser, a valid record must have (in addition to the always required primary key) the user's last name and password. In tblTicket, every field except OrderID is required. In tblOrder, an e-mail address is required, because an order with no customer is invalid. And both fields are required in tblVenue.

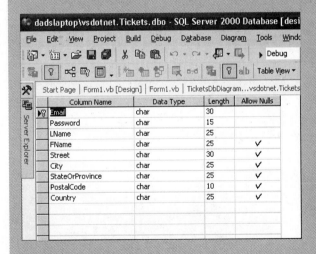

Figure 10-44: Design of tblUser

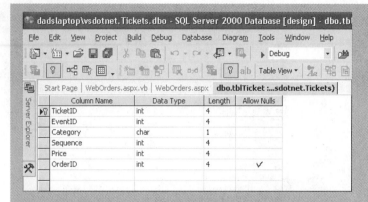

Figure 10-45: Design of tblTicket

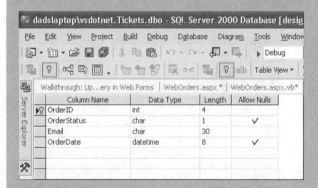

Figure 10-46: Design of tblOrder

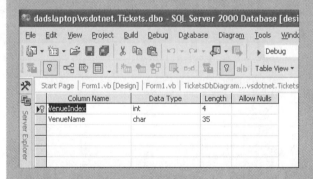

Figure 10-47: Design of tblVenue

4   After you have created the tables, you must establish the relationships among these tables. Create a database diagram for the Tickets database in Server Explorer by expanding the **Tickets** database name (if necessary), right-clicking **Database Diagrams**, and clicking **New Diagram**. In the Add Table dialog box, add all five tables to the diagram, and then click **Close**. Save the diagram as **TicketsDbDiagram**.

5   To modify your initial diagram, which shows all five tables in the Standard view, click inside the diagram but outside any table, then click **Edit | Select All** (note that all five tables are selected), and select **Diagram | Table View | Modify Custom**. Move columns to the left or to the right as needed, so that you end up with only **Column Name** and **Condensed Type** on the right, as shown in Figure 10-48. This view displays each table with the table name, the names of the columns in the table, the data type and length in a combined Condensed Type field, and the designation of the table's primary key. Click **OK**. You have now modified the Custom view, but have not yet applied that view to any table. Now select **Diagram | Table View | Custom**. Lengthen each table so that all columns are displayed. Drag the tables as necessary around the screen so that the tables in the diagram are positioned roughly as shown in Figure 10-49.

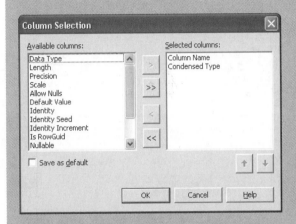

Figure 10-48: Column Selection dialog box

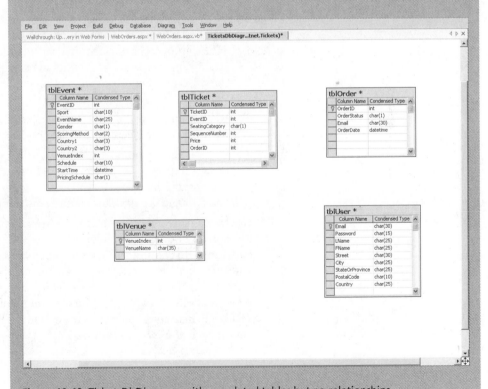

Figure 10-49: TicketsDbDiagram, with completed tables but no relationships

6   To create a relationship between tblEvent and tblVenue, drag the **VenueIndex** field from tblEvent to the VenueIndex field of tblVenue. In the Create Relationship dialog box shown in Figure 10-50, note that the relationship name suggested by Visual Database Tools is FK_tblEvent_tblVenue1, the field VenueIndex in tblVenue is listed for the Primary key table, and VenueIndex in tblEvent is listed for the Foreign key table. Referential integrity constraints are enforced for inserts and updates, but not for deletes. The reason for these settings is threefold:

Figure 10-50: Create Relationship dialog box

1. When a new record is inserted in tblEvent, the referential integrity constraint ensures that the VenueIndex in that new record is either blank (because no venue has been assigned yet) or already exists in tblVenue (meaning the assigned venue is real).

2. If the VenueIndex for a particular venue changes, then the software automatically updates the VenueIndex field of corresponding records in tblEvent.

3. If a particular venue is deleted, the corresponding records in tblEvent should not be deleted. That is, if a particular venue is dropped from the Friendsville International Games, events scheduled for that venue must be reassigned to another venue, not dropped from the Games.

7   Use the same technique—dragging the primary key from one table to tie it to the corresponding field in another table—in order to create relationships between tblEvent and tblTicket (foreign key in tblTicket=EventID), tblOrder and tblTicket (foreign key in tblTicket=OrderID), and tblUser and tblOrder (foreign key in tblOrder=Email). Think about each relationship, and assign referential integrity constraints that seem reasonable. The completed TicketDbDiagram should appear similar to Figure 10-51. Save the diagram and then click **Yes** to continue.

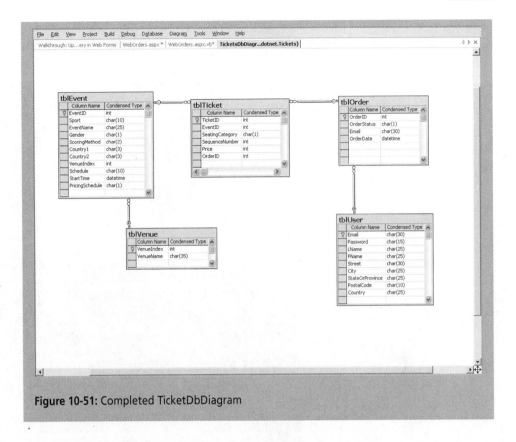

Figure 10-51: Completed TicketDbDiagram

Inserting Records in tblVenue, tblUser, and tblOrder

Because of the referential integrity constraint between tblVenue and tblEvent, you must insert the eight venues into tblVenue (parent table) before you insert the 145 events into tblEvent (child table). You should also create a few records in tblUser and tblOrder so you have some data to work with when you begin developing the FigTickets application. Again, due to the referential integrity constraint between tblUser and tblOrder, the records in tblUser must exist before corresponding records are inserted in tblOrder—that is, a customer must exist before an order for that customer can be placed. This data entry is most easily accomplished manually using Visual Database Tools.

To insert records into tblVenue, tblUser, and tblOrder:

1   In Server Explorer, double-click **tblVenue**, and type in the records shown in Figure 10-52. These are the eight venues for the Games that you have used in earlier tutorials.

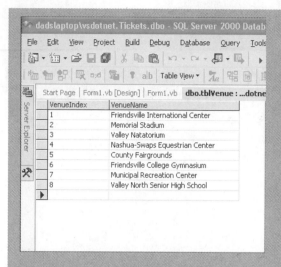

Figure 10-52: Records in tblVenue

2 In Server Explorer, double-click **tblUser**, and type in the records shown in Figure 10-53. These are the records belonging to the FGDT, which you also saw in Tutorial 3. For demonstration purposes, you assume that FGDT members will also purchase tickets to attend the Games.

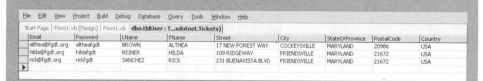

Figure 10-53: Records in tblUser

3 In Server Explorer, double-click **tblOrder**, and type in the records shown in Figure 10-54. In previewing the application at the beginning of this tutorial, these are Hilda's two orders. (At this point, the order details are empty, because tblTickets is empty.)

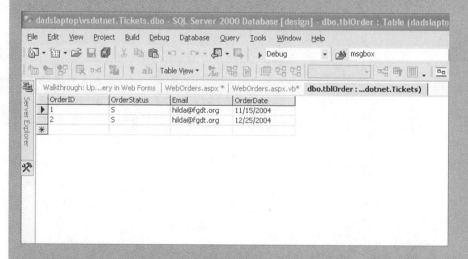

Figure 10-54: Records in tblOrder

Populating a Database from a Windows Forms Application

While you were working in Visual Database Tools on the Tickets SQL Server database, Rick Sanchez began writing a Windows Forms application to populate two of the large tables, tblEvent and tblTicket. The FGDT decided to load tblEvent with all of the Friendsville International Games events that you have been using since Tutorial 5. Rick used Events.txt as it last appeared in Tutorial 8 as his data source. Hilda Reiner suggested that Rick keep the size of tblTicket to a reasonable number for purposes of application development, so Rick chose to create a small tblTicket table consisting of 10 tickets in each of four seating categories for each of the 145 events in tblEvent. When you implement Rick's program, LoadTablesForFigTickets, you must modify the data connection so it points to the Tickets database (or MyTickets database, if you renamed it) on your computer. But other than this small modification, the program works as is.

▶ **tip**
This is another example of code reuse, a recurring theme in this text. Efficient programmers write code that lends itself to reuse. Note that Module1 includes a number of items that are not needed in LoadTablesForFigTickets, but it does include the layout of structEvent, the declaration of pastructEvents(), the procedure that loads pastructEvents(), and the counter pNumEvents. In terms of programmer productivity, the most efficient solution is to simply copy and reuse Module1.vb from the UpClose project in Tutorial 8.

To load and run LoadTablesForFigTickets, in order to populate tblEvent and tblTicket:

1 Open the **LoadTablesForFigTickets.sln** solution in the VB.NET\Student\Tut10\ LoadTablesForFigTickets folder.

2 Open **Module1**, and examine this code. It should look familiar, because this is a copy of Module1 from Tutorial 8.

3 Examine the **LoadEvents()** procedure in Module1. This project also uses Events.txt, copied from Tutorial 8. The LoadEvents() procedure loads the records in Events.txt into pastructEvents(), and stores the number of those records in pNumEvents.

4 Open **Form1** in the Designer as shown in Figure 10-55. By examining this form, you can see that it uses an SqlConnection object, whose ConnectionString property you must modify so that it points to your Tickets database.

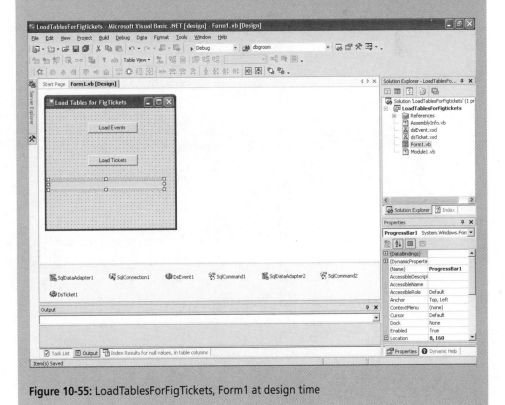

Figure 10-55: LoadTablesForFigTickets, Form1 at design time

NOTE: This GUI is typical of a small utility intended to be used only during project development of a larger project, in this case, FigTickets. Rick did not spend much time making an attractive GUI or properly naming every item. The program is sufficiently intelligible to the FGDT while they are working on FigTickets.

5 Select the **ConnectionString** property of SqlConnection1. Click the **list arrow**. Choose the **Tickets** database (shown in Figure 10-56), which should be visible because you just had this database open in Server Explorer. If you do not see the Tickets database, then click **New Connection**, and, in the Data Link Properties page, enter your computer's **server name** (or select it from the drop-down list), click the **Use Windows NT Integrated Security** radio button, and select your **Tickets** database (by typing or by using the list arrow). Test the Connection to make sure it works. The page should appear as in Figure 10-57 (but with your computer's server name). Click **OK**.

Figure 10-56: ConnectionString property

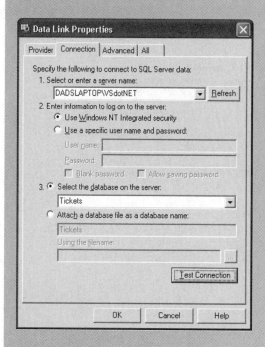

Figure 10-57: Data Link Properties screen

6 Examine the properties of the two SqlDataAdapters, two datasets, and two SqlCommands. SqlCommand1's CommandText object contains an SQL Delete statement that empties tblEvent. SqlDataAdapter1 creates the DsEvent1 dataset, and SqlDataAdapter1's InsertCommand object contains the SQL Insert statement that inserts new records from the dataset into tblEvent in the database when the data adapter's Update() method is invoked. Similarly, SqlCommand2's CommandText object deletes all of the records in tblTicket; SqlDataAdapter2 creates DsTicket1, and SqlDataAdapter2's InsertCommand object contains the SQL Insert statement that loads all of the rows from DsTicket1 into tblTicket in the database.

NOTE: All of these activities could be accomplished with the SqlDataAdapters and datasets; the SqlCommands did not need to be created. All of these activities could also have been accomplished with the two SqlCommands (which delete all of the records in tblEvent and tblTicket), along with two more SqlCommands that would insert records into tblEvent and tblTicket. As you have seen in other examples, data commands operate directly on the underlying tables, whereas data adapters use the disconnected dataset as an intermediary. Rick used both types of objects (that is, data adapters and data commands) in order to demonstrate both approaches to data access. Also notice that Rick used the SQL Data Provider object model for all of these objects, because it is optimized to work with SQL Server. He could just as easily have used the OleDb Data Provider model, which works with any OleDb-compliant data source, but is less efficient.

7 Examine the GUI for Form1. It has just three controls: btnLoadEvents loads tblEvent, btnLoadTickets loads tblTicket, and ProgressBar1 keeps track of the progress as rows are being added to DsTicket1.

8 Open the **Code Editor** for Form1.vb, built on the model for database updates used in Tutorial 9. Figure 10-58 shows the code for loading tblEvent. As you can see, btnLoadEvents_Click() performs the following actions:

- Calls LoadEvents(), the Module1 procedure that loads events into pastructEvents() from the source text file Events.txt
- Calls EmptyEventsDataset(), a procedure that executes SqlCommand1, which deletes the existing records in the tblEvent table of the Tickets database
- Uses a For loop to construct one row in DsEvent1.tblEvent for each record in pastructEvents(), and adds that row to the dataset
- Calls UpdateEventsDataset(), a procedure that uses the Update() method of SqlDataAdapter1 to insert all of the rows from DsEvent1.tblEvent into tblEvent of the Tickets database

```
Private Sub btnLoadEvents_Click(ByVal sender As _
    System.Object, ByVal e As System.EventArgs) _
    Handles btnLoadEvents.Click
  Dim workRow As DataRow
  Dim i, j As Integer
  LoadEvents()
  EmptyEventsDataset()
  For i = 0 To pNumEvents - 1
    workRow = DsEvent1.tblEvent.NewRow()
    With pastructEvents(i)
      workRow(0) = .EventID
      workRow(1) = .Sport
      workRow(2) = .EventName
      workRow(3) = .Gender
      workRow(4) = .ScoringMethod
      workRow(5) = .Country1
      workRow(6) = .Country2
      workRow(7) = .VenueIndex
      workRow(8) = .Schedule
      workRow(9) = DateAdd(DateInterval.Year, _
        1753, .StartTime)
      workRow(10) = .PricingSchedule
    End With
    DsEvent1.tblEvent.Rows.Add(workRow)
  Next
  UpdateEventsDataset()
  MsgBox("Update of tblEvent was successful")
End Sub

Private Sub EmptyEventsDataset()
  SqlConnection1.Open()
  SqlCommand1.ExecuteNonQuery()
  SqlConnection1.Close()
End Sub

Private Sub UpdateEventsDataset()
  SqlConnection1.Open()
  SqlDataAdapter1.Update(DsEvent1)
  DsEvent1.AcceptChanges()
  SqlConnection1.Close()
End Sub
```

Figure 10-58: Procedures that insert records into tblEvent

9 Now examine the code for loading records into tblTicket, which is quite similar to loading records into tblEvent. The only significant difference is that records in tblEvent come from Events.txt, whereas records in tblTicket are constructed inside a set of nested For loops. Figure 10-59 shows the code for loading tblTicket. As you can see, btnLoadTickets_Click() performs the following actions:

- Calls EmptyTicketsDataset(), a procedure that executes SqlCommand2, which deletes the existing records in the tblTicket table of the Tickets database
- Uses a For loop that iterates pNumEvents (that is, 145) times, uses a nested loop that iterates four times, and uses a further nested loop that iterates 10 times; the innermost loop constructs one row in DsTicket1.tblTicket, and adds that row to the dataset
- Calls UpdateTicketsDataset(), a procedure that uses the Update() method of SqlDataAdapter2 to insert all of the rows from DsTicket1.tblTicket into tblTicket of the Tickets database

```
Private Sub btnLoadTickets_Click(ByVal sender As _
    System.Object, ByVal e As System.EventArgs) _
    Handles btnLoadTickets.Click
  Dim workRow As DataRow
  Dim TicketID As Long
  Dim EventID, intSeatCategory, _
    SequenceNumber As Integer
  Dim SeatingCategory As String
  EmptyTicketsDataset()
  For EventID = 1 To 145
    ProgressBar1.Value = EventID
    For intSeatCategory = 1 To 4
      For SequenceNumber = 1 To 10
        TicketID += 1
        SeatingCategory = Chr(intSeatCategory + Asc("V"))
        workRow = DsTicket1.tblTicket.NewRow()
        workRow(0) = TicketID
        workRow(1) = EventID
        workRow(2) = SeatingCategory
        workRow(3) = SequenceNumber
        workRow(4) = 50 * intSeatCategory 'Price
        DsTicket1.tblTicket.Rows.Add(workRow)
      Next
    Next
  Next
  UpdateTicketsDataset()
  MsgBox("Update  of tblTicket was successful")
End Sub

Private Sub EmptyTicketsDataset()
  SqlConnection1.Open()
  SqlCommand2.ExecuteNonQuery()
  SqlConnection1.Close()
End Sub

Private Sub UpdateTicketsDataset()
  SqlConnection1.Open()
  SqlDataAdapter2.Update(DsTicket1)
  DsTicket1.AcceptChanges()
  SqlConnection1.Close()
End Sub
```

Figure 10-59: Procedures that insert records into tblTicket

10 Run the **LoadTablesForFigTickets** application. Click **Load Events**. After about 30 seconds, the message "Update of tblEvent was successful" should appear. Click **OK**. Click **Load Tickets**. A progress bar quickly tracks the creation of rows in the dataset. When the progress bar is complete, wait about 30 seconds for the message "Update of tblTicket was successful" to appear. Click **OK**. Close the application.

11 Now that tblTicket has been populated, you can complete the sample ticket orders for Hilda Reiner. In Server Explorer, open **tblTicket**. Insert OrderID **1** on TicketIDs 1 and 2, and insert OrderID **2** on TicketIDs 98, 99, and **100**. You can now close the **LoadTablesForFigTickets** solution in the IDE.

You have now completed Lesson B. Consider answering the questions and doing the following exercises before proceeding with Lesson C.

SUMMARY

- Robust, scalable, commercial-ready, Internet-based applications offer some of the most interesting challenges in computer program development today.
- A common method of expressing a table design is as follows:
  TABLENAME (<u>PrimaryKey</u>, ForeignKey, NonKeyAttribute(s))
- Visual Database Tools in Visual Studio .NET use the Microsoft Database Engine to create a new SQL Server database.
- You can design tables, add and modify columns, and implement various constraints from Server Explorer. You can easily define relationships with the Database Diagrams facility.
- You can add records manually in Server Explorer. You can also create a Windows Forms application to load records into a database.
- All of these activities can take place behind the firewall, so security is not an issue.

QUESTIONS

1. What objects can be designed through Server Explorer in an existing SQL Server database?

2. What objects can be designed through Server Explorer in an existing Microsoft Access database?

3. What column attributes can be designed through Server Explorer in an existing SQL Server database?

4. Two entities have a many-to-many relationship between them. What is the minimum number of tables necessary to implement the two entities and their relationship?

5. What is the difference between an SqlDataAdapter and an OleDbDataAdapter?

6. The SqlDataAdapter and the OlDbDataAdapter both contain four data command objects. Name these data command objects.

For questions 7–10, use these table designs:

   T1 (p, q, r, s)

   T2 (<u>a</u>, <u>b</u>, c, d, q)

7. The table names are _____ and _____ .

8. The primary keys are _____ in table _____ and _____ in table _____ .

9. The foreign key is _____ in table _____ .

10. The non-key attributes are _____ .

CRITICAL THINKING

At the end of each lesson, reflective questions are intended to provoke you into considering the material you have just read at a deeper level.

1. Consider the design of the Tickets database. What elements must be added to this design in order to make it the basis of the "robust, scalable, commercial-ready" application it needs to be?

2. You have now been exposed to the SQL Data Provider model and the OleDb Data Provider model. When would you choose to use the SQL Data Provider Model for a SQL Server database rather than the OleDb Data Provider model, and when would you choose the latter?

3. You have now been exposed to both the loosely coupled, data adapter and dataset approach to database access, and to the data command approach to database access. When is it more appropriate to use the former, and when the latter?

E X E R C I S E S

1. Using Visual Database Tools, create the structure of an SQL Server database to support student registration at your college. Name the database StudentRegistration. Implement the table designs shown in Figure 10-60. Draw the database diagram for this database, and implement the obvious relationships, enforcing referential integrity. Using Visual Database Tools, populate these tables with five students, five faculty members, five courses, 10 sections, and 10 student registrations.

```
STUDENT (StudentID, Password, LName, FName, Major, Phone)
FACULTY (FacultyID, LName, FName, Office, Phone)
COURSE (CourseID, Title, Dept, Credits)
SECTION (CourseID, SectionNum, Term, Location, Days, StartTime,
      StopTime, FacultyID)
REGISTRATION (StudentID, CourseID, SectionNum, Term)
```

Figure 10-60: Student registrations table designs

2. Using Visual Database Tools, create the structure of an SQL Server database to support the FigEvents application from Tutorial 7. Name the SQL Server database FigEvents. Implement the table designs in Figure 10-61. Draw the database diagram for this database, and implement the obvious relationships, enforcing referential integrity. Using Visual Database Tools, populate these tables with five events, five venues, and 10 venue-seating categories, using the information in the FigEvents application in Tutorial 7.

```
tblEVENT (EventID, Sport, EventName, Gender, ScoringMethod, Country1,
      Country2, VenueIndex, Schedule, StartTime, PricingSchedule)
tblVENUE (VenueIndex, VenueName)
tblSEATS (VenueIndex, SeatingCategory, SeatingCapacity, TicketPriceA,
      TicketPriceB, TicketPriceC)
```

Figure 10-61: Table designs for FigEvents

3. Using Visual Database Tools, create the structure of an SQL Server database to serve the needs of the Friendsville Visitors Bureau. Name the database VisitorsBureau. The bureau will provide information to the public concerning accommodations, restaurants, and visitor attractions during the Games. Implement the table designs in Figure 10-62. Draw the database diagram for this database, and implement the obvious relationships, enforcing referential integrity. Populate these tables with three accommodation categories (A, B, C, with the descriptions budget, moderate, and deluxe) and three restaurant categories (1, 2, 3, with the same descriptions). Insert five visitors, five hotels, five restaurants, and five attractions.

```
tblVISITOR (VisitorID, LName, FName, Street, City, State, ZipCode,
    email, AccommodationsCategoryRequested,
    RestaurantsCategoryRequested, AttractionsRequested)
tblACCOMMODATIONS (FacilityID, Name, Street, City, State, ZipCode,
    email, AccommodationsCategory, MinimumPrice, MaximumPrice)
tblRESTAURANT (RestaurantID, Name, Street, City, State, ZipCode, email,
    RestaurantCategory, MinimumPrice, MaximumPrice)
tblATTRACTION (AttractionID, Name, Street, City, State, ZipCode, email,
    Description)
tblACCOMMODATIONSCATEGORY (AccommodationsCategory, Description)
tblRESTAURANTCATEGORY (RestaurantCategory, Description)
```

Figure 10-62: Table designs for the Friendsville Visitors Bureau

4. Using Visual Database Tools, design a database named Tourney for the intramural beach volleyball tournament in the International Village. Players are identified by AthleteID, and attributes include last name, first name, country code, and TeamID. Teams are identified by a TeamID, with the attributes team name, team colors, and the AthleteID of the team captain. A country is identified by country code, and the only other attribute is country name. There are two athletes on each team. An athlete may come from any country. Create an SQL Server database containing the three tables of this database (tblPLAYER, tblTEAM, and tblCOUNTRY). Create a database diagram, and implement the relationships among these tables, enforcing referential integrity. Load the records for four teams, eight players, and six countries.

5. Design the database to support the procurement function for Dining Services in the International Village. Name this database SupplierFoods. The information in the database includes the foods that Dining Services purchases (tblFOOD), the suppliers they purchase from (tblSUPPLIER), and the list of foods available from each supplier (tblFOOD-SUPPLIER). Note that the relationship between foods and suppliers is many-to-many. That is, a given supplier may offer many foods, and a given food may be available from many suppliers. This is the reason that tblFOOD-SUPPLIER is needed. Use the fields that appear to you to be reasonable and necessary—inventory-related fields for tblFOOD in addition to a description of the food, and address/phone fields for tblSUPPLIER. Make sure that each table has a primary key—a FoodID for tblFOOD, a SupplierID for tblSUPPLIER, and the combination of FoodID and SupplierID for tblFOOD-SUPPLIER. Draw the database diagram for this database, and implement the obvious relationships, enforcing referential integrity.

After completing this lesson, you will be able to:

■ Plan for the design and development of a Web Forms application with interactive update of an SQL Server database
■ Create the Web Forms for the application
■ Create the data access components for the application
■ Write the CodeBehind modules for the application

Interactive Databases on the Web

Planning the Ticket-ordering System

As your computer programs increase in complexity and sophistication, planning and designing the application become increasingly important. FigTickets is an application that needs to be carefully planned prior to beginning its construction.

FigTickets includes four Web Forms, which you will call WebHome, WebLogin, WebUser, and WebOrders. Referring back to the beginning of this tutorial, WebHome appears in Figure 10-1, WebLogin in Figure 10-2, WebUser in Figures 10-3 and 10-6, and WebOrders in Figures 10-4, 10-5, and 10-7. The function of each of these forms is as follows:

■ *WebHome*—This is the application's start-up page; the user selects New User or Existing User.
  ■ If the user selects New User, a hyperlink navigates to WebUser.
  ■ If the user selects Existing User, a hyperlink navigates to WebLogin.
■ *WebLogin*—This is the login page for existing users; when the user clicks Submit, the e-mail address and password entered by the user are stored in global variables, and WebUser is opened.
■ *WebUser*—This is the user information collection and verification page.
  ■ If an existing user's credentials are not found in tblUser, Login Failure is displayed above a blank user's form.
  ■ If an existing user's credentials are found in tblUser, the user's record is displayed under the banner Existing User, and may be updated by the user. If the user clicks Update, data in the form is used to update the user's record in tblUser; if the user clicks Orders, a hyperlink navigates to WebOrders.
  ■ If the user clicks New User on WebHome, a blank user information form is displayed under the banner New User; when the new user clicks Submit, a new user's record is created in tblUser, and WebUser is redisplayed for an existing user.
■ *WebOrders*—This is the main form of the ticket-ordering system; the user creates new ticket orders, and reviews and pays for existing orders. This is by far the most complex form in the FigTickets application.

Data access components are needed in WebUser and in WebOrders. WebUser must retrieve, insert, and update user records in tblUser. WebOrders must access information from tblEvent, tblVenue, tblOrder, and tblTicket.

Software and Help Screens

Visual Basic .NET represents the first release of a new paradigm in Visual Basic. For Microsoft, this software is an ambitious and far-reaching endeavor. As Microsoft developed the software and the extensive Help system to go along with it, the developers and product support engineers could not anticipate all of the questions that developers might have about this software. Furthermore, because development of the product and of the Help system proceeded at the same time, inevitably some details in the product as released differ from the product as experienced by those working on the Help system. Finally, the product does not work seamlessly among all platforms. Although this is true of the entire Visual Basic .NET package, it is especially true of the Help screens dealing with data access in Web Forms. You may discover specific syntax in the Help screens that does not appear to work as advertised on your computer.

To provide additional support to developers, Microsoft maintains and actively manages dozens of newsgroups. You can discover more about these groups at *http://msdn.microsoft.com*. Developers from around the world and Microsoft product support engineers do offer a tremendous resource to help you get answers to your technical support questions. You should avail yourself of that resource, and as you become better versed in the nuances of applications development in Visual Basic .NET, you should peruse the newsgroups of interest to you from time to time, both to see the kinds of questions that others are asking, and to offer your own solutions when someone encounters a technical problem that you have already solved.

Creating the Web Forms for the FigTickets Application

You have a functioning SQL Server database, and you have populated the database with sufficient data to use as a testbed for program development purposes. And you have completed a viable plan for program development. So, now you are ready to begin writing the actual FigTickets Web Forms application.

tip

If this generates an error because FigTickets already exists (which could occur if you installed the deployed FigTickets application in the same location as you are now creating a new project), then call the new project MyTickets instead.

To start a new Visual Basic .NET Web Forms project called FigTickets:

1　From the Visual Studio Start Page, click **New Project**. In the New Project dialog box, select **Visual Basic Projects** under Project Types, and **ASP.NET Web Application** under Templates. Enter **FigTickets** as the Project Name, and click **OK**.

2　In Solution Explorer, rename WebForm1 as **WebHome.aspx**. Add another Web form to the project, naming this form **WebLogin.aspx**. Add a third Web form to the project, naming it **WebUser.aspx**. And add the fourth Web form to the project, naming it **WebOrders.aspx**. The reason for adding all of the Web forms at the beginning is so that you can create the hyperlinks that connect them as you go along.

3　Open **WebHome** in the Designer. Then insert and position the **Label** controls, **Panel** control, and **Hyperlink** controls, as shown in Figure 10-63. Set the **Text** properties and the additional properties shown in Figure 10-64.

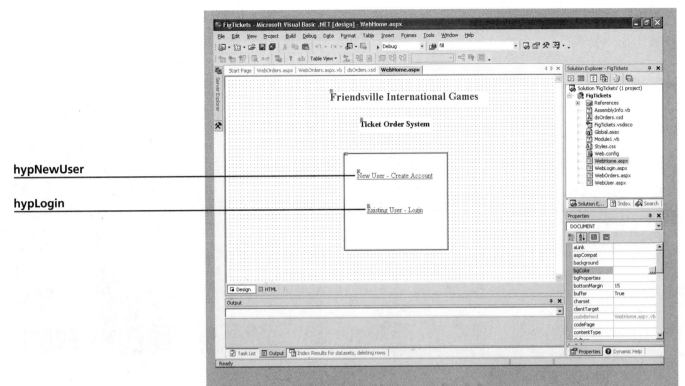

hypNewUser

hypLogin

Figure 10-63: WebHome at design time

Control	Property	Setting
Label1	Font	Large
	ForeColor	Blue
Label2	Font	Medium
Panel1	BorderStyle	Ridge
hypNewUser	NavigateURL	WebUser.aspx
hypLogin	NavigateURL	WebLogin.aspx

Figure 10-64: Nondefault properties of WebHome.aspx

4   Open **WebLogin** in the Designer. Set the **pageLayout** property of the DOCUMENT to **FlowLayout**. Click inside the **form**, and set the **align** property at the insertion point to **center**. Then insert **labels**, **text boxes**, and a **button** as shown in Figure 10-65. Set the **Text** properties and the additional properties shown in Figure 10-66.

txtEmailParameter

btnSubmit

txtPasswordParameter

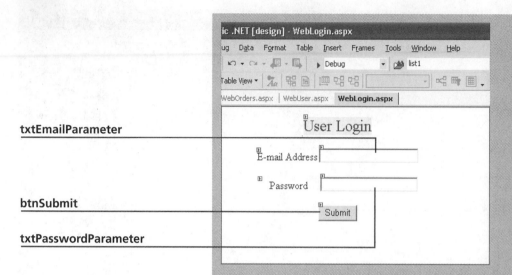

Figure 10-65: WebLogin at design time

Control	Property	Setting
Label1	BackColor	Yellow
	Font	Large
	ForeColor	Blue
txtEmailParameter	TabIndex	1
txtPasswordParameter	TabIndex	2
	TextMode	Password

Figure 10-66: Nondefault properties of WebLogin.aspx

5 Open **WebUser** in the Designer. Insert the **labels, text boxes, buttons,** and **hyperlinks,** as shown in Figure 10-67. In this figure, the Text property of the text boxes was set with the name of the object, so that you would know what to call them. Use these as the names of the objects, but set the **Text** property to **blanks.** Set the **Text** properties of labels, buttons, and hyperlinks as shown in Figure 10-67, and the additional properties shown in Figure 10-68.

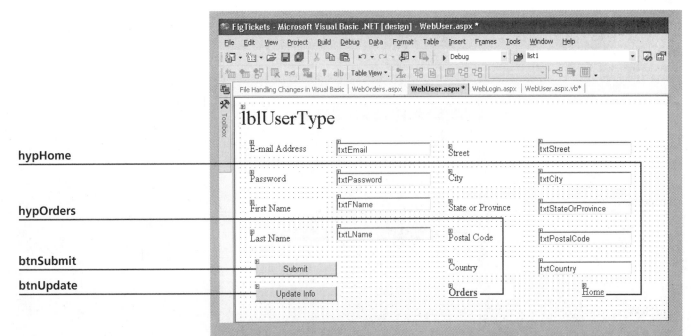

Figure 10-67: WebUser at design time

Control	Property	Setting
lblUserType	Font	X-Large
txtPassword	TextMode	Password
hypOrders	Font	Medium
	NavigateURL	WebOrders.aspx
hypHome	NavigateURL	WebHome.aspx

Figure 10-68: Nondefault properties of WebUser.aspx

6 Open **WebOrders** in the Designer. Insert the **buttons, hyperlink, drop-down list, label,** and **data grids,** as shown in Figure 10-69. Set the **Text** properties and the additional properties shown in Figure 10-70.

btnDone

btnNewOrder

ddlEvents

hypHome

dgrdOrders

dgrdTickets

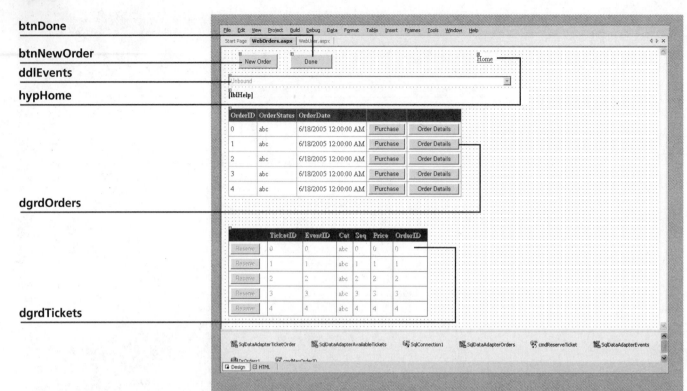

Figure 10-69: WebOrders at design time

Control	Property	Setting
hypHome	NavigateURL	WebHome.aspx
ddlEvents	AutoPostBack	True
	Enabled	False
lblHelp	Font.Bold	True
	Text	<NULL>

Figure 10-70: Nondefault properties of WebOrders.aspx

NOTE: The properties of the two DataGrid controls, dgrdOrders and dgrdTickets, cannot be assigned until the data access components of the form have been added.

7 Run the **FigTickets** application. Although nothing actually works yet, you should see the materialization of WebHome, WebLogin, WebUser, and WebOrders. From WebHome, click the link to **New User,** which should open WebUser. From there, click the link to **WebOrders.** Recall that a data grid is not rendered in a Web page at all if it is empty. From WebOrders, click the link back to **WebHome.** Again from WebHome, click the link to **Existing User,** which should open WebLogin. Close the application and return to the IDE.

Building the Data Access Components of the FigTickets Application

Recall that WebUser.aspx and WebOrders.aspx require data access components. You build WebUser's data access component from SqlCommand objects. WebOrders' data access components are instantiated both from SqlDataAdapters and associated datasets, and from SqlCommand objects. After the data access components of WebOrders are constructed, you configure the two DataGrid controls on that form.

Configuring Data Access Components in WebUser

The WebUser form needs to retrieve a record from tblUser, insert a new record, and update a record. You create SqlCommand objects to accomplish this. All three commands will utilize one connection to the database.

To add data access components to WebUser.aspx:

1   Open or switch to **WebUser.aspx** in the Designer. Drag an **SqlCommand** component from the Data tab of the Toolbox onto the form. Change the Name of the component to **cmdGetUser**. Click the **Connection** property, and choose **New**. In the Data Link Properties dialog box, enter the *server name*, choose **Use Windows NT Integrated security**, and type in the name of your **Tickets** database or select it from the drop-down list. Click the **Test Connection** button to make sure that the database is available. Click **OK**. SqlConnection1 is added to your form.

2   Click the **CommandText** property, and click the **ellipsis** to open the Query Builder. In the Query Builder, first designate the data source(s): add **tblUser**, and close the **Add Table** dialog box. Then build the query, as shown in Figure 10-71. Click **OK**.

Diagram pane

Grid pane

SQL pane

Results pane

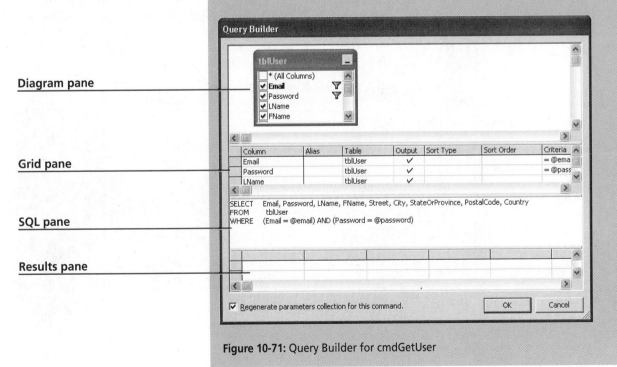

Figure 10-71: Query Builder for cmdGetUser

NOTE: The Query Builder in Visual Database Tools can be used when designing a query, a view, an inline function, or a single-statement stored procedure (these are all possible elements of a database). The Query Builder has four panes: the Diagram pane at the top shows the table(s), view(s), or other data sources for the query, along with any relationships between them. It also shows each field, and displays icons to indicate how that field is being used in the query. Next, the Grid pane displays a spreadsheet showing each field in the data sources and the various options you can select for the query. The third pane is the SQL pane, which displays the actual SQL statement that you are building. The bottom pane is the Results pane, showing the data results the last time a Select query was executed. The Query Builder allows you to work in any of the panes, and the software changes the other panes to match the changes you make. For example, in the present case, if you click the Email column in the Diagram pane, then the Email column is selected for Output in the Grid pane, and the SQL statement reflects the "Email" in the Select statement. You insert a filter in the Criteria column of the Grid pane. (If you are familiar with the Query Designer in Microsoft Access, you will find the Query Builder quite similar. The major difference is that, in MS Access, you must click View I SQL View to see the resultant SQL statement, whereas in Visual Database Tools, the SQL statement is always visible in the SQL pane). Finally, a parameter is designated in SQL Server by using a variable name preceded by the @ symbol, and conventionally the variable name is the same as the field name. So, the parameter for Email is @*email*, and for Password, it is @*password*. You can type these parameters into the Criteria column of the Grid pane. For more information on the Query Builder and its many features, open the Query Builder and press F1. This takes you to the Query and View Designer Help screen, which contains further links to each of the panes in the Query Builder.

3 Drag another **SqlCommand** component from the Data tab of the Toolbox onto the form. Change the **Name** of the component to **cmdInsertNewUser**. Click the **Connection** property, expand **Existing**, and choose **SqlConnection1**.

4 Click the **CommandText** property, and click the **ellipsis** to open the Query Builder. In the Query Builder, add **tblUser**, and close the **Add Table** dialog box. Use the elements of the Query Builder, or just type the SQL statement directly, as shown in Figure 10-72. Click **OK**.

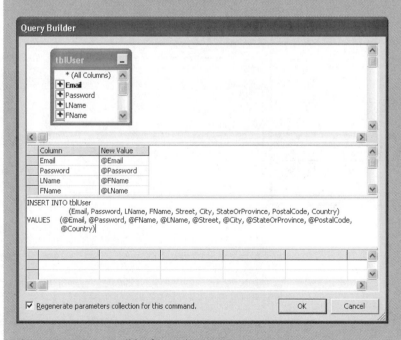

Figure 10-72: Query Builder for cmdInsertNewUser

5 Drag another **SqlCommand** component from the Data tab of the Toolbox onto the form. Change the **Name** of the component to **cmdUpdateUser**. Click the **Connection** property, expand **Existing**, and choose **SqlConnection1**.

6 Click the **CommandText** property, and click the **ellipsis** to open the Query Builder. In the Query Builder, add **tblUser**, and close the **Add Table** dialog box. Use the elements of the Query Builder, or just type the SQL statement directly, as shown in Figure 10-73. Click **OK**.

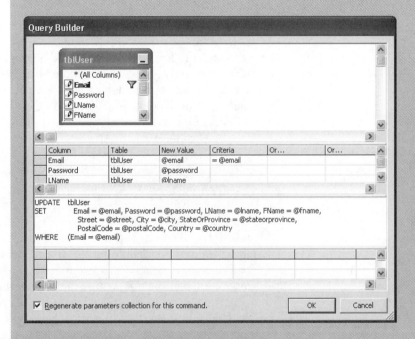

Figure 10-73: Query Builder for cmdUpdateUser

7 Open the **Web.config** file by double-clicking it in Solution Explorer. Insert the following statement on line 5, immediately after `<system.web>`:

```
<identity impersonate="true" />
```

8 Save **Web.config** and close it.

Configuring Data Access Components in WebOrders

Depending on how you decide to provide all of the functionality needed in WebOrders.aspx, at least eight data access components must be added to this form. The approach you take here uses a combination of data adapters and data commands. The complete list includes a connection, four data adapters that all operate against a single dataset, and two data commands. These objects provide the following functionality:

■ SqlConnection1 provides the common connection used by all of the other objects.

■ The dataset DsOrders1 is an instance of dsOrders. It includes three data table objects and two data relations, representing the following:

  ■ *tblOrder*—All of the orders for the current user; this is a subset of tblOrder in the database.

  ■ *tblEvent*—All of the events and venues in the Games; this is a combination (table join) of tblEvent and tblVenue from the database.

- *tblTicket*—All of the tickets available for a selected event, or all of the tickets that make up a selected order; this is a subset of tblTicket from the database.
- A 1:N data relation between tblEvent and tblTicket in the dataset
- A 1:N data relation between tblOrder and tblTicket in the dataset

- SqlDataAdapterOrders generates the tblOrder data table object in the dataset.
- SqlDataAdapterEvents generates the tblEvent data table object in the dataset.
- SqlDataAdapterAvailableTickets generates the version of tblTicket in the dataset that shows all of the tickets for a particular event that have not yet been reserved or sold.
- SqlDataAdapterTicketOrder generates the version of tblTicket in the dataset that shows all of the tickets for a selected order.
- cmdReserveTicket is an SqlCommand object. It inserts an OrderID in a record of tblTicket directly in the database, thereby reserving that ticket to that order, and making the ticket unavailable to anyone else.
- cmdMaxOrderID is an SqlCommand object. It returns the highest OrderID from tblOrder in the database.

To create the data access components for WebOrders.aspx:

1 Open or switch to **WebOrders.aspx** in the Designer. Drag an **SqlCommand** component from the Data tab of the Toolbox onto the form. Change the **Name** of the component to **cmdMaxOrderID**. Click the **Connection** property, and choose **New**. In the Data Link Properties dialog box, enter the *server name*, choose **Use Windows NT Integrated security**, and type the name of your **Tickets** database or select it from the drop-down list. Click the **Test Connection** button to make sure that the database is available, and click **OK** to acknowledge the successful test. Click **OK** in the **Data Link Properties** dialog box; SqlConnection1 is added to your form.

2 Click the **CommandText** property, and click the **ellipsis** to open the Query Builder. In the Query Builder, add **tblOrder**, and close the **Add Table** dialog box. Use the elements of the Query Builder, or just type the SQL statement directly, as shown in Figure 10-74. Click **OK**.

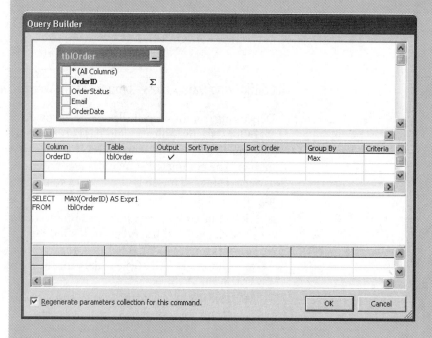

Figure 10-74: Query Builder for cmdMaxOrderID

3   Drag another **SqlCommand** component from the Data tab of the Toolbox onto the form. Change the **Name** of the component to **cmdReserveTicket**. Click the **Connection** property, expand **Existing**, and choose **SqlConnection1**. Click the **CommandText** property, and click the **ellipsis** to open the Query Builder. In the Query Builder, add **tblTicket**, and close the **Add Table** dialog box. Use the elements of the Query Builder, or just type the SQL statement directly, as shown in Figure 10-75. Click **OK**.

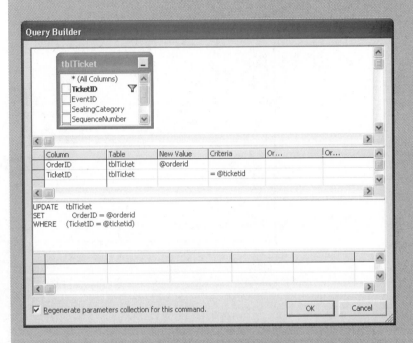

Figure 10-75: Query Builder for cmdReserveTicket

4   Build SqlDataAdapterEvents based on tblEvent and tblVenue in the database. To do this, drag an **SqlDataAdapter** onto the form. The Data Adapter Configuration Wizard opens. Click **Next**, and then click the existing data connection to the **Tickets** database. Click **Next**. Make sure that **Use SQL statements** is selected. Click **Next**, and then click **Query Builder**. In the Add Table dialog box, add **tblVenue**, also add **tblEvent**, and close the **Add Table** dialog box. Then use the elements of the Query Builder, or just type the SQL statement directly, as shown in Figure 10-76. Click **OK**. Click **Finish**. The wizard closes and returns you to the IDE. In the Properties window, change the **Name** of **SqlDataAdapter1** to **SqlDataAdapterEvents**. Below the Properties window, click **Generate Dataset**. Click the **New** dataset radio button. Enter the name **dsOrders**, verify that **tblEvent (SqlDataAdapterEvent)** is selected in the **Tables to add to the dataset** window, and then click **OK**.

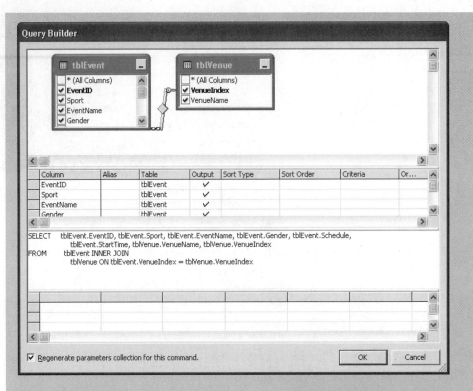

Figure 10-76: Query Builder for SqlDataAdapterEvents

5 Build SqlDataAdapterOrders in a similar fashion. In the Data Adapter Configuration Wizard, select the existing connection to the Tickets database. In the Query Builder, add **tblOrder**, and close the **Add Table** dialog box. Then use the elements of the Query Builder, or just type the SQL statement directly, as shown in Figure 10-77. Click **OK**. Click **Finish**. In the Properties window, change the **Name** of **SqlDataAdapter1** to **SqlDataAdapterOrders**. Below the Properties window, click **Generate Dataset**. Click the existing **dsOrders** dataset. Verify that **tblOrder (SqlDataAdapterOrders)** is selected in the Tables to add to the dataset window, and then click **OK**.

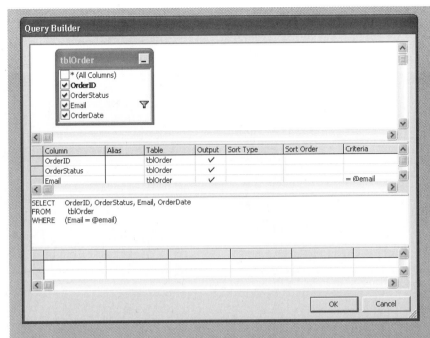

Figure 10-77: Query Builder for SqlDataAdapterOrders

6 Build SqlDataAdapterAvailableTickets in a similar fashion. In the Query Builder's Add Table dialog box, add **tblTicket**. The Query Builder for SqlDataAdapterAvailableTickets should appear as in Figure 10-78. After completing the wizard, rename **SqlDataAdapter1** as **SqlDataAdapterAvailableTickets**. Then click **Generate Dataset**, click the existing **dsOrders** dataset, verify that **tblTicket (SqlDataAdapterAvailableTickets)** is selected in the Tables to add to the dataset window, and then click **OK**.

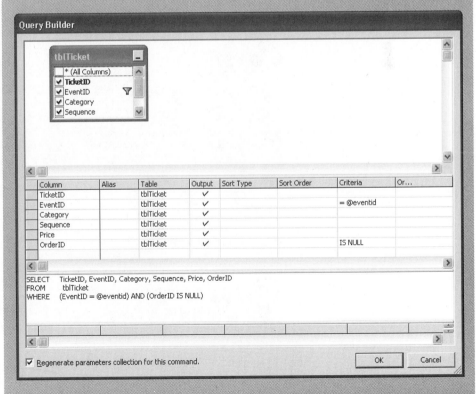

Figure 10-78: Query Builder for SqlDataAdapterAvailableTickets

7   Build SqlDataAdapterTicketOrder in a similar fashion. In the Query Builder's Add Table dialog box, add **tblTicket**. The Query Builder for SqlDataAdapterTicketOrder should appear as in Figure 10-79. After completing the wizard, rename **SqlDataAdapter1** as **SqlDataAdapterTicketOrder**. Then click **Generate Dataset**, click the existing **dsOrders** dataset, verify that **tblTicket (SqlDataAdapterTicketOrder)** is selected in the Tables to add to the dataset window, and then click **OK**.

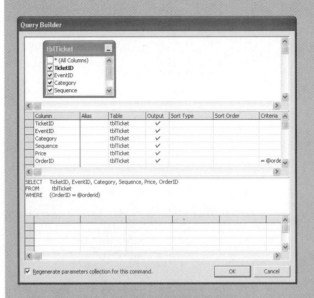

Figure 10-79: Query Builder for SqlDataAdapterTicketOrder

8   Click **DsOrders1**, and click **View Schema** below the Properties window. The XML Designer for dsOrders.xsd opens. Drag **OrderID** from tblOrder to **OrderID** in tblTicket. The Create Relation dialog box opens. Verify that tblOrder is the parent table and tblTicket is the child table. Click **OK**. Similarly, drag **EventID** from **tblEvent** to **tblTicket**. Verify that tblEvent is the parent table and tblTicket is the child table. Click **OK**. The schema for dsOrders should appear as in Figure 10-80.

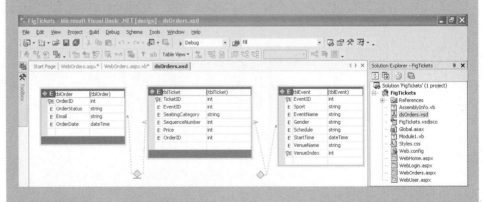

Figure 10-80: Completed schema for dsOrders

Configuring the DataGrid Controls in WebOrders

DataGrid controls are dependent on data access components. You now set the properties of the two DataGrid controls on WebOrders based on the data access components that you have just created.

To configure dgrdOrders and dgrdTickets:

1 Switch to **WebOrders.aspx** in the Designer. Select **dgrdOrders**, and click **Property Builder** at the bottom of the Properties window. In the dgrdOrders Properties pages, in the General tab, click the **list arrow** in DataSource, and select **DsOrders1**. Then, click the **list arrow** in DataMember, and click **tblOrder**. Click the **list arrow** in the Data key field, and click **OrderID**.

2 Click the **Columns** tab. Make sure that the **Create columns automatically at run time** check box is not checked. In the Available columns frame on the left, expand **Data Fields** (if necessary). Select **OrderID**, and click the **arrow** to copy this field to the Selected columns frame on the right. Copy **OrderStatus** and **OrderDate** to the Selected columns frame in the same way. Select **Button Column** in the Available columns frame, and copy it to the **Selected columns** frame. With the Button selected in the frame on the right, type **Purchase** in the **Text** text box, and **btnPurchase** in the **Command name** text box. Change the **Button type** to **PushButton**. See Figure 10-81.

tip

When you select OrderDate and move it to the frame on the right, it would be very nice to be able to format this field. The Property Builder includes a text box for this purpose, into which you can place any format expression recognized in .NET Framework. Unfortunately, it does not work in the first release of Visual Basic .NET.

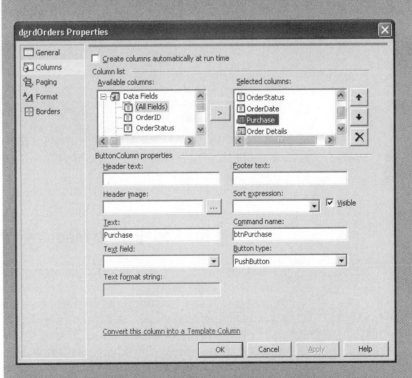

Figure 10-81: Columns tab of the dgrdOrders Properties pages

3 Notice that the Button Column entry in Available columns is expandable. Expand **Button Column** so that you see the lower-level entries: Select, Edit/Update/Cancel, and Delete. You do not need those buttons in this project, but you should know that they are available. Should you create an application that requires the user to select or delete a row, then the corresponding button columns can provide that functionality. If your application needs to permit the user to edit the data in a row, then the Edit/Update/Cancel button column is your answer. An Edit button appears in the column initially. When the user clicks the Edit button at runtime, the Edit button is replaced by two buttons that say Update and Cancel, and text boxes appear in every data field of that row.

4 Select another **Button Column** in the Available columns frame, and copy it to the **Selected columns** frame. With **Button** selected in the frame on the right, type **Order Details** in the **Text** text box, and **btnOrderDetails** in the **Command name** text box. Change the **Button type** to **PushButton**. Click **OK**.

NOTE: If the Create columns automatically at run time check box is checked, the data grid is populated at runtime with all of the columns in the data source, and any new columns added by the programmer appear on the left side of the grid. If you want fewer than all of the columns from the data source and/or additional columns on the right, then you must uncheck the check box, and add each field manually.

5 With dgrdOrders still selected in the Designer, click **Auto Format** at the bottom of the Properties window. Select the **Colorful 1** scheme, and click **OK**.

6 Select **dgrdTickets**, and click the **Property Builder**. In the dgrdTickets Properties pages, in the General tab, click the **list arrow** in DataSource, and select **DsOrders1**. Then, click the **list arrow** in DataMember, and select **tblTicket**. Click the **list arrow** in the Data key field, and select **TicketID**.

7 Click the **Columns** tab. Uncheck the **Create columns automatically at run time** check box. In the Available columns frame, click **Button Column**, and copy a button to the **Selected columns** frame on the right. Type **Reserve** into the **Text** text box, and **btnReserve** into the **Command name** text box. Select **PushButton** as the **Button type**. Click **OK**.

8 With dgrdTickets still selected in the Designer, click **Auto Format** at the bottom of the Properties window. Select the **Colorful 2** scheme, and click **OK**.

9 Click the **Save All** icon.

Writing the CodeBehind Modules for FigTickets

You may very well find the CodeBehind modules for FigTickets shorter than you expected, considering all of the functionality that is built into the application. The simple fact is that a great deal of functionality is provided by ASP.NET and by sophisticated controls like the DataGrid and DropDownList controls and is hidden from you.

These modules include a brief Module1.vb containing the declaration of six public variables, and very brief procedures in WebHome.aspx.vb and WebLogin.aspx.vb. Less than 90 lines of code in WebUser.aspx.vb and under 160 lines of code in WebOrders.aspx.vb complete the application.

Module1.vb

The e-mail address and password must be shared among Web forms, and several forms need to know whether the user is a new user. These items (pstrEmailParameter, pstrPasswordParameter, and pblnNewUser) are declared as public variables in Module1.vb.

In WebOrders.aspx.vb, three module-level variables are needed during several return visits to the page, that is, after round trips between the client and the server. In Visual Studio .NET Web Forms applications, information in the client is automatically preserved through Control.ViewState, and information on the server side can be preserved through the ApplicationState or SessionState. However, for a few simple variables, a less cumbersome approach is to store these variables in a code module. Therefore, pintSelectedEvent, pintNewOrderID, and pblnNewOrderPending are declared as public variables in Module1.vb.

To create Module1.vb:

1 Add a **new module** to FigTickets. Accept the default name of **Module1.vb**.

2 Insert the code shown in Figure 10-82.

```
Module Module1
   Public pstrEmailParameter As String
   Public pstrPasswordParameter As String
   Public pblnNewUser As Boolean = True
   Public pintSelectedEvent As Integer
   Public pintNewOrderID As Integer
   Public pblnNewOrderPending As Boolean = False
End Module
```

Figure 10-82: Declarations in Module1.vb

WebHome.aspx.vb

In WebHome.aspx.vb, the Page_Load() procedure needs to reset the three global variables, to prevent a user from accidentally using the settings from the previous user.

To create WebHome.aspx.vb:

1 Open **WebHome.aspx.vb**.

2 Insert the code shown in Figure 10-83.

```
Private Sub Page_Load(ByVal sender As System.Object, _
    ByVal e As System.EventArgs) Handles MyBase.Load
   pstrEmailParameter = ""
   pstrPasswordParameter = ""
   pblnNewUser = True
End Sub
```

Figure 10-83: Page_Load() procedure in WebHome.aspx.vb

WebLogin.aspx.vb

WebLogin is accessed only for an existing user. Therefore, btnSubmit_Click() sets pblnNewUser to False. It also stores the e-mail address and password entered by the user in the other two public variables. Finally, it opens WebUser.aspx.

To create WebLogin.aspx.vb:

1 Open **WebLogin.aspx.vb**.

2 Insert the code shown in Figure 10-84.

```
Private Sub btnSubmit_Click(ByVal sender As System.Object, _
    ByVal e As System.EventArgs) Handles btnSubmit.Click
  pblnNewUser = False
  pstrEmailParameter = txtEmailParameter.Text
  pstrPasswordParameter = txtPasswordParameter.Text
  Response.BufferOutput = True
  Response.Redirect("WebUser.aspx")
End Sub
```

Figure 10-84: btnSubmit_Click() procedure in WebLogin.aspx.vb

WebUser.aspx.vb

This Web form requires code in support of three events, Page_Load(), btnSubmit_Click(), and btnUpdate_Click():

To insert the three procedures in WebUser.aspx.vb:

1 Open **WebUser.aspx.vb**.

2 Insert the **Page_Load**() procedure shown in Figure 10-85. The Page_Load() procedure must configure the form depending on whether this is a new or existing user, and, if it is an existing user, on whether or not that user's credentials are found in tblUser. The Page_Load() procedure only needs to be executed the first time the page is loaded, which is the reason that all of the code is enclosed in a If Not IsPostBack condition. When retrieving the record for an existing user, this procedure uses an SqlDataReader object, which is a member of SqlClient. The data reader (declared as dreader) should retrieve at most one record, which is the reason for the CommandBehavior.SingleRow parameter. After the record has been retrieved, and if it has been retrieved, the columns of information in dreader are available through an index—that is, dreader(0) is the far-left column in the table, namely, the e-mail address; dreader(1) is the password; and so on.

```
Private Sub Page_Load(ByVal sender As System.Object, _
    ByVal e As System.EventArgs) Handles MyBase.Load
  If Not IsPostBack Then
    SqlConnection1.ConnectionString = "data source = " _
      & pstrInstance & ";initial catalog=Tickets;" & _
      "integrated security=SSPI;" & _
      "persist security info=False;" _
      & "workstation id=DADSLAPTOP;packet size=4096"
    If pblnNewUser Then
      lblUserType.Text = "New User"
      btnSubmit.Visible = True
      btnUpdate.Visible = False
      hypOrders.Visible = False
      pstrEmailParameter = ""
      pstrPasswordParameter = ""
    Else
      lblUserType.Text = "Existing User"
      btnSubmit.Visible = False
      btnUpdate.Visible = True
      hypOrders.Visible = True
      cmdGetUser.Parameters("@email").Value = _
        pstrEmailParameter
      cmdGetUser.Parameters("@password").Value = _
        pstrPasswordParameter
      SqlConnection1.Open()
      Dim dreader As SqlClient.SqlDataReader
      dreader = cmdGetUser.ExecuteReader _
        (CommandBehavior.SingleRow)
      If dreader.Read() Then
        txtEmail.Text = dreader(0)
        txtPassword.Text = dreader(1)
        txtFName.Text = dreader(3)
        txtLName.Text = dreader(2)
        txtStreet.Text = dreader(4)
        txtCity.Text = dreader(5)
        txtStateOrProvince.Text = dreader(6)
        txtPostalCode.Text = dreader(7)
        txtCountry.Text = dreader(8)
      Else
        lblUserType.Text = _
          "Login Failure -- Go back to try again"
      End If
      dreader.Close()
      SqlConnection1.Close()
    End If
  End If
End Sub
```

Figure 10-85: Page_Load() procedure in WebUser.aspx.vb

3   Insert the **btnSubmit_Click()** procedure shown in Figure 10-86. btnSubmit_Click() inserts a new record into tblUser, ensuring that all text fields are in uppercase. This code does not include error checking of any kind. A duplicate e-mail address would cause the program to blow up, for example, and careful checking of the password is not included. The objective was to keep this code to a minimum size, and to let you develop it further on your own. After inserting the new record in tblUser, this procedure modifies the format of the form so that it reflects an existing user.

```
Private Sub btnSubmit_Click(ByVal sender As System.Object, _
    ByVal e As System.EventArgs) Handles btnSubmit.Click
  With cmdInsertNewUser
    .Parameters("@email").Value = UCase(txtEmail.Text)
    .Parameters("@password").Value = txtPassword.Text
    .Parameters("@fname").Value = UCase(txtFName.Text)
    .Parameters("@lname").Value = UCase(txtLName.Text)
    .Parameters("@street").Value = UCase(txtStreet.Text)
    .Parameters("@city").Value = UCase(txtCity.Text)
    .Parameters("@stateorprovince").Value = _
      UCase(txtStateOrProvince.Text)
    .Parameters("@postalcode").Value = txtPostalCode.Text
    .Parameters("@country").Value = UCase(txtCountry.Text)
  End With
  SqlConnection1.Open()
  cmdInsertNewUser.ExecuteNonQuery()
  SqlConnection1.Close()
  pstrEmailParameter = txtEmail.Text
  pstrPasswordParameter = txtPassword.Text
  lblUserType.Text = "Existing User"
  btnSubmit.Visible = False
  btnUpdate.Visible = True
  hypOrders.Visible = True
End Sub
```

Figure 10-86: btnSubmit_Click() procedure in WebUser.aspx.vb

4 Insert the **btnUpdate_Click**() procedure shown in Figure 10-87. btnUpdate_Click() accepts new user information and updates the user's record in tblUser. It does not require a new password, however.

```
Private Sub btnUpdate_Click(ByVal sender As System.Object, _
    ByVal e As System.EventArgs) Handles btnUpdate.Click
  With cmdUpdateUser
    .Parameters("@email").Value = UCase(txtEmail.Text)
    If txtPassword.Text = "" Then
      .Parameters("@password").Value = pstrPasswordParameter
    Else
      .Parameters("@password").Value = txtPassword.Text
    End If
    .Parameters("@fname").Value = UCase(txtFName.Text)
    .Parameters("@lname").Value = UCase(txtLName.Text)
    .Parameters("@street").Value = UCase(txtStreet.Text)
    .Parameters("@city").Value = UCase(txtCity.Text)
    .Parameters("@stateorprovince").Value = _
      UCase(txtStateOrProvince.Text)
    .Parameters("@postalcode").Value = txtPostalCode.Text
    .Parameters("@country").Value = UCase(txtCountry.Text)
  End With
  SqlConnection1.Open()
  cmdUpdateUser.ExecuteNonQuery()
  SqlConnection1.Close()
  pstrEmailParameter = txtEmail.Text
  pstrPasswordParameter = txtPassword.Text
End Sub
```

Figure 10-87: btnUpdate_Click() procedure in WebUser.aspx.vb

WebOrders.aspx.vb

WebOrders.aspx.vb is the most complex code in this application, though it is still rather short. After a set of module-level constant declarations, the procedures include Page_Load(), dgrdOrders_ItemCommand(), btnNewOrder_Click, ddlEvents_SelectedIndexChanged(), dgrdTickets_ItemCommand(), btnDone_Click, and DisplayMsg().

To create the CodeBehind for WebOrders.aspx.vb:

1   Open **WebOrders.aspx.vb**.

2   Insert the module-level constant declarations shown in Figure 10-88. These declarations relate to the messages that appear in lblHelp, and assist the maintenance programmer in understanding subsequent calls to the DisplayMsg() procedure.

```
Const MsgSTART = 1
Const MsgNEWORDER = 2
Const MsgPURCHASE = 3
Const MsgNEWORDERPENDING = 4
Const MsgRESERVE = 5
```

Figure 10-88: Constant declarations in WebOrders.aspx.vb

3   Insert the **Page_Load()** procedure, as shown in Figure 10-89. The bulk of this code constructs an item for ddlEvents, and then adds the item to the drop-down list.

```
Private Sub Page_Load(ByVal sender As System.Object, _
    ByVal e As System.EventArgs) Handles MyBase.Load
  SqlConnection1.ConnectionString = "data source = " _
    & pstrInstance & _
    ";initial catalog=Tickets;" & _
    "integrated security=SSPI;" & _
    "persist security info=False;" & _
    "workstation id=DADSLAPTOP;packet size=4096"
  SqlDataAdapterOrders.SelectCommand.Parameters("@email").Value = _
    pstrEmailParameter
  SqlDataAdapterOrders.Fill(DsOrders1.tblOrder)
  SqlDataAdapterEvents.Fill(DsOrders1.tblEvent)
  If Not IsPostBack Then
    DisplayMsg(MsgSTART)
    dgrdOrders.DataBind()
    Dim workrow As dsOrders.tblEventRow
    Dim s As String
    For Each workrow In DsOrders1.tblEvent
      s = Str(workrow("EventID")) & " "
      If workrow("Gender") = "M" Then _
        s &= "Men's " & workrow("Sport") & " "
      If workrow("Gender") = "F" Then _
        s &= "Women's " & workrow("Sport") & " "
      s &= workrow("EventName") & " - "
      s &= workrow("Schedule") & ", "
      s &= Format(workrow("StartTime"), "h:mm tt") & ", at "
      s &= workrow("VenueName")
      ddlEvents.Items.Add(s)
```

Figure 10-89: Page_Load() procedure in WebOrders.aspx.vb

```
        Next
        ddlEvents.Enabled = True
        ddlEvents.SelectedIndex = -1
        ddlEvents.Enabled = False
    End If
End Sub
```

Figure 10-89: Page_Load() procedure in WebOrders.aspx.vb (continued)

4 The user can take action with respect to existing orders, either purchasing tickets that are on order but not yet purchased, or displaying the details concerning a particular order. When the user clicks a button in a column of a data grid, the data grid's ItemCommand event is triggered. If more that one column of buttons exists in the data grid, you can examine the e.CommandName property to discover the name of the button that was clicked—that will be the name that you type in the Command Name property in the data grid's Property Builder pages. Insert the code for the **dgrdOrders_ItemCommand**() procedure, as shown in Figure 10-90. Recall that you created two item commands in the Property Builder for dgrdOrders: btnPurchase and btnOrderDetails. For a purchase, this code changes the OrderStatus field from Ordered to Sold. For Order Details, the procedure displays the tickets that make up that order, and also displays the event in the DropDownList control.

```
Private Sub dgrdOrders_ItemCommand(ByVal source As Object, _
    ByVal e As System.Web.UI.WebControls. _
    DataGridCommandEventArgs) _
    Handles dgrdOrders.ItemCommand
  Select Case e.CommandName
    Case "btnPurchase"
      If pblnNewOrderPending Then
        DisplayMsg(MsgNEWORDERPENDING)
      Else
        DisplayMsg(MsgPURCHASE)
        Dim key As Integer = _
          dgrdOrders.DataKeys(e.Item.ItemIndex)
        Dim keyrow As dsOrders.tblOrderRow
        keyrow = DsOrders1.tblOrder.FindByOrderID(key)
        keyrow.OrderStatus = "S"
        SqlDataAdapterOrders.Update(DsOrders1.tblOrder)
        DsOrders1.AcceptChanges()
        dgrdOrders.DataBind()
      End If
    Case "btnOrderDetails"
      If pblnNewOrderPending Then
        DisplayMsg(MsgNEWORDERPENDING)
      Else
        DsOrders1.EnforceConstraints = False
        Dim key As Integer = _
          dgrdOrders.DataKeys(e.Item.ItemIndex).ToString
        SqlDataAdapterTicketOrder.SelectCommand.Parameters _
          ("@orderid").Value = key
        DsOrders1.tblTicket.Clear()
        SqlDataAdapterTicketOrder.Fill(DsOrders1.tblTicket)
        dgrdTickets.DataBind()
        If DsOrders1.tblTicket.Count = 0 Then
          Dim workrow As dsOrders.tblOrderRow
          For Each workrow In DsOrders1.tblOrder
            If workrow.OrderID = key Then workrow.Delete()
```

Figure 10-90: dgrdOrders_ItemCommand() procedure

```
            Next
            SqlDataAdapterOrders.Update(DsOrders1.tblOrder)
            DsOrders1.tblOrder.AcceptChanges()
            dgrdOrders.DataBind()
          Else
            Dim workrow As dsOrders.tblTicketRow
            workrow = DsOrders1.tblTicket.Rows(0)
            ddlEvents.SelectedIndex = workrow.EventID - 1
          End If
          DsOrders1.EnforceConstraints = True
        End If
    End Select
End Sub
```

Figure 10-90: dgrdOrders_ItemCommand() procedure (continued)

5 Insert the code for the **btnNewOrder_Click**() procedure shown in Figure 10-91. In addition to acting on existing orders, the user can create a new order. In this procedure, a new record is added to tblOrder, and controls are readied for user selection of an event and the tickets to that event.

```
Private Sub btnNewOrder_Click(ByVal sender As _
    System.Object, ByVal e As System.EventArgs) _
   Handles btnNewOrder.Click
 DisplayMsg(MsgNEWORDER)
 btnNewOrder.Visible = False
 btnDone.Visible = True
 dgrdTickets.Enabled = True
 SqlConnection1.Open()
 Dim dreader As SqlClient.SqlDataReader
 dreader = cmdMaxOrderID.ExecuteReader _
  (CommandBehavior.SingleRow)
 If dreader.Read() Then
   pintNewOrderID = dreader(0) + 1
 End If
 dreader.Close()
 SqlConnection1.Close()
 ddlEvents.SelectedIndex = 0
 ddlEvents_SelectedIndexChanged(sender, e)
 DsOrders1.tblOrder.Rows.Add(New Object() _
   {pintNewOrderID, "O", pstrEmailParameter, Today})
 SqlDataAdapterOrders.Update(DsOrders1.tblOrder)
 DsOrders1.tblOrder.AcceptChanges()
 dgrdOrders.DataBind()
 ddlEvents.Enabled = True
End Sub
```

Figure 10-91: btnNewOrder_Click() procedure

6 Insert the code for the **ddlEvents_SelectedIndexChanged**() procedure shown in Figure 10-92. This procedure displays tickets that are available for the selected event.

```
Private Sub ddlEvents_SelectedIndexChanged (ByVal _
   sender As System.Object, ByVal e As System.EventArgs) _
   Handles ddlEvents.SelectedIndexChanged
  SqlDataAdapterAvailableTickets.Update(DsOrders1.tblTicket)
  pintSelectedEvent = Val(Mid(ddlEvents.SelectedItem.Value, 2))
  SqlDataAdapterAvailableTickets.SelectCommand.Parameters _
   ("@eventid").Value = pintSelectedEvent
  DsOrders1.tblTicket.Clear()
  SqlDataAdapterAvailableTickets.Fill(DsOrders1.tblTicket)
  dgrdTickets.DataBind()
  ddlEvents.Enabled = False
End Sub
```

Figure 10-92: ddlEvents_SelectedIndexChanged() procedure

7 dgrdTickets has one item command, btnReserve, which updates tblTicket to assign an OrderID to a particular ticket. Type the code for the **dgrdTickets_ItemCommand**() procedure shown in Figure 10-93.

tip

Based on various examples in the Help screens, it should be possible to identify a particular row in the DataGrid control, identify the corresponding row in the dataset table, make the prescribed change to the row in the dataset table, and use the data adapter's Update() method to propagate this change back to the underlying table in the database. However, the code examples given in the Help screens to provide this functionality do not execute correctly. That is the reason for the use of an SqlCommand object instead.

```
Private Sub dgrdTickets_ItemCommand(ByVal source _
   As Object, ByVal e As _
   System.Web.UI.WebControls.DataGridCommandEventArgs) _
   Handles dgrdTickets.ItemCommand
  'ItemCommand = Reserve
  DisplayMsg(MsgRESERVE)
  'if the user is selecting tickets from Opening Ceremonies:
  ddlEvents.Enabled = False
  cmdReserveTicket.Parameters("@ticketid").Value = _
   dgrdTickets.DataKeys(e.Item.ItemIndex)
  cmdReserveTicket.Parameters("@orderid").Value = _
   pintNewOrderID
  SqlConnection1.Open()
  cmdReserveTicket.ExecuteNonQuery()
  SqlConnection1.Close()
End Sub
```

Figure 10-93: dgrdTickets_ItemCommand() procedure

8 At runtime, when the user has reserved all desired tickets for an event, the user clicks the Done button. Type the code for the **btnDone_Click**() procedure shown in Figure 10-94.

```
Private Sub btnDone_Click(ByVal sender As System.Object, _
   ByVal e As System.EventArgs) Handles btnDone.Click
  DisplayMsg(MsgSTART)
  btnNewOrder.Visible = True
  btnDone.Visible = False
  ddlEvents.Enabled = False
  dgrdTickets.Enabled = False
  SqlDataAdapterTicketOrder.SelectCommand.Parameters _
   ("@orderid").Value = pintNewOrderID
  DsOrders1.tblTicket.Clear()
  SqlDataAdapterTicketOrder.Fill(DsOrders1.tblTicket)
  dgrdTickets.DataBind()
```

Figure 10-94: btnDone_Click() procedure

```
  If DsOrders1.tblTicket.Count = 0 Then
    Dim workrow As dsOrders.tblOrderRow
    workrow = DsOrders1.tblOrder.FindByOrderID _
     (pintNewOrderID)
    workrow.Delete()
    SqlDataAdapterOrders.Update(DsOrders1.tblOrder)
    DsOrders1.tblOrder.AcceptChanges()
    dgrdOrders.DataBind()
  End If
  pblnNewOrderPending = False
End Sub
```

Figure 10-94: btnDone_Click() procedure (continued)

9   Several procedures display a Help message in lblHelp. These messages are consolidated and controlled by the DisplayMsg() procedure. Type the code for the **DisplayMsg**() procedure shown in Figure 10-95.

```
Private Sub DisplayMsg(ByVal vintMsgNum)
  Select Case vintMsgNum
    Case MsgSTART
      lblHelp.Text = "HELP: Click New Order, Purchase, " & _
        "or Order Details"
    Case MsgNEWORDER
      lblHelp.Text = "HELP: Select an event, click " & _
        "Reserve for each desired ticket, then click Done"
    Case MsgPURCHASE
      lblHelp.Text = "HELP: Thank you for your payment"
    Case MsgNEWORDERPENDING
      lblHelp.Text = "HELP: Complete your New Order first"
    Case MsgRESERVE
      lblHelp.Text = "HELP: Click Reserve for another " & _
        "ticket, or click Done"
  End Select
End Sub
```

Figure 10-95: DisplayMsg() procedure

10   Run the **FigTickets** application, and test all of its features.

Implementation Notes for Building FigTickets4Windows

At the beginning of this tutorial, mention was made of the fact that some students may be unable to implement the FigTickets application due to security restrictions or other limitations of your computer environment. An alternative application called FigTickets4Windows can be developed instead. This alternative is not Web-enabled, and so it would not be suitable as a model for a computer program that sells tickets to the public online. However, it does use the SQL Server Tickets database, the ADO.NET data access components developed for FigTickets, and much of the application logic. So it is a useful exercise for those of you who cannot, for whatever reason, build FigTickets itself.

The instructions for building FigTickets4Windows are in Appendix B.

You have now completed Tutorial 10. Be sure to try out the following exercises before beginning Tutorial 11.

SUMMARY

- Planning and designing an application are important activities before the actual implementation of the selected design is undertaken.

- The worldwide community of Visual Basic .NET developers and Microsoft support engineers provide invaluable technical support through managed newsgroups. Many software bugs, fixes, and workarounds are discovered through these newsgroups.

- A significant portion of the coding for an ASP.NET Web Forms application with interactive database updates is provided by objects in the .NET Framework, requiring little additional coding on the part of the developer.

- The SqlDataProvider model may be the best choice for working with an SQL Server 7.0 or newer database, because the objects in that model have been optimized to work directly with the SQL Server DBMS. However, the OleDb Data Provider model also works with an SQL Server database.

- Data binding of Web Forms controls is one-way by default. That is, bound controls retrieve data automatically, but the ability to update the database must be programmed by the developer.

- The DataGrid control is an especially rich object for displaying and for updating a database.

QUESTIONS

1. To find out about Microsoft's managed newsgroups for developers, visit the _____ Web site.

2. To cause the elements and controls of a Web Form to appear in the middle of the form from left to right as materialized by any browser, you set the DOCUMENT's pageLayout property to FlowLayout, and the form's _____ property to _____.

3. To designate the target address of a hyperlink control, you set the _____ property.

4. By default, the Data Form Wizard uses the _____ Data Provider, regardless of which type of data source is being accessed.

5. The four panes of the Query Builder are _____, _____, _____, and _____.

6. When designating a parameter variable in SQL Server, the prefix is _____.

7. Following this prefix, the conventional variable name is _____.

8. In the Web.config file, the code for implementing impersonations is _____.

9. To open the windows for configuring the DataGrid control, you select the control in the Designer and then click _____ beneath the Properties window.

10. In Visual Studio .NET Web Forms applications, information in the client is automatically preserved through _____, and information on the server side is preserved through _____ or _____.

EXERCISES

Exercises 1 through 5 all relate to the StudentRegistrations SQL Server database that you created in Exercise 1 of Lesson B. Exercises 1, 2, 3, and 4 can each be done independently; Exercise 5 ties all of them together.

1. Create a Web Forms application with one Web Form named webScheduleOfClasses. This form contains two DataGrid controls. At the top of the form, one data grid displays all of the information in the COURSE table, along with a button in each row that says Display Sections. When the user clicks a Display Sections button, all sections of that course in the SECTIONS table appear in the lower DataGrid control. Include all of the elements in the SECTIONS table, but display the last name of the instructor instead of the FacultyID.

2. Create a Web Forms application with one Web Form named webClassRoster. This form offers three text boxes into which the user types the CourseID, section number, and term from the user. When the user then clicks the Get Roster button, a data grid displays the student ID, last name, first name, major, and phone of every student registered for the selected course.

3. Create a Web Forms application with one Web Form named webInstructorSchedule. This Web Form has text boxes where the user enters the FacultyID and the term. When the user clicks a button to Get Instructor Schedule, a data grid with only one row displays the instructor's last name, first name, office, and phone, while a second data grid displays the instructor's class schedule for the selected term, including CourseID, title, credits, section number, location, days, start time, and stop time.

4. Create a Web Forms application with one Web Form named webStudentSchedule. This Web Form has text boxes where the user enters the StudentID and the term. When the user clicks a button to Get Student Schedule, a data grid with only one row displays the student's last name, first name, major, and phone, while a second data grid displays the student's class schedule for the selected term, including CourseID, title, credits, section number, location, days, start time, stop time, and the last name of the instructor. The student can add or drop a course for the currently-selected term by clicking an Add This Course or Drop This Course button after filling in the Course ID and Section Number text boxes created for this purpose. When the student adds or drops a course, the REGISTRATION table is updated, and the data grid is refreshed. (The REGISTRATION table is the only table that can be updated in this entire application, covering Exercises 1 through 5.)

5. Create a Web Forms application with a Web Form named webStart. This Web Form displays hyperlinks offering these options: Schedule of Classes, Class Roster, Student Schedule, and Instructor Schedule. Add the Web Forms that you created in Exercises 1 through 4. Each hyperlink on webStart takes the user to a corresponding Web Form, and a Return Home hyperlink on each of those forms returns the user to the start page.

6. Modify the Web Forms FigEvents application from Tutorial 7 so that it uses the SQL Server FigEvents database that you created in Exercise 2 of Lesson B in this tutorial.

7. Create a portion of a Web Forms application that uses the SQL Server VisitorsBureau database that you created in Exercise 3 of Lesson B in this tutorial. This portion of the application supports the registration of a new visitor, as follows: The Web-based visitor must be able to create a new visitor's record in the database, requesting information about accommodations in a particular category, restaurants in a particular category, and attractions (yes or no). When the new visitor record is created, the system should open a Web form containing the requested information.

KEY TERMS

- 3-tier architecture
- ApplicationState
- authentication
- authorization
- Auto Format property
- basic authentication
- Button Column control
- certificate authentication
- credentials
- database diagrams
- DataGrid Web server control
- digest authentication
- impersonation
- instance name
- Integrated Information Server (IIS)
- IsPostBack function
- Microsoft Data Access Components (MDAC)
- Microsoft Desktop Engine (MSDE)
- NetSDK (instance name of MSDE)
- Property Builder pages
- Server Explorer
- SessionState
- SQL Server DBMS
- SqlClient.SqlDataReader object
- ViewState
- Visual Database Tools
- VsDotNet (instance name of MSDE)
- Windows integrated security, aka integrated Windows security

Error Traps and Help Files

Introducing the Final Version of the Village Housing Application

case ▶ You see the Village Housing application in the Overview at the beginning of this text, giving you a glimpse of the types of applications that you will be able to develop in Visual Basic .NET by the time you reach the end of the course. You then develop the Village Housing application from Tutorial 9. However, the application at that point is still not ready for commercial use, because it lacks adequate facilities for trapping and fixing errors, and it provides only minimal help to novice or confused users. It also lacks any reporting capability. Commercial applications, in general, need to do much better on all these fronts.

The Friendsville Games Development Team has continued to develop and refine the Village Housing application, so that it now incorporates additional features, including error traps and hints, Help files, and two reports generated from Crystal Reports, a report program generator that ships with Visual Studio .NET.

This tutorial also includes some final comments on data access technologies in the Visual Studio .NET platform, and on software configuration management—that is, the discipline of managing changes to software.

Previewing VillageHousing 2.0

This final preview highlights the new features of the Village Housing application. In this preview, you commit intentional errors to test the error trapping and handling capabilities of the application; specifically, you ask for help to test the Help system, and you display and print a report in the Crystal Report Viewer. You start with the error handlers and messages.

To experience the error traps and messages in VillageHousing version 2.0:

1 Create the following folder structure on your computer: **C:\VB.NET\Development\Tut11**. Using Windows Explorer, copy the **VillageHousing2** folder from the VB.NET\Student\Tut11 folder into this new folder.

NOTE: Portions of the preview of VillageHousing2.0 will not work correctly if you do not follow this folder structure precisely.

2 Run **VillageHousing.exe**, available in the C:\VB.NET\Development\Tut11\VillageHousing2\bin folder. Due to the addition of the Help features, a menu has been added to the main form, incorporating the former Load, Update, Cancel All, and Help buttons. Click **File | Load Data** to load the data from the VillageHousing.mdb database. The record for David Simpson appears on the left, and the data grid on the right fills with all of the rooms in the International Village.

3 Change the Room ID assigned for David Simpson to **500** (there is no room whose RoomID=500), and click **Edit | Update**. This action generates the error message shown in Figure 11-1. After reading this not terribly user-friendly error message, click **OK**. (This type of error message is quite informative for developers, but is probably too technical for users.)

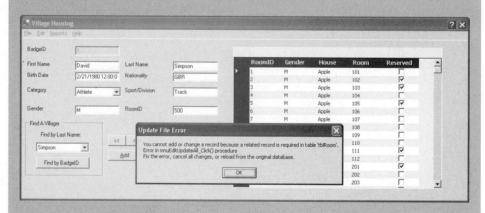

Figure 11-1: Referential integrity exception

The error message first describes the error, a referential integrity exception, because this update requires a matching record in tblRoom and none exists. This exception, first raised within Microsoft Access by a failed attempt to update the record in the underlying table, was passed by Access back to the Village Housing program, where it was trapped in the Try...Catch construct in mnuEditUpdateAll_Click(). The error message indicates which procedure raised the exception (mnuEditUpdateAll_Click())—this portion of the error message might be useful to developers while a program is under construction, but would normally be removed before the program is released for production. The error message goes on to tell the user how to recover from this error.

When working with databases, many possibilities for errors exist. Some scenarios include: the database filename may be incorrect, or the file does not exist; the data connection fails; the data connections are all in use by other users; the specific records being accessed are temporarily locked for update by other users; the data add or update or delete operation violates one of the rules of the database, such as a duplicate primary key or a referential integrity exception. You next intentionally create errors in trying to open the database.

4　Open **Microsoft Access**, open **VillageHousing.mdb** in the VB.NET\Student\ Tut11\VillageHousing2 folder, and open **tblVillager** in Design view. This action places an exclusive lock on that table. Return to theVillageHousing2 application, which is still running (or start it again, if necessary). Try to load the data again by clicking **File | Load Data**. This action raises an exception, shown in Figure 11-2, because tblVillager is locked. Again, the exception is raised within Microsoft Access and returned to the VillageHousing2 application. VillageHousing2 has been programmed to display an error message that indicates the name of the procedure in which the exception was raised. Click **OK** to clear the error. Close Microsoft Access, and then load the data again in VillageHousing2; the load operation works fine. Exit the VillageHousing2 application.

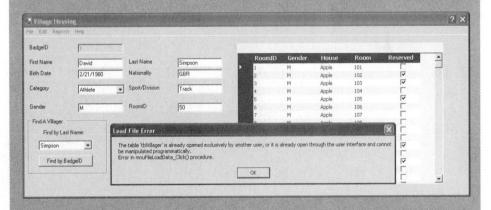

Figure 11-2: Table locked for exclusive use exception

5　Operating system errors can also be trapped. In Windows Explorer, temporarily rename VillageHousing.mdb to VillageHousing1.mdb. Then run VillageHousing2 again, and try to load the data by clicking **File | Load Data**. This time, the error message shown in Figure 11-3 is raised because the operating system could not find the file. (The error message on your computer indicates the folder name where the database is located.) Click **OK** to clear the error. In Windows Explorer, change the **VillageHousing1.mdb** filename back to **VillageHousing.mdb**. Then return to the VillageHousing2 application, and load the data once more; it works fine.

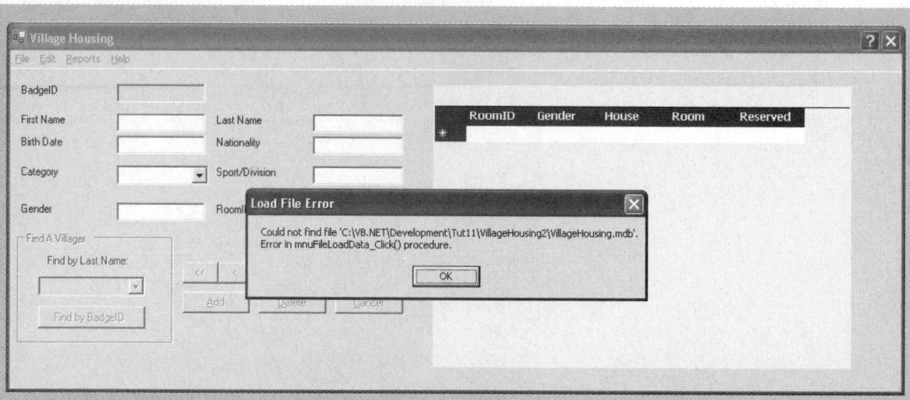

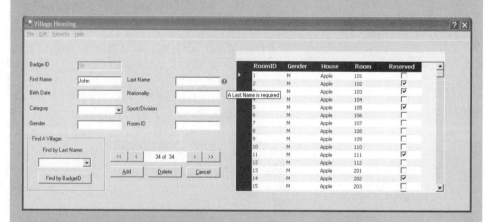

Figure 11-3: File not found exception

6 When possible, errors should be trapped and corrected before attempting to update the database. Click **Add** to add a new villager record. Insert **John** as the new villager's first name, press **Tab** to move the insertion point to the Last Name text box, and press **Tab** again without entering a last name. An error icon appears next to the Last Name text box. Point to the icon with the insertion point, and the message "A Last Name is required" appears in a pop-up window like a ToolTip, as shown in Figure 11-4.

Figure 11-4: Error entering the last name

7 Enter a **Birth Date, Nationality, Category,** and **Sport**, as shown in Figure 11-5, and then enter **q** as the gender, and press **Tab**. Another error icon appears, also shown in Figure 11-5. If you point at the icon, the error message "Enter M or F" pops up. Click the **Cancel** button, and the error icons as well as the input information disappear. The error icons and pop-up error messages are generated from the ErrorProvider control, and btnCancel_Click() clears these errors and the input information.

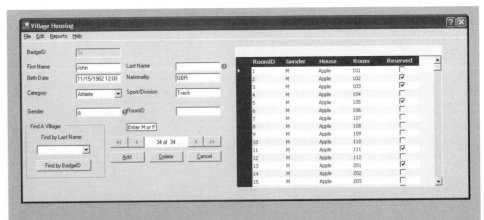

Figure 11-5: Error entering the gender

8   Because you just cancelled an Add record operation, the screen display now shows the last record before the cancelled new record, namely Georgette Simmons, Badge ID 33. Change Georgette's gender to **q**, and press **Tab**. The error icon appears. Change the gender to **F**, and press **Tab**—the error icon disappears. This action demonstrates the fact that correcting the error eliminates the error message—of course, the programmer must program this action.

Next, you will view the elements of the Help system implemented for this application, created largely with the HTML Help Workshop.

To view Help in VillageHousing 2.0:

1   Click **Help | Contents** to see the Table of Contents for the Help system, shown in Figure 11-6. If necessary, expand the Village Housing 2.0 base entry to see the other topics.

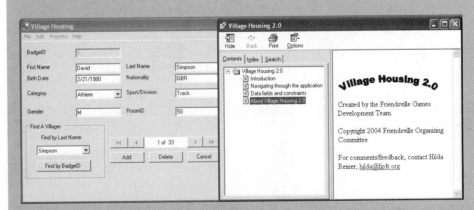

Figure 11-6: Help System—Table of Contents

2   Click **Help | Index** to view the Help index. Enter **Badge ID** as the item to look for in the index, and click the **Display** button to display the Help page that includes Help information concerning Badge ID, as shown in Figure 11-7.

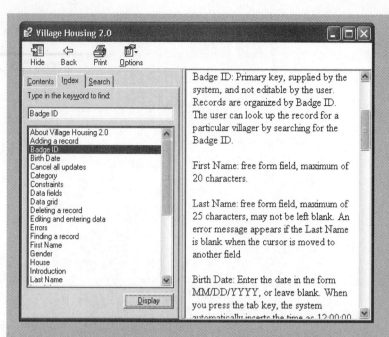

Figure 11-7: Help System—Index, displaying results for Badge ID

3   Click **Help | Search** to see the Help system's Search feature. Enter the word **error** in the search box, and scroll through the results, displayed in Figure 11-8. As you can see, the system highlights each occurrence of the search text in the Help screens.

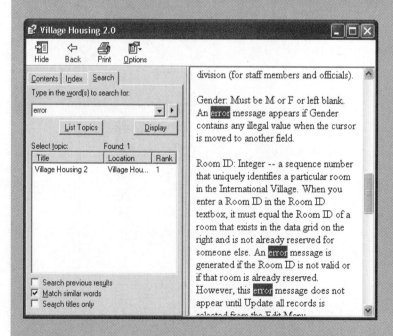

Figure 11-8: Help System—Search feature, looking for the word *error*

4   Click the **Nationality** text box, and press **F1** to see the context-sensitive Help feature, displayed in Figure 11-9. As you can see, the Help Index opens, with Nationality selected. You can click the Display button in the Help Index to display the page that contains information concerning the Nationality text box.

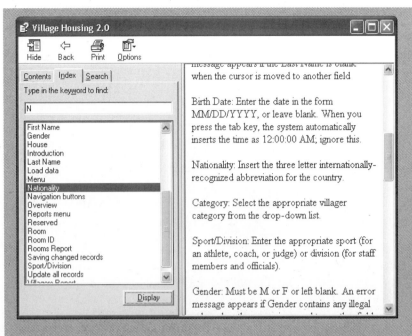

Figure 11-9: Context-sensitive Help, pressing F1 while in the Nationality text box

5   Click the **HelpButton** control ☒ on the right side of the title bar, and then click the **First Name** text box. A ToolTip pop-up displays a Help message, as shown in Figure 11-10. The Help button has also been programmed for the Add and Delete buttons.

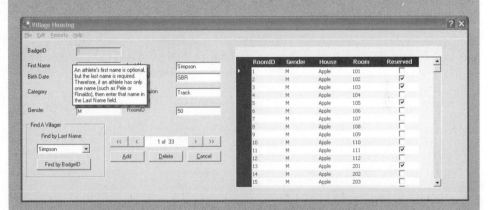

Figure 11-10: Help button ToolTip for the First Name text box

6   To see the final element in this application's Help system, move the pointer to any of the navigation buttons (the arrows that move to the first record, the previous record, the next record, or the last record), and hover over that button. A ToolTip is displayed, from the ToolTip control, as shown in Figure 11-11.

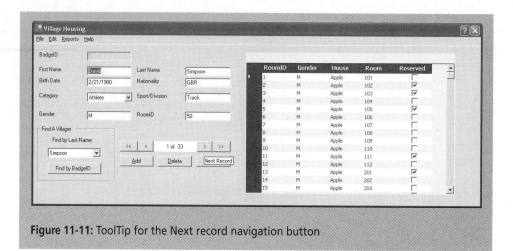

Figure 11-11: ToolTip for the Next record navigation button

Crystal Reports

The third new element in this version of the Village Housing application is the use of Crystal Reports, a product of Crystal Decisions Inc. that ships with Visual Studio .NET. Two sample reports have been written.

To view the sample reports in VillageHousing 2.0:

1 Exit and restart the VillageHousing application, and note that the Reports menu is disabled. To enable the Reports menu, click **File | Load Data** to reload the error-free data from the underlying tables. Then click **Reports | Villagers** to see the report of All Villagers and Their Assigned Rooms, as shown in Figure 11-12. As you will discover later in this tutorial, this is an example of a report based on a query. Note that the report is sorted by the villagers' last names, and that the contents of this sort field appear in a column (called the Group Tree) at the left.

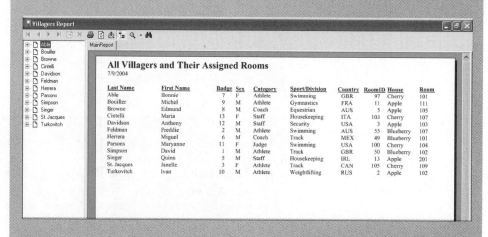

Figure 11-12: Crystal Report showing All Villagers and Their Assigned Rooms

2 Navigation buttons as shown in Figure 11-13 allow you to scroll through a multipage report; however, they are disabled in this report, because the entire report fits on one page. Experiment with the other toolbar buttons. Click the **Print** button, which opens the standard printer dialog box (provided a printer is installed on your computer); click **OK** to print the report, or **Cancel** to cancel printing.

tip
• • • • • • • • • • • • • • •
Double-click any item in the Group Tree—and *presto*—nothing happens at all! But in a multipage report, double-clicking an item in the Group Tree column causes the report page containing that item to be displayed.

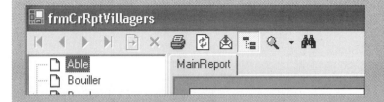

Figure 11-13: Crystal Reports toolbar

3   Click the **Refresh** button to reload the report from the data source.

4   Click the **Export** button to save a copy of this report in a file. By default, the report is saved in Adobe Acrobat (.pdf) format. Click the **Save as type** combo box. You see that the report can also be saved as an Excel spreadsheet (.xls), as a Word document (.doc), or in Rich Text Format (.rtf).

5   Click the **Toggle Group Tree** button, which causes the Group Tree column on the left to disappear or reappear.

6   Click the **Zoom** button. You can now modify display settings for the report if you desire.

7   Click the **Search text** button, and enter the word **Gymnastics** as the search text. If necessary, move the Search text dialog box out of the way of the SportOrDivision column, and click **Find Next**. The first occurrence of the word *Gymnastics* is boxed. Each time you click Find Next, the box moves to the next occurrence of the search text. Continue clicking **Find Next** until no more occurrences of *Gymnastics* can be found.

NOTE: Under the toolbar, you see the Main Report button. This particular report has no subreport, but if it did, a Subreport button would appear, allowing you to toggle between the two reports. For example, you could design a main report showing athletes participating in the Games, and a subreport listing all the events in which each athlete is participating. Clicking the Subreport button in such a scenario would display the list of events for the currently selected athlete, and clicking Main Report would return the display to the listing of all athletes.

8   Close the report. Click **Reports | Rooms** to display the Crystal Report titled Reserved Rooms Report, shown in Figure 11-14. This Crystal Report is constructed directly from the underlying tblVillager, tblHouse, and tblRoom tables. In other respects, it appears similar to the report of All Villagers and Their Assigned Rooms.

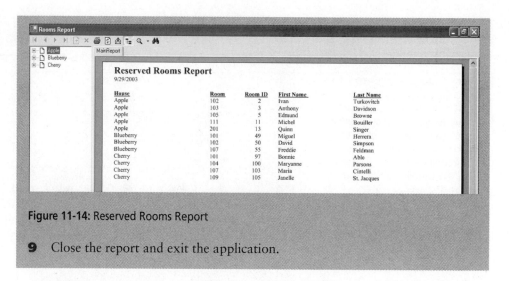

Figure 11-14: Reserved Rooms Report

9 Close the report and exit the application.

The members of the Friendsville Games Development Team—Hilda Reiner, Rick Sanchez, Althea Brown, and yourself—agree that you will have a lot of fun developing this application, and applying the techniques learned here to the whole myriad of programs that the FGDT is responsible for writing.

After completing this lesson, you will be able to:

■ Understand error-handling concepts, including both unstructured and structured exception handling, the Try...Catch control structure, and the ErrorProvider control

■ Describe the components of a Help system for an application, including the HTML Help Workshop, the HelpProvider control, the HelpButton control, and the ToolTip control

■ Describe the report generation functionality of Crystal Reports

■ Compare ADO.NET with the older but still supported ActiveX Data Objects (ADO) data access technology

■ Realize the necessity for software configuration management

Error Handling and Help System Concepts

Runtime Exceptions, Error Traps, Handlers, and Messages

Runtime errors occur for a myriad of reasons, from bad storage media to hardware failures, incomplete transaction processing, user mistakes, and program bugs. When a runtime error occurs, the system is said to **raise an exception** or **throw an exception**. The exception is first reported back to your program with an error number (ErrNum) and an error description (Message). Your program has an opportunity to handle, that is, deal with, the error. You can trap or catch the error, set things aright, and continue processing; or you can let the error stand and let the operating system take over. If your program fails to clear the error, the software issues a supervisor call, and the operating system normally steps in at that point and terminates your program. This is a rather rude result for the user who just happened to press Enter at the wrong time or who tried to save a file on a floppy that was already full. In general, one of your program design objectives is to gracefully handle errors and to avoid the supervisor call that aborts your program.

Unstructured Exception Handling

Although earlier versions of Visual Basic supported most of the concepts of structured programming, one significant area had not been addressed, namely, unstructured error handling.

Structured programming was discussed in depth in Tutorial 3. According to the principles of structured programming, every section of code should consist of sequence, selection, and iteration control structures, which can be nested to any level. An unstructured error handler violates this principle, because (1) the program enters the error handler from wherever an error is encountered, which is not a predictable or controlled location, and acts like a Go To statement—that is, an unconditional branch in program logic, which is illegal in structured programming; and (2) an unstructured error handler provides no assured means of returning whence it came, and even if it does return to the place that caused the exception, the return statement takes the form of another Go To or unconditional branch. By contrast, in a structured error handler, the error is trapped and handled within the confines of a recognized control structure—in this case, a type of selection structure, in which some code block is executed if no error is encountered, while an alternative code block is executed in the event of an error, and in either case execution continues with the next sequential instruction following this selection structure.

If you learned Visual Basic 6.0, you learned to incorporate On Error GoTo error traps into your code, along with rather cumbersome syntax for fixing errors and resuming normal processing (Exit Sub, Resume, and Resume Next). You will encounter unstructured error handling in any legacy commercial application that has not been rewritten from scratch. You should be able to recognize it and know what to do with it. Figure 11-15 provides an example of this type of error handling.

```
Private Sub Button2_Click(ByVal sender As System.Object, _
    ByVal e As System.EventArgs) Handles Button2.Click
  On Error GoTo ErrorTrap
  Dim dblNum As Double
  dblNum = InputBox("Enter a number > 0")
  If dblNum < 0 Then Err.Raise(6)
  dblNum = Math.Sqrt(dblNum)
  lblResult.Text = dblNum
  Exit Sub
ErrorTrap:
  MessageBox.Show(Err.Number & " " & Err.Description)
  dblNum = 0
  Resume Next
End Sub
```

Figure 11-15: On Error GoTo statement

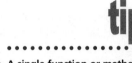

A single function or method can contain structured or unstructured exception handling, but not both.

The unstructured On Error GoTo statement was a holdover from the earliest days of BASIC. Although On Error GoTo is still supported in Visual Basic .NET, most developers welcome the switch to the Try...Catch control structure, borrowed from C++ and Java, which provides structured exception handling.

Structured Exception Handling: Try...Catch

Many program statements in a typical commercial application have the potential for causing runtime exceptions. This is certainly true of any I/O activity involving databases, especially Web-based and multiuser databases, and it also pertains to computational processes that depend on user input. The basic idea of structured error handling is to enclose any risky code in a Try statement (as in, "Try this and see if it works"), then use a Catch statement to catch any errors that might ensue, and then use a Finally statement to execute any code that is necessary whether or not an error was encountered. The Finally clause is optional. The control structure ends with the End Try statement. The syntax of the Try...Catch control structure is shown in Figure 11-16. As shown in Figure 11-16, you can choose whether or not to handle any particular type of exception; and, if you prefer not to deal with it, you can use a Throw statement to throw the original exception again, which allows the operating system to handle the exception as if you had not written an error handler at all.

```
Try
  'Insert the risky section of code.
Catch MyException1 As System.ExceptionClassName1
  'Add your error handling code here.
Catch MyTerminalException As System.ExceptionClassName2
  'Add your error handling code here.
  Throw MyTerminalException 'allow the exception
Catch OtherException As System.Exception
  'Add your error handling code here.
Finally
  'Insert code to be executed whether or not
  'an exception was thrown.
End Try
```

Figure 11-16: Try...Catch...Finally control structure

Figure 11-17 shows a typical application of the Try...Catch control structure. In this case, a user is asked to supply a shipment date and the expected number of days in transit. The program calculates the anticipated delivery date by adding the days in transit to the shipment date, and then displays the result in a DateTimePicker control. In this scenario, user entries can cause three different errors: (1) the shipping date may not be a valid date, so that a type mismatch occurs on the first input; (2) the number of days in transit may not be numeric, so that a type mismatch occurs on the second input; and (3) the sum of the user-supplied shipment date plus the number of days in transit may not be within the range of dates that the DateTimePicker control can handle (January 1, 1753 to December 31, 9999), causing an argument out of range exception. Whether or not an exception is thrown, the Finally code block displays the child form containing the DateTimePicker control.

```vb
Private Sub Button1_Click(ByVal sender As System.Object, _
    ByVal e As System.EventArgs) Handles Button1.Click
  Dim dteShipmentDate As Date
  Dim dteArrivalDate As Date
  Dim intDaysInTransit As Integer
  Dim frm As New Form2()
  Try
    dteShipmentDate = InputBox("Enter shipment date")
    intDaysInTransit = InputBox("Enter expected days in transit")
    dteArrivalDate = DateAdd(DateInterval.Day, _
        intDaysInTransit, dteShipmentDate)
    frm.DateTimePicker1.Value = dteArrivalDate
  Catch exc As Exception When Err.Number = 13 'Type Mismatch
    MessageBox.Show(exc.Message)
  Catch exc2 As ArgumentOutOfRangeException
    MessageBox.Show("The sum of the shipment date and " & _
        "days in transit is invalid")
  Catch
    MessageBox.Show("Other exception: " & Err.Number & _
        " " & Err.Description)
  Finally
    frm.Show()
  End Try
End Sub
```

Figure 11-17: Try...Catch...Finally sample

Whenever an exception is thrown in a running application, Visual Basic .NET sets the properties of the global Err object and creates a new instance of the Exception class (or, depending on the type of error, on a class derived from the Exception class). The Err object is used with both structured and unstructured exception-handling routines. Err.Source identifies the object or assembly that threw the exception. Err.Number identifies the error number. Err.Description is an error message associated with Err.Number, and corresponds to the Message property of the Exception class—the difference being that you can alter the contents of the Message property to create a more user-friendly error message if you want. If you do not assign a value to the Message property, the default is used.

You can intentionally generate a runtime error by using the Raise method of the Err object. This may be useful during program development and debugging—when a certain condition occurs, you want the program to halt and allow you to examine various aspects of the code. The syntax is Err.Raise(ErrorNumber, Source, Description, HelpFile, HelpContextID), where ErrorNumber identifies the exception to be raised, Source designates the location of the error, Description describes the error, HelpFile is the name of a Help file where information concerning this error can be found, and HelpContextID is a specific topic within that Help file. All of the arguments are optional, except ErrorNumber, which is defined as a long integer in the range of 0 to 65535. The numbers from 0 to 512 are reserved for standard Visual Basic .NET errors, so you can define any user error number from 513 to 65535. When you raise a user-defined error, the correct syntax for ErrorNumber is the user-defined error number plus the constant vbObjectError, i.e., `ErrorNumber + vbObjectError`.

A very simple example of the Raise method might be the following scenario: You have a procedure MyProc() in which the variable x must be greater than zero. If x is negative, you want to raise an exception so that you can examine variables and call the stack and determine how you came to this point. Therefore, you insert this statement in MyProc():

```
If x < 0 Then Err.Raise(5, "MyProc", "x is negative")
```

The Exception class also offers StackTrace and HelpLink properties. The StackTrace property contains an array of all function and method calls on the stack at the time the exception was thrown. This can be examined in break mode, so you (or your program) can figure out how you got to the point where the program blew up. The HelpLink property allows you to point to a location in a Help file containing information related to the exception.

Exceptions with Database Access

The Try...Catch construct is especially useful with database activities. Database operations are fraught with unforeseen difficulties: another user may change or delete the record you are trying to change before your operation has a chance to complete; the network connection may fail; or the database itself may be down. Therefore, any operation taken against a database should be inside protected code (that is, within a Try block), and the programmer should take appropriate action if the operation fails.

In building the Village Housing application in Tutorial 9, you used a wizard to construct frmVillageHousing. The wizard created multiple procedures that access the database directly or indirectly, and each of these procedures used the Try...Catch control structure. You can examine one of these procedures carefully to see how it should work and how you can add your own code to enhance its error-handling capability.

Figure 11-18 displays the Sub FillDataSet() procedure. This procedure executes the Fill() method for OleDbDataAdapters 1 and 2. The first action taken in this procedure is not likely to cause an error; the dataset's EnforceConstraints property is set to False. This allows the datasets to be loaded from the database without checking referential integrity (and other constraints) during the load process—because the data is being loaded from the underlying tables, your program can safely assume that the data is internally consistent, and enforcing constraints would likely cause errors during the load process, so the EnforceConstraints property must be temporarily turned off. Turning constraint checking back on is something that should always be done, whether or not the Fill() method works. Therefore, the command to set the EnforceConstraints property back to True occurs in the Finally code block in this procedure. The Try block attempts to fill the dataset. If an exception is raised by that code, that exception is passed to the Catch block. At the moment, this block simply throws the exception again, allowing the operating system to take over with its error handling. But instead, you could program the Catch block to handle the error in a different way. For example, you could display an error message to the user, suggesting that another attempt to fill the dataset be made later. (Rather than using a message box statement, you could display this message with the ErrorProvider control, explained in the next section.) You could make another attempt yourself right away, by enclosing another complete Try...Catch construct within the Catch block. Or you could take any other action you deem appropriate.

```
Public Sub FillDataSet(ByVal dataSet As _
    VillageHousing.dsVillager)
  'Turn off constraint checking before the dataset
  'is filled. This allows the adapters to fill the
  'dataset without concern for dependencies
  'between the tables.
  dataSet.EnforceConstraints = False
  Try
    'Attempt to fill the dataset through
    'the OleDbDataAdapters.
    Me.OleDbDataAdapter1.Fill(dataSet)
    Me.OleDbDataAdapter2.Fill(dataSet)
  Catch fillException As System.Exception
    'Add your error handling code here.
    Throw fillException
  Finally
    'Turn constraint checking back on.
    dataSet.EnforceConstraints = True
  End Try
End Sub
```

Figure 11-18: Sub FillDataSet()

You will discover that commercial applications typically include extensive error handling. If the public at large will be running your code on their own computers, the application needs to be bulletproof: you owe it to your customers to help them avoid any self-inflicted wounds!

The Try-it-again Approach to Error Handling

Especially in multiuser database applications, the reason that an operation may fail is that the particular record or table requested from a database is locked, because it is currently being updated by another user. This is one of several concurrency control issues surrounding multiuser databases, and different database management systems (DBMSs) handle these issues in different ways. For example, Oracle does not permit a **dirty read**—an attempt to read data whose update is pending; hence, the request is refused. In a typical implementation, Oracle also does not wait for the lock to be released, because such an approach can result in a situation called **deadlock**, in which two users each hold a lock on a record that the other needs to complete a transaction. Hence, an attempt to read locked data simply fails, which raises an exception in the calling program.

DBMSs use various locking strategies, but in most instances, a lock is held for only a fraction of a second. Therefore, one useful approach to recover from unsuccessful data access operations in Visual Basic .NET is to attempt the same operation again immediately. You can do this by building another Try...Catch construct inside the Catch block. This approach can be continued indefinitely, producing as many layers of Try...Catch constructs as the developer cares to write. However, the return on investment is limited after the first inner construct, because, if the operation fails twice, it is unlikely that the cause is a locked record or a busy database server.

When more than one layer of Try...Catch constructs exists, the outer layer is called a **wrapper layer**, because it wraps or encloses another error handler inside it. Code in the inner layer is doubly protected. When an exception is thrown, Visual Basic .NET looks for the first Catch statement that traps that error. If none is found, the system then looks at any wrapper Try...Catch construct around the construct that generated the error. The system proceeds through each layer until it finds an appropriate error handler or it exhausts all wrapper layers. If the error has not been handled in any layer of Try...Catch constructs, then the operating system error is generated. Figure 11-19 illustrates this approach.

```
Try
        'first try
        Load a dataset from a table in a database
Catch
        Try
                Load a dataset from a table in a database
        Catch
                Display an error message, advising user to try again later
        End Try
End Try
```

Figure 11-19: Pseudocode for layered Try...Catch constructs

Passing the Error to its Wrapper

The code created by the Data Form Wizard demonstrates another concept similar to the try-it-again approach in building Try...Catch constructs: the Data Form Wizard gives you the ability to write an error handler that traps all exceptions, handles only certain exceptions (or no exceptions), and then, if a particular exception has not been disposed of, simply raises the original exception again. If the original exception is raised again in the Catch block, the supervisor (that is, the operating system) looks for an error handler in the wrapper (if any).

Consider how this concept works, for example, when filling the datasets in frmVillageHousing. Recall from Tutorial 9 that the Data Form Wizard actually creates three levels of procedures for filling the datasets from the database. The click event procedure for loading data, the btnLoad_Click() procedure, calls the LoadDataSet() procedure, and the LoadDataSet() procedure calls the FillDataSet() procedure. The FillDataSet() procedure is where the connection to the database is actually opened, data is extracted from the database, and the data is placed in the datasets. If an error occurs—for instance, if the database connection cannot be opened because the file is not present, or if the data records cannot be accessed because they are locked—the exception is initially raised when the OleDbDataAdapter's Fill method is invoked, which occurs in the FillDataSet() procedure.

Look carefully at Figure 11-20, the FillDataSet() procedure (shown without the comment lines in the original code generated by the Data Form Wizard). In the Try block, the attempt is made to fill the datasets using OleDbDataAdapter1 and OleDbDataAdapter2. If the attempt is successful, execution proceeds to the Finally block. If the attempt fails for whatever reason, the error is handled by the Catch block. However, the Catch block simply raises the same exception again. At that point the supervisor looks for wrapper code to handle the exception, and it finds this wrapper construct in the LoadDataSet() procedure (which had called FillDataSet()). Note that the original exception, with its error number and description, is raised in the wrapper procedure.

NOTE: Some programmers might choose to subdivide FillDataSet() into two Try...Catch blocks, one for invoking the Fill method of each OleDbDataAdapter. In this way, if only one of those fill operations failed, the error handler could discover which one caused the problem.

```
Public Sub FillDataSet(ByVal dataSet As _
    VillageHousing.dsVillager)
  dataSet.EnforceConstraints = False
  Try
    Me.OleDbDataAdapter1.Fill(dataSet)
    Me.OleDbDataAdapter2.Fill(dataSet)
  Catch fillException As System.Exception
    Throw fillException
  Finally
    dataSet.EnforceConstraints = True
  End Try
End Sub
```

Figure 11-20: FillDataSet() Try...Catch construct

Figure 11-21 shows the relevant code extracted from the LoadDataSet() procedure. Recall from Tutorial 9 that this procedure attempts to fill a temporary dataset; it then clears and reloads the main dataset. LoadDataSet() presently contains two Try...Catch constructs, one for filling the temporary dataset (which might not work for all of the reasons that database access is prone to errors), and a second for clearing and merging data into the main dataset (which might not work if for some reason the main dataset became corrupted). The developer can write error-handling code for each case. At present, the automatically generated code from the Data Form Wizard just raises the error again, thereby passing the exception to the next wrapper level.

```
Public Sub LoadDataSet()
  Dim objDataSetTemp As VillageHousing.dsVillager
  objDataSetTemp = New VillageHousing.dsVillager()
  Try
    Me.FillDataSet(objDataSetTemp)
  Catch eFillDataSet As System.Exception
    Throw eFillDataSet
  End Try
  Try
    objdsVillager.Clear()
    objdsVillager.Merge(objDataSetTemp)
  Catch eLoadMerge As System.Exception
    Throw eLoadMerge
  End Try
End Sub
```

Figure 11-21: LoadDataSet() Try...Catch constructs

NOTE: At the end of the LoadDataSet() procedure, the code for loading dsRoom1 appears. You wrote this section of code in Tutorial 9, before studying the Try...Catch construct in detail. This code section begs for inclusion in an error handler, which you will take care of in Lesson B.

The btnLoad_Click() procedure is the wrapper around LoadDataSet(). If an exception was raised in LoadDataSet(), then the LoadDataSet() error handler causes that exception to be raised again in btnLoad_Click(). Figure 11-22 shows the relevant portion of btnLoad_Click(). Note that the error handler does not raise the exception again; rather, it displays a message to the user indicating the nature of the error that was encountered. In this way, the user may have a chance to fix the error or to try the operation again without aborting the application.

```
Private Sub btnLoad_Click(ByVal sender As System.Object, _
    ByVal e As System.EventArgs) Handles btnLoad.Click
  Dim strPath As String
  strPath = System.Reflection.Assembly._
    GetExecutingAssembly.Location
  Dim BeginBin As Integer
  BeginBin = InStr(1, strPath, "\bin")
  strPath = Microsoft.VisualBasic.Left(strPath, BeginBin) & _
    "VillageHousing.mdb"
  OleDbConnection1.ConnectionString = _
    "Provider=Microsoft.Jet.OLEDB.4.0;" & _
    "Password=''; User ID=Admin;Data Source=" & strPath
  Try
    Me.LoadDataSet()
  Catch eLoad As System.Exception
    System.Windows.Forms.MessageBox.Show(eLoad.Message)
  End Try
  Me.objdsVillager_PositionChanged()
End Sub
```

Figure 11-22: btnLoad_Click() Try...Catch construct

In sum, the Try...Catch construct provides structured error handling in Visual Basic .NET. You should use this construct to protect any code that might cause a runtime exception in your programs. You can write multiple layers of error handlers, and you can trap errors with as fine or as broad granularity as you feel necessary for the particular application. Granularity refers to the mesh of a filter: in this case, you can trap all exceptions in one Catch block (broadest granularity), or you can trap every conceivable error in its own Catch block (finest granularity), or anything in between.

The ErrorProvider Control

Both structured and unstructured exception handlers wait for an error to occur, often with some database operation, before they come into play. However, in many instances you can write validation code that checks data prior to executing a database operation that might cause an error. Then, you can warn the user to fix the error with the **ErrorProvider control**. You can trap not only database-related exceptions, but any kind of data entry error.

After you have added an ErrorProvider control to a form, you program each control's Validating event. In this event, you examine the value of the data that the user just typed, and call the ErrorProvider control's SetError method (containing the error message) if the user-provided data is invalid. This causes the error icon to appear next to the control and the message to pop up whenever the insertion point hovers over the control. When the user fixes the error, your code again calls the SetError method, but this time the error message is set to an empty string. This action clears the error message for that control and removes the error icon, as you saw demonstrated in the application preview at the beginning of this tutorial.

A significant advantage of the ErrorProvider control is that, unlike standard error-handling code, the error message does not disappear when the user closes a message box. The error icon remains, and the error message remains available, until the error is cleared.

Designing a Help System

When you offer a computer application to users, the users rightfully expect some instruction in using that application, and some help when their use of the application goes awry. The Friendsville Games Development Team recognizes this mandate, and acknowledges its responsibility to develop a comprehensive Help system appropriate for each of its applications.

When considering the requirements for a Help system for an application, you must keep in mind the different users who may need to know about the system, their level of sophistication, and the accessibility of your Help system to them. For example, you must answer these questions: will the Help system be distributed with the application, or will it be made available on the Web? Can anyone have access to the Help system, or will it require a username and password? Are all users equal, or do some privileged users merit special help? Therefore, your first Help system-related task is to determine the level of required help for an application and the audience.

Visual Basic .NET offers impressive facilities for creating a comprehensive Help system for a Visual Basic .NET application. This section describes the kinds of help that you may develop and offer to users. For each of your applications, you must determine the kinds and levels of help that are needed, and then design your Help system accordingly.

HTML Help Workshop

Microsoft offers a downloadable facility for creating a Help system, called the HTML Help Workshop. To use this facility effectively, you need to download two files, available from *http://msdn.microsoft.com*: htmlhelp.exe and helpdocs.zip. The first file, htmlhelp.exe, installs the HTML Help Workshop software, which you must run to install HTML Workshop on your computer. You should also unzip helpdocs.zip, which contains all of the documentation for HTML Help Workshop.

HTML Help Workshop is a facility for developing and incorporating HTML files into a comprehensive Help system. Though you are using it to support a Visual Basic .NET application, the Workshop software can also be used to create a Help system in support of any application. The HTML Help Workshop software directly supports the creation of four special-purpose files:

- *Project file (.hhp)*—Contains references to the other files that make up a Help system and overall Help system configuration information
- *Table of contents (.hhc) file*—Contains the table of contents for the Help system
- *Index (.hhk) file*—Contains the index to the Help system contents
- *Compiled output (.chm) file*—Incorporates the previous files plus any other HTML files used in the Help system

HTML Help Workshop also includes the HTML Help Image Editor, which facilitates screen captures for inclusion in a Help system.

When you plan for the design of a Help system, you should make two decisions early on. First, will you distribute this Help system with your application, or will you host this Help system at a Web site? Distributing the Help system with your application gives the most direct help to your users, and of course does not depend on users having access to the Internet. However, hosting your Help system on a Web site certainly makes it easier to update or refine the Help system based on your own experience and on feedback from users. Second, you must determine who the audience is for your Help system, and do you have different types or levels of users requiring different kinds of help? For example, the rather rudimentary Help system designed in support of VillageHousing 2.0 is intended to provide an initial introduction to the software for the Village reservations clerks who would use it.

You must also decide what components your Help system should contain. A Help system can contain the project, table of contents, and index files created in the HTML Help Workshop, plus all of the HTML files to which these files give access; or, alternatively, a Help system can be based on HTML files only, without using the HTML Help Workshop at all. Of course, in the latter case, you are responsible for providing whatever Help functionality exists with respect to a table of contents or index, and navigation from one topic to another.

After planning the components and writing the HTML content files, and including internal navigation links, you then use the HTML Help Workshop to build the table of contents and the index (if you have decided to use the workshop facility). The table of contents and the index contain links to all of the HTML files in your Help system. At this time, you also decide whether your Help system will contain a full search capability. You then use the HTML Help Workshop compiler to compile all of the Help system components into one output (.chm) file. This is the main file to which your application will link.

If you have decided to build a series of Help files without the HTML Help Workshop, then you must organize your HTML files in some fashion and determine which of these files is the entry point to the Help system from your application.

When the Help system is completed, you then decide how your application accesses it.

Access to Help from a Windows Application

The Visual Studio .NET Help object contains the Microsoft Windows Help Viewer. The **Help Viewer** renders the familiar Help screen containing Contents, Index, and Search tabs in the left pane, the current topic in the right pane, and a toolbar pane along the top. You have already seen the Help Viewer; it appears in Figures 11-6, 11-7, and 11-8. With the Help object, you can open a compiled (.chm) Help file or another .html file directly, or you can open your Help file via the HelpProvider control.

The HelpProvider Control

The most common access method into your Help system comes from the HelpProvider control, which you add to a Windows Form. The HelpProvider control HelpNamespace property identifies either a .chm file produced by compiling all of your Help files into one file with the HTML Help Workshop, or an .htm or .html file that you have designated as the lead file into your Help system. The HelpProvider control appears in the tray beneath the form to which it is attached.

The left pane of the Help Viewer (containing contents, index, and search tabs) is usually opened from menu selections, which call the Help object's ShowHelp or ShowHelpIndex method.

If you have not created a Help system (either .chm or .htm files), you can still provide limited help using shortcut menus. In this case, you add the HelpProvider control to a form, but you leave the HelpNamespace property blank.

After you have added a HelpProvider control to a form, several Help-related properties are exposed in the properties for each control on the form:

- *HelpKeyword on HelpProvider1*—The particular topic in the index for a Help file related to this control
- *HelpString on HelpProvider1*—The text of a Help message that is displayed in a ScreenTip
- *ShowHelp on HelpProvider1*—The Boolean value that indicates whether context-sensitive help should be displayed for this control

If the user presses F1 when a control has focus, your Help system displays context-sensitive help for that control, provided that the ShowHelp property for that control is set to True. In this case, if the HelpProvider1 HelpNamespace property is blank, then the value of the control's HelpString property is displayed in a ScreenTip. If HelpProvider1's Namespace is not blank, then the designated Help file is opened in the Help Viewer, and the index tab in the Help Viewer is set to the HelpKeyword property.

Help Button

The **Help button** offers an alternate means of providing context-sensitive help. You use a Help button most often when providing help to a user within a dialog box, because a dialog box is modal, and does not allow the display of another form while the modal form is displayed. Therefore, the appearance of the Help button on the VillageHousing 2.0 main form is a bit out of the ordinary (because this is not a modal dialog box); it is included here so that the discussion of Help system options is complete.

Because displaying a Help screen would be impossible from within a modal form, a dialog box or other modal form is usually programmed to display a HelpButton control in lieu of the Maximize and Minimize buttons in the title bar. (Because a dialog box usually is also not resizable, the Maximize and Minimize functions are irrelevant.) You still use a HelpProvider control, and you set the HelpString property with the Help message to be displayed in a ScreenTip. When the user clicks the HelpButton control at runtime, the Help button icon (a mouse pointer with a question mark) is displayed. While the Help button is active, the HelpNamespace property of the HelpProvider control is ignored.

ToolTip Control

Help can also be displayed as a ToolTip by adding a ToolTip component to a form. The ToolTip control appears in the tray underneath the form. (You use only one ToolTip control per form.) When the ToolTip control is present, the ToolTip on ToolTip1 property appears in the Properties window for each control on the form. The text that you type into this property pops up on the screen whenever the mouse pointer hovers over the control at runtime.

Crystal Reports

Crystal Reports is a report program generator from Crystal Decisions Inc. that ships with Visual Studio .NET. Using Crystal Reports in a Windows Forms project is a two-step process.

First, you create a report, using either the Crystal Report Designer or the Crystal Report Gallery (a collection of report-design wizards). The wizard steps you through the design of a basic report with a small number of standard options. The wizard is fairly easy to use, as you will see in Lesson C. By comparison, the Designer allows you to customize your report to a far greater extent than the wizard, but it's also somewhat more complicated to use. Of course, the two approaches can be combined: you use the wizard to design a standard report, and then customize it in the Designer. If you are familiar with the Report Designer in Microsoft Access, you will find this Designer similar. When you create a Crystal Report, you are adding a new item to a project, whose default name is CrystalReport1.rpt (though you should always rename the report to a meaningful name).

Second, after you have completed the report design, you use the CrystalReportViewer control to view the report in your application. The normal procedure is to add a new form to a project, place a CrystalReportViewer control on the form, set the viewer's Dock property to Fill, and set its ReportSource property to the name of the Crystal Report that you have just created. Then you add a menu item to the project's main form, for the purpose of displaying that report. In the menu item's click event, you instantiate the form containing the CrystalReportViewer control, and display the form.

ADO.NET vs. ADO Data Access Technologies

Tutorial 9 mentioned that Visual Studio .NET supports three data access technologies: ADO.NET, ADO, and OLE DB. The third of these, OLE DB, is accessible through Visual C++ .NET and C# .NET, but not through Visual Basic .NET, and so is not relevant to us here. In Visual Basic .NET, you have a choice of using the new ADO.NET data access technology or the older ADO technology, which was introduced in Visual Basic 6.0.

Up to this point, the examples in this book have used ADO.NET exclusively. However, in this last tutorial, the Crystal Report called All Villagers and Their Assigned Rooms was created using ADO—just as a sample of how this technology works.

Though your new Visual Basic .NET applications will most likely use ADO.NET for data access, you are also likely to encounter legacy or upgraded applications that depend on ADO. So it behooves you to have some insight into what that means.

ActiveX Data Objects (ADO) data access is built around the central notion of a recordset. A **recordset** is similar to an ADO.NET dataset in that it is an in-memory store that represents the data stored in one or more underlying tables. It is also similar in that it can be disconnected from (that is, loosely coupled to) those source tables. However, a recordset is unlike a dataset in several important respects:

- If the recordset is disconnected from the underlying tables, then it is usually not updatable. That is, a recordset may contain a snapshot of data in the underlying tables, but changes to the snapshot cannot be propagated back to the database.
- A recordset has no knowledge of relationships between tables. If a recordset contains data from multiple tables, it cannot maintain the distinct identity of the sources. Thus, you can build a recordset from a table join (in Visual Basic .NET) or from the output of a query (in the source DBMS), but this recordset is not updatable.
- If the recordset remains connected to the data source, then it consumes scarce server-side resources. Applications (in any language) that use a technology requiring the maintenance of a connection to the database are not scalable, because the server has a limited number of connections.
- ADO does expose some behaviors that are unavailable in ADO.NET. For instance, an ADO data control may support a scrollable server-side cursor that steps through the records of a table; but, of course, each such cursor uses a connection.

The practical implications are these:

- If an ADO.NET dataset contains two tables and the relationship between them, and if an update capability is required, then implementing the same thing in ADO requires two separate recordsets (one for each underlying table) and the necessary programming to maintain the relationship between them. The coding requirements can easily become prohibitive.
- ADO.NET is only available in managed code applications—those that are fully compliant with the .NET Framework and Common Runtime Library. For native code applications (that is, those written in earlier versions of Visual Basic or C++ and not fully compliant with .NET), ADO is the only choice.

■ ADO is perfectly acceptable for applications that only require access to data and not updates to data, because such applications can take advantage of the loose coupling available within ADO.

Software Configuration Management

A final topic bears mention in an intermediate course in Visual Basic .NET: software configuration management. The Friendsville Games Development Team, with only four developers (Hilda, Rick, Althea, and you), has managed to get by without paying much attention to this topic. But larger and longer projects, and projects involving dozens of programmers at multiple sites, and projects that result in commercial software releases spanning multiple versions over an extended time span, all require careful attention to this topic.

Software configuration management describes the discipline for tracking changes to a software package, especially when multiple programmers are simultaneously working on multiple copies of the software, or when an organization must simultaneously support multiple releases of the software.

You can envision software management headaches even within the small confines of the FGDT. The FGDT may release Up Close 1.0 (from Tutorial 8) to the public, then release a version with a new data file with updated information concerning athletes (named release 1.1), then release a software fix to a bug (Up Close version 1.2), and then release an entirely new version of the software with new functionality (Up Close version 2.0). At that point, users who purchased version 1.0, 1.1, and 1.2 might ask for an upgrade to version 2.0. Suddenly, you have a need to write an upgrade package to version 2.0 for those customers who are running 1.0, those running 1.1, and those running 1.2. And internally within the FGDT, you must keep all of these configurations and releases straight.

You also have the problem of conflicting software changes, when Hilda and Rick are both working on enhancements to the Village Housing application, but each programmer does not know precisely what the other programmer is doing.

In all of these cases, you need to keep track of every software change, the source of that change, the effects of that change, perhaps the approval process for accepting the change, and the status of that change ("Implemented in release 1.2," or "Deferred for version 2.0").

Entire books and doctoral dissertations have been written on the subject of software configuration management. As a Visual Basic .NET programmer, you should at least be aware that this is an issue, and that you will encounter it in the real world.

With respect to Visual Studio .NET, Visual SourceSafe is the component that provides software configuration management functionality. Visual SourceSafe is offered only in the Enterprise Edition of Visual Studio .NET, so it is not covered in this text beyond this brief paragraph.

When you are developing a project that uses Visual SourceSafe, you place each file as you complete it under the control of Visual SourceSafe, where it is backed up to the Visual SourceSafe database. This can include any type of file that you designate to be part of your project—source code, text file, graphics, audio, or video, and so on. Any project file in the database can be accessed by all members of the project team. As each developer makes changes to a file, those changes are recorded and backed up, so that: (1) a chronological record of all changes and who made which changes is maintained; (2) the most recent version of a file is always available; and (3) any previous version can be recovered.

You now have completed Lesson A. Complete the following end-of-lesson questions and exercises before jumping into Lesson B.

S U M M A R Y

- An application is not complete until you insulate the user from execution errors and provide whatever help users may find necessary in using the application.
- Visual Basic .NET supports both structured and unstructured error trapping and handling. The structured error handler is the Try...Catch construct. The unstructured handler is the On Error GoTo construct. Try...Catch is generally preferred in new applications.
- By programming the Validating event and using an ErrorProvider control, you can trap data entry errors as soon as the insertion point leaves a control.
- The HTML Help Workshop is a downloadable facility for creating a complete package of Help files for an application, including a table of contents, index of topics, and full-text search capability. Combined with other HTML pages created for each topic, the HTML Workshop compiles into a single .chm Help file.
- You add Help to an application with the HelpProvider control. You can set the HelpNamespace property to your .chm File or to another HTML file, providing an entry point into your Help system. You can set the HelpNavigator and HelpKeyword properties of individual controls in order to direct the Help system to locate a particular topic or keyword when the user asks for help on that control. Even without an entry in the HelpNamespace property, you can set the HelpString property for a control along with the ShowHelp property in order to display context-sensitive help for a particular control.
- You can add a Help button to a form, which displays a ScreenTip containing help information. A Help button is especially useful on a modal form such as a dialog box, because a modal form permits a ScreenTip, but does not allow any other form to be displayed while the modal form is active.
- You can add a ToolTip control to the form, exposing the ToolTip property for each control on the form.
- Crystal Reports is a report generation facility that ships with Visual Studio .NET. It greatly eases the tasks associated with report creation, especially for reports dependent for input on an external data source.
- For legacy applications converted to Visual Basic .NET and for unmanaged (native) code applications, ActiveX Data Objects (ADO) technology provides a means of database access. ADO is built around the notion of a recordset, an in-memory data store similar to an ADO.NET dataset. The recordset is not aware of internal data relationships. For data relationships to persist in the underlying tables, a recordset must maintain an open connection to the database. A recordset derived from multiple tables is not updatable. Because recordsets are more tightly coupled to the data source, ADO technology is far less scalable than ADO.NET technology. In one respect, ADO is more capable than ADO.NET, because only ADO supports a server-side cursor for scrolling through the recordset dynamically.
- Large, long-term, or commercial computer applications require sophisticated software configuration management, the type of facility offered by Visual SourceSafe in the Enterprise Edition of Visual Studio .NET.

Q U E S T I O N S

1. In structured error handling, suspect code and recovery procedures are encapsulated in a _____ construct.

2. The error-prone code itself is placed in the _____ block.

3. Code that executes in any case, whether or not an error is trapped, is placed in the _____ block.

4. When an exception is raised, control is transferred to the first _____ block that contains a handler for that exception.

5. If the user makes a data entry error, you can display an error icon next to the control and an error message in a ScreenTip. To do this, you add a(n) _____ control to the form, and you program the _____ event for each control whose data you want to check.

6. _____ is a downloadable facility from Microsoft for developing a Help system. Using this facility, you can produce four types of Help-related files:
   a. _____
   b. table of contents (.hhc) files
   c. _____
   d. compiled help system (.chm) file

7. The report generator that ships with Visual Studio .NET is called _____.

8. You can associate a .chm or .html file with a form by adding a _____ control to the form.

9. If a _____ control is added to a form, a property of the same name is exposed for each control on that form. The text in that property appears in a ScreenTip whenever the mouse pointer hovers over the graphical control.

10. The Help button can be added to any form, but it is most commonly added to a _____.

11. The ADO object that corresponds to an ADO.NET dataset is the _____.

12. ADO supports a scrollable server-side cursor, but this cursor consumes a _____.

C R I T I C A L   T H I N K I N G

At the end of each lesson, reflective questions are intended to provoke you into considering the material you have just read at a deeper level.

1. One of the decisions that the FGDT must make concerning its Help systems is where to locate them—with the application software or at a Web site. Where and why would you recommend placing the Help system for the Up Close and Personal application (from Tutorial 8)? The Village Housing application (Tutorials 9 and 11)? The Tickets application (Tutorial 10)?

2. The HelpNamespace property can contain the name of a .chm file or an .html file. When and why would you choose to reference an .html file in lieu of a .chm file?

EXERCISES

The following are paper and pencil exercises designed to ensure that you understand the concepts presented in Lesson A.

1. Examine the code for the LogonManager application that you created in Tutorial 4. Which statements and procedures should be protected by error-handling code? Your answer should include I/O instructions as well as any other instruction that could possibly raise an error in the operating system.

2. Examine the GUI for the LogonManager application that you created in Tutorial 4. Describe how a HelpProvider control could be used to provide explanations for each piece of user-provided data on the forms. Also describe how an ErrorProvider control could trap data entry errors and assist users in entering valid input.

3. Examine the code for the Final Scoring application that you created in Tutorial 6. Which statements and procedures should be protected by error-handling code? Your answer should include I/O instructions as well as any other instruction that could possibly raise an error in the operating system.

4. Examine the GUI for the Final Scoring application that you created in Tutorial 6. Describe how a HelpProvider control could be used to provide explanations for each piece of user-provided data on the forms. Also describe how an ErrorProvider control could trap data entry errors and assist users in entering valid input.

5. Examine the Event Schedule application that you developed in Tutorial 7. Describe the contents of a Help system that could be developed for this application using the HTML Help Workshop.

6. Examine the Up Close and Personal application that you developed in Tutorial 8. Describe the contents of a Help system that could be developed for this application using the HTML Help Workshop.

After completing this lesson, you will be able to:

■ Make preliminary modifications to frmVillageHousing

■ Incorporate the Try...Catch construct in an application

■ Apply the ErrorProvider control on Windows Forms

■ Build a Help system using the HTML Help Workshop

■ Incorporate Help in a Windows Forms application, using the output of the HTML Help Workshop along with the HelpProvider control, HelpButton control, and ToolTip control

Error Traps, Error Handling, and Help Systems

Tasks for the FGDT

The Friendsville Games Development Team has decided to collaborate completely on this last tutorial, although each member of the team has the lead responsibility for a designated aspect of VillageHousing2. After you make the necessary adjustments to the GUI to convert VillageHousing into VillageHousing2, Rick shows the team how to program the Try...Catch construct wherever needed in the application, especially for operations involving database access. Althea demonstrates the ErrorProvider control. Hilda leads the team through the use of the HTML Help Workshop and Crystal Reports. You have the lead on incorporating Help in VillageHousing2, using Hilda's HTML Help Workshop results as well as the HelpProvider, ToolTip, and HelpButton controls. You also have the lead responsibility for creating the Crystal Reports in Lesson C.

Preliminary Activities: Modifying frmVillageHousing

Before embarking on Rick's proposed changes to the code, you must make a few modifications to the frmVillageHousing GUI as it existed in Tutorial 9. The buttons at the top of the form in the Village Housing application (Help, Load, Update, and Cancel All) are replaced by a MainMenu control. The menu also provides for the two Crystal Reports that you will add to Village Housing 2.0, and a complete Help menu.

To initiate the VillageHousing2 project, incorporate a menu in frmVillageHousing, and replace the Help, Load, Update, and Cancel All buttons:

1   The completed VillageHousing project from Tutorial 9 has been provided for you in the VB.NET\Student\Tut11 folder. Rename the folder **MyVillageHousing2**. Open the **VillageHousing** solution, and rename both the solution and the project as **VillageHousing2**. Run the program to ensure that it still works correctly after making these changes.

2   Open **frmVillageHousing** in the Designer. Delete the four buttons at the top of the form: **btnHelp**, **btnLoad**, **btnUpdate**, and **btnCancelAll**.

3 Drop a new **MainMenu** control onto the form (it appears in the tray underneath the form). Type in the **menu items** shown in Figure 11-23, and assign the **menu item names** given in the same figure. Note that several of these menu items represent features that you will incorporate into VillageHousing2 during the course of this tutorial.

Menu items	Menu item names
&File	mnuFile
&Load Data	mnuFileLoadData
E&xit	mnuFileExit
&Edit	mnuEdit
&Update	mnuEditUpdateAll
&Cancel All	mnuEditCancelAll
&Reports [initially disabled]	mnuReports
&Villagers	mnuReportsVillagers
&Rooms	mnuReportsRooms
&Help	mnuHelp
&Contents	mnuHelpContents
&Index	mnuHelpIndex
&Search	mnuHelpSearch
- [separator bar]	MenuItemN [default name]
&About	mnuHelpAbout

Figure 11-23: Menu for frmVillageHousing

4 Open the **Code Editor** for frmVillageHousing. Open the procedure for **mnuFileLoadData_Click**(). Copy into this procedure the contents (excluding the Sub and End Sub statements) of btnLoad_Click(), and then delete the btnLoad_Click() procedure.

5 Open the procedure for **mnuEditUpdateAll_Click**(). Copy into this procedure the contents (excluding the Sub and End Sub statements) of btnUpdate_Click(), and then delete the btnUpdate_Click() procedure.

6 Open the procedure for **mnuEditCancelAll_Click**(). Copy into this procedure the contents (excluding the Sub and End Sub statements) of btnCancelAll_Click(), and then delete the btnCancelAll_Click() procedure.

7 Delete the btnHelp_Click() procedure. The Help dialog box in VillageHousing is replaced by a complete Help system in VillageHousing2.

8 Open the **mnuFileExit_Click**() procedure, and insert an **End statement.**

9 Run the **VillageHousing2** application. Check that all the menu selections (except for the Help menu items) work as advertised. Close the application and return to the IDE.

Using Try...Catch in VillageHousing2

Rick Sanchez has been experimenting with the Try...Catch construct in VillageHousing2. Rick has decided to use this construct to increase the likelihood that the dataset fill and the database update operations will be completed successfully. In a multiuser database application, a user may attempt to access a record or table that is in the process of being updated by another user, causing the data access attempt to fail. Following Rick's guidance, you incorporate an extra layer of Try...Catch constructs into the file load and the database update procedures, so that a failed data access attempt is followed by a second attempt. Further, when two data access attempts fail, Rick suggests a gentle error message to the user rather than an operating system exception that could abort the program. Because this is a new application, Rick also suggests including in the error message an identification of the procedure that generated the error. For purposes of program debugging, lower-level procedures should also include error messages that indicate the nature and location of any exception.

Start by examining how an error is handled in the code generated by the Data Form Wizard before making any changes to it. You create an intentional error by temporarily renaming the database, so that the attempt to load the dataset fails. You make improvements to the error handlers after you understand exactly how the statements in the existing code are processed.

To examine the initial error-handing code in frmVillageHousing:

1   In Windows Explorer, in the VB.NET\Student\Tut11\MyVillageHousing2 folder, rename **VillageHousing.mdb** as **xVillageHousing.mdb**.

2   Run the application, and click **File | Load Data**. The error message indicates that file VillageHousing.mdb could not be found. Click **OK**, and close the running application.

This does tell you that an error occurred and the reason for the error, and it also prevents the application from blowing up. However, it may not give you all the protection that you need in the event of an error, or all the information you need in order to fix the problem. A second level of error handling might be desirable, because the error could be caused by a temporary dropped connection to the database server or some such transient cause. In addition, you might want to know exactly where in your program the error occurred.

3   Next, you discover where in your code the exception occurred. To do this, click the **Try** statement in the **mnuFileLoadData_Click()** procedure, and press **F9** to make that Try statement a breakpoint. Then run the application again, and click **File | Load Data**. The program goes into break mode, with the Try statement highlighted.

4   Select **Debug | Step Into** (or press the short-cut key, **F8** or **F11**) to execute the Try statement and move to the next statement. Press **F8** repeatedly to see each statement that is executed and each exception that is thrown. (These statements are explained in the next section.) After executing the Try statement, the program executes these statements in sequence as you press the F8 function key:

- *Me.LoadDataSet()*—This is a procedure call to the LoadDataSet() procedure. The system pushes the current statement location in mnuFileLoadData()_ Click() onto the stack, and transfers control to the LoadDataSet() header.
- *Public Sub LoadDataSet()*—The procedure header is executed.
- *objDataSetTemp = New VillageHousing.dsVillager()*—objDataSetTemp is assigned as a new instance of dsVillager.

tip

The short-cut key for Step Into is either F8 or F11, depending on which release of Visual Basic .NET is installed.

- *Try*—The Try...Catch construct in LoadDataSet() is entered.
- *Me.FillDataSet(objDataSetTemp)*—This is a procedure call to FillDataSet(), passing objDataSetTemp as a parameter. The system pushes the current statement location in LoadDataSet() onto the stack, and transfers control to the FillDataSet() header.
- *Public Sub FillDataSet(ByVal dataSet As VillageHousing.dsVillager)*—The procedure header is executed.
- *dataSet.EnforceConstraints = False*—Turns constraint checking off while data is being loaded.
- *Try*—The Try block in FillDataSet() is entered.
- *Me.OleDbConnection1.Open()*—The System attempts to open a connection to the (now misnamed) database. The system throws an exception.
- *Catch fillException As System.Exception*—The error handler traps the exception, and names it fillException.
- *Throw fillException*—The only statement in the Catch block simply throws the error again.
- *Finally*—This procedure includes a block of code that must always be executed, whether or not an error was encountered. So, even though the exception has been rethrown, the Finally block is executed before the system deals with the uncleared exception.
- *dataSet.EnforceConstraints = True*—Constraint checking is turned back on.
- *Me.OleDbConnection1.Close()*—An attempt is made to close the connection. Of course, the error in trying to open the connection is still pending.
- *End Try*—This marks the conclusion of the Finally block. However, End Try is not an executable statement. Because the pending error has not been cleared, the system looks for another error handler to deal with it now that the Try...Catch construct in FillDataSet() is concluded. Looking for a wrapper procedure, it pops the stack, returning to the LoadDataSet() procedure and bringing the uncleared exception with it.
- *Catch eFillDataSet As System.Exception*—You find yourself back in the LoadDataSet() procedure, where the pending error from the attempt to open a connection to the database is trapped in the Catch statement. The Catch statement names this error eFillDataSet.
- *Throw eFillDataSet*—The error handler merely throws the exception again. The following statement, End Try, indicates to the system that this Try...Catch construct has no Finally block. Therefore, because the pending error has not been cleared, the system looks for another error handler to deal with it. Looking for a wrapper procedure, it pops the stack, returning to the mnuFileLoadData_Click() procedure and bringing the uncleared exception with it.
- *Catch eLoad As System.Exception*—You find yourself back in the mnuFileLoadData_Click() procedure, where the pending error from the attempt to open a connection to the database is trapped in the Catch statement. The Catch statement names this error eLoad.
- *System.Windows.Forms.MessageBox.Show(eLoad.Message)*—The error message is displayed, indicating that the file was not found. The original error object was regenerated at each level, carrying with it an error number, description, and a series of related parameters. The message that appears to the user was actually caused by the failure to open a connection in the FillDataSet() procedure.

> **NOTE:** The wizard generated the fully qualified reference to System.Windows.Forms.MessageBox. However, because this is a Windows Forms application, the System.Windows.Forms namespace is already included in the project through the list of references in Solution Explorer. Therefore, you can use the MessageBox statement without qualification.

5 If necessary, click the running program on the **TaskBar** to see the error message displayed to the user. Click **OK**.

6 Back in the IDE, click **Debug | Stop Debugging**. Click **Debug | Clear All Breakpoints**.

7 In Windows Explorer, rename **xVillageHousing.mdb** as **VillageHousing.mdb**.

8 Run the application again to make sure that you have not inadvertently introduced any errors during this experiment.

Now that you have seen the error handler in operation, you can take steps to improve it.

To improve error trapping in the fill dataset and update database operations of frmVillageHousing:

1 In the Code Editor for frmVillageHousing, locate the **mnuFileLoadData_Click()** procedure. Replace the **Try...Catch** construct in that procedure with the two-level error trapping procedure shown in Figure 11-24.

```
Try
  'Attempt to load the dataset.
  Me.LoadDataSet()
Catch eLoad1 As System.Exception
  Try
    'Attempt to load the dataset.
    Me.LoadDataSet()
  Catch eLoad2 As System.Exception
    MessageBox.Show(eLoad2.Message & vbCrLf & _
      "Error in mnuFileLoadData_Click() procedure.", _
      "Load File Error")
  End Try
End Try
```

Figure 11-24: Two levels of Try...Catch in mnuFileLoadData_Click()

2 Locate the **mnuEditUpdateAll_Click()** procedure. Replace the entire procedure with the two-level procedure shown in Figure 11-25.

```
Private Sub mnuEditUpdateAll_Click(ByVal sender As _
    Object, ByVal e As System.EventArgs) _
    Handles mnuEditUpdateAll.Click
  Try
    'Attempt to update the datasource.
    Me.UpdateDataSet()
    Me.LoadDataSet()
  Catch
    Try
      'Attempt to update the datasource.
      Me.UpdateDataSet()
      Me.LoadDataSet()
    Catch eUpdate As System.Exception
      MessageBox.Show(eUpdate.Message & vbCrLf & _
        "Error in mnuEditUpdateAll_Click() procedure" & _
        vbCrLf & "Fix the error, cancel all changes, " _
        & "or reload from the original database.", _
        "Update File Error")
    End Try
  End Try
  Me.objdsVillager_PositionChanged()
End Sub
```

Figure 11-25: Two levels of Try...Catch in mnuEditUpdateAll_Click()

3   Click **Build | Build Solution** to ensure that you have not made any syntax errors while typing these procedures.

The click event procedure that initiates the operations for filling the datasets (btnLoad_Click() in Tutorial 9, mnuFileLoadData_Click() in Tutorial 11) calls the LoadDataSet() procedure, and the LoadDataSet() procedure calls the FillDataSet() procedure. The click event procedure that initiates the operations for updating the database (btnUpdate_Click() in Tutorial 9, mnuEditUpdateAll_Click() in Tutorial 11) calls the UpdateDataSet() procedure, and the UpdateDataSet() procedure calls the UpdateDataSource() procedure. You now examine each of these called procedures to see whether and how the Try...Catch constructs should be modified to enhance the error-handling capability of this application.

4   Locate and examine the **LoadDataSet**() procedure, the first portion of which was shown in Figure 11-21. The LoadDataSet() procedure already contains two Try...Catch constructs. If either of these raises an exception, that exception is raised again in the Catch block, which then raises it in the wrapper procedure, mnuFileLoadData_Click(). The error message, if any, indicates the source and nature of the error. No other error handling seems necessary at this point, so Rick decided to leave it alone.

NOTE: Alternatively, you could decide that you absolutely need to know the name of the procedure and type of error at this juncture. If this is the case, then you can insert a message box as the first statement in each Catch block in LoadDataSet(). Both messages indicate that the error occurred in LoadDataSet. The first message would specify that the error occurred when trying to fill the temporary dataset; the second message would specify that the error occurred in the clear/merge operation.

LoadDataSet() includes code at the end of the procedure to load dsRoom1, code which you added to the Data Form Wizard-generated code in Tutorial 9. Loading dsRoom1 certainly should be protected, the same as any other code block that accesses a database. Accordingly, you need to rewrite this last section of the

LoadDataSet() procedure. Like the other two Try...Catch constructs in this procedure, an exception causes another exception to be raised in the Catch block, which causes the exception to be raised in mnuFileLoadData_Click().

5   Rewrite the code in **LoadDataSet**() following the second End Try, as shown in Figure 11-26.

```
Try
  'Now fill dsRoom
  Me.OleDbConnection1.Open()
  Me.OleDbCommand2.ExecuteNonQuery()
  Me.OleDbCommand1.ExecuteNonQuery()
  DsRoom1.Clear()
  Me.OleDbDataAdapter3.Fill(DsRoom1)
  Me.OleDbConnection1.Close()
Catch eRoomException As System.Exception
  Throw eRoomException
End Try
```

Figure 11-26: Protecting the code for loading dsRoom1 in LoadDataSet()

6   Locate and examine the **FillDataSet**() procedure, shown in Figure 11-20. This procedure fills the temporary dataset passed to it using the Fill methods of OleDbDataAdapter1 and OleDbDataAdapter2. Although at first glance you might consider breaking these out into two Try...Catch constructs, this is not really necessary, because the error message (if an exception is raised) identifies which data adapter raised the exception.

7   Locate and examine the **UpdateDataSet**() and **UpdateDataSource**() procedures.

Both of these procedures contain Try...Catch constructs analogous to those in LoadDataSet() and FillDataSet(). In each case, the database access operations are protected and, if an exception is raised by an operation in the Try block, that exception is raised again in the Catch block and thereby passed to the wrapper. Ultimately, an exception is raised in mnuEditUpdateAll_Click(), where the user is notified concerning the error and advised on how to proceed.

8   In the Code Editor for frmVillageHousing, locate and examine the **btnAdd_Click**() procedure. Revise the procedure as shown in Figure 11-27.

```
Private Sub btnAdd_Click(ByVal sender As System.Object, _
    ByVal e As System.EventArgs) Handles btnAdd.Click
  Try
    'Clear out the current edits
    Me.BindingContext(objdsVillager, "tblVillager"). _
      EndCurrentEdit()
    Me.BindingContext(objdsVillager, "tblVillager"). _
      AddNew()
  Catch eEndEdit As System.Exception
    'System.Windows.Forms qualifier is not needed
    'since this is already a Windows form
    MessageBox.Show(eEndEdit.Message & vbCrLf & _
      "Error in btnAdd_Click() procedure")
  End Try
  Me.objdsVillager_PositionChanged()
  editNameFirst.Focus()
End Sub
```

Figure 11-27: Revised btnAdd_Click() procedure

This procedure affects the contents of a dataset, not an underlying database table. Therefore, multiple layers of error-handling code are not called for. If an error condition exists in the local data, repeated attempts change nothing and just generate the same error. Nevertheless, the wizard created the Try...Catch construct, because errors within the dataset are possible. Rick suggests that the wizard-created error message in this procedure be expanded to indicate which procedure generated the error, something that might be of use in debugging. In this procedure and elsewhere in this application, the MessageBox class can be invoked without qualification, because this is a Windows Forms application and the references list already includes System.Windows.Forms.

Applying the ErrorProvider Control

The ErrorProvider control provides a facility for examining user input, and for flagging any errors as soon as they occur. You add an ErrorProvider control to a form, and then program the Validating event for each control on the form whose input you want to validate. You are not limited to database operations or to operations that could raise an exception. In VillageHousing2, Althea uses an ErrorProvider control to validate the fact that the last name field of a villager is not blank and to validate the gender. She shows you how to program the validating event of any control whose contents you want to validate, and how to use the SetError method of the ErrorProvider control to set an error message as well as to clear the error message.

To incorporate an ErrorProvider control in frmVillageHousing:

1 In the Designer for frmVillageHousing, drop an **ErrorProvider** control from the Toolbox onto the form. ErrorProvider1 appears in the tray underneath the form.

2 In the Code Editor, open the Validating event procedure for editNameLast, and insert the code shown in Figure 11-28. This code sets the error string to "A Last Name is required" if, upon leaving the editLastName text box, the text box is empty. However, if the text box is not empty, the error string is set to "", which clears the error.

```
Private Sub editNameLast_Validating(ByVal sender _
    As Object, ByVal e As _
    System.ComponentModel.CancelEventArgs) _
    Handles editNameLast.Validating
  If editNameLast.Text = Nothing Then
    ErrorProvider1.SetError(editNameLast, _
    "A Last Name is required")
  Else
    ' Clear the error.
    ErrorProvider1.SetError(editNameLast, "")
  End If
End Sub
```

Figure 11-28: editNameLast_Validating event procedure

3 Now open the validating event procedure for editGender, and insert the code shown in Figure 11-29. This code allows the Gender field to contain Nothing, "M", or "F"; and it sets an error string if editGender contains anything else.

```
Private Sub editGender_Validating(ByVal sender _
    As Object, ByVal e As _
    System.ComponentModel.CancelEventArgs) _
    Handles editGender.Validating
If editGender.Text = Nothing Or editGender.Text _
    = "M" Or editGender.Text = "F" Then
    ErrorProvider1.SetError(editGender, "")
Else
    ErrorProvider1.SetError(editGender, _
    "Enter 'M' or 'F'")
End If
```

Figure 11-29: editGender_Validating event procedure

4 You should also clear error messages from the ErrorProvider control when the database is loaded, when changes to the current record are cancelled, when all pending changes to the database are cancelled, when a record is added, and when the database is updated. Therefore, insert the two statements

ErrorProvider1.SetError(editNameLast, "")
ErrorProvider1.SetError(editGender, "")

at the end of these procedures: mnuFileLoadData_Click(), btnCancel_Click(), mnuEditCancelAll_Click(), btnAdd_Click(), and mnuEditUpdateAll_Click().

5 Run the application. Load the data, and then click the **Add** button to add a new record. Click on the **Last Name** text box, and press **Tab** without typing anything into the text box. The ErrorProvider control displays the error icon next to the Last Name text box. Point to this error with the mouse, and the ErrorProvider control displays the error message in a pop-up. Click the **Gender** text box, and insert a value other than M or F. Press the **Tab** key. Again, the error icon appears. Point to the error, and note the error message that pops up. Click the **Cancel** button, and note that the error icons disappear.

6 Close the running application, and exit Visual Studio .NET.

Using HTML Help Workshop

The Friendsville Games Development Team decided to implement a Help system for the Village Housing 2.0 application using the facilities of the HTML Help Workshop. Hilda Reiner has the lead responsibility for this task. Accordingly, she is using Microsoft FrontPage to create a series of relatively simple and short HTML files, which will become part of the Help system. She then provides the instructions for using the HTML Help Workshop.

The VillageHousing2 Help system is being built only to demonstrate the FGDT's capacity for constructing a sophisticated Help package. Accordingly, the Web pages used in this Help system are not yet complete. Specifically, Hilda has constructed four small Web pages to include in the demo Help system—the complete Help system to be developed in the coming year will contain many more, larger, and more detailed Web pages, with many internal links. But the purpose here is to demonstrate the use of the HTML Help Workshop within a Visual Studio .NET application, not to develop Web pages *per se*. Hence, this limited set of Web pages is sufficient to demonstrate how a series of Web pages can become part of a single Help system.

Hilda's four Web pages include the following:

- *About.htm*—A standard About page, About.htm, as seen in Figure 11-30 identifies the software name and release, the creator, the copyright holder, and the person (Hilda) to contact for corrections or suggestions.

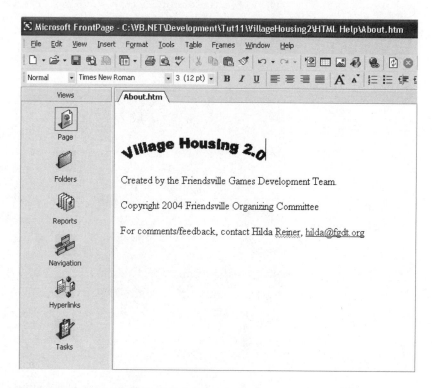

Figure 11-30: About.htm, open in FrontPage

- In the form given to the FGDT, About.htm is the only one of Hilda's four Web pages that calls upon ancillary files, contained in the About_files folder, needed because of the WordArt contained in About.htm. The ancillary files are included in order to show that such files can be compiled into a Help system in Visual Studio .NET. Because you will be using the HTML Help Image Editor to incorporate images into Navigation.htm, you may find it helpful to see how the HTML code implements this WordArt. Figure 11-31 shows the HTML for About.htm; Figure 11-32 displays image001.gif, the graphic image file containing the WordArt; and Figure 11-33 shows the contents of filelist.xml, the xml file that cross-references image001.gif to About.htm. Whenever you insert images into your Help files, the software implements them in a similar fashion.

Figure 11-31: About.htm in HTML view

Figure 11-32: image001.gif

```xml
<xml xmlns:o="urn:schemas-microsoft-com:office:office">
 <o:MainFile HRef="../About.htm"/>
 <o:File HRef="image001.gif"/>
 <o:File HRef="filelist.xml"/>
</xml>
```

Figure 11-33: filelist.xml

■ *Intro.htm*—This page, as shown in Figure 11-34, describes the software in summary form.

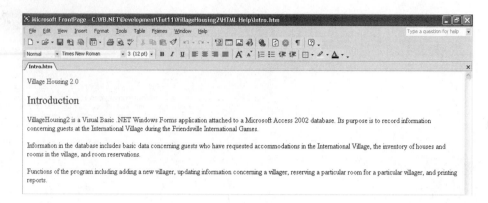

Figure 11-34: Intro.htm

■ *Navigation.htm*—This page, as shown in Figure 11-35, provides summary instructions for navigating among the various windows of Village Housing 2.0. As provided by Hilda, it is missing the screen shots of those windows, because Hilda wants the FGDT to learn how to capture screenshots using the HTML Help Image Editor. Also notice the two flag icons, identifying bookmarks that Hilda has placed in the file.

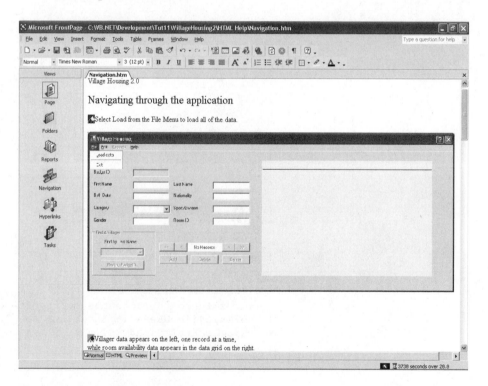

Figure 11-35: Part of Navigation.htm

■ *Constraints.htm*—The Data constraints and best practices Web page, as shown in Figure 11-36, very briefly describes the domain for each field in the VillageHousing database and the rules for entering or updating data values in the user-updatable fields. Note the multiple flag icons, each identifying the location of a bookmark on the page.

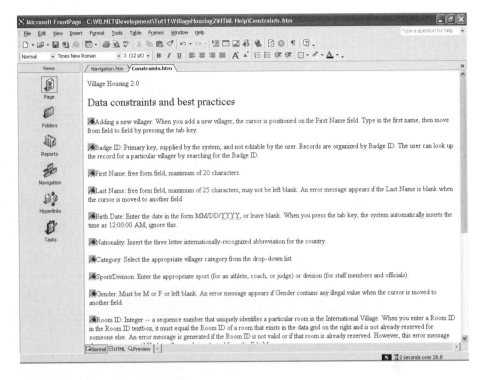

Figure 11-36: Part of Constraints.htm

> **NOTE:** Hilda created these four files using FrontPage, but you could use any software capable of creating .htm or .html files. You could, for example, create simple Web pages in Microsoft Word, and then save each file as a Web page. You can also create HTML files directly in the HTML Help Workshop, but this requires knowledge of HTML itself, because it is only a text editor (with a built-in browser preview capability).

Installing the HTML Help Workshop and Using the HTML Help Image Editor

Your first task is to install the Workshop, and view and enhance Hilda's Web pages.

To install the HTML Help Workshop and use the HTML Help Image Editor:

1   Visit **http://msdn.microsoft.com**. Download and execute **htmlhelp.exe** to install HTML Help Workshop on your computer. Download and unzip **helpdoc.zip**, which contains all of the documentation for HTML Help Workshop. Extract the HTML Help Workshop documentation to the same folder into which you have installed HTML Help Workshop.

2   Open and examine the four **.htm files** created by Hilda Reiner and provided to you in VB.NET\Student\Tut11\HTML files (namely, Intro.htm, About.htm, Navigation.htm, and Constraints.htm). Double-click each one in Windows Explorer to open the file in your default browser. Close each file when you have viewed its contents.

3   Also open and examine the files contained in the **About_files subfolder**, namely **image001.gif** (containing the WordArt) and **filelist.xml** (showing you how image001.gif is cross-referenced to the .htm file).

4   You now use the HTML Help Image Editor to capture screen shots of VillageHousing2, which will be included in Navigation.htm. To view the screens that you need to capture, run **VillageHousing2** again, and click **Help | Contents**. In the Help window, click **Navigating through this application**. As you can see, the four screen shots include the initial frmVillageHousing, frmVillageHousing after data is loaded into the form, and the two Crystal Reports. Close the **Help screen**, but leave the VillageHousing2 application running, because you want to take your screen captures from the running application.

5   Run the HTML Help Image Editor by clicking **Start | All Programs | HTML Help Workshop | HTML Help Image Editor**. In the HTML Help Image Editor main screen, click **Capture | Preferences**. In the Capture Preferences dialog box, click the **Hotkeys** tab, as shown in Figure 11-37. This displays (and allows you to alter) the settings for the only unique keys you need to use in this software: the F11 function key captures the active window, and the F12 function key captures the entire desktop. Click **Cancel** to close the Capture Preferences dialog box. Click **Capture | Using the Keyboard** to initiate the screen capture operation. Click **OK**.

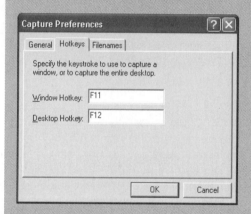

Figure 11-37: Capture Preferences dialog box of the HTML Help Image Editor

6   Ensure that you are looking at the opening screen of VillageHousing2. (If this is not the opening screen, then close VillageHousing2, and run it again.) Move the pointer to the title bar of VillageHousing2, and press **F11** to capture this screen, and return to the HTML Help Image Editor. Save this screen as **Nav1** in the **VB.NET\Student\ Tut11\HTML files** folder—it is saved as Nav1.bmp, a bit-mapped image.

7   Click **Capture | Using the Keyboard** to initiate another screen capture operation. In VillageHousing2, click **File | Load Data**. When the data appear in the form, point to the title bar and press **F11** to capture the screen, and return to the HTML Help Image Editor. Save this screen as **Nav2**.

8   Click **Capture | Using the Keyboard** to initiate a third screen capture operation. In VillageHousing2, click **Reports | Villagers**. When this report appears, point to the title bar and press **F11** to capture the screen, and return to the HTML Help Image Editor. Save this screen as **Nav3**.

9   Click **Capture | Using the Keyboard** to initiate the fourth screen capture operation. In VillageHousing2, close the All Villagers Report, returning the user to the basic application. In the VillageHousing2 main window, click **Reports | Rooms**. When this report appears, point to the title bar and press **F11** to capture the screen. The HTML Help Image Editor reappears, with the Rooms Report. Save this screen as **Nav4**.

10 Close the **HTML Help Image Editor**. Close the **Rooms Report**. Close **VillageHousing2**.

11 Using FrontPage or another HTML editor of your choice, open **Navigation.htm**. Navigation.htm contains four large blank spaces, indicating where each of the four images belongs. Insert **Nav1.bmp, Nav2.bmp, Nav3.bmp**, and **Nav4.bmp** in the appropriate locations within Navigation.htm. Save **Navigation.htm**, and exit **FrontPage**.

Using HTML Help Workshop

You have installed, copied, or modified the ingredients necessary for creating your Help system for VillageHousing2—the HTML Help Workshop, as well as the HTML files containing all of the content. Using HTML Help Workshop, you now create the Help project file (.hhp), table of contents file (.hhc), index file (.hhk), and compiled output file (.chm).

Initiating an HTML Help Workshop Project

Although you can choose to build the complete Help Workshop project in any order, the easiest approach is to start with a project file. However, if you have already created the index or table of contents, or if you are reusing these items from another Help project, the project file can be constructed last.

To begin building a Help system using HTML Help Workshop:

1 Run the workshop by clicking **Start | All Programs | HTML Help Workshop | HTML Help Workshop**. Click **File | New**. A small New dialog box appears. By default, Project is selected, as shown in Figure 11-38. Click **OK**. The New Project Wizard opens. Click **Next**.

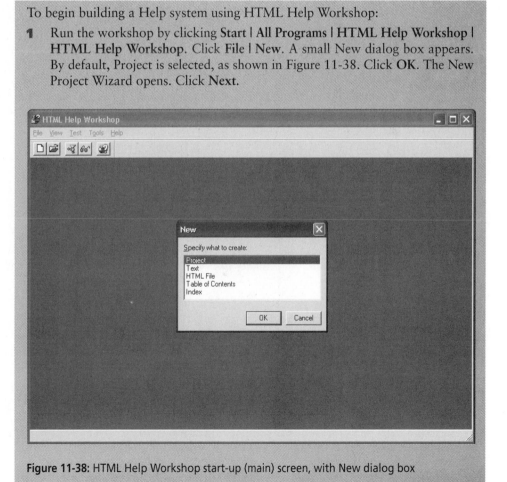

Figure 11-38: HTML Help Workshop start-up (main) screen, with New dialog box

2 In the **New Project – Destination** screen, navigate to the **VB.NET\Student\ Tut11\HTML files** folder, enter the name of the project file, **VhHelp**, and then click **Open**. See Figure 11-39. Click **Next**.

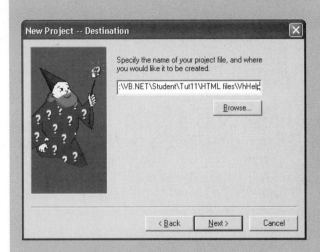

Figure 11-39: New Project – Destination screen

3 In the **New Project – Existing Files** screen, check HTML files, because you already have .htm files to include in this Help project. Leave the other two check boxes unchecked, because you have not yet created a table of contents or an index. Click **Next**.

4 In the **New Project – HTML Files** screen, click **Add**. The Open dialog box appears. Select all four HTML files (**About, Constraints, Navigation,** and **Intro**). Click **Open**. The New Project - HTML Files screen now appears as in Figure 11-40. Click **Next**.

Figure 11-40: New Project – HTML Files screen

NOTE: You do not specify the subfolders About_files or Navigation_files, or the subfolder contents. These folders and the files within them are referenced inside the respective .htm files, and are incorporated into the VhHelp project automatically.

5 The New Project - Finish screen appears. Click **Finish**. The wizard creates the VhHelp.hhp project file, and the HTML Help Workshop main screen appears as in Figure 11-41. On your screen under [OPTIONS], note the name of the compiled file, which should be VhHelp.chm. This file will be created when your help system is compiled, and it will appear in the same folder as the rest of your help files. If the name of the output file is VB.chm, then a help file under that name may be created in the C:\root folder instead.

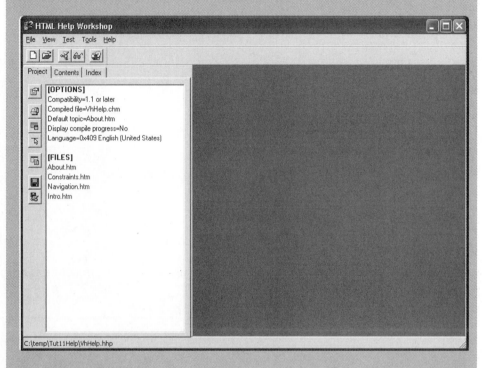

Figure 11-41: HTML Help Workshop main screen, Project tab, after creating the VhHelp project

Note in Figure 11-41 that the HTML files you specified are listed under [FILES]. Certain default project options have also been selected by the wizard, though you can modify any of these. These are listed on the project screen under [OPTIONS]. Of interest here are the name of the compiled output file that the project creates (VhHelp.chm) and the default topic that is displayed if the user asks for help generically without specifying a topic (About.htm). You return to project options later.

Building the Table of Contents
The next task in using the HTML Help Workshop is to create a table of contents and include it in the VhHelp project.

To create a table of contents for VhHelp:

1 In the HTML Help Workshop screen, click the **Contents** tab. The Table of Contents Not Specified dialog box appears, and Create a new contents file is preselected. (Had you created the table of contents file earlier, you could select it here instead of creating a new contents file.) Click **OK**.

2 The Save As dialog box appears, and the default name Table of Contents.hhc is highlighted. Click **Save**.

3 An empty Contents screen appears, as shown in Figure 11-42, allowing you to create your table of contents. Click the button on the left to insert a heading. The Table of Contents Entry dialog box appears. In the **Entry title** text box, type **Village Housing 2.0,** as shown in Figure 11-43. The value in this text box shows how this entry will appear in your table of contents.

Contents properties

Insert a heading

Insert a page

Edit selection

Delete selection

Save file

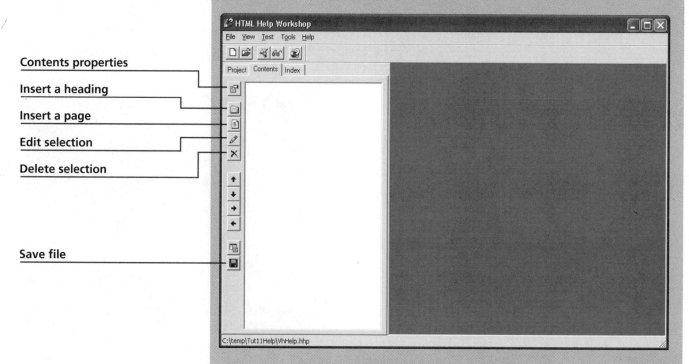

Figure 11-42: HTML Help Workshop main screen, Contents tab selected, with no entries

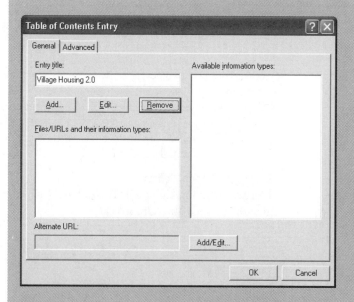

Figure 11-43: Table of Contents Entry dialog box, showing Village Housing 2.0

At runtime, when the user is in the Help system and the user selects an entry in the table of contents (which will appear in the left frame of the Help screen), an associated HTML file should appear in the right frame.

4 In order to associate the Village Housing 2.0 entry with an HTML file, click the **Add** button in the Table of Contents Entry dialog box. The Path or URL dialog box appears, as shown in Figure 11-44. The location and name of your VhHelp project file appears in the Project file text box at the top. (The path to the project file will be different than the path that appears in Figure 11-44.) In the list of HTML titles, Village Housing 2 appears four times, representing the four HTML files in your Help system. Click each of these in turn, and notice that the name of the .htm file appears in the File or URL text box at the bottom of the dialog box. Select the title that corresponds to the name Intro.htm, and click **OK**.

project filename and location (your path will be different)

click each Village Housing 2 HTML title until Intro.htm appears in the File or URL text box

▶ If the titles box does not contain a title associated with Intro.htm, then click the Browse button, navigate to the Intro.htm file, and click OK.

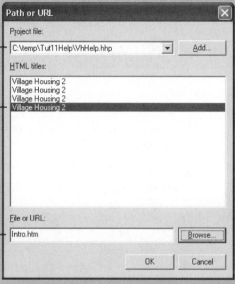

Figure 11-44: Path or URL dialog box

5 The Table of Contents entry now appears as in Figure 11-45. Click **OK**.

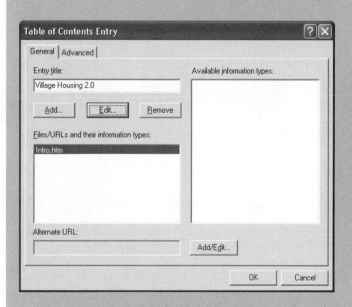

Figure 11-45: Completed Table of Contents Entry dialog box for Village Housing 2.0

6 In the HTML Help Workshop Contents tab, click the button to insert a page. In answer to the question about inserting this entry at the beginning, click **No**. In the Table of Contents Entry dialog box, type **Introduction** in the **Entry title** text box. Again, click the **Add** button to add an associated URL. In the Path or URL dialog box, select the HTML title that corresponds to **Intro.htm**, and click **OK**. Click **OK** again to add this page to the table of contents.

7 In similar fashion, insert three additional pages, assigning the entry titles and corresponding HTML titles and associated HTML files, as shown in Figure 11-46. If any title of an HTML file is missing in the Path or URL dialog box, click the **Browse** button to find and add it to the list. The completed HTML Help Workshop Contents tab should appear as in Figure 11-47. Click the **Save file** button at the lower left of the screen.

Entry type	Entry title	HTML title	File
Heading	Village Housing 2.0	Village Housing 2	Intro.htm
Page	Introduction	Village Housing 2	Intro.htm
Page	Navigating through the application	Village Housing 2	Navigation.htm
Page	Data fields and constraints	Village Housing 2	Constraints.htm
Page	About Village Housing 2.0	Village Housing 2	About.htm

Figure 11-46: Table of Contents entries, titles, and files

Save file

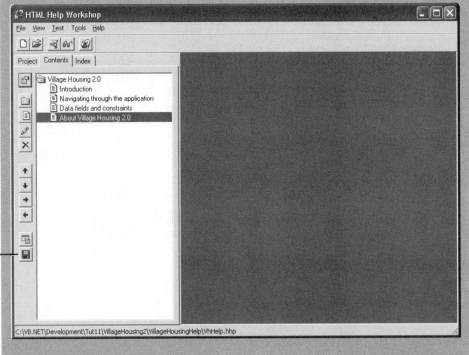

Figure 11-47: Completed HTML Help Workshop Contents tab

Creating a Help Index

You now create an index for your Help system, covering the topics in your HTML Help files; and you include this index in the VhHelp project. Although this sample Help system is small, with limited content and only four brief HTML files, this is sufficient to indicate how the index works and how you can build a very robust Help index as part of a more comprehensive Help system.

To build an index for the Village Housing 2.0 application:

1 On the HTML Help Workshop main screen, click the **Index** tab. The Index Not Specified dialog box appears, and Create a new index file is preselected. This is correct, so click **OK**. The Save As dialog box appears, and the default name Index.hhk is highlighted. Change the name to **MainIndex.hhk**, and click **Save**. The HTML Workshop main screen appears with the Index tab selected, containing a blank index, as shown in Figure 11-48.

Index properties

Insert a keyword

Edit selection

Delete selection

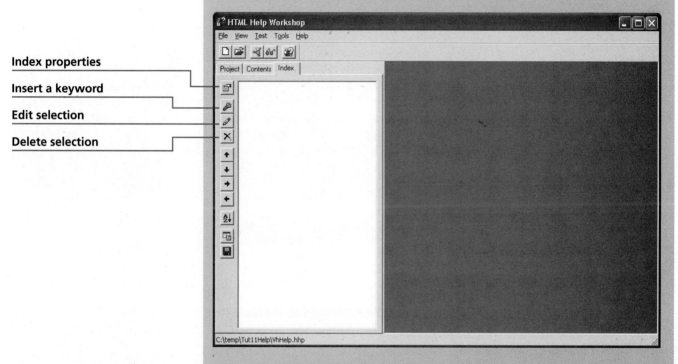

Figure 11-48: HTML Help Workshop Index tab

2 Building the index is quite similar to building the table of contents. Essentially, you enter new keywords into the index, and associate each keyword with an HTML file or URL. If the referenced Web page contains internal bookmarks, these can also be included. Click the key button to insert a new keyword. The Index Entry dialog box appears. In the Keyword text box, type the word **Nationality**, as shown in Figure 11-49.

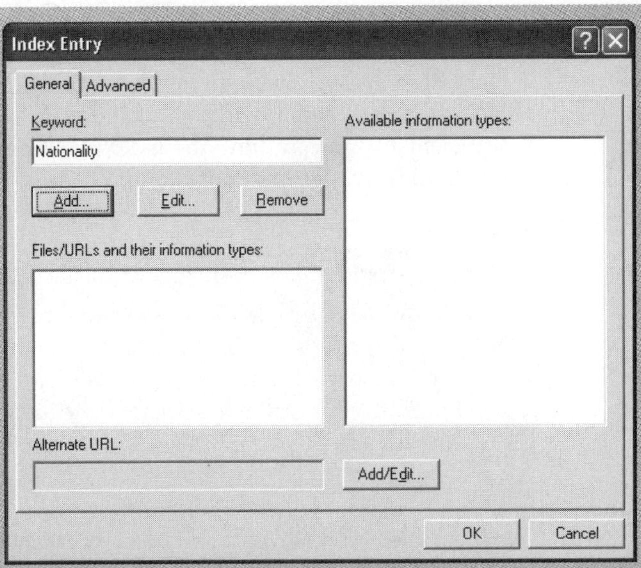

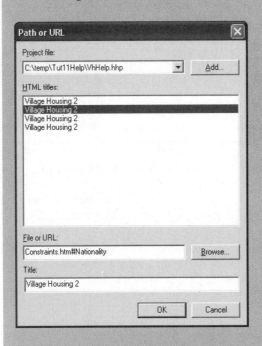

Figure 11-49: Index Entry dialog box

3   To associate this keyword with a file and bookmark, click the **Add** button. In the Path or URL dialog box, click the **Village Housing 2** HTML titles until **Constraints.htm** appears in the File or URL text box. (As was the case with the table of contents, if Constraints.htm is not one of the currently associated files, then browse to find it.) In the File or URL text box, add the bookmark **#Nationality** to Constraints.htm. The completed dialog box should appear as in Figure 11-50. Click **OK**. The completed Index Entry dialog box appears as in Figure 11-51. Click **OK**.

Figure 11-50: Completed Path or URL dialog box

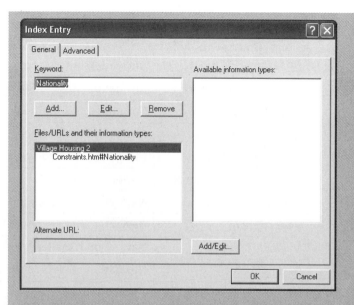

Figure 11-51: Completed Index Entry dialog box

4 In similar fashion, add all of the keywords and associated files and bookmarks shown in Figure 11-52. After you have added all of these items to the index, click the **Sort** button on the lower-left side of the HTML Help Workshop Index tab, so that the index appears in alphabetical order. Click the **Save file** button. The completed Index tab should appear as in Figure 11-53.

Keyword	Files/URL and their information types: Village Housing 2
Add	Constraints.htm#Add
Badge ID	Constraints.htm#BadgeID
First Name	Constraints.htm#FirstName
Last Name	Constraints.htm#LastName
Birth Date	Constraints.htm#BirthDate
Nationality	Constraints.htm#Nationality
Category	Constraints.htm#Category
Sport/Division	Constraints.htm#Sport
Gender	Constraints.htm#Gender
Room ID	Constraints.htm#RoomID
House	Constraints.htm#House
Room (Room number)	Constraints.htm#RoomNumber
Reserved	Constraints.htm#Reserved
Finding a record	Constraints.htm#Find
Data grid	Constraints.htm#DataGrid
Load data	Navigation.htm#LoadData

Figure 11-52: Keywords and files/bookmarks

Keyword	Files/URL and their information types: Village Housing 2
Menu	Navigation.htm#Menu
Navigation buttons	Navigation.htm#NavigationButtons
Adding a record	Navigation.htm#Editing
Cancel all updates	Navigation.htm#Editing
Deleting a record	Navigation.htm#Editing
Saving changed records	Navigation.htm#Editing
Update all records	Navigation.htm#Editing
Reports menu	Navigation.htm#ReportsMenu
Villagers Report	Navigation.htm#ReportsMenu
Rooms Report	Navigation.htm#RoomsReport
About Village Housing 2.0	About.htm
Introduction	Intro.htm
Overview	Intro.htm
Constraints	Constraints.htm
Data fields	Constraints.htm
Editing and entering data	Constraints.htm
Errors	Constraints.htm

Figure 11-52: Keywords and files/bookmarks (continued)

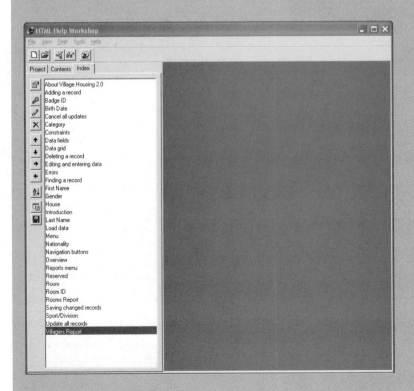

Figure 11-53: Completed HTML Help Workshop Index screen (lengthened to display all entries)

Compiling the Help File

The final task in the HTML Help Workshop is to compile the output (.chm) file. You need to assign a title to the Help file—this is what appears in the title bar of the Help system at runtime. Hilda suggests that a full-text search capability be included in the Help system, so you set this option. After verifying all options and settings, you compile the Help file.

To compile the Help system into a single output file, VhHelp.chm:

1 Click the **Project** tab of the HTML Help Workshop main screen. Click the **Options** button in the upper-left corner of the Project tab. In the Options dialog box on the General tab, enter **Village Housing 2.0** as shown in Figure 11-54. Click the **Compiler** tab. Select the check box to **Compile full-text search information**. Click **OK**. The HTML Help Workshop main screen Project tab appears as in Figure 11-55. Make sure that all files and options are properly configured, as detailed in Figure 11-55.

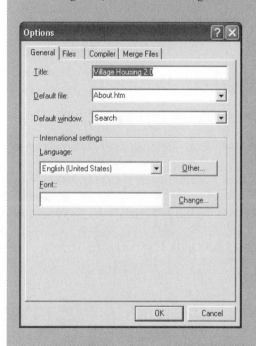

Figure 11-54: Options dialog box, General tab

► You may or may not see Search as an entry in the Default window text box (Figure 11-54) and as a setting in the Options section of the Project window (Figure 11-55). Ignore this discrepancy.

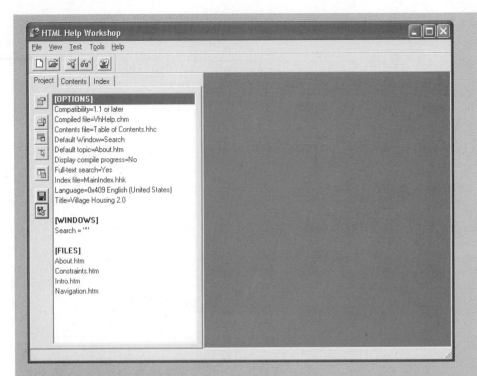

Figure 11-55: Project tab, after all component files have been created and options set

2 Click the **Save all files and compile** button at the lower-left of the Project tab. If no errors are encountered during compilation, the result appears approximately as in Figure 11-56. The compilation statistics on your computer may vary from those shown in the figure. Close the HTML Help Workshop. Note the location and name of the compiled output file, especially if the name is something other than VhHelp.chm, then rename it to VhHelp.chm using Windows Explorer.

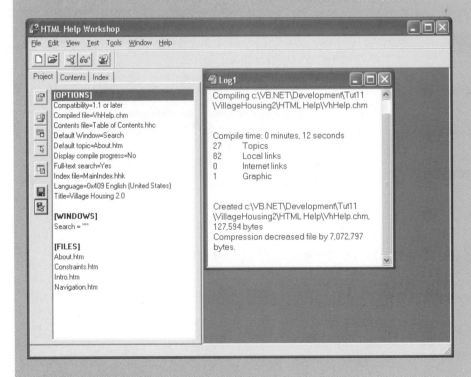

Figure 11-56: Compilation results

NOTE: Any compiler errors are flagged by the compiler, and the output file will not be created.

3 In Windows Explorer, double-click VhHelp.chm to open the completed Help file, shown in Figure 11-57. Experiment with its features and links to make sure that everything is working as you expected. Look up **Nationality** in the Index, and click Display. Perform a search for **Error**, and display the resulting screen. Open a topic in the Table of Contents.

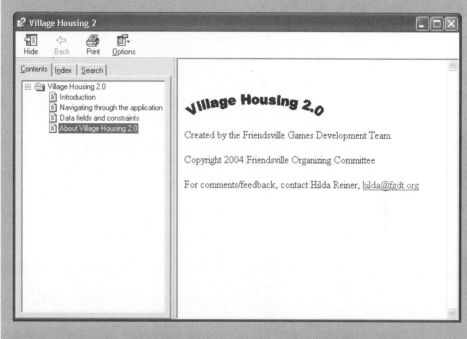

Figure 11-57: VhHelp.chm Contents screen

4 When you are satisfied that your Help system is working properly, copy the output file, VhHelp.chm, to your MyVillageHousing2 folder. You will incorporate this file into the VillageHousing2 application.

Incorporating Help into Your Application

Under Hilda's guidance, you have completed the most difficult parts of building a complete Help system, creating VhHelp.chm from the HTML Help Workshop. You are the FGDT team leader for the remaining tasks: inserting a HelpProvider control, adding a HelpButton control, and finally adding a ToolTip control.

Adding the HelpProvider Control

The HelpProvider control is the vehicle within Visual Studio .NET for incorporating a Help system into a Visual Studio .NET application. You now return to Visual Studio .NET, and add the HelpProvider control to the VillageHousing2 application.

tip

The Microsoft documentation sometimes refers to this as the HelpProvider component rather than the HelpProvider control.

To add the HelpProvider control to VillageHousing2:

1 Open Visual Studio .NET, and open the VillageHousing2 solution. Open frmVillageHousing in the Designer. From the Toolbox, drag a **HelpProvider** control [Fil] onto the form. The HelpProvider control appears in the tray underneath the form.

2 In the Properties window, set the **HelpNamespace** property to the **VhHelp.chm** file. This action makes your Help system available to frmVillageHousing. You now program the Help menu items in frmVillageHousing's main menu to open specific frames in VhHelp.chm.

The HelpProvider control provides a Help object and a Help Viewer, the familiar window for viewing Help screens. The ShowHelp and ShowHelpIndex methods of the Help object instantiate and display the Help Viewer.

3 In the Code Editor, open the mnuHelpContents_Click() procedure. Type the Help.ShowHelp statement for this procedure, as shown in Figure 11-58.

```
Private Sub mnuHelpContents_Click(ByVal sender _
    As System.Object, ByVal e As System.EventArgs) _
    Handles mnuHelpContents.Click
  Help.ShowHelp(Me, HelpProvider1.HelpNamespace)
End Sub

Private Sub mnuHelpIndex_Click(ByVal sender As _
    System.Object, ByVal e As System.EventArgs) _
    Handles mnuHelpIndex.Click
  Help.ShowHelpIndex(Me, HelpProvider1.HelpNamespace)
End Sub

Private Sub mnuHelpSearch_Click(ByVal sender As _
    System.Object, ByVal e As System.EventArgs) _
    Handles mnuHelpSearch.Click
  Help.ShowHelp(Me, HelpProvider1.HelpNamespace, _
    HelpNavigator.Find, "")
End Sub

Private Sub mnuHelpAbout_Click(ByVal sender As _
    Object, ByVal e As System.EventArgs) _
    Handles mnuHelpAbout.Click
  Help.ShowHelp(Me, HelpProvider1.HelpNamespace, _
    HelpNavigator.Find, "About")
End Sub
```

Figure 11-58: Help menu procedures

4 Open the mnuHelpIndex_Click() procedure. Type the Help.ShowHelpIndex statement shown in Figure 11-58.

5 Open the mnuHelpSearch_Click() procedure. Type the Help.ShowHelp statement for this procedure shown in Figure 11-58.

6 Open the mnuHelpAbout_Click() procedure. Type the Help.ShowHelp statement for this procedure, as shown in Figure 11-58.

7 The HelpProvider control exposes help-related properties on each control and on the form. You can program any control to provide context-sensitive help for that form or control. (Context-sensitive help for a control is available at runtime by pressing the F1 function key while the control has focus.) As an example of this capability, set the **HelpKeyword on HelpProvider1** property of the editNationality text box control to **Nationality**.

8 Run the application. Click each of the Help menu items: **Help | Contents**, **Help | Index, Help | Search,** and **Help | About,** closing the Help screen after viewing each instance of Help. Click on **Nationality,** and press **F1** to view the context-sensitive help for that control. Examples of each of these screens appeared earlier in Figures 11-6 through 11-9. Close the running application and return to the IDE.

9 Context-sensitive help can be provided in a ScreenTip even if you have not assigned a value to the HelpNamespace property of the HelpProvider control. To see this capability, temporarily delete the setting of the **HelpNamespace** property of **HelpProvider1.** Then insert the following statement in the **HelpString on HelpProvider1** property of the **editNameFirst** text box: **An athlete's first name is optional, but the last name is required. Therefore, if an athlete has only one name (such as Pele or Rinaldo), then enter that name in the Last Name field.**

10 Run the application, click on the **First Name** text box, and press **F1.** Note that the message you placed in the HelpString property appears in a ScreenTip. **Close** the application. Reinsert the setting of the **HelpNamespace** property of **HelpProvider1** to the **VhHelp.chm** file. Click **Save All.**

Adding the HelpButton control

You just experimented with the use of the HelpString property to provide context-sensitive help when the HelpNamespace property is empty. The HelpString property of a HelpProvider control is also useful in another instance, namely, when providing context-sensitive help on a modal form such as a dialog box, because a modal form does not permit another form to be displayed until the modal form is closed. You set the HelpString property of a control to the Help message that you want to see displayed in a ScreenTip when the user requests help for that control.

> **NOTE:** As mentioned in Lesson A, you use the HelpButton control on frmVillageHousing in order to complete your experimentation with the kinds of Help facilities available in Visual Basic .NET. Because frmVillageHousing is not a modal form, the Help button would not normally be implemented here.

tip

If either the MaximizeBox or MinimizeBox properties is True, the HelpButton property setting is ignored, and the Help button is not displayed.

To incorporate a Help Button control on frmVillagehousing:

1 Set the form's **HelpButton** property to **True,** and set both the **MaximizeBox** and **MinimizeBox** properties to **False** (the convention generally followed on dialog boxes). You have already set the HelpString property for editNameFirst.

2 Set the HelpString property of **btnAdd** to **Click here to add a new villager.**

3 Set the HelpString property of **btnDelete** to **Click here to delete the villager whose record is currently displayed.**

4 Run the application. Click the **Help** button, and then click the **First Name** text box. A message pops up. (This was shown earlier, in Figure 11-10.) Click anywhere on the form to clear the message.

5 Click the **Help** button, and then click the **Add** button. Nothing happens, because the Add button is disabled until the data is loaded. Click **File | Load Data.** Then click the **Help** button, and click the **Add** button. The Help message for the Add button pops up. Click anywhere to clear the message.

6 Click the **Help** button, and click the **Delete** button. The Help message for the Delete button pops up. Click anywhere to clear the message. **Close** the application and return to the IDE.

Adding the ToolTip Control

With a ToolTip control present, you can cause a message to pop up whenever the user's mouse pointer hovers over a control. You now insert a ToolTip control on frmVillageHousing as the final element in the Help package for this application, and you set the ToolTip properties of the four navigation buttons.

To add a ToolTip control to frmVillageHousing:

1 In the Windows Form Designer for frmVillageHousing, drag a **ToolTip** control from the Toolbox and drop it onto the form. ToolTip1 appears in the tray below the form. Note that the **ToolTip on ToolTip1** property is now exposed in the Properties window for every control on the form.

2 In the Properties window for **btnNavFirst**, set the **ToolTip on ToolTip1** property to **First Record**. For **btnNavPrev**, set the **ToolTip on ToolTip1** property to **Previous Record**. For **btnNavNext**, set the **ToolTip on ToolTip1** property to **Next Record**. For **btnLast**, set the **ToolTip on ToolTip1** property to **Last Record**.

3 Run the application. Click **File | Load Data**. Point to **btnNavNext**, and note the ToolTip, which was shown in Figure 11-11. Point to the other three navigation buttons to ensure that the ToolTip appears for those buttons as well. Exit the application and exit Visual Studio .NET.

You have now completed Lesson B. Before you try the final lesson in this text, please answer the following review questions and exercises.

SUMMARY

- Try...Catch constructs should be employed to protect any dangerous or error-prone code. If the code is subject to operational errors because it involves access to a database, it may be useful to build two layers of Try...Catch constructs, so that a failed attempt to access the data is followed immediately by a second attempt.

- You should use the Try...Catch construct to protect any code that could cause an exception, not only data access operations. Commercial applications, especially those intended for use by the general public, require comprehensive and foolproof error-handling procedures.

- The ErrorProvider control provides a good way to check the validity of data entered by the user as soon as the user has entered a piece of data. By programming the Validating event for a control, the developer can highlight an error and provide an appropriate error message. The error message remains available in a ScreenTip until the error is cleared. The Validating event procedure both sets and clears the error message, based on the validity of the data in the control.

- The HTML Help Image Editor facilitates screen captures to be used in HTML documents. Images captured with the HTML Help Image Editor can be inserted into a Web page by using FrontPage or any other HTML editor.

- The HTML Help Workshop is a free, downloadable software package that allows the developer to create a complete Help system for any application. You use the HTML

Help Workshop to consolidate HTML files into a Help system, to build a project (.hhp) file, to create an index (.hhk) file and a table of contents (.hhc) file, to incorporate a full-text search feature, and to compile the entire Help system into a single output (.chm) file.

■ You incorporate a Help system into an application by using the HelpProvider control. You set the HelpProvider control's HelpNamespace property to the name of the .chm file you created with HTML Help Workshop. You then use the HelpProvider control's Help object and Help Viewer to display the table of contents, index, and search frames within a Help Viewer window. By setting the HelpKeyword property for a control, context-sensitive help can be provided as well.

■ If no Help system has been created, you can still provide context-sensitive help in ScreenTips by placing a HelpProvider control on a form, and then setting the HelpString on HelpProvider1 property for each control on the form.

■ For a modal form, the HelpButton control can provide context-sensitive help in ScreenTips. Again, you use the HelpProvider control and set the HelpString on HelpProvider1 property for each control on the form.

■ ScreenTips can also be provided for any control on a form by adding a ToolTip control to the form and then setting the ToolTip on ToolTip1 property for each control.

QUESTIONS

1. Structured error handling in Visual Basic .NET is implemented with the _____ construct.

2. After adding an ErrorProvider control to a form, you program each control's _____ event, where you set or clear an error message.

3. File types created by the HTML Help Workshop are:
   _____ project
   _____ table of contents
   _____ index
   _____ output (compiled help file)

4. The facility for screen captures provided by the HTML Help Workshop is called the _____.

5. To make a compiled Help file available to an application, you set the _____ property of the _____ control.

6. The principle methods of the Help object are _____ and _____.

7. To provide context-sensitive help to a form that includes a HelpProvider control and a compiled Help file, you set the _____ property of each control for which context-sensitive help is desired.

8. To provide context-sensitive help in a ScreenTip to a nonmodal form that includes a HelpProvider control but no compiled Help file, you set the _____ property of each control for which context-sensitive help is desired.

9. To provide context-sensitive help in a ScreenTip to a dialog box or other modal form that includes a HelpProvider control and a compiled Help file, you set the _____ property of the form to True, the MaximizeBox and MinimizeBox properties of the form to False, and the _____ property of each control for which context-sensitive help is desired.

10. To display a ScreenTip whenever the mouse pointer points to a control, you add a _____ control to the form, and set the _____ property of each control on the form for which a ScreenTip is desired.

EXERCISES

1. Starting with a copy of your completed LogonManager application from Tutorial 4, add Try...Catch constructs that protect each file input and output operation. (This does not include the Logon application called from within LogonManager, only the LogonManager application itself.) When an error is encountered, display an appropriate error message to the user, notifying the user that the I/O operation failed, but then allowing processing to continue.

2. Copy Exercise 1. Then modify the copy so that, after displaying an appropriate error message to the user, the program throws the initial exception again.

3. Copy Exercise 1. Then modify the copy so that your program intentionally raises an exception in each Try block in the mnuFileInitialize_Click(), mnuFileBackup_Click(), and mnuFileRestore_Click() procedures.

4. Starting with a copy of your completed LogonManager application from Tutorial 4, add an ErrorProvider control. Program the Validating events for each control that is currently validated by the btnSubmit_Click() procedure. This includes the First Name, Last Name, Work Phone, Home Phone, E-mail Address, Password, and Confirm Password fields. To validate that the user has entered at least one phone number in the Work Phone or Home Phone fields, use the Validating event of txtHomePhone, but set the error (if both phone number fields are blank) on both controls. Use the Validating event of both the WorkPhone and HomePhone controls to clear any errors on both controls, if either control is not Nothing. You do not need to modify btnSubmit_Click(), because a user could inadvertently click Submit without clearing an error. However, if no errors are detected through your ErrorProvider control or all errors are cleared before clicking Submit, then the btnSubmit_Click() procedure should not detect any errors.

5. Starting with a copy of your completed LogonManager application from Tutorial 4, add a HelpProvider control to frmUser. Provide context-sensitive help in a ScreenTip for each control on the form. In addition, in btnSubmit_Click(), if an error is discovered, display a modal dialog box that you create, and include a HelpButton control on this form. (A dialog box is just a form whose FormBorderStyle property is FixedDialog, and whose ControlBox, MinimizeBox, and MaximizeBox properties are set to False. When displaying the dialog box as a modal form, you use the ShowDialog method rather than the Show method.) The dialog box you create should display strings developed in btnSubmit_Click() in a RichTextBox control. The HelpButton control should provide context-sensitive help for the RichTextBox control and the OK button (used to close the form).

6. Using the HTML Help Workshop, develop a complete Help system for the LogonManager application from Tutorial 4. Develop an HTML file for each form in the application. For frmUser, include a definition of each control on the form, and set a bookmark for each definition. Prior to the definitions of the controls on each tab page, include a screen capture of the tab page (captured with the HTML Help Image Editor). The table of contents file created by HTML Help Workshop should include an entry for each HTML file. The index file should include an entry for each control defined in the HTML Help file that you created for frmUser. Include a full-text search capability in the output file, which should be named LmHelp.chm.

7. Starting with a copy of your completed LogonManager application from Tutorial 4 and with the LmHelp.chm file created in Exercise 6, add a HelpProvider control to mdiMain and to frmUser. In the main menu for mdiMain, delete the About entry. Then add a root-level entry called Help. Add menu items under Help for Contents, Index, Search, and About. The Contents entry should display the Table of Contents from LmHelp.chm, the Index entry should display the Index from LmHelp.chm, and the Search entry should display the Search frame from LmHelp.chm. The About entry should display the existing frmAbout. On frmUser, provide context-sensitive help using LmHelp.chm for each control on the form.

Crystal Reports

Designing a Crystal Report

Crystal Reports is a report program generator from Crystal Decisions, Inc., that comes with Visual Studio .NET. Using this facility, you can create simple or sophisticated reports based on data in many types of data sources. You design an initial Crystal Report with the Report Expert from the Crystal Reports Gallery, which is a report design wizard. Using this wizard, you identify the data source and data fields, and specify the basic report layout. Later, you use the Crystal Report Designer to customize the report further to your specifications.

Building the Query for the Report

As you may recall, the Friendsville Games Development Team asked you to take the lead in developing two reports for the VillageHousing2 application, All Villagers and Their Assigned Rooms, and Reserved Rooms Report. The first of these is based on a query stored in the VillageHousing.mdb database, and uses the same ADO.NET technology that you have used in all other database operations in this text. This query lists all of the villagers in tblVillager and includes these fields from that table: NameLast, NameFirst, BadgeID, Gender, SportOrDivision, Nationality, and RoomID. It shows the category from tblCategory that corresponds to the CategoryCode in tblVillager, the Room in tblRoom that corresponds to RoomID in tblVillager, and the House from tblHouse that corresponds to the HouseCode in tblRoom. You now create this query followed by the Crystal Report.

To create the query that will be used for the All Villagers and Their Assigned Rooms Crystal Report:

1 Open **Microsoft Access**, open the **VillageHousing.mdb** database in the MyVillageHousing2 folder, click the **Queries** tab, and double-click **Create query by using wizard**. The Simple Query Wizard opens.

2 In the first dialog box, click the **down list** arrow in the **Tables/Queries** combo box, and select **Table: tblHouse**. Then, in the Available Fields list box, select **House**, as shown in Figure 11-59. Click the **>** button to move the **House** field from the **Available Fields** list box to the **Selected Fields** list box.

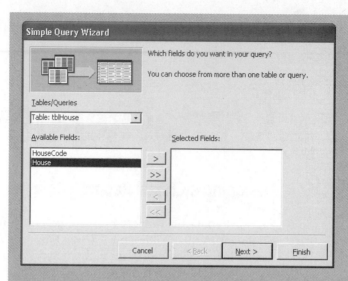

Figure 11-59: Simple Query Wizard, first dialog box

3 Still in the first dialog box, click the **down list** arrow in the **Tables/Queries** combo box, and select **Table: tblRoom**. Then, in the Available Fields list box, select **Room**. Click **>** to move this field to the Selected Fields list box.

4 In the **Tables/Queries** combo box, select **Table: tblVillager**, and in the Available Fields list box, select **NameLast, NameFirst, BadgeID, Gender, SportOrDivision, Nationality,** and **RoomID,** moving each one of these to the Selected Fields list box.

5 In the **Tables/Queries** combo box, select **Table: tblCategory**, and in the Available Fields list box, select **CategoryName**. Move this field to the Selected Fields list box. Click **Next**.

NOTE: The order of tables and fields within tables is not important in designing the query.

6 In the second dialog box, Detail is preselected; click **Next**.

7 In the third dialog box, enter the query name **qryAllVillagersRooms**. Click the **Modify query design** radio button, and click **Finish**. The completed design should appear as in Figure 11-60. Although the order of tables and fields does not matter, make sure that all four tables appear in the top half of the Query Designer, and that all of the necessary fields are present in the lower half of the Designer.

NOTE: If a field that is unnecessary appears in the lower half of the Query Designer, click on that field and delete it. If a necessary field does not appear in the lower half of the Query Designer, double-click that field in the table from which it comes (in the upper half of the Query Designer) in order to add that field to the selected fields in the lower half of the Designer.

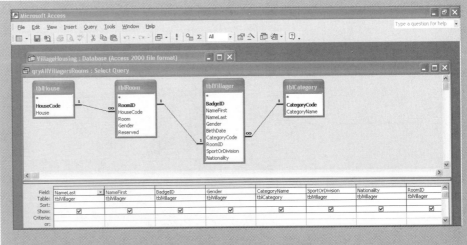

Figure 11-60: qryAllVillagersRooms in the Query Designer

8 Close the **Query Designer**. Run the query to make sure it works. Then close **Microsoft Access**.

Creating the Initial Report

Now that you have the query on which the Crystal Report will be based, it is time to design the initial report.

To create the initial report design for the All Villagers and Their Assigned Rooms report:

1 Open **Visual Studio .NET**, and then open your **VillageHousing2** solution. In Solution Explorer, right-click the **VillageHousing2** project, and click **Add | Add New Item**. In the **Add New Item** dialog box, click **Crystal Report**. In the **Name** text box, change **CrystalReport1.rpt** to **crVillagers.rpt**, and click **Open**. The Crystal Report Gallery opens, shown in Figure 11-61.

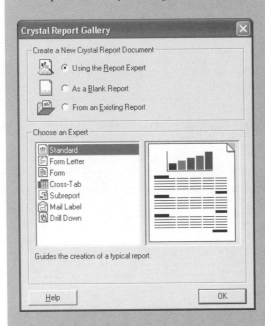

Figure 11-61: Crystal Report Gallery

Note the options available in the Gallery—you can create a new report using the Report Expert (that is, the Report Design Wizard), create a blank report in the Report Designer (which you then design on your own), or base a new report on an existing report. When using the Report Expert, also note the seven different kinds of reports that you can create: Standard, Form Letter, Form, Cross-Tab, Subreport, Mail Label, and Drill Down. Click on each of these options to see the format of the report.

2   For the reports in VillageHousing2, you use the Report Expert to create a Standard Crystal Report. Therefore, with the **Using the Report Expert** radio button selected and the **Standard** report selected, click **OK**. The Standard Report Expert opens.

3   You must first choose data on which to report. Before making your selection, note the variety of data sources supported by Crystal Reports. Expand **Project Data** and **More Data Sources**, as shown in Figure 11-62.

A single Crystal Report can extract data from multiple sources, and these sources can include ADO.NET datasets, OLE DB connections using ADO technology, ODBC using Remote Data Access (an older technology), ADO.NET using XML, or a Microsoft Access or Excel file using Data Access Objects (Microsoft's original data access technology).

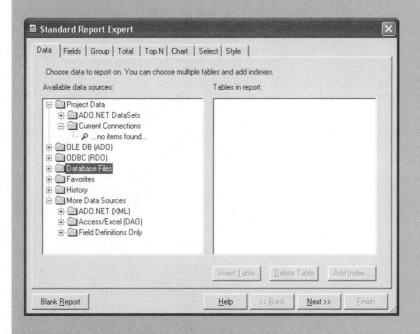

Figure 11-62: Project data possibilities

4   In this case, you are using a query stored in a database as your data source, so expand **Database Files**, and select **VillageHousing.mdb**. Expand **Views**, which displays a list of all queries in the database, select **qryAllVillagersRooms**, and click **Insert Table**, as shown in Figure 11-63. Click **Next**.

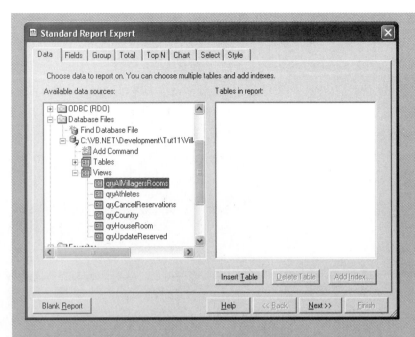

Figure 11-63: Selecting qryAllVillagersRooms for crVillagers.rpt

5 You are still in the same Standard Report Expert window, but you have moved from the Data tab to the Fields tab. (This means that you can move back and forth between tabs if you make a mistake.) In the Fields tab, click **Add All->**. This copies all of the fields in the query from the **Available Fields** list box to the **Fields to Display** list box, shown in Figure 11-64.

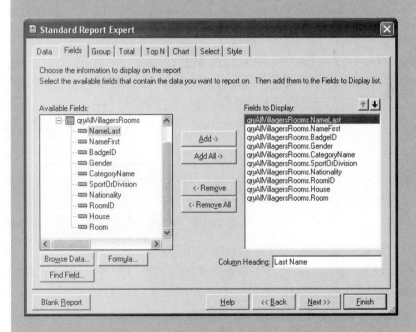

Figure 11-64: Fields tab of the Standard Report Expert

6 From the Fields to Display list, select the field named **qryAllVillagersRooms. NameLast,** and at the bottom of the window, change the **Column Heading** text box to **Last Name,** also shown in Figure 11-64. Then select **qryAllVillagersRooms.NameFirst,** and change the **Column Heading** text box to **First Name.** Similarly, select **BadgeID, Gender, CategoryName, SportOrDivision,** and **Nationality,** changing the column headings to **Badge, Sex, Category, Sport/Division,** and **Country,** respectively. (The main reason for doing this is to shorten the column headings, because the number of columns on this report make it a bit crowded, and the data values in each of these columns fit the shorter headings.) Click **Next.**

7 In the Group tab of the Standard Report Expert, you designate the grouping and sort order of data. Click the field named **qryAllVillagersRooms.NameLast,** and click **Add.** The Sort Order combo box at the bottom indicates that the data will be displayed in ascending order by the currently selected field, which is correct. Click the field named **qryAllVillagersRooms.NameFirst,** and click **Add.** The data will be sorted by last name and then by first name. The completed Group tab appears as in Figure 11-65.

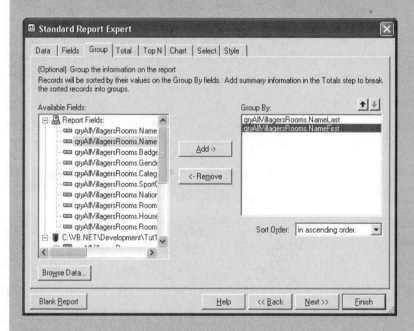

Figure 11-65: Group tab of the Standard Report Expert

8 There are no totals, topN limits, charts, or filters in this report. The only special style consideration is a report title, so click **Next** until you reach the Style tab, or click the **Style** tab directly. On the Style tab, type the report title in the Title text box: **All Villagers and Their Assigned Rooms,** as shown in Figure 11-66.

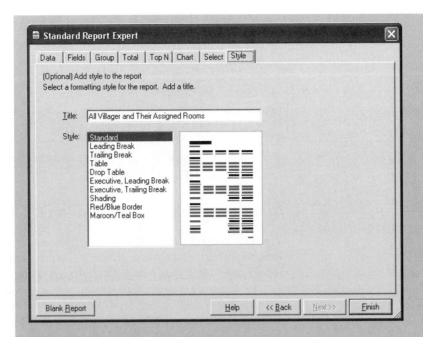

Figure 11-66: Style tab of the Standard Report Expert

9 Click **Finish**. The Standard Report Expert creates the report and closes, and the new report appears in the Crystal Report Designer, shown in Figure 11-67. (The figure shows the Report Designer in Full Screen mode, so that you can see the entire report layout.)

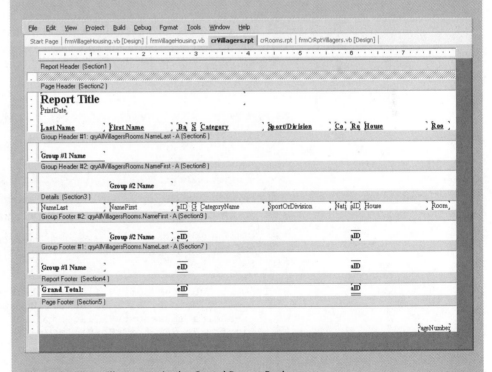

Figure 11-67: crVillagers.rpt in the Crystal Report Designer

Note the several characteristics of the Report Expert, as exemplified by its output. First, when you establish a sort field (in this case, two sort fields, NameLast and NameFirst), the Report Expert marks these as Group fields, and automatically creates a group header and a group footer for each, as well as a grand total. Second, the width of each field is determined by the width of that field in the data source specification, not by the column header. In this case, it is the width of each field in the Field Size property of the Table Designer for each underlying table in VillageHousing.mdb. Hence, if the column header is wider than the detail information in the data source, part of the column header is truncated.

Customizing the Initial Report Design (Part 1)

The initial report design leaves a lot to be desired, especially if you compare it to the runtime report you should create, shown in Figure 11-12. However, the finished report may be somewhat difficult to visualize, especially if you are new to the Crystal Report Designer. Therefore, you suspend your report design activities for the present in order to incorporate the report into the application and see what it looks like in its present form. Then, after viewing the runtime materialization of the report, you return to the design process and customize the report.

Incorporating a Crystal Report into a Windows Forms Application

A report can appear by itself in a form, or it can appear in a part of a form. In this case, you put crVillagers.rpt in a form by itself. The steps for doing this involve creating a new form, adding a CrystalReportViewer to that form, setting the properties of the CrystalReportViewer control, and then instantiating and displaying the form. The details of report generation and layout are handled automatically by the Crystal Report itself, and the details of printing and otherwise manipulating the report are handled by the CrystalReportViewer control.

To incorporate a Crystal Report into a Windows Forms application:

1   Add a new Windows form to the VillageHousing2 project. Name this form **frmCrRptVillagers**. Set its **Text** property to **Villagers Report**, and its **WindowState** property to **Maximized**.

2   Drop a **CrystalReportViewer** control 📄 onto the new form. Set the report viewer's **Dock** property to Fill, and set its **ReportSource** property to **crVillagers.rpt**.

3   Insert a procedure to instantiate and display **frmCrRptVillager** when the user clicks Reports | Villagers, as shown in Figure 11-68.

```
Private Sub mnuReportsVillagers_Click(ByVal sender _
    As Object, ByVal e As System.EventArgs) _
    Handles mnuReportsVillagers.Click
  Dim frm As New frmCrRptVillagers()
  frm.Show()
End Sub
```

Figure 11-68: mnuReportsVillagers_Click()

4 In the mnuFileLoadDate_Click() procedure, insert a statement to enable mnuReports.

5 Run the application. Click **File | Load Data.** Click **Reports | Villagers,** and examine this report carefully, to see the modifications that must be made before the report is complete. The current report appears as shown in Figure 11-69.

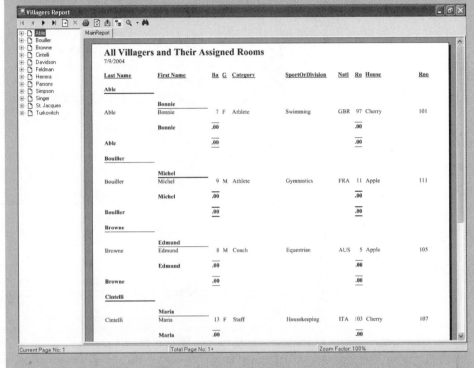

Figure 11-69: All Villagers and Their Assigned Rooms, at runtime (initial report design)

6 Close the report and the running application, and return to the IDE.

Customizing the Initial Report Design (Part 2)

You now need to modify the initial report shown in Figure 11-69 so that it appears like the final report, shown in Figure 11-12. The initial report differs from the final report in the following specifics: the printing of the Group #1 Header, Group #2 Header, Group #2 Footer, Group #1 Footer, and Report Footer (the Grand total line) must be suppressed. (You do not want to actually delete the groups, because this would delete the sorting that you have asked for; you only want to suppress the printing of those lines on the report.) You also need to adjust the width of the following fields, in order to accommodate the currently truncated column headers: Room, RoomID, Nationality, Gender, and BadgeID.

> **NOTE:** If you discover that some of the specifications that you selected in the Report Expert are incorrect, you can return to the Report Expert by right-clicking a blank area in the Crystal Report Designer, and then selecting Report | Report Expert. However, as the warning message when you do this indicates, this action can be dangerous, because when you click Finish in the Report Expert, the wizard re-creates the report from scratch, eliminating any manual changes that you may have made in the Crystal Report Designer.

To customize crVillagers.rpt:

1   Open the Crystal Report Designer for crVillagers.rpt by double-clicking it in Solution Explorer, if necessary.

2   Note that Report Header (Section 1) is already suppressed, indicated by the diagonal lines through that section's data portion. Right-click **Report Header (Section 1)**, and note that Don't Suppress is one of the options. This suggests that printing or not printing a particular section of a report is a toggle switch.

3   Right-click **Group Header #1: qryAllVillagersRooms.NameLast — A (Section 6)**, and select **Suppress (No Drill-Down)**. In the same way, right-click and suppress the printing of **Group Header #2: qryAllVillagersRooms.NameFirst — A (Section 8)**, **Group Footer #2: qryAllVillagersRooms.NameFirst — A (Section 9)**, **Group Footer #1: qryAllVillagersRooms.NameLast — A (Section 7)**, and **Report Footer — A (Section 4)**. At this point, crVillagers.rpt appears in the Report Designer as shown in Figure 11-70; and, if you run the report, it appears as shown in Figure 11-71.

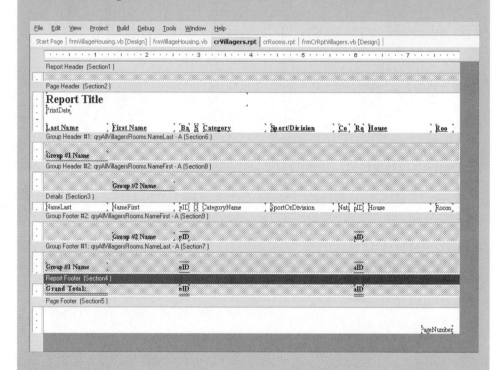

Figure 11-70: crVillagers.rpt in the Report Designer, after suppressing unwanted lines

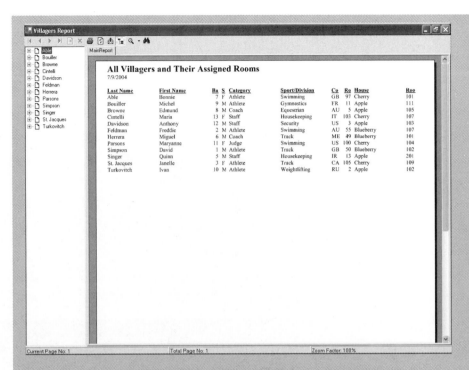

Figure 11-71: All Villagers and their Assigned Rooms, after suppressing unwanted lines

4 The next step is time-consuming, but not unduly complicated. You must adjust the width and position of each field in both the Page Header (Section 2) and Details (Section 3) sections of the report. You may also wish to change the order of the fields—the order should be logical, but need not exactly match the order shown in the figures. You do this in the same way as you would adjust the size and location of any control on a Windows form: select the field, and use its handles to adjust the position when you see the four-headed mouse pointer, and the width when you see the two-headed mouse pointer. You need to run the application and view the report a number of times until the runtime report appears as in Figure 11-12. The result in the Report Designer should appear approximately as shown in Figure 11-72.

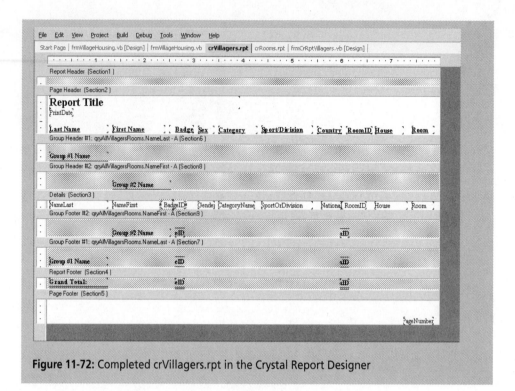

Figure 11-72: Completed crVillagers.rpt in the Crystal Report Designer

Using ADO Technology to Create a Crystal Report

The second report, Reserved Rooms Report, is drawn directly from the underlying tables of the database, and employs ADO technology. Other than specifying ADO technology, the steps in creating the Reserved Rooms Report are analogous to creating the All Villagers and Their Assigned Rooms report.

To create crRooms.rpt:

1 In Solution Explorer, right-click the **VilageHousing2** project name, and select **Add | Add New Item**. In the Add New Item dialog box, select **Crystal Report**. Change the default name **CrystalReport1.rpt** to **crRooms.rpt**, then click **Open**. The Crystal Reports Gallery opens. Click **OK**. The Standard Report Expert opens.

2 Expand **OLE DB (ADO)**. In the OLE DB Provider dialog box, select **Microsoft Jet 4.0 OLE DB Provider**. Click **Next**. In the Connection Information dialog box, browse to locate and select the **VillageHousing.mdb** database. Click **Open**. Click **Finish**. You are returned to the Data tab of the Standard Report Expert.

3 Expand **Tables**, and select tblHouse, tblRoom, and tblVillager by clicking **tblHouse**, then press and hold **Ctrl** and click **tblRoom** and **tblVillager**. Click **Insert Table**. Click **Next**. In the **Links** tab, note that the correct links from tblHouse to tblRoom and from tblRoom to tblVillager have been identified, as shown in Figure 11-73. (Tables in this figure are rearranged so that they are all visible at once.) Click **Next**.

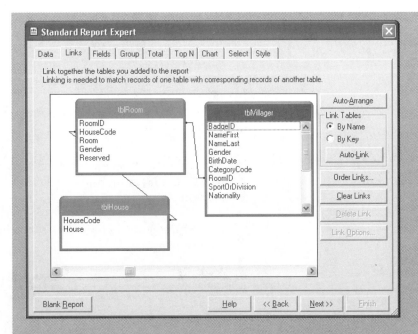

Figure 11-73: Links tab of the Standard Report Expert

4 In the **Fields** tab, tblHouse is expanded—select **House,** and click **Add** to add House to the **Fields to Display** list box. tblRoom expands. Select **RoomID** and **Room,** and click **Add** to add them to the Fields to Display list. Expand **tblVillager.** Select **NameLast** and **NameFirst,** and move them to the Fields to Display list, as shown in Figure 11-74.

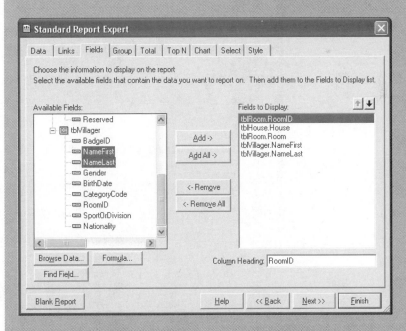

Figure 11-74: Fields tab of the Standard Report Expert

5 In the Fields to Display list box, modify the column headings of **RoomID, NameLast,** and **NameFirst** so that they read **Room ID, Last Name,** and **First Name,** respectively. Click **Next.**

6 In the **Group** tab, select **tblHouse.House** and **tblRoom.Room**, and click **Add** to add these fields to the **Group By** list box. This causes the report to be sorted by house and room number. It also causes group headers and footers to appear in the Report Designer, whose printing you need to suppress.

7 Click the **Style** tab, and insert **Reserved Rooms Report** in the **Title** text box. Click **Finish**. The Standard Report Expert creates crRooms.rpt based on your specifications. The wizard closes, and crRooms.rpt opens in the Crystal Report Designer.

8 Right click **Group Header #1: tblHouse.House – A(Section 6)**, and click **Suppress (No Drill Down)** to suppress the printing of that line. Similarly, suppress the printing of **Group Header #2, Group Footer #2, Group Footer #1**, and **Report Footer**. Adjust the width and position of RoomID and adjacent fields as needed to accommodate all column headers. The final report specification should appear as in Figure 11-75.

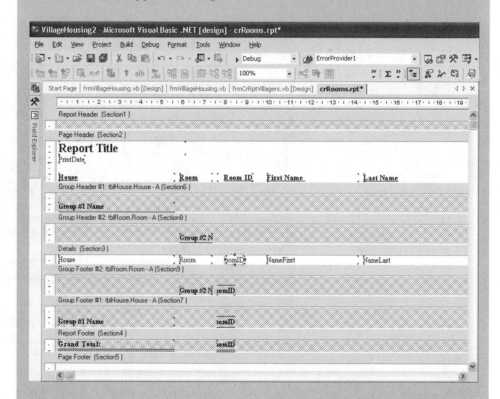

Figure 11-75: Completed crRooms.rpt in the Crystal Report Designer

9 Incorporate crRooms.rpt into the VillageHousing2 application, following precisely the same steps you did for crVillagers.rpt. That is, add a new Windows form to the project, naming this form **frmCrRptRooms**. Set the new form's **Text** property to **Rooms Report**, and set its **WindowState** property to **Maximized**. Place a **CrystalReportViewer** control on the form. Set the viewer's **Dock** property to **Fill**, and set its **ReportSource** property to **crRooms.rpt**. Then program **mnuReportsRooms_Click()** to instantiate and display frmCrRptRooms. When you run the application, the report should appear as in Figure 11-14.

Understanding Error Traps, Help Systems, and Crystal Reports in Web Forms Applications

You will discover that most of the things you have learned in Tutorial 11 apply equally well to Web Forms applications. This section summarizes the similarities and differences between Windows Forms and Web Forms when implementing error traps, Help systems, and Crystal Reports.

Error Traps in Web Forms Applications

The Try...Catch construct itself is exactly the same in Windows Forms and Web Forms. The only differences deal with the GUI and the classes available to each type of application. For example, as you have already learned in Tutorials 7 and 10, Web Forms applications cannot display modal forms, so you cannot use the MsgBox or MessageBox statements. Instead, you must display error messages in some other way—in a frame, in a control placed on the Web page, or in another Web page. But in all other respects, the principles and applications of the Try...Catch construct are the same.

The ErrorProvider control is not available in Web Forms. Instead, Web Forms have a rich variety of data validation controls that actually provide far more extensive error-checking potential. These controls include the RequiredFieldValidator, the CompareValidator, the RangeValidator, the RegularExpressionValidator, the CustomValidator, and the ValidationSummary controls. (These controls are briefly mentioned in Tutorial 7.) A principle advantage of these validation controls for a Web application is that the validation criteria are built into the control's properties and so can be immediately checked on the client side, without requiring a round-trip to the server.

Consider the following simple example: in the LogonManager application from Tutorial 4, you could use an ErrorProvider control to ensure that the Last Name field is not left blank. The code to check for a nonblank entry is written into the Validating event procedure for the Last Name text box. If the LogonManager application were written as a Web Forms application instead, you would use a RequiredFieldValidator control to make sure that a last name is entered. This control does not allow the required field to be blanked out after data has once been entered into it.

To test the RequiredFieldValidator control:

1   Start a new ASP.NET Web application. Place a **text box** on WebForm1, and name it **txtLastName**. Add a second **text box** to the form. Add a **button** with the Text property **Submit**.

2   Place a **RequiredFieldValidator** control on the form, and set its **ErrorMessage** property to **A Last Name is required**. Then set its **ControlToValidate** property to **txtLastName**.

3   Run the application. You can click or tab anywhere on the page without generating an error. If you click the Submit button before entering a value in the Last Name text box, only server-side code can test for the error—but clicking the Submit button causes a round-trip to the server anyway.

4   Enter **your last name** in **txtLastName**. Press **Tab** to move to the next text box. Delete your last name from txtLastName. Press **Tab** to move to the next text box. The error message appears, generated by the RequiredFieldValidator control. This error message is generated on the client side, and requires no round-trip to the server.

5   Close the Web page, and return to the IDE.

Help Systems in Web Forms Applications

The HTML Help Workshop can be used to build a Help system for any application written in any language, and implemented as a Windows Forms or a Web Forms application. Incorporating the Help system into a Web Forms application is somewhat different, however, because the HelpProvider and ToolTip controls have no Web Forms counterpart. To open the Help file, provide a link to it. You can experiment with the VhHelp.chm file that you created for VillageHousing2.

> To experiment with Help in a Web Forms application:
>
> **1** Place a **HyperLink** control on your WebForm1. Set the **Text** property to **Village Housing Help**. Click the **ellipsis** in the **NavigateURL** property, and browse to locate the **VhHelp.chm** file.
>
> **2** Run the application. Click the link to **Village Housing Help**. Your Help file opens in the familiar Help Viewer. Close the **Help Viewer**, and close the Web page. Exit **Visual Studio .NET**.
>
> **NOTE:** Depending on your browser settings, clicking the link to VhHelp.chm may cause a dialog window to open, asking if you wish to open the VhHelp.chm file or save it to your computer, in which case you will need to click Open.

Crystal Reports in Web Forms Applications

The process of creating and incorporating a Crystal Report in a Web Forms application differs very little from the process in a Windows Forms application. You build the report in exactly the same way. Of course, as in all Web-based programs, you must ensure that the data source is available to a user accessing a server. Web Forms controls include a CrystalReportViewer control, which you can drop onto a Web Form. When the Web Form is loaded, the report appears in the CrystalReportViewer control.

You have now completed Tutorial 11. Your journeys through Visual Basic .NET are just beginning. Try this last set of questions and exercises before you embark on them.

SUMMARY

- Crystal Reports provides a comprehensive report generation facility. Seven wizards are available to help you develop an initial report design.
- The Crystal Reports Standard Report Expert guides you in connecting to a data source, selecting tables or views in that data source, selecting fields and column headers, determining the sort order, establishing groups and totals, and selecting a report style.
- The data source(s) for a Crystal Report can include a wide variety of databases and other nonrelational data stores, and can use ADO.NET, XML, ADO, OLE DB, RDO, and DAO technologies.
- The Crystal Report Designer can be used to manually build a report or to customize a report that was first created through one of the wizards. You can add or remove fields, format the report, and suppress printing for certain report sections.
- To incorporate a Crystal Report into a Windows Forms application, Visual Basic .NET includes the CrystalReportViewer control. The viewer can fill part or all of a Windows form. Its ReportSource property identifies the report to be displayed.

■ You write code to instantiate the form containing the CrystalReportViewer control and to display the report at runtime. The viewer includes all of the necessary controls to manipulate and print the report.

■ In Web Forms applications, you employ the Try...Catch construct for error handling in the same way as you use it in Windows Forms applications.

■ Visual Basic .NET offers a rich collection of controls for validating user input in Web Forms applications, including the RequiredFieldValidator, the CompareValidator, the RangeValidator, the RegularExpressionValidator, the CustomValidator, and the ValidationSummary controls.

■ The HTML Help Workshop can be used equally well in Web Forms and in Windows Forms applications. A Web-based Help system facilitates maintenance, because changes can be made immediately available to all users without having to distribute files to all users.

■ Crystal Reports are implemented in a Web Forms application through the CrystalReportViewer Web Forms control. Designing a Crystal Report is the same, regardless of the intended use in a Windows Forms or Web Forms application.

QUESTIONS

1. In the Standard Report Expert, you identify the source(s) of data for a report on the _____ tab.

2. In the Standard Report Expert, the sort order for a report is determined by selecting one or more fields on the _____ tab.

3. In the Standard Report Expert, the report title is entered on the _____ tab.

4. To suppress the printing of a report section, you right-click the section header and select Suppress in the _____.

5. The Windows Forms control that displays a Crystal Report is the _____.

6. You designate which report is to be displayed by entering the name of the Crystal Report in the _____ property.

7. In a Web Forms application, you can ensure that a data field that contains data is not subsequently left empty by using the _____ control.

8. Error handling in a Web Forms application is typically employed in the CodeBehind module by using the _____ construct.

EXERCISES

1. Add a Crystal Report to the VillageHousing2 application to display the contents of tblCountry, sorted by Country.

2. Add a Crystal Report to the VillageHousing2 application to display the name of each villager along with the full name of that villager's country. Use ADO technology for this report. Include the NameLast and NameFirst fields from tblVillager, along with that villager's country from tblCountry. Use grammatically correct column headings.

3. Use the HTML Help Workshop to create a Help system for the EventSchedule application in Tutorial 7.

4. Use the HTML Help Workshop to create a Help system for the FigTickets application in Tutorial 10.

5. Use the HTML Help Workshop to create a Help system for the Up Close and Personal application in Tutorial 8.

6. Starting with your completed Up Close and Personal application from Tutorial 8 and the .chm file you created in Exercise 5, incorporate that Help system into the Up Close and Personal application. Add a main menu to frmStart, and place a Help menu item in the menu, with menu items under Help for Contents, Index, and Search. Also, place a HelpButton control on frmAthlete, and provide context-sensitive help for each control on that form that can receive focus.

KEY TERMS

- ActiveX Data Objects data access technology
- Clear method (with Err)
- Crystal Reports
- Crystal Reports Gallery
- CrystalReportViewer control
- deadlock
- Description property (with Err)
- dirty read
- EnforceConstraints property
- Err object
- Error statement
- error traps
- ErrorProvider control
- Exception class
- HelpButton control
- HelpLink property
- HelpProvider control
- HTML Help Image Editor
- HTML Help Workshop
- Message property (with Exception)
- Number property (with Err)
- On Error GoTo statement
- Raise method
- Report Expert wizard
- Report Section
- ReportSource property
- Resume [Next] statement
- software configuration management
- Source property (with Err)
- StackTrace property
- Standard Report Expert
- structured exception handling
- ToolTip control
- Try...Catch construct

Consolidated Code Listing

The Up Close and Personal Application

This appendix provides a complete listing of the code for frmStart.vb, see Figure A-1; Module1.vb, see Figure A-2; SortModule.vb, see Figure A-3; and frmAthlete.vb, see Figure A-4.

frmStart

```
Public Class frmStart
    Inherits System.Windows.Forms.Form

+Windows Form Designer generated code

  Private Sub frmStart_Load(ByVal sender As Object, ByVal e As _
      System.EventArgs) Handles MyBase.Load
    LoadEvents()
    LoadAthletes()
    LoadNations()
    'CreateBioFiles()
    cboCategory.SelectedIndex = 0
    cboOrder.SelectedIndex = 0
    cboCategory_SelectedIndexChanged(sender, e)
    Dim MyNewLabel As New System.Windows.Forms.Label()
    With MyNewLabel
      .Left = 40
      .Top = 8
      .Height = 16
      .Width = 96
      .TextAlign = ContentAlignment.MiddleRight
      .Text = "Filter Category"
    End With
    Me.Controls.Add(MyNewLabel)
  End Sub

  Private Sub cboCategory_SelectedIndexChanged(ByVal sender As _
      System.Object, ByVal e As System.EventArgs) _
      Handles cboCategory.SelectedIndexChanged
    Dim i, j As Integer
    'clear existing items from cboSubcategory, cboName, and pList1()
    cboSubcategory.Items.Clear()
    cboName.Items.Clear()
    Erase pList1
    ReDim pList1(pNumAthletes)
    Select Case cboCategory.SelectedIndex
      Case 0 'All athletes
        For i = 0 To pNumAthletes - 1
          pList1(i) = pastructAthletes(i)
        Next
        pL1Count = pNumAthletes
        cboOrder_SelectedIndexChanged(sender, e)
      Case 1 'Filter by sport
        For i = 1 To pastrSports(0)
          cboSubcategory.Items.Add(pastrSports(i))
        Next
        cboSubcategory.SelectedIndex = 0
        cboSubcategory_SelectedIndexChanged(sender, e)
      Case 2 'Filter by country
        For i = 0 To NUMNATIONS - 1
          cboSubcategory.Items.Add(pastrNations(i, 0) & " " & _
            pastrNations(i, 1))
        Next
        cboSubcategory.SelectedIndex = 0
        cboSubcategory_SelectedIndexChanged(sender, e)
```

Figure A-1: Consolidated code for frmStart

```vb
        Case 3, 4 'Filter by gender: case 3=Male, case 4=Female
          j = 0
          For i = 0 To pNumAthletes - 1
            If pastructAthletes(i).Gender = _
                IIf(cboCategory.SelectedIndex = 3, "M", "F") Then
              pList1(j) = pastructAthletes(i)
              j += 1
            End If
          Next
          pL1Count = j
          cboOrder_SelectedIndexChanged(sender, e)
      End Select
    End Sub

    Private Sub cboSubcategory_SelectedIndexChanged(ByVal sender As _
        System.Object, ByVal e As System.EventArgs) _
        Handles cboSubcategory.SelectedIndexChanged
      Dim i, j As Integer
      Select Case cboCategory.SelectedIndex
        Case 1 'Filter by sport
          For i = 0 To pNumAthletes - 1
            If UCase(cboSubcategory.SelectedItem) = _
                pastructAthletes(i).Sport Then
              pList1(j) = pastructAthletes(i)
              j += 1
            End If
          Next
        Case 2 'Filter by country
          For i = 0 To pNumAthletes - 1
            If Microsoft.VisualBasic.Left(cboSubcategory.SelectedItem, _
                3) = pastructAthletes(i).Country Then
              pList1(j) = pastructAthletes(i)
              j += 1
            End If
          Next
      End Select
      pL1Count = j
      cboOrder_SelectedIndexChanged(sender, e)
    End Sub

    Private Sub cboOrder_SelectedIndexChanged(ByVal sender As _
        System.Object, ByVal e As System.EventArgs) _
        Handles cboOrder.SelectedIndexChanged
      If pL1Count > 1 Then
        ChooseSort(cboOrder.SelectedIndex)
        If cboOrder.SelectedIndex = 4 Then
          LoadLinkedList()
        Else
          LoadNames()
        End If
      End If
    End Sub

    Private Sub cboName_SelectedIndexChanged(ByVal sender As _
        System.Object, ByVal e As System.EventArgs) _
        Handles cboName.SelectedIndexChanged
      pintAthlete = Val(cboName.SelectedItem)
      Dim frm As New frmAthlete()
      frm.ShowDialog()
    End Sub
```

Figure A-1: Consolidated code for frmStart (continued)

```
    Private Sub LoadNames()
      Dim i As Integer
      cboName.Items.Clear()
      For i = 0 To pL1Count - 1
        With pList1(i)
           cboName.Items.Add(.AthleteID & " " & .FName & " " & _
             .LName & " (" & .Country & ")")
        End With
      Next
    End Sub

    Private Sub LoadLinkedList()
      cboName.Items.Clear()
      Dim Ptr As Integer = pPtr
      Do Until Ptr = -9
        With pList1(Ptr)
           cboName.Items.Add(.AthleteID & " " & .FName & " " & _
             .LName & " (" & .Country & ")")
           Ptr = .Ptr
        End With
      Loop
    End Sub
End Class
```

Figure A-1: Consolidated code for frmStart (continued)

Module1

```
Module Module1
  Public Structure structEvent
    Public EventID As Integer
    <VBFixedString(10)> Public Sport As String
    <VBFixedString(25)> Public EventName As String
    <VBFixedString(1)> Public Gender As String
    <VBFixedString(2)> Public ScoringMethod As String
    <VBFixedString(3)> Public Country1 As String
    <VBFixedString(3)> Public Country2 As String
    Public VenueIndex As Integer
    <VBFixedString(10)> Public Schedule As String
    Public StartTime As Date
    <VBFixedString(1)> Public PricingSchedule As String
  End Structure

  Public Structure structAthlete
    Public AthleteID As Integer
    <VBFixedString(20)> Public FName As String
    <VBFixedString(25)> Public LName As String
    <VBFixedString(1)> Public Gender As String
    <VBFixedString(3)> Public Country As String
    Public DoB As Date
    <VBFixedString(10)> Public Sport As String
    Public Event1 As Integer
    Public Event2 As Integer
    Public Event3 As Integer
    Public Event4 As Integer
    Public Event5 As Integer
    Public RecNum As Integer
    Public Ptr As Integer
  End Structure
```

Figure A-2: Consolidated code for Module1

```
Public Structure structISAM
  Public AthleteID As Integer
  <VBFixedString(1000)> Public Bio As String
  <VBFixedString(50)> Public PicFilename As String
End Structure

Public Const NUMEVENTS = 500 'maximum number of events
Public Const NUMATHLETES = 500 'maximum number of athletes
Public Const NUMNATIONS = 26 'actual number of nations in Nations.txt
Public pastructEvents(NUMEVENTS) As structEvent
Public pastructAthletes(NUMATHLETES) As structAthlete
'pList1 is the list of names to be sorted & displayed
Public pList1(NUMATHLETES) As structAthlete
Public pNumEvents As Integer 'actual number of events
Public pNumAthletes As Integer 'actual number of athletes
Public pL1Count As Integer 'number of names to be sorted & displayed
Public pintAthlete As Integer 'used to identify one athlete
Public pastrNations(NUMNATIONS, 3)
Public pstructBioRec As structISAM 'one record in the ISAM file
Public pPtr As Integer 'points to the first record in the linked list

Public pastrSports() As String = {16, _
  "Baseball", "Basketball", "Boxing", "Diving", _
  "Equestrian", "Fencing", "Field", "Gymnastics", _
  "Shooting", "Soccer", "Softball", "Swimming", _
  "Tennis", "Track", "Volleyball", "Wrestling"}

Public Sub LoadEvents()
  Dim i As Integer
  FileOpen(1, "Events.txt", OpenMode.Input)
  pNumEvents = 0
  Do Until EOF(1)
    With pastructEvents(i)
      Input(1, .EventID)
      Input(1, .Sport)
      Input(1, .EventName)
      Input(1, .Gender)
      Input(1, .ScoringMethod)
      Input(1, .Country1)
      Input(1, .Country2)
      Input(1, .VenueIndex)
      Input(1, .Schedule)
      Input(1, .StartTime)
      Input(1, .PricingSchedule)
    End With
    i += 1
  Loop
  FileClose()
  pNumEvents = i
End Sub

Public Sub LoadAthletes()
  Dim i As Integer
  FileOpen(1, "Athletes.txt", OpenMode.Input)
  pNumAthletes = 0
  Do Until EOF(1)
    With pastructAthletes(i)
      Input(1, .AthleteID)
      Input(1, .FName)
      Input(1, .LName)
      Input(1, .Gender)
      Input(1, .Country)
```

Figure A-2: Consolidated code for Module1 (continued)

```
                    Input(1, .DoB)
                    Input(1, .Sport)
                    Input(1, .Event1)
                    Input(1, .Event2)
                    Input(1, .Event3)
                    Input(1, .Event4)
                    Input(1, .Event5)
                    .RecNum = i
                End With
                i += 1
            Loop
            FileClose()
            pNumAthletes = i
        End Sub

        Public Sub LoadNations()
            Dim i, j As Integer
            FileOpen(1, "Nations.txt", OpenMode.Input)
            For j = 0 To NUMNATIONS - 1
                Input(1, pastrNations(j, 0))
                Input(1, pastrNations(j, 1))
                Input(1, pastrNations(j, 2))
            Next
            FileClose(1)

        End Sub

        Public Sub CreateBioFiles()
            Dim i, j As Integer
            Dim s As String
            FileOpen(1, "Biographies", OpenMode.Random, , , Len(pstructBioRec))
            For i = 0 To pNumAthletes - 1
                With pastructAthletes(i)
                    s = "Biographical Sketch. "
                    s &= .FName & " " & .LName & " was born on " & _
                        Format(.DoB, "MMMM d, yyyy") & ". "
                    s &= IIf(.Gender = "M", "He ", "She ") & _
                                "began the sport of " & .Sport & _
                                " at a very young age, "
                    For j = 0 To 25
                        If .Country = pastrNations(j, 0) Then
                            s &= "and is now proud to represent " & _
                                IIf(.Gender = "M", "his", "her") & _
                                " native country of " & pastrNations(j, 1) & ". "
                        End If
                    Next
                    s &= IIf(.Gender = "M", "His", "Her") & _
                        " favorite event in the Friendsville International Games is "
                    For j = 0 To pNumEvents - 1
                        If .Event1 = pastructEvents(j).EventID Then
                            s &= pastructEvents(j).EventName & "."
                        End If
                    Next
                    pstructBioRec.AthleteID = .AthleteID
                    pstructBioRec.Bio = s
                    pstructBioRec.PicFilename = IIf(.Gender = "M", "misc27.ico", _
                        "misc26.ico")
                    FilePut(1, pstructBioRec, .AthleteID)
                End With
            Next
            FileClose()
        End Sub
    End Module
```

Figure A-2: Consolidated code for Module1 (continued)

SortModule

```
Module SortModule
  Public Sub ChooseSort(ByVal vintOrder As Integer)
    Select Case vintOrder
      Case 0 'sort by AthleteID
        BubbleSort()
      Case 1 'sort by Lastname, Firstname
        SelectionSort()
      Case 2 'sort by Firstname, Lastname
        InsertionSort()
      Case 3 'sort by country
        ShellSort()
      Case 4 'sort by AthleteID in reverse order
        LinkedList()
    End Select
  End Sub

  Private Sub BubbleSort() 'sort on AthleteID
    Dim i, j As Integer
    Dim Temp As structAthlete
    For i = 0 To pL1Count - 2
      Temp.LName = ""
      For j = i + 1 To pL1Count - 1
        If pList1(i).AthleteID > pList1(j).AthleteID Then
          Temp = pList1(i)
          pList1(i) = pList1(j)
          pList1(j) = Temp
        End If
      Next
      'sort is complete if no swap was made
      If Temp.LName = "" Then Exit For
    Next
  End Sub

  Private Sub SelectionSort() 'sort on Lastname, Firstname
    Dim L1Index, LowIndex, L2Index As Integer
    Dim List2(pL1Count) As structAthlete
    For L2Index = 0 To pL1Count - 1
      LowIndex = 0
      For L1Index = 1 To pL1Count - 1
        If pList1(LowIndex).LName & pList1(LowIndex).FName > _
          pList1(L1Index).LName & pList1(L1Index).FName _
          Then LowIndex = L1Index
      Next
      List2(L2Index) = pList1(LowIndex)
      pList1(LowIndex).LName = "ZZZZZ"
    Next
    For L2Index = 0 To pL1Count - 1
      pList1(L2Index) = List2(L2Index)
    Next
  End Sub

  Private Sub InsertionSort() 'sort on Firstname, Lastname
    Dim L1Index, L2Count, L2Index As Integer
    Dim List2(pL1Count) As structAthlete
    L2Count = 1
    List2(0) = pList1(0)
    L1Index = 1
```

Figure A-3: Consolidated code for SortModule

```
        Do Until L2Count = pL1Count
          L2Index = L2Count - 1
          Do Until L2Index < 0 OrElse pList1(L1Index).FName & _
              pList1(L1Index).LName >= _
              List2(L2Index).FName & List2(L2Index).LName
            List2(L2Index + 1) = List2(L2Index)
            L2Index -= 1
          Loop
          List2(L2Index + 1) = pList1(L1Index)
          L1Index += 1
          L2Count += 1
        Loop
        'copy List2 back to pList1
        For L2Index = 0 To pL1Count - 1
          pList1(L2Index) = List2(L2Index)
        Next
    End Sub

    Private Sub ShellSort() 'sort on country abbreviation
        Dim Distance, L1Index, HoldIndex As Integer
        Dim Temp As structAthlete
        'set the initial distance
        Distance = 2
        Do Until Distance > pL1Count
          Distance *= 2
        Loop
        Distance = Distance / 2 - 1
        'main body of the Shell sort
        Do Until Distance = 0
          For L1Index = 0 To (pL1Count - 1) - Distance
            If pList1(L1Index).Country > _
                pList1(L1Index + Distance).Country Then
              HoldIndex = L1Index
              Do While L1Index >= 0 AndAlso pList1(L1Index).Country > _
                  pList1(L1Index + Distance).Country
                Temp = pList1(L1Index)
                pList1(L1Index) = pList1(L1Index + Distance)
                pList1(L1Index + Distance) = Temp
                L1Index -= Distance
              Loop
              L1Index = HoldIndex
            End If
          Next
          Distance /= 2
        Loop
    End Sub

    Private Structure structLink
        Dim RecNum As Integer
        Dim AthleteID As Integer
        Dim Ptr As Integer
    End Structure

    Private Sub LinkedList()
        Dim i, j As Integer
        Dim Temp As structLink
        Dim List2(pL1Count) As structLink
        'sort pList1 by AthleteID (to provide a starting point)
        BubbleSort()
        'load the parallel list
```

Figure A-3: Consolidated code for SortModule (continued)

```
      For i = 0 To pL1Count - 1
        With List2(i)
          .RecNum = i
          .AthleteID = pList1(i).AthleteID
        End With
      Next
      'sort the parallel list in reverse order by AthleteID
      For i = 0 To pL1Count - 2
        Temp.AthleteID = Nothing
        For j = i + 1 To pL1Count - 1
          If List2(i).AthleteID < List2(j).AthleteID Then
            Temp = List2(i)
            List2(i) = List2(j)
            List2(j) = Temp
          End If
        Next
        'sort is complete if no swap was made
        If Temp.AthleteID = Nothing Then Exit For
      Next
      'assign the ptr values to List2
      For i = 0 To pL1Count - 2
        List2(i).Ptr = List2(i + 1).RecNum
      Next
      'load the external pointer and the end-of-list sentinal
      pPtr = List2(0).RecNum
      List2(pL1Count - 1).Ptr = -9
      'sort the parallel list by AthleteID (to match pList1)
      For i = 0 To pL1Count - 2
        Temp.AthleteID = Nothing
        For j = i + 1 To pL1Count - 1
          If List2(i).AthleteID > List2(j).AthleteID Then
            Temp = List2(i)
            List2(i) = List2(j)
            List2(j) = Temp
          End If
        Next
        'sort is complete if no swap was made
        If Temp.AthleteID = Nothing Then Exit For
      Next
      'copy the ptr values to pList1
      For i = 0 To pL1Count - 1
        pList1(i).Ptr = List2(i).Ptr
      Next
  End Sub
End Module
```

Figure A-3: Consolidated code for SortModule (continued)

frmAthlete

```vb
Public Class frmAthlete
    Inherits System.Windows.Forms.Form

+Windows Form Designer generated code


  Private Sub frmAthlete_Load(ByVal sender As System.Object, _
     ByVal e As System.EventArgs) Handles MyBase.Load
    Dim Index As Integer
    DoBinarySearch(Index)
    With pastructAthletes(Index)
      lblAthleteID.Text = .AthleteID
      lblFName.Text = .FName
      lblLName.Text = .LName
      CtrlNation1.SetCountry(.Country)
      lblGender.Text = IIf(.Gender = "M", "Male", "Female")
      lblDoB.Text = Format(.DoB, "MMMM d, yyyy")
      lblSport.Text = .Sport
      Dim Events(5) As Integer
      Dim i, j As Integer
      Events(0) = .Event1
      Events(1) = .Event2
      Events(2) = .Event3
      Events(3) = .Event4
      Events(4) = .Event5
      For i = 0 To 4
        If Events(i) > 0 Then
          For j = 0 To pNumEvents - 1
            If Events(i) = pastructEvents(j).EventID Then
              lstEvents.Items.Add(pastructEvents(j).EventName)
            End If
          Next
        End If
      Next
      FileOpen(1, "Biographies", OpenMode.Random, , , _
         Len(pstructBioRec))
      FileGet(1, pstructBioRec, .AthleteID)
      rtfBio.Text = pstructBioRec.Bio
      pbxPhoto.Image = Image.FromFile(pstructBioRec.PicFilename)
      FileClose()
    End With
  End Sub

  Private Sub DoBinarySearch(ByRef rIndex As Integer)
    Dim Low, Mid, High As Integer
    Low = 0
    High = pNumAthletes
    Mid = Int((Low + High) / 2)
    Do Until pastructAthletes(Mid).AthleteID = pintAthlete
      If pintAthlete > pastructAthletes(Mid).AthleteID Then
        Low = Mid
      Else
        High = Mid
      End If
      Mid = Int((Low + High) / 2)
    Loop
    rIndex = Mid
  End Sub
End Class
```

Figure A-4: Consolidated code for frmAthlete

FigTickets4Windows

This appendix is related to Tutorial 10 and contains a Windows version of the main Web Forms application. It includes a preview of the completed application, followed by step-by-step instructions for constructing it.

Previewing the FigTickets4Windows Application

If you are unable to preview the FigTickets Web Forms application because of security or other restrictions, then you can preview the FigTickets4Windows application instead. This Windows Forms application offers much of the same functionality as FigTickets: it uses an SQL Server database that you create with Visual Database Tools and the Microsoft Desktop Engine, and it includes both data retrieval and data updates. It demonstrates the SQL Data Provider in ADO.NET, using both approaches of data adapters and datasets, as well as data commands and data readers. What it does not do is operate on the World Wide Web, or use the facilities of Internet Information Server (IIS).

To preview the FigTickets4Windows application:

1 Make sure that you have **Microsoft Data Access Components 2.6** or higher running on the computer on which you plan to install FigTickets4Windows. If Visual Studio .NET is installed, then you already have MDAC 2.6 running.

2 You must install the **Tickets** database on your computer. To do this, follow Steps 2 and 3 in the section called **Previewing the FigTickets Web Forms Application** at the beginning of Tutorial 10. Note the *machinename\ instancename* of the SQL Server instance where you install the Tickets database.

3 Run the **FigTickets4Windows** application, located in the VB.NET\Student\AppB folder. Initially, the startup screen prompts you to enter the **machinename\ instancename** of the SQL Server instance. Type in this information, and click the **Save SQL Server machinename\instancename** button. A panel control appears, allowing you to select between New User – Create Account and Existing User – Login. The form now appears as shown in Figure B-1 (although the *machinename\instancename* on your computer will be different from the one shown in the figure). Click **Existing User – Login**. The User Login screen appears. Log in as **Rick Sanchez**, as shown in Figure B-2. Rick's e-mail address is **rick@fgdt.org** and his password is **rickfgdt**. Click **Submit**.

NOTE: As is the case for the FigTickets Web application, the version of FigTickets4Windows that you build in this appendix will not ask the user to type in the SQL Server machinename\instancename. Rather, you will hard code this information into your program. The opening screen will only ask the user to select between a new user and an existing user.

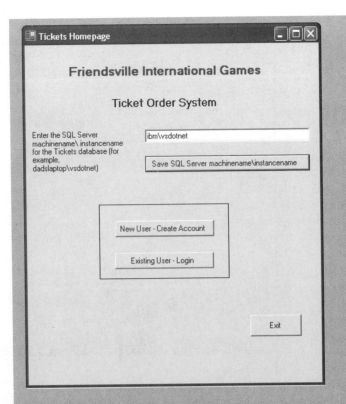

Figure B-1: Opening screen for FigTickets4Windows

Figure B-2: Login screen for Rick Sanchez

4   The Existing User screen is displayed and is shown in Figure B-3. Click **Orders**. On the Orders screen showing the two ticket orders that Rick has placed, click **Order Details** for OrderID 17. The result appears as in Figure B-4. Note at the top of this screen that this ticket order is for the women's softball game between the USA and Japan. In the data grid at the bottom of the screen, you can see that this order is for two $50 tickets. These tickets have been ordered, but not yet purchased.

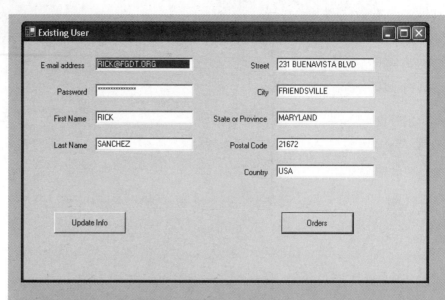

Figure B-3: Existing User screen

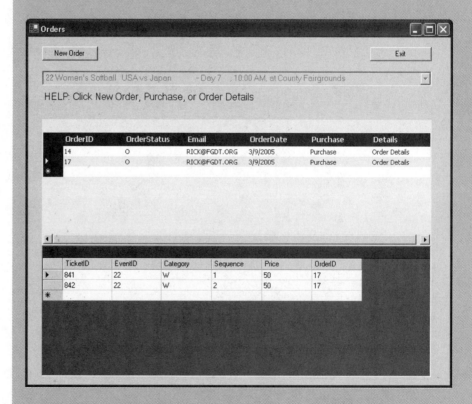

Figure B-4: Orders and Order Details screen

5   Click the **Purchase** button for OrderID 14. A message indicates the change of
status from Ordered (O) to Sold (S), as shown in Figure B-5. Click **OK**.

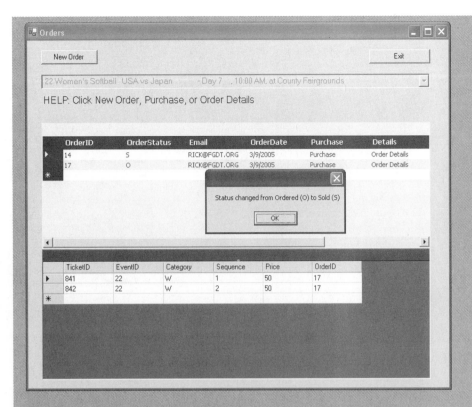

Figure B-5: Purchasing previously ordered tickets

6   Click **New Order**. The Events combo box at the top of the screen becomes enabled, and you can select any event for this new order, as shown in Figure B-6. Select **EventID 15, Closing Ceremonies** from this combo box, after which the combo box is again disabled; all tickets available for this event appear in the tickets data grid control in the bottom half of the screen. Scroll down until you see the $100 tickets, shown in Figure B-7, and reserve (by clicking the **Reserve** buttons) **TicketIDs 571, 572**, and **573**. Click **Done**, and the result appears as in Figure B-8.

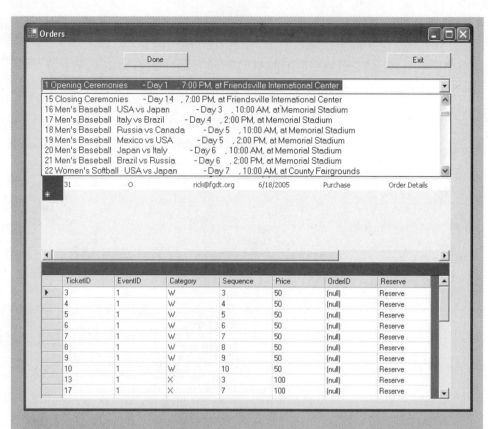

Figure B-6: Selecting any event for a new order

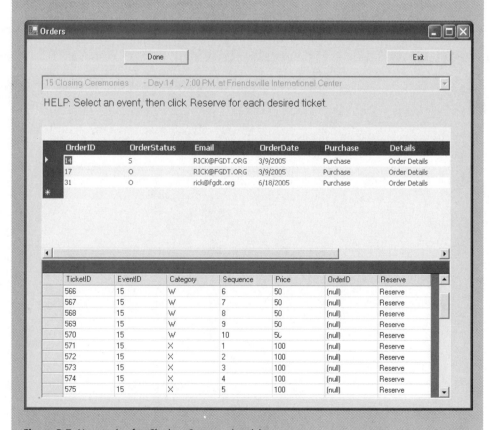

Figure B-7: New order for Closing Ceremonies tickets

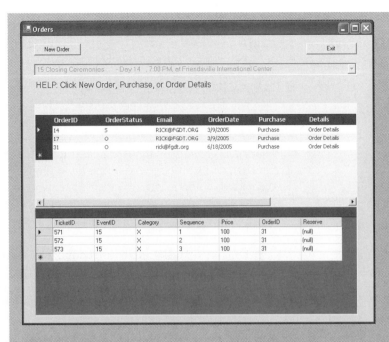

Figure B-8: Completed order for Closing Ceremonies tickets

7 Click **Exit** to close the Orders window and terminate the application.

8 Run the **FigTicket4Windows** application again. This time, from the opening window (shown previously in Figure B-1) click **New User – Create Account.** The New User window opens. Type in the data for Jose Santiago shown in Figure B-9. The password is **Andalucia.** Click **Submit.** The Existing User window appears. Click **Orders.** On the Orders form, click **New Order,** and order two tickets for Jose and his wife to see EventID 129, the women's basketball match between Spain and Portugal.

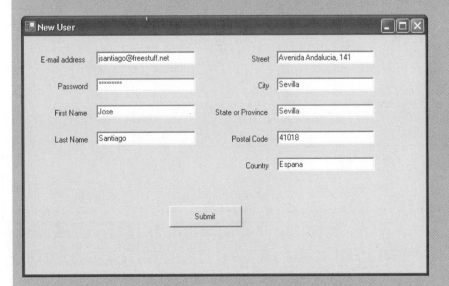

Figure B-9: New User

9 Exit the application.

Building FigTickets4Windows

In following these implementation notes, you will discover that most of the FigTickets application can be implemented in the Windows environment with little modification. Accordingly, the step-by-step instructions here are relatively brief.

The main components of FigTickets4Windows mirror the components of FigTickets. Each Web form has a corresponding Windows form, with the same data access components, most of the same object names, and most of the same application logic. You create frmHome (the Startup object for FigTickets4Windows), frmLogin, frmUser, and frmOrders. You first build the GUI for these four forms, then build the data access components, and then write the code.

Building the GUI for FigTickets4Windows

The first set of tasks for constructing FigTickets4Windows involves starting the project, creating the four forms, and setting the design time properties. Be careful to name objects as indicated in these steps so that the code displayed works properly later. As you will see, most of the object names are copied from FigTickets.

To start the construction of FigTickets4Windows and build the GUI:

1   Start a new **Windows Forms** application called **FigTickets4Windows** in the VB.NET\Student\AppB folder. Rename **Form1.vb** as **frmHome.vb**, set the internal form name as **frmHome**, and designate **frmHome** as the **Startup** object in the project's Property Pages.

2   Design the GUI for frmHome to match Figure B-10, which mimics the design of WebHome, as shown in Figure B-11. frmHome includes three buttons, named **btnCreateAccount**, **btnLogin**, and **btnExit**.

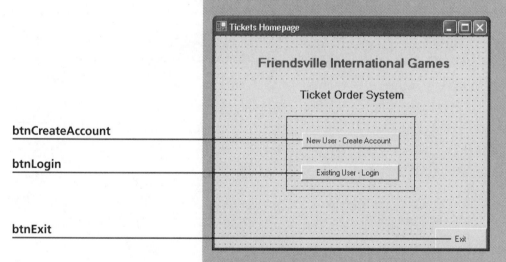

Figure B-10: frmHome at design time

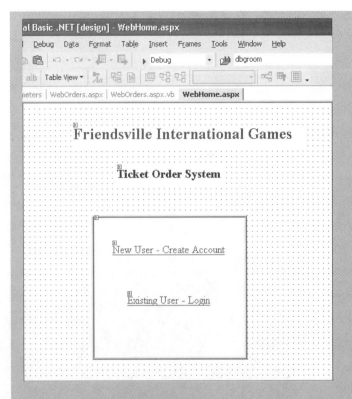

Figure B-11: WebHome at design time

3   Add a new **form** named **frmLogin**. Design the **GUI** for frmLogin to match Figure B-12, which mimics the design of WebLogin, as shown in Figure B-13. frmLogin includes three programmable controls, named **txtEmailParameter**, **txtPasswordParameter**, and **btnSubmit**.

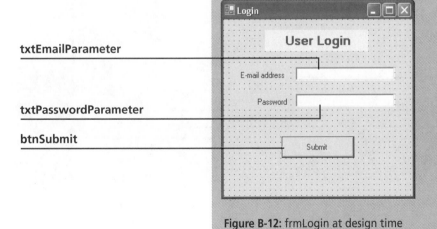

Figure B-12: frmLogin at design time

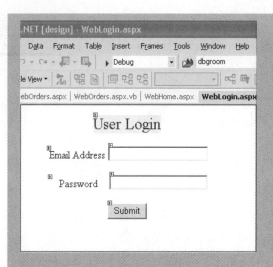

Figure B-13: WebLogin at design time

4 Add a new **form** named **frmUser**. Design the **GUI** for frmUser to match Figure B-14, which mimics the design of WebUser, as shown in Figure B-15. frmUser includes nine text boxes and three buttons. The text boxes are named **txtEmail, txtPassword, txtFName, txtLName, txtStreet, txtCity, txtStateOrProvince, txtPostalCode,** and **txtCountry.** The three buttons are named **btnUpdate, btnSubmit,** and **btnOrders.**

btnSubmit

btnUpdate

btnOrders

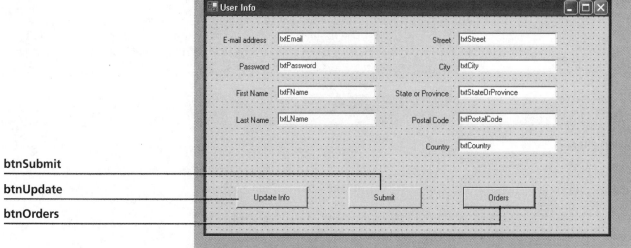

Figure B-14: frmUser at design time

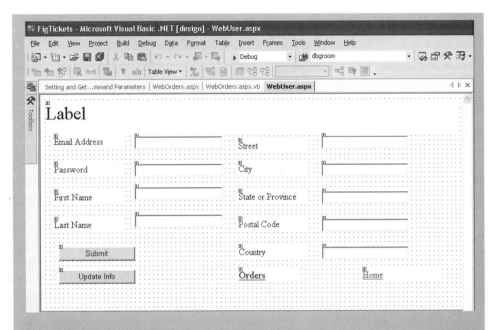

Figure B-15: WebUser at design time

5 Add a new **form** named **frmOrders**. Design the GUI for frmOrders to match Figure B-16, which mimics the design of WebOrders, as shown in Figure B-17. frmOrders includes three buttons across the top (**btnNewOrder**, **btnDone**, and **btnExit**), a combo box (**cboEvents**), a label (**lblHelp**), and two data grid controls (**dgrdOrders** and **dgrdTickets**). Set the following initial properties: **btnDone** is not visible; **cboEvents** and **dgrdTickets** are disabled.

NOTE: The DataSource properties of the two DataGrid controls, dgrdOrders and dgrdTickets, cannot be assigned until the data access components of the form have been added. Figure B-16 shows these two controls after their DataSource properties have been assigned.

btnNewOrder

btnDone

btnExit

dgrdOrders

dgrdTickets

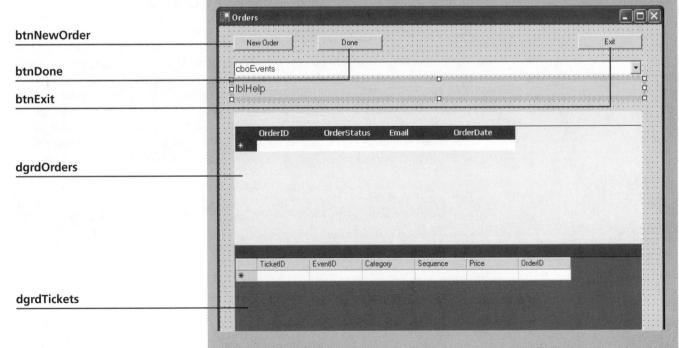

Figure B-16: frmOrders at design time

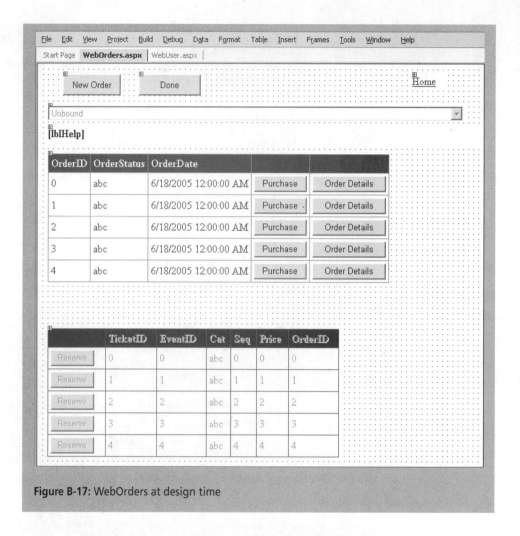

Figure B-17: WebOrders at design time

Building the Data Access Components for FigTickets4Windows

The data access components are the same ones described for FigTickets in Tutorial 10. As a result, you have two methods for constructing the data access components for FigTickets4Windows: (1) you can copy them from FigTickets, or (2) you can create them following the instructions given in Lesson C of Tutorial 10.

If you do not have FigTickets available on your computer, then build the data access components described for WebUser and for WebOrders in Tutorial 10. ADO.NET components work the same in Windows forms as they do in Web forms. The result will be the data access components for frmUser, shown in Figure B-18, and the data access components for frmOrders, shown in Figure B-19.

Figure B-18: Data access components for frmUser

Figure B-19: Data access components for frmOrders

If you have a computer where FigTickets has been constructed, then you can copy the data access components from FigTickets to FigTickets4Windows.

To copy data access components from FigTickets to FigTickets4Windows:

1 Open two instances of Visual Studio .NET. In one instance, open **FigTickets4Windows**; in the other instance, open **FigTickets**. You will be working with the two forms that contain data access components; they are frmUser/WebUser and frmOrders/WebOrders.

2 Open **frmUser** in the Windows Form Designer in FigTickets4Windows, and open **WebUser** in the Web Form Designer in FigTickets.

3 Using copy and paste, copy **SqlConnection1, cmdGetUser, cmdUpdateUser,** and **cmdInsertNewUser** from **WebUser** to **frmUser**.

4 Open **frmOrders** in the Windows Form Designer in FigTickets4Windows, and open **WebOrders** in the Web Form Designer in FigTickets.

5 Using copy and paste, copy **SqlConnection1, SqlDataAdapterTicketOrder, SqlDataAdapterAvailableTickets, SqlDataAdapterOrders, SqlDataAdapterEvents, cmdReserveTicket,** and **cmdMaxOrderID** from **WebOrders** to **frmOrders**. In brief, copy all of the data access components from the tray underneath WebOrders to frmOrders, except for DsOrders1. DsOrders1 is an instance of disorders and cannot be copied directly.

6 Click each data adapter in frmOrders, and click **Generate Dataset** underneath the Properties window. You must repeat this for each of the data adapters, since each data adapter generates only a portion of the dataset. You can find detailed instructions for accomplishing this task in Tutorial 10 under the heading "Configuring Data Access Components in WebOrders."

NOTE: When you copy and paste a data adapter, Visual Studio may identify each data command separately in the tray underneath the form. As a result, the tray may contain myriad objects, as shown in Figure B-20.

NOTE: The DataGrid control is configured later.

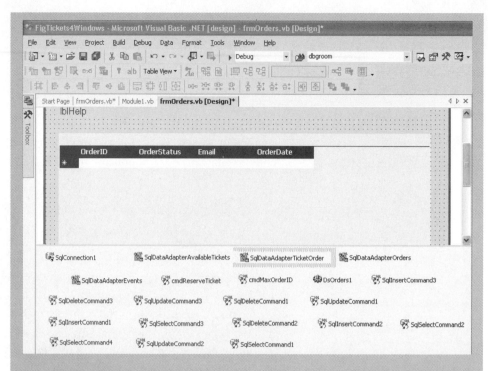

Figure B-20: Myriad data access components after pasting to frmOrders

7   Open or switch to the Designer for frmOrders. In the tray under the form, select **SqlDataAdapterOrders**. In the Properties window, expand the **SelectCommand** property. Select the **CommandText** subproperty, and click the ellipsis. (You may be prompted to login to the SQL Server instance on your computer.) The Query Builder opens. Modify the SQL Pane so that it reads: **SELECT   OrderID, OrderStatus, Email, OrderDate, 'Purchase' AS Purchase, 'Order Details' AS Details FROM tblOrder WHERE (Email = @email)**. Click **OK**.

The reason you changed the Select statement in this manner is to add the Purchase and the Order Details elements to the query, so that these items appear in the dgrdOrders Windows DataGrid control on frmOrders, mimicking the Purchase and the Order Details buttons that appear in the dgrdOrders Web DataGrid control in the FigTickets application. In FigTickets, the Web DataGrid control offers a Property Builder feature, which is used to add these buttons to dgrdOrders. But the Windows DataGrid control does not have a Property Builder feature. You achieve the same functionality by inserting these items in the query, and then programming (later in this appendix) the CurrentCellChanged event of dgrdOrders.

8   Set the DataSource property of dgrdOrders to **DsOrders1.tblOrder,** and set the DataSource property of dgrdTickets to **DsOrders1.tblTicket.** Use the Auto Format feature to spice up the appearance of either or both of the DataGrid controls. In the sample version that you previewed, the Colorful 1 format was chosen for dgrdOrders, while the default format was unchanged for dgrdTickets.

Building the Code for FigTickets4Windows

Again, most of the code was developed for FigTickets. Refer to the section entitled "Writing the Code Behind Modules for FigTickets" in Lesson C of Tutorial 10. The main changes result from slightly different objects. In a Web Forms application, you navigate to a new page, usually from a hyperlink control; in a Windows Forms application, you instantiate a form and show it, usually from a button or menu item control. A dropdown list control in a Web Forms application is a combo box control in a Windows Forms application, and so on. But most of these differences are reasonably apparent to the careful observer.

Because the application logic was explained earlier, it is not repeated here. As was the case with the data access components, you can copy most of this code from FigTickets if you happen to have a machine with FigTickets on it. However, rather than copying all of the code for a form, you should copy the statements within corresponding procedures from the Web form to the Windows form, and then change the names of any objects that are different. This is because the event procedure headers in Web forms are often different from Windows forms headers.

To construct the code for the FigTickets4windows application:

1 Open the **Code Editor** for frmHome. Insert the code shown in Figure B-21.

```
Public Class frmHome
  Inherits System.Windows.Forms.Form

+Windows Form Designer generated code

  Private Sub btnExit_Click(ByVal sender As _
      System.Object, ByVal e As System.EventArgs) _
      Handles btnExit.Click
    End
  End Sub

  Private Sub frmHome_Load(ByVal sender As Object, _
      ByVal e As System.EventArgs) Handles MyBase.Load
    pstrEmailParameter = ""
    pstrPasswordParameter = ""
    pblnNewUser = True
  End Sub

  Private Sub btnLogin_Click(ByVal sender As _
      System.Object, ByVal e As System.EventArgs) _
      Handles btnLogin.Click
    Dim frm As New frmLogin()
    frm.Show()
  End Sub

  Private Sub btnCreateAccount_Click(ByVal sender As _
      System.Object, ByVal e As System.EventArgs) _
      Handles btnCreateAccount.Click
    Dim frm As New frmUser()
    frm.Show()
  End Sub
End Class
```

Figure B-21: Code for frmHome

2 Open the **Code Editor** for frmLogin. Insert the code shown in Figure B-22.

```
Public Class frmLogin
    Inherits System.Windows.Forms.Form

+Windows Form Designer generated code

  Private Sub btnSubmit_Click(ByVal sender As System.Object, _
     ByVal e As System.EventArgs) Handles btnSubmit.Click
    pblnNewUser = False
    pstrEmailParameter = txtEmailParameter.Text
    pstrPasswordParameter = txtPasswordParameter.Text
    Dim frm As New frmUser()
    frm.Show()
    Me.Dispose()
  End Sub
End Class
```

Figure B-22: Code for frmLogin

3   Open the **Code Editor** for frmUser. Insert the code shown in Figure B-23.

```
Public Class frmUser
    Inherits System.Windows.Forms.Form

+Windows Form Designer generated code

  Private Sub frmUser_Load(ByVal sender As Object, _
     ByVal e As System.EventArgs) Handles MyBase.Load
    SqlConnection1.ConnectionString = "data source = " _
      & pstrInstance & ";initial catalog=Tickets;" & _
      "integrated security=SSPI;" & _
      "persist security info=False;" _
      & "workstation id=DADSLAPTOP;packet size=4096"
    If pblnNewUser Then
      Me.Text = "New User"
      btnSubmit.Visible = True
      btnUpdate.Visible = False
      btnOrders.Visible = False
      pstrEmailParameter = ""
      pstrPasswordParameter = ""
    Else
      Me.Text = "Existing User"
      btnSubmit.Visible = False
      btnUpdate.Visible = True
      btnOrders.Visible = True
      cmdGetUser.Parameters("@email").Value = _
        pstrEmailParameter
      cmdGetUser.Parameters("@password").Value = _
        pstrPasswordParameter
      SqlConnection1.Open()
      Dim dreader As SqlClient.SqlDataReader
      dreader = cmdGetUser.ExecuteReader _
        (CommandBehavior.SingleRow)
      If dreader.Read() Then
        txtEmail.Text = dreader(0)
        txtPassword.Text = dreader(1)
        txtFName.Text = dreader(3)
        txtLName.Text = dreader(2)
        txtStreet.Text = dreader(4)
        txtCity.Text = dreader(5)
        txtStateOrProvince.Text = dreader(6)
```

Figure B-23: Code for frmUser

```
            txtPostalCode.Text = dreader(7)
            txtCountry.Text = dreader(8)
        Else
            Me.Text = "Login Failure -- Go back to try again"
        End If
        dreader.Close()
        SqlConnection1.Close()
    End If
End Sub

Private Sub btnSubmit_Click(ByVal sender As _
        System.Object, ByVal e As System.EventArgs) _
        Handles btnSubmit.Click
    With cmdInsertNewUser
        .Parameters("@email").Value = UCase(txtEmail.Text)
        .Parameters("@password").Value = txtPassword.Text
        .Parameters("@fname").Value = UCase(txtFName.Text)
        .Parameters("@lname").Value = UCase(txtLName.Text)
        .Parameters("@street").Value = UCase(txtStreet.Text)
        .Parameters("@city").Value = UCase(txtCity.Text)
        .Parameters("@stateorprovince").Value = _
            UCase(txtStateOrProvince.Text)
        .Parameters("@postalcode").Value = txtPostalCode.Text
        .Parameters("@country").Value = UCase(txtCountry.Text)
    End With
    SqlConnection1.Open()
    cmdInsertNewUser.ExecuteNonQuery()
    SqlConnection1.Close()
    pstrEmailParameter = txtEmail.Text
    pstrPasswordParameter = txtPassword.Text
    Me.Text = "Existing User"
    btnSubmit.Visible = False
    btnUpdate.Visible = True
    btnOrders.Visible = True
End Sub

Private Sub btnUpdate_Click(ByVal sender As _
        System.Object, ByVal e As System.EventArgs) _
        Handles btnUpdate.Click
    With cmdUpdateUser
        .Parameters("@email").Value = UCase(txtEmail.Text)
        If txtPassword.Text = "" Then
            .Parameters("@password").Value = _
                pstrPasswordParameter
        Else
            .Parameters("@password").Value = txtPassword.Text
        End If
        .Parameters("@fname").Value = UCase(txtFName.Text)
        .Parameters("@lname").Value = UCase(txtLName.Text)
        .Parameters("@street").Value = UCase(txtStreet.Text)
        .Parameters("@city").Value = UCase(txtCity.Text)
        .Parameters("@stateorprovince").Value = _
            UCase(txtStateOrProvince.Text)
        .Parameters("@postalcode").Value = txtPostalCode.Text
        .Parameters("@country").Value = UCase(txtCountry.Text)
    End With
    SqlConnection1.Open()
    cmdUpdateUser.ExecuteNonQuery()
    SqlConnection1.Close()
    pstrEmailParameter = txtEmail.Text
    pstrPasswordParameter = txtPassword.Text
End Sub
```

Figure B-23: Code for frmUser (continued)

```
    Private Sub btnOrders_Click(ByVal sender As _
        System.Object, ByVal e As System.EventArgs) _
        Handles btnOrders.Click
      Dim frm As New frmOrders()
      frm.Show()
      Me.Dispose()
    End Sub
End Class
```

Figure B-23: Code for frmUser (continued)

4 Open the **Code Editor** for frmOrders. Insert the code shown in Figure B-24.

```
Public Class frmOrders
    Inherits System.Windows.Forms.Form

+Windows Form Designer generated code
  Const MsgSTART = 1
  Const MsgNEWORDER = 2
  Const MsgPURCHASE = 3
  Const MsgNEWORDERPENDING = 4
  Const MsgRESERVE = 5

  Private Sub frmOrders_Load(ByVal sender As Object, _
      ByVal e As System.EventArgs) Handles MyBase.Load
    SqlConnection1.ConnectionString = "data source = " _
      & pstrInstance & ";initial catalog=Tickets;" & _
      "integrated security=SSPI;" & _
      "persist security info=False;" _
      & "workstation id=DADSLAPTOP;packet size=4096"
    SqlDataAdapterOrders.SelectCommand.Parameters _
      ("@email").Value = pstrEmailParameter
    SqlDataAdapterOrders.Fill(DsOrders1.tblOrder)
    SqlDataAdapterEvents.Fill(DsOrders1.tblEvent)
    DisplayMsg(MsgSTART)
    Dim workrow As dsOrders.tblEventRow
    Dim s As String
    For Each workrow In DsOrders1.tblEvent
      s = Str(workrow("EventID")) & " "
      If workrow("Gender") = "M" Then _
        s &= "Men's " & workrow("Sport") & " "
      If workrow("Gender") = "F" Then _
        s &= "Women's " & workrow("Sport") & " "
      s &= workrow("EventName") & " - "
      s &= workrow("Schedule") & ", "
      s &= Format(workrow("StartTime"), "h:mm tt") & ", at "
      s &= workrow("VenueName")
      cboEvents.Items.Add(s)
    Next
    cboEvents.Enabled = False
    cboEvents.SelectedIndex = -1
    If DsOrders1.tblOrder.Count > 0 Then _
      dgrdOrders_CurrentCellChanged(sender, e)
  End Sub

  Private Sub DisplayMsg(ByVal vintMsgNum)
    Select Case vintMsgNum
      Case MsgSTART
        lblHelp.Text = "HELP: Click New Order, Purchase, " _
          & "or Order Details"
```

Figure B-24: Code for frmOrders

```
          Case MsgNEWORDER
            lblHelp.Text = "HELP: Select an event, then " _
              & "click Reserve " & "for each desired ticket."
          Case MsgPURCHASE
            lblHelp.Text = "HELP: Thank you for your payment"
          Case MsgNEWORDERPENDING
            lblHelp.Text = "HELP: Complete your New Order first"
          Case MsgRESERVE
            lblHelp.Text = "HELP: Click Reserve for another " & _
              "ticket, or click Done"
      End Select
  End Sub

  Private Sub dgrdOrders_CurrentCellChanged(ByVal sender _
      As Object, ByVal e As System.EventArgs) _
      Handles dgrdOrders.CurrentCellChanged
    If pblnNewOrderPending Then
      DisplayMsg(MsgNEWORDERPENDING)
    ElseIf dgrdOrders.Item(dgrdOrders.CurrentCell).ToString _
        = "Order Details" Then
      DisplayDetails()
    ElseIf dgrdOrders.Item(dgrdOrders.CurrentCell).ToString _
        = "Purchase" Then
      PurchaseTickets()
    End If
  End Sub

  Private Sub DisplayDetails()
    DsOrders1.EnforceConstraints = False
    Dim key As Integer = _
     dgrdOrders.Item(dgrdOrders.CurrentRowIndex, 0)
    SqlDataAdapterTicketOrder.SelectCommand.Parameters _
      ("@orderid").Value = key
    DsOrders1.tblTicket.Clear()
    SqlDataAdapterTicketOrder.Fill(DsOrders1.tblTicket)
    If DsOrders1.tblTicket.Count = 0 Then
      Dim workrow As dsOrders.tblOrderRow
      For Each workrow In DsOrders1.tblOrder
        If workrow.OrderID = key Then workrow.Delete()
      Next
      SqlDataAdapterOrders.Update(DsOrders1.tblOrder)
      DsOrders1.tblOrder.AcceptChanges()
    Else
      Dim workrow As dsOrders.tblTicketRow
      workrow = DsOrders1.tblTicket.Rows(0)
      cboEvents.SelectedIndex = workrow.EventID - 1
    End If
    DsOrders1.EnforceConstraints = True
  End Sub

  Private Sub PurchaseTickets()
    Dim key As Integer = _
      dgrdOrders.Item(dgrdOrders.CurrentRowIndex, 0)
    Dim i As Integer
    If key > 0 And DsOrders1.tblOrder.Count > 0 Then
      Dim workrow As dsOrders.tblOrderRow
      For Each workrow In DsOrders1.tblOrder
        If workrow.OrderID = key Then
          If workrow.OrderStatus = "O" Then
            workrow.OrderStatus = "S"
            SqlDataAdapterOrders.Update(DsOrders1.tblOrder)
            DsOrders1.tblOrder.AcceptChanges()
```

Figure B-24: Code for frmOrders (continued)

```
                    MessageBox.Show("Status changed from " & _
                       "Ordered (O) to Sold (S)")
              Else
                 MessageBox.Show("That order has already " _
                    & "been paid for.")
              End If
           End If
        Next
     End If
  End Sub

  Private Sub btnExit_Click(ByVal sender As _
       System.Object, ByVal e As System.EventArgs) _
       Handles btnExit.Click
     End
  End Sub

  Private Sub btnDone_Click(ByVal sender As _
       Object, ByVal e As System.EventArgs) _
       Handles btnDone.Click
     DisplayMsg(MsgSTART)
     btnNewOrder.Visible = True
     btnDone.Visible = False
     cboEvents.Enabled = False
     dgrdTickets.Enabled = False
     SqlDataAdapterTicketOrder.SelectCommand.Parameters _
       ("@orderid").Value = pintNewOrderID
     DsOrders1.tblTicket.Clear()
     SqlDataAdapterTicketOrder.Fill(DsOrders1.tblTicket)
     If DsOrders1.tblTicket.Count = 0 Then
        Dim workrow As dsOrders.tblOrderRow
        workrow = DsOrders1.tblOrder.FindByOrderID _
          (pintNewOrderID)
        workrow.Delete()
        SqlDataAdapterOrders.Update(DsOrders1.tblOrder)
        DsOrders1.tblOrder.AcceptChanges()
     End If
     DsOrders1.tblOrder.Clear()
     SqlDataAdapterOrders.Fill(DsOrders1.tblOrder)
     DsOrders1.EnforceConstraints = True
     pblnNewOrderPending = False
  End Sub

  Private Sub cboEvents_SelectedIndexChanged(ByVal sender _
       As Object, ByVal e As System.EventArgs) _
       Handles cboEvents.SelectedIndexChanged
     If pblnNewOrderPending Then
        DsOrders1.EnforceConstraints = False
        SqlDataAdapterAvailableTickets.Update(DsOrders1.tblTicket)
        pintSelectedEvent = Val(Mid(cboEvents.SelectedItem, 2))
        SqlDataAdapterAvailableTickets.SelectCommand.Parameters _
          ("@eventid").Value = pintSelectedEvent
        DsOrders1.tblTicket.Clear()
        SqlDataAdapterAvailableTickets.Fill(DsOrders1.tblTicket)
        cboEvents.Enabled = False
     End If
  End Sub

  Private Sub btnNewOrder_Click(ByVal sender As Object, _
       ByVal e As System.EventArgs) Handles btnNewOrder.Click
```

Figure B-24: Code for frmOrders (continued)

```
      DisplayMsg(MsgNEWORDER)
      btnNewOrder.Visible = False
      btnDone.Visible = True
      dgrdTickets.Enabled = True
      pblnNewOrderPending = True
      SqlConnection1.Open()
      Dim dreader As SqlClient.SqlDataReader
      dreader = cmdMaxOrderID.ExecuteReader _
        (CommandBehavior.SingleRow)
      If dreader.Read() Then
        pintNewOrderID = dreader(0) + 1
      Else
        MsgBox("Error in cmdMaxOrderID")
      End If
      dreader.Close()
      SqlConnection1.Close()
      cboEvents.SelectedIndex = 0
      cboEvents_SelectedIndexChanged(sender, e)
      DsOrders1.tblOrder.Rows.Add(New Object() _
        {pintNewOrderID, "O", pstrEmailParameter, _
        Today, "Purchase", "Order Details"})
      SqlDataAdapterOrders.Update(DsOrders1.tblOrder)
      DsOrders1.tblOrder.AcceptChanges()
      cboEvents.Enabled = True
    End Sub

    Private Sub dgrdTickets_CurrentCellChanged(ByVal sender _
        As Object, ByVal e As System.EventArgs) _
        Handles dgrdTickets.CurrentCellChanged
      If dgrdTickets.Item(dgrdTickets.CurrentCell).ToString _
          = "Reserve" Then
        'ItemCommand = Reserve
        DisplayMsg(MsgRESERVE)
        'if the user is selecting tickets from Opening Ceremonies:
        cboEvents.Enabled = False
        cmdReserveTicket.Parameters("@ticketid").Value = _
          dgrdTickets.Item(dgrdTickets.CurrentRowIndex, 0)
        cmdReserveTicket.Parameters("@orderid").Value = _
          pintNewOrderID
        SqlConnection1.Open()
        cmdReserveTicket.ExecuteNonQuery()
        SqlConnection1.Close()
      End If
    End Sub
End Class
```

Figure B-24: Code for frmOrders (continued)

5   Module1.vb can be used directly from FigTickets. Add a **Module1** to the project, and type the code shown in Figure B-25.

```
Module Module1
  Public pstrEmailParameter As String
  Public pstrPasswordParameter As String
  Public pblnNewUser As Boolean = True
  Public pintSelectedEvent As Integer
  Public pintNewOrderID As Integer
  Public pblnNewOrderPending As Boolean = False
  Public pstrInstance As String = "dadslaptop\vsdotnet"
End Module
```

Figure B-25: Code for Module1.vb

6 Run the **FigTickets4Windows** application, and test every feature.

Glossary

A

abstract class — a class that cannot be instantiated and must be inherited, because it is incomplete in and of itself

Active Server Page (ASP) — an extended Web page, supporting interactivity and animation; can include server-side code that accepts input from a user (client) and returns output that can be materialized in the client's browser

ActiveX data objects (ADO) data access technology — an alternate data access technology introduced in Visual Basic 6.0 using record sets

ADO.NET — data access technology incorporated in the .NET Framework; emphasizes loosely based datasets and data adapters, but also supports data commands and readers that operate directly on the database

anonymous access — appropriate for publicly accessible applications on the Internet. The Windows machine on which an IIS server is running has an extra Windows user account under the name IUSR_*<machinename>*, where *<machinename>* is the name of the IIS host. When an unknown user sends a request to IIS for access to some resource, IIS impersonates this Windows user account, making the request to Windows under the name *<machinename>*_anonymous

assembly — the package that results from compilation

atomic processing — a rule that a collection of related database changes should be accomplished together, or none of them should be accomplished

authentication — a tier within the security model whereby a user is identified to the system

authorization — a tier within the security model that follows user authentication and determines whether a user is authorized to conduct the requested activity

Autonumber field — in Microsoft Access, an integer field whose value, incremented in each new record, is system-provided

B

back end — the database or other data file that is part of an application and hidden from the user

basic authentication — the very simple authentication prescribed by the Worldwide Web Consortium (W3C) and standard among all Web servers; when basic authentication is prescribed, an unknown user is prompted for a username and password in a standard login dialog

bubble sort (*see also* **waterfall sort**) — an exchange sort that only compares adjacent elements; performs reasonably well on medium-sized arrays ranging from 10 to 100 records

Button control — the standard button, formerly called a command button

C

child node — lower-level node in a parent node

class — the template for a programming object consisting of the properties, events, and methods that define it

code table — additional coded elements that facilitate data entry and enforce standards in a database

ComboBox control — a combination of a text box and a list box; often bound to a column of human-readable values and a corresponding column of codes from one table, while the value selected from the ComboBox is bound to a field in a second table

Common Language Runtime — a set of components and services in Visual Studio .NET that supports all of the Visual Studio .NET languages

component — a class that conforms to a certain standard for interacting with other components. A component may or may not contain a graphical element; a component always contains a code element. A component can provide an easy way to communicate between projects in a solution

concurrency control — the potential problem caused by multiple users attempting to update or delete a record at the same time in a DBMS

connection pooling — sharing a connection among multiple users in order to conserve connection resources

Console application — an application whose user interface is limited to text in a Command Prompt (or MS-DOS) window

context menu — a short pop-up menu that appears when the user right-clicks while the insertion point hovers over a form or control

D

data commands — an element of a database that allows you to remain connected to the database and work with it directly; they are more versatile than data adapters and datasets, but they consume more resources

data definition language (DDL) — a language to define the structure (or schema) of the data in a DBMS

data manipulation language (DML) — a language for manipulating the data after the structure has been defined in a DBMS

data model — a graphical representation of the structure of the data needed to support a particular information requirement. It may be global—an enterprisewide data model—or it may relate to the performance of only one function in one office of an organization. Whatever the scope, the data model is an abstraction of the data requirements that exist in the user's mind

data reader — an element of a database that allows you to remain connected to the database and work with it directly

DataGrid control — control used for displaying all of the columns and rows of a source table, view, or dataset in a grid format

dataset — a data object that contains a disconnected set of data. It usually is filled with data provided by one or more data adapters and normally provides data to bound controls

deadlock — when two users each hold a lock on a record that the other needs to complete a transaction

digest authentication — works the same as basic authentication, except that the information entered by the user is transmitted to IIS in an encrypted form, providing a more secure process

dirty read — an attempt to read data whose update is pending

discover file — a file that contains the URL of a Web site within which the source code for an XML Web service may be dynamically discovered

domain name — correlates to the Internet Protocol (IP) address of the server

Domain Name Server (DNS) — The name for a Web server that usually consists of www, followed by a meaningful domain name, and the top-level domain (TLD) like org, com, or gov

DomainUpDown control — similar in functionality and appearance to the NumericUpDown control; the main difference is that the DomainUpDown control contains a collection of strings, one of which is displayed in the control

Driver Manager — loads the appropriate driver applicable to the data source. Subsequently, the driver parses SQL commands as needed and passes them to the database server; the driver also translates the results coming back from the database and delivers them to the application program; each application language that supports ODBC contains a Driver Manager

E

entity-relationship model (E-R model) — displays the entities and relationships between entities in a database table

ErrorProvider control — validation code that checks data prior to executing a database operation that will cause an error, and alerts the user that an error will occur prior to its occurrence if data is not corrected

eXtensible Markup Language (XML) — a language consisting of a set of tags or markers that define the parts of a document; derived from Standard Generalized Markup Language (SGML) and also related to Hypertext Markup Language (HTML)

F

FlowLayout — placement of controls of a Web form where elements do not have absolute positioning attributes

foreign key — the primary key from the table representing the 1 side of the relationship that is inserted into the table that represents the N side of the relationship in a 1:N relationship

form — one type of class

front end—the graphical user interface (GUI) of an application, what the user sees

FrontPage Server Extensions — enhancements to the Microsoft FrontPage software, required for creating Web Forms Applications in Visual Studio .NET

G

Global.asax.vb — an optional file that provides a common structure for all of the code necessary to maintain session state in a Web Forms application

GridLayout — placement of controls on a Web form in the same way that they are placed on a Windows form, with absolute positioning of each element within its container

H

Help Button — offers an alternate means of providing context-sensitive help; a programmer uses a Help Button most often when providing help to a user within a dialog box, because a dialog box is modal and does not allow the display of another form while the modal form is displayed

Help viewer — renders the familiar Help screen containing Contents, Index, and Search tabs in the left-hand pane, the current topic in the right-hand pane, and a toolbar pane along the top

Hypertext Markup Language (HTML) — a markup language that describes the presentation of data by providing formatting instructions

HTML Help workshop — a facility for developing and incorporating HTML files into a comprehensive Help system

HTML server controls — HTML elements that are converted to controls associated with code that executes on the server

I

impersonation — A tier within the security model that is an optional process in which a Web application pretends to be an authorized user, making it possible to provide access to resources over a public network without requiring every user to log in to the Web server

Index Sequential Access Method (ISAM) file — consists of two portions—the data is stored in a random-access file, ordered by a record key field; then, a separate index file contains a list of all the record keys (column 1) and the record numbers of the associated records (column 2). When the user creates a new record, a new ISAM record is written to the data portion of the file in the correct sequence, and a new entry is also made in the index file

inheritance — properties and methods of an object that are derived from the class upon which the object is based

insertion sort — the only sort routine to allow you to sort elements as they are introduced; it is ideal for sorting new items as they come into existence rather than sorting items in a preexisting array

instance — an object created from a template known as a class; the process of creating an object from a class is called instantiation

Integrated Development Environment (IDE) — the set of windows that you see and services that you use when you are programming; consists of designers, wizards, code editor, toolbox, compiler, debugger, and behind-the-scenes services

Internet Information Server (IIS) — Microsoft network server software; IIS is required for creating Web Forms Applications in Visual Studio .NET

intersection table — a table that is constructed to demonstrate M:N relationships in a relational database design

M

markup languages — instructions that are inserted into a text document and dictate how the content elements are to be displayed (that is, they "mark up" the text). *See* HTML

method — an action that an object can perform

Microsoft SQL Server Desktop Engine (MSDE) — a software package that comes with Visual Studio .NET Professional Edition and that makes it possible for Visual Studio .NET applications to use an SQL Server database directly

module — a reference type, consisting of declarations and procedures only

MonthCalendar control — useful alternative to the DateTimePicker control when you need to display a schedule showing multiple dates or months

multiple document interface (MDI) — a category of a Windows Form application where documents can be opened simultaneously as child forms under an MDI container form

N

namespace — a category or grouping of related classes

navigation buttons — a set of buttons on a data form that facilitate navigation within a dataset

.NET Framework — set of predefined classes and namespaces available to developers in all languages supported by Visual Studio .NET

Node — list of items displayed in a TreeView control

NumericUpDown control — provides a convenient display for a numeric value that the user may need to increase or decrease at runtime

O

object — an instance of a class

object-oriented programming (OOP) — a modern approach to computer programming based on the notions of objects, properties, methods, inheritance, encapsulation, implementation, and polymorphism

OleDbAdapter — an ADO.NET object that retrieves data from a database (using an OleDbConnection), uses it to fill a dataset, and that also sends changes in the dataset back to the underlying database

OleDbCommand — part of an OleDbAdapter that carries out a specific SQL query, such as Select, Insert, Update, or Delete

OleDbConnection — an ADO.NET object that physically connects to a database through an underlying OleDb driver

Open Database Connectivity (ODBC) — a standardized method for correctly translating and parsing all requests in a database

Outlook style interface — A category of a Windows Form application that includes the features of the Explorer style interface as well as containing a third window, often a document of some kind, usually in the lower-right quadrant

Overloads keyword — declares a method that matches the name of an existing member, but contains a different argument list

overriding — requires that the overridden element be declared Overridable, and the overriding element be declared with the Overrides keyword; also requires that the overriding and the overridden elements have the same calling sequence—the elements must be of the same type (function, sub, or property) and have the same name, same number and type of arguments, and the same type of return value

P

packet-switched network — A network where messages are transmitted from node to node in fixed-length message blocks called packets

Panel control — a container for other controls

parameter — a data value required by a method, function, or procedure to accomplish its task

parameterized query — a parameter that configures a dataset and is supplied at runtime through user input

parent node — a node that has a child node

polymorphism — ability of a derived class or instantiated object to provide its own unique implementation of a method declared or defined in the base class

primary key — a unique row identifier in a database table

progress bar — can be used in much the same manner as a scrollbar or track bar, but traditionally it is applied to tracking the progress of lengthy background computer operations, such as file copying, printing, or transmitting data

property — an attribute or characteristic that helps to describe an object

pseudo-ISAM file — has a data portion and an index portion like an ISAM file; the difference is that the programmer (rather than the operating system) is responsible for maintaining both portions, and it is done with two separate files

R

raise an exception (*see also* **throw an exception**) — the handling of a runtime error that is first reported back to the program with an error number (ErrNum) and an error description (Message)

record key — the data item by which the records are organized

recordset — similar to a dataset, an in-memory store that represents the data stored in one or more underlying tables

recursive method — a method that calls itself

reference type — a class does not maintain its own data; rather, data values reside in an object, which references the class definitions

referential integrity constraint — among database tables, if a value exists in a particular row on the child side of the relationship, then that value must exist in the primary key field on the parent side of the relationship

relational model — a model, based on a branch of mathematics called relational algebra and relational calculus, in which data is perceived by the user as consisting of a series of one or more tables, consisting of rows and columns. Each table provides information about one entity (person, place, thing, or transaction) or one relationship. Columns in the table represent the characteristics or attributes of the entity, while rows represent specific instances of the entity

resource constraints — involve memory allocation, file handlers, and number of connections, among other things in a DBMS

RichTextBox control — allows formatting to be applied to any portion of text selected within the control

S

sealed class — in some ways, the exact opposite of an abstract class; a sealed class cannot be inherited, that is, it cannot form the basis for a derived class

search engine — a software program combined with a database, where the database consists of an index of Web pages, and the software program searches through the database looking for matches

selection sort — uses two list areas; the algorithm steps through the first list looking for the smallest value in the list. After passing through the array, the smallest item is then copied to the first position in the second list, while in the first list, the smallest element is assigned a value larger than any other possible value in that list so that it is not again selected as the smallest; this process continues until all the items are sorted

setup project — creates all the necessary files for deployment of your application; the setup project is just another kind of Visual Basic project, like a Windows Forms or Web Forms or Console or User Control project. Visual Studio .NET offers both a Setup Project (for deployment of Windows Forms applications) and a Web Setup Project (for deployment of Web forms applications)

shadowing — a technique related to notions of overriding and overloading a program element; a program element in a derived class can shadow any program element in its base class. This means that the shadowed element is hidden, and any unqualified reference to the element name refers to the shadowing element rather than the shadowed element

Shell sort — Named for its inventor, starts by calculating an optimum distance D between elements to be compared. On the first pass through the table, Table(n) is compared to Table(n+D), and, if these two elements are not in the correct sequence, their values are exchanged. The comparison and swapping continue for n=0, n=1, n=2, and so on, until n+D exceeds the number of elements in the table. This completes the first pass through the table. D is then halved (with the result rounded down, so that half of 15 is 7), and the second pass begins. The process continues until D=0, at which point the table has been sorted

shuttle sort — another version of an exchange sort, this sort proceeds only once through the array, comparing adjacent elements. When it encounters two elements that need to be reversed, it not only reverses those two elements, but also propagates that exchange backwards through previous elements in the array, until the exchanged element finds its proper place among all of the elements that have been sorted so far

single document interface (SDI) — a category of a Windows Form application where each form is independent and contains only one document (text document, spreadsheet, graph, table, or report, etc.); for example, Notepad uses a single document interface

size, location properties — contain, respectively, the Width and Height, and the X (Left) and Y (Top) properties of a graphical object, all measured in pixels

Software Configuration Management — the discipline for tracking changes to a software package, especially when multiple programmers are simultaneously working on multiple copies of the software, or when an organization must simultaneously support multiple releases of the software

standard module — *see* module

StatusBar control — a potentially complex control that is used to display the status of an application

structure — can contain different kinds of data items, each with its own accessibility (Public, Private, Friend, etc.), can contain properties, methods, and events

Style.css — the cascading style sheet for a Visual Basic .NET Web Forms application. This is in the standard format of any XML cascading style sheet. Styles.css provides default values for all necessary styles, which are used unless overridden on individual Web pages

T

table join — a type of query in a database that joins tables together based on a common field

Tables collection — part of a dataset that contains Table objects based on the DataTable class; each Table object contains collections of rows and columns

throw an exception (*see also* **raise an exception**) — the handling of a runtime error that is first reported back to the program with an error number (ErrNum) and an error description (Message)

ToolTip — a small pop-up window that displays text when the user moves the insertion point over a control

TrackBar control — provides a visual display and functionality similar to a HorizontalScrollBar control, a fundamental Visual Basic control ever since the first release of the language

transaction processing — the notion that one physical event can trigger multiple changes to the database

Transmission Control Protocol/Internet Protocol (TCP/IP) — TCP involves creating the packets at the origination end and reassembling the packets into the complete message at the destination end; the IP portion involves the method of switching, storing, and forwarding packets from node to node

U

URL address — consists of the Internet service, the domain name, the path to the Web page (if necessary), and the title of the Web page (if necessary)

user control — controls that you create and define and that inherit from an existing Windows Forms control, from the UserControl class, from a previously defined user control, and from the Control class

V

value type — each variable contains its own data

Visio-based UML modeling — data modeling functionality built into Visual Studio .NET Enterprise Architect Edition

Visual C# .NET — a new programming language, pronounced Visual C Sharp .NET, introduced with Visual Studio .NET

Visual Database Tools — a set of services in Visual Studio .NET that allow you to create and manage an SQL Server 7.0 database, among other things.

Visual J# .NET — a Java-like language implemented for the Visual Studio .NET platform

Visual Source Safe — software configuration management (version control) for programmer teams, provided with Visual Studio .NET Enterprise Edition

Visual Studio .NET project — an application in any of the languages and using any of the templates supported by Visual Studio .NET

Visual Studio .NET solution — a container for one or more Visual Studio .NET Projects

W

waterfall sort (*see also* **bubble sort**) — an exchange sort that only compares adjacent elements; performs reasonably well on medium-sized arrays ranging from 10 to 100 records

WebApplication1.vsdisco — a file that serves as a container for links (URLs) to discovery files that describe the XML Web service

Web browser — allows any Web page to be displayed, masking and accommodating differences among operating systems, monitors, and graphics software

Web.config — A file that sets the system configuration for a Visual Basic .NET Web Forms application, including the compilation language, dynamic debugging option, error trapping, authentication, authorization, tracing, session state options, and globalization

Web Forms application — an application whose user interface appears to the user as Web pages and which is processed on a server

Web service — code that permits two computer programs to communicate over the Internet

Windows Explorer style interface — a category of a Windows Form application that uses two principle controls, a TreeView control and a ListView control

Windows Forms application — an application whose user interface appears in traditional windows

workaround — a creative programming solution whose obvious or straightforward solution is blocked or not supported by the programming language you are using

World Wide Web — the most popular part of the Internet, based on the pioneering work of Tim Berners Lee, who introduced the Web in 1989 as a means for sharing information

wrapper layer — the outermost layer of multi-layer Try...Catch constructs

Z

Z Order property — the graphical order of presentation of overlapping objects. A Z Order value of 0 appears in front of other objects

Index

Symbols

A

S